Creating Environments
for Learning

Birth to Age Eight

Creating Environments for Learning

Birth to Age Eight

Julie Bullard
University of Montana Western

Merrill
Upper Saddle River, New Jersey
Columbus, Ohio

Library of Congress Cataloging-in-Publication Data

Bullard, Julie.
 Creating environments for learning : birth to age eight / Julie Bullard. -- 1st ed.
  p. cm.
 Includes bibliographical references and index.
 ISBN 978-0-13-158579-9
 1. Classroom learning centers. 2. Early childhood education--Activity programs. I.
Title.
 LB3044.8.B85 2010
 372.13--dc22

                         2008053841

Vice President and Editor in Chief: Jeffery W. Johnston
Acquisitions Editor: Julie Peters
Editorial Assistant: Tiffany Bitzel
Senior Managing Editor: Pamela D. Bennett
Senior Project Manager: Linda Hillis Bayma
Production Coordination: Roxanne Klaas, S4Carlisle Publishing Services
Senior Art Director: Diane C. Lorenzo
Cover Images: Photos by Julie Bullard. Art shown in center photo © Kjell B. Sandved, www.butterflyalphabet.com
Cover Design: Kristina Holmes
Media Producer: Autumn Benson
Media Project Manager: Rebecca Norsic
Senior Operations Supervisor: Matthew Ottenweller
Operations Specialist: Susan Hannahs
Vice President, Director of Sales & Marketing: Quinn Perkson
Marketing Manager: Erica DeLuca
Marketing Coordinator: Brian Mounts

This book was set in Times New Roman by S4Carlisle Publishing Services. It was printed and bound by Courier Kendallville, Inc. The cover was printed by Lehigh Phoenix.

Every effort has been made to provide accurate and current Internet information in this book. However, the Internet and information posted on it are constantly changing, so it is inevitable that some of the Internet addresses listed in this textbook will change.

Photo Credits: Julie Peters, pp. 33, 121, 377; Nancy Sheehan Photography, p. 63; Becky Gorton, pp. 109, 264, 337; Lisa Bullard, p. 154; Courtesy of Community Playthings, p. 218; Jeanette Lemieux, p. 236 (bottom right); Terry Murphy, pp. 276, 323; Christopher Bullard, p. 329. All other photos by Julie Bullard.

Pearson® is a registered trademark of Pearson plc
Merrill® is a registered trademark of Pearson Education, Inc.

Pearson Education Ltd., London
Pearson Education Singapore, Pte. Ltd.
Pearson Education Canada, Inc.
Pearson Education–Japan
Pearson Education Australia PTY, Limited

Pearson Education North Asia, Ltd., Hong Kong
Pearson Educación de Mexico, S.A. de C.V.
Pearson Education Malaysia, Pte. Ltd.
Pearson Education Upper Saddle River, New Jersey

Merrill
is an imprint of

www.pearsonhighered.com

10 9 8 7 6 5 4
ISBN-13: 978-0-13-158579-9
ISBN-10:   0-13-158579-7

To my mother, Anne Henderson, whose compassion, love, and respect for all has been an example for both my personal and professional life. Her encouragement and unwavering support have allowed me to pursue my dreams.

About the Author

Julie Bullard is a professor and director of the Early Childhood Education program at the University of Montana Western. During her 30 years in the early childhood field she has been a preschool and elementary teacher, childcare director, Head Start administrator, and has taught adults receiving CDAs, associate degrees, and bachelor's degrees in early childhood as well as students receiving master's degrees in curriculum and instruction. Julie has had a passion for the importance of the early learning environment since completing coursework in architecture more than 30 years ago. She also has a special interest in curricular standards and serves on several state and national committees that are working on developing and implementing standards using play-based curriculum. She is active on the National Education Association for the Education of Young Children (NAEYC) Professional Development Panel and is a national reviewer of early childhood higher education programs. She also serves on an oversight committee for NAEYC/NCATE accreditation. Julie was recently appointed to serve on an NAEYC committee to revise the national early childhood higher education standards. She serves on the National Association for Early Childhood Teacher Education (NAECTE) national board and is also on the National Council for Accreditation of Teacher Education Board of Examiners (NCATE BOE). She has been involved in the development of the Montana early childhood knowledge base, infant-toddler guidelines, preschool guidelines, kindergarten standards, and early childhood and elementary higher education standards. Julie received her doctorate from Montana State University.

Preface

Creating Environments for Learning: Birth to Age Eight is designed for college courses taught at 2- and 4-year institutions that focus on quality early childhood learning environments and curriculum. The book's content spans the birth to age 8 range and is appropriate for teachers-in-training as well as practicing teachers in family childcare homes, childcare centers, preschools, or elementary schools.

How did this book come to be written? Philosophically, I value play as the primary way of learning for young children and have become increasingly alarmed that children's time for play is disappearing. Through play, children construct knowledge by engaging in self-chosen, integrated experiences that are at their ideal level of development. Play is a time-honored, tested, and valued method of learning in early childhood.

Why has play diminished in early childhood settings? I believe this has occurred for several reasons. As we've entered the era of accountability, teachers worry about whether children will be able to achieve all the standards or outcomes if they are involved in self-chosen activities. Additionally, children now spend many more years in group settings. Children may find the same materials present for several years as they stay in the same classroom or even when they move from classroom to classroom. Boredom due to lack of challenging and interesting environments results in children displaying behavioral issues. Teachers often mistakenly reduce the amount of play in favor of more teacher-controlled groups, hoping to control this misbehavior. Finally, in an overemphasis on safety and cleanliness we've often stripped children's environments and lives of many types of experiences and challenges.

In the past, many teachers believed that play was the only catalyst for learning. However, most teachers now realize that children's learning through play is profoundly affected by the social and physical environment they are in. If we want to prevent boredom and help children meet outcomes primarily through play, we need to intentionally design environments that provide children with the materials, tools, and challenges that allow development to flourish. For children to gain the most from play, we also need to be available to scaffold children's learning.

> "... we also need to be available to scaffold children's learning." This means that teachers need to move from primarily managing children's behavior to becoming observant, active facilitators. The environment is crucial in determining the teacher's role. A well-designed environment acts as a "third teacher," reducing behavioral issues and providing learning opportunities. This frees the teacher to spend time scaffolding learning.

I believe that if we want to preserve play, we must assure that teachers are able to effectively integrate developmental and curricular outcomes. To do this, teachers must have a deep understanding of the outcomes they are hoping to achieve, have knowledge of how to design a "rich" environment to achieve the desired outcomes, and understand their role as facilitators. Quality environments are the foundation upon which a quality, play-based curriculum is built.

How do we learn about quality environments? Our Montana early childhood higher education program demonstrates its belief in the importance of the environment by requiring a course on early childhood learning environments. Although we have reviewed and used many different textbooks for this course, we have not yet found a book that meets all our criteria. **We want a textbook that provides basic information on environments, but also helps students to see environmental possibilities.** To enhance children's learning, we believe that teachers must be able to develop "rich" environments, but this can only occur when it is built upon a firm foundation.

We want students to consider early childhood theories, child development, current research, and curriculum standards and outcomes in designing environments. For students to understand the importance of these areas they must be transparent in the textbook, with specific research information and citations. This information must then translate research and theory into practice and be written in user-friendly language. Since many early childhood programs struggle with financial barriers the book needs to contain many practical, inexpensive ideas.

It is also important that the interests, developmental levels, and cultural and geographic backgrounds of the children in the classroom be considered in establishing environments. The book needs to provide information and an abundance of examples that assist students in seeing that every effective early childhood environment will be unique based upon these criteria and that a cookie-cutter approach will not be effective.

Finally, the book needs to cover the entire early childhood age range, from birth to age 8. Even if students will only work in Pre-K programs, they need to understand the range of development since many Pre-K children will be developmentally advanced and ready for more challenging activities. In developing and writing this textbook, I have strived to meet each of these criteria.

Features of This Text

This textbook combines "the basics" or foundational information about how to arrange an environment with an exploration of the characteristics and abundant examples of centers rich with materials and possibilities. Several themes and features are embedded throughout the book.

Go to MyEducationLab and select the topic "Play." Under Activities and Applications, watch the video *Building with Blocks.*

- **MyEducationLab** is a powerful online tool that provides students with assignments and activities set in the context of real classrooms. MyEducationLab is fully integrated in your text and provides practice in an easy-to-assign format. Look for references to video clips and artifacts in the margins of this text.
  - **Assignments and Activities**, linked to every video, help students understand and apply course content.
  - **Building Teaching Skills** exercises provide practice in developing the skills and dispositions that are essential to quality teaching.
  - **Resources** such as a Lesson Plan Builder, practice licensure exams, and links to licensure and content standards provide additional practice, whether students are future teachers or already in the classroom.
- **Content and examples** from each age group—infants and toddlers, preschoolers, and primary grades—in the entire early childhood age span provide information on how to work with a variety of age groups.
- **Color photos** are interwoven throughout the chapters helping to illustrate points and bring theory and ideas to life. **Scenarios about children and teachers in classrooms** introduce each chapter, illustrating how research appears in practice.
- The specific **role of the teacher** in relationship to each center provides information on how to facilitate learning (e.g., promote concept development and develop vocabulary unique to each center).
- **Research citations** help students to understand the knowledge base upon which learning environments and curriculum are built.
- Specific topics and strategies assist students to understand and meet the needs of **diverse learners** such as special sections on English language learners and children with Attention Deficit Hyperactivity Disorder.
- **Curricular standards and children's developmental progression** related to each learning center assist students in understanding the goals and content to be facilitated in each learning center.

- Numerous examples provide information about how teachers consider children's **individual needs and interests** in designing the environment and curriculum.

- Inexpensive **tips** for environmental design and materials provide practical ideas.

- **End-of-chapter exercises** and **Apply Your Knowledge** boxes found throughout the text help students demonstrate their learning.

- Comprehensive **environmental checklists** at the end of each chapter provide a tool to assess early childhood environments and review chapter content.

- Content and examples from **a variety of settings** such as special sections on family child care and afterschool programs allow students to see the application of information to different environments.

Instructor Resources

- **MyEducationLab**. This online resource was designed to reinforce student learning by illustrating and extending chapter content through a collection of online resources, including videos, artifacts, case studies, and strategies. Students can further their understanding of chapter content by answering assignable questions that accompany these resources. Additionally, the site contains exercises to help build teaching skills and dispositions for the classroom, called "Building Teaching Skills and Dispositions." It can be found online at *www.myeducationlab.com*. To start using MyEducationLab, activate the access code packaged with your book. If your instructor did not make MyEducationLab a required part of your course or if you are purchasing a used book without an access code, go to *www.myeducationlab.com* to purchase access to this rich resource.

The following instructor resources are available for instructors to download at *www.pearsonhighered.com*. Click on Educators, then click on the "Download Instructor Resources" link.

- **Online Instructor's Manual**. The *Instructor's Manual* gives professors a variety of helpful resources supporting the text. These include chapter overviews, teaching strategies, classroom activities, and discussion questions.

- **Online Test Bank**. The *Test Bank* contains multiple-choice and essay (short-answer) questions. The items are designed to assess the student's understanding of concepts and application to classrooms.

- **Online PowerPoint Slides**. A collection of PowerPoint slides is provided for each chapter.

- **Computerized Test Bank Software**. Known as TestGen, this computerized test bank software gives instructors electronic access to the Test Bank items, allowing them to create and customize exams. TestGen is available in a dual Macintosh and PC/Windows version.

- **Course Management**. The assessment items in the Test Bank are available in WebCT and Blackboard formats.

Throughout the book you will notice the term teacher. *This is used as an inclusive term to designate providers, educarers, educators, and practitioners whether working with infants, toddlers, preschoolers, or elementary-age children in home, center, or school settings. I hope that this text will be used by current and future teachers as a building block for designing environments where children can learn through play, be challenged to grow, learn needed content, explore friendships, experience wonder and joy, and make new discoveries.*

Acknowledgments

There is a saying that it takes a village to raise a child. The same may be said about writing a textbook. A book is not written by an individual in isolation. Books build upon the research and knowledge of others. Others also provide support, encouragement, critiques, and examples. It would be impossible to list all of those who provided inspiration, support, and encouragement in writing this book. However, I would like to mention a few people who provided outstanding assistance. First, I want to thank my daughter, Lisa Bullard. Lisa reviewed, critiqued, and edited chapters; made trips across the country with me for photo shoots; provided sketches and personal photos; and provided examples of practice from her experience in a range of early childhood settings. Danny, Scott, and Christopher Bullard (my sons), Justin O'Dea (my son-in-law), and Dave Browning (a special friend) also deserve thanks for the many ways they assisted with the book (providing ideas, computer assistance, and photos) and for their patience with my preoccupation and the countless hours that I spent writing.

In addition to my family, many others deserve special recognition. I want to thank Eve Malo, my long-term mentor and friend who edited several chapters and provided wise advice about writing and this book. I wish to thank the following reviewers for their helpful comments: Kimberly Bell, Harford Community College; Patricia Fields, Mineral Area College; Mary K. Fitzgerald, University of Tennessee; Phyllis "Lissy" Gloeckler, University of North Carolina, Greensboro; Lori Harkness, Stephen F. Austin State University; Hengameh Kermani, University of North Carolina, Wilmington; Jared A. Lisonbee, Washington State University; Linda Middleton, Mt. San Jacinto College; Judy Puniwai, University of Hawaii and Hawaii Community College; Sandra K. Regan, Middlesex Community College; Pamela Schmidt, Bunker Hill Community College; and Sandra Snook, Eastern Oregon University/Walla Walla Community College/Blue Mountain Community College. I also wish to thank Janis Bullock, and the University of Montana Western early childhood faculty members, especially Libby Hancock, Lucy Marose, Jen Gilliard, and Pat Adams, who provided thoughtful comments and reviews of chapters. Others who provided important support include Susan Parker and Sheila Roberts. Invaluable input and encouragement were also provided by editor Julie Peters.

There were also many early childhood programs, teachers, and students who provided inspiration for the book. I want to especially thank the programs that allowed me to photograph their settings for this book, including Jen Gilliard's Child and Family Development Institute; Davey Hagland's Starting Small Preschool; Brenna Randall's Little Buckaroos; Cardinal Bernardin Early Childhood Center; Karl Wolf's Central School kindergarten classroom; Elly Drigger's Central School kindergarten classroom; Curious Minds: Early Care and Education Center; Helen Gordon Child Development Center; Mentor Graphics Child Development Center; Silver Bow Montessori; A.W.A.R.E. Inc. Early Head Start Program; Spirit at Play Center; Community Playthings; Cozy Kid's Corner; and Middle Creek Montessori.

Brief Contents

Contents

Contents

Creating Environments for Learning
Birth to Age Eight

chapter 1

Understanding the Importance of the Environment

C *lose your eyes and visualize an environment from your childhood that evoked positive emotions. Remember how you felt when you spent time there. Think of the sounds, smells, and experiences in this place. Now sketch this special space, compose a brief poem depicting this place, or write a list of descriptive words that capture the essence of this environment.*

Over the past years, I have asked hundreds of students to engage in this exercise. There are common threads in the students' descriptions of their favorite places. These special places typically include exploration, rich sensory experiences often involving nature, and freedom to choose activities. This place was a refuge that the student had in some way personalized or made his own. Is this true of your special environment?

Do the children you know or work with today have environments that meet these needs? This book will explore ways that we can create rich environments that become the kinds of places that children will remember as their favorites, places of rich sensory experiences, exploration, choice, freedom—a personalized, pleasant refuge.

Why Is the Environment Important for Children's Learning?

The environment we are in affects our moods, ability to form relationships, effectiveness in work or play—even our health. In addition, the early childhood group environment has a very crucial role in children's learning and development for two important reasons.

First, young children are in the process of rapid brain development. In the early years, the brain develops more synapses or connections than it can possibly use. Those that are used by the child form strong connections, while the synapses that are not used are pruned away. Children's experiences help to make this determination. The National Scientific Council of the Developing Child compares the development of the brain to constructing a house stating, "Just as a lack of the right materials can result in blueprints that change, the lack of appropriate experiences can lead to alterations in genetic plans." They further state, "Building more advanced cognitive, social, and emotional skills on a weak initial foundation of brain architecture is far more difficult and less effective than getting things right from the beginning" (2007, p. 1). Because children's experiences are limited by their surroundings, the environment we provide for them has a crucial impact on the way the child's brain develops (Strong-Wilson & Ellis, 2007, p. 43).

The second reason that the early childhood group environment has such a strong role in children's development is because of the amount of time children spend in these environments. Many children spend a large portion of their wakeful hours in early childhood group settings. For example, a baby beginning child care will spend up to 12,000 hours in the program. This is more time than he will spend in both elementary and secondary school (Greenman, 2005a, p. 1). Children will typically spend another 4,000 hours in kindergarten through third grade classrooms.

The early childhood environment that this baby enters will reflect the teacher's philosophy, values, and beliefs about children and learning through either deliberate design or lackadaisical overlook. It provides messages to all those who enter—children, parents, and staff. Is this a place where I am welcomed and where my physical, social, and intellectual needs will be met? Is this an environment where I am seen as worthwhile and competent? Do I passively receive information in this environment, or am I actively engaging in the construction of knowledge? Does someone think I am special enough to provide a beautiful environment for my benefit? Anita Rui Olds, a well-known environmental designer, believes that we should design our early childhood environments for miracles, not minimums. She states:

> Children are miracles. Believing that every child is a miracle can transform the way we design for children's care. When we invite a miracle into our lives, we prepare ourselves and the environment around us. We may set out flowers or special offerings. We may cleanse ourselves, the space, or our thoughts of everything but the love inside us. We make it our job to create, with reverence and gratitude, a space that is worthy of a miracle! Action follows through. We can choose to change. We can choose to design spaces for miracles, not minimums. (2001, p. 13)

In this chapter we will examine the environment with regard to developmentally appropriate practice, discuss how environments reduce behavioral issues, review environments through the eyes of theorists, examine early childhood approaches that emphasize the environment, and finally examine the teacher's role in the environment. This chapter builds the foundation for the remaining chapters in the book, helping us on our quest to design environments for miracles.

The Environment and Developmentally Appropriate Practice

Drawing upon a variety of theorists, the National Association for the Education of Young Children (NAEYC), the largest early childhood association in the world, wrote a position statement titled, *Developmentally Appropriate Practice* (DAP) *in Early Childhood Programs* (Bredekamp & Copple, 1997; Copple & Bredekamp, 2009). They state, "A broad-based review of the literature on early childhood education generates a set of principles to inform early childhood practice" (Bredekamp & Copple, 1997, p. 9). Several principles set forth in the DAP position statement (Bredekamp & Copple, 1997; Copple & Bredekamp, 2009) relate to the environment. We will explore these principles and relationships.

As you read this section, you will note that each description of how the environment supports the DAP principles discusses the "well-designed environment." This is because the environment can either provide support or act as a hindrance to meeting the principles of developmentally appropriate practices. When the environment is well designed, it supports DAP principles.

Importance of Play

"Play is an important vehicle for developing self-regulation as well as for promoting language, cognition, and social competence" (Copple & Bredekamp, 2009, p. 14). A well-designed environment allows children to participate in in-depth play opportunities. The environment "is the backdrop to play, supplying content, context, and meaning" (Cosco & Moore, 1999, p. 2). The value of play has a long history within early childhood. In the early 1800s, Froebel, often called the father of kindergarten, stated, "Play is the highest expression of human development in childhood for it alone is the free expression of what is in the child's soul" (Froebel, 1912, p. 50). Play continues to be valued in early childhood today as exemplified by its inclusion in the DAP principles.

Play has been recognized globally as not only an important learning tool but also an important right for children. For example, play is included in the United Nations Convention on the Rights of the Child (1989), an international, legally binding instrument. Worldwide, all children engage in play. However, the cultural context determines how play is expressed, the role of adults in the play, the type of play that is encouraged (whether individual or group), and gender roles in play (Johnson, Christie, & Wardle, 2005). Play allows children to practice cultural roles and to try out new roles. "During play, children not only explore and reproduce cultural roles and expectations of gender, race, and class, but also test and resist these cultural conventions as they set up and break down boundaries in their play groups" (Wohlwend, 2005, p. 78).

Through play, children learn the rules for social interaction, build social competence, and practice self-regulation. While playing, they can adopt the persona of another, trying out their role and seeing a new perspective. Play allows children to "construct meaning from emotionally challenging experiences" (Haight, Black, Ostler, & Sheridan, 2006, p. 210). Additionally, play can help to alleviate stress.

Play in a rich environment also provides the vehicle for optimal cognitive development. During play, children actively participate in an integrated activity, often solving complex dilemmas. Because the players control the action and the play script, the play is at the child's ideal developmental level (Johnson et al., 2005). Play also encourages flexibility in thinking and risk taking (Sluss, 2005). Lev Vygotsky, a famous Russian theorist, believed that play served several additional purposes. First, play encourages abstract thought by separating meaning from an object. For example, a building block might become a boat, house, or phone. Second, play allows learning to be supported or scaffolded by more competent peers. Third, play encourages self-talk which leads to greater self-regulation (Johnson et al., 2005).

Play Characteristics. Although there are many definitions of play, the characteristics usually include the following. Play:

- is voluntary,
- requires active involvement of the participants,
- involves symbolic activity (pretend is involved),
- is free from external rules; instead, rules are determined by the players,
- focuses on the **process** rather than the **product**,
- and is pleasurable (Sluss, 2005).

Piaget (1962) described three stages of play. The first stage, called practice or **sensorimotor play** (birth to age 2), is characterized by repetition with children practicing the same activity repeatedly. For example, you might see a toddler fill a bucket and then empty it out, only to begin the cycle again. The second stage is **symbolic play** (age 2 to 7). Piaget further divided this stage into constructive (creating and inventing with materials), dramatic (pretend play where one thing represents another), and sociodramatic play (pretend play with other children involving mutual reciprocity) (Sluss, 2005). During this stage, children use an object to stand for something else. For example, a child might pretend a plastic banana in the dramatic play area is a telephone. Experts stress this is often the beginning of representational thought. Stage three, **games with rules** (ages 7 to 11), such as tag, four-square, board games, card games, and so forth, include clearly defined roles and clear-cut rules (Sluss, 2005).

Social Descriptions of Play. In addition to these cognitive descriptions of play, there are also social descriptions of play. Experts once considered these stages of play. However, some now believe that in addition to development, play styles, temperament, and culture affect the type of play the child engages in (Isenberg & Jalongo, 2001). The social descriptions of play as developed by Mildred Parten (1932) include the following:

- Unoccupied—uninvolved in play.
- Onlooker—the child watches others play and may ask questions.
- Solitary—the child plays alone not interacting with others.
- Parallel—the child plays near others. She may mirror the play of the other child but typically does not engage in conversation.
- Associative—the child begins to play with other children.
- Cooperative—the child plays in a group. This play is characterized by shared, defined goals.

Observing the type of play the child participates in can assist the teacher in establishing an environment that supports their play. For example, if children are engaging in parallel play the teacher would make sure there were duplicate or similar items for mirroring the play of another.

Worldwide there is concern about the opportunity for children to participate in play. Poverty, violence, an over-reliance on media entertainment, inadequate space, and an overemphasis on academics affect children's ability and time for play (Sluss, 2005). In addition, time for play is also reduced by changing cultural values including valuing arranged, structured activities over free play. The International Play Association (1989), in response to these alarming trends, has developed a declaration of the child's right to play. They stress that play is critical for children's physical health, mental health, and education and that we must ensure that children have the opportunity to play in educational, family, and community settings.

Play, engaged in by children throughout the world, is a very important vehicle for children's development. A rich environment can support children's play, providing social, emotional, physical, and cognitive benefits.

Active Learning Is Important

"Always mentally active in seeking to understand the world around them, children learn in a variety of ways; a wide range of teaching strategies and interactions are effective in supporting all these kinds of learning" (Copple & Bredekamp, 2009, p. 14). Children in the early years often need to have concrete experiences to learn. As stated by Bredekamp and Copple (1997), "Children need to form their own hypotheses and keep trying them out through social interaction, physical manipulation, and their own thought processes—observing what happens, reflecting on their findings, asking questions, and formulating answers" (p. 13). A well-designed environment provides children with multiple opportunities to construct their knowledge through first-hand experiences. In addition, the well-designed environment allows multiple forms of interaction (peer to peer, child and teacher, small group) and provides many opportunities for the teacher to scaffold children's learning using a variety of different techniques such as modeling, demonstrating, questioning, and providing direct instruction.

After a family who is Chinese introduced the children to a tea ceremony, the teacher extended their learning with this dramatic play center.

Domains Are Related and Influence Each Other

"All the domains of children's development and learning—physical, social and emotional, and cognitive—are important, and they are closely related. Children's development and learning in one domain influence and are influenced by what takes place in other domains" (Copple & Bredekamp, 2009, p. 11). A well-designed environment can facilitate development across domains. First, it provides experiences that integrate learning. For example, as children build with blocks, they are using both gross and fine motor skills. In addition, they practice cooperative and language skills as they build structures with other children. Furthermore, cognitive skills are used as they problem solve building issues and learn about shapes, weight, and balance. Second, a well-designed environment allows children to be independent, to exercise control, and to build competence and mastery. These skills assist a child in developing a healthy self-concept ("I can do this!"). When children have a healthy self-concept, they are more likely to be successful socially and academically.

Learning Follows Well-Documented Sequences, Becoming More Complex Over Time

"Development proceeds toward greater complexity, self-regulation, and symbolic or representational capacities" (Copple & Bredekamp, 2009, p. 12). In addition, "many aspects of children's learning and development follow well documented sequences, with later abilities, skills, and knowledge building on those already acquired" (Copple & Bredekamp, 2009, p. 11). Within a classroom, you will have children who are at different places in the developmental sequence. For example, in a 4-year-old classroom, you might have a child who can count by rote to 10 but who is unable to count a set of objects, another who can count a set of objects to 20, another who is able to recognize numerals and match them to a set of objects, and still another child who is performing some simple addition and subtraction. The well-designed environment provides math manipulatives at each of these levels.

Development Is Variable

"Development and learning proceed at varying rates from child to child, as well as at uneven rates across different areas of a child's functioning" (Copple & Bredekamp, 2009, p. 11). A well-designed environment provides a variety of materials and activities that meet the needs and interests of individual children. For example, in the manipulative center at Tiny Tots, Jamal and Isabel are both sorting. Jamal is sorting bugs by two attributes (size and type). Isabel is sorting keys by one attribute (type of key). John is completing a 12-piece dinosaur puzzle. Tyrone and Sarah are working together on a 25-piece jigsaw puzzle of a turtle. By having **open-ended materials** (materials that can be used a multitude of ways) such as the keys and plastic bugs, and **closed-ended materials** (materials that can only be used one way) such as the different levels of puzzles, all children in the center are able to choose tasks that interest them and meet their varying abilities.

Social and Cultural Contexts Influence Learning

"Development and learning occur in and are influenced by multiple social and cultural contexts" (Copple & Bredekamp, 2009, p. 13). A well-designed environment assists in cultural understanding by accurately reflecting the lives of children and families in the program. Children see themselves reflected in the classroom materials chosen, in photos of themselves and their families, and in the written and spoken language used in the classroom. Multicultural books, pictures, music, art, manipulatives, and dramatic play props representing children in the classroom as well as other cultures expand the children's understanding (for an in-depth discussion of culture see Chapter 2).

Biological Maturation and the Environment Interact

"Development and learning result from a dynamic and continuous interaction of biological maturation and the environment" (Copple & Bredekamp, 2009, p. 12). The well-designed environment provides a range of challenges so that as a child successfully completes a challenge, another one awaits. For example, after the child has completed the 12-piece puzzles, she can tackle the 18-piece puzzle. The child can work with others or work alone. She controls the amount of time she spends engaged in a particular activity. This freedom allows children to be self-directed learners, learning from both the physical and social world. It also recognizes and honors the individual child's maturational level. As stated by Maxwell (2007), "Physical attributes of the environment may therefore be just as critical a part of a quality childcare program as teacher education and experience" (p. 240).

Practice Advances Development

"Development and learning advance when children are challenged to achieve at a level just above their current mastery, and also when they have many opportunities to practice newly acquired skills" (Copple & Bredekamp, 2009, p. 15). A well-designed environment allows children to practice skills in an authentic way (using skills in a real-life context rather than through drill). For example, children will use their developing writing skills in a variety of centers such as labeling their artwork, creating signs for their block buildings, and creating menus in the dramatic play restaurant. Authentic tasks are more engaging and a more effective way to learn than those same tasks performed through drill or direct instruction (Cooper, Capo, Mathes, & Gray, 2007).

Development Occurs in the Context of Secure, Consistent Relationships

"Children develop best when they have secure, consistent relationships with responsive adults and opportunities for positive relationships with peers" (Copple & Bredekamp, 2009, p. 13). The well-designed environment is a place where children and adults can find sanctuary, nurturance, comfort, compassion, and community (Greenman, 2005a). Relationships flourish as children have the opportunity to play with peers in self-chosen activities. The one-on-one time with an adult that often occurs as children interact in learning centers also facilitates positive relationships.

Experiences Shape Future Dispositions and Behaviors

"Children's experiences shape their motivation and approaches to learning, such as persistence, initiative, and flexibility; in turn, these dispositions and behaviors affect their learning and development" (Copple & Bredekamp, 2009, p. 15). A well-designed environment provides multiple ways of learning the same skill through different learning centers. For example, children might learn math skills as they keep time to the music in the music center, classify in the manipulative center, engage in a math activity on the computer, complete a recipe in the cooking area, or build in the block center. They might represent what they are learning through music, art, dance, or writing. This allows children to choose the learning modality that is most effective for them, while exposing them to a wide range of different learning options. Persistence and initiative are increased when children have the opportunity to learn in ways that are interesting and motivating to them.

Early Experiences Are Critical

"Early experiences have profound effects, both cumulative and delayed, on a child's development and learning; and optimal periods exist for certain types of development and learning to occur" (Copple & Bredekamp, 2009, p. 12). The early years are critical for children's current and future learning. An effective environment is one way that we provide the experiences that children need to develop optimally.

The developmentally appropriate practices principles inform the teacher, the environmental designer. These well-designed environments then support developmentally appropriate practices.

Reducing Behavioral Issues Through Environmental Design

In addition to helping support developmentally appropriate practices, a well-designed environment reduces behavioral issues, allowing the teachers to spend more time scaffolding learning. The environment can help prevent behavioral issues in three ways.

1. Children who are actively engaged in developmentally appropriate, interesting activities that they choose usually display fewer behavioral issues. Because the well-designed environment provides children with many choices at different developmental levels, children's unique skill levels, preferred learning styles, and interests can be addressed.

2. The well-planned environment provides private retreats and activities that assist children to manage emotions.

3. The teacher intentionally designs the layout of the environment to prevent common behavioral issues.

To prevent common behavioral issues:

- Teachers design learning centers (dedicated areas, indoors or outdoors, that have intentional purposes) that allow small groups to work together, without interruption from others.

- Dividers are placed between areas to provide a protected space for play and assist children to stay focused.

- Clear boundaries keep materials in one area from interfering with other areas. For example, shelves are placed between the art and block areas preventing trucks from running under the easels.

This enticing reading area at Helen Gordon Lab School in Portland, Oregon, provides privacy and transparency.

- Fighting over limited resources is prevented by having a sufficient number of materials (for very young children, exact duplicates are often necessary).

- Interesting, enticing materials in every center keep children from all congregating in one center.

- Organized and labeled shelves allow children to keep materials orderly and to locate the materials that they need.

- Materials and books are in good condition and beautifully displayed causing the children to want to take care of them.

- The floor plan is developed to prevent children from seeing it as a racecourse. For example, when an obvious circular path is available it invites children to run (see Chapter 5 for sample floor plans).

- Density, the number of children in a given space, is reduced, since crowding increases the likelihood of aggressive behavior (see Chapter 6 for research and information on density).

- Children's health and safety needs, including restful places to sleep or relax, are planned for (to learn more about this topic see Chapter 4).

If you have behavioral issues in your class, first examine the environment to see if a change could solve the problem. For example, I was a consultant to a program where the following occurred:

The teachers were very frustrated because three children were running their large Tonka trucks (housed in the block area) under the art easels. The day before I arrived, one of the easels had fallen, splattering paint everywhere. The teachers had placed the children involved in time-out, but the next day they again drove the trucks under the easel. At this point, the teachers banned these children from the block area for one week. When I arrived, I observed that there was no clear division between the art and block area. In my opinion, the children crawling on the floor may have been focusing on their play and oblivious to the easels. After our discussion, the teachers redesigned the room, placing clear dividers between the art and block area. This solved the problem where the punitive approach did not.

As stated by Torelli and Durrett, "A developmentally designed environment supports the caregiver-child relationship. It minimizes management and custodial activities, allowing caregivers more time for interaction, observation, and facilitation of children's development" (1996, p. 5).

We have seen how the well-designed environment supports developmentally appropriate practice and how it can reduce behavioral issues. Now we will examine the historical roots of the environment as a key early childhood learning element.

Theorists and Approaches Supporting the Importance of the Environment

Theorists and early childhood approaches and philosophies support the need for a rich environment. Just what does a "rich" environment mean? What are its characteristics? We will begin our discussion with Maria Montessori who is credited with designing and promoting beautiful, child-size environments filled with engaging materials. Maria Montessori's philosophy influenced both Piaget and Vygotsky's theories (Mooney, 2000), which we will examine next. Lastly, we will discuss the perspective of Loris Malaguzzi, who built upon the work of Piaget and Vygotsky as well as other theorists to develop the Reggio Emilia approach (Rankin, 2004). Examining the theorists and approaches assists us in understanding the historical and philosophical foundations for designing learning environments.

Montessori

As we prepare orderly, clean, aesthetic environments using child-size furnishings and beautiful materials, we can thank Dr. Maria Montessori, an Italian physician, who was the first advocate of such settings. The carefully prepared environment is a key component of Montessori's philosophy. She states:

> The immense influence that education can exert through children, have the environment for its instrument, for the child absorbs his environment, takes everything from it, and incarnates it in himself. (1995, p. 66)

According to Montessori (1995), the child must find the environment motivating, so he or she is interested in pursuing the available activities. The child will then want to "conduct his own experiences" (Montessori, 1995, p. 92).

Montessori stressed that the environment needs to liberate the spirit, promote independence, allow activity, and be beautiful, safe, and orderly. It is necessary that the environment be orderly to prevent children from wasting their energy seeking materials (Standing, 1957). Additionally, Montessori believed that when children play in an orderly environment, this desire for order becomes part of the child.

Child-size environments, according to Montessori, not only applied to furnishings but also the proportions within the entire building (windows that are near the ground, low door handles, shallow steps) (Standing, 1957). She promoted using low, open shelves to display self-correcting materials (e.g., knobbed cylinders to seriate by size are placed in a frame that will only allow the correct sized cylinder to fit). Maria Montessori also advocated providing real working tools (knives and scissors that cut, shovels and trowels that actually dig holes, quality paints and clay) to children.

She also believed in beauty. According to Montessori, the environment and materials should be harmonious colors, clean, and shining. However, she also stressed that materials should be practical. For example, she replaced several expensive, beautiful marble tables that had been donated to the Montessori center with more practical, simpler, wooden tables that could be easily moved by the children.

The goal of the environment according to Montessori is, "As far as it is possible, to render the growing child independent of the adult. That is, it is a place where he can do things for himself—live his own life—without the immediate help of adults" (Standing, 1957, p. 267). In this environment the child becomes "increasingly active, the teacher increasingly passive. It is a place where the child more and more directs his own life: and in doing so, becomes conscious of his own powers. As long as he is in a state of dependency on the adult he cannot grow as he should" (Standing, 1957, p. 267). However, Montessori also felt that the teacher plays a very critical role since children only have access to the materials that the teacher provides (Montessori, 1995). In addition, teachers observe children, provide very specific guidance to children on how to use the materials, and support them when needed. However, they show respect for the worker and do not interrupt unless it is necessary. The competent teacher "must make her presence felt by those who are seeking; and hide from those who have already found" (Standing, 1957, p. 280). To learn more about the Montessori philosophy, materials, and the role of the teacher, watch the video *Montessori* on MyEducationLab.

Go to MyEducationLab, at www.myeducationlab. com, and select the topic "Program Models and Theories." Under Activities and Applications, watch the video *Montessori*.

Piaget

Like Montessori, Piaget believed that children learn through play, with curiosity driving their learning. He stressed that children construct their knowledge through active involvement. As stated by Piaget, "Experience is always necessary for intellectual development . . . but I fear that we may fall into the illusion that being submitted to an experience (a demonstration) is sufficient for a subject to disengage the structure involved" (Duckworth, 1964, p. 174).

However, more than just experience is required. "The subject must be active, must transform things, and find the structure of his own actions on the objects" (Piaget, 1964, p. 4). In addition to experimentation, the child must be interested in the learning experience (DeVries, 2004). Without interest, the child will not make the effort to make sense of the experience. Piaget believed that cooperation is also helpful for active learning. Cooperation helps people experience moral dilemmas and conflicts and to become aware of differences in opinions and viewpoints thereby creating cognitive disequilibrium (Bullard & Hitz, 1997). **Disequilibrium** is an uncomfortable state where new information challenges one's existing knowledge, beliefs, or assumptions. When this occurs one might **assimilate** the information, working it into his current thinking and belief system, or the person might **accommodate** or modify her thinking or belief. For example, a child might see a horse for the first time and think "cow," assimilating this new animal into their current thinking. However, if someone tells the child it is a horse she might create a new category of animal, accommodating or changing her thinking. Piaget stressed that, "Active physical and mental interactions of the child with the environment (physical and social interactions) that permit construction are seen as the most important school-related factor in cognitive development" (Wadsworth, 1989, p. 165). Piaget also believed that the child needs to be able to transform space. This includes looking at things from a different angle, such as looking down upon a scene on the classroom floor from a loft.

According to Piaget, the teacher is a guiding mentor, who encourages initiative, experimentation, reasoning, and social collaboration. She arranges safe, supportive environments for spontaneous exploration where learners are free to choose from many alternatives (Bullard & Hitz, 1997). Like Montessori, Piaget believed that to be effective the teacher needs to be a careful observer so that he can set up environments and experiences that challenge children.

Vygotsky

When you think of Vygotsky, you probably think of his best-known theory, the **zone of proximal development.** This zone is the difference between what we can independently accomplish and what we can accomplish with assistance from a more competent peer or teacher. This assistance is called **scaffolding.** Like that of a construction crew this support helps us to reach a higher level.

Like Piaget, Vygotsky also believed that children actively construct their own knowledge and that play is a vehicle for doing so. Both theorists believed that play promotes both cognitive and social learning. According to Vygotsky, play, especially pretend play, should be the leading activity for preschool and kindergarten-aged children (Bodrova & Leong, 2007). Vygotsky defined play as an activity that involves an imaginary situation created by the children in which they take on roles and follow a set of rules related to those roles (Bodrova & Leong, 2007). As children play, they use language to negotiate roles, enact scenes, and determine processes furthering their development (Mooney, 2000).

In addition to play, preschool children should also engage in what Vygotsky called productive activities, such as storytelling, block building, and art and drawing. Pre-academic skills are considered beneficial but only if they emerge from children's interests, are considered meaningful to children, and occur in a developmentally appropriate social context (Bodrova & Leong, 2007). According to Vygotskians, motor activities (statues and stop and start games) can also assist with development, especially self-regulation and attention.

When children enter first grade, learning activities become the leading activity. "Learning activities are adult-guided activity around specific, structured, formalized content that is culturally determined" (Bodrova & Leong, 2007, p. 210). However, children at this age still use models (manipulatives and graphic representations). Vygotskians also stress that children themselves need to understand the learning goal and learn to judge their work according to a standard or acceptable level of performance.

To follow the Vygotskian approach you must be a careful observer who uses the information learned to plan hands-on, interactive environments and to scaffold children's learning. Since Vygotsky believed that learning occurs in a social setting, you would provide opportunities and encouragement for children to work together (Mooney, 2000). In addition, Vygotskians often support the quality of children's play through helping them develop play plans (see Chapter 12 for more information).

Malaguzzi and the Reggio Emilia Approach

Malaguzzi, the "philosophical leader" of the Reggio Emilia inspired approach, scaffolded his approach upon the work of other theorists including Montessori, Piaget, and Vygotsky (Fraser & Gestwicki, 2002, p. 9; Rankin, 2004). Like the previous theorists, he believed that children construct knowledge through active engagement with the environment. Similar to Vygotsky, he stressed the importance of social interaction in developing children's mental constructions.

In the Reggio approach, teachers base the educational environment and activities upon the **image of the child.** The child is seen as unique, curious, capable, competent, having potential, relationship seeking, an active constructor of knowledge, a possessor of rights rather than needs (Fraser & Gestwicki, 2000; Gandini, 2004). This image affects the way that teachers work with children. They view themselves as co-constructors of knowledge or partners in children's learning.

The Reggio Emilia environments are referred to as the "third teacher" (the parents and teachers are considered the other two teachers). Several principles support this concept (Fraser & Gestwicki, 2002; Gandini, 2004). In the Reggio Emilia approach, the environment

- Is aesthetic, containing beautiful materials and spaces. There is intense attention to detail in every environmental feature with no overlooked corner, wall, ceiling, or floor.

- Is highly personalized, reflecting the culture and interests of the inhabitants through photos, materials, artwork, and transcriptions (Gandini, 2004).

- Promotes active learning through abundant **affordances** or opportunities to learn that include many choices, provocative displays, and a variety of open-ended, intellectually stimulating materials. The school is a "workshop for research and experimentation, a laboratory for individual and group learning, a place of construction" (Ceppi & Zeni, 1998, p. 14).

- Encourages interaction with materials through the use of **provocations** (activities, materials, or questions that provoke thought, problem solving, and creativity), many different types of objects (realistic objects, colorful beautiful objects, natural objects, authentic furniture, tools, and utensils), beautiful displays that highlight materials, and mirrors that are placed to see objects in new ways (Strong-Wilson & Ellis, 2007).

- Encourages children to represent their ideas in many different types of media. Each center has an **atelierista** (a trained visual arts teacher) and an **atelier** (shared arts studio). In addition, many classrooms have mini-ateliers. Malaguzzi gave art a new meaning (Rankin, 2004), using art as a tool to express one's ideas, thoughts, and knowledge and also to further one's thinking. As one creates the art, knowledge, ideas, and thoughts become visible and new questions, ideas, and thoughts emerge.

- Welcomes children, families, and teachers and views them as the three subjects of education. As stated by Rinaldi, "everything that happens to one affects the other" (2001, p. 53). The Reggio community is characterized by empathy; close bonds; a sharing of knowledge, fears, and hopes; and a construction of common values and shared meanings (Ceppi & Zeni, 1998, p. 11).

- "Fosters encounters, communication, and relationships" (Gandini, 2004, p. 17) through the design of activities and space. Spaces are available for children to work in small groups and to work individually if they choose. Common areas such as a central piazza encourage children, parents, and teachers from different groups to interact. The environment is also rich in documentation of group efforts. It is a "living testimony to interactions that happen in the environment" (Strong-Wilson & Ellis, 2007, p. 42).

- Provides rich sensory experiences that encourage "investigation and discovery using the whole body." The environment itself (walls, floors, ceilings) is also multisensory with different sensory media so each individual person's needs can be met (Ceppi & Zeni, 1998, p. 8).

- Provides transparency. Light is everywhere, shining through low windows; reflected in shiny mobiles and mirrors hung from ceilings, walls, and lofts; shining from interesting light features; flowing through transparent fabric, beautiful glass objects, colored transparency film in windows and child-created murals on plastic sheets; and explored with light tables (Fraser & Gestwicki, 2002). Children can look from one space to another, outside or into another classroom. It is also a metaphor for openness and transparency in sharing learning through documentation (Fraser & Gestwicki, 2002).

- Brings the outside world in. This includes the natural world and the social world (the community and culture). The program experiences "osmosis with the world outside. A school should not be a sort of counter world, but the essence and distillation of society surrounding it, it is a part of the larger world" (Ceppi & Zeni, 1998, p. 6).

- Supports flexibility and creativity through encouraging children and adults to use objects and space in imaginative ways.

- Provides reciprocity. The environment is not passive; instead it is like a living being, conditioning and being conditioned by children's and adult's actions (Fraser & Gestwicki, 2002; Gandini, 1998).

Go to MyEducationLab and select the topic "Program Models and Theories." Under Activities and Applications, watch the video *Reggio Emilia.*

The Reggio Emilia teacher is a keen observer who is an active listener and interpreter. She uses this knowledge to establish provocations to help children think more deeply, question assumptions, and design flexibly planned curriculum. The curriculum occurs at a leisurely pace and flows naturally from the children's and teachers' ideas (Gandini, 2004). The teacher also collaborates with children, coworkers, families, and the community to form a "community of learners" (Fraser & Gestwicki, 2002). Watch the video *Reggio Emilia* on MyEducationLab to learn more about this philosophy.

Montessori, Piaget, Vygotsky, and Malaguzzi all valued the environment as an important teacher of young children. They each also valued the teacher as an environmental designer and as a scaffolder of children's learning. In the next section, we will further examine the teacher's role in supporting children's learning.

Guidelines for Creating Effective Learning Environments: Role of the Teacher

Teaching effectively through the environment requires the teacher to be concurrently aware of the children in her classroom (their developmental levels, cultural backgrounds, interests, learning styles, dispositions, and behavioral nuances) and the early learning guidelines, curriculum standards, and program outcomes appropriate for her age group. She must use this information to design relevant, engaging environments and to make needed environmental changes as the year progresses. Finally, she must be available as children use the environment to scaffold their learning. In this section, we will discuss the prerequisites for establishing the environment, some key points for environmental design, and the teacher's role once she has designed the environment. Each of these points will be further explained in chapters throughout the book.

Prerequisites for Establishing a Rich Environment

Teachers must have knowledge and skills before even beginning the environmental design. To design the environment you must be aware of

- Child development and developmentally appropriate practices. This knowledge forms the basis for planning and developing curriculum and the environment.

- Individual children's developmental level and interests so that environments can be developed that are meaningful to each child. This is often accomplished through informal assessment techniques such as observation and child interviews and discussions. Interviews with families can also provide important information. One toddler center sent a small plastic bag to each family before the program began and asked them to place pictures or items in the bag that demonstrated their child's interests. The teachers then collected these and used the information as the basis for designing the environment.

- Children's cultural background to assure that experiences and environments are relevant to each child. Garcia states that we must seek information "like an ethnographer" (2003, p. 16), a researcher learning about the culture of the children and families we serve. Being aware of our own culture and how it affects our values, beliefs, and practices is a first step in cultural competence. We are then ready to begin to learn about the culture of others. General information about the culture of the children through activities such as reading, talking to community leaders, and inviting guest speakers to the program can assist us in cultural understanding. Knowing that each family is unique, we can use the general knowledge acquired to talk to each individual family about their specific values and practices (Marshall, 2003). To discover other ways that teachers can learn about families' cultures, watch *Incorporating Home Experiences of Culturally Diverse Students Part-1* on MyEducationLab.

Go to MyEducationLab and select the topic "Diversity." Under Activities and Applications, watch the video *Incorporating the Home Experiences of Culturally Diverse Students Part-1.*

- Curriculum standards and early learning guidelines (what children at different ages should know and be able to do) so that you can develop an environment, and scaffold children's learning in meeting these standards.

- Your own and your program's philosophy. The philosophy we have is often implicit or hidden, but it affects our beliefs and therefore our actions. We each have values and preconceived notions based upon years of our own personal educational experience about the role of the student, teacher, and learning environment. We also have formed beliefs about different cultural and family characteristics. Think about your beliefs in regard to single parents, same-sex parents, grandparents raising children, children who are homeless, children who come from different racial or ethnic backgrounds than you. These beliefs create a lens through which we view the world, families, children, and the classroom. By uncovering our belief system or making our values more explicit, we can examine them to see if they are consistent with early childhood theory and philosophy.

Designing the Environment

After you have met these prerequisites, you are ready to begin the environmental design process. You will need to

- Design your floor plan. If you follow the principles of developmentally appropriate practice, you will typically develop separate learning centers in your classroom (see Chapter 5 for a detailed description).

- Consider design outcomes (aesthetically pleasing, home-like), design elements (softness, texture, color, and lighting), and design palettes (ceilings, walls, and floors). You must also consider noise and the density of children per available space (see Chapter 6 for more information).

- Consider the health and safety of children and adults (see Chapters 4 and 18 for more information).

- Design each learning center, stocking each with an abundance and variety of developmentally appropriate, culturally relevant, interesting, and intellectually stimulating materials. You will want to include both open-ended and closed-ended materials. Children can use open-ended materials, those that have more than one type of use, such as buttons to classify in multiple ways; pieces of fabric to make into capes, headdresses, or doll blankets; or clay to create whatever one can imagine. Closed-ended materials have a specific or a clearly defined use, such as puzzles. Chapters 7 through 17 provide information about designing each specific center.

- Provide an effective context for learning through developing a schedule that allows time for using the centers, designing smooth transitions and routines that support the flow of the day, providing effective grouping methods to meet children's needs, and observing and documenting children's development and interests so you can support children's learning and share their learning with others (see Chapter 3 for more information).

Interacting with Children in the Environment

Of course, the teacher's role does not end with the classroom design. As children use the environment, you will need to be available to support their learning. You will do this in a variety of ways including observing, scaffolding learning, supporting peer interactions, acknowledging them as learners, assisting them to follow rules, keeping them safe, and documenting their learning.

Observing. Observation is critical in helping you to determine children's interests, development, dispositions, and need for support. The information gained assists you in building relationships with children, choosing relevant materials and activities, and evaluating how classroom spaces are used. Close observation will also assist you in determining your immediate role. Is it to observe children's play, to scaffold learning for an individual child or small group, to become a play partner, or to roam the room providing needed assistance?

Scaffolding or Supporting Children's Learning. We can scaffold children's learning in a variety of ways including modeling, asking open-ended questions, providing new language, presenting additional information, offering additional materials, and through being a play partner. However, when we scaffold children's learning, we must always be careful not to inadvertently interrupt or redirect their play (Sluss, 2005). We will examine each of these forms of scaffolding individually.

Modeling. There are many situations where children can be assisted in learning through a more competent model. For example, you might model the use of a tool (spoon, hammer), technique (stacking two blocks, using a slip to join two pieces of clay), social skill (modeling a gentle touch to a toddler, using conflict resolution steps with a preschool child), physical skill (hopping, yoga position), or cognitive skills (using one-to-one correspondence, tagging items as you count them).

Asking Open-Ended Questions. **Open-ended questions** encourage multi-word responses that have more than one correct answer. Open-ended questions invite conversation, require thinking and problem solving, and ask children to share ideas, theories, thoughts, emotions, and reasoning (Kostelnik, Whiren, Soderman, & Gregory, 2009). In contrast, **closed-ended questions** often ask the child to recall factual information, answer a yes or no question, or state a preference. The child typically answers the closed question in one or a few words. Table 1.1 provides examples of both types of questions.

Using Rich, Descriptive Language and New Vocabulary. As you interact with children, you can insert descriptive language and introduce children to new vocabulary. Each center and each activity have unique vocabulary associated with them. For example, when the teacher at Discovery Bay Childcare changed the dramatic play center to a garage, the chil-

Table 1.1 Sample Closed and Open Questions

Closed Questions	Open Questions
What shape is this?	What are the ways that circles and ovals are the same or different?
What color is the bird?	Why do you think the bird is brown?
Should we skip or hop across the room?	What are other ways that we can move across the room?
Is this a moth or butterfly?	How are the butterfly and the moth the same? How are they different?
Will the salt affect the ice?	What are ways that we can make the ice melt faster?
Can you make applesauce from apples?	What are other things that we could make with the apples?

dren learned many new words including *mechanic*, *automobile*, *carburetor*, *dial*, *gear*, and *engine*. When the teacher later changed the area to a hospital, there was a new set of vocabulary: *immunization*, *x-ray*, *anesthesiologist*, and *physician*.

Children begin school with a vast difference in the number of words in their vocabulary. For example, in one study the total number of words children heard before the age of 4 was 13 million for children who were from low-income homes versus 45 million for children from the highest economic group (Hart & Risley, 1995). This has a profound effect on the children's later success in schooling. However, as an early childhood teacher you have the opportunity to help change this statistic by exposing children to rich, descriptive language in the way that they learn best, in an authentic context.

Encouraging Language by Using Parallel Talk, and Expanding and Extending Speech. You can use *parallel talk* with young children to describe what the child is doing or what you are doing. For example, "Oh, you are laying your baby down so it can go to sleep." "You are stacking two blocks." "I am going to get a clean diaper for you now." To increase the child's vocabulary you might also expand the child's sentence. For example, the child says, "Baby sleep," and you might say, "Yes, you are rocking your baby to sleep." When extending the child's speech you add additional information and model appropriate grammar, sentence structure, and pronunciation. For example, when a child says, "I have a truck," you might respond, "Yes; you have a shiny, red, dump truck."

Presenting Additional Information and Enhancing Children's Background Knowledge. When the teacher has background information about a topic, she can naturally introduce information during interactions with children. For example, Tom has a butterfly and moth in his classroom. Garmai and Amberly are looking at them. Tom mentions that the butterfly is called a monarch and that it can fly over 2000 miles. He tells Amberly that this is how far she flies when she visits her grandmother. Amberly says, "But I am in a big plane, and the butterfly is flying with just its own wings. It must get really tired."

Assisting Children to Carefully Observe and Reflect Upon Their Learning. Teachers assist children to observe and reflect in many ways. Tom says to Garmai and Amberly, "Look at the butterfly's and moth's antennas." The children carefully observe through magnifying glasses, noting that the butterfly has a round club at the end of its antenna while the moth does not. Tom lets them know that this is one way that you can tell moths and butterflies apart. Later Tom asks the children if they would like to draw the butterfly and moth, providing the children a way to demonstrate and reflect upon what they learned.

Offering Additional Materials. Children may need additional materials to move to the next step in a project or to think or create in new ways. Julio is building a play guitar at the woodworking center and wants to make the guitar strings. Anne, his teacher, provides some fishing line for him. Jonathon and Saleena are building a multi-level block structure. The teacher provides a pulley, allowing the children to build an elevator in their building. Teachers can also ask the children what materials they think would help them to complete their project.

Being a Play Partner. The younger the child, the more time the adult will spend as the child's play partner. In most cases, you will want to follow the child's lead, engaging in give and take actions and communication (Post & Hohmann, 2000). Azura, a teacher in a toddler classroom, sits with Lisa and Torrence pretending to eat lunch. Lisa pretends to pour Azura and Torrence milk. Azura says "thank you"; Torrence then also says "thank you."

Supporting Peer Interactions. As a teacher, you may need to assist children to solve conflicts they are unable to resolve themselves, to interpret and provide words for children's actions, and to help children enter play. Children who are successful in play entry often begin as onlookers watching the other children play. This allows them to understand the play, the roles, and the plot. They often begin entry by playing next to the group, engaging in a parallel activity. Teachers can assist children to enter play by scaffolding, modeling, giving children desirable props, suggesting roles, or entering the play with the child. There is a more in-depth discussion about peer interactions in Chapter 2.

Acknowledging Learners. We acknowledge learners when we show a sincere interest in what they are doing, document and display their work, and use encouraging language. Encouraging statements reflect the child's effort, provide very specific information, encourage the child's judgment on his work rather than your own, and often lead to further interaction. Encouragement can boost children's self-confidence, persistence, and acceptance of their own and other's efforts (Gartrell, 2007).

In contrast, praise tends to be more generic, focusing on the completed product, and on the adult's judgment about the product. Praise may lead children to feel "conditional acceptance" (Gartrell, 2007, p. 254). Instead of developing intrinsic or internal satisfaction with what one has done, frequent praise can make children dependent on external acknowledgement, making them think they are only worthwhile when someone else states they are. For example, a Head Start teacher, Tanya, shared with me her rude awakening to the dangers of praise. Each day, when Laurie entered the classroom Tanya told her how pretty she looked. When Laurie went to kindergarten, she came home and told her mother "I'm ugly." Her mother was stunned and asked Laurie why she thought so. Laurie said, "Mrs. Taylor never tells me I'm pretty, so she must think I'm ugly." Laurie had become conditioned to praise and without it, she did not feel worthwhile. It is important to acknowledge learners, but to be cautious with praise. Table 1.2 provides examples of praise and encouragement.

Apply Your Knowledge   Two children have spent the entire center time building a multi-floor castle. They are proudly showing the castle to you. What are some encouraging remarks you could say to the children?

Table 1.2 Examples of Praise and Encouragement

Praise	Encouragement
Good job.	This is the first time you've completed the entire puzzle. I bet you feel proud.
I like the way you cleaned up.	You are working very hard putting away all the blocks.
Great artwork.	I see that you put a lot of detail in your picture, like adding all the branches on the tree. That must have taken a long time.

Helping Children Engage in Sustained Play. Some children have a difficult time beginning or sustaining play. It is helpful if teachers have children make a plan before the play period, offer a child a choice between activities, and make sure that there are activities that have high appeal to the child. It is also important to examine the environment to make sure that it is not visually overwhelming, that there are clear divisions between centers to reduce distractions, and that noise levels are controlled.

Reminding Children of the Rules. Reminders of rules may be especially needed when children are new to your classroom. Studies have found that teachers who spend more time at the beginning of the year helping children learn the rules and routines have a greater number of children who are actively engaged later in the year (Guthrie, 2000). Often you will be reminding children of interaction rules. For example, when Nancy grabs Salena's truck, you might say, "Salena is playing with the dump truck right now. Do you want to get a different truck or do you want to ask Salena if you can play with her?" You may also need to remind children of rules that assist in keeping the room orderly, "You need to put the puzzles away when you are done using them." Children might also need reminders about the appropriate use of equipment and materials, "The sand needs to stay in the table. When sand gets thrown it can get in someone's eyes and that really hurts."

Intervening When Needed to Provide for Safe Play. It is important to intervene if children are hurting each other physically or emotionally. You must also make sure that children are not engaging in behaviors that could seriously injure them. However, as stated by Greenman (2005b), we must be very thoughtful about when to intervene.

> The drive to protect our children is profound and easily can lead to cleansing their lives of challenge and depth. Early childhood is a time when children begin to live in the world and hopefully learn to love the world. They can't do this when fenced off from the messy richness of life to live in a world of fluorescent lights and plastic toys, two-dimensional glowing screens, and narrow teaching instruction. Scrubbing and polishing raw experience in the name of health and safety scrapes away the natural luster and meaning of childhood. Many of the wonders and joys of childhood that fuel the best in our adult selves are birthed in the unavoidable messes, bumps, bruises, and tears that come with exuberant exploration. (Greenman, 2005b, p. 7)

Documenting Learning. Another important role of the adult is to document children's individual and group learning. You might capture children's play through anecdotal records (brief, focused descriptions of a situation), photos, transcriptions of their conversations, tape recordings, video recordings, samples of their work, and so forth. Documentation can enhance children's learning by making their learning visible, by demonstrating that we take their ideas and work seriously, and through allowing children and teachers to "revisit" ideas

(Katz & Chard, 1996, pp. 3–4). It promotes teacher's planning and evaluation with children, supplies information for communicating with parents, provides a history of the school, and can become a powerful tool for advocacy (Katz & Chard, 1996).

Enhancing and Extending the Learning Beyond the Learning Center Time

To take full advantage of the environment as a learning tool we need to extend the learning beyond the center time. One technique is to use small- or large-group discussions to enhance the learning. You can use small and large groups to:

Introduce Center Activities and Materials and Build Excitement. Veronica was introducing a bubble center that was going to be in the sensory table. She set out a variety of objects (funnels, sieves, regular spoons, slotted spoons, forks, tea strainer, and potato masher) and asked the children what they thought you might do with these materials. After a lively discussion and many guesses, Veronica brought out a bubble wand and asked again. Several children then guessed that they were going to make bubbles. Veronica then had the children vote on whether each item would make bubbles or not and graphed their answers. Children were eager to see if their hypotheses were correct and to try the different materials. Over the course of the next several days, all the children voluntarily visited the center.

Provide Relevant Background Experiences. Children who have a rich experience base engage in more in-depth play, leading to greater social and intellectual outcomes. Jerry had created a music center with several rhythm instruments, including many from other cultures. However, the children had very little interest in the music area. Jerry realized that the children had never seen the instruments in use. He invited guests to come in and play the various instruments. He also showed a videotape of the cultural instruments being played by a group of musicians. Because of this exposure, the children became interested in using the music center.

Introduce Challenges. Teacher challenges can provide additional interest and assist children to stretch their capabilities. For example, in Chapter 11 you will read a description of a teacher who challenged children to create tall buildings. Another teacher challenged children to create a way to get a doll from the first to the second floor of their block building. By observing you will find opportunities to introduce more challenging tasks for the children you work with.

Plan and Recall Experiences. Both the High/Scope and Tools of the Mind (based on the Vygotskian approach) models emphasize having children make plans before playing and to reflect upon these plans after play. Bodrova and Leong (2007), discussing the Vygotskian approach, stress that planning reduces conflicts and allows children to engage in more mature, focused play. Reviewing their play plans can help children to extend the play the following day.

The High/Scope model encourages beginning planning with toddlers. As discussed by Post and Hohman (2000), planning and recalling can help children to "call up mental pictures of themselves in action, to connect their ideas with actions, to communicate their intentions to others, and to begin to organize their past actions into a simple narrative" (p. 260). To see a teacher guide a group of children through the *plan, do, review* process, watch the video *High/Scope* on MyEducationLab.

Encourage Children to Share Their Work. Sharing work is a way of acknowledging the importance of what children have done. Children get an opportunity to speak in front of a group and to ask each other questions and give suggestions. Additionally, one child's work might spark an interest in another child.

myeducationlab

Go to MyEducationLab and select the topic "Program Models and Theories." Under Activities and Applications, watch the video *High/Scope*.

Synthesize and Discuss Children's Learning. After the children had used the bubble center for several days, Veronica again discussed the bubbles. She and the children reexamined their initial predictions and reviewed what they had found out. Veronica placed all the items that made bubbles in one area and all those that did not in another. She asked the children what was similar about the items that made bubbles. By having this circle, Veronica was able to help children analyze and express what they had learned.

Enriching and Changing Centers as Needed

You will need to continuously observe and monitor centers to enrich and change them as additions and changes can spark children's interest, meet their needs, and provide for more in-depth learning. For example, the children in Jocia's toddler class had become fascinated with an alarm clock that he had added to the dramatic play area. Seeing their interest, he went to a secondhand store and purchased a variety of alarm clocks, wall clocks, and watches for the children to listen to and experiment with.

You might also introduce an **element of surprise.** This is often something that makes children curious, makes them wonder why, and creates new possibilities. Elements of surprise might start a discussion, provoke new ideas, or inspire interest. For example, a teacher might place a crystal in a window, hide "jewels" in the sand table, or place a mirror under a plant so one sees the underside. Min, a Head Start teacher, was studying bones with the children. One day she hid several bones in the outdoor sandbox. As children were digging, they discovered the bones. They were very excited, wondering where the bones came from and what kind of bones they were. All the children busily began to dig, discovering every bone. Elements of surprise cause wonderment, joy, and excitement; gifts that all children deserve.

This light table is enriched with natural (twigs, feathers, pinecones) and recycled items (beads, buttons, fabric, ribbon) allowing children to create designs of their choice. Clear glass containers highlight the materials.

Helping Families Understand the Learning Center Approach

It is also the responsibility of the teacher to assist families in understanding developmentally appropriate practices and to keep families informed about what their children are learning. Families are often concerned about whether their children will be successful in the next level of schooling. Some parents associate worksheets with learning. When they do not see these sent home each night they become worried. Following are several techniques teachers have used to provide information to families.

Jeremy has a family night at the beginning of each year. He introduces the center approach by having the families complete activities in each learning center. Jeremy tries to choose activities that would be appropriate for children and also interesting for adults. For example, in the manipulative area, Jeremy places a collection of office items with a sign asking families to sort them in as many ways as they can think of. One year, four parents became very engaged in this activity and found 50 different ways of classifying the materials. At the end of the evening, the families and teachers gather together to reflect upon what they have learned.

Understanding the Importance of the Environment

Teresa makes signs to place in each center that list skills and knowledge that children acquire through using the center. She also regularly sends "Today I learned" notes to the families. While children interact in centers, she will observe and write a short note to families to tell what their child has learned that day. For example, "Chin used both math and science skills to make a block structure with a turret today. He experimented with many ideas (hypotheses) before solving the problem of how to create a turret that would balance on top of his tower." Teresa has created a check off sheet so that she can easily track who she has sent notes to. By keeping a tracking sheet, Teresa can make sure that she regularly sends notes to each child's family.

Teachers may also send home artifacts (samples of children's "work") and other forms of documentation from center work. These include photos of children participating in an activity, artwork and recording sheets the child has created, or audio recordings of children reading or telling a story. At least occasionally, it is helpful to include information that describes and interprets what children learned. Many teachers save some of this work to place in portfolios. The portfolio will include artifacts with a description and interpretation for each artifact. Portfolios are typically shared with parents during parent-teacher conferences or home visits.

Rhonda, a teacher of kindergarten children, develops a booklet that describes the learning centers in her classroom. There is a photo of each classroom center, a description of what children learn in the center, and the state standards that are addressed in the center. Each year she gives the booklet to each family and the school administrators. She states, "Before I did this, families and the administrators were concerned about whether the children would be ready for first grade if they spent so much time playing. However, now that they understand that children can enjoy school and still be meeting the standards, they have become advocates for this approach."

Programs that use the project approach often have **culminating events** to conclude a project. Culminating events allow the children to share what they have learned with parents and other community members. For example, one program had completed a project on "Our Body," and decided to have their culminating event at a community health fair. They set up displays that included webs of what the children knew before and after the project, questions the children had, art they had created, stories they had written, and materials they had used. Pictures and narratives described the center materials, children's activities, and learning throughout the project. They also invited the public to try out a sensory walk that the children had created. For the sensory walk, the children decorated fourteen flat boxes and placed a different item in each box (e.g., sand, bubble wrap, sandpaper). Participants could walk barefoot through each of the boxes.

Conclusion

In conclusion, teachers play a crucial role in children's learning by designing a rich, stimulating environment, interacting with children as they use the environment, expanding and extending the children's learning beyond the center time period, and changing centers and adding materials to provide for more in-depth learning. In addition, teachers assist parents and administrators to understand the learning center approach. In each chapter of this book, you will find many other examples of specific ways that teachers are involved in children's learning.

In this chapter, we have discussed the importance of the learning environment, how the environment supports developmentally appropriate practices, the crucial role of the teacher, and the recognition by theorists and early childhood founders of the importance of the environment. It seems only fitting to end this chapter with a quote from Maria

Montessori, who first created the child-sized environment and filled it with beautiful, thoughtfully planned learning materials. In discussing children's cognitive development she states, "The first lesson we must learn is that the tiny child's absorbent mind finds all its nutriment in its surroundings. Here it has to locate itself, and build itself up from what it takes in. Especially at the beginning of life must we, therefore, make the environment as interesting and attractive as we can" (1995, p. 97).

Sample Application Activities

1. You began this chapter by imagining your favorite childhood environment. Now think of your favorite environment today. Are there commonalities between your favorite environment as a child and your favorite environment today? What aspects of your favorite environment could you share with children through your classroom environmental design?

2. Visit an early childhood facility. What do you see in the environment that was influenced by Montessori, Vygotsky, Piaget, or Malaguzzi? Observe the teacher and record examples of the ways she is scaffolding the children's learning.

3. You have just been hired to teach a kindergarten class in a public school with K–5 classes. Write a one-page letter to parents describing why developmentally appropriate practices and learning through play are important in kindergarten.

4. Review the Montessori, Reggio Emilia, and High/Scope video clips referenced in this chapter. Using the video clips and information in the text, compare and contrast these three approaches. For additional information see the following websites:

   http://www.montessori-namta.org/NAMTA/index.html

   http://www.reggioalliance.org/narea.php

   http://www.highscope.org/

   http://www.earlychildhoodnews.com/earlychildhood/article_view.aspx?ArticleID=367

5. Review the following Pre-K virtual tour on the Pre-K Now website to see the important characteristics of the physical and emotional environment: http://www.preknow.org/resource/classroomtour.cfm

chapter 2

Establishing an Emotionally Supportive and Equitable Environment

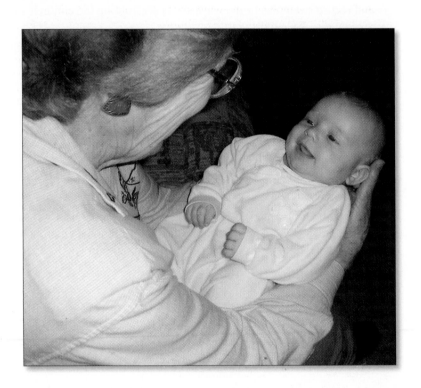

*I*t was November when Kamiko's parents enrolled her in preschool. They had just arrived from Japan to work on a ranch in an extremely isolated, rural, Caucasian community. Alisha, Kamiko's teacher, knew that she should have materials in the environment that reflected Kamiko. However, she could not easily find any books or nonstereotypical images of Japanese children. She finally ordered some books and when they arrived several weeks later, she placed them in the reading area. When Kamiko discovered the books, she was elated. She carried one of the books with her all day, saying "me, me" to everyone she met. She even slept with the book at nap time.

The next day she again carried the book with her, showing the pictures to each parent and child as they arrived.

It was a vivid reminder to Alisha of the importance of having materials and images representing all the children in the classroom. When Alisha saw Kamiko's reaction, she began to examine all the classroom materials. There were multicultural dolls in the dramatic play area, but none were Asian. The same was true for the multicultural figures in the block area. A multicultural poster adorned the wall but again none of the children were Japanese. Alisha replaced the multicultural poster with photos of children in the classroom, she ordered Asian dolls, and she visited with Kamiko's parents to see if they had any materials that she could add to the classroom. The parents brought in some empty food containers, a children's dish set, and a Japanese newspaper for the dramatic play area. This recognition by Alisha of the family's culture helped to build relationships. As the year progressed, Alisha continued to learn more about Kamiko's culture and to build relationships with Kamiko and her family.

Relationships are the heart of an early childhood program. Just as a plant needs to experience both sunlight and rich soil to produce a healthy plant, a child needs to experience both quality *relationships* and quality *instruction* to be successful (Ray, Bowman, & Brownell, 2006). Relationships affect children's social skills, academic success, and brain development (National Scientific Council on the Developing Child, 2004b, 2007; Ray et al., 2006). They also affect children's feelings about the program.

Relationships between staff and children, staff and parents, among children, and among staff define the climate of a program. High quality climates assist children to feel safe, increase positive behavior, and reduce absenteeism from the program. When children are in emotionally supportive environments in the early years, their achievement increases, resulting in higher social, math, and reading scores (Ray et al., 2006). Additionally, supportive relationships positively influence work habits and improve educational resiliency. This is especially true for children who are at risk of school failure (Ray et al., 2006).

Emotional responsiveness (acknowledging and responding to children's emotions and needs), particularly in the early years, even affects brain development and the biochemistry of the brain. Similarly unresponsive care can alter the brain's biochemistry. Here's how this works: when we feel stress, our bodies produce the hormones adrenaline and cortisol. Both hormones help the body to respond to threat. However, when these hormones are activated either frequently or for long periods, they can produce negative effects on the brain. For example, long-term elevations of cortisol can change the architecture of the brain, leading to memory and learning problems (National Scientific Council on the Developing Child, 2004b, p. 3). Because young children's brains are "particularly malleable," stress is especially harmful for this age group (National Scientific Council on the Developing Child, 2004b, p. 2).

The child's early experiences also determine how the stress system reacts to subsequent stress. High levels of stress can result in a stress system that responds at a lower threshold of stress and remains stressed for a longer period of time (National Scientific Council on the Developing Child, 2004b). As stated by the Council, "Like the immune system, which defends the body against threatening infections but can cause autoimmune disease when it turns against the body's own cells, a poorly controlled response to stress can be damaging to health and well-being if activated too often or for too long" (National Scientific Council on the Developing Child, 2004b, p. 2). Elevated stress can lead to an increased vulnerability for stress-related disorders (depression, anxiety, cardiovascular problems, stroke, and diabetes) (National Scientific Council on the Developing Child, 2004b).

However, high-quality care in the early years leads to a lessened stress response (National Scientific Council on the Developing Child, 2004b). In addition, as you will learn in this chapter when a child does experience stress, the responsive teacher can dramatically buffer the child's stress response through her relationship with the child (National Scientific Council on the Developing Child, 2004b).

While teachers have limited influence over the other environments that children are in, they do have control over their classroom. When the classroom environment is emotionally supportive, children not only learn more, but they are more likely to want to come to the program, and absenteeism is reduced.

Circle of Courage: Defining an Emotionally Supportive, Equitable Environment

Realizing the importance of the emotionally supportive, equitable environment, many curriculum developers have designed excellent models to assist teachers. In this chapter, we view the supportive environment through the lens of one of these models, the Circle of Courage. This model, simple to remember and yet profound, provides a unifying theme for services to children in multiple settings. The model, which incorporates resiliency (Brendtro & Larson, 2006) and self-worth research (Coopersmith, 1981), is used worldwide in educational, mental health, youth and family services, treatment facilities, and juvenile justice settings.

The Circle of Courage, based on Native American philosophy, is compatible with beliefs from many cultural groups. The philosophy is based on four needs (the need to belong, to achieve mastery, to be independent, and to be generous). Brendtro, Brokenleg, and Van Bockern (2002), the authors of the Circle of Courage, describe these in the following ways:

- The child who experiences the spirit of belonging knows, "I am loved." This is essential for meeting all other needs. To experience the spirit of belonging children must have mutual connections or positive relationships characterized by deep respect. Since belonging is cyclical, the child who expresses this ideal also knows how to identify and relate to others.

- The child who experiences the spirit of mastery knows that "I can succeed." This includes both academic and social competence. Mastery assists a child to have a positive self-concept.

- The child who experiences the spirit of independence knows "I have the power to make decisions." This provides individual control and inner discipline and allows the child to establish and attain goals. As stated by the authors of the Circle of Courage, "Even when it might be easier for the adults to 'take over,' adults will respect children enough to allow them to work things out in their own manner" (Brendtro, Brokenleg, & Van Bockern, 2002, p. 53).

- The child who experiences the spirit of generosity knows "I have a purpose for my life." Generosity allows the child to take "responsibility for the welfare of others in the community" (Brendtro et al., 2002, p. 59) and to contribute positively to the group through being caring and empathetic.

According to the authors of the model, when these needs are not met or are out of balance, the child becomes discouraged and loses a sense of purpose, leading to a downward spiral (Brendtro et al., 2002). Adults often have a difficult time forming relationships with discouraged, disengaged children and may respond to them punitively. This leads the child to react in an even more discouraged way. However, using the Circle of Courage as a guiding framework for interacting with children, designing our environments, and planning our curriculum can help children to avoid this downward spiral.

Circle of Courage Foundations

To meet the needs of belonging, mastery, independence, and generosity children need foundational skills. These foundational skills include attachment, self-regulation, and social skills (empathy and friendship skills). We will examine each of these foundational skills next.

Attachment

Secure attachment is at the heart of the spirit of belonging. "Attachment describes a strong emotional bond between a baby or young child and a caring adult who is part of the child's everyday life—the child's attachment figure" (Honig, 2002, p. 2). The attachment figure greatly influences a child's beliefs about relationships. These beliefs become internalized templates for behavior and have a "profound effect throughout life" (Honig, 2002, p. 3). Attachment grows over time, beginning at birth and progressing through the early years (Honig, 2002, p. 3). It involves a two-way interaction, with the child affecting the caregiver and the caregiver affecting the child.

Securely attached children use the adult attachment figure as a home base, feeling comfortable to explore or try new things, but returning to the caregiver for reassurance and guidance. Children who are securely attached to at least one adult have better current and future academic and social outcomes. About 70% of young children display secure attachments to one or both parents (Riley, San Juan, Klinkner, & Ramminger, 2008). However, these children also benefit from having a secure attachment to their childcare provider or teacher. There is no indication that the relationship between the child and caregiver negatively affects parental attachment. Instead, outcomes are more positive if the child is attached to both the parents and the early childhood teacher (Riley et al., 2008). Attachment to the teacher is even more crucial for children who do not have a secure attachment with their parents (Riley et al., 2008). While attachment is critical for young children, it is very difficult if they must detach and reattach to important people in their lives. This can cause stress and "enduring problems" (National Scientific Council on the Developing Child, 2004a, p. 4). Therefore, we must try to reduce the number of times that children are moved to new classrooms or programs or experience new teachers within the same classroom. For example, many infant/toddler programs practice *continuity of care* and permit teachers to move with more mobile infants into the toddler room as their teacher when they become ready for this transition.

Attachment is a universal developmental aspect in all cultures. However, the way that responsiveness is demonstrated may differ from culture to culture (Riley et al., 2008). Cultural discontinuity between the child's home and childcare or school setting can cause the child to be vulnerable to stress (Espinosa, 2006). Therefore, it is important that we observe how parents promote secure attachment, so that we can support the child and family by using similar routines and techniques (Riley et al., 2008).

Secure attachment is a critical component of the Circle of Courage, forming the basis for the spirit of belonging. The spirit of belonging is essential for meeting the other needs—mastery, independence, and generosity.

Self-Regulation

Self-regulation is the ability to control one's emotions, actions (impulsivity), and thinking (focusing attention and planning) (Riley et al., 2008, p. 65). The ability to self-regulate predicts both immediate and long-term success. Children who have good self-regulation skills display higher self-esteem, increased academic performance, better social skills, and the ability to handle emotions constructively (Riley et al., 2008, p. 67).

Regulating Emotions. Gaining the ability to regulate emotions is one of the tasks of the early childhood years. By the end of the preschool years, most children are able to anticipate and discuss their feelings. This is very important because, "when children can label a feeling, they can make the leap from unconscious experience to conscious control" (Riley et al., 2008, p. 86). Poorly managed feelings can impair learning, attention, decision-making, planning, and problem solving (National Scientific Council on the Developing Child, 2004b).

Culture affects the way that children display their emotions (Day, 2006). For example, some cultures view it as inappropriate to display anger in public while other cultures do not. In some cultures, physical affection is openly displayed whereas in others this is viewed as inappropriate. Children learn the culturally acceptable ways to display emotions through imitation, feedback, and direct instruction (Kostelnik, Whiren, Soderman, & Gregory, 2009).

Regulating Actions and Thinking. Self-regulation of actions and thinking are also developing during the early childhood years. Self-regulation often involves delaying gratification. This is easier if children are in a predictable environment. I once worked as a houseparent for abused and neglected children. At mealtime, many of the children overate. Even though snacks were readily available, several of them hid food in heater vents, under pillows, and in dresser drawers. They were unable to delay gratification for eating because they had lived in unpredictable environments where food was not consistently available. One successful technique that children often use in delaying gratification is to distract themselves. Self-talk (verbalizing what you are doing or the next steps to take) is another technique that children use to assist in regulating both actions and thinking. A third technique that assists with self-regulation is planning. We can assist children to develop self-regulation skills by providing a predictable environment and routines and by helping children to develop successful techniques such as using distraction, self-talk, and planning. For example, we might incorporate plan, do, review (see information in Chapter 1) as a way of helping children learn planning skills.

Teachers also need to be aware of typical development and to make referrals to specialists where appropriate when development is atypical. Even very young children have deep and intense feelings and can experience severe mental health problems (National Scientific Council on the Developing Child, 2004b). If there are mental health concerns, teachers need to discuss these concerns with the family and refer them to a specialist. Early intervention can be critical for current and future well-being.

Children with parents who are violent, mentally ill, or substance abusers are also at increased risk for difficulties with emotional development. They will need extra support from teachers and may need assistance from counselors (National Scientific Council on the Developing Child, 2004b). Teachers must also be aware of signs of child abuse and must report the abuse if it is present.

Learning to regulate one's emotions, thoughts, and actions are important goals for the early childhood years. Self-regulation is a foundation for achieving mastery and independence, and for interacting successfully with others or displaying generosity. To learn more about this important topic, watch the video *Parental Involvement in the Emotional Development of Toddlers* on MyEducationLab.

myeducationlab

Go to MyEducationLab and select the topic "Family/Parent Involvement." Under Activities and Applications, watch the video *Parental Involvement in the Emotional Development of Toddlers.*

Social Skills

Children's social skills build upon their self-regulatory skills. Researchers contend that social skills and knowledge are as important for school success as academic skills (Ray et al., 2006). To form and maintain successful relationships, children must identify, regulate, and manage their feelings in a constructive manner. In addition, they must develop empathy and friendship skills (National Scientific Council on the Developing Child, 2004b).

Developing Empathy. To develop empathy, children must first be able to engage in social perspective-taking (understanding another's wants and thinking) and emotional perspective-taking (understanding another's feelings). With empathy, the child experiences an emotional response as he views things from the other's perspective (Riley et al., 2008). When 2-year-old Julian sat down and cried next to his friend, Kirsten, who was sad that her mother had left, he was displaying perspective-taking and empathy. He understood Kirsten's feeling of loneliness and demonstrated an emotional response to her sadness.

Developing Friendship Skills. To make friends children must learn communication, negotiation, and play entry skills. In addition, they must demonstrate the attributes of a friend. Children often learn these attributes, such as cooperation, faithfulness, and loyalty, from more competent peers or adults.

Even during the first year of life, children begin to recognize another child as a social partner. As toddlers, they begin to have reciprocal social interactions (Honig & Thompson, 1994). For example, Tabi and Tenile were washing dolls in the water table. Tabi said, "Baby wet." Tenile handed her a towel and said, "Dry baby." Tabi said, "Thank you." The friendships formed in the toddler and preschool years can be quite stable over time (Dunn, 2004). One study found that 50% to 70% of children's friendships lasted through the next year (Howes, 1989). The concept of friends changes from preschool to elementary school to adolescence. However, children typically choose friends that are similar to themselves in race, gender, behavioral characteristics, play behaviors, and attitudes (Kostelnik et al., 2009).

"The quality of peer relationships in early childhood predicts later success in intellectual growth, self-esteem, mental health, and school performance" (Riley et al., 2008, p. 42). But, why do friendships affect children's outcomes? While interacting with friends, children develop interaction skills, practice reciprocity and fairness, and learn to value other's feelings. Research also indicates that children's interactions with groups of friends are more positive than when they interact with other peers. In addition, a group of friends is often pursuing a mutual goal, leading to discussion, negotiation, and cooperation. This leads to more problem solving and complex thinking (Riley et al., 2008, p. 43). Friends can also be helpful in coping with new situations. For example, when children move to a new classroom at the same time as a friend, the transition is easier. Having a friend in an established group also helps pave the way for other friends to join the group.

However, the peer group rejects some children. Rejected children often exhibit inappropriate social skills (Honig & Thompson, 1994), particularly communication skills (Hazen & Black, 1989). Children who are not popular are more likely to perform poorly in school and ultimately to drop out (Riley et al., 2008). Children who do not have friends are also at serious risk for detrimental developmental effects (National Scientific Council on the Developing Child, 2004a, p. 3).

Teachers have a responsibility to assist children in developing the foundations for the Circle of Courage: attachment, self-regulation, and social skills. But, how do they do this? We will examine the teacher's role in assisting children to develop these skills in the next section.

The Teacher's Role in Supporting the Circle of Courage

The teacher plays a crucial role in helping the child to feel a sense of belonging, mastery, independence, and generosity. The teacher models these characteristics, establishes an environment that assists children in achieving these values, and supports children through informal and formal techniques.

Creating a Spirit of Belonging

The teacher sets the stage for the child to feel a sense of belonging by displaying a warm, accepting attitude. This helps the child to form an attachment to the teacher. She also creates a welcoming, caring, classroom community. Finally, she is responsive to all children, including those who are from cultures different from her own, children who come from low-income families, and children with disabilities.

Forming an Attachment with Each Child. "Throughout the early childhood years, most learning depends on the formation of a nurturing relationship" (Riley et al., 2008, p. 8). Children are more likely to form attachments to adults who are sensitive, warm, and nurturing (Riley et al., 2008), adults who show unconditional positive regard for the child (Gartrell, 2007). To help form attachments the adult needs to show genuine interest in the child and to spend quality time with him. For example, the adult converses with the child, listening attentively as he speaks, and asks questions to get to know the child's preferences. As the child and adult spend time together, they learn to "read each other" and it becomes easier for the adult to know how to assist the child (Riley et al., 2008). In addition, children gain their feelings about their own self-worth from the adults in their environment. When the adult is warm and responsive, the child feels valuable and worthwhile. Children who experience warmth from their caregiver display greater social competence, have fewer behavioral issues, achieve more academically, and show increased reasoning skills. They are more excited about school and are more self-confident (National Scientific Council on the Developing Child, 2004a).

In addition to displaying warmth, the adult must also be responsive to the child. The responsive adult treats children with respect, responding quickly to their needs. For example, the infant teacher responds to a baby's cries. She also uses appropriate pacing during interactions, taking cues from the baby (Riley et al., 2008). For example, when the baby looks away, the teacher realizes that he is trying to escape the stimulation and respects this. The teacher creates a responsive environment and schedule that allows time and space for positive interactions.

It takes time for attachments to develop. Secure attachment is more likely when there is an ongoing sustained relationship between the caregiver and child (Honig, 2002, p. 22). Unfortunately, high teacher turnover rates in early childhood programs can negatively affect attachment by not allowing time for the attachment to develop and by creating negative impacts when the attachment ends. In addition, frequent moves from classroom to classroom can also have negative impacts for the child. There is a relationship between the number of lost caregivers and socially withdrawn or aggressive behavior on the part of the child (Howes & Hamilton, 1993). The child who loses a person he is attached to may act depressed and have difficulty forming new relationships. Many programs that are aware of the importance of attachment are designing policies that assist children to attach with caregivers. In addition to reducing turnover, programs provide time for relationship development by assigning primary caregivers and keeping children with the same caregiver for multiple years (Riley et al., 2008). Smaller child/adult ratios also assist with attachment.

The morning meeting is a component of the Responsive Classroom, an approach developed by the Northeast Foundation for Children. It is comprised of four parts: greeting each other by name, sharing personal news (often children who wish to share sign up ahead of time), a group activity to build cohesion, and classroom news and announcements (Kriete, 2002). The purpose of the meeting is to make each member feel welcome, develop a sense of community, and learn social skills. In many cases, the meetings are child led.

Figure 2.1
Developing a Sense of Belonging Through the Morning Meeting

Developing a Classroom Community. We often hear about the need to develop a sense of community, but exactly what does this mean? When there is a sense of community, there is an emotional connection among members. They encourage, support, and influence each other. Members depend on each other and feel like insiders within the group. To create a sense of community teachers can

- Make sure that all staff, children, and families are represented in the classroom displays and materials.
- Help children get to know each other and to bond together as a cohesive group. Many programs begin the year with "All About Us" where children learn about themselves and others in the classroom. This time is also devoted to many group-building activities.
- Allow time for children to systematically share with each other (see Figure 2.1) and to spend time interacting in both formal and informal small groups.
- Set up the classroom environment to encourage children to work together. For example, provide two phones in the dramatic play area, multiple earphones to listen to a CD, two doll buggies for strolling together, wagons for pulling each other, rocking boats and swings, easels side by side with paint that is shared, two chairs at the computer center, large floor puzzles, and board games.
- Be realistic about sharing. Even adults have difficulty sharing favored possessions or items they are using. Make sure that you have duplicate materials and enough materials so that all children can be actively engaged using materials that interest them.
- Develop activities where children work together to complete a goal. For example, children might create a garden, paint a mural, build a house from straw bales, move together like a centipede, or make a ball bounce on a parachute.
- Develop a unique sense of place in the program, one that represents the children, adults, and community in which you live. To create a sense of place, teachers can display staff, children's, and family's photos, treasures, and work. Also, provide materials that reflect the uniqueness of the environment in which you live. For example, if you live near a beach your playground might include driftwood that children can use for building. Many programs develop a special sense of place by encouraging children to name the classroom and develop a class mascot.

Being Responsive to Children from All Cultures. "Culture is defined by the values, traditions, social and political relationships, and worldview shared by a group of people bound together by a combination of commonalities that include one or more of the following: history, geographic location or origin, language, social class, or religion" (Wolpert, 2005, p. 53). Culture is learned, often being passed on from generation to generation. However, members are embedded in the cultural group to different degrees (Day, 2006, p. 29).

Culture is dynamic, changing over time due to influences from cultural members, as well as outside forces (Day, 2006; Johnson et al., 2005). However, there is also cultural stability. The desire of a system to maintain the status quo tends to prevail over change (Day, 2006, p. 29). Culture is a template that influences all aspects of our lives: our goals, expectations, relationships, values, roles, and perspectives. Through our culture, we learn rules that govern the way we think, act, and feel, allowing us to behave in ways that are acceptable to the group (Day, 2006, p. 29). It is critical that we understand the children's and families' cultures in our classrooms.

When there is a mismatch between the teacher's culture and the child's, there is the possibility that misunderstandings will occur (Ray et al., 2006). The difference in cultural lens, or the way we view the world because of our culture, may cause teachers to misinterpret children's abilities or behaviors and negatively affect the teacher's ability to establish rapport with the child. It might also make it more difficult to understand the child's needs and interests affecting the ability to deliver effective curriculum. In addition, *cultural discontinuity* (a difference in the learning preferences, practices, and behaviors valued at home and school) can cause children to have a more negative perception of themselves as learners, readers, writers, and speakers (Garcia, 1993).

In the United States, the population of children is becoming more diverse. For example, over 30% of Head Start children (Office of Head Start, 2008) and 20% of school-age children speak a language other than English at home (Federal Interagency Forum Child and Family Statistics, 2005). Additionally, statisticians estimate that by the year 2020, 50% of children in the United States will be black or brown (Ray et al., 2006). However, the population of teachers does not reflect this same diversity with 87% of elementary teachers being Caucasian. The typical elementary teacher is also female, middle income, and monolingual, speaking English only (Ray et al., 2006).

In addition to concern about lack of continuity between the children's home and school culture, there is also danger from bias. According to Day (2006), "Institutional bias that are manifested in monocultural, monoracial assumptions and representations in books, materials, testing, and tracking for example can cause repeated and cumulative harm to children's growth, development and academic achievement" (p. 30).

The mismatch between teacher and children's culture as well as individual and institutional bias can contribute to some children being less successful in the classroom. Achievement gaps occur between children who are black, Latino, and Native American and their white peers (Day, 2006, p. 23). For example, fewer children who are African American, Latino, or poor graduate from high school or attend college (Ray et al., 2006). As reported by Linda Espinosa, an early childhood researcher and professor, the Latino population, the largest and fastest growing ethnic minority in the United States, is the group with the lowest academic performance. She states that children who are Latino start kindergarten behind their white peers in reading and math, and these differences continue to widen as children progress through school, leading to high drop-out rates. So how can we reverse this trend?

To change these statistics, we must provide an equitable education and help children experience a sense of belonging in our classrooms. We begin by examining our own cultural beliefs. This helps us to uncover our own template or our own lens for viewing the world. We are then ready to learn about the children's cultures. Teachers can learn about the cultures of the children in their classrooms in a variety of ways. They can interview community members; review research and other written materials; observe children and their families; discuss goals, beliefs (for example, about routines, celebrations, family roles, gender roles, food, discipline), and traditions with children and families; and ask parents and children to share songs, stories, food, customs, and family activities with the class (Ray et al., 2006).

As we learn about culture, we must remember that there is great variety within a particular culture. Children and their families are also individuals, and we must be cautious about attributing specific characteristics to them simply because they belong to a particular cultural group. In other words we must not stereotype. Listen to one teacher describe her experience in making an assumption based on a child's culture by watching the video *Explode Stereotypes* on MyEducationLab. As stated by Day (2006) and reinforced by the video clip, "Because we are human we share predictable, universal patterns of change with all other humans; because we are social beings, we share predictable patterns of behavior with members of our group or groups; and because we are individuals, each of us is unique and idiosyncratic" (p. 24).

We can use the information we have learned about individual children and their culture to arrange inclusive environments, plan appropriate activities, and adapt our interaction styles. This is critical, if we are going to help all children to succeed.

myeducationlab

Go to MyEducationLab and select the topic "Diversity." Under Activities and Applications, watch the video *Explode Stereotypes*.

Culturally Relevant Materials. Johnson et al., (2005), in discussing culturally relevant materials, state that many classroom materials, are culturally neutral, such as balls, blocks, and math manipulatives. They emphasize, "Efforts to make such materials relevant to specific groups of children are humorous at best and potentially counterproductive" (p. 234).

However, many materials are not culturally neutral. It is critical that books, posters, play people, dramatic play props, puzzles, and other materials that reflect cultures be inclusive. These materials need to reflect the diversity within the program (for example, race, ethnicity, family structure, age, disabilities, gender, occupations). In addition, we want to expose children to diversity they might not regularly experience (Wardle & Cruz-Janzen, 2004). In evaluating toys and materials for multiculturalism, consider the following (Johnson et al., 2005):

- Materials should expose children to many forms of diversity (for example, race, ethnicity, family structure, disabilities). Teachers need to integrate the materials into the environment and curriculum, rather than using them only occasionally or in an isolated way.

- Materials need to portray the child's culture and all cultures in a positive, authentic, and realistic light. For example, you would not want to portray American Indians as only living in teepees and wearing headdresses since this is not an accurate portrayal either historically or currently for many American Indians.

These hand puppets are an example of multicultural materials.

- Materials should never convey that one group is better than another group. "Unfortunately, if certain people are not represented in play materials, this invisibility is a powerful indicator of lack of importance" (Wardle & Cruz-Janzen, 2004).

- Materials need to challenge all forms of stereotypes, such as only men or only women can have certain careers, or because you are from a particular race, you have a specific talent.

- Materials need to emphasize individual differences and the diversity within large groups. Just because you belong to a specific group (female, male, African American, Caucasian, Asian American, and so forth) does not mean that you think, act, or have the same talents as every other member of the group. Many children are multiracial and multiethnic. It is important to have materials that reflect this as well.

Throughout the book, you will find examples of ways teachers have made their environments culturally relevant.

Apply Your Knowledge Throughout this chapter, we have been reading about how essential it is to affirm each child and her culture. As a frequent volunteer in my daughter's first grade classroom, the teacher asked me to help with a Halloween party. I noticed that Sarah did not participate in the costume parade, play the games, or eat the treats. Instead, she sat quietly at her desk with tears streaming down her face. I thought that perhaps she was ill and asked the teacher what was wrong. She said that Sarah belonged to a religion that did not celebrate Halloween and her parents should have kept her home for the day. What message did Sarah receive from this experience? What message did the other children learn? What are ways that we can respect all members in the classroom when we conduct celebrations?

Many programs do not celebrate holidays for several reasons. First, many teachers believe that since families have different religious and cultural beliefs about what holidays to celebrate and the appropriate way to celebrate or not celebrate, the celebrations are best done in the child's home or church. Secondly, since children are typically exposed to an extensive amount of holiday celebration outside the classroom, many teachers feel it is not necessary to also celebrate within the classroom. Holiday periods can be very stressful for both children and families. The early childhood setting may be the only setting where normal routines and activities are occurring. Third, teachers are also often concerned about whether "holiday curriculum" is the best use of children's learning time. Instead, these programs may celebrate the end of a long-term project with a culminating event, or celebrate an author's birthday (such as Dr. Seuss) after studying the author.

Early Childhood Programs as a Culture. While it is critical that the school reflect the culture of the children, families, and community, the school itself also forms a unique community and culture. The school not only translates culture but creates the "culture of childhood," helping all to appreciate and value this time (Rinaldi, 2001, p. 53). The culture of childhood is formed partially by the adult's view of children and childhood. For example, if adults view childhood as a time of wonder, joy, and exploration, then they will set up experiences and environments where this is a focus. This will affect the way children experience and remember their childhood. The school culture, like all cultures, is influenced and influences those who participate within it.

Being Responsive to Children with Special Needs. Children who have special needs are often, although not always, at special risk. They are more vulnerable to academic failure, due to both the disability and lack of support and services to be successful. They might also experience a lack of social success, including peer rejection (Odom, Zercher, Li, Marquart, Sandall, & Brown, 2006) and being a more frequent target of bullies than their peers who are nondisabled (Sveinsson & Morris, 2006). Additionally, frustrated teachers sometimes increase the child's difficulties through reacting inappropriately to challenging behaviors.

It is critical that the teacher establish a warm, nurturing, respectful relationship with the child who has special needs and his family. The teacher will also need to help other children accept the child with special needs. You might help children understand the child's disability through discussions, reading books, and allowing children to try special equipment the child uses. If children have questions, you will want to offer the child who is disabled the opportunity to determine how to answer the questions. The child may choose to answer the question himself, choose to tell the child that he does not wish to answer the question, or choose to refer the question to you to answer. You will also want to make sure your environment reflects children with disabilities (for example, dolls with disabilities and assistive devices in the dramatic play area, pictures in the room that include children with disabilities, books that show children with disabilities).

To help children to relate positively with those who have special needs you might invite guest speakers with disabilities to visit your classroom. As a classroom teacher, I invited Jason, a neighborhood man who was paraplegic, to visit my program. The children had many questions. "What happened?" "Do your legs hurt?" "Can you walk?" "How do you get out of the wheelchair?" "Can you do a wheelie?" They were especially interested in how Jason drove. He showed them the brake and gas pedal on the steering column and gave them rides on the wheelchair lift. After the initial visit, Jason became a frequent volunteer enriching all our lives.

Making Modifications. In addition to establishing positive relationships, it may be necessary to make modifications to help the child with a disability to be successful. Sandall and Schwartz (2002) have developed a successful model, called Building Blocks (see Figure 2.2), that can help teachers with a process for inclusion. This process is effective whether the child has challenging behaviors, a specific disability, or an undiagnosed special need. The foundation of the model is a "high quality early childhood program," one that they define as having "engaging interactions, a responsive and predictable environment, many opportunities for learning, teaching that is matched to the child and activity, developmentally appropriate materials, activities, and interactions, safe and hygienic practices, and appropriate levels of child guidance" (p. 11). This base is necessary for all children, regardless of whether they have special needs. It is crucial because without it other interventions will not be effective.

If the child is not successful within the classroom even with this solid early childhood base, the teacher moves to the next block, curriculum modification. This is any modification that allows the child to participate fully in the classroom. For example, you might alter the schedule, environment, or materials; simplify activities; provide special equipment; or provide additional peer or adult support. To determine the modifications, it is important

---

In providing for successful inclusion of children with special needs the teacher would use the following as steps. Many children with special needs can be served simply through providing step one. Each step becomes increasingly intensive but is needed by fewer children.

1. Provide a developmentally appropriate program.
2. Modify the curriculum through altering the schedule, environment, or materials; simplifying activities; providing special equipment or materials; or providing additional peer or adult support.
3. Embed opportunities to meet the child's goals within ongoing activities and experiences.
4. Provide child-focused strategies such as set-aside time to work individually with the child.

Figure 2.2
Building Blocks for Inclusion
Source: Based on *Building Blocks for Teaching Preschoolers with Special Needs,* by S. R. Sandall and I. S. Schwartz, 2002, East Peoria, IL: Paul H. Brookes Publishing Company.

to observe the child so that you can clearly define the difficulties. Parents, previous teachers, and specialists often know what modifications have been successful in the past to alleviate issues. At times, it will also be necessary to brainstorm and experiment with different solutions. For example, Daniel, who had cerebral palsy, was unable to hold a paintbrush. Torrence, his teacher, first tried placing a pencil grip on the brush. However, this did not work. He then put a foam curler around the paintbrush for Daniel to try. With a happy grin Daniel said, "I can do it."

If the child is still having difficulties after curriculum modifications are made, you will move to the next level of support called "embedded learning opportunities" (Sandall & Schwartz, 2002, p. 12). These short teaching episodes occur as part of the regular classroom activities and routines.

If this is still not successful, then you will move to the final building block, providing "explicit, child-focused instructional strategies" (Sandall & Schwartz, 2002 p. 13). These are more systematic, frequent, and carefully planned than embedded learning opportunities. While the other interventions occur within the normal class activities, these may require specific set-aside time on the part of the teacher and child. Throughout the book, we will be looking at meeting the needs of children with disabilities using the Building Blocks model.

Being Responsive to Children in Poverty. Children in poverty are another group who are particularly vulnerable and as such need the highest quality early childhood program. Yet, research indicates that when there is a high concentration of poverty in a program, the teachers are less sensitive and the quality of instruction is poorer (Pianta, Howes, Burchinal, Bryant, Clifford, Early, & Barbarin, 2005).

Thirty-nine percent of all children in the United States live in low-income families (Douglas-Hall & Chau, 2007). Children of color and those who are immigrants are disproportionately represented in this number (Ray et al., 2006). For example, 63% of American Indian, 61% of Latino, and 60% of African American children live in poverty (Douglas-Hall & Chau, 2007).

Poverty is a risk for children that exposes them to stressors including inadequate and unstable housing, unsafe neighborhoods, and deficient prenatal and ongoing health care (Bowman, 2006; Ramsey, 2003). Studies have found that cortisol levels, a method of measuring stress, is elevated in children with lower socioeconomic status (SES)(National Scientific Council on the Developing Child, 2004b). As we learned earlier in this chapter, prolonged or frequent stress in young children can negatively affect the architecture of the brain. Children who are from low income families are also at greater risk for developmental and behavioral problems, particularly if there are other risk factors as well (such as inadequate parenting, substance abuse or violence in the home, or disabilities) (Bowman, 2006). Unfortunately, early childhood programs sometimes add to children's stress when there is a mismatch between the child's home and school culture or conflicts between children and the teacher, and when activities and environments are set up that allow children to fail (Bowman, 2006).

As teachers, we have limited control over society's inequities. However, we can do many things within our programs and classrooms. We can develop respectful, responsive relationships with low-income children and their families. As teachers, we can

- Establish classrooms that allow all children to experience success.
- Help ensure that our classrooms and curriculum represent children of all income levels. For example, a study of homes might include discussion about homeless shelters.
- Reflect upon our program policies and requests from the perspective of a low-income family. For example, is it reasonable to ask families to donate money

for their child to go on the class field trip, to provide a t-shirt for tie dyeing, to provide a gift for an exchange, or to transport their child to attend Early Head Start (a program specifically designed for low-income children and their families)?

- Provide needed services within our programs whenever possible (school breakfasts, after-school care, transportation, access to social services).
- Learn about community services and, when appropriate, refer families for needed assistance.
- Advocate for needed services for all children and families.
- Be conscious of parent work schedules, and transportation and childcare needs when setting up family events.
- Examine our own biases and cultural lens and make sure that our biases do not negatively affect the child.

It is sometimes difficult for those who have some financial security to understand the profound effect of poverty (Ramsey, 2003).

Amelia, a child in my classroom, often came to class smelling bad with unwashed hair and dirty clothes. Unfortunately, this affected her interactions with her peers and even with the adults in the classroom. Even though I visited with the mother about Amelia's grooming, there was no change. I presumed that the mother was deliberately ignoring Amelia's needs. However, 2 weeks later when I went on a home visit, I found the sewer in the house backed up and the water turned off. The sewer smell seeped into the clothing and furnishings in the house. The family hauled all the water they used up a steep hill in buckets, making water for bathing or washing clothes a luxury. Even though the family had talked to the property owner repeatedly, he refused to fix the water or sewer saying he was "planning to tear the house down and was not willing to put any money into it." The family, who lacked a deposit to move elsewhere, felt they had no other options but to stay in the inadequate housing. I found that my assumptions were biased and inaccurate. Due to my own upbringing and past experiences, I had not pursued why Amelia was dirty. Instead, I assumed the family did not care about her. Through the home visit, I learned the reason for the grooming issues and was able to refer the family (with their permission) to an agency that could assist them. With the agency's help, they were able to move into different housing and Amelia's grooming immediately changed.

To make children feel that they belong in our classrooms, we must form an attachment to every child. This begins with unconditional, positive regard for each child and family, and the establishment of a warm, respectful relationship. To demonstrate respect for children and families, we need to understand their values, beliefs, and culture and to use this knowledge to create effective environments. We must make special efforts to meet the needs of those children who are most vulnerable, children who are from a nondominant culture, children who have disabilities, and children from low-income families.

Helping Children Achieve Mastery

Responsive care also forms the basis for assisting children to develop the spirit of mastery or the attitude that "I can succeed." When a child's needs are met, they develop the attitude that "the world will treat me well, that my needs will be met in the future, and that I have some control over my environment." However, when no one responds to children's needs they give up the expectation that they will get what they need, and "lose confidence in themselves and their abilities" (Bowman, 2006, p. 53). One day, when I was a houseparent for children who had been abused and neglected, a caseworker brought a 9-month-old baby to us with a very severe, infected burn on his little toe. Although he had to be in excruciating pain, he did not cry or show any emotion. Eventually, the toe needed to be amputated. He learned to walk and run. However, in the time he was with us, even if he was hurt he never learned to cry. His early experiences had taught him that crying did no good; he could not expect others to meet his needs. In early childhood settings, we would expect never to see this extreme type of abuse. However, meeting children's needs for attention can sometimes be difficult when you are caring for many children. If adults leave children to cry when they need us, they too will learn that the world is a harsh place, where no one will meet their needs.

We must also help children to achieve mastery and develop **self-efficacy** (a person's belief about her competence in a given situation). A wide body of research indicates that a person's self-efficacy strongly influences her performance and motivation (Bandura & Locke, 2003). For example, a mega-analysis (a review of several research studies) showed that 11% to 18% of a child's academic performance is due to his self-efficacy (Cohen, 1988; Schunk, 1989). Children with higher levels of self-efficacy are more motivated to try tasks and show increased persistence in completing tasks. So how can we promote self-efficacy? Following are several ways:

- Provide challenges in a variety of domains—climbing to the very top of the climber and ringing the bell, matching the numerals with a number of objects, reading a picture book.
- Whenever possible use individual and small-group activities rather than large-group activities. Individualized and small-group activities are more likely to meet children's current level of development since teachers are able to scaffold each child's learning more effectively.
- Provide materials at increasing difficulties so that children can see their skills improving. Sandra provides math games with colored dots demonstrating the level of difficulty. Children in her room are excited when they can successfully complete the activity at the next level.
- Teach children skills they need to be successful. As an example, demonstrate how to hold scissors correctly, how to use a specific art tool, how to tag or point to items when you count them.
- Provide choices of activities to meet all children's interests and developmental levels.
- Make encouraging remarks. "I see you are working very hard on completing the puzzle. You only have four pieces left."
- Assist children in setting and meeting individual goals. Even very young children have goals, as demonstrated by a baby learning to crawl. You can assist children to verbalize their goals or, for very young children, verbalize the goal for them, making the goal more visible.
- Recognize when children have met their own personal goals ("I know that you had a goal to climb the climbing wall all by yourself. You did it.").
- Avoid group competition. Instead, encourage children to master their own goals. Group competition can discourage children. As a result, they may avoid the activity. Without practice, their skills continue to fall behind their peers.
- Continue to improve your own self-efficacy. A teacher's self-efficacy, or his belief in his ability to teach, affects his interactions with children and the way he designs learning experiences. This in turn affects children's academic performance (Bandura, 1993).

Responsive care is the foundation in assisting children to experience a sense of mastery. We must also cultivate self-efficacy by providing challenging activities that children can successfully master, giving skill and goal-setting support, and encouraging children's efforts.

Assisting Children to Become Independent

Being independent allows the child to have individual power and autonomy (Brendtro et al., 2002). The amount of independence adults expect from children is culturally based (Day, 2006). Therefore, it is important to consult with parents in determining the goals for independence in the classroom. There are many ways that the teacher can encourage independence. These include the following:

- Setting up the environment to encourage independence (materials available and accessible, children taught how to use materials, and dependable routines).

- Allowing children to do what they can for themselves and to make decisions they are capable of making.

- With assistance from children, establishing clear and consistent guidelines or rules. When rules are clear and consistent, children are able to be more independent and self-regulating (Riley et al., 2008). When they assist in creating the rules, they feel more ownership and therefore will respect the rule more (Gartrell, 2007). The guidelines or rules should be worded in a positive way, letting children know what to do rather than what not to do. However, beware of creating too many rules. Wien (2004) worked with a group of childcare centers in establishing rules. The programs agreed that all rules had to pass the following test. Did the behavior harm the child, other children, or property? If not, the rule was not needed. Using these criteria, teachers discarded many rules such as restricting the number of children in a learning center and forbidding toys from home. As the teachers discarded the rules, the setting was less stressful, quieter, and calmer; teachers spent less time monitoring and more time interacting; and the children became more independent and exercised more control over their own behavior (Wien, 2004).

- Allowing children to make choices and learn from the results. At some point, children will be required to make decisions that can have life-altering consequences. Providing children opportunities to make developmentally appropriate choices allows them to be independent and gives them experiences in making choices.

Allowing children to develop culturally appropriate independence and autonomy assists children to feel powerful and experience inner discipline.

Assisting Children to Display Generosity

The spirit of generosity reflects the ability to be caring, empathetic, and willing to share time and possessions with others. However, to demonstrate caring and empathy, we must be able to recognize and manage our feelings, control our behavior, and use pro-social skills to interact with others.

Helping Children to Recognize and Control Their Own Feelings. Helping children to control their emotions begins with reducing their frustration through setting up a developmentally appropriate environment and schedule. We need to create an environment that provides many options (spaces for physical activity and areas for quiet relaxation; spaces for being in groups but also spaces for being alone; a range of challenging, interesting activities; and enough materials so that all children are engaged). To support children we need a schedule that alternates quiet and active activities, that allows time for restful relaxation, but does not require children to stay on mats when they are unable to sleep. The schedule needs to limit large-group activities, instead focusing on individual and small-group activities.

We also need to help children learn skills. One of the skills young children need to learn is to identify their emotions. You can assist them through

- Labeling their feelings ("You look excited that your mama is coming").
- Using feeling words to describe your own emotions ("I feel worried when the water is spilled all over the floor because I'm afraid someone will slip and get hurt").
- Interpreting the feelings of others for the child ("Rainey looks sad because you took her toy") (Riley et al., 2008).

Learning to identify and use words to describe feelings is one way that children learn to manage emotions. You can also assist children in finding other ways to deal with strong emotions. At times, they will need to deal with the strong emotions before they engage in problem solving to resolve the issue (someone took their toy). At other times, the child has no control over the situation, and can only deal with his feelings (parents getting a divorce). Different techniques might work better for different problems. In addition, some children respond more favorably to some techniques than to others. Marie-Élise, a teacher at Pinewood kindergarten, developed a poster to remind children of different calming techniques (see Figure 2.3).

Lisa, a teacher of toddler children, has a poster that shows children expressing different emotions. When children are unable to verbalize their feelings, they are sometimes able to point to the way that they are feeling. Julie, who teaches preschool, makes a "dial a feeling" for each child's cubby. When children enter the program each morning, they set their dial. This allows Julie to know immediately if there are children who might need some additional attention.

As you get to know individual children, you will learn what techniques are most helpful for each of them and you can then help remind them of strategies that have been successful for them in the past.

Helping Children to Manage Their Behavior. If we want children to interact positively with others, we need to help them manage their behavior. However, we need to make sure the techniques we are using are consistent with the respectful way that we want the children to interact with others. For example, if we want children to talk to each other respectfully, then we need to use a respectful tone and words ourselves even when we are frustrated.

Figure 2.3
Calming Techniques

When I am upset, I can:
- Work it out by hammering nails into the stump or squeezing squish balls
- Talk it over with a friend or the listening doll
- Act it out with the doll house or puppets
- Breathe it out by taking five deep breaths
- Draw about it or write about it

When I am too excited, I can:
- Listen to music
- Play in the water table
- Read quietly in the alone box
- Do yoga in the physical center
- Use the sand tray to make a design

Listed below are some positive discipline techniques that can be effective in managing behavior and are at the same time respectful of the child.

Active or Reflective Listening. When using active listening, the adult reiterates what the child has said. When actively listening, you refrain from giving advice. Instead, you simply repeat what the child has said, paraphrase the message, or reflect the feeling behind the statement. If reflecting the child's feeling, use a tentative voice to avoid sounding like a mind reader. For example, Jamaar says, "I'm not going to circle." Using a questioning tone you state, "You really don't like circle?" Jamaar then explains that Andre won't sit by him and that Andre says he isn't his best friend anymore and he can't come play at his house. By using reflective listening in this case, you were able to unveil Jamaar's real issue. Active listening encourages further conversation, validates the child, and helps the child to clarify his thoughts and feelings, often resulting in the child solving his own problem. Additionally, just discussing a problem or issue can often be therapeutic.

I Messages. You use an "I message" to express your own feelings about children's behavior. An "I message" typically contains a word describing how you feel, the specific behavior that caused you to feel this way, and how the behavior affected you. "I feel worried when blocks get thrown because I'm afraid someone will get hurt." Both adults and children are usually less defensive when they hear an "I message" rather than a "you message."

Natural Consequences. These consequences occur with no intervention from you. For example, a child who goes outside without mittens in the winter may get cold hands. Natural consequences allow children to learn from their behavior and the accompanying results. They are a very effective technique that teachers can use when the consequence is not harmful or dangerous for the child or others. In addition, for natural consequences to be effective, you must be able to accept the results. For example, unwashed paintbrushes will get hard and unusable. However, you may feel that this natural consequence is not appropriate for the program or other children in the classroom. Therefore, you would not want to use the natural consequence in this case.

Logical Consequences. These consequences clearly relate to the behavior, but do not occur naturally. For example, if you rip a book, you need to fix it. If you hurt someone's feelings, you need to figure out ways to make them feel better.

Redirection and Substitution. This technique may involve distracting a very young child with a more appropriate activity (Marion, 2007). For example, a baby is crawling toward the electrical outlet and you give him a ball to play with. When redirecting an older toddler or child, the teacher provides an acceptable substitution for the behavior (Marion, 2007). For example, if a 3-year-old child is climbing on a shelf, you might redirect her to the climber if it appears the child's goal is to climb. If the child's goal is to reach something that is out of reach, you might substitute a safer way to obtain the material.

Problem Solving or Conflict Resolution. Problem solving or conflict resolution involves assisting the child or children to solve a problem using the following steps:

1. Define the problem—Use active listening and I messages to determine the underlying issue.
2. Explore alternatives—Brainstorm all possible solutions. It is important to accept all solutions and to write them down or tape-record them for later analysis.

3. Choose a solution—Go through your brainstormed list of solutions. If anyone has any objections to an alternative, then cross the alternative off. Choose a solution that is mutually agreed upon. This may be a combination of the initial brainstormed alternatives.

4. Obtain a commitment from everyone who is involved—Agree who is responsible for implementing the solution, when it will be implemented, and how it will be implemented.

5. Set up a time to discuss how the solution worked.

Initially, children need a lot of practice and support to use this method. However, once children learn the technique they will be able to handle more problems independently and will also have acquired a lifelong skill.

We can help children to manage their behavior by using these respectful techniques. We are also modeling effective techniques that they can use in interactions with others.

Assisting Children to Develop Pro-Social Skills. In the early childhood years, children are developing skills for getting along with others. We help children develop these skills through having clear goals for our classroom, modeling, taking advantage of teachable moments to coach children, and through intentionally designing activities.

Establish Pro-Social Goals. Two overarching rules for the pro-social classroom are:

1. We treat everyone with respect.
2. We live peacefully with each other.

Children ages 3 to 6 effectively use the peace table at Curious Minds Early Childhood Center to resolve conflicts.

In addition to not physically or verbally hurting or bullying someone else, respect involves being friendly to others. Gartrell (2007) emphasizes that there is a difference between friendliness and being friends. Children need to have the right to choose their friends. However, they need to be friendly to all members of the class. The class can determine what being friendly means in their classroom through having in-depth discussions.

To live peacefully with each other children need to learn to solve conflicts. To learn conflict resolution skills children need both modeling and direct teaching. It is also helpful to have a special place to go to work on the conflict if it cannot be immediately resolved. Many programs have established a peace table or peace chairs. For example, Curious Minds Early Childhood Center has a peace table. The teacher posted the different steps to resolving a conflict (listen to each other, brainstorm ideas to solve the problem, choose a solution, and try the solution out). She also provided a book with pictures and words to remind children of possible solutions. Puppets are also available since some children find it easier to express themselves through the puppet. Even 3-year-olds at Curious Minds successfully use the table and the steps to resolve conflicts.

When the conflict affects most of the class members, you might have a problem-solving circle. Anyone in the classroom can call a meeting. The teacher or child begins the meeting by describing the situation that needs to be solved. Then the class uses the conflict resolution steps to solve the issue (Gartrell, 2007).

Model Pro-Social Skills. As a model for pro-social living, we must develop a positive relationship with each child in our care. As stressed by Bowman (2006), "Just as children must interact verbally with adults in order to get language, they have to interact emotionally and socially to develop relationships" (p. 53). Positive adult relationships help children develop insights into others' thoughts and feelings and helps them learn to positively interact with others. This sets the stage for current and future relationships. We can help make modeling even more powerful when we make our actions explicit, verbalizing what we are doing and thinking. For example, when Carletta was crying, her teacher said, "I wonder what would help Carletta feel better?" "Maybe she would like a hug, I'll ask her."

Use the Teachable Moment to Coach Children on Pro-Social Skills. For example, this might be encouraging toddlers to "Use gentle touches" as they play with the baby. You might provide specific words a child might use. "Terrence, you can say, 'Stop, give back my truck.'" An important role of the teacher in the early childhood years is to assist children with group entry skills and play skills, that is, learning techniques for successfully joining a group of children and maintaining play. Begin by observing children's strategies that are unsuccessful and assist them to try other techniques. Some common ways that you might assist a child include

- Encouraging the child to watch other children to determine what the children are playing and the roles that each have.
- Assisting the child by suggesting a role for the child.
- Encouraging the child to play alongside the other children using similar materials.
- Inviting children to play together with you; then, as the children begin to play, you can remove yourself from the play situation.
- Providing the child with a highly desired prop to ease play entry.

The teacher should also notice socially appropriate behavior and encourage it. For example, "Rosie and Tanya, I see you are sharing the truck."

Intentionally Design Activities to Help Children Learn Pro-Social Skills. In addition to modeling and taking advantage of teachable moments, you will need to intentionally design activities to encourage pro-social skills and to assist children in understanding others' perspectives. You might do this through

- Reading books about feelings that solve social dilemmas, or where children see something from a new point of view.
- Enacting and discussing real and hypothetical situations. One way to do this is to develop a dilemma and have the children determine the ending. You might use role-playing, puppets, dolls, or play figures to tell the story (Gartrell, 2007). Some classrooms have designated characters that always tell these types of stories. You might create a dilemma around a situation you have observed in the classroom. For example, Maria developed the following story based on a classroom incident. She told the story using puppets and a shiny, red car as a prop.

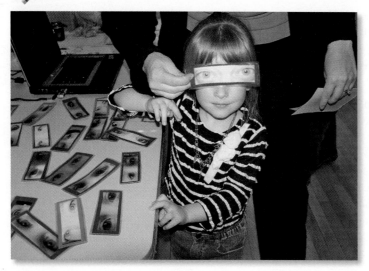

These digital photos help children to focus on the similarities and differences in their classmates' eyes.

"One day the children came to school and there was a brand new, shiny toy car in the block area. Tim could not wait to play with it. All morning he waited. Finally, Bruce set the car down. But, before Tim could reach it, Mark picked the car up. Tim went to Mark and grabbed the car. He had waited a long time and thought the car should be his." The children and Maria then discussed the feelings of Mark and Tim and discussed what each child might do.

Assist Children to Become Culturally Competent. We have discussed the importance of the teacher being culturally competent. It is also important that we help children to develop cultural competence. We need to help children to have knowledge of, comfort with, and respect for people of varying cultural backgrounds so that they can engage in effective interactions and reject unfair treatment of others (Kostelnik et al., 2009, p. 4). You can help children to become more socially competent by reading books and sharing music from other cultures and by creating opportunities for children to interact with people who are different from themselves (for example, diverse guest speakers, volunteers, and field trips). You can also provide diversity materials (books, games, clothing, posters, and artifacts) in the classroom. In addition, it is extremely important to discuss hurtful comments and biased statements and to immediately address any such statements in the classroom or program. Children need to learn how to recognize such statements and how to respond when they hear them.

Pro-social skills are necessary for children to make friends and to succeed in the world. In addition, they help to assure that our classroom will be a welcoming place for all.

How the Physical Environment Supports the Circle of Courage

The physical environment presents an immediate message of either belonging or exclusion. It can provide opportunities for success and mastery, or failure and boring repetition. It can provide an arrangement of space and materials so that children can be independent, or it can be set up where teachers are the "material brokers." It can provide spaces and activities for developing community or be so noisy, crowded, and chaotic that this is impossible.

Children at Mentor Graphics Child Development Center learn about skin colors through interacting with this display, where they can read a book and match their skin color to the paint chips and small jars of dried beans.

The well-designed physical environment can support the Circle of Courage, helping children to develop a sense of belonging, mastery, independence, and generosity. When designed as the "third teacher" the environment is also less stressful for both adults and children, allowing teachers to spend more time in positive interactions with children.

We can establish a positive social environment that leads to courage rather than discouragement through supporting the Circle of Courage in our classrooms. When we make decisions about individual children, create changes in our environment, or adopt new curriculums we can ask, "Will this assist the children to develop a sense of belonging, mastery, independence, and generosity?" When we reflect upon our interactions we can ask, "Am I interacting with children in a way that lets them know they belong, they can achieve, they can make independent choices, and they can have and be a friend?" In establishing a Circle of Courage classroom, these and similar questions become our compass.

Sample Application Activities

1. Think about your own culture. How has your culture influenced your values (e.g., what constitutes mealtime; is it different on weekends; what is everyone's role in preparation, serving, cleaning up) and beliefs (e.g., the role of children, the role of adults, how people should express emotions, and your goals)?

2. Think about institutional racism. What are examples you have witnessed or experienced?

3. Observe in a classroom. Find evidence where the teacher or children are demonstrating the Circle of Courage: spirit of belonging, mastery, independence, and generosity.

4. How skilled is the teacher in the classroom you are observing in using coaching to teach children pro-social skills?

5. Use the environmental assessment (Figure 2.4) to evaluate the social-emotional environment of a classroom.

6. To view a list of children's books, scripted stories, and activities to support social-emotional development, visit the following website:
   http://www.vanderbilt.edu/csefel/practicalstrategies.html#teachingskills
   This site also includes modules and video clips on social-emotional development for teachers.

7. To learn more about teaching tolerance, order a free book and video, *Starting Small*, from the Southern Poverty Law Center. The video also shows the use of a peace table.
   http://www.tolerance.org/teach/resources/index.jsp

8. To find a list of multicultural children's books, see
   http://www.education.wisc.edu/ccbc/books/detailLists.asp?idBookListCat=1

9. To find a list of children's books stressing all types of diversity, see
   http://www.fpg.unc.edu/~pfi/pdfs/diversity_booklist.pdf

10. To practice your teaching skills in regard to conflict resolution, go to MyEducationLab and select the topic "Preschool." Under Building Teaching Skills and Dispositions, complete the exercise "Resolving Conflicts Among Preschoolers."

believing myself.

Figure 2.4 Environmental Assessment: The Emotionally Supportive, Equitable Environment

The teacher develops a warm, nurturing relationship with each child in the classroom through

- ☐ treating every child with respect and responding quickly to his needs.
- ☐ observing and responding to children's verbal and nonverbal cues.
- ☐ spending quality time alone with each child.
- ☐ advocating for ongoing sustained relationships between children and caregivers.

The teacher creates a welcoming caring community by

- ☐ developing an inclusive physical and social environment.
- ☐ expecting friendliness between children.
- ☐ representing all staff, children, and families through classroom materials.
- ☐ providing activities to help children get to know each other and to bond together as a cohesive group.
- ☐ allowing time for children to systematically share with each other.
- ☐ providing time for children to work in informal and formal small groups.
- ☐ setting up the classroom environment to encourage children to work together.
- ☐ being realistic about sharing, providing duplicates of popular materials and toys and enough interesting materials that all children are engaged.
- ☐ developing activities where children work together to complete a goal.
- ☐ developing a unique sense of place in the program.

The teacher provides materials that reflect the diversity within the program and exposes children to diversity they might not regularly experience. Materials

- ☐ expose children to many forms of diversity (such as race, ethnicity, family structure, age, disabilities, gender, occupations).
- ☐ portray the child's culture and all cultures in a positive, authentic, and realistic light.
- ☐ are integrated into the environment and curriculum, rather than being used only occasionally or in an isolated way.
- ☐ challenge all forms of stereotypes, such as only men or only women can have certain careers, or because you are from a particular race, you have a specific talent.
- ☐ emphasize individual differences and the diversity within large groups.

The teacher assists children to learn about and manage feelings through

- ☐ setting up an environment that reduces frustration (spaces for physical activity and quiet relaxation; spaces for being in groups but also spaces for being alone; a range of challenging, interesting activities; and enough materials so that all children are engaged).
- ☐ developing a schedule that reduces frustration (such as allowing time for restful relaxation but not requiring children to stay on mats when they are unable to sleep).
- ☐ labeling their feelings.
- ☐ using feeling words to describe her own emotions.
- ☐ interpreting the feelings of others for the child.
- ☐ providing activities that help children to identify feelings.
- ☐ providing activities such as woodworking and puppetry to help children handle strong emotions.
- ☐ using positive child discipline (active listening, I messages, natural and logical consequences, redirection, and conflict resolution).

The teacher assists children to develop pro-social skills through

- ☐ establishing pro-social goals.
- ☐ modeling.
- ☐ coaching children on pro-social skills (providing words, helping with group entry and play skills).
- ☐ teaching children conflict resolution skills.
- ☐ noticing and encouraging pro-social skills.
- ☐ intentionally designing activities to help children learn pro-social skills.
- ☐ assisting children to become culturally competent.
- ☐ immediately addressing hurtful and biased statements.

paraphrase
try to analyze

Figure 2.4 Continued

The teacher assists children to achieve mastery through providing

- ☐ challenges in a variety of domains.
- ☐ materials at increasing difficulties so that children can see their skills improving.
- ☐ choices of activities to meet all children's interests and developmental levels.
- ☐ individual and small-group activities for the majority of the day.
- ☐ skills children need to be successful.
- ☐ encouraging remarks.
- ☐ assistance to children in setting and meeting individual goals.
- ☐ recognition when children have met a goal.
- ☐ individual rather than group competitions.

The teacher helps children to achieve independence by

- ☐ setting up the environment to encourage independence (materials available and accessible, children taught how to use materials, and dependable routines).
- ☐ allowing children to do what they can for themselves and to make decisions they are capable of making.
- ☐ establishing clear and consistent guidelines or rules with the children.
- ☐ allowing children to make choices and learn from the results.

---

building relationship
Teachers role

Emergent curriculum

the plan what

due what the child is interest

this is specially

for the infant

my assignment paper

Establishing an Emotionally Supportive and Equitable Environment

chapter 3

Establishing a Context for Learning

Designing Schedules, Transitions, Groupings, and Assessments

*S*ophia was a new teacher who wanted to make sure that the children in her class were well prepared for kindergarten. The children began the day with a half hour large-group time, which Sophia used to emphasize a concept for the day. For example, she taught one letter a week. During group time, children would sing a song about the letter and think of items that began with that letter. The children next had selective choice. Sophia divided the children into groups and assigned them to a learning center. Every fifteen minutes a bell rang and children moved to the next center. After selective choice, it was small-group time. Again, children were assigned to a group and rotated through three tables, each containing a small-group activity. After group time the children went to the gym for exercises, ate lunch, and then went home.

Schedules: Structuring Time

In the opening vingette, Sophia is using a rigid production schedule where time is viewed as a limited resource that must be strictly controlled by the teacher (Wien, 1996, 2004). In this view of scheduling, it is not the needs of the individual children but the clock that takes precedence, with both teachers and children rushing throughout the day (Wien, 1996, 2004). Many teachers believe that short periods for play cause children to be more occupied, thus creating less boredom. However, research indicates the opposite is true. Short play periods result in less in-depth play and more onlooker and unoccupied play (Christie & Wardle, 1992; Tegano & Burdette, 1991). As stated by Doris Fromberg, a well-known early childhood professor and author, "Scholarship takes time" (2002, p. 70). Only with adequate time will children be able to engage in cooperative play such as ne-gotiating roles, acting out a plot, or developing a complicated block structure (Christie & Wardle, 1992; Fromberg, 2002; Tegano & Burdette, 1991). Play may be negatively af-fected by limiting the overall center time and also by rotating children through centers.

Apply Your Knowledge   In addition to limiting opportunities for in-depth play, how could assigning children to centers and rotating them every 15 minutes negatively affect their learning?

Daily schedules are necessary to provide consistency and psychological stability, and to allow children to know what is expected. When children become familiar with the routines, they become less anxious, freeing their attention for higher order learning (Bowman, Donovan, & Burns, 2001). They can predict what comes next, allowing them to feel more competent, to build self-control, and to learn emotional and behavioral reg-ulation (Butterfield, 2002). Effective daily schedules are also a proactive discipline tech-nique. "Thoughtfully designed caregiving routines can incorporate helpful buffers against the development of behavior problems among children with inherited vulnerabil-ities by providing opportunities for choice, relational warmth, structured routine, and other assists" (Shonkoff & Phillips, 2000, p. 44).

It is important to base schedules on early childhood philosophy. Early childhood phi-losophy dictates that children have extended blocks of time to engage in active exploration (Bredekamp & Copple, 1997). Research indicates that when there are frequent schedul-ing changes, children's internal motivation to complete tasks is decreased, their attention spans are reduced, and they show increased dependency on the teacher (Gareau & Kennedy, 1991). In contrast, large blocks of time allow children the time needed to work individually or collaboratively to plan and implement activities. Children increase their attention span as they are engaged in meaningful learning. They also learn to manage their own time rather than relying on the teacher. Additionally, large blocks of time reduce tran-sitions, allowing more time for learning.

By planning large blocks of time that are predictable from day to day, children and staff can have the security of knowing what comes next and what behavior is expected during this time. The schedule should be used as a guide rather than as a rigid time sched-ule so that children's needs and interests can be honored.

Outdoor time was just ending at the Inquiring Minds Child Care when the children noticed a flock of birds had landed in a nearby tree. The children were very interested in these unique migrating birds. Instead of rushing inside, the teacher and children examined the birds, discussing the colors, size, beak, tail feathers, and feet. One of the teachers went inside to collect the digital camera and the sketch books. Children made sketches of the birds and took digital pictures. When they went inside, the children and teachers were able to use their sketches, digital pictures, and the bird guidebook to determine the type of birds they had seen.

Because this teacher believed in the teachable moment and using the schedule as a guide rather than as a rigid framework, the children had a unique learning opportunity. **Teachable moments** are spontaneous educational opportunities usually based on an unplanned experience or question. To effectively manage a classroom, we must plan daily schedules that include large blocks of time for active engagement. We must then use this schedule as a guide, allowing for teachable moments. What other criteria must be considered in planning the effective schedule?

Tips for Planning Effective Schedules

Planning the optimum schedule is a time-consuming process that requires the teacher to consider multiple and sometimes conflicting needs and criteria. The teacher must consider the philosophy of the program, the needs of the children, the wishes of parents, and the criteria for effective scheduling such as alternating quiet and active activities. We will examine each of these areas.

Reflect Early Childhood Philosophy and the Philosophy of the Program.

Early childhood philosophy, informed by our current knowledge about child development, stresses that teachers need to allow children to learn through a play-based experiential process and to make choices among different activities (Bredekamp & Copple, 1997; Copple & Bredekamp, 2009). For example, teachers need to plan integrated in-depth curriculum (Bredekamp and Copple, 1997; Copple & Bredekamp, 2009). Teachers who understand the philosophies of early childhood education and theories of child development, and who are striving to put these understandings into practice, would usually be uncomfortable seeing separate times for each subject area (such as 30 minutes for science, followed by 30 minutes for social studies). Instead, in a developmentally appropriate setting, children will learn these subjects through using learning centers and participating in integrated projects.

In Nauala's kindergarten class, children were studying grasshoppers. Grasshoppers had invaded nearby fields and were a topic of interest to the children. Children developed a list of questions about grasshoppers and sought answers through observation, experimentation, reading, and visiting with experts. For example, they read factual and fictional stories about grasshoppers, developed and tested hypotheses about what grasshoppers ate, measured how far grasshoppers jumped, visited multiple sites to determine where grasshoppers preferred to live, talked to farmers and examined the effect of grasshoppers on the crops, wrote their own book about grasshoppers, made diagrams and models of grasshoppers, and created artistic renditions of grasshoppers. Literacy, social studies, science, math, and creative art were all integrated into this project.

Program philosophy also affects scheduling. For example, High/Scope uses a method called "plan, do, and review" (Hohmann & Weikart, 2002). Each of these components will be evident in the schedule for a program that follows the High/Scope model. For example, the schedule might show that children spend 10 to 15 minutes in small groups making plans for what they will do during center time. The children will then have 45 to 60 minutes to use the centers and implement their plan (children might also engage in unplanned activities). Following this they will spend 10 to 15 minutes in small groups reviewing and reflecting upon their learning.

Respect Children's Needs (Attention Span, Varying Levels of Development, Differing Interests). The younger the children, the more individualized their schedules will be. For example, in an infant room children need to eat and sleep on their own schedule (Bredekamp & Copple, 1997). As children get older, they will be able to eat and sleep at more predictable times. However, even for toddlers and preschoolers, it is important to individualize these routines when necessary. For example, you might have crackers available for a child who is very hungry to snack on or have a quiet place where a child can take a morning nap if she is tired.

Many teachers are flexible in following the schedule, allowing children's interests to determine when to move to the next phase of the day. For example, if the children are all highly engaged in using learning centers, this time might be extended.

Include Scheduled Times. There are parts of the day over which the teacher has limited personal control, such as use of gym or playground. This varies depending upon the program. In some programs, outdoor time is scheduled so that several classrooms are not on the playground at once. In other programs, lunch is delivered at a specific time. It is essential to begin developing your schedule by listing these time periods. However, it is important that the program day not be so interspersed with rigid scheduled times that having large blocks of time is compromised (Greenman, 2006). If children's needs are being negatively affected by these set times, it is important to problem solve ways to meet the children's needs in your classroom while still meeting the needs of the entire program.

Provide a Balance of Child-Initiated and Adult-Initiated Activities. **Child-initiated** means that children are allowed to make choices among many different activities. This allows children to choose activities that are at their appropriate developmental level, and that are interesting and relevant to them. For example, it is center time at the Learning Garden. Two children are in the art center. One child is drawing a picture of the vase of flowers sitting on the art table. She has not only helped to grow the flowers but also has just helped the teacher to pick them. Another child is creating a card for her sister who has just come home from the hospital. Although both children are drawing, they are more deeply engaged because the activities are personally meaningful to them.

The schedule will also need to provide time for **adult-initiated** activities. For example, scheduled small- and large-group times are typically teacher initiated. Adult-initiated activities might also occur during center time. For example, during center time at the Learning Garden one of the teachers was sitting with a small group of five children providing guided exploration with clay.

The schedule in this kindergarten classroom varies slightly each day based on scheduled time with music, art, library, and computer specialists. Therefore, the teacher has created a schedule for children in a pocket chart that can be updated on a daily basis.

Establishing a Context for Learning

Children were following the teacher's suggestion that they try to "pull legs" from their chunk of earth clay. This choice activity helped children to learn an important clay skill (Topal, 1983, p. 35).

Provide a Balance of Individual, Small-Group, and Large-Group Activities. The younger the child, the more time will be spent in individual activities. As children become toddlers, the teacher might begin to provide some group activities that children can voluntarily attend. Preschool schedules will typically include some large-group time. However, according to the Child Development Associate Classroom Observation Instrument, even during the preschool years, large-group times should be limited to 10 minutes (Council for Professional Recognition, 1995). Regardless of age, children in the early childhood years should spend most of their time in individual and small-group activities.

Alternate Quiet Activities with Active Activities. **Quiet activities** are those that have little physical movement, for example, nap time, story time, or lunchtime. **Active activities** might include outdoor time or gym time. It is important that we alternate quiet and active activities particularly when they are teacher directed and where children are required to participate. For example, children who sit through a morning circle, then sit through a small-group literacy activity, and then sit during morning snack may become restless and inattentive. When participating in learning centers, children are typically allowed to move freely and choose their own level of activity. In most classrooms, centers include quiet as well as more active activities.

Allow Adequate Time for Routines (Resting, Mealtime, Tooth Brushing, Clean-Up Time). Routine times are learning experiences for young children, if enough time is allowed for children to fully benefit from the activity. For example, contrast the two approaches to lunchtime at ABC Child Care Center and Spirit at Play.

At ABC Child Care, children go through a lunch line, where the adults prepare the children's plates. The children then sit quietly and eat. Teachers feel that it is important for children to finish eating quickly so that they can move on to learning experiences. Therefore, they have implemented a "no talking" policy. Teachers spend most of the lunch period reminding children to "eat, not talk." As the teachers rush through the routines, they not only hinder learning opportunities but also treat the children disrespectfully.

At Spirit at Play, teachers realize that mealtime provides the perfect opportunity to engage in meaningful learning and in-depth conversations. On any given day, you might hear lively discussions about the food they are eating ("Can we grow lettuce in a pot in the window or does it have to be planted outside?"), the activities that they completed in the morning ("How can we get the block tower to reach above our heads without crashing?"), anticipated events ("I wonder what we will see when we walk to the beach?"), and joys or concerns ("Where will daddy live if he doesn't live with us?"). Children eat family style, getting their own food. This allows children to learn self-help skills, reflect upon what foods they like and dislike, determine proper proportions, and learn about sharing with others. Teachers eat with children, modeling social skills. The teachers also use the mealtime as an opportunity to increase knowledge and skills; for example, pointing out that the oranges are cut into fourths as a way of assisting children with math skills and vocabulary. The children and teachers at Spirit at Play are all familiar with the mealtime routine and expectations. The mealtime at Spirit at Play provides a rich learning experience and is a positive experience for both the teachers and children. Further, the teachers have modeled a respectful way of interacting with others.

Teaching children the classroom routines can be time-consuming, particularly when children first begin a program. However, teachers who spend more time teaching routines at the beginning of the school year have children who are more engaged in learning activities and need less assistance later in the year (Bohn, Roehrig, & Pressley, 2004).

Plan Transitions. Transition times, or the time spent changing from activity to activity, consume as much as 20% to 30% of the child's day (Berk, 1976; Sainato & Lyon, 1983). Therefore, it is important to make sure these times are learning experiences. This is more likely to occur when the schedule allows unrushed time for transitions. Detailed information about how to plan effective transitions is included later in this chapter.

In addition, you will want to minimize the number of transitions whenever possible. For example, some programs have children individually prepare and eat their snack during center time, eliminating the need for large-group transitions to and from snack. Small-group time and special activities can also be incorporated into center time.

Include a Daily Time to Be Outdoors. During outdoor time, children have the opportunity to participate in activities often not present in the indoor environment. Outdoor time allows for boisterous play, loud voices, and large motor engagement. In addition to exercise, the outdoors provides other health benefits including less concentrated infectious disease organisms and exposure to sunlight, which allows children to produce Vitamin D (American Academy of Pediatrics, American Public Health Association, National Resource Center for Health and Safety in Child Care and Early Education, 2002). Outdoor play also allows children to be involved firsthand with nature and to experience the many aspects of weather. Many programs further enhance children's learning by developing their outside environment into an outdoor classroom containing a variety of learning centers. Children need to be outdoors everyday, unless it would be a health risk to do so (wind chill below 16 degrees, heat index above 89 degrees) (American Academy of Pediatrics, American Public Health Association, & National Resource Center for Health and Safety in Child Care and Early Education, 2002, p. 51; NAEYC, 2005). It is important to have alternate plans when children cannot go outside. See Chapter 17 for a variety of indoor large motor ideas.

Include Extended Center Time for Engaging in In-Depth Learning. Learning center time should be a minimum of one hour to allow for deep involvement in play (Bredekamp & Copple, 1997, p. 126; Copple & Bredekamp, 2009, p. 153). This time period, called work-play, self-selection, project time, free choice, center time, or activity time in different programs, is an opportunity for children to participate in individual and small-group learning. During this time, children choose between the many available learning centers. These centers will vary depending upon the age group of the child but often include dramatic play, blocks and construction, art, music, sensory, literacy, math, science, and manipulative centers. In addition, special small-group activities are often included during this time period, such as cooking projects, special art activities, and activities that support ongoing project work.

Children in a rural program were completing a project on tractors. After an in-depth study that included visiting an implement dealer, the children decided to create their own tractor. Each day during center time, several children worked on constructing a tractor from a large refrigerator box. Often they revisited a video they had taken of the tractors at the implement dealer, reviewed sketches they had made of tractors, consulted books and posters, and had lively discussions as they gained a more in-depth understanding of tractors.

Large blocks for center time allow children to make a variety of decisions, learn to plan and manage their time, and work at their own pace. During this time, children can choose whether to work individually or in small groups, and whether to engage in quiet or more active activities. They can also control the tempo of their work, determine how long to spend on an activity, and decide whom to interact with. In many programs, these large blocks of time also allow for some spontaneity. For example, a teacher and a small group of children might take a trip to a nearby library when children need additional information for a project.

Include a Developmentally Appropriate Large-Group Time. The younger the children, the shorter the group time should be and the more choice children should have in whether or not they participate in the group. Group times are most effective when children are actively involved such as participating in music and drama activities, story telling, puppetry, or interactive story reading. Group times are also used to introduce new centers, discuss the day's events, share learning, review teacher's and children's joys and concerns, and discuss classroom situations and brainstorm solutions. Since group times are short, there is typically only time to focus on one or two of these activities.

In planning group times, the teacher needs to first consider the goals for the activity and then whether the large group is the best way to achieve these goals. As might be expected, children are more off-task in large groups than small groups (Rimm-Kaufman, La Paro, Downer, & Pianta, 2005; McWilliam, Scarborough, & Kim, 2003).

Katie, a teacher at Northern Head Start, read a book to the children each day during large-group time. She wanted to introduce children to a variety of literature and to teach pre-reading skills such as prediction and phonological awareness. However, when Katie reflected upon her group time she realized that she spent much of her time managing the group, interrupting the book to ask children to sit quietly. When she asked questions some of the children answered quickly and others rarely seemed to respond. Children also complained about not being able to see the book. Katie decided to reexamine her circle time and try a variety of strategies. First, she divided the class into small groups so that each child would be able to have more opportunities to see and interact with the book by asking and responding to questions. She also carefully chose books to read aloud, making sure that they were age-appropriate, quality books with pictures that were large enough to be seen by the children. She tried to make her stories more interesting by using a dramatic voice, bringing story props, and occasionally telling the story with puppets. Katie also strived to more actively involve the children in the stories by reading stories the children could dramatize, encouraging children to repeat phrases as she read predictable books, and asking children relevant questions as she read the book (What do you think will happen next? Why do you think he did that? What else could he have done?).

Determine Needs for a Small-Group, Teacher-Directed Time. While small-group activities are often incorporated into center time, many programs also include a separate time for small groups. During this time, teachers might set up many different types of learning experiences. These might include special cooking projects, project planning or implementation, math or science activities, small-group reading activities, or writing in journals and sharing their journals with the group. In some programs, small groups may also be child led. For example, in the Helena K-3 classroom, a circle that focused on joys and concerns was led by a child each day. If a concern was introduced, the child facilitated the group in problem-solving solutions.

Meet the Needs of Families. When developing schedules, it is important to consider the needs of the families in your program. For example, do most of the children eat breakfast before they arrive? If so, you might want to consider a breakfast bar, where children who have not had breakfast can help themselves to a bowl of cereal and a piece of fruit rather than having everyone sit down for breakfast. If parents and children need to spend extended time in the car commuting after child care, you might want to plan your schedule so that the child has had an opportunity to participate in active activities before leaving.

Make the Schedule Visible. Schedules are typically posted so that children, teachers, families, and volunteers can anticipate the next event. For younger children, the schedule is often displayed in picture form. See the picture at the beginning of the chapter for an example of a picture schedule.

Regularly Analyze the Schedule. Teachers need to regularly assess the schedule to assure that it is meeting the needs of children, families, and teachers. The schedule is not an end in itself but instead is designed to meet children's needs and to allow program goals to occur.

Establishing an effective schedule provides a framework that allows a community of learners to engage in rich learning opportunities. Each teacher is a decision maker in developing a schedule based upon the needs and unique characteristics of the children, staff, families, and philosophy of the program. However, in developing schedules it is sometimes helpful to examine what others have done. Following are sample daily schedules.

Sample Daily Schedules

Each of the following sample schedules is designed for a different age group. In addition, each of the schedules vary based upon the detail they provide and the terms they use for common areas of the day (work-play, selective choice).

Sample Infant Schedule. The understanding of parental everyday routines is very important, particularly to provide continuity and meet the cultural needs for infants and toddlers. Shonkoff and Phillips, in *Neurons to Neighborhoods* (2000), discuss behavioral inheritances, stating that they are "embodied in the 'scripts' that characterize everyday routines for such common activities as sleeping, feeding, and playing" (p. 867). For example, are infants rocked to sleep or do they fall asleep on their own? How independent are infants expected to be? It is important that parents and teachers work closely to meet infants' and toddlers' needs (Butterfield, 2002).

In planning for infants, individual schedules are followed. However, during the day each child needs to have the opportunity to:

- Have undivided adult attention and interaction during routine times such as feeding and diapering. This time provides a prime opportunity to engage in individualized, meaningful communication.
- Be read to.
- Listen to music.
- Engage in floor time.
- Have one-on-one interaction with a teacher around individualized learning goals.
- Explore materials in the classroom.
- Engage in gross motor activities both indoors and outdoors.

During arrival and departure time, teachers and parents share news about the child and written communication sheets regarding the child's sleep, eating, and diaper changes. Special instructions and daily anecdotes are also discussed and often written on communication sheets.

Sample Toddler Schedule. Toddlers have developed more self-regulation in comparison with infants and can therefore have a more group-oriented rather than individualized schedule. Since children at this age are seeking greater independence, more time needs to be planned for individualized transitions. For example, toddlers may take a long time putting on a coat or shoes. The schedule also needs to allow ample time to explore and discover.

7:45 Arrival—Special table time activities and books. Individualized hand washing.

8:30 Breakfast—Children who are hungry eat breakfast family style. As children finish eating, they wash their hands and go to centers.

9:00 Center time—Choice of dramatic play, art, music, manipulative, blocks and construction, sensory, gross motor, and book nook. Teacher-planned special activities (art, literacy, music, project). Diaper checks and changes.

10:00 Clean up and transition outdoors.

10:20 Outdoors—Gross motor activities and interaction with the natural environment.

11:10 Transition indoors—Wash hands for lunch, sing songs.

11:30 Lunch—Children and a teacher sit in small groups sharing food and conversation. As children finish lunch they wash hands, brush teeth, and have their diaper changed.

12:15 Naps—Children look at books or listen to teachers telling stories until they fall asleep.

2:15 As children wake, they have their diaper changed, eat snack, and engage in quiet center time activities (books, manipulatives, media, art).

3:10 Clean up and transition outdoors.

3:30 Outdoor—Gross motor activities and interaction with the natural environment.

4:00 Transition indoors.

4:15 Centers—Choice of dramatic play, art, music, manipulative, blocks and construction, sensory, gross motor, book nook plus teacher planned special activities (music, movement, creative drama), diaper checks (in warm weather, teachers set up outdoor centers and this time is spent outside).

5:30 Departure.

Sample Preschool Schedule. You will note that in this schedule snack time is included as part of the center activities. This technique allows children to eat when they are hungry and can free up time for other activities. You will also note that not all children are required to lay down on a mat. Instead quiet time for non-nappers involves participating in quiet activities. It is important that naptime be planned based upon the need of the child and family. Some families request that their child have a nap so that they will have more time together as a family in the evening.

A playground is adjacent to this classroom. In the afternoon, children have the choice of using the outdoor or indoor learning centers.

7:45 Arrival—Children and parents sign in. Work jobs (individualized and small-group tabletop activities). Individualized hand washing.

8:30 Breakfast—Children and teachers eat family style—conversation, social skills, and self-help skills are stressed. As children finish breakfast they go to the circle area to dictate stories, write, or draw in their individual journals.

9:10 News and views small group—Children are divided into two groups. Teachers share information about new materials, centers, and activities for the day. Two children each day share journals. Children and teachers make plans for activities and projects.

9:30 Transition to outdoors—Children are individually released from the circle using self-concept boosting activities (description of the child, photo of child engaged in an activity or with a special person, happygram describing something the child did the day before, etc.). Time is allowed for toileting, gathering materials for outdoor play, and putting on coats.

9:50 Outdoors—Choice of outdoor centers (climbing, balancing, swinging, art, music, woodworking, Zen garden, sand and water, gardening, dramatic play) or participating in teacher-planned special activities. In bad weather, gross motor activities are set up indoors.

10:30 Gross motor transition—Children use gross motor skills to enter the building (hop, skip, crawl through tunnel). Children put coats away, wash hands, use toilet, and so on.

10:40 Work-play—Children choose from literacy, math, manipulative, sensory, science, dramatic play, block and construction, woodworking, music, and creative art centers or teacher-directed individual and small-group activities. Snacks are available for children who are hungry.

11:40 Clean up—As children complete clean up they go to small-group story areas and look at books.

11:50 Small-group story—Teachers read books to small groups of children.

12:10 Concept transition—Children are released individually to wash hands using a concept-based transition (addresses, full names, colors, patterns, etc.).

12:15 Lunch—Children and teachers eat family style with an emphasis on conversation, social skills, and self-help skills.

12:45 As children complete lunch they brush their teeth, wash their hands and face, and get out their mats.

1:00 Quiet time/nap time—Children lay down on cots and listen to stories told by the teacher or look at books. Non-nappers go to a separate area and have quiet alone time for half an hour during which time they look at books, draw, or write in journals.

2:00 Indoor and outdoor learning centers—As children awake or finish quiet time they can participate in indoor or outdoor learning centers. During this time, children also prepare their own individual snack by following simple picture recipe cards.

4:30 Clean up and movement—Children put away materials in indoor and outdoor centers and assist in cleaning the center for the day. Each child is assigned a chore (e.g., watering plants, cleaning paint containers, emptying the water table, putting balls away, etc.). As children finish cleaning they join a circle where one teacher is leading the group in movement activities.

5:00 Closing circle—Children and teachers meet in small groups to share joys and concerns. Children dictate daily news. The teacher writes the news on chart paper and displays it for parents to see.

5:15 Departure.

Sample Kindergarten Schedule. The teacher in this program has posted the state standards that children are meeting as they engage in each of the learning centers.

8:45 Opening circle—Self-concept activity and daily announcements (new centers, activities planned for the day, news from home).

9:05 Work stations—Children participate in literacy-infused learning centers—literacy, math, cognitive manipulative, science, dramatic play, block and construction, woodworking, music, creative art, plus teacher-directed individual and small-group activities.

10:15 Transition—Clean up and wash hands to prepare for snack.

10:30 Snack—Children and teacher eat in small groups; informal conversation is encouraged.

10:45 Physical skills—Large motor and movement activities (indoor or outdoor movement centers, teacher-led activities).

11:10 Circle time—Science, math, and literacy instruction.

11:30 Small group—Children engage in small-group, teacher-directed learning activities focused on science, math, literacy, social science, and project work.

11:55 Transition to lunch.

12:00 Lunch and outdoor time—As soon as children finish lunch they go to the playground where they use gross motor equipment or participate in dramatic play or teacher-organized or child-initiated games.

1:05 Transition indoors.

1:15 Literacy activities—Children read books, write in journals, and participate in author's circles.

1:45 Work stations—Children participate in literacy infused learning centers—literacy, math, cognitive manipulative, science, dramatic play, block and construction, woodworking, music, creative art, plus teacher-directed, individual and small-group activities.

2:30 Clean up—As soon as children finish cleaning up they go to the circle area and complete a quick daily evaluation (mark on a sheet of paper the favorite thing they did that day, fill in a circle indicating how well they got along with friends, and indicate what activities they completed at centers).

2:45 Closing circle—Summarize and evaluate the day.

3:00 Departure.

First- Through Third-Grade Schedule. This classroom emphasizes the project approach to learning. During the afternoon, students conduct research on their project using the many centers and integrating the different subject areas. For example, this group is currently studying our bodies. They have many questions about the skeletal system and body organs. In the art center, they are using different materials to construct a body; in the science center, they are examining X rays and identifying different bones using research books; in the manipulative center, children are dissecting an owl pellet finding bones that they hope to reconstruct; and several children are writing a research book on what they are learning about their bodies.

8:15–8:45 Morning meeting (morning messages, group sharing, community-building activity, daily announcements, and planning).

8:45–9:45 Literacy workshops and centers.

Reading—Mini lessons, reading conferences, independent and partner reading, author's chair.

Writing—Mini lesson, author's chair, writing conference, prompted writing.

Centers—Games (spelling and word games), listening center, writing center, book center, computer center.

9:45–10:00 Clean up centers—prepare to go outside or to the gym.

10:00–10:30 Outdoor time or gym.

10:30–11:15 Math skill groups.

11:15–11:40 Read aloud—chapter book.

11:45–12:30 Lunch and recess.

12:30–1:00 Individual or buddy reading.

1:00–3:00 Projects, centers, special guests.

Centers—literacy, manipulative, math, dramatic play, construction, science, art, music, puppetry, special project center.

3:10 Closing meeting—self-reflection on day, joys and concerns.

3:25 Dismissal.

You will note that in some of the previous samples, the teacher has noted her transition times and transition activities on the schedule. Well-planned transitions help bring closure to an activity and to move children smoothly to the next part of the day. As the preschool example illustrates, these can also be learning times if well designed. The next section will discuss how to plan for effective transitions.

Designing Effective Transitions

Nicole carefully planned her morning activities with the group of 3-year-old children that she was teaching. Although she normally planned carefully, today she had planned with extra deliberation because she was being observed by her early childhood college professor. Her morning had gone perfectly. Nicole and the children were completing a project on caterpillars and during free time the children were involved in many activities relating to the project that Nicole had planned. During circle time the children all listened attentively when she read The Very Hungry Caterpillar *by Eric Carle. The children even helped to tell the story as she read. Then everything fell apart. After circle when she told the children it was time to wash up for lunch, they all jumped up and began a stampede for the sink to wash their hands. Before she knew it, three children had been pushed on the way to the sink (one of the children was on the floor and two other children were crying). There were several children all trying to wash their hands at once who were shouting at each other. The college professor had to stop observing to help restore order.*

Transition times, the process of changing from one activity to another, can be difficult for adults and for children. Children are expected to listen to the teacher's instructions, end one activity, follow multiple-step directions, and begin another activity all while filtering out distractions from peers. If not well planned, transition times may also involve children congregating in one spot and waiting with nothing to do. These times can be difficult for all children. But, for children with disabilities such as Attention Deficit Hyperactivity Disorder (ADHD), characterized by difficulties with attention, impulsivity, and hyperactivity, the reduced structure and multiple demands during transition times can make coping extremely difficult (Buck, 1999). This is all further complicated by the fact that during transition times, adults are often multi-tasking, trying to assist children to move through the various stages of the transition while also facilitating the next activity. Like Nicole, many early childhood practitioners fail to plan for transitions, making the transition process even more difficult (Sainato, 1990).

Effective transition times are particularly important when one considers that a typical program in early childhood can include 12 to 15 transitions (Rogers, 1988) and as mentioned earlier, transitions may account for as much as 20% to 30% of the child's day (Berk, 1976; Sainato & Lyon, 1983). Well-planned transitions not only decrease frustration and behavior problems but can turn wasted time into educational opportunities, allowing both adults and children to feel competent. How do we plan effective transitions?

Tips for Effective Transitions

Following are several techniques that can help make transitions effective and educational.

Determine if It Is Necessary to Have a Transition. Could the number of times that children need to make transitions be reduced by rearranging your schedule? In many cases activities can be incorporated into selective choice. For example, instead of children all engaging in a group art activity, the special art project could be available throughout selective choice. This creates fewer transitions, smaller group sizes, and child choice of when to participate.

Visualize How the Transition Would Look if It Was Successful. What would the children be doing? What would the teacher be doing? Using the visualization as a goal, develop a concrete plan to achieve it (Buck, 1999). For example, Nicole, the teacher in the scenario, must plan a transition for children to wash their hands. She must also think about what the children will do after they wash their hands. Will they go directly to the lunch table? Will they sit wherever they wish or will the children sit in designated spots? If they go directly to the table, can they begin to eat immediately or must they wait until everyone is seated?

Place Transition Times on the Daily Schedule and on the Daily Plan. This acknowledges the importance of these times and is more likely to result in the time being planned. It is important to realize that transitions take time. Rushing through transitions can cause stress for children and adults while diminishing the opportunities for learning that can occur during these times (Greenman & Stonehouse, 1996).

Predetermine the Roles and Responsibilities of Each Adult During Transitions. For example, Nicole could ask her assistant to be by the sink. She could then release the children individually or in small groups to wash their hands.

Reduce the Waiting Time That Often Accompanies Transitions. In addition to wasting valuable time and increasing the likelihood of behavior problems, requiring children to wait with nothing to do is disrespectful. As stated by Davidson (1982), "Adults who often make children wait for them or the group, or who otherwise waste children's time convey a basic lack of respect for children which may well have a detrimental effect on the way that children view themselves" (p. 16). Additionally, teachers may inadvertently punish children who conform to their expectations by making them wait until all the children are finished before beginning an activity. This often occurs after clean up. To prevent this, make sure that an activity starts as soon as a couple of children are finished cleaning up. Children can listen to and follow an activity or a finger-play tape, or look at books. It is important to plan activities that children can easily become involved with as they join the group. For this reason, most teachers avoid reading stories during this time. Other ways to avoid waiting time is to have everything ready for an activity before the children begin. Moving children in small groups rather than large groups also reduces waiting time. For example, as soon as some of the children are ready, they go outside with a teacher rather than waiting for the large group to be ready.

Use Any Wait Time in Transitions Wisely and Effectively. If children must wait, it is important to provide transition activities. For example, you might sing songs, play language games, tell a story, complete finger plays, clap patterns, write or draw in journals, exercise, or perform creative movement activities. Jeareal, a preschool teacher, plays a game, "what it is, and what it isn't" when there is waiting time. Using any object, children list what it is and then what it isn't. For example, a pencil might be pointed, round, red. It is not a pen, stick, or elephant. Some beginning teachers make a list of ideas to use while waiting that they post on the wall or keep in their pocket so they are always prepared.

Make Transitions Predictable. Some teachers have a specific song they play for cleaning up or they might say the same chant every time they leave the playground to go inside. These routines provide stability and add an opportunity for rituals that are enjoyable for the teacher and children (Greenman, 2006).

Give a Warning Before the Start of a Transition. For example, "In five minutes, we will be cleaning up so that we can go outside." As adults, we would be insulted and likely resistant if a friend were to say, "You need to stop what you are doing and put everything away because we are going outside now." Giving a warning demonstrates that we have respect for children and their work. The time between the warning and the transition allows children to bring closure to the task they are engaged in and to begin planning for the next event. This often results in children being more cooperative. Whenever possible, it is helpful to allow children to complete the task they are involved in before they transition to the next activity.

State or Review Expectations Before the Transition Begins. In addition to giving children verbal instructions, some teachers have directions in pictures showing the children performing each of the tasks for the transition. This technique has been used effectively with children who are hard of hearing or who have autism. It is important that the expectations are necessary and developmentally appropriate. For example, some teachers require children to sit quietly before they are released from circle. Although this may be the traditional way that circle releases have occurred in the program, teachers need to ask themselves if there is a reason this is important. For many children, sitting quietly is very difficult and not developmentally appropriate.

Engage in Active Supervision During Transition Time. Researchers have found that those teachers who engage in the active supervision skills of scanning, moving, and interacting increase appropriate behavior (Colvin, Sugai, Good, & Lee, 1997). Scanning involves looking frequently around the room and noticing children's behaviors. Moving involves walking in unpredictable patterns, using proximity to control and reinforce behavior. Interacting includes modeling, conversing with children, reinforcing behavior, and reminding children of expectations when needed (McIntosh, Herman, Sanford, McGraw, & Florence, 2004). Since transition times can be difficult for children, it is important for every teacher in the room to be actively engaged in assisting and supervising children. It is best if materials needed for the next activity are set up before the transition begins.

If Needed, Adapt the Transition Expectations for Children with Special Needs. Children with disabilities may need extra assistance during transition time.

Sean, a 4-year-old child with ADHD, had difficulty with the transition from outside to inside. Moving from the playground to the classroom involved walking down a steep flight of steps. Sean, who was extremely hyperactive and anxious to get inside, had on more than one occasion accidentally pushed the child in front of him. The teachers, after brainstorming options, decided to have Sean come into the classroom before the other children. Not wanting to make Sean feel like he was being punished, they decided to let Sean be the lunch helper. Sean was excited to perform this role.

There are many strategies that assist children with special needs to effectively negotiate transitions. The most important, as illustrated in the example, is to problem solve solutions based upon the specific need of the child. Some children may need additional time to make the transition, fewer multiple-step directions, a picture card showing the sequence of the transition, or a student buddy.

Make Transitions Educational. Transitions can be made educational in a variety of ways. For example, children can be released from circle through emphasizing a new skill they are learning such as recognizing their first and last name, colors of clothing, or addresses. They can improve listening skills, vocabulary, and observation skills when they try to guess which classmate the teacher is describing. Physical skills can be enhanced as children kick an imaginary ball as they move from the playground to the classroom. Creativity and problem solving can be emphasized when teachers ask children to find their own unique way to move down the hall.

Helpful Hints for Different Types of Transitions

There are some daily transitions that present especially difficult challenges. Following are some of these transitions along with ideas to help make these transitions run smoothly.

From Home to Program. This is often a difficult transition for several reasons. The transition not only involves the child and teacher but also the parent, making it unclear who is responsible for the child during this time. The teacher's time is often divided between welcoming parents and children and attending to children who are already present. Both the child and the parent might be grieving the need to be apart.

It is important that the teacher be available to aid in the transition. Teachers might encourage parents to stay at the program until they and their child feel comfortable parting. When the parent does leave, the teacher needs to support the child until they engage in an activity. For example, the teacher might support the toddler by holding the child, walking to the door or a window, and waving good-bye to the parent. Some programs have low "good-bye windows" at the infant and toddlers level that they can crawl to and look out.

To assist in the transition, it is helpful if the teacher has engaging activities immediately available for the child. These activities should take a minimum of teacher attention and be highly desirable to the children. There needs to be enough materials so that all the children who wish to can participate. For example, some teachers have a clay table with a variety of tools. Others have a basket of books, a set of puzzles and games, or work jobs (individual fine motor and cognitive activities) that are used only at this time of the day.

Because change is especially difficult for certain children, some programs encourage them to bring a security item from home to assist them in bridging their two worlds. Other programs have developed individual family photo albums that children can look at when their parents leave.

Moving from Place to Place in a Group. It is difficult for children to move in a group. The temptation is to get there quickly by running ahead of the teacher. Teachers can assist children by giving them something specific to do as they walk. For example, children might play follow the leader. They can walk in different ways—walking like a rag doll, walking stiff legged, walking on toes, or walking heel to toe. Children can move like different animals or forms of transportation (car, plane, bus). They can practice different gross motor skills like hopping, jumping, or skipping. The teacher can give children certain landmarks or items to find along the path. Children and teachers can also sing a song while moving to the beat.

Moving from Indoors to Outdoors. In cold climates, preparing to go outside can involve putting on hats, coats, boots, mittens, and snow pants. Rainy climates can also necessitate dressing in a variety of gear. In many programs, all the children are preparing to go outside at once, resulting in crowded conditions. Because children have different skill levels and clothing that varies (for example, rain pants that pull on versus rain pants that zip), they are ready to go outside at different times. Therefore, this transition is more effective when children get ready to go outside individually or in small groups. The children who are ready earlier can help other children who might need assistance in zipping a coat or pulling on boots. As soon as the small group is ready, they can go outside with a teacher. Coming inside from outdoor play also necessitates a transition. To see how one teacher assists children with this transition watch *Transitioning from Outdoor Play to Circle Time* on MyEducationLab.

Go to MyEducationLab and select the topic "Guiding Children." Under Activities and Applications, watch the video *Transitioning from Outdoor Play to Circle Time.*

Transitioning to Nap Time. In setting up the nap time transition and routine you will first want to make sure you have realistic expectations. Children should not be required to lie on their mats for long periods of time (more than half an hour) when they are not asleep. Nonsleepers can relax by participating in quiet activities.

For children who do lie down to nap, you will want to set the stage for napping by helping children to relax. You can help children to calm down by having them move to their mats in a slow way such as pretending to be turtles, snails, or toys that are winding down (Pica, 2004). Once on the mats, children can engage in progressive relaxation exercises such as being a rag doll, limp noodle, or melting ice cube (Pica, 2004). You can also lead children in guided imagery such as being a cloud floating in the sky or a stream flowing through the mountains.

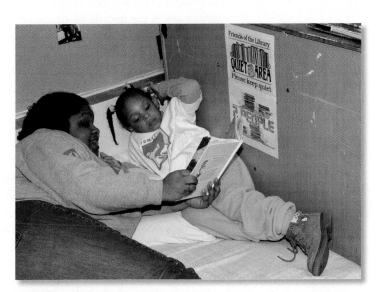

This teacher creates a pleasant nap time transition by reading the child a favorite book. Lying down right next to the child places the teacher at the child's eye level, in an informal, comfortable position.

Teachers can also assist children to relax by teaching them deep breathing techniques. For example, they might pretend to blow up a balloon. Playing relaxing music, dimming lights, and giving children back rubs also helps children to relax and fall asleep. Puppets can also be used effectively for transitions. For example, a sleepy-time puppet can be brought out each day to tell the children a special story as they lie on their cots. Finally, you might provide books for children to look at as they prepare for sleep. By teaching children relaxation skills and modeling the establishment of a relaxing atmosphere, we can help provide a more pleasant transition for children and adults. In addition, we are teaching children a lifelong skill.

From Clean Up to Circle Time. Cleaning up can be an overwhelming job, particularly if children have not been cleaning up as they have been playing. To aid in cleaning up, a small group of children can be given a specific area to clean. Often these are the children who were last playing in the area. Children are often more cooperative when they are given choices of what to pick up within the area. "Would you like to pick up the large blocks or the small blocks?" Teachers can also make clean up a game. "You be the bulldozer and push the blocks to the shelves, I'll put the blocks on the shelf." Playing an energizing song that children dance and move to while cleaning up is another technique. This not only accomplishes the task but also encourages physical movement. Many teachers have chants or songs that they use to signal the beginning of clean up.

School to Home. Leaving the program might be difficult for some children, particularly those who have a difficult time with change. Children are often engaged in an activity when parents arrive and may be reluctant to discontinue it. Often children have not received a warning that they will be leaving. Additionally, parents, teachers, and children are all tired at the end of the day.

Just as children might bring a transition object from home to ease entry into the program, a transition object from the center might ease the exit. For example, children might check a book out from the center that the parent will read to them at home. Teachers can also make a conscientious effort to warn children that their parents are coming soon. If children are in the middle of an activity, such as eating snack or finishing an art project and the parent is unable to wait, the teacher might want to send the unfinished snack or art project home to be completed.

Through carefully planned transitions, teachers can reduce stress and behavioral issues, limit wasted time, and increase learning opportunities. Children can learn independence and inner control, learn to use time wisely, and acquire the skills needed to make successful transitions throughout their schooling careers and life.

 Apply Your Knowledge Jeremy and Sarah, co-teachers of toddlers, struggle each day to get all the children ready to go outside. Most of the children need a lot of assistance to put on coats, snow pants, boots, hats, and mittens. In addition, some of the parents forget to bring the needed clothing. Jeremy or Sarah then have to dig through the program extras to find ones that will fit. While Jeremy and Sarah are helping the ten children get ready, the children that are already dressed are waiting, pushing, or wrestling with each other, and saying they are hot. The teachers worry about children getting overheated and sweating while waiting and then going outside in the cold. How can Jeremy and Sarah make this transition more effective?

In addition to planning the schedule and transitions, programs need to think about the number of children in the classroom. The number of children in the group affects the amount of classroom space required and classroom dynamics.

Planning Successful Groups

There are many decisions in establishing classroom groups including whether to have single or multi-age groups, effective size of classroom groups, and whether it is important to have stability in the group over time. Within-class grouping also needs to be considered.

Should groups be homogeneous or heterogeneous, stable or constantly changing? What is the best size for groups? Although it is not possible to address all these questions in this chapter, we will focus on guidelines for group size, in-class grouping, and one promising practice, looping or continuity of care.

Group Size

Group size has become a concern in infant/toddler, preschool, and elementary school classrooms. Smaller group sizes are associated with increased developmental outcomes and more positive interactions (American Academy of Pediatrics, American Public Health Association, & National Resource Center for Health and Safety in Child Care and Early Education, 2002).

Group size for infants, toddlers, and preschool children is often governed by state licensing regulations. In addition, recognizing the importance of group size to children's developmental outcomes, national bodies, including NAEYC and the National Health and Safety Performance Standards have also developed standards. NAEYC Accreditation Standards recommend maximum group sizes of 8 for infants, 12 for toddlers, 20 for preschoolers, and 24 for kindergarten children (2005). These numbers are based upon meeting other quality indicators including well-trained staff. The National Health and Safety Performance Standards in some cases recommend even lower group sizes (e.g., a maximum of sixteen 4- to 5-year-old children) (2002, p. 4) setting standards for the industry rather than only those programs that are accredited. According to these standards, group size and teacher-child ratio are considered two of the most important areas to regulate.

As the nation tries to "leave no child behind," reducing class sizes in elementary school has become a political issue with both the federal government and several state governments passing legislation to reduce class sizes (Crosser, 2005). Many studies have been conducted regarding the impact of class size on achievement in elementary schools. One well-designed *longitudinal study* (observing the same subjects over a long period of time) was conducted by the State of Tennessee and included 6,300 children (Crosser, 2005). Results showed that children who were in smaller classrooms (15 children) had significant increases in achievement in all areas compared with students in larger classes (20 or more), even when the larger classes contained a teacher's aide. The more years the children were in the smaller classes, the greater the achievement difference. These effects were long-term, lasting into high school and beyond, with students who had been in smaller classes displaying lower drop-out rates, higher grades, and less grade retention. Effects of small class sizes are especially positive for low-income and minority students (Biddle & Berliner, 2002; Crosser, 2005; Finn & Achilles, 1999).

When there were fewer than 15 children in a group, the children were also more cooperative and compliant, there was less wandering behavior, and there were fewer arguments (Ruopp, Travers, Glantz, & Coelen, 1979). As might be expected, teachers spent more time interacting with children and less time managing the group (Ruopp et al., 1979).

There have also been many studies that have examined within-class groupings. According to a meta-analysis that analyzed 51 studies of within-classroom groupings, small groups benefit all ability levels, especially if the teacher is trained in cooperative learning strategies (Lou, Abrami, & Spence, 2000). Groups often function most effectively when they contain 3 or 4 members (Lou et al., 2000).

Promising Grouping Strategy: Looping

One strategy that has produced promising outcomes is a practice described as looping when referring to elementary schools, and continuity of care when discussing infant/toddler, and preschool programs. This is the process whereby a teacher stays with a group of children for two or more years.

Looping enthusiasts and researchers describe several advantages to looping. Looping provides stability and continuity for children, resulting in less anxiety when a new year begins (Chirichello & Chirichello, 2001; Grant & Johnson, 1995; Hanson, 1995; Hegde & Cassidy, 2004). Looping results in more in-depth, positive relationships between children and teachers. For example, teachers have fewer discipline problems and use more positive forms of discipline (Chirichello & Chirichello, 2002; George, Spreul, & Moorefield, 1987; Hegde & Cassidy, 2004). Because they know the children better, teachers are able to meet the needs and interests of individual students more effectively and the curriculum tends to be more child centered rather than subject centered (Hampton, Mumford, & Bond, 1997; Hanson, 1995). Looping also promotes a greater sense of community among students (Chirichello & Chirichello, 2002). Family–teacher relationships also improved and parent involvement increased when looping was implemented (George et al., 1987; Hegde & Cassidy, 2004).

Looping also allows the "gift of time" meaning that time is saved due to the efficiency of looping (Hegde & Cassidy, 2004; Krogmann & Van Sant, 2000). Advocates state that looping adds an additional month to a school year each succeeding year it is used (Burke, 1996; Hanson, 1995). According to teachers who loop, time is also used more effectively because there is less duplication, improved teacher-student relationships, and greater knowledge of a student's skills, interests, and dispositions (Simel, 1998). The "gift of time" also refers to the flexibility to allow extra time to learn. The teacher can cover material another time if needed and wait to introduce concepts until she feels students are developmentally ready. Time allows the teacher to establish emotional and social support systems needed for lifelong learning (Chirichello & Chirichello, 2001), to try a variety of interventions for a particular student (Krogmann & Van Sant, 2000), and to see the late bloomer blossom (Mazzuchi & Brooks, 1992). Looping is seen as one alternative to grade retention (Jimerson, Pletcher, Graydon, Schnurr, Nickerson, & Kundert, 2006). Countries that often use looping report significantly less retention (Reynolds, Barnhart, & Martin, 1999).

Several studies have compared the achievement of students in looping and nonlooping classrooms. Studies demonstrate that students in looping situations score substantially higher in reading (Bogart, 2002; Krogmann & VanSant, 2000; Yang, 1997) and math achievement tests (Hampton et al., 1997; Yang, 1997) than their peers in nonlooping situations. This was true even when both the looping and comparison groups were taught by the same teacher (Hampton et al., 1997).

Looping is not without difficulties. Although looping or continuity of care is promoted as being important for quality care for children, particularly infants and toddlers, one large study found that it rarely occurs (Cryer, Hurwitz, & Wolery, 2001). In addition, even in programs that promote looping, high teacher turnover might make the procedure ineffective. Looping can make scheduling more difficult, particularly when children are entering and exiting the program at different times. However, some programs have found that if they use mixed age groupings, these scheduling issues can be resolved. The strong bonds between children, and between the teacher and children, can also make it more difficult to end the relationship at the end of the looping cycle (Hegde & Cassidy, 2004; Simel, 1998).

Research supports looping or continuity of care as allowing the gift of time, raising achievement levels, and enhancing relationships between children, the teacher and child, and the teacher and parent. However, programs in the United States still rarely engage in this practice.

Determining the number of children in the classroom and how children will be grouped are important considerations in establishing a context for learning. Also important is assessing children's knowledge, skills, and dispositions so that environments and experiences can be designed to meet children's needs.

Assessing and Documenting Children's Learning

To design engaging, developmentally appropriate learning environments and materials it is necessary to continually assess and document children's development, learning, and interests. There are many assessment tools we can use, each having their own strengths and limitations. Table 3.1 provides information on several different types of assessments. To be effective, teachers must be intentional about the information they wish to collect and have a plan for how they will collect the information.

Daily Discoveries, a preschool, uses a variety of assessment techniques during center time. A skills checklist is developed to use with the work-jobs. When a child demonstrates a skill (such as counting by rote to ten and matching numerals with the correct number of objects), it is recorded on the list. Teachers also hang clipboards in each center so they can easily record anecdotal records. At the end of the week, teachers cut the anecdotal records apart and place them in individual children's files. At times, a tape recorder is placed in a center. The teacher then listens to the tape and/or has volunteers transcribe the tape. This information provides valuable insight into children's thoughts,

Table 3.1 Descriptions, Advantages, and Disadvantages of Different Types of Assessment Techniques

Type of Assessment	Description	Advantages	Disadvantages
Anecdotal records	Short descriptive detailed narrative about a specific event.	Flexible, open ended.	Time consuming. May be difficult to determine group needs without careful analysis.
Running record	Sequential narrative spanning a longer period of time than an anecdotal record.	Flexible, open ended.	Time consuming. May be difficult to determine group needs without careful analysis.
Time sampling	Observation of what happens during a given period of time often using tallies.	Objective, can observe several children simultaneously.	Closed ended, lacks behavioral and contextual detail.
Checklist	A list of behaviors or traits that the teacher checks off.	Easy to use, time efficient, can be used to examine entire group.	Closed ended, lacks behavioral and contextual detail.
Frequency counts	A tally of each time a behavior occurs.	Can document change over time. Effective in determining if interventions or other changes have produced results.	Closed ended, lacks behavioral and contextual detail.
Analyzed work samples	Tape and video recordings, photos, and artifacts (e.g., Venn diagrams, KWHL charts, webs, handwriting samples) that show children's current work and thinking.	Authentic. Can be used to show both progress and accomplishments.	May be difficult to determine individual or group needs without careful analysis. Analysis can be time consuming.

This kindergarten teacher provides documentation of children's learning through the display of the sunflower mural the children created. A story about the process written by the children further documents their learning.

language, and social skills. Teachers also assess children informally as they interact with them.

Children are also active participants in documenting their own learning using recording sheets, tape recorders, and digital cameras. They complete recording sheets by writing, drawing, or circling answers. For example, in a sink and float center the teacher includes a sheet that has a picture of each item the child is testing. Children circle the items they think will float, then they test each item, and then go back and correct their predictions. Children tape record themselves reading, telling a story, singing, or playing a musical instrument. A digital camera is available for children to take pictures of block structures, sand creations, and pattern block designs. Children also use the camera to show the process of their work over time. For example, children created a car from a cardboard box. They took several pictures showing the various steps.

Some teachers, particularly in K through third-grade classrooms, require that children visit certain centers or complete some mandatory center activities during the week. The children are often given a checklist of required activities. The tracking sheets that document the completion of the activities then become one more piece of assessment evidence.

Throughout this book, we will be examining ways of assessing individual children's learning as well as assessing different learning environments. Here, we will examine three different types of artifacts or work samples that one might use in assessment—webs, KWHL charts, and Venn diagrams.

Webbing

Webbing is a way of organizing and structuring ideas and information. We can web to capture children's knowledge and ideas, to identify misconceptions, to document and organize children's questions, and to record children's learning. Webbing can also be used for creating a tentative curriculum plan and for documenting what has been accomplished.

In creating a web, one writes the topic in the center of a sheet of paper and then creates subtopics around the topic. Ideas or activities continue to web outward. Webs can be completed by individual children, groups of children, or the teacher. In Figure 3.1, you will see an example of a web created by a teacher. The web shows the children's questions about a chicken and activities that might help to answer the children's questions.

KWHL Charts

KWHL (what we know, what we want to know, how we will find out, and what we learned) charts are used to elicit student's prior knowledge, determine their questions, plan ways to answer their questions, and allow them to reflect upon their learn-

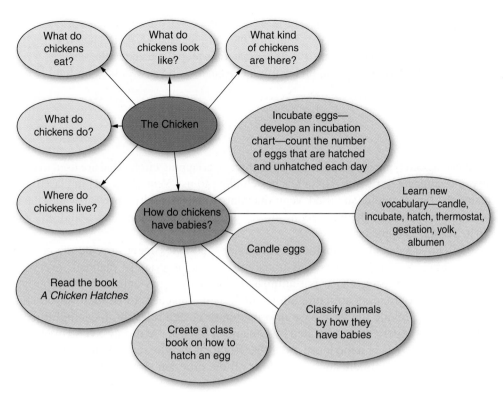

Figure 3.1
Example of a
Teacher-Created
Web for "Chicken."

ing. This information can also be used for curriculum planning. For example, Tamia, a first-grade teacher, was planning a study of insects. She used the KWHL to determine the children's current knowledge and questions, so that she could design relevant experiences for them. See Table 3.2 for the KWHL that one of the children, Sabrina, created.

Table 3.2 Sabrina's KWHL Chart on Insects

What I Know	What I Want to Know	How I Will Find Out	What I Learned
There are many insects.	Are spiders insects?	Look at a bunch of spiders.	
They all have eight legs.	What happens if a poisonous insect bites you?	Look in a book. Ask my dad.	
Some insects bite.	How long do they live?	Ask insect scientist.	
Some insects fly and some crawl.	How far can they fly?	Look in a book.	
	What do they do in the winter?	Ask insect scientist.	
Sabrina is a first-grader. When she finishes her investigation she will fill out the "What I Learned" section.			

Apply Your Knowledge You will note from Sabrina's KWHL chart that she has a misconception about insects. What materials might you add to the science center that will assist her to clear up her misunderstanding and answer her questions?

Venn Diagrams

A Venn diagram typically consists of two or three overlapping circles that are used to classify and compare attributes. Nissa teaches children to use Venn diagrams in classifying materials. For example, she used Venn diagrams to have children predict which items would sink or float. In the intersecting area of the circles were items that would sink and float. See the example in Figure 3.2.

Effective schedules, transitions, group size, and assessment provide the context for learning. When schedules and transitions are appropriately planned, everyone knows what to expect, chaos is diminished, and learning is enhanced. Appropriate group size and grouping structure allow children and teachers to be more successful. Assessments provide the necessary information to design relevant, meaningful environments and experiences. As stated by Greenman (2006), "Avoiding a rigid order that chokes or constricts or a too loose order that frightens or intoxicates generally requires a thoughtful and complete analysis of how all the program structural elements interact" (p. 56).

Figure 3.2
Children's Float and Sink Predictions on a Venn Diagram

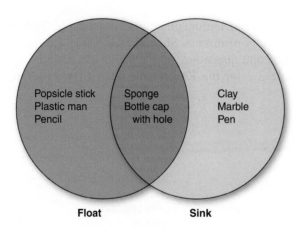

Sample Application Activities

1. Develop a list of finger plays, songs, and activities that you can use for transitions. Combine your ideas with your classmates and create a booklet of transition ideas.
2. Visit an early childhood program. Use the transition critique found in Figure 3.3 to assess at least one transition.
3. Examine each of the schedules in this chapter. Determine the degree of detail that you would use in designing a schedule.

Schedules

☐ Is the schedule developmentally appropriate for the age group? For example, individualized schedules for infants, no required group times for young toddlers?

☐ Is the schedule consistent with the program philosophy?

☐ Is a schedule posted for both children and adults to follow?

☐ Are quiet and active activities alternated?

☐ Is there a developmentally appropriate balance of large-group, small-group, and individual activities?

☐ Does the schedule provide a balance of child-initiated and adult-initiated activities?

☐ Does the child have at least one hour of center time each day?

☐ Is there an outdoor time scheduled each day (or a gym time for bad weather)?

☐ Are routine times included in the schedule?

☐ Is the schedule explained in enough detail that you can understand what children are expected to do during this time period?

Transitions

☐ Are times for transitions listed on the schedule and the lesson plans?

☐ Is there evidence that the transitions are planned?

☐ Is there a limited amount of waiting time during transitions?

☐ If waiting time is necessary, are children engaged in a meaningful activity?

☐ Are transition times used to increase children's knowledge and skills?

☐ Are children given enough time to make transitions so that they are not rushed?

☐ Are children given advance notice that an activity is changing?

Figure 3.3
Environmental
Assessment:
Schedules and
Transitions

Source: Permission is granted by the publisher to reproduce this figure for evaluation and record-keeping. From Julie Bullard, *Creating Environments for Learning: Birth to Age Eight.* Copyright © 2010 by Pearson Education, Inc. All rights reserved.

4. Develop a schedule for an infant/toddler, preschool, or early elementary classroom. Use the schedule critique in Figure 3.3 to assess your schedule.

5. Use a Venn diagram, KWHL chart, or web as a way of preassessing children's knowledge before planning an activity.

chapter 4
Creating a Healthy, Safe Environment

*B*ecky, a teacher for many years, was the owner of the only preschool in the small town in which she lived. She often told parents that her number one concern was child safety. To prevent injury, she eliminated any potentially hazardous material from the preschool. For example, Becky had read that the number one injury in early childhood settings was due to falls. Therefore, she did not have any climbing equipment either inside or outside. She also made sure that there were no sharp or breakable items in the room. Children were only allowed to use "unsafe items" like scissors when an adult was present.

When her business expanded, Becky hired a new co-teacher, Deleena. Deleena was concerned that many of the safety rules had a negative impact on children's development. In addition, she felt that when children were not given opportunities and exposure to common materials, toys, and equipment that they were not learning necessary safety skills. For example, in the setting Deleena had worked in previously, *glass was used to display many of the manipulative and art materials. Children handled these materials carefully, realizing that they could break. It was extremely rare that a glass dish or container was broken. However if it did occur, the staff used it as a teaching opportunity. Deleena pointed out to Becky that the children typically have exposure to many of these materials in their home environments, which are often less closely supervised than in the preschool. Learning to use the materials safely could reduce injuries in other environments. Due to the extreme conflicts in teaching beliefs, the teaching partnership did not last.*

Apply Your Knowledge (1) Examine your state's licensing requirements. What guidance is provided that could resolve the above dilemma? (2) Examine *Caring for Our Children: National Health and Safety Performance Standards: Guidelines for Out-of-Home Child Care* at http://nrc.uchsc.edu/CFOC/index.html. What safety guidance do these standards provide? (3) Explain whether your beliefs about safety align more with Becky's or Deleena's beliefs.

While early childhood professionals agree that health and safety are important, as the above scenario illustrates there is often disagreement about what constitutes a hazard. However, national and state health and safety standards can assist in resolving these issues. Professionals often use these standards to provide guidance in developing program procedures. Yet in a large-scale study examining 749 early childhood classrooms throughout the United States, researchers found that in everyday practice, many providers did not follow the health and safety rules and policies they had established. Therefore, they exposed children to health and safety risks and did not meet the minimal levels of care particularly for diapering, toileting, and meals (Cryer & Phillipsen, 1997).

This chapter will examine ways of reducing both short- and long-term illness in early childhood settings through hand washing, cleaning, sanitation, improved air quality, and reduced pesticide use. We will examine ways to prevent common safety risks. Finally, we will explore how it is possible to meet health and safety standards and still have interesting, aesthetic toileting, diapering, and sleeping areas.

Preventing Illness in Early Childhood Settings

In a group setting, it is especially important to take extra care in preventing illness. Children in early childhood programs are more susceptible to illness than children who are not exposed to groups, especially during the child's initial group exposure. Although at any age group settings increase the risk of illness, for children this risk is greater. First, many children have had limited exposure to others and therefore have not developed antibodies to the variety of germs they encounter, resulting in lower immunity. Additionally, young children's behaviors such as putting toys in their mouths, wiping noses with hands, and close physical contact with others also increase the spread of disease (Marotz, 2009).

The most common method of disease transmission in group settings is airborne when tiny droplets of fluid are passed from one individual to others during talking, sneezing, and coughing. The second most common source of infectious disease is fecal-oral transmission caused by contamination from adult's and children's hands or indirect objects such as sink faucets, computer keyboards, and toys (Marotz, 2009).

There are many ways that early childhood teachers can help to keep children healthy. Listing every potential way is beyond the scope of this book. Therefore, we will focus on sanitary practice because this is the primary way to reduce illness. Because asthma is rapidly increasing in the United States, we will also examine air quality since this has such a direct link to asthma. Additionally, we will look at pesticide use, since the damage resulting from exposure to pesticides can have lifelong effects.

Hand Washing, Cleaning, and Sanitation to Reduce Illness

Researchers have identified frequent hand washing as one of the most effective ways to reduce germs in a group setting (Kotch et al., 2007). They recommend that children and adults wash their hands when they arrive at the program; before and after eating food or engaging in water or sand play; and when using media such as play dough or clay. Hand washing also needs to occur after any contact with bodily fluids or after touching an animal. Both adult's and children's hands must be washed after diapering or using the bathroom. Since germs can be harbored under chipped nail polish and under rings (Moolenaar et al., 2000; Trick et al., 2003), some professionals recommend that these not be allowed in an early childhood setting (Marotz, 2009).

Cleaning and sanitation also play a critical role in preventing disease in early childhood programs. According to the National Association for the Education of Young Children (NAEYC) Accreditation Standards (2006), the following standards are important in reducing germs and illness:

- Any surface with bodily fluids, including diaper-changing tables, needs to be cleaned and sanitized immediately. It is essential to wear gloves when touching bodily fluids that contain or may contain blood to prevent the possibility of spreading AIDS or other blood-borne diseases. Having gloves conveniently located throughout the classroom and any other areas used by children is necessary to assure this occurs.

- Cooking and eating surfaces need to be cleaned and sanitized before and after use.

- Floors, sinks, faucets, toilets, counters, doors, cabinet handles, door knobs, soap dispensers, table tops, toilet bowls, and all areas around the toilet need to be cleaned and sanitized at least once a day and whenever they are soiled.

- Toys, dress-up clothes, combs and brushes, cribs, sheets, and mattresses need to be washed weekly and whenever soiled.

- Blankets and cubbies need to be washed monthly and whenever soiled.

- When children put toys in their mouths, the toys need to be sanitized before being used again.

- Mops and cleaning rags need to be sanitized before and after use.

Infants and toddlers are especially susceptible to communicable diseases due to their immature immune systems, the additional risk of germs spreading when wearing diapers, and engaging in behaviors such as putting toys in their mouths (Slack-Smith, Read, & Stanley, 2002). Therefore, extra diligence is crucial to protect this vulnerable group. For example, Playcare, a program serving infants and toddlers, has established systems to make healthy practices easier. They hang several mesh bags on walls throughout the play area to collect any mouthed toys. At the end of the day, they dip the bags of toys into bleach water and hang them to dry.

TIP   Bleach solutions can be created by adding one-fourth cup household bleach to one gallon of cool water or one tablespoon bleach to one quart of cool water. To be effective the solution must be on the surface a minimum of 2 minutes. The solution needs to be made fresh each day (American Academy of Pediatrics, American Public Health Association, and National Resource Center for Health and Safety in Child Care and Early Education, 2002).

Improving Air Quality to Reduce Illness

Poor indoor air quality (IAQ) is consistently listed as one of the top five environmental risks by the Environmental Protection Agency Science Advisory Board and the National Resources Defense Council (EPA, 2000; Mott, 1997). Levels of indoor air pollutants are often up to 100 times higher than those found outside (EPA, 2000). Schools and child-care programs are especially susceptible to poor air quality due to having a greater concentration of people per square foot than other buildings. In addition, the age of buildings can contribute to poor air circulation. For example, studies conducted in American schools reveal that 15,000 schools suffer from IAQ (Indoor Air Quality) problems. This affects one in five schoolchildren (General Accounting Office, 1995; Schneider, 2002). Children who are from racial minority groups and/or from families who are low income are disproportionately affected by poor air quality since they often are in home and school environments with high levels of both indoor and outdoor pollutants. This has led some writers to suggest there is a lack of environmental justice (Schneider, 2002).

Poor air quality can cause and contribute to both long-term and short-term health problems (EPA, 2005) and because children breathe more air per body weight than adults they are often more adversely affected (Kennedy, 2001). Reported symptoms include upper respiratory infections, nausea, dizziness, headaches, fatigue, allergic reactions, irritated eyes, nose, and throat. (EPA, 2005; Schneider, 2002). Poor air quality results in increased absenteeism and poorer student performance (Mendell & Heath, 2005). It can also contribute to asthma, resulting in American children missing 12.8 million days of school a year (ALA, 2007; Schneider, 2002).

How can we improve air quality in early childhood settings? We can reduce contaminants, control humidity, and adequately ventilate the classroom. Contaminants include carbon dioxide from people breathing, building materials containing formaldehydes, bacteria, smoke, car exhaust, dust, dust mites, mold, and household products (such as cleaning supplies, scented shampoo and soaps, perfumes, candles) (Schneider, 2002). Whenever possible these materials should be eliminated. Some programs are now using "green" building materials, cleaning supplies, and grooming products as a way of reducing contaminants. For example, teachers might use vinegar and baking soda for cleaning rather than more toxic cleaning supplies. Other programs are reducing dust and dust mites by eliminating carpets.

Humidity plays an important role in air quality. Ideally, humidity should range between 40% and 70% (Schneider, 2002). High humidity causes mold, contributing to poor indoor air quality and allergic reactions (Schneider, 2002). However, low humidity reduces children's natural mucus, one of their lines of defense against illness.

It is also critical to assure adequate ventilation. In addition to delivering fresh air, ventilation can dilute or remove contaminants. You can ventilate buildings by either opening windows or through ventilation systems. For example, in a childcare study in Sweden, air-cleaning technology statistically reduced absenteeism caused by illness (Rosen & Richardson, 1999).

Reducing Pesticides to Protect Children's Health

Pesticides (chemicals used to kill a variety of types of pests) are listed as another of the top five environmental threats to children by the National Resources Defense Council (Mott, 1997). "Exposures to pesticides can produce cough, shortness of breath, nausea, vomiting, headaches, and eye irritation" (The National Institute for Occupational Safety and Health, 2007, p. 1). Chlorpyrifos (CPFs), the most investigated ingredient in insecticides, "kills neurons, causes defects in neural cell migration, and reduces connections among brain cells" (National Scientific Council on the Developing Child, 2006, p. 4). The National Scientific Council on the Developing Child (2006) states that even "modest changes in brain architecture caused by exposure to CPF can lead to measurable problems in learning, attention and emotional control" (p. 4). As a result of early exposure to pesticides, children are also more prone to cancer, neurodevelopment impairment, immune dysfunction, and reproductive problems in adulthood (National Research Council, 1993; The National Institute for Occupational Safety and Health, 2007), so it is critical to prevent this exposure from occurring.

Children are exposed to pesticides through inhaling contaminated air, by eating or drinking contaminated food, by skin absorption from handling contaminated materials, and from contamination on the child's hands that comes in contact with the mouth (Wilson, Chuang, Lyu, Menton, & Morgan, 2003). For example, one study showed that after spraying a pesticide just once, the chemical remained on the children's toys and other hard surfaces for two weeks. While the safe level set by the EPA for this chemical was 3 micrograms per kilogram of body weight per day, this study demonstrated that children may have been exposed to 208 micrograms through skin absorption as they played with the toys. Children who display high levels of hand-to-mouth activity may have absorbed as much as 634 micrograms per kilogram of body weight through both oral and skin absorption (Gurunathan et al., 1998).

Pesticides can also be tracked in on shoes and deposited on floors and carpets in early childhood settings. This is especially harmful for young children who play on the floor and breathe the dust that is contaminated or have hand-to-mouth contact.

But, what can you do? There are several steps that can be taken to reduce children's exposure to both pests and pesticides in schools and childcare settings. While it is important to control pests because they may inflict painful bites, spread disease, and cause allergic reactions, many programs are accomplishing this through implementing integrated pest management (IPM). Some legislative bodies such as Michigan's have even enacted regulations requiring IPM (National Scientific Council on the Developing Child, 2006). Programs using IPM first identify pests and try to eliminate them through prevention. For example, programs might eliminate pests' access to food, water, and shelter by removing crumbs and emptying all garbage cans regularly or blocking their access to the building by placing screens on all windows and plugging all holes where pests might enter. Next, the program might use nonchemical methods such as traps or power washing. If these steps do not work, chemicals might be used. However, those following the IPM philosophy use the least toxic chemical available and use targeted spot treatments rather than whole building treatments or treatments based on a predetermined schedule. In addition, to prevent pesticides from entering classrooms on shoes, some programs have providers and children remove shoes when they are in the classroom. This is a requirement for infant programs in the NAEYC Accreditation Standards (2006).

Based on a review of 43,000 research tests, the following produce were determined to be the highest and lowest in pesticides.

Produce highest in pesticides:	Produce lowest in pesticides:
Peaches	Onions
Apples	Avocados
Sweet bell peppers	Sweet corn (frozen)
Celery	Pineapple
Nectarines	Mangos
Strawberries	Sweet peas (frozen)
Cherries	Asparagus
Lettuce	Kiwi
Imported grapes	Bananas
Pears	Cabbage
Spinach	Broccoli
Potatoes	Eggplant

Figure 4.1
Produce Highest and Lowest in Pesticides
Source: Environmental Working Group (EWG). 2006. *Shopper's Guide.* Retrieved on 11/9/2008 from http://www. foodnews.org/

Eating organic fruits and vegetables reduces pesticide risk from ingestion (Environmental Working Group, 2006). The EWG recommends that at a minimum you should buy organic versions of fruits and vegetables that are typically highest in pesticides. Carefully washing all produce and choosing produce low in pesticides can also reduce ingestion. See Figure 4.1 for a list of the produce highest and lowest in pesticides.

There are several steps that the early childhood teacher can take to improve both children's and adults' short- and long-term health in early childhood settings. These include proper sanitation, air quality awareness, and reduction of pesticide exposure.

Safety in Early Childhood Environments

After children reach one year of age, accidental injuries are the largest cause of death in the United States (National Center for Health Statistics (NCHS) Vital Statistics System, 2001; National Safety Council, 2001). Therefore, reducing injuries when working with this age group is a major concern. A longitudinal study of more than 1,200 children followed from birth through first grade found that children who spend more time in child care have a slightly reduced risk of injury compared with children spending more time in their own homes (Schwebel, Brezausek, & Belsky, 2006). Additionally, the majority of injuries (87%) that do occur in child care are minor. Only 1% are considered severe. However, because so many children in the United States are in child care, there are still a large number of children accidentally injured in these settings each year. For example, in one year, 31,000 children, 4 years old and younger were treated in U.S. hospital emergency rooms as a result of injuries sustained in child care. At least 56 children died in child care during the 1990s (U.S. Consumer Product Safety Commission, 1999). The majority of deaths were due to suffocation from nursery equipment or soft bedding. Most injuries (74%) in early childhood settings are due to playground accidents (see Chapter 17 for more information on this topic).

It is important to be continually alert for safety dangers in the environment. A large-scale national study conducted by the U.S. Consumer Product Safety Commission (CPSC) found that two-thirds of the childcare settings they examined had at least one safety hazard. The CPSC warns that there is a potential for children being injured, even seriously hurt, in these environments. The study looked at cribs, safety gates, window blind cords, drawstrings in children's clothing, recalled children's products, and ground coverings (U.S. Consumer Product Safety Commission, 1999). Listed below are some of the most important environmental concerns in keeping children safe:

- All materials should meet the standards of the Consumer Product Safety Commission (CPSC).
- To protect against falls, stairways, windows, and elevated surfaces should meet the American Society for Testing and Materials (ASTM).
- Children should be protected from electrical outlets with specially designed outlets or safety caps.
- Electrical cords should not be within reach of children.
- Emergency phone numbers need to be posted near each telephone (poison control, fire department, emergency contact numbers for parents and others, and the child's doctor).
- Make sure there are adequate fall surfaces under both indoor and outdoor equipment and that toys are not left in fall zones. Continually examine the environment for tripping hazards.
- To prevent poisoning, make sure all cleaning supplies and medications are in locked cupboards, there are no poisonous plants on the premises, and that children do not have access to purses or offices where adults might store personal medication.
- Toys need to be safe by being age and developmentally appropriate for the group. For example, all toys for infants and toddlers or children who are still mouthing toys need to be choke resistant. They also need to be lead free and nontoxic. Finally, one must examine toys to make sure that they cannot lead to strangulation.
- Buckets and tubs containing water need to be closely supervised and emptied when not in use since small amounts of water can be a drowning hazard for young children.
- All equipment, including railings on stairs, need to be examined for possible strangulation risk. Window blind cords and drawstrings on children's clothing can also create safety issues.
- A daily safety check and maintenance is critical to keep equipment and the child's environment safe.
- Children need to be safe from other children who are aggressive. See Chapter 2 for more information on this subject.

Even if the environment meets safety guidelines, supervision is critical in ensuring child safety. The majority of injuries (60%) that occur in early childhood settings are due to child behavior rather than environmental causes (Alkon et al., 1999); for example, a child tripping and falling, colliding with objects, or one child pushing another as they go down a set of stairs. Most states have established child/staff ratios to assist in providing adequate supervision. It is critical that programs maintain these ratios. In addition, it is important that adults actively monitor children. Many programs require staff to maintain visual contact with children as they play. Low classroom dividers can help children to feel a sense of privacy, while still allowing adults to adequately supervise children.

Although severe injuries are rare in early childhood settings, it is important to be alert to and to immediately correct safety dangers. It is also important to assure children remain safe through adequate supervision. Can we keep children healthy and safe and still develop aesthetic environments?

Designing Healthy, Aesthetic Bathrooms, Diaper-Changing Stations, and Sleeping Areas

This section will examine bathrooms, diaper-changing stations, and sleeping areas. Teachers typically design these to be functional with close attention to safety and health. How can they also be aesthetic?

Healthy, Aesthetically Pleasing Bathrooms

Bathrooms in early childhood settings, designed for functionality and ease of cleaning, often include harsh lighting, cold, hard surfaces, rule-oriented posters, and unpleasant smells. However, bathrooms can be aesthetic, provide an opportunity for learning, and still meet health and safety codes. As stated by Greenman (2005a), "It is important to keep in mind the concept of the primal importance of the bathroom experience to young children, as we determine the aesthetics and functionality of bathrooms" (p. 194).

At Middle Creek Montessori, this wash center, located in the bathroom, provides children many learning experiences.

In Reggio Emilia preschools, Gandini reports that "Bathrooms have mirrors of different shapes, and the children can make faces and see their bodies in a playful way. There are often green plants there, and collages made by the children. . . . In some schools, I have seen very complicated pipes with colored water inside that the children can use for experiments. Even the ceilings are used for hanging sculptures and mobiles built by the children from unusual materials, at times transparent and colored to catch the light" (Bartlett, 1993, p. 31).

Mentor Graphics Child Development Center near Portland, Oregon, decided to beautify their bathrooms. They added sculptures created by the children and draped transparent fabric at the tops of the toilet stalls to soften the space. Serenity School features full-length windows that look into a small enclosed garden surrounded by a high fence. Discovery Preschool uses clear plumbing pipes below the sink so that children can see what happens to the water when it drains.

Ideally, bathrooms are located in the classroom. This allows children who are developmentally ready to independently take care of their own personal needs (Maxwell, 2007). You can also assist children to be independent by providing color or picture codes for the hot faucet and cold faucet, and by posting pictures of the proper hand-washing procedures.

Many programs use half doors and partial walls in bathrooms for preschoolers. This allows a feeling of privacy while still providing for safety and supervision (Greenman, 2005a). When children reach kindergarten

Transparent fabric beautifies and softens the metal stalls in this bathroom. The bathroom also features child-created sculptures.

age or older, they no longer need the close supervision and often desire a higher degree of privacy, so experts recommend full partitions (Greenman, 2005a).

To prevent the spread of infection, it is important for children to wash their hands, using liquid soap and disposable towels. Because frequent hand washing can lead to dry, cracked skin, lotion should also be available. Choose soap and lotion carefully, avoiding any ingredients children or adults in the classroom are allergic to.

Healthy, Aesthetic Diaper-Changing Stations

Diaper changing is a frequent, important part of the care routine in infant/toddler rooms. This space needs to be functional and sanitary. Yet, since so much time is spent in this environment it will be beneficial to the staff and children if it is also aesthetically pleasing.

The routine of changing diapers provides the ideal opportunity for a tranquil, personal one-on-one time between the adult and child. To allow for relaxed time and to ensure safety, adults should not have their back to the other children while changing diapers (Greenman, 2005a). If this is absolutely necessary, mirrors can be strategically placed to see the rest of the room.

To reduce the risk of back strain, which is the leading cause of worker's compensation claims for childcare providers (Pardee, 2005, p. 23), the height of the diaper changing area needs to be comfortable for the adult. Another way to reduce back strain and to provide for toddler independence is to provide steps to the diaper-changing table.

Diaper-changing tables can be a breeding paradise for germs (see Figure 4.2). Therefore, it is important to use the following procedures when changing diapers. Provide a separate diaper-changing facility and sink for each group of children (Aronson, 1999). Clean and sanitize the changing surface after each use and make sure it is constructed from a smooth surface that does not allow penetration of liquids or soil. The *National Health and Safety Performance Standards: Guidelines for Out-of-Home Child Care Programs* (American Academy of Pediatrics et al., 2002) recommends that in addition, you cover the changing table with a nonabsorbent paper liner that is discarded at the end of the diaper change. To help protect yourself from disease, wear disposable gloves. When you change the child's diapers avoid contamination with other surfaces by having everything prepared ahead of time. For example, before beginning to change the diaper, remove the disposable wipes you will be using to avoid contamination of the container. Dispose of the diaper in a covered, lined, hands-free garbage can. After the child is changed, wash the child's hands and your hands for at least 10 seconds with liquid soap and running water (NAEYC Accreditation Standards, 2006).

Figure 4.2
Fecal Contamination

Studies commonly find that fecal contamination of the environment is frequent in centers and is highest in infant and toddler areas, the risk of diarrhea is significantly higher for children in centers than in age-matched children cared for at home or in small family childcare homes. The spread of infection from children who are not toilet-trained to other children in childcare facilities or to their families is common, particularly when Shigella, rotavirus and other enteric viruses, *Giardia lamblia, Cryptosporidium,* or hepatitis A virus (HAV) is the causal agent.

Source: American Academy of Pediatrics et al., 2002.

It is also important to be continually aware of safety. To reduce the danger of falls there should be a lip on the changing table and the adult should always keep one hand on the child. Experts recommend avoiding using safety straps because they harbor germs and can give the provider a false sense of security.

> TIP   If space in the bathroom is an issue in a home child care, a removable diaper-changing table that is placed above the tub can be a solution.

Like bathrooms, diaper-changing areas can meet all the safety and health requirements and still provide an interesting, aesthetic environment. Mirrors on the ceiling and beside the changing table can allow children to look at themselves and to see what the adult is doing. Mobiles, pictures, photos, or skylights can provide interesting viewing and points for discussion. Exhaust fans or open windows for ventilation can keep the environment more pleasant smelling. Some programs even install disposal shoots to the outside of the building.

Tina, a teacher of infants/toddlers, provides an example of improving the ambiance in her environment. She adds a fresh bouquet of flowers (donated by a local floral shop) to the diaper-changing area. See Figure 4.3 for an illustration of a diaper-changing area.

Healthy Napping and Sleeping Areas

Sleeping environments can be challenging in early childhood settings since they need to be arranged to provide for the differing sleeping needs of children. It is disrespectful, agonizing, and developmentally inappropriate to require children who are not sleeping to lay quietly for more than a few minutes. While separate napping rooms are ideal, many programs do not have this luxury. Unless there is abundant space, it is generally better to use program space for multi-purposes. If the classroom has to be used for napping, you might place the children that are most likely to sleep in one area of the room. Nonsleepers often rest and then use the classroom's quiet centers. To provide additional quiet activities, Lisa, a teacher of preschoolers, has a special box of books and materials that she only brings out at this time of day. Angelo provides individual manipulative and cognitive activities for

Figure 4.3
Diaper-Changing
Station

children to work on during quiet time. Dim lights, drawn shades, quiet music, and backrubs can help to relax both sleepers and nonsleepers. If needed, lamps can be used to give additional light for those working on quiet activities.

To provide for children's health and safety needs while sleeping, the cots need to be placed at least 3 feet apart. Bedding cannot be shared by children or stored so that one child's bedding touches the bedding of other children (American Academy of Pediatrics et al., 2002). Some programs accomplish this by storing bedding in pillowcases and then placing them in children's individual cubbies.

Because infants and young toddlers sleep on their own schedule, it is important to have a sleeping area within the classroom. This allows children to be visually supervised as they sleep.

Babies must be put to sleep on their backs to help prevent Sudden Infant Death Syndrome (SIDS). SIDS is the leading cause of death in babies that are 1 to 12 months of age (Center for Disease Control and Prevention, 2006). Of these deaths, 17% to 25% occur when the child is receiving child care (Moon, Sprague, & Patel, 2005). In 50% of these cases, the childcare provider placed the child on his or her stomach to sleep (Moon et al., 2005). Placing babies on their stomach to sleep, particularly when it is an unaccustomed sleeping position, raises the risk of SIDS by 18% to 20% (American Academy of Pediatrics, 2005). In spite of numerous campaigns, one study revealed that 20% of programs still continue to place babies on their stomach when sleeping (Moon, Weese-Mayer, & Silvestri, 2003). Unless a doctor orders otherwise, babies should always be placed on their backs to sleep. Firm mattresses and an uncluttered sleeping area (no soft bedding, bumper pads, stuffed animals) are also important in decreasing suffocation risks. When children are able to roll over on their own, it is not necessary to reposition them if they roll onto their stomach.

It is crucial that health and safety rules be followed. It is also important to develop an environment that is conducive to sleep.

Tracey, who worked in an Early Head Start Center, wanted to change the hard lines, harsh lights, and bright white walls that gave the napping area an institutional feel. She painted the room a pale blue with fluffy white clouds on the ceilings and draped a soft cloth over the florescent lights (after first checking with the fire marshal). Some of the cribs were no longer being used and these were removed to create additional space. She then had room to add a rocking chair to the area. A sound machine that played calming ocean and other environmental sounds was also added.

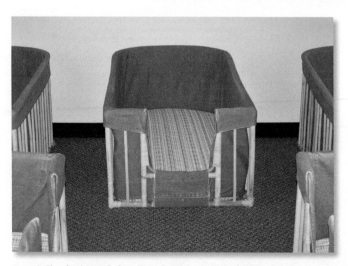

Specially designed sleeping baskets allow babies the freedom to crawl out when they awaken. Adults are always nearby.

Instead of the traditional crib, the Helen Gordon Lab School in Portland, Oregon, uses specially designed baskets for children to sleep in. This allows children the freedom and independence to crawl out of the basket when they wake up. The baskets are aesthetic and also save space.

To totally safeguard a child one would need to place him in a padded room, provide no materials, and allow no contact with others. However, while this severely deprived environment would keep the child safe and physically healthy, it would not allow the child to develop needed social and cognitive skills. Nevertheless, it is important that risks of injury or illness be minimized in early childhood settings through the establishment and maintenance of safe and healthy environments. With thoughtful analysis, it is possible to accomplish these goals while still providing an aesthetic environment that allows children to take risks and display childhood exuberance.

Sample Application Activities

1. Examine the air quality and pesticide regulations in your early childhood state licensing standards.
2. Observe an early childhood setting. What safety problems were prevented through close monitoring of children by teachers? Did any problems occur due to lack of supervision?
3. Design a plan for an aesthetic, yet healthy, early childhood bathroom.
4. Investigate one of the following websites:

   http://www.oeconline.org/kidshealth/ehcc/ (Oregon's Eco-Healthy Child Care)

   http://cfpub.epa.gov/schools/top_sub.cfm?t_id=44&s_id=4 (indoor air quality in schools)

   http://nrc.uchsc.edu/CFOC/index.html (National Resource Center for Health and Safety in Child Care and Early Education)

   http://schoolipm.ifas.ufl.edu/toolbox.html (National School IPM)
5. To learn more about diapering and effective diapering stations, go to MyEducationLab and select "Health, Safety, and Nutrition." Under Building Teaching Skills and Dispositions, complete the exercise "Diapering."

chapter 5

....

Arranging an Effective Environment

A consultant was asked to visit a multi-grade K–3 grade classroom to assist Dana, the teacher, with children who Dana described as "out of control." As the consultant entered the room, she found numerous items hanging from the ceiling. All the walls in the classroom were plastered with posters, children's work, written rules, transcribed stories, and a variety of store-purchased signs. The children sat in desks in the center of the room. On the outskirts of the room were shelves that were overflowing with material. Stacks of books filled much of the remaining floor space.

During work time, children worked individually or in small groups using the materials off the shelves while other children met in small groups with the teacher. Children often interrupted the teacher because they could not find the materials they were looking for. Some of the children became distracted by the activities of the other children. This necessitated the teacher leaving the group she was working with to help these children get back on-task.

Dana was surprised when the consultant suggested that changing the classroom environment might meet her goal of allowing children to work effectively in individual and small groups while also providing a solution to the out-of-control behavior.

Guidelines for Creating a Room with Learning Centers

Our classroom environment either promotes or distracts from our learning goals, encouraging or discouraging success for all children. The environment needs to reflect our beliefs and theories about how children learn. Do you believe in children working cooperatively in small groups? Do you believe in the teacher as a facilitator of learning? Do you believe in meeting children's individual learning styles and needs? Do you believe in children being highly engaged with learning materials? Do you believe in children having choices? Do you believe in children learning through hands-on activities? Do you believe that learning should be active and student centered?

When these questions were posed to Dana, she immediately answered "yes" making her a perfect candidate for the learning center approach. Dana reorganized her classroom and materials into several learning centers and removed materials no longer needed. The centers allowed small groups of children to work together without interruption. Barriers between centers helped the children to concentrate. Children were also more easily able to locate materials and so could work independently.

A learning center is a self-contained area with a variety of hands-on materials organized around a curriculum area or topic. Well-designed learning centers respect children's learning styles and interests, and allow them choices, thereby fostering their self-esteem and decision-making abilities (Rushton, 2001). All children, especially those with emotional or behavioral difficulties, who are given choices of activities are more self-directed, have less disruptive behavior, and are more engaged in tasks (Dunlap et al., 1994).

Each learning center helps students develop unique content knowledge, skills, and dispositions while promoting different social skills and work habits. For example, the dramatic play and block centers may encourage cooperative play, while the science center may encourage individual investigation.

Learning centers are also referred to as interest centers, learning stations, work stations, or activity areas. Because learning centers are so consistent with early childhood philosophy, most early childhood teachers choose this method of arranging their rooms.

A high-quality learning center is planned with a purpose in mind. It is inviting and aesthetically pleasing, containing an abundance of developmentally appropriate, relevant, interesting, and interactive materials. Learning centers that are high quality are planned to encourage independent use by children. We will discuss each of these criteria in more depth.

Clearly Establish Goals Based on the Children's Backgrounds, Interests, Development, and State and National Standards

What are the goals for the center? What specific skills, knowledge, and dispositions do you want to promote through this center? In determining goals you will want to examine program, state, and national standards and early learning guidelines. It will also be important to examine children's background knowledge and interests to develop environments that are relevant and developmentally appropriate.

Supply the Center with an Abundance of Interesting, Interactive Materials

In resource-rich environments, children are more engaged in independent learning activities (Moore, 2002). However, there must be a balance of clutter and abundance. If the shelves have too many materials, children may have a difficult time making choices or locating the materials they want. However, if there are too few materials, children have limited choices and may waste time waiting for materials to become available. The lack of resources can also cause increased fighting. Additionally, children's ability to reach their full potential may be hindered. For example, Pardee recommends that a preschool classroom contain a minimum of 225 blocks (2005). With an abundance of blocks, several children can work at once creating elaborate block structures. Running out of blocks before a structure is completed can stymie the child's creativity, attention span, and problem solving. Eventually children in these classrooms learn to build quick, less complicated structures.

Determining the exact quantity of materials will require you to closely observe the children in your group. If children are waiting for toys or fighting over toys either there are not enough materials or duplicates of popular materials may be needed. This is especially important for toddlers who are often engaged in parallel play, using identical play materials (Legendre, 2003). If children are wandering rather than engaging in play, there may be too few materials available or children may be overwhelmed because there are too many choices.

Sometimes teachers reduce the number of materials so that children can clean up the area more quickly. However, it is important to reflect upon your goals. Is your goal to create an optimum learning environment? Then you would not want to reduce materials simply to decrease the time needed to clean the center.

Other teachers may eliminate any toy that children fight over. However, this often increases rather than decreases fighting behavior because there are fewer toys. Teachers might instead add duplicate toys.

Choosing the right materials is also important. The materials need to be developmentally appropriate for the children in the classroom. They need to be challenging, but not so difficult that children cannot be successful. If materials are too easy, children become bored. On the other hand, if the materials are too challenging, children become anxious (White, 2004). When materials are slightly above the child's current level of functioning, they can act as a scaffold to assist children to reach the next level of development (Maxwell, 2007; Vygotsky, 1986). Children gain knowledge, skills, and confidence when they successfully negotiate challenges.

Children also need variety in materials and room design (Maxwell, 2007). Too little variety leads to boredom (Maxwell, 2007). However, if the environment is too complex children experience cognitive fatigue, and learning and competency is compromised (Maxwell, 2007). According to Maxwell (2007), an expert in environmental design, children need the opportunity to recover from cognitive fatigue through activities that do not require focused attention such as sitting and watching fish or birds (p. 232).

One way to create a range of challenges is to use open-ended materials. While some materials in the classroom will be closed materials that can be used in only one way (puzzles), open-ended materials or materials that can be used in multiple ways also need to be available. Open-ended materials meet the needs of a range of developmental levels, maintain the interest of children for a longer period of time, and invite creativity and deeper thought. For example, when a jar of old buttons was placed on a manipulative shelf in a kindergarten classroom, children became very interested. They postulated about where the different buttons came from, discussed which buttons they liked best, classified (or sorted) the buttons in multiple ways, seriated the buttons arranging them from largest to smallest, and counted the buttons.

At times children and teachers may create a display of materials to emphasize a particular concept. For example, a toddler teacher created a display of yellow items to emphasize the color. However, it is important that most displays and materials contain interactive components. Young children learn best when engaged in hands-on activities (Bredekamp & Copple, 1997).

Assure Materials Are Developmentally Appropriate and Culturally Relevant

A quality learning center contains materials that are developmentally appropriate and relevant to the children in the classroom.

A teacher in a small rural area in the northwest was changing her dramatic play area. After looking through activity books, she decided to create a circus, complete with tumbling mats, balls to juggle, a hoop to jump through, circus clothing to wear, clown face paint, stuffed circus animals, cages for the animals, and a canopy for the circus tent. However, none of the children had ever been to a circus. Since they had no idea what to do with the materials, they rarely used the center. After reflecting on why the children were not using the center, the teacher decided to establish a center that would be more relevant to the children. After thoughtful contemplation, she decided on a fishing center. Her community contained blue ribbon trout streams, drawing anglers from all over the country. One of the children's parents was a fishing guide and many of the children had gone fishing with their parents. All the children had seen people standing by the river fly-fishing or floating down the river dragging a fishing line. The fishing center contained a rubber raft surrounded by a blue plastic tarp (the water), paddles, life jackets, children's fishing poles, paper fish, fishing net, tackle box containing lures with the hooks removed, waders, a fishing vest, a cooler, and a campfire ring and frying pan (for cooking fish). Because the center was relevant, children spent many weeks engaged in this center.

It is also important to make sure that all materials in the classroom are anti-bias. The challenge, as described in *Anti-Bias Curriculum*, is "reflecting children and adults of color, those who are differently abled, and who are engaged in nonstereotypic gender activities; and to eliminate stereotypic and inaccurate materials from daily use" (Derman-Sparks, 1989, p. 11).

Display Materials in an Inviting and Aesthetically Pleasing Way

What do you want children to notice? An engaging display can invite us to become involved. It catches our eye, provokes our interest, and entices us to look and to touch. In speaking about arranging the Reggio Emilia environment, Lella Gandini states, "it is very suggestive to the children for what they could do, because the material is attractively arranged and inviting. If you have transparent containers, and you have seeds and dried flowers and pieces of colored paper, and you have buttons, and marbles, and things like that, they all look like precious things" (Bartlett, 1993, p. 32). The way materials are displayed shows the value or importance we place on them and by extension the importance we place on children's learning. As the quote illustrates, even items that are often thrown away can become enticing treasures when displayed attractively.

Design the Center for Independent Use

To use learning centers independently, materials need to be available and organized. Children also need to know how to use the materials. To be accessible, materials need to be placed within children's reach and located in the center where they are used. This typically means that materials are stored on low, open shelves. Materials need to be organized and labeled so that children can easily locate them and return them to the proper place when they are done. Teachers can label shelves with digital photos, pictures out of a supply catalog, an outline of the item, and/or a word designating the item. Collections of items might be placed in baskets and labeled by categories of materials, for example zoo animals or farm animals.

Closed materials (those that have a right answer) should be self-correcting. For example, a teacher created a matching sound game by placing different ingredients (buttons, sand, paper clips) in film canisters. He then placed stickers of the item on the bottom of the canisters. As a result, children could check to see what item was in the container and to see if they had paired the sound jars correctly.

If children are going to use materials independently, they also need to know how to use the center and the materials appropriately. One way to accomplish this is to introduce materials. In some classrooms, the teacher introduces materials to individual children as they are ready to use them. Typically, children in these classrooms are allowed to use the materials only after they have been introduced. In other classrooms, teachers introduce the materials to children during group time. Introductions allow the teacher to build interest in the materials, while establishing ground rules for use. For example, in introducing the fishing center, the teacher built interest by showing the children a short video clip of some people fishing. She then let the children preview each of the new materials that were being added to the center and discussed how the material should be used. For example, she demonstrated how to use the paddles while emphasizing the need to keep the paddles in "the water." At times, it will also be necessary to remind children of the rules as they use the materials.

Another way to assist children in using centers independently is to create task cards using words or pictures or both. For example, children in a kindergarten classroom made clay boats as part of a sink and float center. They designed their clay boats and then tested them to see how many pennies they would hold. See Figure 5.1 for an example of a picture task card. Children recorded their data and continued to try to design boats that could hold more pennies. They then discussed the similarities and differences between the boats, determining the characteristics that allowed the boats to hold more weight.

Figure 5.1   Make a Clay Boat

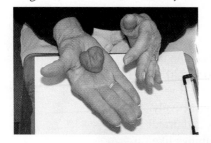 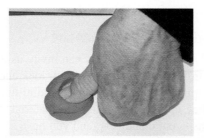 

sorted) the buttons in multiple ways, seriated the buttons arranging them from largest to smallest, and counted the buttons.

At times children and teachers may create a display of materials to emphasize a particular concept. For example, a toddler teacher created a display of yellow items to emphasize the color. However, it is important that most displays and materials contain interactive components. Young children learn best when engaged in hands-on activities (Bredekamp & Copple, 1997).

Assure Materials Are Developmentally Appropriate and Culturally Relevant

A quality learning center contains materials that are developmentally appropriate and relevant to the children in the classroom.

A teacher in a small rural area in the northwest was changing her dramatic play area. After looking through activity books, she decided to create a circus, complete with tumbling mats, balls to juggle, a hoop to jump through, circus clothing to wear, clown face paint, stuffed circus animals, cages for the animals, and a canopy for the circus tent. However, none of the children had ever been to a circus. Since they had no idea what to do with the materials, they rarely used the center. After reflecting on why the children were not using the center, the teacher decided to establish a center that would be more relevant to the children. After thoughtful contemplation, she decided on a fishing center. Her community contained blue ribbon trout streams, drawing anglers from all over the country. One of the children's parents was a fishing guide and many of the children had gone fishing with their parents. All the children had seen people standing by the river fly-fishing or floating down the river dragging a fishing line. The fishing center contained a rubber raft surrounded by a blue plastic tarp (the water), paddles, life jackets, children's fishing poles, paper fish, fishing net, tackle box containing lures with the hooks removed, waders, a fishing vest, a cooler, and a campfire ring and frying pan (for cooking fish). Because the center was relevant, children spent many weeks engaged in this center.

It is also important to make sure that all materials in the classroom are anti-bias. The challenge, as described in *Anti-Bias Curriculum*, is "reflecting children and adults of color, those who are differently abled, and who are engaged in nonstereotypic gender activities; and to eliminate stereotypic and inaccurate materials from daily use" (Derman-Sparks, 1989, p. 11).

Display Materials in an Inviting and Aesthetically Pleasing Way

What do you want children to notice? An engaging display can invite us to become involved. It catches our eye, provokes our interest, and entices us to look and to touch. In speaking about arranging the Reggio Emilia environment, Lella Gandini states, "it is very suggestive to the children for what they could do, because the material is attractively arranged and inviting. If you have transparent containers, and you have seeds and dried flowers and pieces of colored paper, and you have buttons, and marbles, and things like that, they all look like precious things" (Bartlett, 1993, p. 32). The way materials are displayed shows the value or importance we place on them and by extension the importance we place on children's learning. As the quote illustrates, even items that are often thrown away can become enticing treasures when displayed attractively.

Design the Center for Independent Use

To use learning centers independently, materials need to be available and organized. Children also need to know how to use the materials. To be accessible, materials need to be placed within children's reach and located in the center where they are used. This typically means that materials are stored on low, open shelves. Materials need to be organized and labeled so that children can easily locate them and return them to the proper place when they are done. Teachers can label shelves with digital photos, pictures out of a supply catalog, an outline of the item, and/or a word designating the item. Collections of items might be placed in baskets and labeled by categories of materials, for example zoo animals or farm animals.

Closed materials (those that have a right answer) should be self-correcting. For example, a teacher created a matching sound game by placing different ingredients (buttons, sand, paper clips) in film canisters. He then placed stickers of the item on the bottom of the canisters. As a result, children could check to see what item was in the container and to see if they had paired the sound jars correctly.

If children are going to use materials independently, they also need to know how to use the center and the materials appropriately. One way to accomplish this is to introduce materials. In some classrooms, the teacher introduces materials to individual children as they are ready to use them. Typically, children in these classrooms are allowed to use the materials only after they have been introduced. In other classrooms, teachers introduce the materials to children during group time. Introductions allow the teacher to build interest in the materials, while establishing ground rules for use. For example, in introducing the fishing center, the teacher built interest by showing the children a short video clip of some people fishing. She then let the children preview each of the new materials that were being added to the center and discussed how the material should be used. For example, she demonstrated how to use the paddles while emphasizing the need to keep the paddles in "the water." At times, it will also be necessary to remind children of the rules as they use the materials.

Another way to assist children in using centers independently is to create task cards using words or pictures or both. For example, children in a kindergarten classroom made clay boats as part of a sink and float center. They designed their clay boats and then tested them to see how many pennies they would hold. See Figure 5.1 for an example of a picture task card. Children recorded their data and continued to try to design boats that could hold more pennies. They then discussed the similarities and differences between the boats, determining the characteristics that allowed the boats to hold more weight.

Figure 5.1   Make a Clay Boat

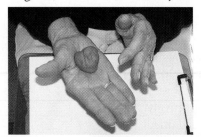
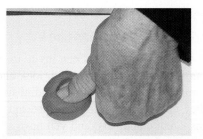

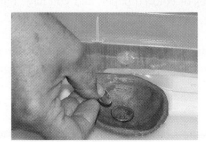

Apply Your Knowledge During learning center time, many of the children in Keith's multi-age preschool classroom do not engage in play but rather wander from activity to activity. Keith is considering eliminating learning centers because he feels they are not working. Before he does this, he speaks to his colleague, Christine, about the issue. Christine says that she will observe his classroom and investigate what might be the cause of the problem. What are possible causes of the children's wandering behavior that Christine should examine?

Teachers need to carefully think about and design each individual center. They also must consider the entire room arrangement. Are there common criteria teachers must consider in arranging classrooms regardless of age? What learning centers should be placed next to each other? Are some arrangements of space more effective than others?

Guidelines for Developing Effective Room Arrangements and Floor Plans

There are some guidelines that apply to all early childhood room arrangements (infants, toddlers, preschool, and early elementary). These include considering how to define individual centers and how to group centers, and the traffic paths between centers. Other common characteristics that need to be considered for all age groups include establishing an effective entry space, providing places to gather as a group, providing retreat or alone areas, and providing a variety of centers.

Develop Effective Entry Spaces

Entry spaces have a variety of purposes. When well designed they provide a place for:

- Families and children to observe what is happening in the classroom.
- Children to make a gradual transition to the classroom (there may be a place for children and families to read books before entering the classroom).
- Informational displays.
- Daily interaction between families and staff.
- Conveying important messages about the program.
- An enticing element to attract children and make them excited about coming to the program (Pardee, 2005).

Entries into programs vary, some children enter long institutional halls while other children may enter directly into their classroom. Regardless of the entry point, the entry area conveys a message. The question is whether the message being given is consistent with the philosophy of the program.

At Aware Early Head Start, an infant/toddler program, teachers analyzed their entryway for the message it was conveying. They noted that the bulletin board was covered with required notices, such as workers compensation flyers, mandatory child abuse reporting requirements, parental notification of illness guidelines, and a poster discussing what to do in case of lice. They also noted that while the space contained a child check-in system, there was no avenue for two-way communication between families and teachers.

This entry is beautiful. It is also practical, providing individual cubbies and places for children to sit to put on or remove boots.

The staff felt like the entry created an institutional, rule-bound, rather frightening feeling (this is a place where you might get sick or injured). The teachers made several changes. They first removed all items from the bulletin board, replacing them with children's photos and matted children's artwork. They added a basket of books and a bench where families could read to their children as they were entering and leaving the program. To create a mechanism for reciprocal written dialogue, they provided a two-way communication book. A joys and concerns box was also added so that families could have the option of sharing information anonymously. Since one of the families was Spanish speaking, teachers wrote all information in both English and Spanish. To make the area appealing to the infants and toddlers, the teachers added a variety of different types of mirrors at the children's eye level. The entry now conveys an entirely different message than before, letting families and children know "you belong here and your input in valued."

There are many other ways to make your entry welcoming. The Diana School, a preschool in Reggio Emilia, features a disguise closet in their entryway. The closet is full of interesting costumes that allow children to change their appearance before entering the classroom. As one child stated, "You get in like one person and come out like another" (Bondavalli, Mori, & Vecchi, 1993). Lella Gandini describes the Diana School entry in this way:

> Already with the entrance, the hallway gives an introduction to the school; to show who are the teachers there, what is the plan of the school, what are the scheduled events. Often there is a message on the ceiling, . . . there is also communication with the children. At a low level there are little mirrors that open like books, so that when they come in they can make faces or play with each other. They also invite adults to reflect on what image of children they have. And then there are illustrations of recent activities of the children with photographs and things they have done, things they can relate to, and that show their work is valued. In this way the space of the school even in the hallway gives a strong message of welcome, and shows that children, teachers and parents are equally important. (Bartlett, 1993)

Provide Well-Established Boundaries Between Centers

To be effective, centers need a well-defined area with boundaries that still allow children to see the options available to them (Olds, 1989b). Boundaries provide both physical and emotional security for children. Research indicates that children in well-defined areas are more task-oriented and engage in more positive interaction, cooperation, and greater exploration (Moore, 1986). Probably because children are more engaged in both activities and positive peer interactions, teachers are less controlling and spend their time in more active involvement with children when areas are well defined (Moore, 1986).

Teachers can create boundaries from low bookshelves, furniture, sheer curtains, or low dividers that are made from fabric, colored Plexiglas, lattice, or pegboard. Whenever possible, the dividers should be designed to be portable, thus allowing for a flexible room arrangement that can change as children's interests change.

Teachers can also use different color rugs or masking tape to create boundaries, or hang fabric or parachutes from the ceiling to create a separate area. However, these are not as effective since they do not provide protection from visual stimulation.

Plan Coherent Circulation or Traffic Paths

Paths need to be unobstructed and wide enough to accommodate children, including children in wheelchairs. They also need to provide clear access to a door or fire exit. However, classrooms also need to be designed so there are not long or circular paths for running. As stated by White, children look at environments for the "affordances" they provide (2004). Long paths afford the opportunity to run (White, 2004). In planning your classroom, it is important to think about how children will negotiate through the room. "Coherent circulation paths are one of the physical characteristics that encourage exploration and discovery" (Maxwell, 2007, p. 232). Have you ever gone into a department store that is divided into a confusing maze of departments? It can be frustrating and rather frightening if you feel trapped and unable to find your way out. We want to develop our classroom so that it makes logical sense to the young child and does not appear to be a confusing maze.

Provide a Variety of Learning Centers

The number and type of learning centers will vary based on the ages of the children, the space in the room, and the interests of the children and staff. In addition to the typical centers found in classrooms (literacy, dramatic play, creative art, music, manipulative, sensory, computer, science, math, and blocks) many programs will provide special centers. These might include carpentry, cooking, games, sewing, or research centers. Some of these centers, for example the sewing center, might be portable and brought out only during certain times of the day.

Strategically Group the Centers

In planning the arrangement of learning centers, it is important to consider the fixed features in the room, whether activities in the center are quiet or noisy, and how materials in adjacent centers might be used to enrich play.

Fixed or permanent physical features include windows, electrical outlets, sinks, and floor coverings. These fixed features need to be considered in choosing the most feasible locations for each learning center. For example, the art center is best in an area with an easily cleanable floor surface, near a sink. The computer center needs to be near an electrical outlet. Natural lighting is important for close work, so the art area and reading area might be best near windows. Shelves that house materials and the workspace for using the materials need to be located close to each other. When they are not, children are less likely to use the materials (Maxwell, 2007).

To allow children to effectively concentrate and engage in conversation, centers need to be grouped according to whether they are quiet or active areas. Typically, the literacy, art, computer, science, math, manipulative, and sensory centers are considered quiet areas. These centers should be located in the most protected part of the room, usually away from doors (Olds, 2001). The music, block, dramatic play, gross motor, and woodworking centers are considered active or noisier centers and can be grouped near each other.

A final consideration in grouping areas is to think about what learning centers might be used together to create opportunities for more enriched play. These centers can be placed adjacent to each other. For example, teachers in a toddler center moved the block and dramatic play areas next to each other. One of the children made a platform with the large blocks. Another child, who was in the dramatic play center wearing a fire hat, saw the platform and said "fire truck." She brought another fire hat to the block area and both children sat on the block platform making fire truck noises. It is unlikely that this scenario would have occurred if the dramatic play and block areas were not adjacent.

Provide Places to Gather as a Group

Classrooms for toddlers, preschoolers, and early elementary children need to have a place where children and the teacher can gather as a group. Because classrooms are often small, it is important that this space be multi-purpose. Belinda, a teacher of preschool children, uses the music and dance center for her group area. She covers the shelves housing the musical instruments with a sheet during group time to reduce distractions.

Develop Retreat Areas or Places to Be Alone

"At times all children feel an acute need for privacy" (Lowry, 1993, p. 58). Yet adults in early childhood programs often do not respect this need (Readdick, 1993). Readdick states, "In many instances the only provisions for solitary pursuits are the bathroom stall and the time-out chair" (1993, p. 60).

Solitary retreats provide children the opportunity to think and dream, engage in uninterrupted concentration, regain control of emotions, and unwind after intense periods of interaction. In examining early childhood centers with and without alone spaces, researchers found that when there were no places to retreat, children interacted less with peers, engaged in more wandering behavior, and were more hostile and aggressive (Sheehan & Day, 1975). Research also indicates that having places to be alone or retreat from the group are linked to later enhanced cognitive development (Moore, 2002). Too much stimulation can negatively affect optimal development (Lowry, 1993). Although it is tempting for teachers in crowded environments to eliminate alone areas as a way of saving space, when children are in a more dense situation, there is an even greater need to be alone.

This inviting alone area gives the children a sense of privacy, while still allowing supervision.

Alone spaces need to be situated in a quiet space away from popular activities (Maxwell, 2007). They also need to be enclosed. Studies indicate that when children are given a choice of a more open or closed area, they choose the more enclosed area (Lowry, 1993). "The essential feature . . . lies in the encapsulations of a relatively small amount of space into which a child can enter and experience variable degrees of sensory discontinuity from the larger surrounding environment" (Gramza, 1970, p. 177).

Since children have little control over leaving an environment to seek solitude, it is crucial that adults develop areas within the classroom where solitude can be found. There are many ways to create retreat areas. What you choose will depend upon what the children in your group find calming and relaxing. Teachers might put a basket of books next to a pillow-filled bathtub. They might place a small tent with camping equipment in the room, create an enclosed art area with clay and tools for one child, or develop a quiet "office" by cutting the side out of a refrigerator box and adding a desk and writing materials. Lisa, a teacher of toddlers, created a magical space in her classroom by decorating a refrigerator box with shimmery gold paper, adding a sheer gold curtain for a door, painting the inside of the box black, and adding a flashlight and glow-in-the-dark chalk. It was a favorite place for children to spend some time alone. Teresa also created a unique alone area. From the ceiling of her classroom, she suspended a hula hoop on which were hung sheer curtains reaching to the floor. Removing a closet door and installing a sheer curtain provides a similar type of retreat (Weinberger, 2006). Other teachers have created alone areas using inner tubes, tunnels, or cable spools with some of the slats removed.

As part of a study on recycling, the children and the teacher created this alone area from recycled gallon milk containers.

Sample Room Arrangements

When planning room arrangements, consider the physical features of the room, the size of the furniture and equipment, the developmental levels of the children, the learning centers that you wish to include, and the guidelines listed previously for planning effective room arrangements. Because of these many variables, each room arrangement is usually unique. However, the following room arrangements can provide ideas.

Infants

When planning a room arrangement for infants, there are several things to consider. These include providing a comfortable, pleasant location for mothers to nurse their babies; enough room for individual cribs or baskets in a quiet area; a diaper-changing area with a sink large enough to bathe a child and an adjacent counter to hold supplies; convenient storage for strollers; and easy access to food preparation. Because infants spend much of their time on the floor, you must plan for a "plopping place" that allows adults to sit with several infants at once (Olds, 2001, p. 305). This needs to be accompanied by comfortable places for adults to sit on or near the floor such as stacking back seats, canvas sling chairs, or stadium seats (Olds, 2001).

Figure 5.2 Infant Room Arrangement

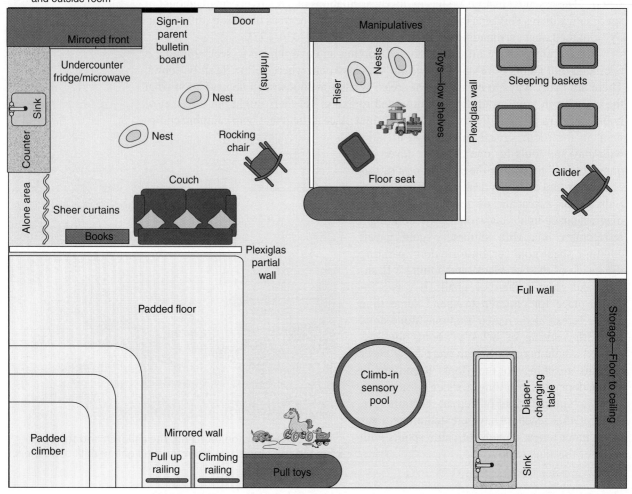

Because infants are developing gross motor skills, they need space and a variety of surface levels to practice on. For example, you might have a carpeted riser that is 4 to 12 inches off the floor, or a small loft that is 2 to 4 feet off the floor (Olds, 2001). Ramps and steps provide additional climbing opportunities. Infants also need an open area to play with balls, and push and pull toys. Low, secure shelves containing manipulatives such as rattles, activity boxes, dump and fill items, cause and effect toys, puzzles, musical items, and safe household items also need to be available (Bredekamp & Copple, 1997). A book area containing sturdy books for the infant to look at is also important in the infant environment. See Figure 5.2 for an example of an infant room arrangement.

Toddlers

Toddlers are still mastering movement and so need room for gross motor activities and uneven surfaces to practice climbing up and down. Platforms for this age group can be 36 inches off the floor (Olds, 2001, p. 312). The toddler room will need to include a diaper-changing table with steps to provide independence and to protect adults' backs.

Figure 5.3 Toddler Room Arrangement

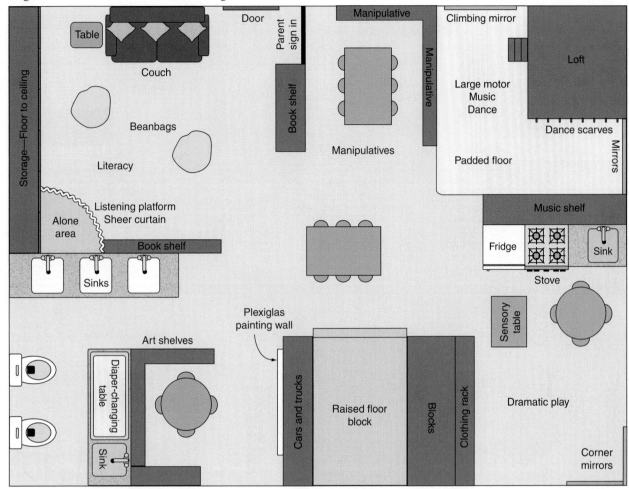

It is also important to have storage for small cots, strollers, and car seats. Learning centers for this age group should not be totally enclosed. When children are able to see the teacher they use more of the room (Legendre, 1999). Centers that are typically found in toddler rooms include dramatic play, creative art, literacy (reading, writing, and listening), music, sensory, manipulative, alone areas, and a block and construction center. Figure 5.3 shows an example of a toddler room arrangement.

Preschool

The preschool classroom needs to provide for long-term work, children's physical needs, and a variety of learning centers. For example, because children this age engage in projects over an extended period of time, it is important to provide enough room for storing ongoing projects.

Some children at this age take naps, while others do not. Therefore, it is necessary to provide a place for both sleepers and nonsleepers. Bathrooms are also important in preschool rooms; they let children be independent but still allow supervision from an adult.

At a minimum, learning centers in preschool classrooms should include dramatic play, creative art, literacy (reading, writing, and listening), music, sensory, computer,

Figure 5.4 — Preschool Room Arrangement

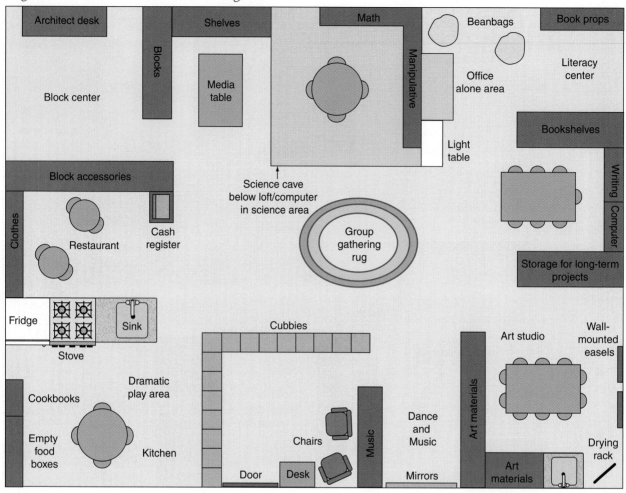

manipulative, science, math, alone areas, and a block and construction center. Figure 5.4 shows one preschool room arrangement. You can see another by watching *Room Arrangement: Preschool* on MyEducationLab.

K–3 Classrooms

In the past, many K–3 grade classrooms contained desks in straight rows. However, recognizing the importance of cooperative and active learning has caused many teachers to rethink this arrangement. In a study of 294 grade K–5 classrooms, 76% used a small-group cluster design in their classrooms. In another study, 94% of teachers surveyed also used this design (Patton, Snell, Knight, & Gerken, 2001). In planning K–3 classrooms, it is important to consider the increasing role of technology in education. K–3 classrooms should include, at a minimum, the following centers: social science, math manipulative, literacy (reading, writing, and listening), science, music, drama, creative art, computer and research, alone areas, and a block and construction center.

In addition to developing the floor plan, teachers must also consider the furniture and dividers. The floor plan and furniture play a reciprocal role. For example, the size of the furniture and the type of dividers affect the room layout. But as Figure 5.5 shows, the floor plan also dictates the need for furnishings and dividers.

myeducationlab PEARSON

Go to MyEducationLab and select the topic "Environments." Under Activities and Applications, watch the video *Room Arrangement: Preschool*.

Figure 5.5   K–3 Room Arrangement

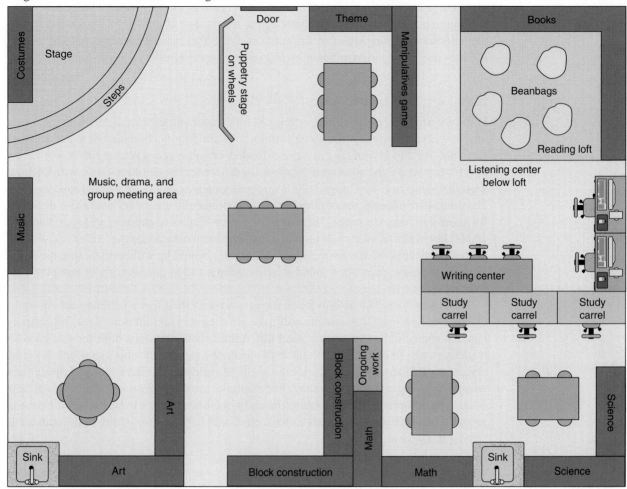

Furniture and Dividers

Furnishings reflect the program's values and can either support or impede the program's philosophy and curriculum. For example, in most programs infants are placed in cribs to sleep. When they wake, they must wait for the adult to remove them. However, some programs, wanting to allow infants greater independence and control, are using baskets instead. The baskets sit on the floor and have an entryway at the end that allows the infant to crawl in and out. Furniture needs to provide for learning opportunities. It also needs to be ergonomic and comfortable for all inhabitants of the space, safe, and aesthetically pleasing.

Provides for Learning Opportunities

To provide for optimal learning, the environment must accommodate a variety of learning styles (Burke & Burke-Samide, 2004). This includes having an array of seating and learning arrangements (Burke & Burke-Samide, 2004). There should be places for children to sit alone, to sit with peers, and to share with a teacher. Providing cozy, comfortable stuffed chairs, beanbag chairs, hammocks, rocking chairs, wooden chairs and tables, and stadium chairs allows children and teachers to find areas that are conducive to their current activity and comfortable for them. For example, when given a choice of where to sit during silent sustained reading, some third-grade students chose to remain in their desks, others got out mats and laid on the floor, and still others sat in beanbag chairs. One child read best when rocking in the rocking chair. Recognizing the importance of classroom design in meeting the individual learning styles of students, one New York school district mandated that all teachers provide a variety of learning and seating spaces (Burke & Burke-Samide, 2004).

Ergonomic and Comfortable for All Who Inhabit the Space

Furniture needs to be ergonomic—designed for comfort, efficiency, and to meet the user's physical needs. For example, when furniture for children is child size, it is not only ergonomic, but children engage in more extended, complex play (White, 2004).

Chairs need to be adjustable to allow for differences in children's size, with shallow seats that slant back. McDougall (2006) argues that plastic chairs and desks found in many classrooms are not only uncomfortable and ergonomically incorrect but are also designed for short-term use. He states, "Between the age of 5 and 16, children will spend around 16,000 hours sitting on a chair intended for short term occasional use" (2006, p. 49). He further challenges readers to consider whether they would be willing to swap their office chair for a plastic chair often found in schoolrooms and to do this without reducing performance.

Children should be able to touch the ground with their feet when they are sitting in chairs. Because many classrooms will have children that are different sizes, it is important that chairs in the classroom reflect this. Tables should be waist high and designed so that chairs will fit easily under them with plenty of room for the children's legs. It is important for teachers to also consider the needs of children who have physical disabilities when purchasing and using furniture. For example, can tables accommodate a wheelchair or does inappropriate furniture cause the child in the wheelchair to be excluded from the group? The classroom also needs to have comfortable places for adults to sit, with adult seating throughout the room.

Safe Furniture

In addition to being ergonomic, furniture must be safe. To prevent accidental tipping, shelves and furniture must be stable. Rounded corners on furniture are important to help prevent injury if children fall. Because the furniture will need to be sanitized frequently, the surface must be designed to withstand sanitizing solutions. "Proper furniture surfaces also can lessen the effects of glare and direct sunlight, and can minimize eye strain that can be caused by high contrast between the work surface and reading materials" (Waldecker, 2005, p. 2).

Aesthetically Pleasing Furniture

Furniture either contributes to or detracts from the aesthetics in the classroom. The condition of the furniture, the color and texture, the materials it is made from, the way it reflects light, and the furniture lines all contribute to aesthetics.

Furniture should be in good condition. If it is not, you might consider a slipcover for a couch or chair or a tablecloth to cover a shelf or table.

Shelving is a visible, important element in classrooms, providing a backdrop for materials that are placed on them. It is important to avoid bright primary colors that compete with the materials (Pardee, 2005, p. 22). Instead, consider using light wood shelving or shelves painted white or a very pale color. Shelving and tables can either reflect or absorb light. "Although furniture can't bring more light into the classroom, it can help maximize daylight that already comes into the room. Selecting furniture with lighter surfaces, for example, creates ambient light, accentuating incoming natural light and brightening the room" (Waldecker, 2005, p. 2).

The choice of materials for shelving and tables can also affect aesthetics. While plastic will often get dingy with age, wood ages gracefully (Olds, 2001). Some programs incorporate old wooden furniture (often purchased at garage sales) into their classrooms, combining functionality with unique lines and characteristics. For example, one program used a beautiful rolltop desk as a sign-in area. The multiple cubicles in the desk served as parent mailboxes.

Furnishing a classroom is a long-term investment. It is estimated that it will cost $700 to $1,000 per preschool or elementary school-age child to furnish a new classroom and $1,500 per child to furnish an infant/toddler room. In addition, $125 to $150 per child should be budgeted each year for toys, books, and materials (Pardee, 2005, p. 26). To protect our investment, we must have adequate storage for the materials that are not currently in use.

Storage

Appropriate storage can help to reduce clutter, save time, make materials accessible, enhance the rotation of toys and equipment, and maximize the use of resources (Greenman, 2005a). Because storage is so important, Greenman recommends that a minimum of 10% of the square footage of a program be devoted to storage (2005a).

Several different types of storage are necessary in an early childhood program. Child-accessible storage space is needed for toys and materials that are currently being used by the children. To meet this need, storage is often provided on low, open shelves that are located throughout the classroom. It is hard for children to independently obtain materials and to determine choices when materials are placed in stacks or left in boxes (Greenman, 2005a). For this reason, they are often placed in labeled baskets or containers. Containers for children's materials can affect the aesthetics of the room. "They can reduce the amount of primary color and the visual clutter in a room, or add to it if the containers themselves are primary colors. The use of wood and wicker containers adds to the warmth and textural richness of the environment and reduces the amount of plastic overload. Fabric and metal containers add to the texturescape" (Greenman, 2005a, p. 213).

Children and teachers also need personal storage. Cubbies or low coat hooks and baskets often provide for this need. Personal storage acknowledges that each person is important in the room, while safeguarding private materials and possessions.

The final type of storage is typically off-limits to children. It includes storage for toys, materials, and supplies needed for replenishment and rotation; teacher supplies and materials; and cooking, cleaning, and medical supplies. This storage is often in closed cupboards or closets. Open cupboards are frequently hung with curtains to clearly differentiate the storage as off limits and to reduce the appearance of clutter. To save space, many programs place teacher storage cupboards high on the wall. This leaves the bottom portion of the wall available for classroom use. While much of the storage will be unlocked, it is crucial that all toxic materials be placed in locked cabinets.

This program builds teacher storage above the children's block shelves, saving the limited floor space for play.

In planning your storage, carefully consider whether you want the materials to be child accessible. For example, do you want children to access extra art materials to assist in replenishing an area or do you only want teachers to do this? Child-accessible materials need to be within the child's reach. If the materials are only to be used by teachers, it is important to have this clearly distinguished.

To allow for easy access, the storage of materials should be close to their intended use. For example, one program wanted to make sure that they took needed science supplies on discovery walks. However, this usually did not occur because the materials were on shelves in the teacher's supply room. The teachers decided to create a science bag that they hung on a hook by the door. The bag included magnifying glasses, a tape measure, plastic bags to gather specimens, clay to make casts of objects such as tree trunks, field guides, paper and pencils, and so forth. Because the science bags were readily accessible, the teachers and children took them each time they went for a walk. These tools for investigation greatly enhanced children's learning.

Storage areas need to be well organized. Labeling shelves, containers, or bags will allow multiple users to find things. Disorganized storage can be costly in terms of staff time, program quality, and money. Staff may spend an inordinate amount of time finding materials, become discouraged and purchase new supplies, or just not bother to rotate toys or replenish needed materials when storage areas are disorganized.

Because most programs have limited storage, it is important to take full advantage of all the storage that is available. For example, you might store materials under cribs, lofts, tables, or window seats. Backs of doors or cabinets might also be used for storage. Some teachers create a storage area by cordoning off a corner of the room with a curtain or screen.

Inexpensive storage units can be made by wiring together milk crates or creating a shelving unit with a PVC frame and wooden shelves. Some teachers use labeled, sturdy boxes covered with fabric or contact paper for infrequently used materials. They place the boxes on high classroom shelves or stack them in the classroom. Space might be saved by placing some materials in labeled plastic bags (for example, collage materials), reducing the space taken by containers.

As they develop their room arrangement, it is important to consider storage. Organized storage is a critical component of an effective program.

High-quality learning centers and room arrangements; comfortable, functional furniture; and appropriate storage all contribute to an effective environment. Effective environments can enhance relationships and support program goals, leading to increased learning, independence, and competence in children. Furthermore, the environment can welcome participants by providing a comfortable, joyful place to learn and work.

Sample Application Activities

1. Use the Environmental Assessment found in Figure 5.6 to assess the learning centers and room arrangements of several early childhood programs.
2. Develop an action plan for at least one of the classrooms you assessed, detailing what changes you would make to meet the criteria.
3. Develop a floor plan for your ideal classroom.
4. Develop a new learning center that meets the criteria found in this chapter.
5. Build skills on developing an appropriate room arrangement. Go to MyEducationLab and select the topic "Environments." Under Building Teaching Skills and Dispositions, complete the exercise "Developing a Preschool Room Arrangement."

Learning Centers

- ☐ Is the purpose of the center evident?
- ☐ Is the center inviting and aesthetically pleasing?
- ☐ Is there an abundance of materials—enough so that children do not have to wait or get stymied in their attempts to create?
- ☐ Are materials developmentally appropriate, providing challenges but not being so difficult that children become frustrated?
- ☐ Are there materials for a wide range of developmental levels?
- ☐ Is there an abundance of open-ended materials?
- ☐ If the materials are close ended, are they self-correcting?
- ☐ Do the materials reflect cultural diversity?
- ☐ Are there materials that reflect the lives of children with disabilities?
- ☐ Are materials anti-biased?
- ☐ Are materials located in the centers where they are used?
- ☐ Are materials readily available and within reach of the children?
- ☐ Are materials organized?
- ☐ Are shelves labeled so that children can easily find items and know where to put them away?
- ☐ Do children know how to use the materials?

Room Arrangement

- ☐ Do the centers have well-established boundaries?
- ☐ Are centers the size needed to accommodate the number of children and the activity occurring in the center?
- ☐ Is every area of the room being effectively utilized?
- ☐ Are the boundaries movable so they can be changed as needed?
- ☐ Are traffic paths wide enough to accommodate a child in a wheelchair?
- ☐ Do traffic paths allow clear access to a door or fire escape?
- ☐ Is the arrangement of centers transparent to children and adults, so they can easily navigate the space?
- ☐ Is the room arranged to prevent long or circular paths that encourage running?
- ☐ Are centers placed to take the best advantage of physical characteristics of the room (outlets, lighting, sinks, flooring, etc.)?
- ☐ Are centers grouped according to whether they are quiet or active?
- ☐ Are centers that might combine to contribute to more in-depth play adjacent to each other?
- ☐ Is the entry space welcoming for parents, children, and staff?
- ☐ Does the entryway provide an effective transition area into the program?
- ☐ Are there places in the room to gather comfortably as a group?
- ☐ Are there places to be alone?
- ☐ Are there a variety of clearly designated learning centers?

Figure 5.6
Environmental Assessment: Learning Centers and Arrangements

chapter 6
Design Considerations

Imagine two environments. One environment is a coffee shop. It has many different forms of lighting, the rich smell of coffee, quiet music playing in the background, small tables for two to four people to visit, plants, local artist's paintings displayed on the walls, and a bookshelf with games and magazines.

The other environment is a large department store during a huge sale. The store is crowded with shoppers and shopping carts. Shelves contain items packed from floor to ceiling. The local radio station is playing music with an occasional interjection from the store loudspeaker promoting store ads.

Environments such as the two just described evoke emotions and establish a mood. The ambiance that is created may be unintentional or deliberately designed with a specific purpose in mind. One only needs to watch a television program on one of the channels dedicated entirely to this purpose to find information on changing environments to create your mood of choice. Since children and teachers often spend 8 to 10 hours a day in an early childhood environment, it is important to intentionally design this setting. Design experts recommend that different parts of the environment be designed to promote different moods. "As areas vary in size, function, and layout, so too should they vary in mood, so that children go from place to place within the four walls of a room and experience spaces that are soft and hard, dark and light, cold and warm, and colorful and bland" (Olds, 2001, p. 16). One must also consider the lighting, noise level, density or crowdedness, and design elements and principles when establishing the ambiance. "Through application and manipulation of design elements (color, light, texture, shape, form, and space) and design principles (balance, rhythm, proportion, and scale), advocates of quality child care have the potential to create stimulating, harmonious, and organized childcare environments" (Read, 2003, p. 233). Improvement in facilities benefits children, families, and staff. For example, research suggests that facility improvement can improve staff retention as much as increases in pay (Buckley, Schneider, & Shang, 2004).

Desired Design Outcomes

What kind of ambiance should early childhood programs try to achieve? Two outcomes that are frequently mentioned by early childhood design experts are an aesthetically pleasing design and a homelike environment.

Aesthetically Pleasing, Homelike Environments

Homelike. Many experts recommend that early childhood teachers strive to create a homelike ambiance (Butin, 2000; Curtis & Carter, 2005; Olds, 2001; Torelli, 2002; Trancik & Evans, 1995). However, in practice this is often not the case. As Curtis and Carter (2005) state, "Now most early childhood programs have a school or institutional feel to them, filled with look-alike supplies in primary colors, plastic, and prefabricated games and materials. . . . All programs are starting to look like an early childhood catalog. Centers do not reflect the identity of the families and communities they serve" (p. 34). Gandini (1984), known for her work with the Reggio Emilia schools, states, "Even though we may value individuality in children and adults, we rarely build environments which have personality" (p. 17).

Homelike environments can help to establish a sense of belonging, easing the transition between home and school. Individualized environments, personalized for the inhabitants, also leads to place identity. When one has place identity, she has a greater sense of belonging and ownership over the environment leading to increased self-esteem and happiness (Fisher, 2006). Following is a list of characteristics to consider in developing an environment that is homelike:

- Welcoming
- Divided into usable space for different functions
- Includes private places to escape
- Includes places for people to gather together
- Provides comfortable furniture and different types of seating
- Contains different types of lighting
- Filled with real, functional items (dishes, pottery, pots and pans, tools)

This horse swing reflects the place identity of this rural community, which frequently hosts rodeos.

Soft furniture, pillows, a plant, a wall hanging, and a lamp all assist in providing a homelike ambiance in this reading area.

- Contains objects that have personal meaning such as framed art and collections of natural items (seashells, rocks)
- Filled with images of the inhabitants through photos and mirrors
- Includes living things (plants, flowers, animals)
- Contains softness (rugs, throw pillows, wall hangings, curtains, tablecloths)
- Provides richness of texture and color without being overwhelming
- Provides attention to detail
- Contains beauty
- Reflects values of inhabitants
- Reflects the inhabitants' culture and ethnicity
- Reflects the surrounding social and cultural community
- Reflects geographic location
- Personalized by the inhabitants

The ability to personalize the environment creates a sense of belonging and control. There are several ways this can be achieved in an early childhood setting. Teachers can add open-ended materials that children can use to create a unique space. For example, children can use large pieces of fabric to create a tent, instantly transforming the environment. Items that children have collected or brought from home can be displayed. Children can also help choose what is placed on the walls.

Designing the environment so that children can change some aspects such as seating arrangements or lighting makes the space more functional and also allows children to exercise some control. "Allowing a child to personalize the environment encourages them to claim ownership, form attachments and become familiar with their surroundings" (Trancik & Evans, 1995, p. 52).

Aesthetically Pleasing. To create an aesthetically pleasing, harmonious environment, one must not only think of each of the design elements in isolation, but must also think of them in unison. As stated by Olds (1989b), "To design for aesthetic richness, the building's or room's elements (floors, walls, ceilings, horizontal and vertical supports, objects, forms, and architectural details) all should be conceived of as interactive surfaces to be sculpted, painted, draped, and molded much the way artists sculpt, paint, and mold wood, clay, canvas, fibers and colors" (p. 8). In the aesthetic environment, each of these elements is designed to create beauty and harmony (Bartlett, 1993). The environment is clutter-free and is thoughtfully organized with attention given to details (Bartlett, 1993). In addition, the program is filled with "sensory delights." Olds describes these as "pleasant aromas; delightful sounds; interesting colors, plants and live moving creatures (fish, pets); changing light and shadows; and wonderfully varied tactile experiences" (2001, p. 303).

Design Elements

Elements of design that are important to consider in early childhood environments are softness, texture, color, and lighting. When planned carefully, these elements can help to establish an aesthetically pleasing, homelike environment.

Softness

One thing that clearly distinguishes an institutional environment from a home environment is softness. Although softness is often eliminated in early childhood programs due to the desire to have an antiseptic environment, softness is important in creating an environment that is cozy, comfortable, cuddly, and homelike. Softness is also critical in reducing noise levels and reverberation. Children can experience softness through upholstered furniture, pillows, beanbag chairs, covered mattresses on the floor, and throw rugs. Teachers can also create the appearance of softness by adding tablecloths, curtains, drapes, canopies, and wall hangings.

Texture

Although our skin is the largest body organ, touch is the most ignored sense in planning early childhood environments (Olds, 1989b, p. 10). According to Olds (1989b), texture contributes more to overall ambiance than any other design element. "The view that childcare facilities should be antiseptic and childproof, and therefore replete with smooth, washable surfaces, deprives children of the textural richness they enjoy and deserve" (Olds, 2001, p. 232).

Anyone who has the irresistible desire to touch a rich velvet drape, run their hand along a bumpy brick wall, or feel a cold marble countertop knows the sensory pleasure derived from textures. Textures in classrooms cause light to reflect differently, creating interest. They also provide for a more complex environment, creating opportunities for children to compare, contrast, and experiment (Olds, 2001). According to Ceppi and Zini (1998), sensory experiences not only assist in learning, but the lack of sensory input negatively affects our future abilities to learn through our perceptions.

> Children are born with an immense genetic capacity that enables them to explore, discriminate, and interpret reality through their senses. Neurobiological research has clearly demonstrated the co-protagonism of the senses in the construction and processing of knowledge and individual and group memory. It follows that an unstimulating environment tends to dull and deafen our perceptions. Studies have shown that this is true even for very young children, and therefore schools must be capable of supporting and nourishing the sensory perceptions in order to develop and refine them. (p. 7)

Textures also contribute to a more homelike environment that can help reflect the lives and cultures of children. On a practical note, textures help to control sound and to create space definition.

Different textures are also necessary because each person experiences perceptions differently. The environment needs to be rich in a variety of tactile stimuli, allowing each person to have her needs met (Ceppi & Zini, 1998).

Textures can be incorporated through more permanent design features, such as adding different floor, ceiling, and wall surfaces. These can include a variety of materials such as brick, wood, metal, glass, ceramic tile, rubber, and bumpy plaster designs. Different textures can also be added to environments through furniture, drapes, canopies, pillows, wall hangings, tablecloths, baskets, sensory tables, and play materials, and by creating texture walls. Everyday items used in a different way can also add new tactile experiences.

A teacher in an Early Head Start infant room placed a rubber bath mat below the sink to prevent slipping. One day one of the infants pulled back the edge and found the bumpy suction cups on the underside of the mat. She became fascinated, touching the suction cups with her hands, arms, legs, and feet. Soon several children gathered around, experimenting with the bath mat. Seeing the children's interest, the teacher developed a texture crawl, taping together items with different textures such as velvet, bubble wrap, corduroy, and burlap.

Color

Like texture, color in the classroom can be used to create a differentiated space. Color can also be used to emphasize physical features of a room, to create an illusion of more or less space, and to make a room more attractive. Color affects the luminosity in the room by reflecting or absorbing light. There is also evidence that color evokes moods. However, it appears that this is culturally based rather than biologically based (Ceppi & Zini, 1998) and that it is not only the color but also the value and saturation that influence emotions (Manav, 2007). Perhaps this is why, after examining 200 studies of school environments, Higgens, Hall, Wall, Woolner, & McCaughey (2005), came to the conclusion that there "is conflicting evidence, but forceful opinions on the effects of colour" (p. 22) with studies producing inconsistent results.

In determining the best color to paint an environment, you should consider whether you want the space to look larger or smaller. Dark colors will make a space look smaller. If ceilings are high, you might want to paint them darker to make them appear lower. If the room is long and narrow, you can make the distant wall appear nearer by painting it a darker color.

Many design artists and early childhood specialists recommend using visually demanding bright colors only for accents (Bredekamp & Copple, 1997; Olds, 2001; Torelli & Durrett, 2000). Bright colors on shelves and furniture can cause overstimulation especially when we consider all the color that will be added to the environment by the toys, materials, items on the walls, and even the children's clothing. Instead, experts recommend that neutral colors be used, with learning centers being painted different but harmonious colors to differentiate the space (Olds, 2001). The neutral background allows the emphasis to be placed upon the toys, materials, and inhabitants of the space. In *Children, Spaces, and Relations,* Ceppi & Zini (1998) emphasize that the walls should be a basic background allowing those using the space to exercise their own creativity in applying a "second skin" (p. 63). Varieties and ranges of colors in materials can then add needed complexity, variety, and richness to the environment. This gives children the opportunity to learn about, compare, contrast, and experiment with color. This philosophy is in opposition to the often-found practice of using bright primary color schemes or pastel nursery themes that are based upon a simplified viewpoint of children (Ceppi & Zini, 1998). However, all considerations of color should be thought about in relationship to contemporary and cultural beliefs, since the early childhood setting needs to reflect the society it resides within rather than be an isolated entity.

Lighting

Lighting affects the aesthetics of the room as well as the visual acuity and mental health of the occupants. "Creating good lighting is not just a matter of having 'enough' lighting . . . . Good lighting is ultimately a matter of achieving a desired look and feel. Light can shape our moods. It can soothe the mind and invigorate the body. Light, in all its manifestations, has the power to not only illustrate what we see, but influence how we see it, even to make it beautiful" (Karre, 2003, p. 5).

Whenever possible, it is important to have natural light. As stated in the General Services Administration (GSA) handbook (2003), a set of regulations that govern all federal government childcare programs, "Natural lighting is essential in childcare centers. It is the hallmark of nurturing, quality environments" (p. 5–2). To help reduce glare, natural light should come from at least two directions (GSA, 2003; Olds, 2001).

Windows not only provide light but also allow access to the world outside, creating a "spirit of place" (Olds, 2001). Children can observe nature and the elements, and feel like they are part of the community surrounding the classroom. The room can feel larger when one can view the outside. If windows are strategically located, children can see what is occurring in the building before they enter, helping them to build anticipation and ease the transition (Moore, Lane, Hill, Cohen, & McGinty, 1994). Unlike artificial light, natural light from windows is dynamic, changing throughout the day.

Learning may also be enhanced with natural lighting. Researchers claim that natural lighting can improve achievement by 20% or more (Earthman, 2004; Heschong Mahone Group, 2003). Poor lighting, on the other hand, can cause "headaches, eye strain, and fatigue" (Higgens et al., 2005), negatively affecting learning.

Natural lighting also reduces energy costs, decreasing the needs for electric lights (Al-Mohaisen & Khattab, 2006). Electric lights consume energy and also produce waste heat energy. This is a problem in warm climates, causing an increase in the use of air conditioners (Al-Mohaisen & Khattab, 2006, p. 13).

However, it is typically not practical to rely totally on natural light. When natural light is not possible, full-spectrum lights are recommended (GSA, 2003; Olds, 2001). Some researchers indicate that full spectrum lights result in better physical health (Graves, 1985; Hathaway, Har-

This fixture provides lighting while adding visual interest and beauty to this area.

greaves, Thompson, & Novitsky, 1992; Graves, 1985). However, others claim that these benefits have not yet been proven (Gifford, 1994).

It is also recommended that classrooms have a variety of different types of lighting (track, pendant, recessed, dimmer controlled, lamps) to create "a distinctive atmosphere" in different areas of the room (Torelli, 2002). "A tapestry of light and dark areas in rooms and buildings adds to their comfort, interest, and spirit of place" (Olds, 2001, p. 192). "Pools of light facilitate special orientation, draw people together, and provide objects and people with definition and relationships. Pools of light affect people's attention, behavior, and their impressions of spaciousness or enclosure" (Olds, 2001, p. 191).

Different types of lighting allow for different needs. For example, dimmer-controlled lighting for sleeping areas allows low light when children are napping while still allowing supervision. Different types of lighting also allow children to have some control over their environment. For example, a lamp with a three-way bulb in the reading area allows children to adjust the degree of lighting according to their needs.

To get the best advantage of your lighting, ceilings and walls should be painted with a high light reflectance value (LRV) paint. High LRV can lead to a 25% reduction in needed lighting fixtures (Fielding, 2006). Mirrored ceiling tiles can also achieve this effect.

Design Palettes

Just as the artist uses a palette to draw or paint on, the early childhood teacher and children use the ceilings, walls, and floors as the design palette for the classroom.

Ceilings

Ceiling height provides a sense of your significance within the environment, helps to establish the type of activity expected, and impacts noise reverberation. Perhaps you have entered a cathedral or courtroom with very high ceilings. In this environment, you may feel small and insignificant. For this reason, some researchers suggest that ceiling height be lowered for children's spaces, to promote security and self-esteem (Moore et al., 1984; Weinstein, 1987).

Ceilings less than 8 feet high suggest quieter types of play and greater intimacy (Moore et al., 1984; Olds, 2001). In one study, more cooperative behavior was found when ceiling heights were lowered (Read, Sugawara, & Brandt, 1999). Higher ceilings promote active play. However, they also introduce more formality (Moore et al., 1984; Olds, 2001). Creating varied ceiling heights can also help reduce noise reverberation (Olds, 2001).

Some teachers reduce high ceilings through hanging canopies or draping fabric from the ceiling. Others lower ceilings by horizontally suspending large sheets of foam panels or sheets of lattice. The illusion of a lower ceiling can also be created by hanging kites or banners. In determining what items to hang, it is important to consider visual clutter.

Walls

Walls can be solid or transparent, be partial or reach to the ceiling. Transparent walls help to block sound while enhancing light. They also keep children from entering an area while still allowing visual access. Programs may place transparent walls or windows between classrooms, between the kitchen and classroom, or into halls. Infant/toddler classrooms frequently place transparent partial walls between the classroom and diaper-changing area.

Backdrop for Displays. Walls often form the backdrops for displays. In the article, *Aesthetic Codes in Early Childhood Classrooms,* Tarr (2001) discusses the typical early childhood environment. She describes the walls as "a visual bombardment of images" (p. 1) plagued with primary colors and simplified, flat figures that are cartoonish or of greeting card quality. Children's work in these environments is often displayed on brightly colored backgrounds with commercially made borders. Other walls are crowded with items such as large calendars, weather charts, ABC's, and number lines. Rather than reflecting the culture and society, this is an environment that would only be found in a school or childcare setting. Tarr (2004), in another article, discusses how this type of environment can silence children. "The mass of commercial stereotyped images silence the actual lived experiences of those individuals learning together. An overload of commercial materials leaves little room for work created by the children—another kind of silencing. Finally, children are muffled when what is displayed does not accurately reflect who they are in terms of gender, culture, and ethnicity but rather in stereotyped ways" (p. 3). Olds (2001) also emphasizes the need to avoid stereotyped images, specifically mentioning Disney, television, and fairy tale characters. She states that they "tend to be 'Cutesy' and are often used to make a place appear child-oriented when everything else is not" (Olds, 2001, p. 248).

Purpose of Displays. When planning how to use wall space, teachers must think about the purpose of the display. Displays can provide an impetus for imagination and creativity, expose children to beauty, spark interest in a topic, and become interactive learning materials. Most importantly, walls form the backdrop for children's work and photos.

Provide Inspiration. Pictures can provide inspiration, thereby promoting children's learning. For example, when Tessa placed pictures of different famous architectural buildings on the wall in the block center, children in her preschool classroom went from creating basic wooden constructions to creating elaborate block structures. Mrs. Sampson hung a selection of flower paintings by Georgia O'Keeffe exposing children to a beautiful display and also providing inspiration. As a result, the kindergarten children began painting flower pictures, which were also used to create a display.

This display is made more attractive by the black fabric background. A picture that was provided for inspiration, photos of children creating the art, and a written description of the process provide a context for the viewer.

Vertical Learning Surfaces. Walls and bulletin boards can become interactive displays or "vertical learning environments" (Readdick & Bartlett, 1995). For example, a teacher in a toddler program used two posters of children showing a variety of different emotions to create an activity. The teacher made a matching game by cutting up one of the posters and adding Velcro. In an elementary school, a teacher used the bulletin board to create a display titled "100 Ways to Use a Plastic Bag." As children thought of new ideas, they wrote them on cards that they added to the board.

Display Children's Work. And, of course, walls are used to display children's work. It is important to display children's products respectfully, with the primary focus on the creation itself. You must be careful not to overpower the child's creation with the border and background (Tarr, 2004). In some preschool and elementary schools, each child is given an individual space on the classroom wall to display his choice of work. This allows children to choose what they want to highlight, while allowing them to learn about design and experiment with creating attractive displays. The Learning and Belonging (LAB) preschool uses a different approach. Rather than hanging up all the children's artwork, they have three frames hung on their bulletin board. Children's artwork rotates through these frames. Teachers are careful never to hang work that was created at the same time in the frames, believing that the uniqueness of each child's work is highlighted when the pictures that are hung use different media and subjects. They also believe that displaying all the children's work at once, even when the work is individualized, diminishes the work of each individual child.

Provide Images of Children, Families, and Staff. Walls should also contain photos of current children, families, and staff. Photos of children engaged in activities can help children, staff, and parents revisit and reflect upon an experience. When our walls contain pictures of children, families, and staff in the program, it also illustrates that we view them as being important. Pictures can also help us to get to know each other better.

Photos can be included in a variety of ways. Pictures of current children participating in relevant activities may be hung in the different learning centers. Instead of purchased posters, current children's pictures can be used to illustrate hand-washing steps or the daily schedule. Photos of the artist may be displayed with the child's artwork. One program makes a family quilt each year that displays pictures of the children and their families. Parents and children choose photos to include. These often contain the family pet, favorite places, and their homes. Many programs provide framed photos and short biographic sketches of the teachers in the program to help families identify and get to know staff better. Pictures for children should be hung at their eye level. For example, very low bulletin boards covered with Plexiglas can contain pictures at the eye level of infants and toddlers. The Plexiglas protects the pictures while allowing children the opportunity for a close look.

Avoid Visual Bombardment. It is also important to avoid having too many items on the walls. When the walls are crowded with materials, even if they are appropriate items, it can create a visual sensory bombardment. Like wallpaper, the individual items become part of the background. Additionally, items that are intended for the children need to be hung at their eye level. If hung too high, materials add to visual clutter while serving no useful purpose.

Walls in early childhood programs have the potential to become overcrowded because of the multiple users, such as teachers, assistants, children, and administrators. To help decide what is placed on walls, it is helpful to develop a set of guiding principles. For example, the Learning and Belonging (LAB) Preschool's guiding principles state that materials placed on walls must be authentic, have a defendable function, provide a balance of form and function, and be current. Materials are considered more authentic if they are concrete or related to the current group of children. For example, a photo of a current child building a block structure is considered more authentic than a picture from a book. There must be a sound rationale for placing the item on the wall—a defendable function. In examining the balance of form and function, teachers determine if the space the item requires is worth the function it will provide. For example, large birthday calendars are often found on early childhood walls. While knowing and acknowledging children's birthdays is very important in many programs, the form or space occupied by the large display might not be an appropriate balance. Instead, teachers in one program make a special class birthday book. Each child has a page in the book containing a current picture and baby picture of the child, her birth date, and a list or picture of some of her favorite things. The materials on the wall must also be current, reflecting the children and adults in the group.

Floors and Different Surface Levels

Flooring Materials. A variety of flooring materials provides children the opportunity to learn through comparing and contrasting. For example, how fast will a toy truck roll on a carpet versus a waxed wooden floor? Floor surfaces can be flat or inclined, rough or smooth (Trancik & Evans, 1995, p. 49). They can be made from a variety of materials. While in the past wall-to-wall carpeting was a popular flooring choice, many programs today are installing linoleum, tile, or wood floors. Teachers then add area rugs where soft surfaces are desired. Throw rugs of different types of materials add variety to the setting and can reflect the culture of the community (bamboo mats, braided rugs, hand-woven rugs, cotton rag rugs, or Oriental rugs). Rugs allow for more flexibility in arranging space, are easier to clean, and are more eco-healthy than wall-to-wall carpeting. The Eco-Healthy Child Care Awards (2007), developed in Oregon, include elimination of wall-to-wall carpeting as one of their criteria. In installing wall-to-wall carpeting, toxic glues and adhesives are used. It is more difficult to clean carpets than a hard surface, which allows the build-up of pesticides or other materials that are carried in on children and adult's shoes. Carpet can also harbor allergens, including mold and mildew.

Experts recommend that floors be neutral colors (Bredekamp & Copple, 1997; Ceppi & Zini, 1998). Torelli (2002) urges programs to avoid teaching rugs such as ABC rugs or number rugs because they add to the visual clutter.

Varied Surface Levels. Different surface levels can help to differentiate space, reduce noise levels, add interest to the room, create intimate areas, allow a new view, increase usable space, provide gross motor activity, and help children to feel powerful. There are many ways to create different surface levels including lofts, risers and stages, platforms, and areas that are recessed.

Lofts can provide a variety of possibilities. For example, they can be equipped with rope ladders, stairs, fire poles, knotted ropes to climb, ramps and slides, ball rolls (like a marble roll), and buckets and pulleys to transport items into the loft.

Lofts can also be used for a variety of purposes. In one elementary classroom, children and the teacher developed a constitution regarding loft usage and rules. The loft became a mini-library, a performing stage, a place for private conferences, a puppet stage, and an area for small-group work at various times throughout the year (George, 1995). In another classroom, each child received the use of the loft for one week. During this week, children decorated the loft and chose how the loft would be used. In a K–3 multi-grade classroom, children were studying space. The loft became a space ship, with instruments created by the children. One preschool program built small lofts by modifying bunk beds. These cozy lofts, which increased the space in the small classroom, were just the right size for one or two children. It is important when planning lofts that you examine licensing regulations and make sure you comply with safety standards.

A puppet stage in the bottom of the loft, and a reading area above, provide an appealing literacy environment in this kindergarten classroom.

Special Design Considerations

Two critical design considerations for early childhood programs are density and noise. Both can have significant influences on stress levels and learning opportunities.

Crowding or Density

Impact of High Density. Density levels or the number of children per square foot of space can have profound effects upon children and adults. High density levels can increase stress, aggression, destructive behavior, and withdrawal and decrease positive social interactions, achievement and attention span in children. (Kantrowitz & Evans, 2004; Legendre, 2003; Maxwell, 1996, 2003).

Although many state standards require 35 square feet per child, many design experts recommend a minimum of 50 square feet (White & Stoecklin, 2003). The GSA National Standards for Child Care Facilities, the United States Department of Defense, the Head Start Technical Assistance Centers, and the Easter Seal Child Development Centers all recommend 45 to 50 square feet per child. Legendre (2003) found that when toddlers had less than 5 meters (53.8 square feet) for play, their cortisol levels increased. Cortisol is a hormone that is linked to stress in children. There is concern that children's development might be adversely affected by frequent or extended periods of stress (Shonkoff & Phillips, 2000). Cortisol levels decreased when toddlers had more than 54 square feet for play.

High density levels also increase aggression and destructive behavior in some children (Kantrowitz & Evans, 2004; Maxwell, 1996) while leading to withdrawal in other children (Kantrowitz & Evans, 2004). Children in high-density classrooms engage in more solitary play and have fewer positive social interactions (Evans, 2001; Legrendre, 2003). They also display shorter attention spans during play (Kantrowitz & Evans, 2004). Studies of elementary students indicate lower levels of achievement in classrooms with greater density (Maxwell, 2003).

Crowding can be especially detrimental for children with special needs, for example, children who are hyperactive, have anxiety, or are impulsive (Kantrowitz & Evans, 2004; Loo & Kennelly, 1979). The behavioral effects of high density in early childhood programs are magnified when children also experience crowding at homes (Maxwell, 1996).

High density levels may also affect teachers. Studies indicate that high density can cause attentional overload in adults (Saegert, 1978).

Reducing Density. If the room is small, the teacher will need to evaluate ways of increasing space. For example, could the teacher's desk be removed? In addition to housing coats, could the cubby room be used for a center? Could a loft be added? Could a closet have the door removed and become an area for a center? Could some furniture be removed? It is recommended that at least one-third to one-half of the floor space be free from furniture to allow for play (Teets, 1985).

In addition to considering crowding in relationship to classroom size, one must also consider crowding because of daily usage patterns. The teacher needs to carefully plan the space each learning center requires. When a popular center is too small, crowding within the center can occur. Some teachers control this by having a sign-in system for each center. For example, to use a center, children might hang their nametag on a hook by the center. When all the hooks are full, there is no more room in the center. Limiting required accessories is another way to control numbers. For example, only two goggles may be available at the woodworking table or four aprons at the water table. Children realize that when these props are in use, then they need to find another place to play. It is imperative that children have several choices for play spaces. As a rule of thumb, you will want one-third more spaces in centers than there are children in the classroom.

Other teachers analyze each center for usage patterns and, in any center that children are not using, they make changes to increase its appeal, thereby decreasing density in other centers. In other situations, the size of a center might need to be adjusted. Because the need for different amounts of space change as the year progresses and children's interests or projects change, it is important to have movable boundaries.

Problems with density can also occur when areas of the classroom are used for limited purposes. For example, children might only use an area of the room for group time, naptime, or lunch, or for certain projects. In a large room, this might still allow enough area for the children to use the rest of the day. However, in most classrooms, it is important to use the entire room during the majority of the day, creating areas in the classroom that are multi-use.

Impact of Low Density. While high density is often the concern in early childhood programs, low density can also be an issue causing more onlooking behavior and less interaction between children (Smith & Connolly, 1986). Programs experiencing reduced interaction due to a large space may want to block off sections of the room to increase the density.

Noise

Impact of Noise. There is growing concern about children's exposure to noise, with 25% of 8 to 10 year-olds in the United States exhibiting some hearing loss (Kilgore, 2005). While many teachers realize that high noise levels can cause hearing loss, there is also a need to regulate lower levels of noise. Lower levels of noise can negatively affect memory, attention, use of language, and academic achievement especially reading and speech development (Evans & Maxwell, 1997; Maxwell & Evans, 1999, 2000). Exposure to noisy environments also leads to elevated stress levels and increased blood pressure (American Academy of Pediatrics, American Public Health Association, & National Resource Center for Health and Safety in Child Care and Early Education, 2002; Evans, Hagge, & Bullinger, 1995). Noise level is affected by both the background noise and the reverberation in the room.

While noise can come from outside sources, the major source of noise is the children themselves (Shield & Dockrell, 2003). Several studies have found that even when children are engaged in quiet activities, the noise level in the classrooms is typically high enough to interfere with speech development, understanding of language, and letter/number recognition (Kryter, 1985; Maxwell & Evans, 2000; Shield & Dockrell, 2003). Children in quieter preschool classrooms have higher attentional levels, higher levels of language skills, and perform better on language tests (Maxwell & Evans, 2000). While noise levels impact all learners, they pose a greater threat to those learners with visual, hearing, or central nervous system disabilities (Doctoroff, 2001). For example, hearing aids may amplify all noises, including background noises, making it more difficult to hear relevant speech in a noisy room. Even intermittent hearing loss may cause problems. If a child has fluid in the ears, it is equivalent to increasing the noise level in the room by 35 decibels (American Academy of Pediatrics et al., 2002).

Exposure to noise also leads to elevated stress hormones (Evans, Hygge, & Bullinger, 1995). Blood pressure is also increased in noisy environments (American Academy of Pediatrics et al., 2002).

High levels of noise have a greater impact on younger children since they have limited control over the environments they are in and have reduced ability to tune out irrelevant background noise (Wohlwill & van Vliet, 1985). These findings are especially troublesome when one considers the rapid pace of learning and the effect of stress on the developing brain in the early childhood years.

Noise also affects teachers, causing additional emotional and physical stress and affecting relationships. Both childcare and elementary teachers have a higher incidence of voice disorders than colleagues in other professions (Sala, Laine, Simberg, Pentti, & Suonpää, 2001; Smith, Lemke, Taylor, Kirchner, & Hoffman, 1998). High noise levels can also impact psychosocial well-being in teachers. Teachers in classrooms with higher levels of noise display increased withdrawal and disruptions in personal relationships (Grebennikov & Wiggins, 2006).

The National Health and Safety Performance Standards (American Academy of Pediatrics et al., 2002) state that for at least 80% of the time, noise levels need to be below 35 to 40 decibels. This is the level where a person can be clearly understood in a normal conversation without raising her voice level.

Noise Reduction. Noise may come from equipment such as projectors in the classroom, and heating and air conditioning (Nelson, Soli, & Seltz, 2003). Malfunctioning fluorescent lights are another source of noise. Keeping equipment in good repair and only using when necessary can reduce noise.

There is more noise found in classrooms that are situated adjacent to loud rooms, have mainly hard surfaces, have walls that do not reach the ceiling, or have high ceilings (Maxwell & Evans, 1999). In addition, noise may come from adjacent streets or buildings. Noise can be reduced by adding acoustical ceiling tiles; ceiling hangings; and soft elements like carpets, pillows, and curtains (Maxwell & Evans, 1999). Walls and backs of bookcases can be covered with acoustical panels, textured wall hangings, divider drapes, or carpet (Olds, 2001). While acoustical tiles can be expensive, teachers can make their own sound-proofing panels by covering fiberboard with eggshell foam and then adding fabric (Wien, Coates, Keating, & Bigelow, 2005). Sound dampers can be added to furniture legs. Because children and furniture are close to the floor in early childhood classrooms, 50% of a room's volume is empty. This allows noise to travel unimpeded and increases reverberation (Olds, 2001, p. 182). Using partitions, different ceiling heights, lofts, and climbers can help solve this problem.

Teachers can also take several other actions to decrease noise, including separating noisy and quiet areas, designing quiet alone spaces, and providing earphones for music and computers. Teachers can make a conscious effort to decrease noise whenever possible. For example, many programs have music playing in the background. While this is often intended to reduce noise levels, it may instead add to the noise level as children and teachers talk over the music. It is also important to avoid loud toys. A recent study found that many toys, including toy cars, exceed the safety standards for noise (Kilgore, 2005).

Teachers can also assist children to use lower voices. Vincent (1999), in a book describing multi-age elementary classrooms, described a noise meter. The noise meter has a dial that the teacher can turn to indicate the noise level for a given period of time. This includes no voices, buddy voices (only heard by the person next to me), table voices (heard at a table full of children), and classroom voices (heard across the room). Teachers can model using lower voices by reducing the space between the teacher and child when talking. When talking to large groups, some teachers are using sound amplification systems to assure that all children hear.

By reducing noise and density, both children and teachers can live in an environment that is less stressful and produces better learning outcomes. Through careful planning and intentional design, teachers can also produce a homelike, aesthetic environment that is a welcoming place for every person that inhabits the space.

Sample Application Activities

1. Examine a variety of pictures from architectural magazines. What mood does each environment evoke? Compare your reactions to others. Determine what specific characteristics of the environment creates the mood you are experiencing.
2. Visit an early childhood environment and analyze the environment using the environmental design checklist found in Figure 6.1.
3. Develop a list of criteria that will govern what is placed on the walls of your current or future early childhood program.

☐ Is the environment homelike?
- welcoming
- divided into usable space for different functions
- includes private places to escape
- includes places for people to gather together
- provides comfortable furniture and different types of seating
- filled with real, functional items (dishes, pottery, pots and pans, tools)
- contains objects that have personal meaning such as framed art and collections of natural items (seashells, rocks)
- filled with images of the inhabitants through photos and mirrors
- includes living things; plants, flowers, animals

☐ Is the environment aesthetic?
- beautiful
- clutter free
- sensory rich
- thoughtfully organized
- attention given to detail

☐ Does the environment reflect the inhabitants of the program (lives, families, culture, ethnicity, geographic location, interests)?

☐ Are there ways that children can personalize the environment?

☐ Is there an abundance of natural lighting coming from at least two directions?

☐ Are distinctive atmospheres created through different types of lighting (track, pendant, recessed, dimmer controlled, lamps)?

☐ Does the environment contain a variety of soft elements?

☐ Are a variety of textures found in the room?

☐ Are neutral or pale colors used for most walls and shelving?

☐ Do the walls contain a few carefully chosen items or is there a visual bombardment of images?

☐ Are materials on the wall authentic and related to the current group of children?

☐ Is there a defendable purpose and a balance of form and function for each of the items that are on the wall?

☐ Are there different surface levels in the classroom (lofts, risers)?

☐ Is the flooring a neutral color?

☐ Is there a variety of flooring surfaces?

☐ Is there a minimum of 50 square feet of space per child in the classroom?

☐ Is all the available space being used (unless there is low density)?

☐ Are children distributed evenly throughout the space during center time?

☐ Can individuals be clearly heard and understood in a normal conversation without raising their voices?

Figure 6.1
Environmental Assessment: Design Considerations

Source: Permission is granted by the publisher to reproduce this figure for evaluation and record-keeping. From Julie Bullard, *Creating Environments for Learning: Birth to Age Eight.* Copyright © 2010 by Pearson Education, Inc. All rights reserved.

4. Brainstorm a list of interactive bulletin board ideas for children of different ages.

5. Visit an early childhood classroom and pay special attention to the noise level. What steps is the teacher taking to reduce the noise level? What additional steps could she take?

6. Learn more about reducing noise level by visiting the Quiet Classrooms website at http://www.quietclassrooms.org

7. To learn more about design visit the National Clearinghouse for Educational Facilities at http://www.edfacilities.org/rl/classroom_design.cfm

chapter 7

Developing Literacy Centers

*E*vangeline noted that few children were using the reading area during center time. She discussed this concern with a co-teacher, wondering if she should assign children to centers. Her coworker suggested that instead Evangeline consider ways of emphasizing this area and enticing children to want to read.

Evangeline began by analyzing the current exposure children had to books. Each day they read a story during a whole group circle. Reflecting upon this experience, Evangeline realized that much of the time was spent managing the group rather than emphasizing reading enjoyment. Because of the group's inattentiveness, she often read the story as quickly as possible, rarely pausing to ask questions or seek input from the children.

A pleasurable reading experience became Evangeline's first goal. She divided her circle activities into two groups, with the assistant taking half of the children. They pre-planned each story time, thinking about ways to engage the children. Typically *when reading they would pique children's interest by discussing the cover of the book, asking prediction questions, relating the content to the children's lives, and encouraging children to ask questions. At times, they became storytellers and dressed as a character in the story. At other times, they read audience participation books such as predictable books where children recited part of the story along with the teacher. They often brought in props that related to the story, such as flannel boards, stuffed animals, and puppets.*

At the end of each story time, they placed the books and props in the reading area. Children began to look forward to story time and frequently read the modeled books and used the props in the reading area.

Early literacy skills are critical in laying the foundation for current and later success in oral and written language. In addition, literacy skills often play a crucial role in learning content in other areas.

Oral language involves a symbol system where the word represents an object or idea. "Writing and reading with an alphabetic system involve an extra layer of symbols, where the phonemes are represented by letters" (Roskos, Christie, & Richgels, 2003, p. 5). The ability to master these symbolic systems is critical, since the child's literacy skills at the end of the preschool years are predictive of later reading and academic success (Farran, Aydogan, Kang, & Lipsey, 2006). For example, children who have low vocabularies often continue to struggle throughout their schooling (Hart & Risley, 1995). As children mature, this foundation affects their future careers and ability to function in a democratic society.

It is important to create a print rich environment by having functional print throughout the classroom. This can include written directions, written schedules, labels for parts of the room and for materials, written morning messages, and signs (exit). Functional print should be written in English and in other languages spoken by the children in the classroom. To see many examples of how teachers can create print rich environments, watch the video *Creating a Print Rich Environment* on MyEducationLab.

While functional print, books, and writing materials should be available in all centers in the classroom, it is also important to have an area primarily devoted to literacy. In a study examining the unique characteristics of K–2 teachers who were nominated as effective in enhancing literacy, 100% of the kindergarten teachers, 85% of first-grade teachers, and 73% of second-grade teachers had a literacy center in their classroom (Pressley, Rankin, & Yokoi, 1996).

myeducationlab

Go to MyEducationLab and select the topic "Early Literacy." Under Activities and Applications, watch the video *Creating a Print Rich Environment.*

Stages of Literacy Development

Reading and writing acquisition is a developmental continuum that begins at birth (IRA/NAEYC, 1998, p. 5). From birth, children are primed to learn language, recognizing their parent's voices and preferring speech to other sounds (Berger, 2006). By the age of 2 months, they can make a range of different meaningful noises such as cooing, laughing, and crying. One-year-old children are able to make sounds from their native language and often are speaking their first words. Beginning at about 18 months of age, after children learn their first 50 words, they go through what is referred to as a naming explosion. During this time, they gain 50 to 100 new words per month. Most of these beginning words are nouns (Berger, 2006). This growth in vocabulary is an important predictor of reading success (Epstein, 2007). Children's rapid growth in vocabulary and sentence length continues through the early childhood years. See Table 7.1 for average sentence length and vocabulary of children ages 24 to 60 months.

Table 7.1 Child's Age, Average Sentence Length, and Receptive Vocabulary

Child's Age	Average Sentence Length	Number of Vocabulary Words Understood
24 months	2–4 words	500–2,000 words
36 months	4–5 words	1,000–5,000 words
48 months	5–6 words	3,000–10,000 words
60 months	6 or more words	5,000–20,000 words

Sources: CDC, 2007; Berger, 2006.

Written language also progresses rapidly in the early years, proceeding through the following stages (MacDonald, 2006):

- Random scribbles.
- Controlled scribbles—Children begin to use linear scribbles to represent print.
- Letter-like forms—Children begin to create mock letters with letter-like forms. They separate writing from drawing.
- Letter and symbol relationship—Children begin to write their names and copy words in their environment.
- **Invented spelling**—Children begin to write their own words, spelling them phonetically or according to the sounds of the speech. Words will often contain consonants but may not contain vowels. This is a meaningful, important phonemic process. It often occurs before children know the names of all the alphabet letters or have mastered phonemic awareness (Richgels, 2001; Roskos, Christie, & Richgels, 2003).
- Standard spelling—Children begin to use conventional spelling.

Literacy skills (reading, writing, speaking, and listening) develop concurrently rather than sequentially (Epstein, 2007, p. 24) and continue to increase throughout the early childhood years. By the third grade, most children can read fluently using a range of word strategies, write expressively, edit their work, and use a rich and varied vocabulary (IRA/NAEYC, 1998).

How the Literacy Center Enhances Children's Development

In a well-developed literacy center, children get the opportunity to practice important skills needed to become effective speakers, listeners, readers, and writers.

Oral Language

Speech is a crucial tool in expressing oneself. Oral language is also considered a building block or foundation for reading and writing (Searfoss, Readence, & Mallette, 2001). Through oral lan-

What stage of writing is Emera displaying?

guage, children gain essential background knowledge, experience language sounds that lead to phonological awareness, learn new vocabulary, and learn about the uses and conventions of language (Halle, Calkins, Berry, & Johnson, 2003, p. 2).

Listening Skills

Children spend 65% to 90% of their time listening while in school settings (Gilbert, 2004, p. 20). However, of all the language arts, teachers place the least emphasis on helping children develop listening skills (Smith, 2003; Timm & Schroeder, 2000) causing some to call it the "forgotten language art" (Tompkins, 2005). A well-developed literacy center can help develop these important skills.

Print Awareness

Print awareness allows a child to understand the organization of print and that print carries meaning. This includes concepts of print such as the distinction between a letter, word, sentence, or paragraph. Also included is that print has a direction (left to right, top to bottom in the English language) and occurs in a particular order (beginning, middle, and end in a story). Another important component of print awareness is that print can be used for a variety of purposes. For example, to give direction and information, to provide pleasure, and to communicate with others (Searfoss et al., 2001).

Phonological Awareness

"The term **phonological awareness** refers to a general appreciation of the sounds of speech as distinct from their meaning" (Snow, Burns, & Griffin, 1998, p. 51). This includes learning that oral language is composed of sounds that can be segmented (divided) and blended. Children usually begin this process with learning about rhyming, then sentence segmenting, syllable segmenting and blending, onsets (initial word sounds) and rime (middle and ending word sounds), and finally individual **phonemes** (smallest unit of sound) (Chard & Dickson, 1999).

Alphabet Principle and Phonemic Awareness

The **alphabet principle** and **phonemic awareness** is the understanding that there is a relationship between letters and sounds and that words have a structure made of sounds and sound patterns (Epstein, 2007).

Positive Attitude Toward Reading

To become proficient in using literacy, children must have a positive attitude toward reading and writing. Positive attitudes often result in increased motivation to read and write. As children engage in additional practice, they typically become more proficient. Children who like to read have often had an abundance of positive experiences being read to. They view reading and writing as pleasurable and something that they are successful at. For example, to persist at reading, children need to experience a 90% to 95% rate of success (Neuman, Copple, & Bredekamp, 2000).

Enhancement of Other Curricular Areas

In addition to learning specific literacy skills in the literacy center, children also have the opportunity to

- increase knowledge in all curriculum areas.
- learn about new worlds, both real and imaginary.

Go to MyEducationLab and select the topic "Early Literacy." Under Activities and Applications, watch the video *Individual Story Time: Preschool*.

● cope more effectively with difficulties. Stories can help children realize that others have had similar experiences. Books can provide information on coping strategies and answer questions that children might have. They can also act as a springboard to open dialogue about a difficult situation. For example, watch *Individual Story Time: Preschool* on MyEducationLab to see how a story helps one child cope with a difficult situation. In addition to stories, you might have children draw or write about their feelings. Tessa begins each day with "emotional literacy." Children draw or write about their emotions and experiences. For example, one child was happy because they got a new puppy. Another child was sad because they missed a grandfather who died.

● improve social interactions. Children learn literacy skills through social interaction and social skills are enhanced by increased language skills.

● be entertained and experience enjoyment.

Through using an effective literacy center, children gain skills in literacy and other curricular areas. But how does one design an effective center?

Designing an Effective Literacy Center

A rich, effective literacy center provides a comfortable, enticing place for children to engage in reading, storytelling, listening, writing, and manipulating and playing with letters and words. Each of these different activities may be included within one center or divided into smaller centers such as reading, writing, and listening areas. If they are divided into separate centers, they should be placed in close proximity to each other, since activities in one area of literacy often provide inspiration for other areas. For the sake of clarity in this chapter, we will examine each of these areas separately.

Designing an Effective Reading Area

To design an effective reading area the teacher must think about the appropriate placement of the center; the size of the center; how to create an enticing, inviting environment; and what books and props to include in the center.

Placed in a Quiet, Well-Lit Area of the Room.   Since reading is often a quiet activity, the center should be located in the quiet area of the room. It is important to have adequate lighting in this area. Having a three-way light bulb allows children to adjust the lighting according to their needs.

Clearly Defined.   The literacy center may be in a loft, on a riser, or divided from the rest of the room by bookshelves and dividers. A clearly defined, separated area reduces distractions and encourages more in-depth experiences.

Large Enough Area to Accommodate Five to Six Children.   In planning the reading center, you need to consider the number of children that might be using the center at any point in time. Morrow (2001), a well-known literacy expert, recommends that the center should accommodate a minimum of five or six children. In addition, there should be at least one very private, quiet place to read. For example, I once had a classroom with a bathtub filled with pillows that was just right for an individual reader. Ecole, a Head Start teacher, created a reading hut by laying a shelf on its side.

- Blank books—Blank blue exam books or teacher-created books (books can be cut into shapes to suggest writing about a certain topic).

- Book-making supplies so children can create their own books—These include different types of paper, materials for covers (fabric, wallpaper samples, construction paper), and materials to hold the books together (staples, yarn, hole punch, wide arm stapler, brads).

- Clipboards for writing and drawing in other areas.

- Alphabet strips or cards (since children's ability to quickly focus their eyes from near to far vision is still developing, it is easier for young children to use print that is located closer to them rather than an alphabet that is posted on the wall).

- Sample words and letters

  • Words to trace or use as models—Teachers at the Early Childhood Learning Center place an index card containing a word and a picture illustrating the word into a plastic bag and organize the words by topics using a round metal ring to hold each collection of words together.

  • Word walls (see Figure 7.2 for more information).

  • A book of writing samples containing a list, poem, story, letter, and thank-you note.

  • Individual word banks—Index cards with words written on them that the child has written or dictated (store them in index card boxes or plastic bags) (Morrow, 2002). Alternatively, children can write words on sticky notes and insert them into their own personal dictionary.

  • Picture dictionaries, both commercial and child made.

This aesthetic writing area allows an individual child to concentrate as he or she composes.

Figure 7.2
Word Walls

Word walls are organized collections of words that are displayed for children to use. Depending upon the purpose, words might relate to the current unit, project, or theme; be high-frequency words; be commonly misspelled words; or be words chosen for word analysis such as rhyming families. Some teachers develop an "interesting words" wall. Children choose words they find interesting to add to the wall. Depending on the age group, these words might be color coded by parts of speech (for example, red for adjectives).

Many word walls are organized by placing the alphabet on the wall and placing the words under the proper letter. Kieff (2004) recommends only adding about five new words per week and moving older words to word banks. By doing this, the wall will not contain so much print that it will be difficult to locate the sought-after word.

To be effective, words need to be large enough and posted low enough that children can easily see them. Preschool word walls often contain a photo or illustration next to the word.

To increase usage, teachers should engage children in interactive word wall activities. For example, they might focus on the words during circle or small-group time (pointing out similarities, clapping syllables, finding words that rhyme, etc.). Some teachers establish word walls that children can manipulate (word cards can be placed on a magnetic background or in a pocket chart).

- Pictures and photos to stimulate writing or to use in child-created books.
- Folders for children to store their own writing and a filing system for easy retrieval of the file.
- Ways of sharing writing with others such as bulletin boards for displaying writing, mailboxes, or message boards. Children's written dictations and stories can be placed in the reading area as another way to share.
- Special highlighted activities to promote learning and to keep children interested and motivated to write.
- Labeled shelving for holding writing materials.
- Labeled containers for organizing and storing paper (stacking trays), journals, individual children's writing files, and pencils, crayons, markers, and other writing implements (cans, glasses).

Special Activities in the Writing Area. Preschool and early elementary age children might complete many special activities in the writing center. In choosing special activities, teachers need to consider the children's interests and developmental levels. Often the writing center special activities are presented during group time and then the materials are placed in the writing center for children to pursue during center time. With modifications most of the activities listed are appropriate for pre-K–3rd grade. For example, while a preschool child might create a "Feelings Book" by drawing and labeling pictures, a third-grade child might write and illustrate poems or short descriptive essays about feelings. Some ideas for special activities include the following:

- Write an individual or class book about ourselves (All About Me Book, What I Can Do Book, Feelings Book, My Wishes Book).
- Write a factual book on a topic that has been studied.
- Make an individual or class alphabet book (pre-K–K)—The teacher should provide a variety of alphabet books to use as models. High-quality alphabet books have one letter per page, pictures that children recognize, and a fast-paced story, words that rhyme, or some other interesting story element (Beaty, 2005, p. 6). You might also provide stickers and pictures for creating the books. One kindergarten class made a very personalized alphabet book by forming their bodies into alphabet letters. The teacher took photos and the children used these to create their book.
- Create a book modeled after a published storybook, poem, or song. Children can use the published storybooks for inspiration and as starting points for creating their own similar stories (e.g., "Willoughby Wallaby Woo," a poem by Dennis Lee; *Mr. Brown Can Moo! Can You?* by Dr. Seuss; *Are You My Mother?* by P. D. Eastman; *Brown Bear, Brown Bear, What Do You See?* by Eric Carle).
- Make a pictionary (a picture dictionary).
- Create a book of **environmental print** (print such as signs, food wrappers, and other print found in the environment).
- Create an environmental print bulletin board.
- Write a rebus story (a story where some of the words are pictures) using stickers or a computer program such as KidPix or KidWorks.
- Write daily news reports of classroom happenings to share with parents (this is often one of the rotating, assigned children's jobs).
- Write greeting cards to parents and to sick classmates.
- Write thank-you notes to class guests or field trip hosts.

- Create invitations to an event being held at the school.
- Create announcements of different classroom events (hamster had babies, child lost his first tooth).
- Make a class newspaper containing pictures and script from class members.
- Create an ad for a favorite book (Morrow, 2001).
- Develop a roll story with a friend.
- Draw a comic strip.
- E-mail parents or pen pals.
- Take a classroom poll.

For children kindergarten through third grade you might include a help board in the writing center. The board often includes the following (Diller, 2003):

- A list of ideas for writing.
- Models of different forms of writing (list, letter, poem, instructions, story).
- A list of where to go for help (word wall, friend, pictionary, teacher).

To promote writing at home, some teachers provide a writer's briefcase that can be checked out. The briefcase contains paper, writing implements, and ideas and inspirations for writing (Jalongo, 2003).

Designing an Effective Listening Area

A listening center is one important way to encourage and enhance listening skills. Following are materials and criteria to consider in establishing the listening center:

- Provide a tape recorder or a CD player with multiple headphones. If children are not yet reading, it is helpful to label the on and off button so children can operate the machine independently.
- Provide a variety of stories, activity tapes, finger plays, music, and listening games. Provide some of these in different languages. One way to provide additional languages is to have children listen to stories on the computer. Many children's stories have options for changing the language. You can also ask families to record favorite stories in their culture's language.
- Provide comfortable listening places such as beanbag chairs or pillows.
- Label tapes and CDs so that children can easily locate them.
- Encourage active listening by having children do the following:
  - Listen to activity songs and do the actions as they are sung.
  - Read along in a book and turn the pages when indicated. Providing multiple copies of books allows several children to actively follow along.
  - Act out the story using puppets, flannel board figures, or other props. You might create figures to match the story by cutting out pictures from the dust jacket or by photocopying pictures from the book, laminating the figure, and making a stand from Styrofoam to create standing paper dolls (Beaty, 2005).
  - Use story sequence cards to display the part of the story that is being read.
  - Identify different sounds (such as household sounds) on a tape by putting pictures of the items producing the sound in the correct order. Children can turn the cards over to check the numbering to see if they are correct.

- Listen to a story and discuss it afterwards with a friend who has listened to the same story. Teachers can also create tapes that ask questions during the story. The child stops the tape and discusses the question with his or her partner.
- Play listening games such as Simon Says . . .
- Respond to the story by drawing a picture or writing about it.

● Keep tapes and props stored together in a plastic bag or basket.

● Provide blank tapes for each child so they can record their own stories or create stories to go with their pictures.

Special Considerations for Infants and Toddlers

To promote infant and toddler literacy, adults need to provide an environment rich with books, pictures, language, and experiences. The environment also needs to provide comfortable and cozy places for interacting. For example, an infant/toddler reading area needs to include comfortable places for adults and more than one baby to snuggle and read (love seats, a baby crib mattress placed against a wall, a hammock). There should also be places for toddlers to read on their own. This might be an individual reading place, such as a decorated appliance box. A low canopy or children's tent can also provide an intimate reading space. A small swimming pool or fishing boat with a sheepskin rug or pillows are other options for a comfortable reading area. As with reading areas for older children, this area should be in a quiet, contained space.

Books need to be within children's reach. Providers can prop books on the floor for very young infants. They can place books on very low bookshelves or in plastic see-through pockets attached to the wall for mobile infants and toddlers. Books for infants and young toddlers are often cloth, plastic, or board books. Although they are sometimes difficult to find, it is important to provide high-quality books. The content should be relevant to the lives of the children and appropriate for the age group. They should be either wordless or contain a simple text with few words. Since children are trying to learn about and make sense of the world, it is important that illustrations are realistic (no pink elephants). The size of the book should be small enough to manipulate by little hands and durable enough to handle some rough exploration. Magazines such as *Babybook* and store catalogs featuring many pictures might also be included.

It is also important to provide personalized books. Practitioners can make these using small photo albums or plastic sandwich bags that are hooked together on a ring. Books can be created about class happenings, families, pets, or common words the child knows. Books of individual children participating in different activities can also be interesting for children. Individual books can also help children deal with sadness and loneliness. Seamus, a young toddler, had a father who lived in another state. To help with the separation, his grandmother created a book of Seamus and his father doing a variety of activities together (flying a kite, taking a walk, riding in the stroller, throwing rocks, sleeping) called *Daddy and Me.* She wrote a simple story to accompany the pictures that Seamus enjoyed hearing repeatedly. Teachers can also create individualized group books. Lisa, a teacher of toddlers, created a book, based upon *Brown Bear, Brown Bear, What Do You See?* She used children's names and photos (Zinnia, Zinnia what do you see? I see Terrance looking at me).

The book area for infants and toddlers should contain a variety of different books, with several books per child. Expect that toddlers will carry books around with them to different areas since they often enjoy reading a book to their baby doll or showing another child a picture in a book.

In addition to books, it is helpful to provide laminated picture cards or postcards that children can carry around, manipulate, or match to the actual object (Miller, 2005). These can be placed in a small basket or can be attached to a wall with Velcro. Another way to use walls for infant/toddler literacy is to mount pictures behind a sheet of cardboard with doors that open to reveal a picture underneath (Isbell & Isbell, 2003). Pictures can also be taped on the floor (Isbell & Isbell, 2003). Very young infants can have pictures propped around them to look at. For example, soft fabric blocks can be created that contain a plastic viewing window. You can also purchase these from toy companies such as Discovery Toys.

Although it is unusual to find a separate writing area in infant/toddler environments, even very young children enjoy making marks on paper. Therefore, it is important that paper and a variety of writing implements be available somewhere in the environment.

It is crucial that infants and toddlers hear an abundance of language. From birth, adults need to read and sing to children. Adults should use language to describe what the child is doing, to name objects and feelings, and to describe what the adult is doing. Since many hours with very young children are consumed in routine care such as feeding and diapering, it is very important that adults take this opportunity to visit with children. Describing to children what you are going to do as you diaper them or move them from place to place is also a way of showing respect for the child. Adults also need to respond to all efforts the child makes to communicate, responding to children's coos, engaging in conversational give and take, and expanding and extending children's speech as they begin to use words.

Teachers' Facilitation of Learning in the Literacy Center

Teacher involvement in the literacy center is critical to assist children to meet their potential. Children participate in more literacy behaviors during center time when teachers introduce the materials and then interact with the children during the center time (Morrow & Rand, 1991). In addition to establishing an environment that values children's language and allows children to use literacy in authentic ways, the teacher supports children's literacy learning in many other ways.

Provide Opportunities for Children to Gain Background Knowledge

"Reading involves comprehending written texts. What children bring to a text influences the understandings they take away and the use they make of what is read" (Strickland & Riley-Ayers, 2006, p. 3). It is the adult's responsibility to provide rich environments and experiences. To increase vocabulary and background knowledge, children need an abundance of concrete, varied experiences with people, places, and things.

Expand Children's Language

Teachers can increase children's vocabulary acquisition by adding information to what the child has said ("See the ball." "Yes, it is a very big blue ball.").

Intentionally Use Rich Language and New Vocabulary Words

There is a strong relationship between the child's vocabulary and his reading achievement and comprehension (Strickland & Riley-Ayers, 2006). It is important to not only use common words but to also include rare or sophisticated vocabulary that goes beyond the 8,500 most common words when you are talking with children (Strickland &

Riley-Ayers, 2006). Children need multiple opportunities to hear a new word used in context before they learn it (Justice, 2004). While intentional vocabulary development is crucial in developing desired literacy outcomes (Justice, 2004), research indicates that teachers in early childhood settings often do not use rich vocabulary (Girolametto, Hoaken, Weitzman, & van Leishout, 2000). Since teachers often have multiple focuses as they interact with children, it is sometimes difficult to think about rich vocabulary during the actual time of interaction. Therefore, teachers need to be intentional and pre-plan new vocabulary words they want to use with children. Some programs post vocabulary words on the walls that they wish to stress, so all adults remember to use them. These words might relate to a new center, material, or topic that is being introduced.

Model Active Listening

To actively listen, you must give the child your full attention. We do this by being at the child's eye level; making appropriate eye contact; not interrupting or changing the subject; giving verbal and nonverbal feedback; focusing on the message, the underlying meaning, or the emotion being conveyed; showing our understanding by reflecting what the child has said; and asking open-ended relevant questions (Jalongo, 2008). Teachers must provide the needed time to listen to children. Although this is sometimes difficult for teachers to do, especially with children who stutter or are hard to understand, it is critical. Teachers sometimes want to assist the child by guessing what the child is trying to say. However, effective teachers allow children to finish their own sentences rather than interrupting and finishing sentences for them.

Ask Appropriate, Open-Ended Questions

Open-ended questions increase children's language since they usually take more than a one-word answer, tend to increase dialogue, and often ask for thoughts, opinions, or feelings. Open-ended questions often begin with how, why, what, when, or where. In classrooms, 80% of teacher interactions are task-oriented (instructions, giving information, providing corrections) (Jalongo, 2008). When teachers do ask questions, only 7% to 12% are open-ended (Jalongo, 2008; Wittmer & Honig, 1991). Since asking open-ended questions does not come naturally to many teachers, it is necessary to intentionally plan questions to ask. It is also important to actively listen to children's responses. To revisit information on open-ended questions see Chapter 1.

Support Peer Interactions and Discussions

In social contexts, children learn new words and get an opportunity to use the words they know. In the literacy center, teachers might support peer interactions by encouraging buddy reading, placing two or three chairs at the computer, and encouraging activities that children co-produce (such as producing a puppet show or jointly writing a rebus story).

Read Books to Children

"The single most important activity for building the understandings and skills essential for reading success appears to be reading aloud to children" (IRA/NAEYC, 1998, p. 5). Center time is an ideal time to read aloud to individual and very small groups of children. This time allows an intimacy between the children and teacher and the opportunity to interact with the book in a way that is often not found in larger groups. See Figure 7.3 for interactive ways to read books to children.

Figure 7.3
Interactive Ways to
Read a Book

Interactive reading is critical to obtain the maximum learning experience (Morrow & Gambrell, 2001). It is "the talk that surrounds the reading that gives it power, helping children to bridge what is in the story and their own lives" (IRA/NAEYC, 1998, p. 5). Interactive reading occurs before you read the book (building interest, asking for predictions, discussing and introducing the topic, relating the book and topic to children's experiences). It occurs during book reading (asking open-ended and prediction questions, asking children to share personal experiences that relate to the book, encouraging children to ask questions and make comments). It is also important to have discussions after reading the book (reflecting upon, discussing, and responding to the book's plot and characters; for example, you might ask "What would you have done. . . ?"). Some teachers have children respond to the book through writing in their journals, drawing a picture, or completing an activity related to the story.

Teachers also scaffold children's literacy learning as they read (Roskos, Christie, & Richgels, 2003). For example, they might teach new vocabulary, print conventions, phonological awareness, print recognition, and book concepts. However, this must be done in a very thoughtful manner so it does not negatively affect the story (Roskos et al., 2003).

Story time needs to be a pleasurable experience. This is often more likely to occur when reading to individuals or small groups. This allows the child more opportunities to actively engage with the text, which prevents boredom and misbehavior. Teachers can also tailor the book and the interaction to meet the needs and interests of the child or children participating.

Teachers should preread books they plan to read aloud, read the book with expression, set the stage, and show enjoyment for the book and the reading experience.

Develop Interest in Books

Teachers help children develop interest in reading by providing an engaging, enticing literacy center. As the opening scenario illustrated, children also become interested in books when there are interesting story times. See how one creative teacher builds interest in a book in *The Story Teller: Ms. Joan and Her 3-Year-Olds* on MyEducationLab. This book was later placed in the literacy area and became a favorite of the children.

Convert Words to Text

Teachers can help children understand the conversion of words to text by creating class experience stories, putting children's favorite songs and finger plays into writing, and writing down children's individually dictated sentences and stories. You can also record and then transcribe children's oral storytelling.

Model the Use of Reading, Writing, and Storytelling Props

During the day, teachers have many opportunities to model reading and writing. At times, it might be helpful to verbally state what you are modeling. "Oh I see that the glue bottles are almost empty. I'm going to write glue on my shopping list, so that I remember to buy it."

The use of props also needs to be modeled so that children will understand how they can be used. If the teacher does not model the use of the props, children often will either ignore the props or use them inappropriately.

PEARSON
myeducationlab

Go to MyEducationLab and select the topic "Early Literacy." Under Activities and Applications, watch the video *The Story Teller: Ms. Joan and Her 3-Year-Olds.*

Offer Individual and Group Instruction for Reading and Writing

Teachers support children's reading and writing by offering individual and group instruction as needed. For example, Sarah's kindergarten class had visited the fire station. She used this opportunity to teach children about the conventions of thank-you notes. During center time, Sam was writing an individual thank-you card. He wanted to know how to spell firefighter. His teacher showed him how to find the word on the word wall. Sam then wrote the word in his own individual word bank.

It is also important to model and encourage correct pencil grip and paper placement. Correct pencil grip and paper placement assists children to write more legibly and effectively (it is not as tiring for the hand). You should encourage children to hold the paper with their other hand as they write. It is also important to teach children to use the correct slant for their papers so that they are keeping their wrist straight as they write. If the child is left-handed, the left corner of his paper should slant upward.

Meet the Needs of All Learners

We need to meet the needs of all learners in our classroom by providing a wide range of developmentally appropriate, interesting reading, writing, manipulative, and oral language materials and activities. In this section, we will address two groups of children that research indicates are at special risk in the area of English literacy: children who are learning English as a second language and children who are from low-income backgrounds.

Supporting Children Who Are Learning English as a Second Language. More than 9% of the school population is learning English as a second language (Kindler, 2002), making it critical that teachers understand second language acquisition. As a starting point, teachers should view the second language as additive (adding to the child's first language), rather than in a negative light. Teachers should never attempt to replace the child's home language with the second language. "Children's identities and senses of self are inextricably linked to the language they speak and the culture to which they have been socialized" (Genessee, Paradis, & Crago, 2004, p. 33). Additionally, the development of a strong base in the child's first language assists him in acquiring a second language by providing background knowledge, vocabulary, and concepts about print (IRA/NAEYC, 1998, p. 6). To support children and their relationship to their parents and culture, we need to continue to support children in learning and maintaining their home language and make sure the school environment includes literacy materials that represent the home language (IRA/NAEYC, 1998, p. 6). We can ask families and community members to bring objects from their culture, ask families and community members to tell stories in their language and tape them, and provide authentic children's literature reflecting the culture and experiences of children in the group. If at all possible, we should speak at least some words from the child's home language or find others who can do so. "The earliest interactions between a child and the significant others around him communicate to the child what types of language are valued" (Espinosa, 2006, p. 40). Using children's native language shows respect for the child and his culture, helps the child to gain knowledge and feel pride, helps to establish parental rapport, and encourages parental involvement (Lucas & Katz, 1994). For a further discussion about how to value children's culture watch *Incorporating Home Experiences of Culturally Diverse Students in the Classroom-Part 3* on MyEducationLab.

We also need to assist the child to learn English. It is important to use gestures, manipulatives, and visual aids to assist children to grasp the words we are saying. We should also speak clearly and slowly. According to second language acquisition theory, children go through stages as they learn and use a second language. It is important we understand these stages. For example, children might understand hundreds of words in a second language before they begin to speak the language.

myeducationlab

Go to MyEducationLab and select the topic "Diversity." Under Activities and Applications, watch the video *Incorporating Home Experiences of Culturally Diverse Students-Part 3.*

- Stage 1: Silent/Receptive—During this stage children may not speak. However, they may understand up to 500 words and will respond nonverbally.

- Stage II: Early Production—Children in the early production stage have developed around 1,000 words that they can understand and use. They often speak in one- or two-word sentences at this stage.

- Stage III: Speech Emergence—Children at this stage speak in short phrases and sentences using approximately 3,000 words.

- Stage IV: Intermediate Language Proficiency—At this stage, children can use 6,000 words and speak in complex sentences.

- Stage V: Advanced Language Proficiency—To acquire advanced proficiency can take 5 to 7 years. Children at this stage are able to use grammar and vocabulary similar to same-age native speakers (Reed & Railsback, 2003, pp. 15–17).

Supporting Children From Families with Low Socioeconomic Status. Statistically, children who live in low socioeconomic (SES) households have lower vocabularies, fewer literacy skills such as recognizing alphabet letters and writing their names, and poorer background knowledge when entering kindergarten than their higher income peers (Neuman, 2006). This is especially troubling since those children who begin with poor skills often do not catch up. For example, in a classic study, Juel (1988) discovered that if a child is a poor reader at the end of grade one, there is an 88% chance that the child will still be a poor reader at the end of grade four.

So what causes this knowledge gap? It appears to be experience with words. Statistically, the accumulated experience with words is much lower for children who are low income (13 million for 4-year-old children who are low income, 45 million for 4-year-old children from the highest economic group) (Hart & Risley, 1995). Not surprisingly, the majority of words that children use are part of the parent's vocabulary. In addition the size of the vocabulary also parallels that of the parents (Hart & Risley, 1995).

Children who are low income also often have disparate print opportunities. They may lack opportunities to read books because there are often fewer books in the home, public libraries in the area are often open fewer hours, and many school libraries are closed (Neuman, 2006). Statistically, low-income children are read to less before entering kindergarten than their middle-class peers (25 hours versus 1,000 hours) (Adams, 1990).

Many low-income parents also have fewer economic and emotional resources for enhancing background knowledge and literacy development. For example, children who are low income have fewer opportunities for high-quality child care, lessons, camps, and outside activities (Neuman, 2006). Parents are also more likely to experience depression and have concerns that affect the quality of interaction with their children (Neuman, 2006).

It is important that early childhood programs provide children with literacy opportunities that will enhance their skills. Children need to hear high-quality books, increase background knowledge through many experiences, engage in rich conversations, and hear many vocabulary words. Some programs help to assure that children have more opportunities to be read to by having "foster grandparents" or volunteers come into the program during free choice to read to children.

To produce better results for children who are low income it is also necessary to encourage parents to talk with and engage in reading and storytelling with their children. Providing book and writing briefcase checkout programs is especially important in low-income neighborhoods.

Observe and Document Individual Children's Learning

Children's literacy learning can be assessed in a variety of ways, including observation, anecdotal records, analysis of written and oral samples, and vocabulary and reading inventories. Teachers and children might create individual literacy albums or portfolios that contain writing samples, tapes of children reading and telling stories, lists of books that the child has read or listened to, and transcripts of a conversation as a way of documenting their achievements. Children often assist in choosing artifacts to include and reflect upon why they want this particular entry to be included. These reflections can also become part of the literacy album or portfolio.

Teachers can gain an extraordinary amount of knowledge about children through careful observation. Following are some questions that can guide you in observing children in the literacy center.

- Does the child know how to handle a book (turns pages one at a time, starts at the beginning of the book, holds book right side up)?
- Does the child look at or read books voluntarily?
- Does the child listen attentively when being read to individually, in a small group, and in a large group?
- Does the child demonstrate the ability to comprehend stories (can retell a story, can add information, can answer open-ended questions, is able to talk about the story and make predictions)?
- Is the child able to name alphabet letters? Which ones?
- Does the child demonstrate concepts about print (English is read from left to right and top to bottom)?
- Can the child identify words (sight words, environmental print, frequently used words, own name and names of friends)?
- Can the child read a book (telling story from the pictures, memorizing the book, reading some words in the story, reading all the words in the book)?
- Is the child able to tell or retell a story (story told in sequential order, story involves characters, setting, problem to be solved, plot, resolution)?
- Does the child demonstrate phonemic awareness?
- Is the child able to clap the number of syllables in a word?
- Can the child give examples of rhyming words?
- Does the child scribble, draw, or write voluntarily?
- Can the child record her ideas through pictures and words?
- What book genre is favored by the child?
- What writing conventions does the child use (left to right, top to bottom, space between words, capital letters at the beginning of a sentence, uses punctuation)?
- What stage of spelling is the child in?
- Does the child engage in conversations (takes turns, uses appropriate eye contact, initiates conversations, responds to other's initiations)?

TIP   Some teachers provide a system so that children can keep track of which books they have read or have had read to them. For younger children individual picture charts can help them to document the books they have read. These charts then become part of the child's literacy portfolio.

Teachers are critical in designing effective literacy environments and then scaffolding children's learning as they interact in these environments. Early childhood teachers can set the stage for children's lifelong love of reading and writing.

Literacy in the Outdoors

The outdoor playground can provide many authentic opportunities for integrating literacy. For example, in the Little Explorers playground, the following are available:

- Signs label each playground zone.
- A chalkboard is hung inside the playhouse with a bucket of colored chalk nearby.
- A basket of books sits beside the porch swing.
- Along the bike path are stop signs, yield signs, and arrows indicating the direction of travel.
- Clipboards, paper, and a variety of pencils and crayons are available for writing or making sketches.
- Guidebooks for identifying bugs and birds are accessible.

All the materials are organized and stored in a locked cupboard that is opened when the children are outdoors. Providing the storage saves teachers' time and helps to assure that the materials are available on a daily basis.

Events in the outdoors can also enhance oral language.

One day the children at Kid College arrived to find that the basement of their center had flooded, and rainwater continued to flow into the building. Some of the children began to experiment with ways of stopping the water from entering. As they worked, they discussed and debated many different options. Sherri, a 5-year-old, watched the efforts for a while and then became a news announcer describing the flood and the efforts to stop it. When Sherri ran out of ideas for continuing the narrative, her teacher suggested that she interview others about the flood. Sherri continued as a news announcer for nearly an hour.

Outdoor events such as the flood at Kid College, finding a worm, seeing a bird visit the bird feeder, or finding the first flower in bloom are experiences that most children want to exuberantly share with others. Outdoor activities also encourage social interaction and language as children swing, climb, run, and play together.

Effective literacy centers allow children to use reading, writing, and listening for authentic purposes; to interact with others; and to make sense of the written word that surrounds them (Searfoss et al., 2001). In the literacy center, teachers can introduce the magic of books, share the power of language, and lay the foundation for future success.

Sample Application Activities

1. Critique an early childhood literacy environment using the environmental assessment found in Figure 7.4. What could be added to make the environment richer?

2. Learn more about early childhood literacy by visiting the NAEYC Early Childhood Literacy website at http://www.naeyc.org/ece/critical/literacy.asp.

3. Tape record yourself reading a book to children. Critique yourself using the information found in Figure 7.3.

Figure 7.4
Environmental Assessment: Literacy Center

Source: Permission is granted by the publisher to reproduce this figure for evaluation and record-keeping. From Julie Bullard, *Creating Environments for Learning: Birth to Age Eight.* Copyright © 2010 by Pearson Education, Inc. All rights reserved.

Reading, writing, listening, and literacy manipulatives may be combined in one center or may be in separate centers.

☐ Is the literacy center in a quiet, well-lit area of the room?

☐ Is the literacy center clearly defined (in a loft, separated from the rest of the room by bookshelves)?

☐ Is the center a large enough area to accommodate five to six children (Morrow, 2001)?

☐ Is the center comfortable and aesthetic?

☐ Is the area enticing (book-related displays, objects to go with highlighted books, interesting entry)?

☐ Is the center engaging, providing props and materials for active reading and storytelling involvement (Reutzel & Morrow, 2007, p. 38)?

☐ Is the center well stocked with five to eight quality books per child?

☐ Are books in good condition (no torn pages or missing covers)?

☐ Are featured books displayed with their fronts showing?

☐ Are additional books organized on shelves or baskets?

☐ Are books high quality (quality illustrations, award-winning authors, interesting stories)?

☐ Are new books and props added on a regular basis?

☐ Are the books responsive to the needs and interests of the children in the group (variety of difficulty levels, range of topics and genres, in languages spoken by the children)?

☐ Are the books representative of a variety of cultures and families?

☐ Are there developmentally appropriate literacy manipulatives that promote oral skills, alphabetic awareness, phonemic awareness, and knowledge of words?

☐ Is there a table and chairs for several children to sit and write?

☐ Is an author's chair available?

☐ Is there an assortment of writing implements?

☐ Is there a variety of materials to write on, including transitory writing surfaces?

☐ Are there labeled shelves and containers for organizing writing materials?

☐ Is there a computer with installed writing software and a printer so children can print their own stories?

☐ Are there journals or blank books available?

☐ Are book-making supplies available?

☐ Are there clipboards for writing or drawing in other areas?

☐ Are there models for children to use in their writing (such as alphabet strips or cards, word walls, writing samples, picture dictionaries)?

☐ Is there a system for children to store and easily retrieve their writing?

☐ Is there evidence in the room that children are sharing their writing with others (mailboxes, message boards, bulletin boards with experience stories, child-created stories in the reading area)?

☐ Are there special highlighted activities to promote learning and to keep children interested and motivated to write?

☐ Is there a tape recorder or a CD player with multiple headphones?

☐ Are there a variety of stories, activity tapes, finger plays, music, and listening games (in English and the children's native language) for children to listen to?

☐ Is there a comfortable listening place such as beanbag chairs or pillows?

☐ Are tapes and CDs labeled so that children can easily locate them?

☐ Are there props and materials for active listening?

☐ Are the tapes and props stored together in a plastic bag or basket?

☐ Are there blank tapes so each child can record her own stories?

☐ Is there print throughout the room?

☐ Are there books in several classroom centers?

☐ Are there writing materials in several classroom centers?

4. Tape record yourself having a conversation with children. Analyze what type of questions (open or closed) you asked and how often you expanded or extended the child's speech.

5. Make a list of environmental print found in an early childhood learning environment.

6. Critique a random sample of five books found in the early childhood environment. Do they meet the standards for high-quality literature found in Figure 7.1?

7. Assist a child to create a book using ideas from this chapter. Place the book in the reading center when it is completed.

8. Complete an online exercise that will help you review and apply your knowledge of literacy. Go to MyEducationLab and select the topic "Early Literacy." Under Building Teaching Skills and Dispositions, complete the exercise "Building Strong Literacy Practices."

chapter 8
Developing Manipulative and Sensory Centers

*A*rmelia, a teacher in an urban Early Head Start center, noticed that the infants in her room were very interested in textures. Wanting to give the children a whole body sensory experience, she put a small rubber blow-up boat in the classroom and placed a variety of pieces of cloth inside, including cotton, velveteen, satin, burlap, nylon, and chiffon. At the end of each day, Armelia washed and dried the fabric to have it clean for the next day. The babies climbed into the boat and crawled on the material, laid on the fabric, and even sometimes fell asleep in the "textured nest." They also used their developing manipulative skills to pick up the fabric, place it over their heads, and rub it between their thumbs and fingers. The babies seemed to develop their own fabric preferences, digging the desired cloths out of the pile. As the year progressed, Armelia changed the materials in the boat to meet the children's new interests. For example, the children became intrigued with the suction soap dish when they found it on the floor one day.

Armelia responded by putting suctioned bath mats (suctions facing up) into the boat that the children used to sit on, walk on, and crawl on. She also placed other suction items (suction balls, suction soap dishes) for child experimentation into the boat. Through the sensory boat, the infants were able to develop sensory, manipulative, gross motor, and cognitive skills.

The Manipulative Center

The manipulative center includes materials to develop children's fine motor skills. Fine motor skills consist of coordinating movements in the fingers, hands, and arms (Trawick-Smith, 2006, p. 208). They are necessary for writing, drawing, assembling puzzles, and performing self-help skills like eating with utensils, buttoning, zipping, and tying shoes. Fine motor skills are influenced by perception, the nervous system, cognition, motivation to accomplish a task, and environmental support (Feldman, 2007).

Children who have difficulty with fine motor skills are more dependent on others and may have trouble with many school tasks. They are often teased by classmates and may experience a poor self-concept (Losse, Henderson, Elliman, Hall, & Knight, 1991; Wehrmann, Chiv, Reid, & Sinclair, 2006). Teachers often view these children more negatively, wrongfully believing the child's messy paper is due to carelessness or laziness (Rosenblum, Weiss, & Parush, 2003). Children with poor fine motor skills may engage in avoidance behaviors, reinforcing other's beliefs that they are unmotivated (Thorne, 2006).

The early childhood years set the stage for children's future success. For example, children who have neat handwriting receive higher grades on their work even when the content is very similar and the writing is not supposed to influence the scoring (Sweedler-Brown, 1992). In one study, scorers received training to try to reduce this bias. However, even with training there was evident scorer bias toward more neatly written papers (Sweedler-Brown, 1992).

So much time is spent in fine motor activities during preschool and elementary school that children who have fine motor difficulties are at an extreme disadvantage (see Table 8.1). Think of the time that you engage in fine motor activities each day. How is your life impacted by your skill level in this area?

So what can we do in the early childhood years to enhance children's fine motor skills? This chapter will review environments, materials, and teacher interactions that can assist all children to develop these needed abilities.

Table 8.1 Children's Age and Percentage of Time Spent in All Fine Motor Tasks and Only Paper/Pencil Tasks

Children's Age	Percentage of Time Engaged in Fine Motor Tasks	Percentage of Fine Motor Time Devoted to Pencil and Paper Tasks
Head Start (preschool)	37%	10%
Kindergarten	46%	42%
Elementary	30% to 60%	85%

Sources: Marr, Cermak, Cohm, & Henderson, 2003; McHale & Cermak, 1992; Rosenblum, Weiss, & Parush, 2003.

Stages of Fine Motor Development

Children make incredible strides in fine motor skills in the early childhood years. Quinell, who is 4 months old, is picking up things with her entire hand. By 8 months, like 50% of other children her age, she is able to use the pincer grasp (using her finger and thumb) (Feldman, 2007, p. 130). Her fine motor skills will continue to develop as her neurological and physical system matures. However, she will also need experiences to gain fine motor skills. Throughout the early childhood years, Quinell, like most children, will develop the needed manipulative skills through involvement in purposeful, self-chosen activities, using a variety of tools and objects (Exner, 1992). With practice, the use of the tool typically becomes automatic. For example, controlling a pencil becomes automatic for most children as they grow older, allowing them to concentrate on other aspects of the writing process (Rosenblum et al., 2003).

As we plan developmentally appropriate experiences, it is important to remember that motor skills typically develop from the head downward (cephalocaudal trend) and from the inside out (proximodistal trend). For example, the child gains control of the arm, the hand, and then the fingers (McDevitt & Ormrod, 2007).

How the Manipulative Center Enhances Children's Development

The well-planned manipulative area can be a rich source for learning. Children use fine motor and perceptual skills, practice motor planning and execution, and engage in eye-hand coordination in this center. Most of the materials found in the manipulative area also enhance cognitive skills.

In addition, children increase their attention span and self-discipline as they participate in activities. For example, children often continue to work until they complete an entire puzzle or match all the lids to the jars. They often experience a sense of satisfaction as they complete a challenge for the first time (matching all the nuts and bolts). While many activities in this area are designed to be accomplished alone, some are designed for two or more children (floor puzzles, games). These activities help children learn to work cooperatively with others and to develop skills of turn-taking.

Designing an Effective Manipulative Center

Children develop fine motor skills in many areas of the early childhood classroom (literacy, block, math, science, cooking, and art centers). However, most early childhood programs also include a designated manipulative center where the primary purpose is the development of fine motor and self-help skills.

It is important for the teacher to focus on the skills to be developed and to carefully choose materials that will enhance these skills. In one study, researchers presented kindergarten children with more than 50 manipulative activities to use as one option during center time. The researchers chose materials that were self-corrective and attractive and that focused on the pincer grasp. For example, in one activity children used a spoon to move "diamonds" from a beautiful bowl to a decorated egg carton that had a blue velvet pillow glued inside each compartment (Rule & Stewart, 2002, p. 10). The activities were introduced either by the teacher or by a tape recording. The children in the control group also had opportunities to use manipulative activities and spent the same amount of time as the experimental group engaged in these activities. However, in spite of this, the children in the experimental group outperformed the children in the control group in an authentic fine motor task. This study underscores the need for thoughtful planning and for introducing each activity (Rule & Stewart, 2002). Some important criteria in developing the manipulative center include

- A quiet, uninterrupted area for children to work.
- An area that is well lighted, preferably with natural light.

- Low, open, labeled shelves to hold materials. Many teachers label shelves and trays with pictures and/or words. This allows children to practice literacy skills and enables them to return materials to a designated space.

- Trays or baskets to hold all the materials needed for each discrete activity. Trays also help children to define the workspace when using the table (Texas Child Care, 2005). If using baskets to hold materials, you might use carpet squares for defining the child's workspace.

- Storage for additional materials. Since materials for fine motor skills need to be rotated frequently to meet the developmental needs and interests of children, it is important for teachers to have accessible, convenient storage. Classroom storage also allows teachers to meet the immediate needs of an individual child or small group of children.

- Horizontal surfaces including tables, chairs, and floor space (for completing large floor puzzles).

- Vertical surfaces. Occupational therapists stress the importance of using vertical surfaces such as white boards, flannel board, or magnet boards hung on walls or placed on easels (Benbow, 1990; Myers, 1992). Vertical surfaces naturally cause children to properly position their wrist and to use thumb opposition (Myers, 1992). Working on a vertical surface also assists with wrist extension, which supports balanced use of hand muscles and aids in shoulder and arm muscle development (Benbow, 1990). As stated by Myers (1992), "Switching activities from a horizontal to a vertical orientation can transform an ordinary or mediocre activity into a powerful tool for encouraging fine-motor skill development" (p. 48).

- Using attractive materials. In both the Reggio Emilia and the Montessori approaches, the importance of using beautiful materials is stressed. The following quote describes the Montessori philosophy. "In selecting trays, pitchers, and other utensils for Practical Life exercises, look for the most attractive materials that you can find and afford. Design activities that will draw the child's interest and create a prepared environment that is harmonious and beautiful. If possible, avoid using plastic pitchers, bowls, trays, and other materials . . . . Children respond to the beauty of wood, glass, silver, brass, and similar natural materials" (Seldin & Wolff, 2007). (See Chapter 1 for more information about the Montessori and Reggio approaches.)

- Using enticing materials that are interesting to the range of children in the group. Tina noticed that Terrance, a boy who struggled with fine motor control, very rarely used the manipulative center. However, Terrance was always the first to notice a bug in the play yard or classroom. Tina capitalized on this interest by adding several plastic bugs, small bug houses, and different-sized spoons for picking up and moving the bugs into the bug houses. When Tina introduced the bugs, she stated that they were pretending that these bugs were very fragile and should only be carefully lifted with a spoon. Terrance was fascinated with the new activity, telling the names of each type of bug to his classmates as he carefully categorized the bugs into the bug houses.

- Diverse materials that are developmentally appropriate, meeting individual children's needs. The teacher needs to understand the developmental sequence of fine motor skills, activities that help enhance development, and the specific developmental

Attractive containers filled with colored water entice children to practice pouring.

skills of the children in her group to design a developmental manipulative center. Since there will be children at a variety of levels, it is important that the center include some open-ended activities such as a variety of nuts to sort into trays, or waffle blocks to build with. A variety of complexity levels should be made available for closed-ended activities. For example, the diamonds activity described earlier would be easier with a larger spoon. Having more than one size of spoon allows children to be successful while providing them the opportunity to increase the challenge, as they are ready.

- Enough developmentally appropriate materials to provide four to six children with several choices each.
- High-quality tools such as scissors. To reduce frustration and encourage scissor practice, scissors should be sharp and should cut paper easily. The holes should be small, just the right size for the thumb and finger (Myers, 1992). Both right- and left-handed scissors need to be available and labeled in an obvious way. It is important that children be taught safety rules when using scissors. For example, Amy, a teacher of 3-year-old children, has the following rules for scissors. "Scissors need to be held down and away from you when you are carrying them." "You always use walking feet when you are carrying scissors." "Scissors are for cutting paper or other art materials."

Appropriate Materials for the Manipulative Area

When you plan materials for the manipulative area, it is important to consider the different manipulative skills young children are learning. These include the development of the pincer grasp, strength in grasp, bilateral coordination, eye-hand coordination, wrist swivel, wrist stability, finger dexterity, and development of the hand arches. In this chapter, materials are listed under each of these skills. While the materials primarily address the skill under which they are listed, they may assist with other manipulative skills as well. For example, stringing beads develops bilateral coordination but it also develops eye-hand coordination and the pincer grasp.

Materials to Develop the Pincer Grasp

Learning to use the pincer grasp (where children use the thumb and index finger to pick up a small item) is a critical fine motor skill. When children use the pincer grasp, it is important that the web space or the space formed by holding the thumb and finger together be rounded. This allows the child to hold a pencil or other tool in a way that is less tiring for the hand. The pincer grasp can be developed by materials such as

- A sieve with colored toothpicks for inserting through the holes (using colored toothpicks allows children to classify by color if they wish).
- Colorforms or stickers to place on paper.
- Eyedroppers to move water from one container to another.
- Tweezers, tongs, or spoons to move glass marbles, beads, shells, or pinecones from one place to another.
- Wooden chopsticks that are tied together at the top with a rubber band to pick up pompoms.
- A Lite Brite.
- Pins to push into a paper with a cork board underneath to punch out a design of choice.
- Buckles to open and close and shoes to tie (at Bright Beginnings Preschool an actual shoe is nailed to the wall for children to lace and tie).

- A sunflower with tweezers to remove the seeds.
- A rubber band ball for removing and adding rubber bands.

Materials to Strengthen Grasping and Squeezing

Following are some materials to enhance grasping and squeezing:

- A plant sprayer and colored paper so that children can spray a design on the paper.
- A paper puncher, many different types of paper, and a beautiful container to hold the punches. The punches can be used for other activities.
- A turkey baster and cotton balls (the child can blow the cotton ball across the table with the baster).
- Squeeze toys such as toys whose eyes bulge when squeezed.
- Clothespins that are used to attach items to a clothesline (the clothesline can be placed on the wall of the manipulative area).
- Sponges and basters. In a Montessori program, the manipulative shelves included a tray furnished with a baster, a pitcher of colored water, and two glasses. Children pour the water into one of the glasses and use the baster to move the water to the other glass. Another tray includes a pitcher of water, two small bowls, and a sponge. The child pours the water from the pitcher into one dish and then uses the sponge to move the water from that dish to another one.
- A nutcracker with nuts to crack (nuts can later be eaten for snack).

Materials to Strengthen Bilateral Coordination

Bilateral coordination is using both hands together or using one hand for one thing while using the other for something else (holding paper with one hand while cutting with the other). Following are manipulative materials that enhance bilateral coordination:

- Cotton balls to pull apart (these can then be used to glue onto a picture or to make a project).
- Beads to string into necklaces.
- Pop beads to put together and pull apart.
- A stapler and paper.
- Lacing cards.
- Cards that show a clapping rhythm for children to imitate.
- A child's shirt to practice buttoning (Joanne, a preschool teacher, took the shirt and placed it over a frame, making it easier to button).
- Two clear jars (one containing colored water) and a funnel on a tray. Children can pour water from one jar through the funnel into the other jar.
- Paper for folding airplanes or origami.
- Newspaper for tearing (the newspaper can be used for collages, paper mache, or other art products).
- Beautiful small coin purses to unzip and find the treasure.

Materials to Strengthen Eye–Hand Coordination

This refers to focusing and coordinating eye movement and the processing of visual input to control and direct the hands to accomplish desired tasks (Johansson, Westling, Bäckström, & Flanagan). Some materials that encourage eye–hand coordination are

- Golf tees, with clay or Styrofoam to pound the golf tees into.
- Nails and a wood stump to hammer nails into.

- Poker chips and a covered potato chip can with a slit in the lid for inserting the chips.
- A variety of items to pour (water, aquarium gravel) and dishes to pour them into.
- A wire strainer, pebbles, and two dishes for transferring the pebbles from one dish to another.
- Peas to shell (these can later be used for lunch or snack).
- Nesting dolls to stack together.
- Games such as Pick Up Sticks, Barrel of Monkeys, Operation, Bedbugs, and Don't Spill the Beans.
- Small building materials such as 1 inch blocks, legos, tinker toys, gears, Lincoln logs, bristle blocks, marble rolls, and erector sets.
- A variety of types of puzzles.

> TIP You can create your own puzzles by gluing a picture onto foam board or thick cardboard and then cutting the picture into a puzzle design. Some teachers create personalized puzzles using pictures of the children, their families, or class activities. Labeling the back of each puzzle piece with a symbol unique to that puzzle can assist with clean-up if puzzle pieces get mixed up.

Materials to Enhance Wrist Rotation

Wrist rotation includes being able to perform a twisting motion with the wrist. This is necessary for everyday activities such as opening doorknobs. Some materials that promote wrist rotation include

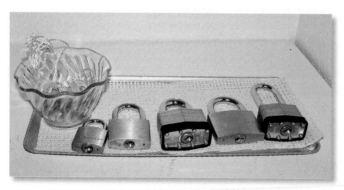
The padlocks and keys develop wrist rotation. The different sizes also encourage seriation.

- Lids and jars to match (provide a variety of different interesting jars and lids).
- Nuts and bolts to screw together.
- Padlocks and keys to open and close (provide several different padlocks).
- Screws, wood to screw them into, and screwdrivers.
- Items to take apart (hair dryer, toaster, carburetor) with a screwdriver or nut remover.
- An Etch-a-Sketch.
- A flashlight for taking apart and reassembling.

Materials to Enhance Wrist Stability

Children's wrist stability is enhanced by using a vertical surface. Make sure your manipulative area includes some vertical surface work. If there is not room on the walls, consider tabletop easels.

> TIP You can create your own tabletop easel to increase children's opportunities with vertical surfaces by cutting diagonal cuts on two opposite sides of a box. Then tape cardboard to the open side.

Materials to Enhance Finger Dexterity or Moving Individual Fingers in Isolation

Children often develop finger dexterity while performing finger plays. To extend this activity to the manipulative area, you can add finger puppets (one for each finger) that the child can use to retell a familiar story, song, or finger play. Providing a typewriter for children ages 4 to 8 can also allow children to develop finger dexterity but only if they are using all the fingers as they type.

Materials to Develop the Arches of the Hand (General Hand Development)

There are several materials that are used in therapy to help develop the arches. These can also be used in an early childhood setting with preschool and K–3 children. These materials include

- Small tongs or clothespins to pick up small objects, such as beads or cotton balls. Children can classify these objects into sorting trays.
- Small items (pennies, marbles, plastic bugs) with teacher-created cards. The card contains a picture of the type of item and the number of items to hold in your cupped hand. The child draws a card and completes that challenge.
- Games that include dice (the child shakes the dice in her cupped hands until she reaches a number spun on a dial).
- Sock puppets (the child can make the puppet "talk" by opening and closing her hand).
- Plastic packing bubbles to pop with the fingers and palm.
- Tomy Waterfuls (games where the top is filled with water and you move small objects by pushing a button) (Myers, 1992).

Materials to Enhance Cutting

Cutting may occur in the art area, writing area, or the manipulative area. Children typically progress through developmental stages in cutting. They are first able to cut play dough with a plastic knife or scissors, next snip paper into small pieces, then fringe paper, and finally cut lines (creating strips for paper chains or cutting out newspaper comic strips). At the next stage, children are able to cut out geometric shapes, turning the paper with their holding hand. It is easier for children to cut with high-quality scissors using paper that is card weight.

Special Considerations for Infants and Toddlers

Some of the previously mentioned materials are appropriate for infants and toddlers such as pop together beads or colorforms to place on and pull off surfaces. Infant manipulative materials may be in baskets on the floor with each basket containing groups of similar items. It is recommended that toddlers age 2 or older have a formally designed manipulative area (Texas Child Care, 2005). Some manipulative materials that are suitable for infants and toddlers include

- A basket of different types of rattles.
- An assortment of small boxes to open and close, each filled with a surprise (stuffed toy, unbreakable mirror glued inside, jewelry, shiny key chain).

TIP   Many of the previous examples use everyday and found items instead of expensive store bought items to develop manipulative skills. This helps families to understand that everyday items in their homes can be used for learning experiences.

- Nesting boxes, bowls, or butter tubs to stack.
- Pots and pans with lids to take off and on.
- A decorated coffee can or hot chocolate can with a hole in the top with items that fit through the hole (the items can be changed when children lose interest in the current items).
- An empty tissue box with scarves to pull out.
- Simple puzzles.
- Busy boxes.
- Duplos or other snap-together building blocks.

Marlis, a teacher of infants, decorated a hot chocolate can. She cut a round hole in the plastic lid and placed an unstitched nylon mesh bath scrubby in the can. Children enjoyed pulling the nylon mesh out of the can and then stuffing it back in.

Special Considerations for Older Children

Teachers often abandon the manipulative center as children enter elementary school. However, it is important to continue to provide this center particularly since 10% to 34% of children experience handwriting difficulties (Rosenblum et al., 2003). Manipulative materials can assist children in developing the skills they need for handwriting and other fine motor tasks. Many of the activities listed previously are also appropriate for children in K–3 classrooms. Some additional, more challenging materials include

- Model building.
- Sewing (create costumes, clothing for dolls, pillows for dramatic play).
- Knitting.
- Weaving with a loom.
- Beading with small beads.
- Creating products with carpentry hand tools.
- Creating designs with nails.
- Making string art.
- Braiding.
- Yo–yos and hacky sacks.
- Folding origami and paper airplanes.
- Jacks and marbles.
- Playing string games like Cat in a Cradle.

This manipulative center for K–3 children is full of high-appeal materials. Note how informative books are also included.

Teachers' Facilitation of Learning in the Manipulative Center

Some teachers believe that the manipulative center might be one area in the classroom where children can learn on their own without teacher intervention. However, research indicates that teacher presence in the manipulative area is associated with more engagement in both the center and the materials

(Tomes, 1995). Some roles that teachers use to scaffold children's learning in this area include the following.

Introduce New Materials

Teachers might introduce materials to children as a group or individually as a child demonstrates readiness and shows interest. Introducing the materials assists children in knowing how to use them and also builds interest.

Keep the Center Interesting

Teachers keep the center interesting by adding new materials and removing materials children are no longer using. It is important that children have the opportunity to master materials and tools before teachers remove them.

Provide Encouragement and Recognition

Teachers can provide encouragement and recognition of children in the manipulative area by noticing what they are doing, making encouraging remarks, discussing their progress with them, and documenting their learning. Many teachers also provide a place for children to display products created in the center. For example, Tessa helped children in her afterschool program create a mobile from some of the paper airplanes they had created.

Provide Challenges

Many of the manipulative materials can be made more challenging. For example, if children have moved water from one cup to another using a baster, challenge them to move the water using an eyedropper, or to think of other ways they might move the water.

Teach Children the Correct Way to Use Tools

As children are developmentally ready, it is important to help them learn to use tools in the correct way. For scissors, the child should have the thumb and middle finger in the holes of the scissors and use the index finger to stabilize the scissors. While it is common that children hold the scissors with the thumb and index finger, this does not allow for the needed control (Myers, 1992). Proper scissor positioning and the opportunity to cut can enhance many areas of fine motor and hand development (Myers, 1992).

Provide Assistance to Children Who Are Struggling

Observe children. If they are struggling, it might be helpful to provide different tools or materials. For example, a child who is left-handed may be trying to cut with right-handed scissors. Providing left-handed scissors will allow the child to be successful. Another child may be unsuccessfully trying to cut tissue paper and becoming increasingly frustrated. If the child's goal is to cut, then providing a firmer paper will assist the child. If the child wants the tissue paper to be smaller, you could suggest tearing it.

Scaffold Children's Learning

There are several ways that teachers can scaffold children's learning. For example, a child may become frustrated when she is not able to complete a puzzle and might want you to complete it for her. Observe the child to determine what strategies she is currently using. This allows you to suggest other strategies she might try. For example, you might suggest she turn over each puzzle piece so it faces upright, find the outside edges first, look carefully at each piece, think about which puzzle pieces might be at the top of the puzzle, and look at the picture on the box.

Assist the Child with Proper Positioning

It is important to have proper body position for many fine motor activities. For example, it may be more difficult to cut effectively while leaning over to cut something placed on the floor than it is to sit at a table and cut at a waist-high level.

Encourage the Child to Cross the Midline

To cross the midline, the child must move a hand over the middle of the body. You can encourage children to do this by placing the activity on his dominant side with the container on the other side. Crossing the midline is an important task that children need to master in the early childhood years.

Be Aware of the Effects of Object Size

Children are more likely to use more advanced in-hand manipulation when using small-sized objects (½" to 1") (Exner, 1992). However, if you are working with infants and toddlers or any other children who mouth objects, you must make sure that any materials you are using will not pose a choking hazard.

Participate in Conversations with Children

The manipulative area often provides an ideal opportunity to engage in reciprocal conversations with individual or small groups of children. Conversations might include discussion of the materials or strategies the child is using. In addition, as children sit and put puzzles together or build with Legos they often will initiate conversations unrelated to the materials at hand.

Meet the Needs of All Learners

Children with Disabilities. While there are many disabilities, such as cerebral palsy, that are classified as physical disabilities, many other disabilities are not primarily physical but often co-occur with perceptuomotor deficits. This includes Attention Deficit Hyperactive Disorder (ADHD). In Nordic countries, a special diagnostic category recognizes this relationship, DAMP (deficits in attention, motor control, and perception) (Yochman, Ornoy, & Parush, 2006). Children with DAMP are slower and less accurate when performing fine motor tasks. The severity of the ADHD predicts the severity of fine motor skills. Other disabilities that often co-occur with poor fine motor control include Down's syndrome and Fetal Alcohol Syndrome (Bruni, 1998).

According to Losse et al., (1991), who studied the long-term effects of children with motor difficulties, it is crucial that even children with minor motor problems receive intervention in the early childhood years (1991). It is very important to intervene early since perceptuomotor activities greatly influence children's current and future learning (Yochman et al., 2006). In addition, support is necessary so that children can be successful in many everyday activities such as dressing, tying shoes, and using a fork to eat. Instruction and practice can assist children to improve their skills (Bruni, 1998). Unfortunately, children often do not choose to engage in activities they are poor at (Walsh, 2007). For example, kindergarten children who have difficulty with penmanship may avoid writing, thereby increasing the problem. Rather than having the child practice writing repeatedly, it is helpful to provide other activities that enhance fine motor control. These materials should appeal to the child's interest, so that he will choose to use them. Teachers should also provide appropriate materials so that the child can experience success. Providing needed assistance based on individualized observation is also important. For example, a child may have difficulty writing because she is not holding the paper with her non-writing hand. After observing this, the teacher can model how to hold the paper while

Scott was a 6-year-old child who had been diagnosed with ADHD and perceptual motor disabilities. His teacher first provided a variety of different types of pencil grips for Scott to experiment with. However, he continued to struggle with writing. Writing was tortuously slow and full concentration was required to write each letter. At an Individual Education Program (IEP) meeting, there was discussion about the negative effect of the fine motor deficit on Scott's overall learning. The team (Scott's mother, teacher, special education teacher, principal) decided on several modifications. They included

- Providing extended time for written and fine motor tasks.
- Reducing the amount of fine motor tasks by allowing verbal and tape recorded answers.
- Teaching Scott to type.
- Encouraging fine motor tasks that do not involve writing, such as model building.

Figure 8.1
Meeting Scott's
(a child with ADHD)
Needs

writing. Occupational therapy can also be an effective method for improving fine motor skills, especially when it includes teacher and family consultation and teacher training (Wehrmann et al., 2006). See Figure 8.1 to learn about other helpful strategies.

Children Who Come from Diverse Backgrounds. Children come to early childhood programs with vastly different experiences relating to fine motor skills. Children's interests and dispositions, resources available, and cultural values influence the amount of time children have devoted to this area. Since fine motor skills are so crucial in preschool and K–3 settings, it is important that teachers provide many opportunities for children who have less developed fine motor skills. Materials that reflect children's cultural backgrounds, especially items they see family members use, often have high appeal. For example, Puanani created an activity in her manipulative center in Hawaii with chopsticks, rice spoons, small seashells, and wooden sorting trays. Debbie, who has several children in her classroom whose parents are mechanics, added small engine parts for disassembling to her manipulative center. Both teachers found that children participated in manipulative activities more when these high-interest materials were available.

Children Who Are Left-Handed. Children who are left-handed face special challenges in a right-handed world. Between 8% and 10% of children are left-handed (Giagazoglou, Fotiadu, Angelopoulou, Tsikoulas, & Tsimaras, 2001). In one study, 90% of the children who were left-handed also had family members who were left-handed, suggesting a genetic link (Giagazoglou et al., 2001). Children who are left-handed often score more poorly in fine motor tasks (Giagazoglou et al., 2001). In the past, drastic efforts such as tying the left hand behind the child's back were made to change the hand dominance of children who were left-handed. However, we now recognize that this is inappropriate. Instead, it is important to provide tools, such as scissors, that are designed for children who are left-handed and to teach children the proper ways to position tools and materials to be successful.

Observe and Document Children's Learning

Unlike other areas such as art and writing that might produce a product that is saved, the manipulative center often does not produce a permanent product. Therefore, it is even more important to note children's progress, struggles, and accomplishments through techniques such as photos, checklists, or anecdotal records. For example, Samantha documents the progress of children in her kindergarten class by creating a checklist of items in the manipulative area. She then checks off an item if she sees the child successfully complete it. When Josyan matched all the nuts and bolts, she checked that item on her list. For ease of use, the checklist is hung on a clipboard in the area. To protect confidentiality, Samantha places a paper listing the skills that children learn in the manipulative area on top of the list. This provides information for families and other visitors. Other teachers document accomplishments and struggles with anecdotal records and with photos. Some questions you might want to consider in assessing and documenting children's learning include the following:

- Which hand does the child use?
- Does the child consistently use the dominant hand?
- Can the child use the pincer grasp?
- Is the web space rounded?
- Can the child effectively use both hands (bilateral coordination)?
- Can the child move individual fingers without the other fingers also moving?
- How does the child hold scissors?
- What is the child's skill level in cutting?
- Can the child effectively use the materials in the center?
  - String beads
  - Place nuts on bolts
  - Put together puzzles
  - Pour without spilling
- What type of strategies does the child use when completing puzzles or other activities? For example, does the child use trial and error or does he use more intentional methods?
- What is the child's attention span in using the manipulative materials?
- What type of materials does the child choose to use?
- What ideas do children have for using materials?

Manipulative skills are critical for children's current and future schooling success as well as for their quality of life. We know that a child's fine motor skills are partially based on her development. However, children also must have appropriate experiences to develop to their full potential. Therefore, as early childhood teachers, we have the obligation to provide children with rich, abundant, developmental, relevant, and interesting fine motor materials and experiences.

The Sensory Center

The sensory center, sometimes called a sand and water area or media table, is an area that is soothing, tension releasing, and open-ended, thereby making it failure proof for children (Koch, n.d.). Since the 1920s, when Margaret Lowenfeld introduced sand play, this area has been considered therapeutic. Sand, when combined with miniature people, animals, and houses, allows children to recreate and have control over their world (Stevens, 2004). Like the manipulative center, the sensory center also provides children the opportunity to develop fine motor and cognitive skills. In addition, the sensory center "fosters curiosity, imagination, and experimentation" (Crosser, 1994, p. 28) and, since children often use the center with others, social skills and language are also enhanced.

Designing an Effective Sensory Center

The focus of the sensory center is often a water or media table. While there are advantages to store-bought media tables including ease in draining, wheels for ease of moving, a lid to close the table when it is not in use, and a design that is the correct height for children,

Figure 8.2
Recipes for Sensory
Exploration

Three sensory materials that are popular with children are flubber, goop, and play dough.

Flubber Recipe
Mixture 1
1⅛ cups very warm water
2 teaspoon Borax (can be found in the laundry section of a grocery store)
Stir mixture 1 until Borax is completely dissolved. Set aside.

Mixture 2
1½ cup very warm water
2 cups Elmer's glue
Liquid watercolor
Thoroughly blend mixture 2.
Pour mixture 1 into mixture 2 and mix with hands until fully combined. Flubber is created by a chemical reaction. Use vinegar to clean up flubber. It dissolves the mixture.

Goop Recipe
Add one box of cornstarch to 1½ cups of water. Add water to the cornstarch until semifirm. If the mixture becomes too hard, add more water. You might want several boxes to provide enough mixture for a water table. You can also use this mixture in a cake pan or tray. To clean up goop from the floor, let it dry and then vacuum or sweep it up.

Play Dough Recipe
2 cups flour
1 cup salt
2 tablespoons alum
1 cup boiling water
2 tablespoons oil

Mix flour, salt, and alum in a large bowl. Make a dip in the center and add the oil and water. Mix together, adding more flour if too sticky or more water if too firm. Many teachers add Kool-Aid to the dough for the scent and the color.

there are many options for creating other sensory play environments (Koch, n.d.). These include the following:

- A wading pool or blow-up boat for whole body sensory experiences
- Homemade water tables
- Dishpans
- Baby bathtub
- Cardboard box for dry sensory play
- Serving tray for flubber, goop, or play dough (see Figure 8.2 for recipes)

Additional suggestions to create an effective sensory center include the following:

- Place the sensory table away from the wall so that children can access all sides of the table. Because children in the sensory center usually have their backs to the surrounding centers, it is not as necessary that the center be separated from the rest of the room by dividers.
- Provide low storage shelves on which to place baskets or tubs full of materials. A low pegboard on a nearby wall can also be helpful for hanging the clean-up tools and smocks.

Even a bowl, a washcloth, and a small amount of water provide sensory play for Seamus.

- Place the sensory center near a sink so that it is easy to fill and empty the water table. It is helpful to be able to run a hose directly from the sink faucet to fill the table. Specially designed tables also allow one to screw a hose onto the drain for emptying it. Olds (2001) recommends that the table be permanently connected to a water source and plumbed into a drain for ease of cleaning.

- Provide an easy to clean floor. If you have carpet you might consider duct taping a shower curtain or plastic runner under the table.

- Supply long-sleeved waterproof smocks that are easily accessible to children. These might be hung on hooks at the end of the water table or on a wall that is nearby.

- Include a battery operated hand-held vacuum, small broom and dustpan, and small sponge mops so that children can clean up the area when there is a spill or at the end of free play.

- Provide a variety of props to choose from that meet the children's interests. Begin by having children explore the media without props. When children have fully explored the media, add props to sustain interest and to provide new opportunities for exploration and learning.

- Add literacy materials—Contextual print and photographs can be used to label items in the area (to identify where the broom is kept or what is placed in the basket or tub). You can also add books to support the play of the children. For example, Mrs. Ames's kindergarten class visited a farm as part of a study on mammals. Many of the children had little previous exposure to farm life and were interested in recreating, in the sandbox, what they had seen. Mrs. Ames added farm props along with books about farm life to expand their experience. Children used the books as a reference as they created their own farm.

- Provide a safe and healthy experience. According to the National Health and Safety Standards (2002), to prevent the spread of infectious diseases it is important to observe the following precautions:

  - Water needs to be emptied after each group of children is done playing, and the tub and the toys must be washed and sanitized daily.

  - Make sure that children with cuts, scratches, and open sores do not use the table or that they wear disposable rubber gloves.

  - Children should wash their hands both before and after playing in the sensory table.

  - Be aware of children's allergies in your classroom and avoid any materials that the children might be allergic to.

  - Do not use materials that pose a choking hazard if working with younger children.

  - Clean up the floor when spills occur so that the floor is not slippery.

  - Make sure that bleach is not added to the water.

While following these rules may seem daunting, many teachers involve the children in assisting with clean-up. For example, at Kid's World Preschool children enjoy helping to fill and empty the water table. They also use child-size cleaning tools to keep the floor clean and dry. Their teacher, Alexandria, has found that the time required to maintain the table is worth the effort since children are so engaged with the media.

Appropriate Materials for the Sensory Center

The sensory table can be filled with a variety of media. The most common are water, sand, dirt, and a combination of these. However, your imagination is the only boundary in thinking of other safe sensory materials with which to fill the table. Props add additional play and learning opportunities. While you might find many of these same materials in the science area, the primary purpose in this center is to provide sensory stimulation. However, as children explore the media, they will also be developing concepts.

Water

As children play in water, they gain therapeutic, social, physical, and cognitive benefits. They also have the opportunity to learn many scientific concepts, such as water flows when it is poured, water takes on many forms, water dissolves some materials, and water takes the form of the container it is in. Some materials float in water while other items sink. Some materials absorb water while others are water resistant. Water can be used for cleaning objects (Schwarz, 2007). Your goals for water play and the children's interests will help determine the materials that you will add. For example, you can add

- Different herbs or other scents.
- Colored dye.
- Ping-pong balls, shells, and small plastic fish with tongs, aquarium nets, or scoops.
- Ice cubes with tongs.
- Bubbles mixture and materials for creating a variety of bubble-making wands.
- Soap flakes, eggbeaters, and hand whisks.
- Materials for sinking and floating experimentation (for example, children can collect a variety of seeds to see which will sink and float—coconuts, rose hips, nuts in shells) (Crosser, 1994).
- Corks, Styrofoam, and tinfoil to create boats.
- Sponges, wash cloths, and baby shampoo for washing dolls.
- A clothesline, clothespins, and doll clothes for washing the clothes and hanging them to dry.
- Plastic animals and toys.
- Play dishes, pots, and pans with dishrags, sponges, and a drying rack.
- Cars and trucks with a chamois for drying them.

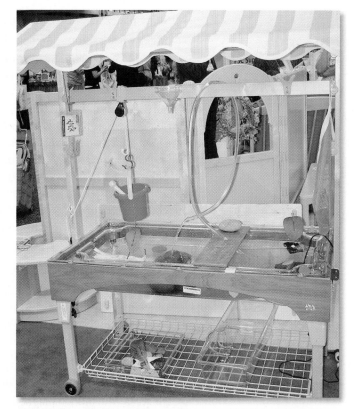

Leaves, twigs, and bark become boats in this water table. Note also how the cross bar on this water table creates many possibilities for using pulleys, funnels, and tubing to learn science concepts.

- Magnetic fish with a magnet hook hanging from a child-size fishing pole.
- Ice blocks—allow children to choose a container to fill with water and freeze. These different sizes of ice blocks can be placed in the water table. Children can also freeze items in the ice such as small plastic animals, figures, bugs, or flowers.
- A block of ice with a squirt bottle of colored salt water, plastic knives, small rubber hammers, and safety goggles for creating ice sculptures.
- Basters, eyedroppers, ladles, spoons, pitchers, sponges, and water cans for moving water.
- Tubing, PVC pipe, accordion tubing, marble works, and funnels for developing more advanced means for moving water. You might want to suspend the funnel over the table to enhance interest and give children a starting point for their experimentation.
- Pumps such as bilge pumps, kerosene pumps, and pumps found in liquid soaps (Chalufour & Worth, 2005).
- Different sizes of containers and measuring cups for experimenting with conservation.
- Shiny plates and bowls to experiment with reflections.
- Water wheels (store-purchased or child-created).
- A bubble wall made by attaching a hook in the ceiling and adding a pulley, PVC pipe, and rope (school-age children).

Children in Katie's classroom were very interested in experimenting with water flow. She moved the water table near a wall and placed a piece of metal between the wall and the table. She added items with magnets on the back that children could use for their water flow experimentation (funnels, water jugs that included spigots, small pieces of rain gutter). She also added magnetic clips that children could use to hold cups or plastic containers. The children would place the water jug on the top of the metal backdrop and then experiment with the arrangement of the other items. By opening the spigot on the water jug, they could observe how the water flowed through the objects.

Sand

Sand is another natural material that is therapeutic and provides many learning opportunities. Following are some concepts that children can learn while playing with sand: Sand can be dry or wet. It absorbs water. Wet sand is heavier than dry sand. You can mold wet sand. Different types of sand have different textures. Objects can be hidden and found in sand (Schwarz, 2007). You can add the following materials to enrich sand play:

- Small cars, dump trucks, bulldozers
- Magnets with hidden magnetic treasures to find in the sand (Hill & Berlfein, 2000)
- Magnifying glasses to closely examine grains of sand (Hill & Berlfein, 2000)
- Sand wheels
- Small rakes and combs for creating designs
- Sifters and funnels of different types
- Shovels, scoops, spoons
- Play dishes, small empty food boxes, egg cartons

Children at Livingston Head Start visited the Museum of the Rockies to see the life-size dinosaur exhibit. They also witnessed and were fascinated by the paleontologist who was painstakingly removing rock from around a bone. Later, their teacher, Cathy, hid bones encased in plaster of paris in the sand table. When children discovered them, they requested tools to remove the bones. Cathy provided toothbrushes and small plastic knives for the children.

Sand and Water

"Patting and poking, piling and smoothing, the children's eager hands turned the sand area into a fairyland of shapes" (Hill & Berlfein, 1977, p. 18). To enhance play with sand and water, add the following:

- People, houses, and animals for creating habitat
- Stones, sticks, and other loose parts for expanding the habitat
- Rocks and wood for making islands and bridges
- Pie tins, muffin tins, and other smooth-sided containers to use as molds

Other Tactile Items That Can Be Added to the Sensory Table

Different media have unique attributes providing varied possibilities for children's sensory experiences. Some potential materials include snow (add gloves), dirt, clean mud, leaves, cedar chips, pine needles and boughs, shredded paper or paper punches, paper scraps, sawdust, goop, cotton, used dried coffee grounds, scraps of different kinds of fabric, aquarium or pea gravel, seashells, animal food or bedding (if studying a certain animal), Styrofoam peanuts, flubber, recycled items (plastic pieces, juice can lids, old CDs), or items with different textures.

Teachers' Facilitation of Learning in the Sensory Center

As in all areas of the classroom, it is important that you, as the teacher, take cues from the children about the degree of your involvement with them in the sensory center. Sometimes involvement can be as unobtrusive as observing and recording children's play. At other times, you may join in the activity, particularly with very young children. It may be helpful to have a chair to sit in, so you are at the same level as the children. Following are a variety of ways that teachers may be involved in the sensory center.

Extend Children's Learning

Teachers can extend children's learning by adding relevant props and materials. For example, Jeremiah observed that the children were creating roads in the sand table. He added small wooden traffic signs from a toy train set along with some buildings. The children began to incorporate these into their play, expanding their learning.

Create New Puzzlements

Children have the desire to make sense of their world (Piaget, 1954). Therefore, "puzzling, novel situations can promote learning" (Crosser, 1994, p. 28).

The toddlers in Corentine's classroom had been playing with cups, filling them with water, and pouring the water into a bowl. Corentine added two new cups to the area. One had one hole punched in the bottom and the other had three holes punched in the bottom. The toddlers were intrigued by the new cups. Aaron began to experiment to see if he could still scoop the water with the new cup and place it in the bowl. Alicia watched Aaron for a few minutes and then filled the cup that had three holes. Using it as a sieve, she held it above the bowl. Both Aaron and Alicia watched the water drain into the bowl. Aaron then began to fill the new-found sieve with water from a cup that did not have holes.

Promote New Vocabulary Acquisition

Incorporating new vocabulary within conversations is an effective way to help children to learn new words. You can label tools (colander, sieve, funnel, eggbeater, ladle), processes (strain, flow), and characteristics of the media (coarse, grainy, gritty). Often positional words (above, below), words that express relationships (larger than, less than), and other mathematical terms (none, numerals) can also be stressed.

Ask Open-Ended Questions

Encourage children to problem-solve and predict what will happen by asking open-ended questions. For example, you might ask, "How many cups will it take to fill the container?" "Will both containers hold the same amount of water?" "How much cargo (small plastic boxes) do you think your boat will hold?" "What are other materials you might use?"

Create Challenges

When children are interested and developmentally ready you might create a challenge. For example, you might challenge children to create a boat, a bridge, or a water wheel.

Facilitate Pro-Social Play

There are several ways that teachers can promote pro-social play in the sensory center. Teachers can help children to understand another child's point of view: "Terrence gets upset when you take the boat he is playing with." Modeling pro-social language is another way to encourage pro-social play: "Anita wonders if she can share the waterwheel with you." Encouraging children to work together on a project such as designing a bridge over their river can also help children to develop pro-social skills.

Create Limits and Simple Rules

Because of the limited space around the sensory table, too many children can limit play opportunities and may lead to aggression. Therefore, many teachers place limits on the number of children allowed at the table. If they find that more children want to use the area, they set up individual tubs on tables that are nearby. Some teachers help children to remember the limits by only providing four aprons and requiring that all children using the table wear an apron. Other rules for successful use of the center are typically developed with the children. For example, "The water and sand stay in the table."

Meet the Needs of All Learners

"Water play is developmentally appropriate regardless of the child's physical condition, mental condition, age, language, gender, culture, or exceptionality" (Crosser, 1994, p. 28). This is true for all sensory materials. However, make sure that the water table is the correct height for the children that are using it. Children usually stand when they are using a media table. But if you have a child in a wheelchair, the water table will need to be lower. Tennille built a stair step water table. One end was the right height for someone who was sitting, while the other end was the right height for a child who was standing. This allowed Natalie, who used a wheelchair, to access the water table. It also allowed other children the option of standing or sitting while using the table.

The sensory center is especially important for children who have sensory integration dysfunction (SID), a neurological condition where children have difficulty receiving information from their senses. Children with this condition may be under or overly sensitive to sensory stimulation. This area allows the child who desperately seeks physical sensory stimulation to receive it. It can also be helpful to the child who is overly sensitive to stimulation. These children feel constantly bombarded by stimulation over which they have no control. In the sensory area, they are in control of the sensory input they receive. They also gain the therapeutic benefits of the play.

Observe and Document Individual Children's Learning

Observing and documenting children learning at the sensory center assists teachers in learning about and documenting individual children's development. It also assists teachers to know what types of materials or experiences could be added to the center to meet individual children's needs. Some questions you might answer while observing in the sensory center include the following:

- What tactile activities does the child engage in?
- How does the child interact with the material? For example, does the child cautiously touch the media only with her fingertips or does she use her whole hand and arm?
- What type of play is the child engaged in—unoccupied, onlooker, solitary, parallel, associative, or cooperative (See Chapter 1 for definitions of each type.)
- What strategies does the child use to enter play with others?
- What type of scenarios does the child role-play?
- What fine motor, problem-solving, math, and science skills do you see the child using?

Special Challenges in the Manipulative and Sensory Center
Families Who Do Not Want Their Children to Get Dirty

Some people believe that their parenting skills are being judged by the clothes that their children are wearing. Therefore, they send children to early childhood programs in their best clothes, warning children to stay clean. You can use several strategies in this situation. In some cases, providing information to the parents about the value of "messy" activities and asking them to send children to school in play clothes produces results. In other cases, providing smocks that totally cover the child's clothing is sufficient. In still other cases, children might change into play clothes after they reach the center.

Children Who Are Overly Sensitive to Stimulation or Concerned with Getting Their Hands Dirty

Some children who display sensory defensiveness (an intolerance of many normal sensory experiences) might not want to touch the media. Other children may not wish to get their hands dirty. In these cases, it is often helpful to offer the child nonlatex gloves to wear when using the media. This allows the child to play with messy materials, while respecting her personal needs. You might also provide props so the child can experience the play without actually touching the media. Modeling play with sensory materials might also provide encouragement for the child to use sensory media. However, it is important to never force a child to use the materials.

Outdoor Manipulative and Sensory Play

Children gain many manipulative and sensory experiences outdoors. While there is often not a specific manipulative center, most programs provide outdoor sand and water play. Many of the ideas mentioned for indoor sand and water play are also appropriate on the

Sand play is enriched in this outdoor area through the addition of props. Pay special attention to how the props are stored.

playground (see Chapter 17 for additional suggestions in this area). Other ideas include the following:

- Establish a car wash—add sponges, spray bottles, and chamois for children to wash bikes, trikes, and other riding toys (Crosser, 1994).

- Provide large paintbrushes and water so children can paint the side of buildings and sidewalks.

- Spray paint a sheet with colored water.

- Add gutters to the sand area—Sue Dinwiddie (1993) describes using rain gutters with pre-school-age children. She states that three or four gutters cut into different lengths (5, 3⅓, 7½, and 2½ feet) were sufficient for in-depth play. Children used the gutters to transport sand, water, mixtures of sand and water, vehicles, and balls. They experimented with slope and angles, different mixtures and solutions, and different ways of transporting the solutions.

- Add a variety of molds and props to the moist sand area for making sand castles. Molds can be made with any type of open container with smooth sides (yogurt containers, milk cartons with the tops cut off). Feathers, sticks, rocks, shells, and other natural materials can enhance creations. You might also want to add signs or materials to create signs for children who want to save their sand castles (West & Cox, 2001).

Sand and water are basic elements of the earth that can soothe the soul while providing many learning opportunities. All age groups enjoy sensory play, from the youngest baby who is interacting with a sensory quilt to the 90-year-old grandmother walking barefoot on a sandy beach. In today's busy, fully scheduled world, children need the opportunity to experience messiness and open-ended materials.

In both the manipulative and sensory center, children can successfully engage in either individual or group play. A well-developed center gives children the opportunity to use fine motor skills, practice eye–hand coordination, and at times create imaginary worlds.

Sample Application Activities

1. Observe children using a manipulative center. What specific fine motor skills are they demonstrating? What additional materials could you add to further enhance these skills?

2. Review the opening scenario. Make a list of additional sensory or manipulative materials the teacher might add to the boat for infants or toddlers.

3. Assess a manipulative or sensory center using the environmental assessment found in Figure 8.3.

4. Experiment with different media. What words would you use to describe the materials? What other new vocabulary words could you introduce?

In assessing the manipulative center, consider the following. Does the center contain

☐ a quiet, uninterrupted area to work?
☐ an area that is well lighted, preferably with natural light?
☐ low, open, labeled shelves to hold materials?
☐ trays or baskets to hold all the materials needed for each discrete activity?
☐ enough materials to provide four to six children with several choices each?
☐ storage for additional materials?
☐ horizontal surfaces, including tables, chairs, and floor space?
☐ vertical surfaces?
☐ aesthetic materials?
☐ materials of high interest to the children?
☐ materials that meet the children's developmental needs?
☐ high-quality tools such as scissors?

In assessing the sensory center, consider the following. Does the center provide

☐ a sensory table placed so children can access all sides?
☐ storage for materials to use in the center?
☐ a nearby sink or other water source for easy cleaning?
☐ an easy to clean floor?
☐ long-sleeved waterproof smocks that are easily accessible to children?
☐ child-size cleaning implements?
☐ a variety of interesting props?
☐ a safe and healthy experience?
  • water emptied after each group of children is done playing
  • tub and toys washed and sanitized daily
  • children with cuts, scratches, and open sores do not use the table or they wear rubber gloves
  • children and adults wash their hands both before and after playing in the sensory table
  • any materials, that the children in the classroom might be allergic to are avoided
  • materials do not pose a choking hazard (if younger children are in the classroom)
  • floor is cleaned when spills occur
  • water is bleach free
☐ literacy materials, including contextual print?

Figure 8.3
Environmental Assessment: Manipulative and Sensory Centers

Source: Permission is granted by the publisher to reproduce this figure for evaluation and record-keeping. From Julie Bullard, *Creating Environments for Learning: Birth to Age Eight.* Copyright © 2010 by Pearson Education, Inc. All rights reserved.

5. Observe different children using the media table. What primary purpose (social interaction, sensory, problem solving, reenacting a familiar scene, dramatic play) do they appear to be achieving through the play?

6. Review one of the following websites to gain additional information about topics in this chapter.

Learn more about sensory integration at the Sensory Processing Disorder Foundation at http://www.spdfoundation.net/

Learn more about children's physical developmental milestones at the National Center on Birth Defects and Developmental Disabilities at http://www.cdc.gov/ncbdd/autism/actearly/

chapter 9
Developing Science Centers

*O*ne day several children in Kelly's class of 3- to 6-year-olds found caterpillars on the playground. After examining them, Kelly and the children decided that they would like to find out more about caterpillars. They began their research by studying caterpillar habitat. Kelly and the children observed where the caterpillars lived in their playground, looked through books, and invited an expert on insects to visit. They then developed habitats for the caterpillars that they placed in the science center. One of the children's parents found cocoons in their yard and these were also added to the science center. Kelly added journals to *the center so that children could draw and record their theories and their findings. For example, children drew their theories on metamorphosis, drew their observations of the different stages, and drew sketches of moths and butterflies based on observation. Through discussions and by examining the pictures children drew, Kelly could see what current ideas and misconceptions the children held. This helped her to plan relevant experiences. Kelly also added a life-cycle seriation game, a self-correcting classification game featuring insects and noninsects, and both nonfiction resource books and children's fictional books about butterflies, moths, and other insects to the science center.*

Kelly carefully thought about the concepts she hoped children would develop as part of this study. She chose two "big concepts" to stress: (1) basic needs of living things and (2) life cycles. She also developed a list of facts specifically related to insects and butterflies that she posted in the center, so that she and other adults in the classroom could share the information with children as they were interacting and discussing the insects in the science center. Two interesting facts she discovered were that insects comprise about 53% of animal life in the world (Danoff-Burg, 2003, p. 33) and that 90% of bugs go through metamorphosis. She also made a list of vocabulary words that she wanted to stress (chrysalis, cocoon, larva, metamorphosis, pupae, egg, silk, thorax, abdomen, caterpillar, entomology) and posted these in the center. Again, she and other adults intentionally used these words both in individual discussions with children and during group times.

*At the beginning of the project, Kelly and the children made a KWHL chart about butterflies and moths (what I **k**now, what I **w**ant to know, **h**ow I will find out, and what I **l**earned). This helped to activate children's prior knowledge and discover questions they had. It also served as documentation of learning at the completion of the center. The children and Kelly frequently revisited their questions during group time to see what questions had been answered and to add new questions. Some of their questions included, "Do all caterpillars make the same kind of butterfly?" "Do all caterpillars turn into butterflies?" "What does the pupa eat?" Whenever possible, they found out their answers through experimentation. For example, they found caterpillars in their yard and watched to see if they all spun cocoons. They experimented with what the pupa ate by offering them a variety of different types of food. In addition to revisiting their questions during group times, Kelly used this time to read books about insects that she then placed in the science center. Children developed plans for their experiments and discussed new things they had discovered while interacting in the science center. Kelly also used group times to focus on the "big ideas," life cycles and basic needs of living things. They discussed their own basic needs as well as the needs of the butterflies. Each of these group times served to reinforce the children's hands-on learning in the science center.*

By the end of the study, children were actively using several of the vocabulary words in their discussions. They were able to discuss habitat requirements for butterflies and compare them to their own needs. They were able to sequence the life-cycle seriation game and to describe metamorphosis. They also knew several facts about butterflies and moths: Butterflies are insects and insects have six legs, an outside skeleton, three parts to their body, and a pair of antennae. Children also discovered through careful observation that butterflies have an elongated knob on the end of their antennae and that moths do not. Through this center and the accompanying activities children learned science process skills, concepts, and content.

Apply Your Knowledge   If you were Kelly, how would you further develop children's knowledge of living things and life cycles?

Children are scientists who are naturally curious and biologically primed to learn about the world around them (French, 2004). They use the information they gain through their everyday experiences to develop theories about how the world works. For this reason, the early years are recognized as "years of promise" in the area of science (Carnegie Task Force, 1996). However, as children try to make sense of the world, they may also develop misconceptions.

History of Science Education

Science curriculum began to appear in American schools in the late 1800s. However, in the past sixty years there has been an increased interest in science due to international competition and the increased needs of the workforce.

In 1957, when the Soviet Union launched Sputnik, it was the first country to launch a satellite into space. This event created a flurry of interest in science curriculum in the United States. Curriculum interest and reform has also been prompted due to ongoing concern about how American children fare in international science and math comparisons. For example, children in Japan and China are approximately one year ahead of middle-class American children. American middle-class children are one year ahead of American low-income children (Prentice Starkey in National Research Council, 2005).

There also has been an increased interest due to the need for a scientifically literate workforce. As stated by the Glenn Commission, "At the daybreak of this new century and millennium . . . the future well-being of our nation and people depends not just on how well we educate our children generally, but on how well we educate them in mathematics and science specifically" (2000, p. 6).

The foundation for scientific knowledge begins in early childhood. Since children are trying to make sense of the world, they develop their own theories about how the world works, whether accurate or inaccurate. As stated by Karen Lind (1998) (an early childhood science author), one of the strongest themes in the national standards is "that all children can learn science and that all children should have the opportunity to become scientifically literate. In order for this learning to happen, the effort to introduce children to the essential experiences of science inquiry and explorations must begin at an early age" (p. 73).

Children's Development of Scientific Concepts

The development of scientific concepts is crucial to the understanding and use of scientific knowledge. Researchers have written more than 7,000 journal articles during the past thirty years about children's development of scientific concepts (Gelman, 1999, p. 50). This research has challenged previous thinking about children's concept development. The following four themes have been identified:

- Concepts are tools that have powerful implications for children's reasoning—both positive and negative.

- Children's early concepts are not necessarily concrete or perceptually based. Even preschool children are capable of reasoning about nonobvious, subtle, and abstract concepts.
- Children's concepts are not uniform across content areas, across individuals, or across tasks.
- Children's concepts reflect their emerging 'theories' about the world. To the extent that children's theories are inaccurate, their conceptions are also biased. (Gelman, 1999, p. 50)

As we develop science centers, it is important that we try to understand children's current theories. We also need to help children link what they are learning to larger concepts. Concepts help children organize information. They also act as building blocks for learning. Concepts help children with cognitive tasks such as "identifying objects in the world, forming analogies, making inferences that extend knowledge beyond what is known, and conveying core elements of a theory" (Gelman, 1999, p. 51).

How the Science Center Enhances Children's Development

"The cognitive skills in mathematics and science displayed by young children are not only the roots of later literacy in those areas, they are the building blocks in the development of the capacity to comprehend complex relationships and reason about those relationships" (National Research Council, 2005, p. 4). Through science, children also learn skills that transfer to other curriculum areas. For example, they improve their ability to observe, problem solve, collect and organize data, and to create hypotheses and test them. They add to their vocabulary and learn to communicate information. They develop concepts about the world around them. As they engage in science, children often use math and literacy skills in authentic ways. For example, children in Kelly's classroom used math skills as they counted the number of butterflies that hatched each day and created a graph of what the pupa liked to eat. They used literacy skills as they learned new vocabulary, wrote stories about the butterflies, read the fiction and nonfiction books about insects, and created a class metamorphosis book.

Children are naturally curious. Well-designed science centers and activities build upon this curiosity promoting children's wonder, joy in experimentation, and love of exploration.

But what specific content and skills should children learn in the early childhood years? The process skills children need to learn are fairly clear (National Research Council, 2005). Children need to learn to observe, compare, classify, measure, quantify, represent data, interpret representations, predict, and communicate. In a preschool curriculum called ScienceStart, Conezio and French (2003) have broken these process skills into a four-step cycle.

- Ask and reflect—What is the question? What do we already know about it?
- Plan and predict—How will you address the question? What is the plan? What do you predict will happen?
- Act and observe—Put the plan into action. Observe the results.
- Report and reflect—Share information with others (tell someone, dictate, draw, make a chart, create a song, put on a skit). (p. 11)

However, appropriate science content is limitless and it is not clear what content is critical or important in the early years (National Research Council, 2005). Many believe that what children specifically study is not as important as linking what is studied to the "big picture" or to "big ideas" (Klein, Hammrich, Bloom, & Ragins, 2000). "A big idea can be described in two ways: as involving an enduring principle that transcends its origins, subject matter or place in time; and as a linchpin idea—one crucial to a student's ability to understand a subject" (Wiggins & McTighe, 1998, p. 113). Big ideas can be understood by both novices and experts but at different levels. As one studies "big ideas" new questions often arise.

Designing an Effective Science Center
Purpose of the Science Center

While science can occur throughout the classroom, it is important to provide a focus on science by having a science center. In the science center, children can spend intensive time observing, predicting, experimenting, using scientific tools, practicing processes, and learning content. However, in one study, only 50% of the early childhood classrooms had a science center (Tu, 2006). Tu found that even when there were items that lent themselves to science discussions, often none occurred. For example, while 70% of the classrooms had plants in the room, there was no discussion or child involvement with the plants (Tu, 2006).

Types of Science Centers

Science centers may focus on a current theme or project or be isolated from other current curriculum. They may be organized in different ways.

- Some teachers develop science boxes that are available throughout the year. Each box contains materials around a different topic and children have the choice of choosing from many different activities. For example, Sherwood (2005) develops ABC science shoeboxes. Each box is created for an individual or a small group. For example, Sherwood's (2005) "A" box contains materials (eyedroppers, water cup, materials to test for absorption, record sheet for drawing results) on the concept of absorption, "B" contains a variety of toys emphasizing the concept of balance, and "M" contains magnet activities. The National Science Education Standards published by the National Science Teachers Association (NSTA) stress the need for depth over breadth of topics covered. The approach described above exposes children to a variety of science activities. It also may be a way to allow children to follow up on previously introduced activities or centers. However, it may be difficult to provide the needed depth for optimum learning when there are so many concepts to focus on.

- Science centers can also focus on inquiry, where children are encouraged to focus on a question or questions to answer. After a local oil spill that coated birds' feathers in oil, teachers and children in one school explored the following questions: "What happens to a duck feather when it is coated with oil?" "What will remove the oil from a bird's feather?" Duck feathers (some that were coated in oil) and a tub of water were placed in the center. The center also contained a variety of tools and substances to remove the oil (brainstormed by the teacher and children). Children kept track of their experiments with a picture chart where they circled any item that cleaned the oil and crossed out any item that did not (Charlesworth & Lind, 2007). Like scientists, as children engage in these in-depth inquiries they use science process skills (developing and testing hypotheses and communicating results) while answering their questions. When the inquiry is relevant to children, these centers can be highly motivating, building upon children's natural curiosity. The teacher in this approach to centers will often introduce the inquiry at a large-

or small-group circle and then place the materials in the science center for children to use during center time.

- A science center can also be a discovery center (Charlesworth & Lind, 2007) where children, instead of pursuing an answer to a specific question, might be exploring scientific concepts. A discovery center will often have less specific outcomes than an inquiry center. For example, at a preschool center children were completing a long-term project on cars. The science center contained a variety of car parts that children could examine, explore, disassemble, and reassemble. The teacher helped children to explore the concept of how tools help us as they tried to disassemble parts with and without tools and using different types of tools. The children also explored pulleys and gears.

- Science centers can also contain inquiry tools that children can use throughout the classroom. For example, children might use measuring tools to determine if the plants growing by the window grow faster than the plants that do not have the natural light. They might be building structures in the block area and be using the pulley to design an elevator that will carry items from one floor to the next.

Setting Up the Science Center

Regardless of the type of center you choose to create, it is important that the center

- Is in an enclosed area in the quiet area of the classroom, allowing for uninterrupted work and concentration.
- Is near a sink since many of the activities might require water for experiments and clean up.
- Is large enough to accommodate several children and the teacher.
- Is near a window (if possible) since many explorations need natural light.
- Provides an organized, labeled science table and shelving to highlight and store materials.
- Provides adequate work space, often a table and chairs, since many times children will need to spread out materials housed on the science table or shelf to complete them.
- Contains a bulletin board for posting science information and findings.
- Is designed to encourage cooperation and communication between learners (Charlesworth & Lind, 2007).
- Is enticing. Kelly provides lab coats to make the science center more interesting to the children in her room. Rene uses visors with "scientist" written on them to designate the number of children in the center and to assist children in assuming the scientist's role. Some teachers develop an enticing science enclosure such as a tent or cave for a science lab. Many teachers introduce the center to the group at circle time, building interest through a teaser.

Choosing Materials and Activities for the Science Center

To effectively meet children's needs and help them to acquire scientific knowledge, skills, and dispositions, we need to choose materials and activities for our science center that meet the following criteria:

- It is designed for action rather than just for looking (Charlesworth & Lind, 2007). Young children learn through active engagement with materials and ideas. For example, in the butterfly center Kelly provided journals for sketching

This science center houses child-collected natural materials such as feathers, pinecones, rocks, shells, and bones. Different strengths of magnifying glasses provide an interactive feature, keeping the center from only being a display. The binoculars are another tool that encourages children to view the world differently.

the butterflies' transformations, graphs to record the number of days in each stage of metamorphosis, and magnifying glasses for closer examination of the pupae and butterflies. If she had not provided these materials, children would have had limited engagement other than just looking at the butterflies. As stated by Greenman, "A creative science area is more laboratory than museum" (2005a, p. 269).

- It is relevant to the children in the classroom. The emphasis in science centers for this age needs to be on things that children can actually touch and feel. For example, in Hawaii this might include tide pools, oceans, volcanoes, rain, local flowers, and native insects. Children are curious about the world outside the classroom that affects their immediate lives. As they have relevant experiences with the world surrounding them, it allows for the joy of discovery and active experimentation.

- It is built upon current knowledge, background, and previous activities so that it is developmentally appropriate for the group of children using the center.

- It encourages "what if" statements (Charlesworth & Lind, 2007). One way of encouraging this is to provide open-ended materials that allow for different variations so that children can extend their experiments. For example, if experimenting with connected tubes to create a marble roll activity, the child should be able to take the tubes apart and assemble them in different ways. Different weights or sizes of marbles can also be provided for more variability. Other types of tubing can also increase the amount of variation.

- It stresses process skills (ask and reflect, plan and predict, act and observe, report and reflect) (Conezio & French, 2003, p. 11) by providing materials needed to perform these tasks such as ways of recording ideas and plans, materials for close observation, and ways of reflecting what the child has learned.

- It exposes children to specific content related to the topic being studied.

- It ties into bigger overriding concepts or "big ideas." For example, in studying any topic relating to biology, some big ideas that can be stressed are life cycles and living versus nonliving. Even one- and 2-year-old children are "adept at concept acquisition." This helps them to organize information and prevents the world from being a chaotic place (Gelman, 1999, p. 50).

- It allows for individual differences by providing open-ended material or a variety of tasks at different levels.

- It allows children to use the center independently:
  - all needed materials are available
  - materials are arranged in a logical order or sequence

- there is a clearly designated place for each item
- materials are within the children's reach
- if there are directions for completing an activity, they are provided through pictures, written, tape recorded, or introduced at circle time

- It encourages children to represent their knowledge (paper, graph paper, tape recorders, journals, recording sheets, clipboards, pencils, and markers).
- It contains resource materials such as books, posters, videos, and a computer.
- It contains inquiry tools such as magnifying glasses of different types, microscope, Petri dishes, scales, eyedroppers, pulleys, tweezers, twine, clay for imprints, specimen bags and boxes, and nets.
- It includes science content background sheets and a list of vocabulary to be stressed so adults can scaffold children's learning. The background sheets should also include the "big ideas" or overriding concepts being stressed.

Perhaps because so many early childhood teachers are uncomfortable with science, science centers are often lacking or not fully developed in early childhood settings. It is important when developing a science center to make sure that it provides tools, resources, and materials needed for active engagement and for documenting learning. Children need time for in-depth exploration. It is unnecessary and counterproductive to change the center each week. However, it is important that the teacher adds materials and changes the center to answer new questions emerging from the children.

Science Center Environments That Support Children's Learning

In this section, we will examine some possible science center materials and activities for preschool and early elementary grades in the areas of science tools, physical science, life science, and earth and space science. We will examine the big ideas or concepts that the activities and materials promote, the standards that are being addressed by the materials and activities, and when applicable some common misconceptions that children might hold. These centers are typically introduced to the children during a small- or large-group activity. Children then complete the explorations during center time.

Using Science Tools

The "big idea" or overriding concept in studying science tools is that "tools such as thermometers, magnifiers, rulers, or balances often give more information about things than can be obtained by just observing things without their help" (American Association for the Advancement of Science, 1993, p. 10).

For example, Kendis and her class of kindergarten children studied magnification. During the study, children

- Compared different strengths of magnifying glasses
- Compared different types of magnifying glasses to determine which were easier to use for different purposes
- Explored different types of machines that magnify (overhead projector, telescope, binoculars)
- Explored water drop magnifiers by placing waxed paper over a newspaper and adding different sizes of drops over the letters

In addition to containing the different magnification tools, the science center contained books on magnification, interesting small items to examine with the magnifying glasses (a collection of coins, different kinds of bugs, assortment of rocks), graphs for recording results, and prediction charts. Kendis also prepared a fact sheet on magnification and a list of vocabulary words relating to magnification. She posted these along with the overriding concept on the wall in the center. Kendis scaffolded children's learning at the center by listening carefully to their theories. The children believed that the larger the magnifying glass, the more powerful it was. They had found that to be true by examining the magnifying glasses in the center. To dispel this misconception, Kendis introduced some new, even larger (but weaker) magnifying glasses. By continuing their exploration, the children found that their theory was not accurate. Through this activity, the children learned about tools and magnification, engaged in science process skills (making and testing predictions), and used literacy (read books) and math skills (developed graphs).

Physical Science Standards

Physical science is the study of nonliving things. For early elementary age children the goals in this area are to study

- The properties of objects and things
- Position and motion of objects
- Light, heat, electricity, and magnetism (National Academy of Science, 1996, p. 123)

Worth and Groller (2003, p. 68) have further clarified the standards for preschool children to be the study of

- Properties of solids and the properties of liquids
- Position and motion of objects
- Properties and characteristics of sounds and light

Physical Science Learning Center Activities

Some sample activities for science centers that allow children to gain an understanding of physical science include liquids, bubbles, float and sink, movement, and magnets.

Liquids. Two important concepts that children can learn relating to liquids are that (1) liquids have different properties that can be described and (2) liquids take the shape of the container they are in. To help children explore liquids, teachers might provide pictures or written task cards and materials so that children can do the following:

- Drop (dish soap, oil, honey, water, corn syrup, and vinegar) onto paper towels or coffee filters to examine the absorbency of different liquids.
- Drop a liquid onto different materials (cloth, newspaper, waxed paper, aluminum foil, construction paper) to see the absorbency of different surfaces.
- Look at the drops with a magnifying glass.
- Make the largest drop possible (children can use straws, basters, and eyedroppers).
- Make the smallest possible drop that can still be seen, using toothpicks.
- Add water to the different liquids to see what happens. Will the water mix with the other liquid?
- Drop color into the different kinds of liquids.

- Put water and oil in a bottle to examine density (vegetable oil floats because it is less dense than water; corn syrup sinks because it is more dense than water). Will the other liquids float or sink? What will happen if colored salt water is added to plain water?
- Classify several different kinds of liquids in jars by fluidity (i.e., how easy the substance flows).
- Discuss the characteristics of a liquid.
- Sort objects by whether they are a liquid or solid.

Bubbles. A bubble is a film of liquid surrounding a gas or air pocket. Two concepts that children can learn about bubbles are that (1) bubbles have air inside them and (2) air takes up space. Some bubble activities that children could complete in the science center to help them understand these concepts include the following:

- Divide objects into things that will make bubbles and things that will not make bubbles. Provide a variety of objects that might be used to make bubbles such as strawberry baskets, slotted spoons, sieves, funnels, wire bent into a closed circle, and wire bent into an open circle. Also provide laminated sorting sheets labeled with pictures and words for children to use in sorting the objects into those that will make bubbles and those that will not.
- Hold up the bubbles to the light to determine what colors can be seen.
- Make a pile of bubbles by using a straw to blow into the bubble mixture. Task cards might ask children to see what shapes are in the bubbles and to look at just one of the bubbles to see how many flat sides there are.
- Experiment to find out if different types of objects produce different shapes of bubbles (provide a variety of objects with holes in them such as sieves, square bubble blowers, tea strainers, funnels, and strawberry baskets).
- Create a bubble maker (provide wire, straws, string).
- Experiment with different bubble solutions (using different types of detergent, adding sugar to the bubble solution, adding glycerin to the bubble solution, adding white corn syrup to the bubble solution) to determine which makes the longest lasting bubble.

You will want to encourage children to record their experiments and write or draw what they did, dictate their findings to an adult, or share their finding at circle time.

Float and Sink. Floating and sinking combines the study of liquids with the study of solids. One of the "big ideas" for floating and sinking is that solids have properties. One of these is whether they sink or float in water. The teacher might introduce activities, or challenges, during group time or she might draw or write challenges on task cards for children to follow. These can be explored over a period of days or even weeks. Some activities for exploring this concept of sinking or floating include the following challenges:

- Divide the objects into those that will float and those that will sink. (Provide a variety of items, including items that are similar but different weights such as a ping-pong ball and a golf ball. Also, provide laminated sheets with pictures and words for sink and float that the children can use for their predictions.)
- Put the objects in the water to see if the predictions were correct.

- What are the similarities in the objects that sink? What are the similarities in the objects that float?
- Will a plastic film canister float? Does it float if you fill it with water? Does it float if you fill it with clay?
- Make a boat out of clay that will float. How many pennies can the boat hold?
- Make a boat out of tinfoil the same size as the clay boat. How many pennies can the boat hold?
- Redesign the boats so that they can hold more pennies.
- Can you make a straw sink?
- Predict which baby food lid will sink first (provide baby food lids with different sizes and patterns of holes).
- Design an object that will float for one minute and then sink.

Some common misconceptions that children have in regard to buoyancy is that objects float because they are lighter than water, they sink because they are heavier than water, wood floats and metal sinks, and all objects containing air float (Operation Physics, 1998). Buoyancy is determined by density, which is the mass divided by volume. If the item weighs more than the water it displaces, it will sink. As teachers, it is important that we understand these misconceptions, so that we can avoid reinforcing them when we work with children. We need to assess children's understanding and scaffold their learning as needed. For example, we might want to include materials that help children to see that their misconceptions are not accurate (for example, a metal boat).

Movement. Some concepts that children learn about movement include "There are ways to make something move and to change the way that something is moving" (AAAS, 1993, p. 89). They are also learning that tools make work easier by altering the way the work is done. Children can learn about these concepts by moving water. Provide children with basters, eyedroppers, pumps, siphons, tubing, and funnels. Allow them to discover ways to move the water. In the beginning, it might be helpful to provide some examples to spark interest and provide some early success.

Children can explore many other movement activities to discover that "Things move in many different ways, such as straight, zigzag, round and round, back and forth, and fast and slow" (AAAS, 1993, p. 89). There are ways to make something move and to change the way that something is moving. "Things near the earth fall to the ground unless something holds them up" (AAAS, 1993, p. 94). Some of the materials you can add to the science center to help children explore the concept of movement include

- Marble rolls
- Lengths of rain gutters so that children can create ball rolls
- Pulleys, baskets, and ropes so that children can experiment with different ways of moving objects
- A pendulum
- Moving cars with an incline, placing different surface materials on the incline to experiment with the effects

Magnets. Two of the "big ideas" for magnets is that "magnets can be used to make things move without being touched" and that "forces can act at a distance with no perceivable substance in between" (AAAS, 1993, p. 94). Children can also learn specific information about magnets such as magnets attract some things and not others, magnets vary in strength, magnets can be a helpful tool. Below are some activities for exploring magnetism with preschool and early elementary age children.

- Explore a variety of items (screws, paper, buttons, aluminum foil, pennies, paper clips, rubber bands, scissors, eraser, dime, bottle cap) predicting and then testing theories about what is attracted to the magnet.

- Make a rule about the objects the magnet attracts.

- Determine which is the strongest part of a magnet by trying to pick up paper clips with different parts.

- Experiment with different magnets (bar, horseshoe, ring, rod) to see which is strongest. How many linked paper clips will each magnet pick up? Record results.

This preschool magnet center provides a prediction sheet, items for experimentation, factual books, and an informational sheet for teachers.

- Move metal shavings with a magnet. How far away can you be and still move the shavings?

- Will a magnet move a paper clip that is in water? Will it move a paper clip through a layer of cloth, through a piece of paper, or through a piece of wood? Complete a recording sheet. Circle the smiling face if yes, the magnet can move the paper clip, and a frowning face for no, the magnet cannot move the paper clip. Teachers can design the sheet by either drawing or taking a picture of someone conducting each experiment. For example, take a picture of a paper clip that is on top of a red piece of cloth with a magnet underneath. Place a smiling face and a frowning face beside each picture, so the child can circle the correct one.

- Find things in the classroom that are attracted to the magnet. Draw a picture of each thing you find.

- Experiment with toys that are magnetic (magnetic building blocks, magnetic sculpture, magnetic marbles, Magna Doodle toy). Teachers can also create their own toys with magnets. For example, attach a magnet to the bottom of a toy duck and place the duck in a shallow pan of water. The children can move the duck around in the water. Tie a magnet to a small tow truck and let the children tow the steel cars.

When choosing materials or activities to explore magnetism, it is important not to reinforce misconceptions. Common misconceptions that children have regarding magnets are that all metals are attracted to magnets, all silver colored items are attracted to magnets, all magnets are made of iron, and large magnets are stronger than small magnets (Operation Physics, 1998, p. 7). For example, Cora had placed magnets and a variety of materials in the science center. As she observed children using the center, she discovered that they had developed a hypothesis and, after testing their hypothesis, had concluded that shiny materials are attracted to the magnets. Cora then added some shiny objects to the center that were not attracted to magnets. This allowed children to reexamine their hypothesis. She also added a book that provided information about magnetism. Teachers can help children look up information when they have questions that they cannot answer. However, as this case illustrates, it is important that the teacher is knowledgeable enough about the topic to recognize children's misunderstandings.

Life Science Standards

Life science is the study of living organisms and their relationship to each other and their environment. For children in the early elementary grades the National Academy of Science (1996, p. 127) has defined the standards for this area as being

- Characteristics of organisms
- Life cycles of organisms
- Organisms and environments

Worth and Grollman (2003) have further defined life science goals for the preschool years as being

- Physical characteristics of living things
- Basic needs of living things
- Simple behaviors
- Life cycles
- Recognizing variation and diversity in living things
- Relationship between living things and their environments
- People (pp. 26–29)

Life Science Learning Center Activities

Animals. In addition to the life science standards listed above, concepts for studying animals include "All animals have offspring, usually with two parents involved" and "Animals have features that help them live in different environments" (AAAS, 1993, p. 102). "People need water, food, air, waste removal, and particular range of temperatures in their environments, just as other animals do" (AAAS, 1993, p. 128).

Too often class animals are relegated to the top of a shelf or corner of a room with children displaying little interest. One year when I was teaching preschool, we bought gerbils for our classroom. The children named the gerbils, and each day one of the children was responsible for feeding the gerbils. However, other than that, no one paid much attention to the class pets. The gerbils were master escape artists. One night when they escaped, they fell in the fish tank and drowned. The children discovered them in the morning and for the first time displayed a lot of interest in the gerbils. In reflecting upon this experience, I became aware that I had assumed that simply placing the animals in the classroom would create science opportunities. However, I had done nothing to promote this.

While classroom pets can serve different purposes (some animals might provide a therapeutic outlet), for pets or animal visitors to provide science opportunities teachers need to think about the science learning they are trying to promote. For example, teachers can help children to learn about habitat by having children study and design the habitat for the class pet or visitor. To tie this to a "big idea," teachers and children can discuss what other creatures need the same type of habitat. What are some things that all animals need as part of their habitat? What are unique characteristics that help animals live in different habitats?

Teachers can encourage focused observations of the animal or insect through asking questions, providing recording materials, and including tools in the center. For example, Meiying and the children in her class had just returned from the pet store with a dozen crickets. They developed a KWHL chart listing their current knowledge and questions.

The children had many questions that they were interested in investigating. "What makes the cricket chirp? How does the cricket move? How do they make the chirping sound? Where do they spend their time while in the cage? What are their antennas like? Are they the same as the bumblebee that we studied earlier?" These questions helped to guide children's investigations. Having books and resource materials available assisted the children in finding answers to their questions when they could not be answered through direct observation. Meiying also showed the children a cricket cage that she used as a child in China. The children were fascinated and became interested in building their own cages. She also told them about the cricket songs, stories, and beliefs from her native land, increasing their interest and cultural knowledge.

Because of their abundance and relatively short lives, insects such as crickets, butterflies, and mealy worms are interesting to study. They are ideal for studies of life cycles and biological change.

Another way that children can be engaged with classroom animals and insects is to conduct simple experiments. For example, they might provide different types of foods to determine which ones the animal or insect eats. Children could provide different types of bedding materials to see which a hamster prefers. Or they might create a house without windows and one with windows to see which one a cricket goes into.

Plants. Some "big ideas" or concepts in studying plants include these: Organisms have needs that must be met by the environment, organisms have life cycles, plants and animals affect each other. Specific information that children might learn about seeds and plants include the following: Seeds differ in appearance (size, shape, color, texture); each seed grows into a specific kind of plant; seeds grow into flowers, shrubs, trees, fruit, and other kinds of food; some plants come from seeds, and others come from roots and stems (Lind, 2005, p. 212). Following are some activities that could be placed in a science center that would allow children to explore seeds and plants.

- Sort, classify, and identify a collection of seeds.
- Examine a variety of kinds of fruits and vegetables. Find their seeds (cucumber, ear of corn, green beans, nuts, apricots, apples, oranges).
- Remove seeds from a variety of different types of pods such as peas or sunflowers.
- Conduct experiments such as planting seeds in different types of soil, placing plants in different light or heat conditions, or planting seeds different depths and seeing how long it takes them to grow. While these activities will often be completed as a small-group activity, the experiments can then be placed in the science center for children to observe, sketch, and graph data.
- Examine the root structures of plants by planting a seed between two pieces of Plexiglas or in glass jars, or by sprouting beans in plastic bags.
- Collect, closely examine, identify, and sketch common plants found in the local area. The children and teacher might collect a variety of plants from their homes and then place them in the center with magnifying glasses, sketch books, and identification cards. Teachers might want to create their own identification cards containing the picture and name of each plant that is in the center. This will be easier for children to use than a guide book, since it contains only the plants that are present and shows pictures of them in their present form. Guide books can also be present for children to look through.
- Grow a dish garden by cutting off the top inch of carrots or beets. Keep the tops in a dish with water. Keep track of the results by carefully observing and keeping records in a journal.

Earth and Space Science Standards

Earth and space science is the study of the earth, the climate, the solar system, and the universe. The National Academy of Science (1996, p. 130) identifies the standards for early elementary grades for earth and space science as

- Properties of earth materials
- Objects in the sky
- Changes in earth and sky

Worth and Grollman (2003) further clarify these standards for preschool classrooms as being

- Properties of earth materials
- Weather and climate
- Pattern of movement and change of the moon and the sun (p. 144)

One of the big ideas in earth science is that humans and the environment impact each other.

Earth and Space Science Learning Center Activities

In this section, we will examine soil, rocks, and water and ice. Another common topic of study in this area is the examination of seasons.

Soil. Some concepts in studying soil are that soils can be classified based on color, texture, and consistency; that soils can retain water and help plants survive (Lind, 2005, p. 240); and that animals, plants, and humans can cause changes to soil. There are several center activities that children can complete to learn about soils.

- Children can visually examine different types of soil, examine the soil with a magnifying glass, classify the soils, and see if any items in the soil are attracted to magnets. To make the activity more interesting each child can bring a soil specimen from his own backyard.
- Children can add one cup of water to a jar of each of the different types of soil. The soil will separate into layers. Encourage children to first predict what they think will happen. After they have added water, encourage children to draw the layers in their journals.
- Let the children experiment with the different mixtures (clay, humus, and sand that have had small amounts of water added to them). Encourage children to share their observations. The clay will be able to be formed into a ball, humus will clump slightly, but sand will not.
- Examine worms in soil. How does the soil change over a period of time?
- Plant the same type of flower in different soils. Does the plant grow differently based on the type of soil?

Rocks. Some concepts relating to rocks are that rocks are formed in different ways (Lind, 2005, p. 240); rocks are nonliving things (Lind, 2005, p. 240); rocks can be classified based on common characteristics. In studying rocks in the science center, you might provide a variety of different types of rocks for children to classify by size, color, and hardness; by whether they are layered or not layered, whether they are magnetic, or whether they sink or float. You will want to provide tools for testing and examining the rocks, including a scale for measuring, magnifying glasses for close examination, sorting trays, magnets, water for determining whether they sink or float, and nails and pennies to scratch the rock. It will also be important to provide data charts to record information and resource books for identifying the rocks.

Nathan's class began a study of rocks when the children became interested in the huge decorative rocks that the contractors moved in next to their school. The children collected rocks and brought rocks from home to classify. During circle times, Nathan introduced the different tests that could be conducted on the rocks. Materials for the tests and the rocks were placed in the science learning center. Children kept records of the tests using a picture table that Nathan had prepared. When the children had spent extensive time exploring and sorting the rocks, Nathan introduced information on the classification of rocks into sedimentary, metamorphic, and igneous. He showed how the tests helped to determine what kinds of rocks they had in the classroom.

Apply Your Knowledge   What age of children do you think Nathan was working with? Would rocks be an appropriate topic for other early childhood age groups? If so, what modifications in the activities should be made?

Water and Ice. An important concept that early childhood children need to learn concerning water and ice is that, "Water can be a liquid or a solid and can go back and forth from one form to the other. If water is turned to ice and then the ice is allowed to melt, the amount of water is the same as it was before freezing" (AAAS, 1993, p. 67). Some learning center activities involving ice include:

- Experiment with different ways to make colored ice melt faster. Provide tools such as hammers to crack the ice, containers of water, squirt bottle with salt water, a hair dryer, and other tools that the children think of. The color will assist in keeping track of the different experiments that are occurring.
- Examine the ice with a magnifying glass.
- Encourage children to place ice in different areas of the room to see which will melt the fastest.
- Have children design containers to preserve the ice without putting it in the refrigerator or freezer. Provide a variety of different materials that the children have brainstormed.

We have examined a variety of learning center activities for preschool and early elementary age children. Is it important to have a science center for infants and toddlers? What science concepts are infants and toddlers learning?

Special Considerations for Infants and Toddlers

From birth, children actively investigate their environment using observation and prediction to make sense of their world. While infant and toddler programs often do not have a specific science center, materials that help children learn science concepts are incorporated into other classroom centers. The important science concepts children are exploring at this age group are

- Using their senses to explore the physical properties of materials
- Becoming aware of cause and effect ("If I turn this switch the light will come on.")
- Recognizing real and not real (a live animal versus a stuffed toy animal, a real rock versus a plastic replica of a rock)
- Making simple classifications (Miller, 2004, p. 25)

To learn concepts, children need to have hands-on experiences. This is particularly true for infants and toddlers.

Many years ago, I was a houseparent for children who were abused and neglected. One day a social worker brought a 2-year-old child, named Jay, to live with us. Jay loved horses. He played with toy horses, we read horse books repeatedly, and he only wanted to wear the horse print pajamas. The county fair was coming to town and I was excited to take Jay to see the horses. However, when we went he was very afraid. He didn't know that horses were big, that they made loud noises, or that they had a smell. He came home and never again asked to read a horse book, to wear the pajamas with horses, or to play with the toy horses.

As illustrated in the vignette, only through hands-on experience can children gain complete knowledge. Some materials for hands-on science explorations with infants and toddlers include

- Natural materials—leaves, pinecones, rocks, feathers, seashells, water, dirt, snow, ice, wet and dry sand, mud
- Items to explore natural materials—sand wheels, scoops, sifters, shovels, buckets, spray bottles
- Living things such as dogs, cats, worms, and bugs along with their food and the materials used to care for them
- Items to explore how things move—ball rolls, toy cars, tubes, ramps
- Materials to compare and contrast, such as rough and smooth
- A variety of objects to group and classify
- Cause and effect materials—pop-up toys, music boxes, activity boxes
- Bubbles

Infants and toddlers are learning about the people, animals, and plants in their environments, including how each should be treated. One teacher of toddlers adds pots of herbs to her classroom. She calls these "petting plants." Children can carefully touch the plants and smell the fresh herbs on their hands.

How do you know which science activities to choose for your group of children? What is the role of the teacher as children use the materials? We will examine these questions next.

Teachers' Facilitation of Learning in the Science Center

To promote children's scientific knowledge, teachers must establish an effective science center and determine the activities and materials for the center. It is also crucial that we interact with children before, during, and after they use the center. Interacting with children has a significant effect on children's science learning and the way they use materials

(Heath & Heath, 1982; Iatridis, 1984). Following are some of the important roles that teachers have in promoting science through a center approach.

Determine Concepts to Be Taught

"Concepts are building blocks of knowledge: they allow people to organize and categorize information" (Lind, 1999). Concepts for young children in science might include life cycles, biological change, physical change, systems and interactions, cause and effect, differences between animate and inanimate objects, physical properties of objects, and learning that material can be classified. Choose concepts to be taught based upon children's interests, development, national and state standards, and the surrounding environment. Also, be cautious of ideas listed in activity books that might not be related to science concepts. For example, one time-honored activity often listed in activity books is creating a volcano by mixing soda and vinegar. While this activity could be used to teach about chemical reactions, when we use it as a volcano activity we may be inadvertently teaching misinformation. Are volcanoes caused by chemical reactions?

Choose Developmentally Appropriate Concepts and Activities

It is important to consider children's developmental understandings in planning science activities. They must be able to have at least an elementary understanding of the scientific explanation underlying the activity. If not, they come to view science as magic and their scientific learning is insecure.

Determine Children's Current Knowledge and Theories

Children have preconceived notions that may or may not be accurate (Miller, 2004). To determine children's current knowledge, theories, and misconceptions, you might have children explain their version of a phenomenon. Bonita does this by having children complete a KWHL chart. Jeri has each child draw his or her theories. Other teachers find out children's misconceptions through careful questioning. While misconceptions can be resistant to change, providing "hands on" experience that allows children to learn other explanations is extremely helpful.

Introduce Materials and Develop Interest

Diego was introducing a sink and float center to the children. First, he took a round ball of clay and asked the children if they thought it would float or sink. After the predictions, he dropped the clay in water to see what happened. The children described their theories about why the clay sank. He next built a clay boat. Again, he asked the children to predict whether it would sink or float and to discuss why they thought so. After the predictions, he told children they could find out what would happen by experimenting in the science center. To see an example of how another teacher introduces a science center, watch the video *Science* on MyEducationLab.

Go to MyEducationLab and select the topic "Math, Science, and Technology." Under Activities and Applications, watch the video *Science*.

Assist Children to Develop a Mental Structure

Children can build upon mental structures as they learn new information or observe phenomena (Gelman & Brenneman, 2004; National Research Council, 2005). "Once a mental structure is in place . . . children are much more likely both to notice new data that fit with what they have already learned and to store data in such a way that they can build on it in the future. Conversely, when children lack a mental structure for organizing particular domains of knowledge, the significance of new data is not evident to them and they must either construct a new structure to accommodate it or fail to benefit from it" (Gelman, 2005, p. 6). To assist children to develop mental structures and to add to existing structures, we can link new knowledge to previous schemas, mental structures, and big ideas. For example, what we know about a cat can be linked to what we know about other animals. When we have developed a schema about animals and are introduced to a new animal, even one that we have never met, we know that it can breathe, eat, reproduce, and move by itself (Gelman & Brenneman, 2004, p. 3).

Teach Children Scientific Vocabulary

Language and science go hand in hand. "The importance of language within a domain suggests that one should not 'cheat' on vocabulary: terms such as respiration, nutrients, and the concepts to which they apply belong in the preschool classroom, both because children learn words at an astonishing rate during these years and because proper vocabulary is part and parcel of conceptual growth" (Gelman & Brenneman, 2004, p. 4). As you interact with children, use scientific vocabulary. Some teachers keep a list of vocabulary they want to stress posted in an obvious spot in the classroom, so they remember to emphasize those words.

Provide Background Knowledge

To effectively help children develop background knowledge on the topic being studied, we need background information ourselves. Without background knowledge, we are unable to take full advantage of teachable moments, such as when a child asks why the leaves are falling. In addition, we might not recognize children's misconceptions or we might be inadvertently teaching misconceptions ourselves. We can gain knowledge by seeking professional development opportunities. We can also improve our knowledge one topic at a time by researching the topic the class is currently investigating. It is important to prepare background information on the topic of study so that others in the room can also improve their knowledge.

When we have background knowledge on the topic, we can share this information with children and enhance their learning. We might share information during individual conversations with children, with a group of children at circle time, or when children ask questions.

Ask Open-Ended Questions

When asking questions, we must be careful not to act like a quiz show host. The goal in questioning is to have a two-way, in-depth conversation. The purpose of asking questions should be to understand children's current level of thinking and to help them, through careful questioning, to think more deeply about a topic or theory. You can also use questions as a way to provide new challenges and provocations. For example, you might ask, "Why do you think that happened?" "How can you test out that idea?" "What do you think would happen if . . .?"

Encourage Children to Reflect Upon Their Learning

Language helps children to express and represent their knowledge (French, 2004). Through reflecting and communicating, children learn to recall information, generalize what they have learned, analyze their findings, and solve problems as they discuss with others (Klein et al., 2000).

Encourage and Model Curiosity, Inquiry, and Enjoyment of Science

Unfortunately, many adults have had poor experiences in relationship to science education. We need to be careful not to pass this dislike of the subject on to children. Children are naturally curious. When we capitalize on this curiosity, we can develop science centers that children will enjoy, and perhaps we can learn to enjoy science ourselves.

Implement Group Science Talks

During group science talks, teachers can introduce materials, pique interest, and encourage children to share their current ideas, predictions, and theories. As children continue to work within the center, they can record their learning in many ways—photographs, drawings, models, emergent writing—and share this with other children at circle time. Discussion among the students can lead to greater learning opportunities as they challenge each other's thinking. These challenges can lead to increased knowledge and revised theories. To see an example of one teacher leading a small-group science talk, watch *A Scientific Investigation in Preschool: Tadpole to Frog* on MyEducationLab.

myeducationlab

Go to MyEducationLab and select the topic "Math, Science, and Technology." Under Activities and Applications, watch the video *A Scientific Investigation in Preschool: Tadpole to Frog.*

Meet the Needs of All Learners

It is important that all children have access and encouragement to learn science in the early childhood years. The early childhood years provide the foundation for later science learning. By becoming scientifically literate, we can better understand the world. Scientific reasoning can help us to make better decisions. In addition, like math, science can be an equalizer or a gatekeeper for later success. Historically, research shows that girls, children of color, children with disabilities, and children who are poor "have been excluded from the science pipeline to higher education and the science/math related jobs of the future" (Sprung & Froschl, 2006, p. 7). For example, "in 2002, only 12% of science, math, and engineering degrees were awarded to African Americans, Latinos, and American Indians" (Sprung & Froschl, 2006, p. 8). Women hold only 15% of the jobs in science and engineering in the United States (Sprung & Froschl, 2006). Although nearly 5% of college students have disabilities, only 0.0001 receive degrees in math or science (Sprung & Froschl, 2006).

How does the data apply to the early childhood years? According to many researchers, if we want to change these statistics and provide science equity to all groups, we must begin in the early childhood years (Sprung & Froschl, 2006). What are steps we can take to help all children succeed in science? We can do the following:

- Use inquiry-based science. "Inquiry-based science is a wonderful way to level the playing field for all students. Students who are less verbal or English Language Learners can shine in a hands-on environment; students with disabilities can utilize the problem-solving skills they hone through everyday living; and girls can engage in cooperative learning, a style that research shows works well for them" (Sprung & Froschl, 2006, p. 8).

- Make sure to include books and posters in the science center that show underrepresented groups engaged in science.

- Invite guest speakers who are from underrepresented groups.

- Honor what children know and bring to the classroom. 5-year-old Jeramiah had never traveled outside a twenty-mile radius from home. He'd never been to a lake, mountain, zoo, science center, water park, or museum. However, his grandfather and grandmother had taught him about all the native plants (their names, which you could eat, how they could be used for medicine) and animals on the reservation. His teacher began the year with a study of plants and encouraged Jeramiah and his family to share their knowledge.

- Provide open-ended materials in the science center to meet all developmental levels.

- Provide pictorial directions in the science center. If you include written directions, include the primary languages of all the children in the classroom.

- Most importantly, we must believe that all children can be successful in learning science.

Observe and Document Individual Children's Learning

Assess Interests. As mentioned previously, it is important for teachers to assess children's interests so they can plan experiences that are relevant to them. Teachers can do this by interviewing children, listening to their questions, or observing how they spend their time. Some teachers ask parents about their children's interests. At the beginning of a new school year in a toddler program, teachers gave parents a plastic bag and asked them to place an object, drawing, or photo of something their child was interested in into the bag. When the bags were returned the majority contained rocks. Teachers were then able to begin the year with a relevant topic—rocks.

Assess Prior Knowledge. Once a topic is determined, children's prior knowledge and theories need to be assessed. This can be done by asking open-ended questions and recording the results. For example, Kelly began her butterfly center by asking what children knew about butterflies. Throughout the discussion, she continued to ask open-ended questions finding out children's theories about how butterflies get their food, how they have young, and so forth. Answers can be recorded in a list, a web, or a KWHL. Gallenstein (2005) recommends using concept maps with preschool and early elementary age children. A concept map is similar to a web but often uses words to show the relationship between items. Gallenstein recommends using actual objects or pictures of objects and arrows with words for the early childhood years. For example, in developing a concept map of the five senses, she begins with a picture of a child with arrows pointing to each sense. She then has the children place a plastic mouth, ear, eye, nose, and hand where they believe they belong. Next, she adds items or pictures of items to taste, smell, hear, see, and touch. Again, the children place them where they believe they belong. Finally, the children describe what they have done and how the objects relate to each other. Gallenstein uses this information in planning curriculum.

Assess Learning. Artifacts such as drawings, constructions, writing, photographs, graphs, tables, and record sheets are important in documenting children's ongoing learning about the science topic. Their verbal descriptions can continue to be a rich source of information about their changing ideas and theories. If a web was initially created, a post-web can show growth in children's knowledge. Likewise, completing the "what I learned" on a KWHL chart can indicate increased competence.

As teachers engage in ongoing assessment of children's learning, they use this information to plan sequential learning activities and to add relevant materials to the science learning center.

Teachers play a critical role in developing science centers and interacting with children to help them develop competence in science. However, science does not only take place indoors. The outdoor science area can also provide rich science opportunities.

Outdoor Science Centers

Outdoors is the perfect place for exploring and learning about many science topics. For example, children can

- Explore wind with kites, pinwheels, windsocks, wind ribbons, paper airplanes, and feathers.
- Learn about plants by gardening (see Chapter 15 for more information).
- Observe bugs and animals in their natural habitats.
- Create elaborate water systems using the garden hose and PVC pipe.
- Conduct simple experiments. For example, if you have ants in your playground children might take a plate and divide it into several sections, placing a different potential food item in each section (sugar, grass, bird seed, crumbs of bread, a larger slice of bread) (Williams, Rockwell, & Sherwood, 1987). Which foods are the ants attracted to?

An outdoor sorting table encourages children to collect and classify materials.

- Learn what birds prefer eating by setting up a variety of types of bird feeders.
- Observe the weather and record information at a weather station.
- Learn about shadows by experimenting with their own shadows or by creating a sun dial.

Teachers can support this learning by providing the tools and resource materials needed to fully explore the topic. Some teachers create science inquiry bags or totes that can be taken outside with them. These contain reference books or laminated sheets for identifying birds and bugs, measuring tools, various magnifying glasses, insect nets, jars and sacks for collecting specimens, and clipboards and paper for documenting information.

Children are naturally curious. From birth, they are continually forming hypotheses and testing them. By providing rich experiences, we can capitalize on this interest and assist all children to learn scientific processes and knowledge that will become the building blocks for future success in science.

Sample Application Activities

1. Observe children during center time to see what science activities they are engaged in.

2. Develop a booklet of science fact sheets for common early childhood topics.

3. Brainstorm a list of science vocabulary words for different common science topics.

4. Critique a science center using the science environmental assessment found in Figure 9.1.

Figure 9.1
Environmental Assessment: Science Center

Source: Permission is granted by the publisher to reproduce this figure for evaluation and record-keeping. From Julie Bullard, *Creating Environments for Learning: Birth to Age Eight.* Copyright © 2010 by Pearson Education, Inc. All rights reserved.

☐ Is the science center large enough to accommodate several children?

☐ Is the center designed to encourage cooperation and communication (Charlesworth & Lind, 2007)?

☐ Does the center allow for uninterrupted work?

☐ Is the center near a sink, if possible?

☐ Is there adequate work space?

☐ Does the center contain organized, labeled shelving to store materials?

☐ Does the center contain a bulletin board or other surface for posting information and findings?

☐ Is there adequate lighting in the center?

☐ Is the center near a window, if at all possible?

☐ Is the center enticing and inviting?

☐ Is the center designed for action rather than just for looking (Charlesworth & Lind, 2007)?

☐ Does the center encourage children to develop "What if" statements?

☐ Does the center stress process skills (ask and reflect, plan and predict, act and observe, report and reflect) (Conezio & French, 2003, p. 11)?

☐ Does the center stress specific content related to the topic being studied?

☐ Does the center tie into larger overriding concepts or "big ideas"?

☐ Does the center include science content background sheets and a list of vocabulary to be stressed so adults can scaffold children's learning? The background sheets should also include the "big ideas" or overriding concepts being stressed.

☐ Does the center build upon current children's curiosity, interests, knowledge, background, and previous activities?

☐ Does the center allow for individual differences by providing open-ended material or a variety of tasks at different levels?

☐ Does the center allow children to use the center independently?
  • Directions for the center are provided in pictures, written, tape recorded, or introduced at circle time.
  • All needed materials are available.
  • Materials are arranged in a logical order or sequence.
  • There is a clearly designated place for each item.
  • Materials are within the children's reach.

☐ Does the center encourage children to represent their knowledge (paper, graph paper, tape recorders, journals, recording sheets, clipboards, pencils, and markers)?

☐ Does the center contain resource materials (books, posters, videos, computer)?

☐ Does the center contain inquiry tools (magnifying glasses of different types, microscope, Petri dishes, scales, eyedroppers, pulleys, tweezers, twine, clay for imprints, specimen bags and boxes, and nets)?

5. Review information at the National Academies Press website to learn more about the national science standards: http://www.nap.edu/catalog.php?record_id=4962

6. Review the National Child Care Information and Technical Assistance Center website for information about a variety of science topics in early childhood at http://nccic.org/

7. To improve your science background knowledge, view free science videos at the Annenberg Media website at http://www.learner.org/resources/browse.html For example, see "Essential Science for Teachers: Earth and Space Science."

8. Develop a science center using the criteria discussed in this chapter. Make sure you introduce your center.

9. Learn more about how to design science activities based upon the interests and current knowledge of children on MyEducationLab. Select the topic "Math, Science, and Technology." Under Building Teaching Skills and Dispositions, complete the exercise "Promoting Inquiry in Curriculum."

chapter 10
Developing Math Centers

*J*uanita, a teacher at Brighter Future Preschool, was eager to implement what she learned at a preschool math workshop. However, the presenter had stressed that you must begin by observing the skill level and interests of the children in your room. Therefore, Juanita developed a checklist of mathematical skills based on the math standards and then carefully observed the children to determine their current level of mathematical knowledge and understanding. While observing, she noted that few boys used the math center. Instead, they spent all their free time playing with the cars in the block center. Following the observations, she began to enrich her environment. For example, since many of the children were learning to classify, she placed several items in the math area including small cars, beautiful small colored rocks, and pinecones to sort. To pique the boys' interest she also added wrenches to seriate *(arrange from large to small). She created a game where children matched cars and garages based on a numeral and the correct number of dots. Juanita was pleased to discover that the children, including several of the boys, became more engaged in using math manipulatives.*

Math manipulatives, the heart of the math center, have a rich and ongoing history in early childhood. In the nineteenth century, Froebel, considered the father of kindergarten, developed mathematical manipulatives or "gifts" for young children. This emphasis on using math manipulatives continues to be considered best practice in the twenty-first century.

Children in a developmentally appropriate classroom have numerous opportunities to learn mathematical skills and concepts as they play with materials. For example, children learn many geometry skills while they play with blocks (see Chapter 10 for more information). As children cook or play in the media table, they often practice measuring skills. Materials in the manipulative center encourage the use of one-to-one correspondence and counting. However, experts recommend that a specific math center be established for preschool and elementary classrooms to further develop these skills (National Research Council, Bowman, Donovan, & Burns, 2001). Having a separate math center encourages teachers to place an intentional focus on this area. It also makes the emphasis on math evident to staff, families, and children.

How Children Learn Math

Children first learn math content and process skills informally. From infancy, they use mathematics in everyday activities and to solve problems. As stated by Vygotsky (1978), "children's learning begins long before they enter school . . . they have had to deal with operations of division, addition, subtraction, and the determination of size. Consequently, children have their own preschool arithmetic, which only myopic psychologists could ignore" (p. 84). According to Ginsburg, an expert on early childhood mathematics (2006), "despite its immaturity, young children's mathematics bears some resemblance to research mathematicians' activity. Both young children and mathematicians ask and think about deep questions, invent solutions, apply mathematics to solve real problems, and play with mathematics. Clearly then, one of our goals should be to encourage and foster young children's *current* mathematical activities" (p. 158). Children use math to help make sense of the world. Teachers need to build upon this natural interest, providing children with in-depth opportunities and time to use math materials and ideas (NAEYC/NCTM, 2002).

However, while children intuitively use math to solve problems, according to Piaget, the only way that they can learn **social-arbitrary knowledge** is from adults or more competent peers. Social-arbitrary knowledge consists of "arbitrary truths agreed upon by convention and rules agreed upon by coordination of points of view" (DeVries & Kohlberg, 1987, p. 21). For example, in math the names of the numbers, signs, and shapes are examples of social-arbitrary knowledge. Teachers must support children's learning as they use mathematical materials, helping them learn social-arbitrary knowledge.

By the time children begin kindergarten, they have typically learned some social-arbitrary knowledge. For example, more than 90% of children are able to count to 10, recognize shapes, and read numerals. More than half of the children can count beyond ten and 20% can read two-digit numbers (West, Denton, & Germino-Hausken, 2000). However, it is important that they not only are able to count or read numerals, but that they are able to use this knowledge with purpose and meaning.

How the Math Center Enhances Children's Development

While interacting in a well-developed math center, children have the opportunity to learn about the mathematical standards as defined by the National Council of Teachers of Mathematics (NCTM). These are numbers and operations, geometry, measurement, algebra, and data analysis. Although the early childhood teacher needs to provide experiences relating to each of these standards, the primary emphasis for pre-K through second-grade children is numbers and operations, geometry, and the measurement standards.

In addition, children in the early childhood years need to develop math process skills including problem solving, reasoning, communicating, connecting, and representing (NCTM, 2000). These process skills transcend mathematics, involving lifelong skills that children need to be successful in all areas of their lives. For example, in early childhood classrooms we can find many examples where children need to use problem-solving skills (planning a fair way to share a toy with a friend, determining a way to keep a tower of blocks from falling, or keeping a pool of water from sinking into the sand). We will explore each of these math processes in more depth.

Problem Solving

Common steps for problem solving involve understanding the problem, making a plan for solving the problem, implementing the plan, and reflecting to see if the solution works or the answer makes sense (Copley, 2000). Problem solving not only entails learning and practicing these steps but also acquiring dispositions to problem solve. "An effective problem solver perseveres, focuses his attention, tests hypotheses, takes reasonable risks, remains flexible, tries alternatives, and exhibits self regulation" (Copley, 2000, p. 31).

Reasoning

When children reason they "draw logical conclusions, apply logical classification skills, explain their thinking, justify their problem solutions and processes, apply patterns and relationships to arrive at solutions, and make sense out of mathematics and science" (Charlesworth, 2005, p. 142).

Communicating

Children share their mathematical ideas in a variety of ways. They may communicate verbally or nonverbally (charts, tallies, and drawings). Even very young children display their mathematical knowledge (holding up two fingers when asked their age).

Connecting

"The most important connection for early childhood mathematics development is between the intuitive, informal mathematics that students have learned through their own experience and the mathematics they are learning in school" (NCTM, 2000, p. 132). As discussed earlier, children naturally use math to solve problems they encounter in their natural world. Unfortunately, as children begin school and use formal mathematics, they often begin to view math as a set of rules and procedures rather than as a way of solving everyday problems. Teachers can help children to avoid this by using familiar manipulative materials to teach math, making children's natural mathematics visible by using math vocabulary to describe their activities, and using examples from children's experiences when introducing a math concept.

Representing

Representing assists children in organizing, recording, and sharing information and ideas (NCTM, 2000). Children might use fingers, make tallies, create diagrams, produce graphs, make maps, or draw pictures to represent their knowledge (Copley, 2000).

When developing the math center, it is important to consider the appropriate math standards. Equally important is helping children use the math process skills as they use the materials. For example, Carmen was enjoying sorting rocks into groups by color. Juanita pointed out that Carmen was classifying the rocks (tied mathematical language to an informal math activity). She asked Carmen how she was grouping the rocks (stressed mathematical communication). When Carmen had completed the classification, Juanita asked her if she could think of other ways that she might classify the rocks (encouraged problem solving).

Designing an Effective Math Center

The math center provides children the opportunity to independently use manipulatives that will assist them in developing their natural math skills. The center also houses tools, such as measuring devices, that might be used as resources in other centers. For example, Sofia and Carlos used a yardstick from the math center to measure their "tall block skyscraper." An effective math center provides the following:

- A clearly designated space in the quiet area of the room
- A large work area that allows children to explore the math manipulatives
- A rich variety of developmental math manipulatives relating to the different math standards (numbers and operations, measurement, geometry, algebra, and data analysis)
- Organized shelves with a clearly designated place for each item
- Aesthetically pleasing containers that allow children to see what is available and that keep all needed materials together
- A place to display completed and in-progress work such as a bulletin board, the top of a shelf for three-dimensional work, and a three-ring binder for sketches and photos of work

Individual trays containing all the needed manipulative materials for each math activity are attractive and easy to carry to the table.

Appropriate Materials for the Math Center

In addition to carefully planning the placement and layout of the math center, it is important to choose appropriate math materials. Appropriate materials allow for active manipulation, have a clearly defined mathematical purpose, are either open-ended or self-correcting, and are based on assessments of children's knowledge and skills. Materials need to be rotated to meet the developmental needs and interests of the children. We will examine each of these criteria in more depth.

Provide for Active Manipulation of Concrete Materials

Children must have abundant opportunities to learn through active manipulation of concrete materials before using abstract ideas. Children can often memorize information but not understand unless they have had experiences with concrete objects. For example, when my son Christopher was a second grader, he exclaimed proudly at supper one evening that four cups make a quart and that four quarts make a gallon. However, later in the meal when I asked him about the size of the gallon milk carton on the table, I was met by a puzzled stare.

Have a Clearly Defined Mathematical Purpose or Goal

It is important that teachers are familiar with national and state standards and use this knowledge when choosing materials. At Bright Beginnings, teachers post an index card on the shelf next to each math manipulative. The index card includes the standard, the purpose of the material, how teachers can scaffold learning, and how to assess the learning. At first, the teachers felt that preparing cards might be too much work. However, they found that it helped them to be more intentional in choosing materials. It also provided helpful information for other teachers and volunteers.

Open-Ended or Self-Correcting Materials

Children can correctly complete open-ended materials in many ways. There are many right answers. For example, Amanda provided children with a variety of buttons to classify. Children could classify these by the number of holes in the button, color, shape, or material the button was made from. Any of these would be correct or right. A closed-ended activity, however, has a right answer. For example, if you have a puzzle where children place numbers 1 to 10 in order, there is only one correct answer. This is an appropriate activity for children who are developmentally ready for this step. For example, many 4-year-olds will be beginning to learn numerals and their order. How can you make it self-correcting? One way would be to make it into a puzzle so the child would know immediately whether the numerals were in the correct order. Why does this matter? Let's look at the experience that one child, Joan, has in the math center. Joan plays with the number line every day. However, it is not self-correcting. Each day she places the numbers in this order 1, 2, 4, 3, 5. Teachers are supervising and assisting many children during center time and do not notice this error. Each time she incorrectly completes the activity, it reinforces her misconception. Besides creating a puzzle, there are many other ways to make materials self-correcting. For example, Jeri observes that children in her classroom are ready to match a number of items to the correct numeral. She takes a round pizza cardboard and divides it into six sections, placing one dot in one section, two in another, and so on. She then takes wooden clothespins and writes numerals on them. The children are to clip the correct clothespin to the right area on the pizza cardboard. Jeri can color code the clothespins and dots (very obvious) or she can color code just the back side of the pizza circle. For example, all dots on the front are blue, but the clothespins are different colors. The yellow clothespin has a numeral 1 on it. Children turn the game over when it is complete and look to see if the yellow clothespin is by the yellow dot.

Based on Assessment of Children's Mathematical Skills and Knowledge

Open-ended materials will meet a variety of developmental levels. However, since children can only successfully complete closed-ended materials in one way, it is even more crucial that the material matches the child's skill level. Just as we would not give children who were completing 10-piece puzzles a 50-piece puzzle, we should not give children who are learning one-to-one correspondence a number line to complete. Even if you have a single age level in the classroom, you will have children at many different developmental levels. Some teachers code closed-ended math and manipulative materials so that children know which materials to choose. For example, Cindy, a kindergarten teacher, places colored dots on the items. Children know which dots match their skill level.

Relate to Children's Interests

While many items can be used for counting, sorting, patterning, and classifying, as the opening scenario illustrates, children are more likely to use the materials if they relate to their interests. Children at Loving Care School became very interested in insects. Their teacher found a variety of realistic plastic bugs that she placed in the math center. Two children who were interested in bugs but had never before engaged in patterning activities spent most of their selective choice time making patterns with the bugs.

Rotated to Meet Children's Changing Developmental Needs and Interests

Many programs make one of two errors. Either teachers never rotate materials, or they have a rotation pattern but change materials without consideration of children's skill levels or interests. Instead, changes in the math center need to be made based upon the observation and assessment of the children's skills and interests. If children are still using materials, you will generally want to leave the materials in the center. Allowing children opportunities for repetition encourages concept formation. When the materials are changed, it is important to still keep a range of materials that address the different math standards as discussed next.

Center Materials Related to the Math Standards

As discussed earlier, the National Council of Teachers of Mathematics (NCTM) has identified five mathematical standards for pre-K through second grade. We will examine possible learning center materials in relationship to each of these standards. The specific materials you choose will be based upon the developmental readiness and interests of the children in your classroom.

Materials to Support the Numbers and Operations Standard

Mathematicians consider the numbers and operations standard to be the most important of the standards for the early years (Clements, 2004). Operations include not only addition, subtraction, division, and multiplication but also "counting, comparing, grouping, dividing, uniting, partitioning, and composing" (Clements, 2004, p. 17).

Counting. Children typically begin counting by memorizing the number words. Depending upon the environment, this may begin as early as the age of 2 (Clements, 2004). However, number words are more difficult than other words for children to learn due to their function as a grouping rather than an individual item. Numbers are also a concept rather than a noun (Mix, Huttenlocher, & Levine, 2002).

To count items successfully children must understand **one-to-one correspondence** or that there is one number word for each item they are counting. They must learn to keep track of items as they count them and to tag or count each item only once. It is often easier to do this if children touch each item they are counting. Finally, they must understand that the final number that they count represents the number of items in the collection. This concept forms the basis for all future work with numbers and operations (Clements, 2004). When you assess children's understanding of numbers, it is important to look at each of these steps. By doing so, you can determine what skills the child will need to work on to progress to the next level. For example, Sabrina could count by rote to 10. She recognized small sets (up to four) without counting them. However, if the set was larger, she seemed unable to determine how many items there were. While observing Sabrina counting money in the dramatic play area, the teacher noted that Sabrina did not tag each coin as she counted it and therefore recounted several of the coins. The teacher demonstrated how to organize and tag the coins to count them.

One-to-One Correspondence. It is easier for children to use materials that are less abstract for one-to-one correspondence. Therefore, teachers should first provide real objects, then cutouts, then pictures, and finally symbols and patterns (Charlesworth, 2005). Following are several materials that you could place in the math center to assist in developing one-to-one correspondence.

- Outline game—Outline interesting items and place the outline and the items in a box. Children can match each item to the correct outline.
- Match groups of items—For more advanced one-to-one correspondence, create matching games of items that go together (fork and spoon, nut and bolt, and mitten and hand).
- Pegs and pegboards—These come in a variety of sizes, so they can be chosen based upon the fine motor development of the children in the group.
- Jars and lids—Collect a variety of different types of jars with matching lids that children can put together.
- Cars and garages (as in the opening scenario)—Initially children might drive a car into each garage. As children become more proficient with one-to-one correspondence, this task can become more difficult by adding a different number of dots to each car and the corresponding garage allowing children to match the dots. Finally, numerals can be added to the cars, which are then matched to the dots on the garages. To make the task self-correcting, add matching colored dots to the bottom of the car and the top of the garage.

The nests and eggs are enticing to the children at Little Raskals who have been studying birds.

Recognizing Numerals. Following are materials that you can add to the math center to help children recognize numerals.

- Objects with numerals, including calculators, adding machines, playing cards, magnetic numbers, and puzzles.
- Games where children match numerals. For example, use two old calendars that have similar size grids. Cut one apart and place magnetic tape on the back of each number. Attach the intact calendar to a cookie sheet or magnetic file cabinet. Children can match the appropriate number to the intact calendar. For another simple-to-create game, take a deck of cards and cut the top and bottom apart. By using a different type of cut for each card, the cards can be self-correcting.
- Sandpaper numerals. Add a blindfold that children can use if they wish. Children can feel the number

and try to guess which numeral it is. Make sure to add dots to the other side of the card so children can check their answers.

- Play dough, clay, or wire for children to use to form numbers. You can add a spinner to add interest. The child spins the dial to determine which numeral to create.

- Numerals from burlap or other textured surface glued on a card. Children can place paper over the numeral and make a rubbing.

- Number sewing cards (write a numeral on burlap with black permanent marker; use a large sewing needle and yarn to sew around the numeral) (Brown, 1982).

- Beanbag toss. Children throw a beanbag and then identify the numeral that the beanbag lands on. Include the numeral, number name, and dots to meet the developmental needs of more learners. When children have mastered the numerals, they can throw more than one time and add the results.

Writing Numerals. You can assist children to learn to write numerals by providing the following materials:

- Zip-lock plastic bags filled with hair gel or other items for a transitory writing slate. Children can write numbers and then erase them and start over.

- Laminated number cards to trace or use as a model for writing numerals.

- Lined and unlined paper and different types of pencils and markers to use for writing numbers.

- Individual number books with a numeral on each page and materials such as stickers, stamps, pictures, or cutouts for children to use in completing their book.

This private area at Davey's Preschool encourages children to write their numbers in the attractive sand container.

- Old calendars with large squares that children can use to practice writing their numbers (Seefeldt & Galper, 2004).

Counting and Matching the Correct Number of Items to the Numeral. There are many materials you can add to your center that allow children to practice identifying numerals and matching these to the correct number of objects. Following are a few suggestions:

- Materials where children actively manipulate the objects they are matching to the numeral. For example, they might place golf tees into predrilled holes in a wooden numeral or the correct number of gems into a bowl.

- Number games. When children are exposed to number games, they make significant gains in numeracy compared with children who do not have this opportunity (Young-Loveridge, 2004). Games should have an element of chance to keep them interesting and to prevent only the most skilled children from winning. Some appropriate games include Go Fish with a deck of cards, Math Bingo, Candy Land, Dominoes, Number Concentration, and Chutes and Ladders.

- Number books. Researchers have found that using number books is also associated with larger gains in numeracy skills (Young-Loveridge, 2004). When you add counting books, make sure you also add props so that children can actively manipulate them as they read the book. For example, you might add flannel pieces or pretend pieces of fruit to manipulate when reading *The Very Hungry Caterpillar.*

- Fishing game. Add string to a dowel with a magnet at the end. Create fish from cardboard and add a paper clip to their mouth. Write a numeral on the side of the fish. Children draw a card with a number of dots and then "catch" the fish with the correct numeral. To make it easier to find the correct fish, fish with larger numbers can be larger.

Adding to or Taking Away. One experiment found that children as young as 3 can add and subtract sets up to 10 by first predicting and then counting (Zur & Gelman, 2004). To assist children to add and subtract, provide the following materials:

- Objects from songs, finger plays, or books that stress addition or subtraction. Teachers can introduce these activities during circle time and then place the props in the math area for children to use. For example, if telling a story involving a baker who added ingredients to create different dishes, you could add both the baker's hat and the flannel board pieces to the math center (Zur & Gelman, 2004).

- Cuisenaire rods that children can use to create equal combinations (for example, two 5 cm rods equal one 10 cm rod). Cuisenaire rods are wooden, colored manipulative sticks, ranging in size from 1 to 10 cm, that children can use for a variety of math activities.

- Addition and subtraction games. Play games with two dice. Children add the dice and move that many spaces on the game board.

- A money center. Based upon the children's developmental level, challenges can be created. For example, "How many different ways can you find to equal a nickel, a dime, a quarter, or a dollar?"

Materials to Support the Geometry and Spatial Awareness Standard

Children in the early childhood years are learning to name and describe shapes. They are also learning to transform shapes and describe spatial relations. As children become familiar with shapes they are able to form mental images (NCTM, 2000). When providing materials for geometry and spatial awareness, it is very important to be aware of children's common misconceptions. This is especially crucial for early childhood teachers because concepts of two-dimensional shapes (whether right or wrong) become stable as early as age 6 (Clements, 2004). So what are the common misconceptions?

Because children are often introduced to only prototype shapes such as an equilateral triangle, they often mistakenly believe that any triangle that does not display the same orientation or symmetry is not a triangle. To prevent this misconception, it is very important to give children a variety of examples of each type of shape (shapes that are different sizes and that have different orientations). Children also need to see both examples and nonexamples (Clements, 2004). For example, when you are introducing triangles, include many types of triangles (acute, right, obtuse, and equilateral), but also include nontriangles (three-sided objects with a wavy line, or a three-sided object with an opening).

Another common misconception occurs when teachers teach squares and rectangles separately instead of teaching that squares are a special type of rectangle. Rectangles are a type of parallelogram. Parallelograms are a specific form of a quadrilateral. Obendorf and Taylor-Cox (1999) advise that we first introduce children to quadrilaterals by encouraging children to explore a variety of four-sided forms. Then have children classify these forms into different categories. Discussions should focus on sides and points. Below are sample activities to enhance geometric thinking:

- Games—Create a "belongs and does not belong" game where children sort objects or cards by a certain attribute such as circle/not a circle. Other games that involve shapes include concentration with different types of shapes, shape bingo, or twister.

- Feeley box shape activity—Create a feeley box by cutting a hole in a heavy cardboard box and adding a sock cuff to the hole. Place differently shaped objects into the box. Children can draw a shape card and try to find an object in the feeley box that matches that shape.

- Picture shape cards and materials for children to use in creating shapes (clay, Tinker Toys, toothpicks and plasticine, a geoboard). Varying the items used to create shapes enhances interest. Children draw a card and then create the shape using the materials.

- Legos, Unifix cubes, Cuisenaire rods, pattern blocks, tangrams, and parquetry blocks along with graphics and diagrams for children to create pictures and objects (Golbeck, 2005). In addition to premade cards, at Burlington Little School, preschool children take digital pictures of their designs. These are printed and placed in a three-ring binder allowing children to recreate their own and others' designs.

- Mirrors so that children can explore the **line of symmetry** (the line where both halves are the same).

Materials to Support the Measurement Standard

In international comparisons, children in the United States score lower in measurement than in other mathematic standards. Their scores are also lower than their peers' scores in other countries (National Center for Education Statistics, 1996). Since the roots of learning measurement take place in the early years, it is important that we provide children measurement opportunities (Clements & Stephan, 2004).

In learning about measurement, children go through the following five stages (Copley, 2000; Herbert, 1984). They

- Learn that objects have measurement properties that can be described
- Compare objects using measurement terminology (heavier, shorter, etc.)
- Determine a process and unit to use for measuring different types of items
- Use standard units for measuring such as rulers and yardsticks
- Create and use formulas (Copley, 2000, p. 126)

Measurement is a set of complex skills and concepts that completely develop over a period of many years (Clements & Stephan, 2004). Typically, children are not able to successfully use all measuring tools or to create and use complex formulas until they are in the upper elementary grades. Research indicates that it is best if measurement activities begin with learning about length, developing concepts of "shorter," "longer," and "equal in length." Children should first explore the concept of length through making direct comparisons between objects—for example, deciding which string of pop-together beads is longer by holding them side by side. After children understand length, you can introduce other measurement attributes, including weight, volume, area, time, and temperature.

Comparing. Help children to learn about comparing properties of items and to use comparison vocabulary through the following materials:

- Items of different sizes to seriate such as nesting dolls to order from smallest to largest.

- Weight canisters to match (these can be created by using black or gray film canisters and placing different items in them). Make these self-correcting by placing identical stickers on the bottom of the canisters that match.

- Several identical jars with different amounts of liquid so children can seriate the jars by volume.

Exploring Measuring Tools. When exploring measuring tools children need to understand the concept of a measurement unit and learn techniques for accurate measurement such as accurate alignment and not leaving gaps when measuring. In the past, it was considered best practice to avoid giving children standard measuring tools such as rulers until they were proficient at measuring using nonstandard measurement tools (measuring with feet, unifix cubes, paper clips). Research now indicates that at any age children benefit from using standard measurement tools (Clements, 2004). If you do use nonstandard measurement items, it is important to use only one type. For example, you would not want to use unifix cubes to measure one day and paper clips to measure the next day. "Research does not support using multiple nonstandard units" for teaching children about measurement (Clements & Stephan, 2004, p. 308). Following are materials that you can add to your math center to enhance measurement skills:

- Variety of measuring tools with several objects and ingredients to measure. For example, provide a household scale, balance scale with weights, and a kitchen scale for measuring weight. Supply measuring cups, quart and gallon jugs, graduated cylinders, and measuring spoons for measuring liquids. Provide a tape measure, ruler, wheel measure, yardstick, and meter stick for measuring length. Make clocks and different types of timers available for exploring the measurement of time. It is important to fully explore each measurement tool before introducing other tools. When children become proficient with the various tools, they can experiment with which measurement tool works best for different objects.

- Pumpkins, gourds, or squash to measure (circumference, weight, length, height). The vegetables can be measured both before and after cooking.

- Heavy strips of cardboard that children can use to make their own rulers.

- Balance scale and a series of oral, written, or pictorial challenges. As children become more proficient, they can create challenges for each other.

  - How many teddy bear counters weigh the same as one small unit block?

  - How many pennies does it take to equal the weight of one small toy car, one small doll, etc.?

  - Which weighs more—the toy boat or the toy car?

  - How many items can be found in the classroom that weigh the same as one penny?

- Variety of containers and a bucket of sand. Add tall, thin containers as well as fat, short containers that have the same volume.

- A scale and several similar-sized balls (nerf ball, baseball, softball, plastic ball) that weigh different amounts.

- Measuring box with a variety of measuring tools (tape measure, ruler, folding yardstick, meter stick) that children can use throughout the room when they wish to measure.

- "Beat the clock" games. Provide a timer and direction cards with pictures and words. For example, how many times can you hop before the timer runs out? How many screws and bolts can you put together in one minute?

- Mounted wall clock with a paper clock below it so that children can match the hands (Houle, 1984).

- Stopwatch for elementary age children to use in determining how long it takes to complete common activities (tie your shoe, write your name).

TIP Calendar Debate

Although calendars are a time-honored tradition in early childhood programs, many early childhood professionals question whether they are developmentally appropriate. As stressed by Ethridge and King (2005), "The concept of time is ambiguous, socially constructed, and abstract" (p. 292). Children under the age of 6 have typically not acquired the developmental level to understand the calendar (Ethridge & King, 2005; Schwartz, 1994). In fact, many are still grappling with the concept of today, yesterday, and tomorrow. Realizing this, some teachers use the calendar for patterning or counting activities. However, Beneke, Ostrosky, and Katz (2008) recommend that instead these math skills be taught in an individualized, meaningful context, such as through learning center activities. Time devoted to calendar can instead be used more wisely in group "math talks." See the discussion of math talks in this chapter for more information.

Materials to Support the Patterns and Algebra Standard

Before children can create patterns, they must be able to sort and classify. One of the goals for pre-K through second-grade children is to "sort, classify, and order objects by size, number, and other properties" (NCTM, 2000, p. 90). Teddy bear counters, for instance, allow children to classify by color or size. Contrast this to intellectual kits created by a long-time early childhood teacher, Eve Malo. These kits, created around a theme such as kitchen gadgets or office desk items, provide endless opportunities for classifying objects into sets. Additionally, children's interest is often piqued by classifying objects they see the adults in their lives using.

Children also need trays to sort sets into (muffin tins, deviled egg plates, egg cartons). To add interest and a sense of importance to the activity, teachers can use aesthetically pleasing sorting trays (wooden manacala trays, crystal relish dishes).

As children become more proficient in classifying objects, introduce the concept of Venn diagrams. Venn diagrams are used to identify common attributes between different sets. Two or three overlapping circles can be created with plastic tubing, string, or inner tubes.

Patterning. Making patterns begins with understanding the unit (AB). Either the unit repeats (ABABAB) or it grows (ABAABAAAB). Teachers designing pattern activities can plan color, shape, size, and spatial orientation patterns (Taylor-Cox, 2003). Some patterning materials for young children include the following:

- American Indian beads for duplicating or creating patterns (Sgarlotti, 2004). For a less expensive option, make pattern necklaces or bracelets out of pieces of colored straws cut into ¼" segments.

Figure 10.1
Items to Sort, Classify,
Count, and Pattern
Source: Gallenstein, 2004;
Seefeldt & Galper, 2004.

shells	bottle caps	watches
rocks	fabric samples	leaves
keys	wallpaper samples	pinecones
feathers	nuts and bolts	rocks
leaves	small toy animals	picture cards (such
toy cars	marbles	as animals with
beads	different types of	and without hair)
buttons	bells	
coins		

- Manipulatives (seashells, unifix cubes, small blocks, or paper chains) and pattern cards.
- Stamps for creating patterns.

After children have mastered the recreation of a pattern and the creation of their own unique patterns, they are ready to describe or read their patterns, draw their patterns, and finally to record their patterns using numbers or letters. A variety of different items can be used for sorting, classifying, counting, and patterning. See Figure 10.1 for some ideas. You will want to choose the material based upon the children's interests and their level of development. Rotating the items can spark new interest and present new classifying and patterning challenges.

Materials to Support the Data Analysis Standard

In teaching graphing, it is important to begin by using physical objects. For example, all children wearing red stand on the floor graph. Then teachers should proceed to manipulatives, followed by picture graphs (an example of a picture graph is shown in Figure 10.2), then line plots, and finally bar graphs. By second grade, children should be able to analyze data and create their own picture graphs, line plots, and bar graphs (Russell, 1991). Sample graphing materials for math learning centers include the following:

- Real objects for children to graph—For example, graph a collection of dolls on a floor graph. You can create floor graphs by using a tablecloth (use a flannel-backed tablecloth to prevent slipping on carpeted floor or place a nonslip rug pad under it for linoleum floors) and dividing it into columns with colorful tape.
- Small manipulative objects and ice cube trays for graphing (Copley, 2000).
- Pictures of children to use for graphing—Place a digital picture of each child on a juice can lid and provide a magnetic graph. Children can then use these for many different teacher- or child-initiated graphing activities (e.g., gender, hair color, eye color, prefers dogs or cats).
- Clothespins with each child's picture and name on a clothespin. Children can interview their classmates and clip the clothespin on a cardboard graph based upon the answer (Baratta-Lorton, 1972).
- Graph paper for children who are more proficient in graphing.

Special Considerations and Materials for Infants and Toddlers

Infants appear primed to learn mathematics. Even from birth, infants are able to discriminate between small sets (one to three items). For example, when researchers repeatedly showed one-day-old infants sets with two items they became bored and looked away. However, when they were then shown sets with three items they became interested, demonstrating that they saw this set as different (Caulfield, 2000; Mix et al., 2002). Infants are also able to anticipate quantitative transformations (Berger, Tzur, & Posner, 2006; Mix et al.,

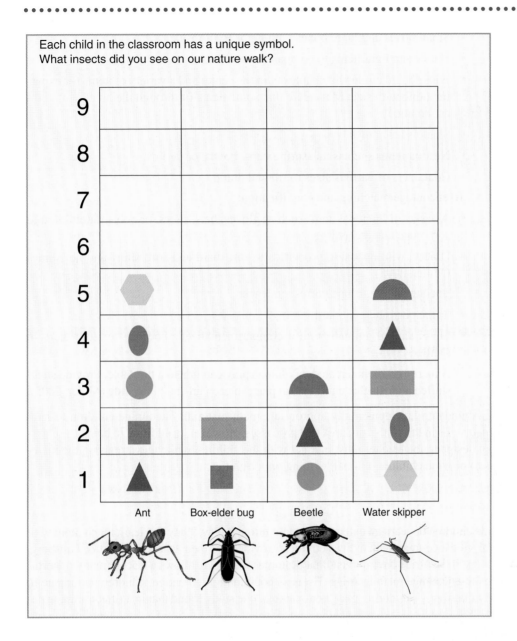

Each child in the classroom has a unique symbol.
What insects did you see on our nature walk?

Ant   Box-elder bug   Beetle   Water skipper

Figure 10.2
Picture Graph

2002). For example, if infants watch you place two items behind a screen and then see you place one more item behind the screen, they expect to see three items when the screen is removed. If there are two items or four items instead, they act surprised (Clements, 2004; Cooper, 1984). These studies help us to realize that infants have mathematical knowledge that we can expand upon as teachers.

Some of the materials mentioned previously in the chapter are appropriate for infants and toddlers. For example, many of the classification materials would be appropriate as long as they do not pose a choking hazard. While you will typically not have a separate math center in infant and toddler classrooms, math manipulatives can be integrated into other centers. Following are materials that you can provide to infants and toddlers to emphasize math.

- To assist children to learn early geometric skills:
  - A big and little center with a collection of big and little items to play with, compare, and contrast such as big and little balls, cars, dolls, and spaces (Isbell & Isbell, 2003).

Developing Math Centers

- Small boxes and large boxes with items to fit inside.

- Heavy and light items to compare and contrast.

- A cardboard circle with a hole cut in the center and a variety of items for experimenting with size. Make sure that some items fit through the hole, while others do not.

- Shape-sorting toys.

- Nesting items such as measuring cups, bowls, or jar lids.

- Containers of various sizes to fill and dump.

- To encourage matching and classification:

  - A basket of identical items such as gloves, hats, shoes, or boots for children to sort, match, and classify.

  - Objects with opposing properties to sort (hard and soft, shiny and not shiny) (Miller, 2005).

- To encourage one-to-one correspondence:

  - Large pegs and pegboards.

  - Small stuffed animals with a compartmentalized shoe bag to store them in (Miller, 2005).

  - A merry-go-round created by gluing spray can lids to a turntable. Provide small stuffed animals that children can place in each lid and give a ride (Miller, 2005).

Abundant, developmentally appropriate math materials encourage children to gain needed skills in the math standards and processes. However, in addition to being the classroom designer, the teacher must interact with the children while they are using the materials to provide children optimal learning opportunities.

Teachers' Facilitation of Learning in the Math Center

While children do learn an extensive amount through play, "they can learn much more with artful guidance and challenging activities provided by their teachers" (Seo & Ginsburg, 2004, p. 103). A rich environment that promotes math play allows a teacher many opportunities to encourage math learning. Even without adult intervention, children participate in many math activities during play. For example, one study found that in a fifteen-minute period, 88% of the children engaged in some form of math activity. The amount of math used in play was similar across income levels and gender, suggesting that math concept formation is naturally embedded in play (Seo & Ginsburg, 2004). Imagine how this play is enhanced in a mathematically rich environment supported by a teacher who scaffolds learning.

To scaffold learning, teachers need to engage children in formal and informal math discussions. As teachers interact with children they can model mathematical language, ask questions to help children reason, suggest ideas for materials, ask children to communicate their thinking, build on children's intuitive knowledge connecting this to formal mathematics, and encourage children to solve problems. While children use the math materials, the teacher will also be assessing and documenting children's learning, making sure that the needs of all children are being met.

Engage Children in Formal, Preplanned Math Talks

Math talks can be used to introduce and build interest in materials, to discuss math concepts, and to share math learning. Kristi, a Head Start teacher, taught the children the finger play, "Five Little Monkeys." She then discussed addition and subtraction while reading the book, *No More Monkeys Jumping on the Bed*. Next, she introduced an activity where children matched plastic monkeys to numerals. After circle time, she placed the activity and the book in the math center. Because of the interest built during circle time, the majority of children chose to use the materials.

Marlis, a teacher of multi-age preschoolers, designated a "math talk" circle each day. During "math talk" she scaffolded children's learning through discussing and introducing math concepts. For example, for 2 weeks she introduced different patterning activities using materials from the math center. Each week she also had an estimation jar. The children would guess how many items were in the jar during choice times and then at the end of a week they would take the items out at circle time and count them.

Representing and communicating are two of the math process skills. Taurean encourages children in her kindergarten classroom to share their tallies, charts, diagrams, and drawings with the class during their "math talks" as a way of acknowledging and supporting these skills.

Engage Children in Informal Math Talk

The amount of teacher talk about math is significantly related to children's achievement in math, with those teachers who use the most math talk having children with the highest math skills at the end of the year (Klibanoff, Levine, Huttenlocher, Vasilyeva, & Hedges, 2006). Better outcomes are obtained when the teacher talk is focused on reciprocity, where "adults make overtures to children that are in tune with their current attentional focus, building on the children's activities, prior knowledge, and skill level" (National Research Council et al., 2001, p. 44). Informal math talk can be used to address the needs of individual or small groups of children.

Model Mathematical Language

"Although children exhibit many quantitative skills before they know the words for numbers or mathematical concepts, acquiring mathematical language opens the door to new ways of thinking and complex skills" (Mix et al., 2002, p. 135). Emphasize mathematical vocabulary by including directional words (such as near, far, over, under, above), names of shapes, and numeral names. Use mathematical terms such as not, if-then, all-some, equal, none, sets, points, sides, flip, turn, add, subtract, divide, and multiply to develop concepts and vocabulary (Copley, 2000). Daniel posted a list of math vocabulary words on the wall in the math center so that he would remember to use them with children.

Ask Questions to Assist Children in Reasoning

"The use of questions and demonstrations can help draw out existing knowledge and build on it, contributing to a restructuring of the child's understanding" (National Research Council et al., 2001, p. 43). Ask questions that encourage children to reason and to think more deeply. Reasoning is one of the process skills emphasized by the NCTM. For example, you might ask, "I wonder what would happen if . . . ?" "How do you know . . . ?" "Can you show me another way to sort the objects?" "What other ways can you make the number 10?" "Describe your pattern." (Copley, 2000). For an example of a teacher assisting a child reasoning about their classification of seashells, watch the video *Intelligence* on MyEducationLab.

Go to MyEducationLab and select the topic "Child Development." Under Activities and Applications, watch the video *Intelligence*.

Suggest Ideas for Materials

Carmella, a teacher of kindergarten children, observed two boys rolling cars down a ramp. They were discussing which car traveled the furthest. Because one of the cars had traveled straight and one had curved, they were having a difficult time deciding. Carmella took advantage of this teachable moment, suggesting that they measure the distance. The boys brought over the measuring tote and tried the different measuring tools to see which would work the best. They ultimately used the sewing tape and were able to answer their question. Carmella's suggestion allowed the children to use mathematical tools to solve a real-life problem.

Ask Children to Communicate Their Thinking

When children communicate their thoughts, they think more deeply about what they have done. For example, research shows that when teachers ask children to justify their categorization of shapes they categorized them more accurately (Hannibal, 1999). It also allows the teacher to assess a child's understanding. Judy observed that Ella, who is four, had divided all the shiny buttons and a couple of flower buttons into one tray and all the other buttons into another. She presumed that Ella was dividing using "shiny" and "not shiny" and had made an error with the flower buttons. However, when she asked Ella to explain the grouping, Ella told her "pretty" and "not pretty."

Connect Children's Intuitive Math Knowledge and Formal Mathematics

"Play does not guarantee mathematical development, but it offers rich possibilities. Significant benefits are more likely when teachers follow up by engaging children in reflecting on and representing the mathematical ideas that have emerged in their play" (Ginsburg, 2006, p. 25). As children are engaged in using math in their play it is important to label it as such, thus assisting children to make the connection between informal and formal mathematics. Additionally, you can record their work (photos, video, or transcriptions) and, after children have completed playing, you can show them the recordings and ask them to reflect upon what they were doing. This also allows you to point out the skills they were using in mathematical terms.

Encourage Children to Problem Solve

Teachers need to actively teach children steps to use in problem solving (to understand the problem, to make a plan to solve the problem, to implement it, and then to reflect to see if the plan worked). As discussed at the beginning of the chapter, this is one of the process skills emphasized by the NCTM. We also need to encourage the dispositions to problem solve and to try alternatives. For example, you might ask, "What else might you try?"

Assess and Document Individual Children's Learning

You will want to assess and document children's mathematical knowledge, skills, and dispositions to determine their progress and learning needs (NAEYC/NCTM, 2002). This allows you to plan activities and materials that will scaffold children to the next associated concept. Assessment and documentation can also assist you in reflecting upon your own effectiveness. Teachers can use many tools when assessing children's math skills. These include anecdotal records, checklists, inventory of activities completed, work samples, and student interviews to determine children's thinking.

Janisa, a teacher of a multi-age preschool classroom, developed math jobs for children. Each of these individualized, hands-on activities emphasized unique math skills. Janisa numbered each math job and created a chart with children's names and numbers so that anyone witnessing a child attempting or successfully completing the math job could annotate the chart. It was easy for Janisa to then transfer this information to the child's file. This information also helped Janisa to plan subsequent activities.

Meet the Needs of All Learners

The child's long-term academic success is built on the mathematical foundation that is established in the early childhood years. It is crucial that we meet the needs of all learners in our classrooms so they have an equitable opportunity for mathematical success. Math equity is one of the principles that NCTM has developed to guide math education (NCTM, 2000). The area where nonequity is especially pronounced in the early childhood years relates to socioeconomic status. Research indicates that children from middle and higher socioeconomic status have higher levels of math achievement than children from lower socioeconomic backgrounds when they begin kindergarten (Klibanoff et al., 2006). The difference in math levels is one of degree. Children from lower socioeconomic backgrounds travel the same learning trajectory or course in regard to mathematical understandings and strategies as their higher income peers. However, they are delayed on this path. For example, "In a number knowledge test, low-income 5- to 6-year-olds performed much like middle-income 3- to 4-year-olds" (National Research Council et al., 2001, p. 81). This gap often has devastating effects, becoming more pronounced in elementary school (Denton & West, 2002) and continuing throughout high school (Braswell et al., 2001). Lack of math skills often contributes to students not attending or not persevering in college. For example, algebra is a "gatekeeper subject" for higher education (Taylor-Cox, 2003, p. 14). Those who do not have this skill are generally unable to acquire a college education.

This gap does not appear to relate to intelligence, since research shows that nonverbal calculation skills are not related to socioeconomic status (Jordon, Levine, & Huttenlocker, 1994). Instead, the gap is probably related to opportunities to learn social-arbitrary knowledge.

In addition, the kinds of materials used to learn math might be biased toward some groups. In one study, children in a third-world agricultural community who did not attend school were compared with children in an urban area in the United States who did attend school. When the math task involved seeds and grain, the children in the agricultural community outperformed the children from the United States. However, when colored disks were used to perform the same tasks, the U.S. children did better (Lantz, 1979; National Research Council et al., 2001).

It is especially important that teachers assist children from low-income backgrounds to acquire math skills. Teaching children conventional knowledge and mathematical language, and providing a rich mathematical setting, are all important. It is also important to use familiar, interesting manipulatives.

In addition, it is vital to meet the needs of children at a variety of developmental levels. Caroline, a 5-year-old girl with Down's syndrome, attended a Head Start center. Nancy, her teacher, was concerned about whether the materials in the different centers in the classroom met Caroline's learning needs. Using the Building Blocks model described in Chapter 2, Nancy began by first checking to make sure she was offering a high-quality program for all the children in the classroom. In examining the math center, she found that all the materials were closed-ended and would be appropriate for only a few of the children. Nancy developed several new activities for the math center that were open-ended, including many materials to sort, classify, pattern, and count. The center was now more appropriate for Caroline and her classmates. Since one of Caroline's goals was to match shapes, Nancy also added a shape sorting ball to the center.

Teachers need to provide opportunities for all children to gain the skills to be mathematically successful in numbers and operations, measurement, algebra, geometry, data analysis and math processes. To do so, we must assess children's development and intentionally plan high-interest, developmentally appropriate materials, opportunities, and interactions that will challenge children to grow mathematically.

Outdoor Math Centers

The outdoors provides many opportunities for authentic math experiences. Through thoughtful planning, teachers can enhance these opportunities. Some examples of outdoor math materials include

- Measuring cups and containers of all sizes for the sand and water area.
- An easily accessible measurement tool kit. When materials are readily available, it encourages both teachers and children to use them. For example, children at Tiny Tots found a worm and got out the tape measure to measure it. They had a small journal in the tool kit where they recorded the length of the different worms they found. This was the longest worm found up to this time, causing great excitement.
- A jumping pit with a built-in measuring tape.
- Graphs for collecting data (number of birds or type of birds visiting a bird feeder or how many times you need to fill the bird feeder each week).
- An outdoor weather station with a windsock, rain gauge, thermometer, sundial, and cloud cards. One of the children's rotating jobs can be to check, record, and share information from the weather station. Provide a journal in a sealed plastic bag where children can record their findings.

To function in society today it is crucial that all children gain knowledge and skills in math. The foundation for this learning begins in the early childhood years. Unfortunately, so do the inequities in learning opportunities. To prevent children's futures from being negatively impacted by this gatekeeper subject, we must provide all young children with rich experiences in math. One way we do this is to provide well-designed math centers that contain an abundance of developmentally appropriate math materials. As teachers, it is crucial that we interact with children as they use these materials to scaffold their learning.

Sample Application Activities

1. Observe children during center time to see what mathematical activities they are engaged in.
2. Develop some math games for the age you currently teach or plan to teach. Try to develop the game so it can be adapted to meet the changing development needs of children. For example, you might have different dice, some with dots and others with numerals.
3. Critique a math center using the environmental assessment in Figure 10.3. What changes could be made to enhance the center?
4. Tape record yourself in the math area or observe another teacher. How is the teacher facilitating children's learning? What math terminology is the teacher using? Are there examples of missed opportunities for facilitation?

☐ Is there a clearly designated math area in the quiet area of the room?

☐ Does the center provide a variety of developmental math activities in each of the different math standards (numbers and operations, measurement, geometry, algebra, and data analysis)?

☐ Are shelves organized with a clearly designated place for each item?

☐ Does the center contain aesthetically pleasing containers that allow children to see what is available and keep all needed materials together?

☐ Is there a large space to work?

☐ Is there a place to display completed work such as a bulletin board, a three-ring binder for sketches and photos, and top of a shelf for three-dimensional work?

☐ Are materials or activities in the math center
  • concrete materials that allow for active manipulation?
  • based on a clearly defined purpose or goal?
  • open-ended or self-correcting?
  • based on assessment of the current group of children's skills and knowledge?
  • related to children's interests?
  • rotated to meet children's changing developmental needs and interests?

Figure 10.3
Environmental Assessment: Math Center

5. To learn more about the National Council of Teachers of Mathematics (NCTM) national math standards visit the following website.

   http://www.nctm.org/standards/default.aspx?id=58

6. To read the NAEYC/NCTM Early Childhood Math Position Statement see
   http://www.naeyc.org/about/positions/psmath.asp

7. To see a library of video clips of K–4 teachers teaching math see
   http://www.learner.org/resources/series32.html

chapter 11

Developing Block and Building Centers

A *dalina, a teacher of 5-year-old children, attended a workshop on blocks at an early childhood conference. She returned to her program very motivated to develop a rich block environment for children in her classroom. Although she had always had a block area in the classroom, Adalina, like many teachers, approached it with a "laissez-faire" attitude (Bruce, 1992). In the past, she randomly cycled props through the center, she rarely interacted in the center, and she never went beyond individual discussions with a builder to enrich, extend, or discuss the learning that occurred in the block area.*

Adalina began her block area transformation by closely observing the children to determine their stage of building. She also noted what they were building. She saw that many of the children were building houses and that some of the children were representing actual structures they had seen. To expand the children's background knowledge, Adalina decided to invite an architect and a carpenter to the classroom. The architect showed the children a picture of the studio where she worked, blueprints she had designed, and photos of the houses made from the blueprints. The carpenter discussed how he used the blueprints and showed the children some of the tools he used. The children were fascinated.

Next, Adalina made changes to the environment. She added a small drafting table with a gooseneck light and different types of paper so children could develop their own blueprints. She laminated blueprints and hung them with Velcro on the wall. Children could easily move the blueprints closer to their building area, if desired. During circle time, Adalina and the children talked about different kinds of houses and realized that their blueprints were only for stick-built single-family dwellings. The children decided to create blueprints for other types of housing (a duplex, an apartment, and a trailer house). One of the children, who had attended a pow-wow the summer before, decided to create a blueprint for a tepee. Adalina added books and magazines on different types of houses to the block area. The children and Adalina spent several circle times examining, comparing, and discussing the blueprints children were developing.

Adalina also enriched the block area with some of the tools that the carpenter had discussed, including a level and tape measure. Many of the children began measuring and comparing buildings. Adalina developed a graph where children could record their measurements.

The increased use of the block area caused Adalina to reexamine the block area rules, one of which was that all blocks needed to be put away at the end of center time. As children became more involved in in-depth building experiences, they often could not complete the projects in one day. Therefore, Adalina and the children decided to let the structures remain as long as they were actively being built or used. Paper and markers were added to the center so that children could create signs to label or to save their structures.

Additional props were added as needed, including linoleum and carpet samples, different sizes of Masonite (for roofs and floors), and pulleys (for building an elevator). Adalina and the children continued to closely observe buildings as they went for walks, creating a book of photos of surrounding structures. Parents also became involved, bringing in not only pictures of their own homes and places they worked, but also photos of houses they had seen on travels.

As a result of these changes, children engaged in more literacy, math, and science activities. Adalina also observed more cooperative building activity and reluctant builders becoming involved with block building.

 Apply Your Knowledge   What specific math and literacy skills did children have the opportunity to learn in the block area created by Adalina? What other curriculum areas were being addressed in this block area?

With the help of a child, blocks of wood come to life. "Blocks become airports or empires. Blocks become stadiums and skyscrapers, houses and hovels, castles and, today, even condominiums. Out of the imaginings of a child, blocks become everything! Lacking imagination, blocks revert to chunks of wood . . . waiting to become again" (Cody, 1989,

p. 109). These open-ended materials provide a multidisciplinary curriculum where children of all developmental levels can engage in many skills simultaneously (Miller, 2004; O'Hara, Demarest, & Shaklee, 2005). As Adalina illustrated, with close observation and intentionality, teachers can greatly enrich and extend these learning opportunities.

History of Blocks

Block building has a rich history within early childhood. Friedrich Froebel (the father of kindergarten) is credited as being the first to use blocks as part of a systematic curriculum (Gura, 1993). Maria Montessori also used blocks as part of her materials. In both these cases, blocks were used in a prescribed way. For example, one set of Montessori blocks is designed as cubes that are to be placed in increasingly smaller sizes to create a tower (Provenzo & Brett, 1983). In 1915, Caroline Pratt, desiring blocks that would allow children to have the freedom to design and build what they wished, developed the unit block. The unit blocks are designed mathematically (two smaller blocks equal a larger block). Unit blocks are still used in early childhood settings throughout the United States (Provenzo & Brett, 1983). They are also found in schools throughout the world (Cartwright, 1988).

Stages of Block Building

Harriet Johnson, who worked with Caroline Pratt, studied the children's use of unit blocks. Based on this study she developed stages of block building. Like the unit blocks, these stages are still used today to assess children's block building skills.

- Stage 1—Prebuilding: In the prebuilding stage children often experience blocks as a sensory material. They may physically examine the blocks, bang blocks together, taste the blocks, and fill containers with blocks and either dump them out or carry them around. This is an important stage, assisting children to learn about the weight and properties of blocks.
- Stage 2—Rows and Towers: In this stage, children build horizontal or vertical rows. As is characteristic of children this age, there is much repetition. As children first begin to build, they typically place the blocks directly in front of each other. Blocks are placed side-by-side in rows or stacked in towers (Reifel, 1984). As children advance in this stage, they may make adjoining towers that are connected by a row of blocks. The children may use the row of blocks as roads. By age 3, most children will be exhibiting this stage or beyond (Johnson, 1996; Reifel, 1984).
- Stage 3—Bridging: This stage refers to children placing two blocks close together and then balancing another block as a roof between the blocks (Johnson, 1996, p. 14).
- Stage 4—Enclosures: As the name implies this stage involves enclosing a space. Most children will be building en-

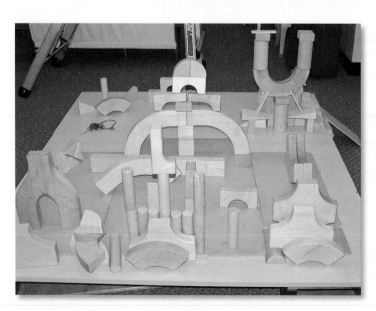

What stage of block building is being exhibited?

closures by age 4 (Johnson, 1996). At this stage, children will be able to clearly differentiate indoor and outdoor space.

- Stage 5—Patterns: In this stage, children begin to use symmetry in their building and decorative patterns may emerge.

- Stage 6—Naming of Structures and Early Representation: Children at this stage use all they have learned at previous stages. Unlike earlier stages, where children may name a structure due to an inquiry by an adult, children at this stage have an intention in mind as they begin to build. They also begin to use the building for dramatic play.

- Stage 7—Reproduction: Children in this stage actually reproduce buildings and structures they have seen. As in stage 6, children at this stage use their structures in dramatic play. By age 7, most children have progressed to the point that they can coordinate interior space with interior objects. They also can include exterior landmarks that are of appropriate scales and that portray relationships with the building (Reifel, 1984).

With ample opportunities to build, some children may progress through these stages quickly (especially stages 2 to 5). They may also cycle back to earlier stages at times. Older children who have never had experience with blocks still proceed through each of the stages. However, they might advance through them even more quickly than younger children (Johnson, 1996).

The more time and experience the child has, the more complex the block play becomes (Hanline, Milton, & Phelps, 2001; Johnson, 1996). For example, children who have more experience tend to use more dimensions, building three-dimensional rather than one- or two-dimensional structures (Reifel, 1984).

Observe a group of boys during block play by watching the video *Building with Blocks* on MyEducationLab. What stage of block building are the boys displaying? How do the props support their play? What are they learning as they build?

Go to MyEducationLab and select the topic "Play." Under Activities and Applications, watch the video *Building with Blocks*.

How the Block Center Enhances Children's Development

Block play provides rich opportunities. While children build with blocks they develop mathematical skills, use symbolic representation, practice science skills, make use of literacy, exhibit social-emotional skills, demonstrate aesthetic awareness, and practice geography.

Mathematical Skills Developed in the Block Area

The block center may be one of the most important areas in the classroom for creating opportunities to experiment with quantity and number sense and to increase spatial awareness and knowledge of geometric concepts. These two math standards are often viewed as the most crucial for children in the early years (Clements & Sarama, 2000a).

There is a strong relationship between spatial skills and mathematics (Casey & Bobb, 2003). Block building enhances spatial skills. For example, children who performed well in preschool block building take more math classes (these are more likely to be honor classes), receive higher standardized math test scores, and have better math grades in middle and high school than children who were less competent preschool block builders (Wolfgang, Stannard, & Jones, 2001). This was especially true for higher-level math skills such as geometry (Wolfgang et al., 2001). The correlation between block building skills and higher performance in later mathematics was true even when considering gender, intelligence, and social class (Wolfgang et al., 2001).

Blocks give children the opportunity to learn geometric concepts (Piaget, 1967). Some of the geometric concepts that children develop through block building are the ability to

- "Recognize, name, build, draw, compare, and sort two and three dimensional shapes" (Clements & Sarama, 2000a, p. 82)
- "Describe attributes and parts of two and three dimensional shapes" (Clements & Sarama, 2000a, p. 82)
- "Investigate and predict the results of putting shapes together and taking them apart" (Clements & Sarama, 2000a, p. 82)
- "Describe, name, interpret, and apply ideas of relative position in space" (Clements & Sarama, 2000a, p. 83)
- "Describe, name, interpret, and apply ideas of direction and distance in navigating space" (Clements & Sarama, 2000a, p. 83)
- "Find and name locations with simple relationships, such as 'near to'" (Clements & Sarama, 2000a, p. 83)
- "Use coordinate systems, such as those in maps" (Clements & Sarama, 2000a, p. 83)
- Recognize and apply slides, flips, and turns (NCTM, 2000, p. 96)
- Recognize and create shapes that have symmetry (NCTM, 2000, p. 96)

Children's spatial skills increase when they play with blocks, learn spatial language (such as above, below, beside), and engage in spatial planning where they develop images of structures they plan to build (make a blueprint for their building). With experience and a higher level of thinking, children's understanding of shapes deepens. For example, they are able to relate a square to a rectangle (Clements & Sarama, 2000c). Most preschool children can accurately identify circles and squares. They identify triangles correctly 60% of the time and identify rectangles correctly 54% of the time, not always recognizing that rectangles need right angles (Clements & Sarama, 2000c). Children's ideas about shapes, while not always accurate, often stabilize by age 6 (Clements & Sarama, 2000c). Surprisingly, little is learned about shapes from preschool to middle school (Clements & Sarama, 2000c). In their research, Clements and Sarama (2000c) found that the opportunities to learn are more important than developmental levels in children's knowledge of shapes.

Blocks can also increase children's knowledge of quantity and number sense (Chalufour, Hoisington, Moriarty, Winokur, & Worth, 2004). "Quantity or number sense may be as important to math development as phonemic awareness is to emergent literacy" (O'Hara et al., 2005, p. 4). For example, classifying, seriating, and using conservation in block and construction play relates to higher standardized achievement test scores in kindergarten and in first grade (Pasnak, Madden, Martin, Malabonga, & Holt, 1996; Pasnak, McCutchen, Holt, & Campbell, 1991).

In some programs, block building is dominated by boys. Because of the rich opportunities for mathematical as well as other learning, it is important to encourage girls as well as boys to use this area. When girls have equal block building opportunities, they are as competent as boys in block building skills (Gura, 1993; Hanline et al., 2001).

In Brianna's classroom, the girls very rarely used the block area. She decided to try having a girls' block building week, where only girls could use the area. Because several of the girls enjoyed playing in the dramatic play area, she added miniature props to the block area (people, furniture, dishes). Most of the girls chose the block building area during the week. Following this girls' only week, the girls frequently used the block area. Brianna stated, "I wondered if it was the right thing to do. I've never before restricted an area. However, the girls had somehow gotten the idea that the block area was only for boys. I think they were intimidated by the block area, as well. Having this block week seemed to give them confidence and change their attitude."

Symbolic Representation in the Block Area

By age 3, most children represent symbolically with blocks (Reifel, 1984). According to Piaget (1962), symbolic representation is one of the most important cognitive achievements of the preoperational years. In the beginning stages of block building, children might first show symbolic representation as they use the block to represent another object such as a car or phone. As children become more proficient builders, they are able to intentionally represent their ideas and their concepts of different types of structures. To do this they must attend to the differences and similarities between the different types of structures and think about the purpose of the structure. As children represent their thinking, their ideas and concepts become visible to themselves and to others. This allows further discussion and engagement in understanding the concept. For example, Ricardo and Daniel were building stores. Ricardo said, "You didn't make a store, stores always have windows in the front. You don't have a window." Daniel answered, "It is a store. Not all stores have windows." Adelaida, their teacher, overheard the conversation. She and the boys discussed why stores might or might not have windows. They each decided that they would look at stores as they traveled through the neighborhood, looking to see if all the stores had windows.

Science Skills Developed in the Block Area

Block play helps children learn about the properties of materials, stability, and balance (Chalufour et al., 2004). "Accumulation of experience in building all kinds of structures provides a child with a good idea of what can or cannot be done with the material. A child learns to work with a cause-and-effect approach and to predict the structural stress resulting from the forces of gravity interacting on various parts of a building" (Moffitt, 1996, p. 31). The block area also provides many opportunities to learn other scientific content. Children can learn about force and motion as they build roads and ramps and use them with toy vehicles (Miller, 2004). As children become more advanced builders, they may also learn about other simple machines such as pulleys or wheels and axles.

While children learn science and math process skills in many centers, blocks are a "medium that is particularly well adapted for children to use these processes" (Moffitt, 1996, p. 27). Skills such as questioning, problem solving, analyzing, reasoning, communicating, investigating, and creating and using representations can be practiced as children play with blocks (Chalufour et al., 2004).

Literacy Skills Developed in the Block Area

The block area is a natural area for promoting literacy (Vygotsky, 1976). During block building, children practice many skills needed in reading, including visual discrimination and oral language (Stroud, 1995). While building, they practice fine motor skills and coordination that they need for writing (Stroud, 1995). The block area, when enriched with literacy materials, also gives children authentic opportunities to read and write for a purpose (Wellhousen & Giles, 2005).

Visual discrimination is needed to distinguish differences in letters and words (such as the difference between a *b* and a *d*). As children use blocks of different sizes and shapes, they use visual discrimination to create structures that are the same on both sides or display symmetry. Even as children are putting blocks away on shelves, they are practicing these skills (placing the triangle block on the shelf so that it matches the outline).

Since block building is often a cooperative activity, children have many authentic opportunities to use oral language. One study found that children produced more oral language and exhibited greater diversity in vocabulary in the block center than in the dramatic play area or a theme-based area (Isbell & Raines, 1991). In the block area, children have the opportunity to use language to explain an idea. This is a crucial aspect in the development of thought (Bodrova & Leong, 2007).

Children in the block area practice fine motor and coordination skills as they build with blocks and as they carefully decorate and use their buildings. These are important skills in handwriting, as well.

Finally, children have many authentic opportunities to practice reading and writing in the block area. However, this will only occur if the teacher is intentional in providing materials and in modeling and encouraging literacy activities. When the block area was enriched in a first-grade classroom, children increased the number of literacy behaviors. While children engaged in rich oral language before the block area was enriched, other literacy activities rarely occurred. When literacy materials such as stickers, paper, writing tools, books, pictures, posters, rulers, and sign-making materials were added to the block area, literacy activities dramatically increased. Further, when the adult interacted with children in the block area, discussed what children were doing, introduced materials, and modeled the use of print during play, literacy activities exploded to more than 50 separate literacy incidents in one week (Pickett, 1998). Adults in the study were careful not to direct play. Instead, they played alongside children, discussing ideas, asking questions when appropriate, and at times making suggestions. For example, the teacher suggested placing a sign on the store that a child was building so everyone would know what type of store it was. After this, several other children began to develop signs to identify their buildings.

Social-Emotional Skills Developed in the Block Area

Block building allows children to develop relational skills, express and deal with emotions, and develop a feeling of competence. While playing with blocks, children have the opportunity to negotiate, interact, and cooperate (Pickett, 1998). Blocks also provide children the opportunities to scaffold the learning for others (Vygotsky, 1978). In a study examining interactions during block building, Johnson-Pynn and Nisbet (2002) found that children as young as three spontaneously engage in peer tutoring. During peer tutoring, children most often give nonverbal cues such as demonstrating, modeling combinations of blocks, pointing, or selecting the correct block and handing it to the other child. When peers give verbal cues, they often ask the novice to look at some aspect of the block or building, discuss the shape or color, or describe the novice's actions. There was no difference found in the types of aid offered by older versus younger block building experts.

Block building can also be an avenue for expressing and dealing with emotions. While block building, children can enact scenes and confront fears. They have the power to act out their feelings and even change endings if they choose.

Additionally, while playing with blocks, children develop a feeling of competence. Block building allows children to become the "physical master over their environment, which may in turn give them a greater sense of control, empowerment and self-confidence" (Miller, 2004).

Development of Aesthetic Awareness in the Block Area

Block building is a form of transitory art. While building, children learn about balance, symmetry, shape, and design (MacDonald & Davis, 2001). They critique their own and other's buildings, developing artistic appreciation. As children build, they often add aesthetic details that are not needed for functionality alone. Block building also allows for individual creativity and thinking outside the box (O'Hara et al., 2005). Teachers can assist children to develop aesthetic awareness by providing materials children can use to decorate their structures, and by encouraging children to discuss and critique building details.

Geography Skills Developed in the Block Area

As children create in the block area, they often build homes or other structures found in the community. Church and Miller (1990) discuss several ways that teachers can extend this learning, including:

- Going on neighborhood walks and having children document what they see through sketches and photographs.
- Facilitating discussions. For example, discussing similarities and differences in homes, different types of structures, purposes of different types of structures.
- Displaying pictures and books of different kinds of homes, including pictures of the children's homes and homes in the neighborhood.

Children may use blocks to develop models and maps of their classroom, school, and community.

Designing an Effective Block Center

To develop an effective block center you must provide an appropriate space with an adequate supply of blocks and accessories. These materials need to be stored in an accessible manner.

It is very important that the block area be large enough so that it can easily accommodate the number of children using the space. This will allow children room to build elaborate structures. It will also reduce conflict and help prevent accidental structure destruction. Since it is recommended that preschoolers and elementary-age children be allowed to save their structures, it is also important to consider this when planning your space.

To provide protection for the builders and structures, the block center needs to be in a semi-enclosed area protected from the traffic path. Many teachers develop a "no building zone" bordering the shelves. This allows children to get blocks off the shelves and return them without disrupting other builders. To be effective, the "no building zone" needs to be at least 2 feet wide. If accommodating a wheelchair, the zone will need to be 4 feet wide (MacDonald & Davis, 2001).

The block center needs a stable building surface. A flat carpet or rug can provide a stable surface to build on while providing some protection from excessive noise as blocks fall.

To provide a rich building experience, it is critical that there are enough blocks. The exact number of blocks needed will be based on the number of children in the block area at one time and the children's stage of block building. At a minimum, the *Block Book* (1996) recommends the following number of unit blocks:

- 586 blocks for 3-year-old children
- 748 blocks for 4-year-old children
- 980 blocks for children who are 5 years and older

To make blocks easily accessible, they need to be stored on open shelves. The shelves should be labeled with an outline of the correct size block. Outlines can be painted on the shelf, made with contact paper, or drawn with a marker. You can also add a label that gives the name of the block (unit, double unit).

Blocks need to be arranged on the shelves to illustrate the mathematical relationship. For example, a quadruple unit block on the bottom shelf, with the two double unit blocks arranged on the shelf above them, and four unit blocks on the shelf above that. For an illustration, see the photo at the beginning of the chapter. The longest blocks need to be placed on the bottom shelf. This helps to stabilize the shelf, making it easier and safer for children to get the blocks on and off the shelf (MacDonald & Davis, 2001).

In addition to unit blocks, many programs add other types of blocks (blocks created from tree branches, foam, cardboard) to the area. This can increase the total number of blocks, allow children to experiment with different properties, and provide different building opportunities.

Block accessories should be available. These are typically stored in baskets and bins on open shelves, and labeled with pictures and/or words. For example, there may be a basket of zoo animals and one of farm animals.

Appropriate Materials for the Block Center

Appropriate materials for the block area will be based upon the children's stage of block building and their interests. In addition to blocks, you will typically add block play accessories, motivational materials that provide ideas and information, and writing materials.

Note the aesthetic way these natural building materials are displayed.

A display of natural materials encourages building.

Block Play Accessories

Carefully observe, sketch or take photos, and analyze children's work in the block area (Miller, 2004). This process will assist you in determining what accessories and materials to add to enrich the children's learning. Materials must be appropriate for the age group, authentic (found in an adult setting), and functional (practical and useful) (Neuman & Roskos, 1990).

To be practical and useful, the items need to be added when children are developmentally ready to use them and when the materials promote the children's current interests. For example, if children are creating towers and roads, you might add pictures of towers and roads, and toy vehicles. If children are making enclosures, you might add toy people (variety of ethnic groups as well as some people who have disabilities), furniture, animals, sign-making materials, and pictures of houses (Newburger & Vaughan, 2006). You might also add a variety of open-ended materials to be used for flooring, roofs, decorations, and for child-created accessories. If children are beginning to add doors and windows to their structures, you and the children might create some doors and windows from wood and transparency film that can become part of the props.

Following are some suggestions of materials that might be added to the block area, based upon the children's interests and level of development.

Children might visit local businesses to collect some of the samples, providing an opportunity to learn more about building while also receiving materials to use in the program.

Open-ended materials

- Pieces of wood and masonite (samples of wallboard are an appropriate size)
- Cardboard tubes
- Empty cans
- Empty thread spools
- Linoleum and carpet samples
- Wallpaper samples
- Countertop samples
- Ceramic tiles
- Cone-shaped hats or cups
- Popsicle sticks
- Natural items—pinecones, rocks, boughs, trees, stones
- Aluminum foil
- Bottle caps
- Small boxes that can become buildings
- Clay (to keep signs up, to provide stability for fences made out of Popsicle sticks, to create people)
- Plastic tubing
- Hay (if children are creating farms)
- Sheer curtains
- Pieces of fabric
- Rain gutters (for making car ramps)
- Plastic berry containers
- Meat trays
- Packing peanuts
- Materials for connecting (tape, duct tape, string, rope, yarn, twine)

Teacher or child-created materials

- Child-created stained glass windows—Create by taking tissue paper and gluing to waxed paper using liquid starch. When the creation is dry, you can trace around each piece of tissue paper with a black marker if you wish. Cut the stained glass windows into desired shapes and laminate them for durability (MacDonald & Davis, 2001, p. 141).
- Doors and windows (often created with Popsicle sticks and transparency film)
- Current children's pictures pasted on cardboard and cut out
- Digital pictures of children or buildings on paper towel tubes
- Signs
- Newspaper or magazine pages rolled into sticks to use as logs for building
- Blown-up street maps that are laminated

Purchased materials

- Vehicles (cars, boats, busses, trains)
- People (multiethnic, nonbiased)
- Dollhouse furniture
- Animals
- Traffic signs
- 1-inch blocks for decoration
- Landscaping materials (trees, bushes)
- Pulleys
- Electrical circuits, lights, switches (to create lighting for a town)
- Dress-up clothes (especially if children are in block building stage 6 or 7)
- Measuring tapes, carpenter tape, yardstick
- Mirrors to explore symmetry and see different perspectives
- Graph paper to design buildings

Motivational Materials to Provide Ideas and Information About Structures

Children's ideas for building come from a wide range of sources. Most often, these are from the curriculum theme, television, and peers (Reifel & Yeatman, 1991). You can provide additional ideas by supplying the following:

- Cards with pictures of structures
- Architectural magazines
- Travel magazines
- Art books of bridges and buildings
- Calendars that feature buildings (MacDonald & Davis, 2001)
- Photo album of local buildings
- Books about structures and building

Writing Materials

The reason children usually write in the block area is to designate ownership of their building, identify their buildings (for example, bakery), and to save structures (Stroud, 1995). In addition, children may make blueprints for structures they plan to build or sketches of completed structures. Teachers can add materials so that children can complete these tasks. These can include materials such as

- Paper of various sizes
- Sticky notes
- Adding machine tape
- Markers, pencils, and crayons
- Masking tape and string to attach signs to buildings
- Scissors

In addition, teachers can add authentic literacy materials that architects and carpenters use in their work. These could include

- Invoices
- Order forms
- Envelopes
- House plans
- Blueprints
- Pictures of roads, architectural features, different kinds of buildings

Some teachers also add a block center journal (Wellhousen & Giles, 2005). Children can sketch and write or dictate stories about their structures as a way of documenting their building experiences.

The teacher provides additional writing opportunities when she allows children to save structures from day to day. Children will often write signs letting others know that they wish to keep their building. When children have ample building time over a period of days, they often will add signs identifying their building, as well.

Special Considerations for Infants and Young Toddlers

It is important to begin block building in infancy (Reifel, 1984). Infants and young toddlers should be provided a variety of blocks that are different sizes and types. For example, blocks that are similar sizes but made from different materials (sponge and wood) allow children to explore weight. Infants and young toddlers also need many different-sized containers to put blocks into, assisting them to discover concepts of space and shape (Newburger & Vaughan, 2006). Since young toddlers enjoy moving materials from place to place, you can also provide small wagons or carts. Many of the accessories mentioned earlier would also be appropriate for infants and toddlers (cars, people, animals).

The block center can provide valuable learning opportunities for children when it is well designed and contains an abundance of appropriate materials. There are several other ways that the teacher can enhance children's learning. We will explore these next.

Teachers' Facilitation of Learning in the Block Center

Teachers can enhance the learning in the block area by providing background experiences, acknowledging builders, establishing rules that are conducive to building, interacting with individual and small groups of children as they play, and implementing group block talks, challenges, and provocations. It is important that the teacher also meet the needs of all learners. She must also regularly assess the center as well as observe and document individual children's learning.

Provide Experiences

Children often build and create what they know from experience. To provide these experiences, teachers can take children for walks, explore structures, and talk about building features (Reifel, 1984). You can also take children on field trips to visit different types of buildings. Like Adaline who we met at the beginning of the chapter, you can invite guests such as carpenters and architects to visit the classroom.

Acknowledge Block Builders

Kuschner (1989), in an article titled "Put Your Name on Your Painting: But the Blocks Go Back on the Shelves," discusses the lack of visibility and acknowledgment that often occurs in the block area. For example, artwork is labeled and displayed in the classroom, admired, sent home to parents, and collected for portfolios. The work is permanent and the owner is acknowledged. Block building, on the other hand, is often transitory. The teacher might make a quick comment and the building is destroyed. There is not a sense of ownership or permanency. Permanency is important because it allows the opportunity for further reflection on one's work. When work is not publicly acknowledged, the message we may be sending to children and parents is that block building is not valued. We can assist block builders to gain visibility and acknowledgment by

- Photographing or sketching block structures.
- Displaying block structure photos and sketches.
- Sending block structure photos and sketches home to parents.
- Including block structure sketches and photos in portfolios.
- Labeling structures with the builder's name. When a name is connected to something a child has done, it creates a sense of pride and a valuing of the activity (Kuschner, 1989).
- Encouraging the child to reflect upon and discuss the structure.
- Allowing block builders to keep their structure until they are finished building and using it.
- Encouraging children to write about their structure.

Establish Rules That Are Conducive to Building

It is important to establish rules that help children work successfully together. For example, "Structures are only destroyed by the builders." "A structure remains standing until all the builders agree that it should be torn down." Many teachers also establish rules regarding safe ways to build high structures.

However, it is also important to evaluate the necessity of rules. For example, two rules that may interfere with block building are, "Everything needs to be placed back on the shelf at the end of center time," and "All materials must remain in their respective centers." As mentioned previously, in-depth block building takes time and if it is at all possible, structures should be allowed to remain standing until children are done using them. In the past, the block area was often used as a space for circle time. Many experts no longer recommend this practice since it interferes with keeping block structures.

This elaborate block animal train was built over a period of several days, becoming larger and more extensive as time went on.

Allowing children to bring items from other areas often enriches the children's play experience. For example, Heisner (2005) describes an observation where a child wanted to bring a chair from the housekeeping area to the block area. At first, the teacher told the child to return the chair but later the teacher acquiesced, allowing the chair to be brought into the block area. The child used the chair as a captain's command post, giving orders for building and directions on using the block-built spaceship. In this case, the chair was an important prop that conveyed the power of the captain's position.

Interact with Individual or Small Groups of Children as They Play

In a rich environment, children learn through their own explorations. They also learn from their peers both through observation and through peer teaching (Johnson-Pynn & Nisbet, 2002). However, scaffolding by an adult can increase these learning opportunities. Some of the ways that teachers interact with children during block play include the following:

- Listen to children's explanations about their buildings.
- Ask questions to help children think more deeply. By asking thoughtful questions, the teacher can assist children to reflect upon their building process. This can include discussing reasons the children used certain techniques, their building intentions, the materials they used, the difficulty they had carrying out their plans, and the ideas they have for changing, modifying, and revising their building (Kuschner, 1989, p. 53). As children discuss and reflect upon their building, they think more deeply and may draw new conclusions.
- Name the type of block being used (unit, double unit, half unit, etc.), which helps children recognize the mathematical relationships between the blocks. See Figure 11.1 for a sketch and name of each type of unit block.

- Use spatial and mathematical vocabulary as you discuss the process and structure (add, subtract, more, less, greater than, fewer, equal to point, side, line, angle, surface, plane, symmetry). You might also use ordinal order (first, second, third), cardinal numbers (1, 2, 3), and names of shapes (triangle, square) to describe the structure.

- Increase vocabulary related to building and structures through using new words when talking with children. The vocabulary the teacher stresses will vary depending upon the developmental level of the child. An infant and toddler may be learning basic words like roof, floor, window, and door. As children get older, they can learn more advanced architectural terms and features (arch, column, dome, dormer, eave, and gable) (Miller, 2004). School-age children may be ready to go more in-depth, learning words that more accurately describe each type of feature (round arch, triangular arch, and gothic arch). To help themselves remember to use enriched vocabulary, some teachers post vocabulary words on the wall in the block area.

- Provide correct information. Teachers often pass on their misconceptions to children (Clements & Sarama, 2000b, p. 485a). Some of these misconceptions are that all diamonds are squares, a square is not a rectangle, and a square cut in half always makes a triangle (Clements & Sarama, 2000b, p. 485a).

- Help problem solve a building dilemma.

- Make suggestions when children appear to be "stuck."

- Sketch and photograph buildings.

- Help measure buildings.

- Model interacting together to create a building.

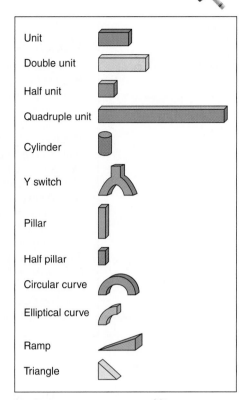

Figure 11.1
Unit Block Names and Sketches

When interacting with children, be careful that you do not take over the children's play, which can result in children spending less time in the play experience (Heisner, 2005).

Implement Group Block Talks

Group block talks can be used to motivate and provide inspiration, extend learning, and recognize block builders (Chalufour et al., 2004). Some ideas for group talks include the following:

- Show pictures of interesting buildings and discuss the architectural features.

- Provide information through guest speakers.

- Extend learning or motivate new building with books (see Figure 11.2.) One teacher reads a story during circle time using the props (animals, people) found in the blockbuilding center. She then places the props back in the block center along with the book. The result is increased dramatic play in the block area as well as increased time spent in block play (Heisner, 2005).

- Introduce new building materials.

Figure 11.2
Children's Books
Related to Building

Block City by Robert Louis Stevenson and Daniel Kirk
Building by Philip Wilkinson
Changes, Changes by Pat Hutchins
Bridges Connect: A Building Block Book by Lee Sullivan Hill
Blocks by Jay Allen (Board book)
Building by Elisha Cooper
Building a House by Bryon Barton
Building an Igloo by Ulli Stelzer
Building Big by David Macaulay
How a House Is Built by Gail Gibbons
Homes by Fionna MacDonald
Jobs People Do: A Day in the Life of a Builder by Linda Hayward
The Lot at the End of My Block by Kevin Lewis
This House Is Made of Mud by Ken Buchanan
This Is My House by Arthur Dorros
Skyscrapers by Judith Dupre
If You Take a Mouse to School by Laura Numeroff
Albert's Alphabet by Leslie Tryon
Traditional classics such as *The Three Little Pigs* and their modern alternatives the *Three Little Wolves and the Big Bad Pig* by Eugene Trivizas (Wellhousen & Giles, 2005)

- Make plans for block projects.
- Examine photos and sketches of children's current block building and discuss design elements and what worked or didn't work.
- Conduct a walkabout where the group examines each other's block structures and discusses them (Chalufour & Worth, 2004).
- Facilitate a builder's circle (similar to a writer's circle) where a child shares his work with others, describing what he created, problems he faced, and his future plans.
- Discuss and problem solve building dilemmas (such as how to keep blocks from toppling when they reach a certain height).
- Use blocks to demonstrate or teach a lesson (science lesson on simple machines—lever, incline plane, wheel and axle; math lessons on naming the blocks, carefully examining and discussing the shapes—their sides, points, and angles, and asking children to discover different combinations of blocks that equal the unit block) (Sprung, 2006).
- Use blocks for prediction and problem solving (such as what are all the possible combinations of blocks that would equal a unit block, how many blocks would it take to cover a 2-foot area with blocks).
- Discuss and analyze block data (such as a graph showing the heights of the children's structures).

Introduce Block Challenges and Provocations

Teachers can also create block challenges and provocations. While the challenges are often related to children's current block play, in some cases, particularly with older children, they may be new provocations created by the teacher. Challenges cultivate curiosity, create interest, help to improve children's block building skills, and may encourage reluctant builders to participate (Andrews, 1999; Casey & Bobb, 2003).

Following are some examples of block challenges.

- Casey and Bobb (2003) describe posing mathematical problems that arise out of a character's adventure, such as those posed by *Sneeze Builds a Castle.* To assist Sneeze, children participate in mapmaking, build enclosures and archways, create a tower three levels high, and develop an entire castle complex.

- One kindergarten and first-grade classroom created structures from a book called *Block Building for Children* (Walker, 1995). Although children began with a plan shown in the book, they often changed, improved, and modified their block buildings. Children who had not used the center previously began to build with the blocks, particularly the girls (Andrews, 1999).

- One class read *Albert's Alphabet* and created each of the alphabet letters out of blocks. They took photos of the block-created letters and placed these on the wall in place of pictures of alphabet letters (Andrews, 1999).

- Chalufour and Worth (2004) describe challenging children to build a tower as high as possible using one kind of block.

- Many teachers have children use blocks to create maps of their school, neighborhood, town, or city. According to Clements and Sarama (2000a), even preschoolers as young as 3 can build and understand very simple maps. Mapmaking with blocks allows children to gain perspective as they examine their map from various points of view.

- Dreier (1996) describes a third-grade class that created a city out of blocks and then used it to enact community life. Each child created a building found in a city and then added accessories, including a miniature representation of herself. The children used their block city to role-play city life. This created a need for more in-depth exploration and deeper understanding. As children "lived" in their block city, they became aware of the need for city services, taxation, group interdependence, and many other concepts.

- Other challenges involve asking children to devise ways to get people from the first floor to the second floor of a block building or to make their building accessible for someone in a wheelchair.

Meet the Needs of All Learners

It is important to consider children's levels of ability and their cultural and experiential backgrounds in planning the block environment. Hanline et al. (2001) compared block building of children with and without disabilities (physical, speech, language, and autism). They found that children with disabilities progressed through the same block stages as children without disabilities, although at a significantly slower rate. However, for all children, both with and without disabilities, the time spent in block play was significantly related to growth in block building, block building scores, and complexity of structures.

It is important that all children have the opportunity to build with blocks and that their needs be accommodated. Typically, this will involve problem-solving adaptations for each child. Following are some suggestions that might be a starting point for problem solving.

- Children who have visual impairments may be assisted by sandpaper or cardboard block outlines on shelves or by labeling shelves with braille. Children should be encouraged to use both hands to fully explore the blocks. Because children learn block skills by observing their peers, it is helpful to verbally describe other children's block building solutions or ask children to do so.

- Horizontal building might be most successful for children who have involuntary movement problems (Church & Miller, 1990).
- Children who are in wheelchairs may be able to be removed from their wheelchair for block building or they may need a wheelchair-accommodating table that they can build on.
- Experiment with a variety of different positions for children who have physical disabilities. For example, a child might be most comfortable propped on her stomach to build (Wellhousen & Kieff, 2001).

It is important that block accessories reflect diversity. For example, you might add vans that are marked as handicap accessible, handicap parking signs, seeing eye dogs, and figures using wheelchairs, mobility canes, hearing aids, and glasses (Wellhousen & Kieff, 2001, p. 163). You will also want to add people and accessories that reflect different racial and ethnic groups. It is important that all materials be closely examined to make sure they do not reflect gender or racial bias.

Children in all cultures use blocks or other construction materials (Wellhousen & Crowther, 2004). These materials differ based upon the culture and upon the building materials available. In developing culturally relevant environments, we need to include accessories and pictures from the children's culture. In a childcare center on a Montana American Indian reservation, the teachers added animal skins, natural building materials such as sticks and small stones, and materials to make small tepees to their block area. Children often made tepees with a floor of animal skins. In front of the tepee would be a fire ring made out of the stones. Since some people still lived in tepees and others used tepees during pow wows, these accessories honored the children's culture and allowed them to portray their experiences.

We can also introduce children to new cultures through pictures, photos, books, and accessories. For example, when showing different structures, we can show a variety of dwellings, including straw huts, high-rise apartment buildings, trailer houses, and open-air houses.

Assess and Make Changes to the Area as Needed

It is important that we continually assess the block area to make sure that it is providing the needed materials to enhance children's development and provide for their interests. This will include carefully observing the stages of block development the children are displaying as well as examining what they are building.

Observe and Document Individual Children's Learning

Many developmental areas can be assessed while observing children in the block area. Following is a list of questions that you might use as a guide in assessing children's development in this area.

1. What stage of block building is the child engaged in (prebuilding, rows and towers, bridging, enclosures, patterns, early representation, reproduction)?
2. What are the child's interests? What is the child building? Does the child build the same thing repeatedly or do his structures vary?
3. What problem-solving approaches does the child use (trial and error, asking others, observing others)?
4. How do children describe what they are doing (physical description of their building, problems they are encountering, their building intentions)?

5. How does the child interact with others (engage in solitary play, build parallel buildings, build cooperative structures)?

6. Does the child engage in peer tutoring (verbal or nonverbal)?

7. If another child is using materials desired by a child, how does the child obtain the materials? For example, does the child take the materials from another child, offer an exchange, verbally negotiate, or ask the teacher?

8. What math skills is the child demonstrating (classifying shapes, counting, putting shapes together to create another shape, describing and naming shapes, measuring, graphing, using mathematical equivalents—there is not a unit block available so the child uses two half-unit blocks in its place)?

9. What science skills is the child demonstrating (balance, symmetry, use of simple machines)?

10. What writing skills is the child demonstrating?

11. Does the child examine books, photos, sketches, or blueprints in designing his building?

12. Does the child sketch her building or create the building in another media after it is completed?

13. Does the child draw blueprints as a way of planning her building?

14. What vocabulary (spatial and architectural) does the child use?

15. What new discoveries, concepts, or developmental abilities has the child recently shown (Church & Miller, 1990)?

There are many different tools you might use to assess children in the block area, including observation, checklists, tape recordings of children discussing their structures, anecdotal records, work samples, photographs, or videos.

The teacher plays a crucial role in the block area by establishing the conditions for learning—creating an effective block area that meets the needs of all learners, providing background experiences, establishing rules, and continually assessing the block area and the children's use of the area, making changes as needed. It is also critical that teachers enhance children's learning by encouraging and acknowledging them, interacting with them as they build, providing block talks and challenges, and assessing their skills.

Special Challenges in the Block Area

To provide an effective block center, teachers must also overcome challenges as they arise. Three challenges that we will discuss are difficulty with cleaning up, children not using the center, and an insufficient number of blocks.

Cleaning Up

When children build elaborate structures using all the blocks on the shelf, putting blocks away can be time-consuming. In addition, because block structures may be developed by many children, no one wants to take ownership when it is time to pick up. Following are some strategies that might assist clean up:

- Recognize that clean up will take time. Fantastic learning experiences are worth the time it takes to clean up.
- Acknowledge the child's construction. Take a picture of the structure with the builders, label the construction with the builder's names, and discuss the construction with the child or children.

- Allow block structures to remain standing until they are no longer in use.
- If blocks must be put away, give an advance warning so builders can complete what they are working on.
- Make clean-up a game—Create tickets showing a number and type of blocks to pick up and have children draw tickets out of a basket. Have some children be bulldozers and push all the blocks to the shelf, have other children be cranes who lift the blocks onto the shelves and put them away. Use toy vehicles to move the blocks to the shelves.
- Model putting the blocks away and cleaning up by assisting children with this task.
- In some programs, the entire class helps to clean the block area. This technique provides all children the opportunity to handle the blocks, learn about the properties of blocks (weight and size), and experience mathematical ideas and classification.

Children Not Using the Block Center

If children are not using the block center, begin by assessing the block center to make sure that it is arranged properly and is designed around children's interests and needs. Also, consider whether there is enough time to devote to block building. Without enough time it may seem to children that the time needed to clean up is not worth the effort to build. If the environment and schedule are conducive to block building and children are still not using the block center, you might consider the following strategies:

- Read books about block building.
- Invite guests who are builders.
- Take field trips to visit structures.
- Begin a "starter" building (Church & Miller, 1990).
- Sit in the center; your presence will draw children to this area.
- Acknowledge block structures that children create.

An Insufficient Number of Blocks

A set of hardwood unit blocks will last longer than most items in your classroom. However, they are expensive. As this book went to press, unit blocks from Constructive Playthings for example, were priced at $840 for 644 blocks or $427 for 322 blocks. They are guaranteed against breakage or splintering and will last for many, many years. Some programs have special fund-raising events for buying blocks. Others make their own blocks from white pine. Bakawa-Evanson, Oesterreich, and Ouverson (1995) state that you can make 77 blocks using one 8-foot long 2×2 and two 8-foot long 2×4s. Read their article for a detailed description on how to make your own unit blocks. You can also make a variety of other homemade blocks. These include creating blocks from

- Milk cartons—To create these blocks, trim the tops of two milk cartons and slide them together facing each other.
- Boxes—Paint or cover boxes of different sizes with contact paper. To make the boxes stronger, stuff them with shredded paper.
- Cans—Cover different sizes of cans with contact paper.
- Trees—Create blocks by cutting up sections of tree branches.
- Sponges—Use a variety of dense sponges as blocks. These can be covered with fabric.

Outdoor Block and Building Centers

The outdoor area allows children the opportunity to build forts and interact in larger, even life-size structures. The micro-world unit blocks give way to the life-size world of large blocks (Cartwright, 1990, p. 41). In addition to all the skills gained by inside block building, outside building provides more opportunities for large motor development and often demands more cooperation to complete a structure.

Outdoor environments are perfect for building forts, an activity engaged in by children in all societies (Elkind, 2006). Forts allow children to make and shape their world and to fulfill their need for independence, privacy, and self-sufficiency (Elkind, 2006, p. 10; Sobel, 1993). Forts can be built from a variety of materials.

Large hollow blocks are frequently used as building materials outside, but can also be used indoors, if space permits. Cartwright (1990) recommends a minimum of 20 blocks and 10 boards for a group of children. Accessories such as miniature sawhorses, small ladders, and cloth or tarps can assist in creating forts and other structures. Dramatic play can be enhanced by adding hats, clothing, and props. Observation will help to determine the props that might be most helpful. For example, if children are creating vehicles, a steering wheel might be a useful prop.

Kindergarten and first-grade children in one school were studying different types of housing. They took a field trip to several different homes, including a straw-bale house that was in the process of being constructed. After the visit, the children became excited about creating their own straw-bale house. They developed plans, talked to builders, contacted a farmer to supply the bales, and eventually built their house. Each day a group of preschool children walked by the playground and watched the development of the straw-bale house. They too wanted a straw-bale house in their playground. Again, the process was repeated. The preschool teacher was able to locate smaller bales of straw. However, it still took three or four children to lift each bale and much problem solving to determine how to get the straw bales to the top level. Both the preschool and early elementary children were proud of their accomplishment, showing their house to parents and visitors. The straw-bale houses were also used for an extended time in dramatic play.

There are many other open-ended materials that can be used for outdoor building, including

PVC pipe and joints

pieces of wood

willow poles (Cuppens, Rosenow, & Wike, 2007)

stones

logs, tree stumps, or tree cookies (slabs of trees)

plastic milk crates

wooden telephone wire spools

wooden shipping crates

As mentioned previously, accessories need to relate to children's interests and level of development. Some possible outdoor accessories include

pieces of fabric, sheets, tarps, or blankets

carpet squares

heavy-duty cardboard cylinders

hats

license plates

steering wheels

large traffic signs

large toy vehicles

play dishes

old headphones

flashlights (Church & Miller, 1990)

As with indoor building, it is important that the outdoor building space be located in an area with limited interference from other areas. For example, you don't want children building in the zone that is used for swinging or hauling materials through this zone to reach the building area. Providing storage immediately adjacent to the outdoor building area also saves time in removing materials and cleaning them up. When it is inconvenient to retrieve materials, they may not be used. You might consider having a locking box to store materials rather than having to return materials to a storage shed that is located across the playground.

"Blocks respond to children's need (to carry, to build, to balance, to imitate, to fantasize) and respects their uniqueness" (Cody, 1989, p. 111). With the help of the builder, inert pieces of wood come to life, allowing children to create a world of their choosing. While children are creating their worlds, they are engaging in math, science, and literacy. They are developing aesthetic awareness and social skills and expressing themselves emotionally. Through intentional environmental design and thoughtful interaction, the teacher expands children's learning opportunities.

Sample Application Activities

1. Use the Environmental Assessment in Figure 11.3 to critique a block area.
2. Observe children while they are playing in the block area. Determine their stage of development and interests. What block accessories could the teacher add to assist their play?
3. Examine a block area to determine what accessories are available that would encourage literacy, math, and science.
4. Observe center time at an early childhood program. How are adults interacting with children? Are they expanding knowledge? Do you observe missed opportunities? Are adults too intrusive? How are children's block buildings being acknowledged?
5. Use a digital camera to photograph several classroom block areas. Analyze them by the standards described in the text.
6. To learn more about blocks and their impact on learning, visit the Yale-New Haven Teachers Institute and read http://www.yale.edu/ynhti/curriculum/units/1993/1/93.01.01.x.html
7. Learn more about Friedrich Froebel by visiting this website: http://www.froebelweb.org/webindex.html

□ Is there a designated block area?

□ Is there a stable surface to build the blocks on?

□ Is the block area in a secluded area of the room?

□ Is the block area situated so that it is not in a traffic area?

□ Is there adequate room for children to build?

□ Are unit blocks available (except for infants and young toddlers)?

□ Are there enough unit blocks to create the structures that children wish to make (586 blocks for 3-year-olds, 748 blocks for 4-year-olds, 980 blocks for children 5 and older)?

□ Are accessories available?

□ Do accessories support the stage of development and children's interests?

□ Are there some open-ended materials so that children can create their own accessories?

□ Are there motivational materials (such as books, pictures, photos) to provide ideas and information about structures?

□ Are there writing materials available (preschool and early elementary)?

□ Are the blocks arranged mathematically on open shelves?

□ Are the shelves labeled with block outlines?

□ Does the schedule allow enough time for children to engage in in-depth building?

□ Are the accessories effectively grouped and organized?

□ Over a course of time, are all children involved in the block area?

□ Are pictures and accessories anti-bias?

□ Do pictures and accessories portray a variety of different cultures?

□ Do pictures and accessories reflect children who have disabilities?

Figure 11.3
Environmental
Assessment: Block
Center

Source: Permission is granted by the publisher to reproduce this figure for evaluation and record-keeping. From Julie Bullard, *Creating Environments for Learning: Birth to Age Eight.* Copyright © 2010 by Pearson Education, Inc. All rights reserved.

chapter 12

Developing Dramatic Play Centers

*C*hristine Ferguson, a teacher of kindergarten children, took her class to visit a pet store. The store manager gave the children a tour of the store, discussing the different pets. The children helped to feed the pets and observed their different habitats, behaviors, and eating habits. In many cases, this would have concluded the visit. However, Christine had asked the store manager to show the children different aspects of a pet store employee's job especially as it related to literacy. The store manager showed the children the store signs, labels, coupons, and price tags and the pet books they sold in the store. She described and demonstrated how the cash register worked and showed how she wrote receipts for the customer. At the conclusion of the visit, she gave the children a variety of items (blank store signs, flyers, coupons, store sacks) so they could create their own classroom pet store. After the visit, the children helped to design a pet store in their dramatic play center. They brainstormed a list of items they would need to create the center. The children then collected, created, and brought items from home (stuffed animals; boxes and cans of pet food; animal treats, toys, and books). They also designed *the physical layout of the center using blocks to create shelves and using the classroom puppet center to hold the cash register. The children played in the center for several weeks, reenacting what they had seen in the pet store and extending it with their own ideas. One day, one of the children said her stuffed dog was hurt and needed to see a doctor. In response to the child's comment, the teacher arranged a visit from a veterinarian who showed the children how she brushed dog's teeth, examined animals, and wrote prescriptions to make the animals healthy. The vet provided play materials for the children (empty syringes, prescription pads, stethoscope) and the idea of a veterinarian's hospital was born (Ferguson & McNulty, 2006).*

This story illustrates several elements needed for creating a successful dramatic play center. The children shared a common first-hand experience when they visited the pet shop. The visit allowed them to learn about pet stores and also about the work of the pet store employee. This shared experience helped children in developing the "scripts" they used in their sociodramatic play. Group dialogue and discussion during subsequent circle times extended their group knowledge about pets. Interest in the pet store was extended by having the children actually design the sociodramatic center. An abundance of props supported the children's play and also reminded them of different aspects of the pet store employee's role (for example, making signs). An observant teacher saw the opportunity to expand the learning by introducing the veterinarian to the children.

Apply Your Knowledge   What props might the teacher and children create or collect for the veterinarian center? In addition to the visit from the veterinarian, what are other ways the teacher might help children to gain background information about veterinarians?

Dramatic play allows children to "become representers of their experiences" and also to create new imaginative realities (Brown, Sutterby, & Thornton, 2001, p. 1). This highly motivating activity has been linked to social, emotional, cognitive, and physical growth (Calabrese, 2003).

Development of Dramatic Play

Children's dramatic play ability is enhanced as their development allows them to use symbolic representation and to engage in cooperative play with others. Very young children under the age of 2 often need realistic objects for pretending. However, around the age of 2, they begin to use less realistic objects where an item might be a symbolic representation for something else (a block may be used for a telephone). By the age of 3, most children are capable of pretending with imaginary objects and events even when props are not present (Elias & Berk, 2002).

Children's ability to play with others is also developing during the infant and toddler years. Between the ages of 1 and 2, children begin to demonstrate reciprocal imitation during play (Shonkoff & Phillips, 2000). They will imitate another child and then will build upon what the other child is doing, expanding their repertoire for acting out roles. For example, Paul and Samantha were cooking. Paul used a large spoon to stir the pretend mixture in his pot. Samantha imitated Paul with her own pot and spoon. She then got a small plate and used the spoon to put some mixture on the plate. Paul imitated Samantha by dishing the pretend mixture onto his plate. Toddler play is also often characterized by repetitive activity, where children will reenact the same scene repeatedly.

When children become preschoolers, the number of players expands (Shonkoff & Phillips, 2000) and dramatic play becomes a cooperative activity where players work together to carry out a predefined theme (Smilansky & Shefatya, 1990). This is often referred to as sociodramatic play. For play to be considered sociodramatic, several components must be present. The child must (a) engage in role-playing (pretends to be another person, animal, or object); (b) make believe with actions and objects; (c) have verbal and social interaction with at least one other person to coordinate roles and plot; and (d) have a play theme that persists for 5 minutes or more (Smilansky & Shefatya, 1990). In the next section, we will examine why sociodramatic play is important.

How the Dramatic Play Center Enhances Children's Development

"In the Vygotskian tradition, dramatic play is accorded a special place in the development of young children" (Bodrova, Leong, Hensen, & Henninger, 1999, p.1). As stated by Vygotsky, "In play the child is always behaving beyond his age, above his usual everyday behavior; in play he is, as it were, a head above himself" (1978, p. 74). Play scaffolds or supports learning, providing the optimal context for development (Bodrova et al., 1999, p.1). Dramatic play allows children to practice skills they learned in real-life situations, to assimilate information, and to try to make sense of it (Brown et al., 2001). While engaging in sociodramatic play, children gain literacy, self-regulatory, cognitive, social, emotional, and creative skills. These benefits are enhanced when children participate in mature dramatic play as they create an imaginary situation, use language to create the pretend scenario, form explicit roles and implicit rules, and enact play for an extended time frame (Bodrova et al., 1999, p. 1; Bodrova & Leong, 2007).

This child-created dramatic play area contains a child-decorated sign; an eating area complete with tablecloth, flowers, and menus; and a waiting area complete with magazines to read. What does this area tell you about the children's concept of restaurant?

Literacy Development

Sociodramatic play is an especially powerful medium for supporting literacy development. Play promotes oral language as children become "storytellers of pretend events" (Brown et al., 2001). During sociodramatic play, children must negotiate play scripts and roles with their peers. They must also determine the meaning of props. In addition, they act out the role using different voices, inflections, and rich verbal exchanges (Elias & Berk, 2002). In this age of curriculum standards and accountability, some teachers and programs are adopting more teacher-directed activities to promote language skills. However, research indicates that this may be the wrong approach. When children participate in sociodramatic play, they use more elaborate narratives than when they are engaged in a more teacher-directed story telling activity (Kim, 1999).

Dramatic play also is important in reading and writing. To read or write, children must understand that the written word is a symbolic representation of an object or idea. Often, the first place that children encounter and understand symbolic representation is during dramatic play, when children use an item to stand for something else. In addition to this, dramatic play in an enriched environment allows children to practice writing and reading in an authentic, highly motivating context (Bodrova et al., 1999). For example, children playing restaurant might read menus, signs, and cookbooks. They might write orders, signs, recipes, and menus.

Self-Regulation and Cognition Development

Sociodramatic play may be especially important in the development of self-regulation, particularly for children who are impulsive (Elias & Berk, 2002). As discussed in Chapter 2, self-regulation is the ability to control one's emotions, actions, and thinking (Riley, San Juan, Klinkner, & Ramminger, 2008, p. 65). Self-regulation assists us in regulating our social and cognitive processes, allowing us to develop goals, make plans to achieve them, monitor our learning, implement our ideas and plans, and use reflection. According to Vygotsky (1978), dramatic play is the ideal arena for learning self-regulation, because it is a highly motivating activity to practice rule-bound behavior. In addition, the imaginary situation helps children to separate their thoughts and behaviors from what is going on around them and to use their internal ideas to guide their behavior. During dramatic play, children use self-regulation to keep the play script going, to be flexible with others, and to control themselves. Children also use more private speech (using self-talk to control behavior) while engaged in dramatic play than when playing in other classroom centers (Krafft & Berk, 1998). Private speech is associated with self-regulation.

In addition to the development of self-regulatory skills, dramatic play allows children authentic opportunities to use many other cognitive skills. For example, one study that examined the dramatic play of 18-month to 4-year-old children found that they used a variety of everyday mathematics skills while playing. These skills included using spatial awareness, classification, fractions ("half for you and half for me"), counting, simple addition and subtraction, patterns, and geometrical knowledge.

Play appears to be circular, meaning that those who are intellectually competent participate in more advanced play. Advanced play leads to greater intellectual competence, creativity, and problem solving (Trawick-Smith, 2006). Dramatic play, like art and writing, is also a way that children represent their knowledge.

Social Development

Dramatic play allows children to practice social skills and to "gain culturally valued competencies" (Elias & Berk, 2002, p. 219). Researchers have found that children participate in more complex social interactions in dramatic play than in other centers in the classroom (Petrakos & Howe, 1996). While playing in this area, children negotiate roles, take turns, and resolve interpersonal relationships. Through their negotiations and discussions, they begin to understand their own and other's family and cultural beliefs, practices, and values. For example, Tina and Sylvia were role-playing cooking and eating a meal. Tina said, "Let's pretend the bookcase is a TV." Sylvia was confused about why they needed a television for their meal. This exchange led to a discussion about the differences in mealtime at their two homes. As illustrated by this example, "children bring to the play experience their cultural background and lifestyle as sources of information" (Kostelnik, Whiren, Soderman, & Gregory, 2009, p. 277). During dramatic play, children also take on the roles of others, allowing them to gain an understanding of the role, experience another's perspective, develop empathy, and engage in rehearsal for life.

Emotional Development

Dramatic play can act as a cathartic release (a way to discharge emotion). It also allows children to act out fears and traumatic events in a safe environment. Through play, children have the power to control what happens and to change the endings if they wish. They can practice solving dilemmas and use play as a form of communication (Brown et al., 2001). For example, they can "use toys to say things they cannot verbalize, to do things they would otherwise feel uncomfortable doing, and to express feelings and emotions they might be reprimanded for expressing in other contexts" (Brown et al., 2001).

Creative Development

Through dramatic play, children practice skills needed for creativity. For example, children use their imagination for fantasy and make believe. "The children's imaginativeness is a dimension of creativity" (Saracho, 2002, p. 436). The quality of the child's pretend play also is linked to the child's ability to use divergent thinking (generate multiple ideas), which is another aspect of creativity (Russ, Robins, & Christiano, 1999).

While using the dramatic play center, children also use drama skills such as developing scripts and assuming roles. They imitate other's mannerisms, language, and behavior, and often use materials and props in creative ways.

Dramatic play provides rich opportunities for children to develop literacy, cognitive, self-regulation, social, emotional, and creative skills. As Christine in our opening scenario demonstrated, we can enhance children's dramatic play by establishing an effective dramatic play center.

Designing an Effective Dramatic Play Center

Although children participate in dramatic play even with few props, we can enrich their experiences with thoughtfully designed environments. To assist children in achieving optimal development, the dramatic play needs to be available on a daily basis. Teachers must also effectively arrange and supply the center to provide rich experiences. An effective dramatic play center has the following characteristics:

- It is in a well-defined area such as a separated corner of the room. Some experts suggest a special entry to the play area such as an arch to set it apart from other classroom centers (Pardee, 2005). You might also think about the ceiling height. Research shows that children participate in more cooperative play when the ceiling height is lower (Read, Sugawara, & Brandt, 1999). Some teachers use cloth drapes in the dramatic play area to lower ceilings and to further define the play space.

- It provides sufficient space for at least four to six children to play.

- It is located next to the block area to increase the movement of materials between the two centers. For example, the children at Bright Beginnings had just ridden around the city as part of a transportation unit. Marlis, the teacher, had placed bus driver uniforms and hats in the dramatic play center. The children donned their hats and uniforms and decided they needed a bus. They went to the block area, used the large hollow blocks to create the bus, and then commenced to role-play.

- It contains familiar and authentic items that allow children to represent their experiences. For example, in Reggio Emilia centers children use the same pottery and dishware that they would find in their homes. The dramatic play center also contains real food that would be found in kitchens (dried beans, pasta in different shapes) (Gandini, 1984, p. 19); see controversy about using food for play on p. 267. Adding materials that children can use for "cooking" can often enhance their play. At Birge Nest, an infant/toddler classroom, the teachers moved the sandbox into the dramatic play area. They also added play dough. The children's play included more social interaction, was more in-depth, and lasted for a longer period of time after these items were added. Several children who had previously not played in this area began to participate.

- It contains materials that reflect all the members of the classroom—children with disabilities, from all types of family groupings, and from all ethnic and cultural backgrounds. Both boys' and girls' interests are promoted through the center theme and materials.

- It includes materials that represent many cultures (even those that are not in the classroom). One way to include different cultural materials is to ask parents in the classroom to donate items they are not using. For example, when one teacher asked families to bring in materials, she received a bamboo steamer and a Chinese tea set from one family. You might also receive donations from ethnic restaurants and stores. It is important to represent many cultures. "When teachers fail to include a wide variety of multicultural and nonsexist props in their dramatic play areas, they unconsciously reinforce monocultural ideas about how a business or home setting is 'supposed' to look" (Boutte, Scoy, & Hendley, 1996, p. 34).

- It is aesthetic. In our home environments many of us strive to create an aesthetic environment that reflects our individual style. Many early childhood programs also strive to create aesthetic dramatic play areas using beautiful materials (copper pots and pans, china dishes, vases of flowers, plants, tablecloths, rugs, fabric, and throw pillows).

- It contains clothing or pieces of fabric for children to create their own clothing. Clothing helps children "step into the role" (Bafile, 2004).

- It contains full-length mirrors so children can see themselves.

- It contains a variety of props to support rich play opportunities. Props often suggest play themes; for example, a stethoscope in a doctor's kit will encourage listening to each other's heartbeats. While less-realistic toys or props result in more varied play, the play is often shorter in duration (Pellegrini, 1985). Real items are often sturdier and less expensive, and might do more than their play counterparts (Bafile, 2004). For example, when real stethoscopes rather than play stethoscopes were used, children had the opportunity to actually listen to each other's heartbeats.

- It includes duplicates of props so children can participate in parallel play (shopping carts, doll strollers). This is particularly important for younger children.

- It includes authentic math props. For example, in a home living area you might find a calendar on the wall, watches in the jewelry box, clocks, receipt books, calculators, cell phones, and food items that are sorted and classified in the cupboard.

- It includes authentic and appropriate literacy props. For example, if the dramatic play area was established as a home living area you might add cookbooks in the kitchen area; note pads, pens, and a telephone book by the telephone; magazines by the child-size couch; recipe cards with pictures and words and blank recipe cards for children to create their own recipes; grocery list paper, store coupons, and empty checkbooks.

- It includes some loose parts so children can develop what they need (Brokering, 1989). For example, rug samples, blankets, boxes, and boards can become magic carpets, forts, or doghouses with some imagination. Pieces of fabric can become capes, sarongs, head wraps, doll blankets, dancing scarves, baby slings, or tablecloths.

- It provides ways to make clothing and prop choices available and organized. For example, it might include hooks or hangers for clothing, a labeled basket or hat rack for hats, coat racks for displaying purses, and a jewelry box for jewelry. Baby clothes and props can be placed in a chest of drawers with picture and word labels. Outlines made from contact paper can be placed in the cupboard so children know where dishes and pots and pans belong. You might put plastic fruit in labeled baskets. As children put items away, the area not only stays neat but children are also practicing one-to-one correspondence and classification.

- It contains needed equipment (wooden shelving, stove, fridge, sink, cupboard, tables and chairs). Wooden equipment is more expensive but is also more durable. The equipment needs to be the proper size for the age group.
- It is dynamic, being changed or added to as needed to sustain rich play opportunities.

Teresa's Home Living Center

At the beginning of the school year, many teachers establish a home living center in the dramatic play area. Teresa, a teacher of preschool children, sent a note to parents before the school year began asking them for empty food boxes, clothing, baby items, utensils, pictures, magazines, and other items that would represent their culture. With the parent's assistance, Teresa began the year by providing dramatic play props representing the cultures in her classroom. This allowed the children to participate in dramatic play using some familiar props and introduced them to their classmates' cultures. When the children started school, they were excited to find items in the classroom that they had in their homes and were proud to show other children how to use the materials. As children became familiar with these materials, Teresa slowly began introducing and adding materials from cultures that were not represented in the classroom.

She also drew on the children's background knowledge and elicited their ideas to help plan materials to add to the area. For example, when one of the boys in her room suggested that they needed materials for pets, several other children agreed. So pet props were added to the area. Following is a list of materials that Teresa had in her dramatic play center:

- Child-size furniture including tables and chairs, cozy chair, couch, rocking chair, stove, fridge, sink, cupboard, closet, chest of drawers, hat rack
- Child-size broom, mop, dustpan
- Sponge, dishtowels, and potholder by the play sink
- Mirrors
- Multicultural dolls, doll bed and doll basket, doll clothes (unisex), diapers, receiving blankets, doll toys, empty powder and shampoo containers, adaptive doll equipment, strollers, front baby packs, and baby slings
- Dress-up clothes for boys and girls including clothing, shoes, boots; two pairs of Chinese traditional children's shoes and a dragon pattern suit donated by a parent; used cowboy boots and cowboy hats from a family; and colorful sarapes donated by another family
- Jewelry boxes containing necklaces, earrings, rings, bracelets, eyeglasses, and sunglasses
- Briefcase, purse, billfold, keys, diaper bag, lunch box, tool belt, and suitcase
- Real nonworking phones (two to encourage children to talk to each other)
- Pets and pet props (water dish, dog bones, dog toys, empty container of dog food)
- Pots, pans, dishes, and utensils (small cast iron frying pan, wok, bamboo tongs, tortilla press, tortilla warmer, mortar and pestle, Mexican wood molinillo [chocolate stirrer], Chinese tea set, forks and spoons, chopsticks, Chinese soup spoons)
- Play food, empty food containers (parents brought in empty cans, boxes, and spice containers, providing cultural variation)
- Placemats and tablecloths with real flowers (donated each week from a flower shop)
- Adaptive equipment (crutches, wheelchair lent by a local business)
- Literacy props (Chinese, English, and Spanish newspapers and magazines, different ethnic cookbooks, notepad and paper near phone)

- Clock hanging on the wall with a paper clock below it so that children could set the paper clock to match the real clock
- A separate sitting room with child-size couches and chairs, CD player, magazine rack, plants, reading glasses, table, a lamp and a beautiful rug that a parent brought back from China when she visited her family

By involving the families, Teresa was able to set up a rich dramatic play area that was culturally relevant to the children in her classroom.

Watch the video *Emergent Curriculum Built on Children's Interests: Hospital Project* on MyEducationLab to see another example of a dramatic play center.

Go to MyEducationLab and select the topic "Projects and Themes." Under Activities and Applications, watch the video *Emergent Curriculum Built on Children's Interests: Hospital Project.*

TIP   If you use life-size baby dolls you can supply the doll with an inexpensive wardrobe by using authentic newborn baby clothes. You might obtain newborn baby clothing at thrift stores, garage sales, or through donations.

Special Considerations for Infants and Toddlers

Children's early pretending is context driven, suggested by the objects that are available in the environment (McCune-Nicolich, 1981). To enhance their ability to make-believe, it is important that children have access to a range of materials that support pretending. Unfortunately, in a large-scale study, it was found that many infant/toddler classrooms did not have adequate materials and props for pretend play (Cryer & Phillipsen, 1997).

As with older children, toddlers practice adult roles as they play. As soon as children begin to walk, they need a dedicated area for dramatic play. It is important to have familiar centers (home living) and realistic props (pots and pans, baby dolls). Because sharing is difficult for infants and toddlers, it is crucial that there be duplicates of popular items. Duplicate items will also allow children to copy each other as they participate in parallel pretend play (Howes, Unger, & Seidner, 1989).

The lamp, tablecloth, and framed mirrors make this an aesthetic dramatic play environment. Pieces of transparent fabric allow children to use their imagination to create headdresses, slings to carry dolls, clothing, or even tents.

Many of the items that Teresa included in her home living center would be appropriate for infants and toddlers. However, in planning for this age group you will want to carefully consider their development. Dress-up clothing and baby doll clothing needs to be easy to get on and off with Velcro, large buttons, or elastic so that children can be successful. Jewelry and other materials need to be large enough to prevent a choking hazard. Also, consider children's interests in making your plans. Many toddlers enjoy pushing items, so baby buggies are popular. They enjoy equipment with knobs that actually turn and doors that open, so it is important that play equipment provides these options.

This stage provides a backdrop for the fairy tales this group of children have been reenacting.

At this age, children may need more adult modeling and suggestions to support them in using pretend play. For example, adults may suggest that the child put gas in her play car or feed her baby (Bedrova & Leong, 2007).

Special Considerations for School-Age (K–3) Children

As children become school age, they continue to participate in sociodramatic play. However, organized games with rules become important and their sociodramatic play often changes to reflect this focus. I once witnessed children in an after-school program spend the entire hour of center time negotiating their play script. Fortunately, at this age they are also able to keep their scripts going over a longer period of time (Kostelnik et al., 2009). These children continued to organize their script over the next several days, eventually enacting it. Elementary-age children will reenact stories, movies, and their own narratives. Some teachers provide a stage or a puppet theater to encourage children's reenactments. Other teachers use the dramatic play center to support curriculum units. For example, they develop prop boxes to support social studies. The study of historical events can come alive as children have the opportunity to dress up, use props, and assume the role of someone from another time period.

Changes to the Dramatic Play Center

Whether teaching infants, toddlers, preschoolers, or elementary-age children, it is important to carefully observe children's play to determine when to add props or change the center. If children do not seem interested in dramatic play even with the addition of new props, it is time to discuss

This center designed by the teacher and children after visiting a veterinary clinic includes stuffed animals, a file for each animal, a cash register, phone, prescription pads, clothing, and veterinary props.

As illustrated in this picture, the veterinary center allows children to experiment with new roles.

Stores
Pet store
Farmers' market
Bakery
Flower shop
Grocery store
Shoe store
Music store
Restaurant
Pizza parlor
Clothing store

Community Services
Bank
Post office
Hair salon
Repair shop
Garage-mechanics shop
Gas station
Office
School
Fire station
Library
Theatre

Farm
Horse stable

Medical Services
Hospital
Dentist
Optometrist
Veterinarian

Transportation
Airport
Bus or train station

Activities
Skiing
Camping
Fishing camp
Fitness center
Dance studio
Skating rink
Beach (add tide pool with small wading
  pool)
Boating

Children's Fantasy Ideas
Dragon's den
Living on Mars

Teachers can enrich centers by shining a scene on the wall using an overhead projector. For example, Dabria was changing her center into a train. She shone a picture of a local train station on the wall. Transparencies of photos can be created using color copying machines or colored printers. Make sure you buy transparency film that is designed especially for the machine that you are using.

Figure 12.1
Dramatic Play Center Possibilities

with children ways of changing the center. Changing the center allows children to experiment with new roles, explore new scenarios, and use additional vocabulary. The change may also spark interest in children who have not previously used the center. For ideas on possibilities for the dramatic play center, see Figure 12.1.

Children can assist in planning changes to the dramatic play center. For example, they can brainstorm the types of play centers and props. As illustrated in the opening scenario, children can help to collect and make the props and physically arrange the center. This level of involvement can assist in building interest, provide additional materials and props, and help children to think about and share their knowledge in relationship to the proposed center.

> TIP   If you are removing the house center, it is helpful to have a dollhouse with furniture and props so that children can still act out events in their lives.

Prop Boxes

Many programs develop prop boxes. The advantage of prop boxes is that they save time, volunteers can help create them, and classrooms can share them. Often when teachers share them, they pool their resources so the prop boxes have a greater quantity and variety of props than one teacher alone would have access to. In some areas, organizations such as local childcare associations, NAEYC chapters, or museums create prop boxes that members can check out.

Developing Dramatic Play Centers

Prop boxes can be used in different ways. Often they are used for teacher convenience, as the starting point for changing the dramatic play center. However, Amanda lets the children use the prop boxes, having a variety of prop boxes on shelves for children in her afterschool program to choose from. Carrie fully develops the dramatic play center following the children's lead, but adds two or three related prop boxes to the center that children can use to enrich their play.

When creating prop boxes, it is helpful to begin with similar-sized sturdy boxes or totes for easy stacking and storing. To obtain the needed materials, you can send out a list to parents, go to inexpensive stores (secondhand, dollar), and go to the stores or community services that are being represented.

To be effective, prop boxes need to be developmentally appropriate and relevant to the group of children using them. They need to contain authentic props whenever possible, enough materials for a small group of children, and literacy materials (Barbour, Desjean-Perrotta, & Rojas, 2002). Prop boxes also need to be nonsexist and contain multicultural materials.

Teachers can add new centers, provide new materials, or include prop boxes as ways of enriching play. What other roles does the teacher play in supporting children's learning in the dramatic play center?

Teachers' Facilitation of Learning in the Dramatic Play Center

To promote high-quality dramatic play, teachers need to support children by providing background experiences, planning effective centers, building and maintaining excitement and interest in dramatic play, and facilitating children's play skills.

Provide Rich, Shared Experiences

A shared background of experiences can enrich children's dramatic play (Bodrova & Leong, 2007; Sacks, Goldman, & Chaille, 1984). Often this is accomplished through a field trip. Bodrova and Leong (2007) suggest that the adults you are visiting model the "actions, words, and social interactions" associated with the role (p. 148). They also recommend that several different roles be modeled to allow children to play out the script. It is important that children see people performing their roles and that the tour guide at the location is prepped for the age of the group of children you are bringing. It might be helpful to give the person a sense of what the children are interested in, questions they may have, and the depth of their current understanding. For example, if visiting a grocery store, it is important to see the variety of vegetables and also to see the produce manager unpacking the vegetables, cleaning them, setting up the display, creating signs, and describing how to sell the produce to an interested customer. You might help children remember the trip and the roles people play by having each person wear a distinctive article of clothing that represents what he or she does. For example, one classroom took a trip to a grocery store. The florist wore brightly colored gloves to keep thorns from poking her. The baker wore a tall baker's hat to keep flour out of his hair. The butcher wore an apron. The teacher then placed these props in the dramatic play center to remind children of the different roles at the grocery store. Children can also learn about roles from guest speakers, puppet shows, stories, and short videos.

Plan Centers That Encourage Active Engagement

When planning the dramatic play center, teachers must think about children's play opportunities. Each time you change the center or add new materials to the center, ask yourself the following questions:

- What will the children do in the center?
- What roles can be carried out?

- How do the props support the roles?
- Are the children knowledgeable about the roles?

Changes in the center need to lead to active engagement for children. For example, a student teacher spent many hours creating a dramatic play backdrop that included a fireplace, each brick having been drawn by hand. Much to the disappointment of the teacher, the children had no way of interacting with the backdrop, so they did not play in the area.

Build Excitement

Teachers can build children's excitement and interest in the center in many ways. For example the teachers in the beginning scenario had children help to construct the center. In another program, the teacher built excitement in a grocery store by first setting out the grocery bags full of store items. Then she put out a sign stating "Grand Opening." On the opening day, a ceremony was held that included a ribbon cutting and free samples (Rybczynski & Troy, 1995, p. 9).

Keep Interest Alive Through Providing a Dynamic Center

The effective dramatic play center is rarely static. Instead it is dynamic, changing to meet children's interests and expand their learning. While the teacher is an observer who builds on children's interests by adding props and changing the center as needed, she also may at times be a protagonist. For example, the teacher who developed the grocery store kept children's interest alive by adding new store specials each week and continuing to provide free food samples along with picture recipes to create the food (something that would happen in a real store).

Provide Adequate Time for Dramatic Play

There needs to be adequate daily center time for dramatic play. Developing the scenario, choosing and negotiating roles, and selecting props is a time-consuming process. For older children, this process usually takes place even before the children actually participate in dramatic play. The amount of time needed will vary depending upon the age of the children. However, for preschool and kindergarten children, a minimum of one hour for center activities is necessary to allow for this type of in-depth play (Copple & Bredekamp, 2009).

Introduce Materials and Teach Mini Lessons as Needed

It is helpful to introduce materials and teach mini lessons to support children's play (Rybczynski & Troy, 1995). For example, you might introduce and model the use of a prop, especially one that the children might not be familiar with. You might also introduce unfamiliar literacy materials such as checkbooks. When teachers introduce and make suggestions about literacy props, children engage in a greater quantity and a greater variety of literacy activities (Morrow, 1990). Mini lessons about joining and sustaining play are also helpful. For example, you might give a puppet show where one puppet wants to join in the dramatic play and tries a variety of unsuccessful and successful approaches.

Extend Play

With younger children, you might extend children's play by being the play partner, but as children begin to play cooperatively with peers, it is important for children to determine and enact their own story line (Calabrese, 2003). Unless it is absolutely necessary, you should not redirect the play. "Redirection gives control of the learning situation to the teacher, not the student; thus, the situation loses some of the motivational power of play" (Rybczynski & Troy, 1995, p. 10).

Instead of being a play partner, you might assist preschool and early elementary children to deepen and extend their play through a play plan (Bodrova & Leong, 2007). To produce a play plan the child writes or draws what he plans to do during the dramatic play period, including the imaginary situation and the roles. The teacher can ask open-ended questions to help children think more deeply about the roles and about the story line, as well as suggesting new roles. She can also remind children about their previous script and help them to extend it. Children using play plans spend more time participating in mature dramatic play, recall more details of their play, and argue and fight less while playing (Bodrova & Leong, 1998, 2007). Bodrova and Leong (2007) suggest that children reflect upon their dramatic play at the end of the play session, determining if they want to continue the script the next day. It is also important that they review the plan immediately before beginning the play, helping them to recall their previous ideas. Although play plans are often first initiated by the teacher, children typically adopt the idea of play plans and begin to use them independently not only in dramatic play but in other areas of the classroom as well (Bodrova & Leong, 1998).

Assist Individual Children to Join Play

Teachers play an important role when they teach children successful strategies for joining play. To be effective in helping children to join play, teachers must first understand the play-entry strategies successful children use. Successful peer entry begins with the child participating in low-risk behavior (low risk of being rejected). This includes observing the other children at play and engaging in parallel play. The child then moves to high-risk behavior (risk of rejection higher) such as asking a question or suggesting a role that he might play. If granted entry into play, the successful child causes minimal disruption to the group (Beilinson & Olswand, 2003). It is important to observe the child who is unsuccessful in peer entry to determine the area of difficulty. Then you can teach the child the needed strategy to be successful. In addition to teaching these strategies, the teacher might:

- Interpret the child's behavior to the group, "Josie is cooking spaghetti just like you."
- Assist by suggesting a role to the group that the child might fill, "Perhaps Josie could be the big sister."
- Give the child a highly valued prop to help ease the entry (Beilinson & Olswand, 2003)

Assist Individual Children to Sustain Dramatic Play Episodes

After children have gained entry to the dramatic play, they must be able to sustain the play. To assist children having difficulty sustaining play, observe and document their play to determine what specifically is causing them problems. Does the child not understand her role or how to use a prop? Does she not want to play the role she has been assigned, or not understand the play script? There are many ways that adults can thoughtfully intervene in children's play, including the following. From least to most intrusive, these are:

- Visually looking on and offering assistance only if needed
- Using nondirective statements to describe what the child is doing such as "You are feeding the baby because the baby is hungry."
- Asking questions such as "What will you do next?"
- Giving directive statements, such as "Now you can help to set the table for dinner."
- Entering the play for a short time to demonstrate a prop or role (Levy, Wolfgang, & Koorland, 1992, p. 250)

Enrich the Dramatic Play by Incorporating Materials from Other Centers

Incorporating materials created in other learning centers allows children to make new props, use their products for an authentic purpose, and integrate skills learned in other areas with dramatic play. For example, children's artwork can be framed to decorate the walls in the dramatic play area. Children can use the writing center to create signs, checkbooks, and blank tablets or the art center to create wallets, jewelry, and crowns. Clothing and pillows might be created in the sewing center while small stools can be built in the woodworking area. Each of these props can enrich the dramatic play center. In addition, creating props can help children to develop an interest in this area.

Facilitate Children Acting Out Their Fears

"Through play, children can explore stressful experiences in a safe environment, helping children understand and gain some control over them" (Huffman, 2006, p. 3). Teachers can facilitate children acting out their concerns and fears by learning as much as they can about the children in their classrooms and any stressful situations they might be facing. The teacher can then provide the needed props to assist the child in role-playing the event. For example, if the child is having a medical procedure you can learn as much as you can about it and add books, pictures, props, medical clothing, and medical materials to the center (Huffman, 2006, p. 4). For toddlers, it might be helpful if the adult can take the role of the child and model coping strategies. Another strategy is to ask open-ended questions as the child plays with the props. For example, if the toddler is role-playing the doll going to the hospital, the adult can ask how the doll feels and ask the child to describe ways that we might make the doll feel better, thereby understanding how the child wishes to be comforted (Huffman, 2006).

Older children are often able to enact scenes without adult intervention. However, sometimes the teacher needs to take the time to understand what the children are trying to accomplish through their play before negating it with rules. One day in Nancy's Head Start class, the children began to move all the furniture to another part of the classroom. When Nancy asked the children about this, they stated that they were being evicted. If Nancy had stated the rule, "All furniture stays in the housekeeping area" she would never have understood the need of the children to reenact the scene that so many of them had experienced. The children role-played this scene over several days, each time moving everything from one area to another. Finally, they asked to permanently move the dramatic play center to the new area of the classroom and after they did, the eviction play ended.

 Apply Your Knowledge At times children may play out life experiences that are foreign to you or that you are uncomfortable with. Brainstorm a list of possible dramatic play topics that would fall in this category. How can you validate children's experiences and their lives in situations such as these?

Meet the Needs of All Learners

Supporting Children from All Cultures. It is important to represent each child's culture in the dramatic play area. The dramatic play area also offers the opportunity to teach children about cultures that are not represented in the room. While many programs now have multicultural dolls, it is important to think of multiculturalism in relationship to all aspects of the dramatic play center. For example, when planning a home living center we can include doll props, cooking utensils, eating utensils, dishes, clothing, hats, shoes, books, pictures, fabric, play food, and print representing different cultures. When introducing unfamiliar items to children it is important to weave the familiar and the unfamiliar together. Whenever possible, let the children see the object being authentically used. For example, before you introduce a tortilla press, you might invite a guest to demonstrate how to make tortillas and then eat them for snack. Visiting ethnic sections of a grocery store and ethnic restaurants are other ways to gain experiences (Huber, 2000). Family members can also be a great resource for such enrichment. Pictures on the wall can also help children to learn about different forms of dress, food, eating utensils, and ways of cooking food (Huber, 2000).

In our eagerness to add multicultural props, we must also be cautious about not inadvertently teaching children misconceptions and stereotypes. These misconceptions can occur if we teach children that everyone from the same culture has the same beliefs, lives in the same style of housing, or wears the same type of clothing. Customs within the same culture often differ based on personal beliefs, age, income level, and geographic area of the country.

Misconceptions can also occur when we place an emphasis on traditional rather than modern life. For example, when we add a kimono to the dramatic play center we need to help children understand that most Japanese wear western clothing in public. However, the kimono might be worn at home or on special occasions.

> TIP When buying multicultural dolls, make sure that they not only have various skin tones but also different facial features, and a variety of hair and eye colors. Include both male and female dolls.

Supporting Children with Disabilities. To support children with disabilities it is important that the center be accessible, that materials reflect the children who are disabled, and that the children receive the coaching and support they need to successfully interact with peers. To be accessible, the child not only needs to be able to enter the center but also must be able to reach and use the materials. Accommodations will vary depending upon the child's needs. For example, if a child needs to lean against the toy stove to play with it, it is important that the stove be anchored securely so it will not tip. If the child has difficulty picking up the kitchen utensils, a foam hair curler might be inserted over the handle to provide a better gripping surface.

Children with disabilities also need to see themselves reflected in the materials and props in the dramatic play center. Assistive devices such as hearing aids, wheelchairs, and glasses can be available for dramatic play. Assistive devices for doll play can also be added.

Children with disabilities may engage in more solitary and less cooperative play at the same age as their peers (Hestenes & Carroll, 2000). While children with mild disabilities tend to go through the same stages of play as their peers, they make the transitions from one stage to the next at a later age (Guralnik & Hammond, 1999).

How can we assist children with disabilities to interact with their peers? Some experts advocate script rehearsal where the teacher or other adult participates in a play scenario, coaching the child as they interact (Neeley, Neeley, Justen, & Tipton–Sumner, 2001). The adult uses direct teaching, models a script, uses script words, and finally prompts the child to act out the role using the script words she has learned. After the child is successful in interacting with the adult, another child is invited into the play session. Finally, the child joins the regular playgroup. After preschool children participated in this intervention, their solitary play was reduced from 49% to 6% and group play increased from 14% to 61% (Neeley et al., 2001).

Observe and Document Individual Children's Learning

Assessing and documenting children's play in the dramatic play center can help you understand their level of play, play interests, common scripts, and ability to interact with others. You can also observe many other skills in this area (language, math, science, emotional, social, self-regulatory, and creative). You might use anecdotal records, running records, artifacts such as their play plans, video recordings, or audio recordings to assess children's learning in this area. Some questions you might ask while observing are:

- What type of play does the child typically engage in—solitary, parallel, associative, or cooperative (see Chapter 1 for definitions of each play type)?
- Is the child able to enter a dramatic play situation with others?
- Whom does the child prefer to play with?
- Does the child role-play, pretending to be another person, animal, or object (Smilansky & Shefatya, 1990)?
- Does the child make believe with actions (Smilansky & Shefatya, 1990)? If yes, give an example.
- Does the child make believe with objects (Smilansky & Shefatya, 1990)? If yes, give an example.
- Does the child create make believe situations (Smilansky & Shefatya, 1990)? If yes, give an example.
- Does the child verbally interact with at least one other person (Smilansky & Shefatya, 1990)? If yes, describe the interaction.
- Does the child interact with others to coordinate the roles and the plot (Smilansky & Shefatya, 1990)? If yes, give an example.
- Can the child maintain the play theme for 5 minutes or more (Smilansky & Shefatya, 1990)?
- What type of literacy behaviors does the child demonstrate?
- What types of mathematical skills does the child use in the dramatic play area?
- What scripts does the child enact?
- What role does the child prefer?
- Is the child a leader or follower in developing and maintaining the play script?
- Is the child able to successfully use the different props in the center?
- Can the child negotiate successfully with others?

Special Challenges in the Dramatic Play Center

Superhero and War Play

Should superhero and war play be banned? Teachers are often concerned about safety, the limiting nature of the play, and what children are learning by enacting violent scenes from superhero play (Levin, 2003). However, it often does not work to ban gun and superhero play because this type of play allows children to feel powerful and to face their fears. Many children have a strong need for this. Additionally, when teachers try to ban this type of play, children may defy the rules, hiding their play or declaring that the play is not superhero or gun play (Levin, 2003). Furthermore, banning the behavior does not give the children the opportunity to work through their issues (NAEYC, 2006). To diminish violent play while still meeting children's needs to feel powerful and face their fears, you can do the following:

- Promote imaginative play rather than imitative play by observing the children and helping them to expand on their play script (NAEYC, 2006). Since superhero play or war play often has a very limited story line, it might also be helpful to have children write or draw a play plan to expand their play.

- Redirect children to accompanying play behaviors. For example, several children were playing pirates pretending to have sword fights. The teacher suggested they problem solve other ways they could escape from the boat. The children also became involved in making costumes, boats, and hideouts.

- Focus on the helping behaviors of superheroes (such as making a list of the ways that Batman helps other people). At times, you might be able to provide additional information about the character. When Ninja Turtles were popular one teacher told children about the famous artist, Michelangelo. Two boys who had been playing the Ninja Turtle named Michelangelo became very interested and decided to see what it would be like to paint laying on their backs. They taped paper to the bottom of a table and spent a significant amount of time painting their ceiling (Gronlund, 1992).

- Focus on real-life heroes, fairy tales, and folk tales to give children alternative powerful figures to act out.

- Help children to understand the difference between real and imaginary characters and behaviors.

- Provide additional outlets for facing and describing fears including drawing and writing. Also provide ways for dealing with an abundance of high energy, including plenty of outdoor time and opportunities for indoor physical activities (tumbling, pounding nails into a tree stump).

- Provide additional ways for children to feel powerful; for example, through the accomplishment of physical feats and challenges.

It is also important to guarantee the physical and emotional safety of all children in the group. One way of accomplishing this is by having the children help to establish rules surrounding this type of play, such as "Only play with those who want to play" and "Superhero play occurs only in a certain area" (NAEYC, 2006).

Outdoor dramatic play is encouraged through providing props and materials. This golf cart is just the right size for children.

Outdoor Dramatic Play Centers

Dramatic play is often ignored when planning playgrounds (Brown et al., 2001). While dramatic play takes place on playgrounds even when specific places are not established, an encapsulated site increases the length and the depth of children's play (Frost, Wortham, & Reifel, 2001).

There are many potential dramatic play areas, including a lean-to, playhouse, grotto, platform, and even vehicles such as golf carts or old rowboats. Children can also help to create their own play sites. For example, children and adults can build snow caves, straw houses, and sandbag houses. They can plant climbing peas or sunflowers to create an enclosed area.

Outdoor dramatic play can be enriched with natural materials found on the playground such as flowers, dirt, leaves, branches, and water. When natural materials are available, children often use the materials to maintain play episodes (Brown et al., 2001). Loose parts (boards, tarps, blankets) can also extend play opportunities.

Through dramatic play, children can enact and transform reality, while increasing their cognitive, social, literacy, self-regulatory, creative, and emotional skills. When teachers design rich dramatic play areas and scaffold children's learning, the quality and quantity of dramatic play increases, leading to increased learning across the curriculum.

Sample Application Activities

1. Develop a prop box. You can find ideas by visiting http://www.childcarelounge. com/caregivers/propbox.htm or http://www.allthedaze.com/drama5.html

2. Choose a theme or topic and brainstorm a list of props.

3. Think of the dramatic play area. What would you do to make sure it represents all cultures?

4. Brainstorm a list of different kitchen utensils, dishes, and cooking pots that could give children experience with different cultures.

5. Observe children entering a sociodramatic play episode that is already in progress. What skills do the different children use in entering the play?

6. Visit a center and evaluate their dramatic play area using the environmental assessment found in Figure 12.2.

7. Observe an individual child and use the questions in the chapter as a way of assessing and observing their dramatic play activities.

8. Build your skills in enhancing dramatic play by completing an exercise on MyEducationLab. Select the topic "Dramatic Arts." Under Building Teaching Skills and Dispositions, complete the exercise Supporting Informal Drama in a Preschool Classroom.

The effective dramatic play center

☐ Is in a well-defined area such as a separated corner of the classroom or outdoors in a "cave," boat, den, playhouse

☐ Provides sufficient space for at least four to six children to play

☐ If indoors, is located next to the block area to increase the movement of materials between the two centers

☐ Contains relevant and familiar items that allow children to represent their experiences

☐ Contains materials that represent all members of the classroom—cultural materials, assistive devices, different family groupings

☐ Includes materials that introduce children to many cultures and family groupings (even those that are not represented in the classroom)

☐ Is aesthetic

☐ Contains clothing, or pieces of fabric for children to create their own clothing

☐ Contains full-length mirrors

☐ Contains a variety of props to support rich play opportunities

☐ Includes duplicates of props so children can participate in parallel play

☐ Includes authentic math props

☐ Includes authentic and appropriate literacy props

☐ Includes some loose parts so children can develop what they need

☐ Provides ways to make clothing and prop choices available and organized

☐ Contains needed equipment such as a toy stove for a home living center

☐ Is dynamic, being changed or added to as needed to sustain rich play opportunities

Figure 12.2
Environmental Assessment: Dramatic Play Center

chapter 13
Developing Art Centers

It is National Arbor Day, and three early childhood programs nestled in the Rocky Mountains have responded by including activities focused on trees. At Kiddie World, the teacher has substituted pine boughs for paintbrushes at the easel. She has also added pinecones to the collage materials. At ABC Academy, the teacher is instructing small groups of children to follow her directions in drawing evergreen trees by overlapping a series of triangles. At the Nature Preschool, children are drawing their own evergreen trees. They first examined the tree growing outside their program by touching and smelling the needles, sap, and bark. They made casts of the bark and then used magnifying glasses to explore the bark, needles, and sap more intimately. Finally, they sat outside and made pencil sketches of the tree.

Through the arts we decorate, communicate, and express ourselves aesthetically (Koster, 2005). Art is also a tool for thinking and inquiry, allowing children to "make their theories and ideas visible, take new perspectives, represent and explore emotions, and to study properties of the physical world" (Pelo, 2007, p. 110). As children create and share art, they also learn about other's perspectives and ideas (Pelo, 2007).

Visual arts are basic to humanity, existing in all cultures and dating back to prehistoric cave drawings (Koster, 2005). Art influences all aspects of our lives, including the design of our clothing, buildings, vehicles, and toys.

Approaches to Art

In the opening scenario, the programs demonstrate three approaches to art: noninterventionist, production-oriented, and art as inquiry.

Noninterventionist Approach

The teacher at Kiddie World is using a noninterventionist approach to art. In this approach, the teacher provides a variety of materials and encourages free exploration. Children are totally in charge of what they produce, with the process being the focus. The teacher views her primary role as providing encouragement and support for individuality. The belief underlying this approach is that children, given the right environment, will naturally develop artistic skills (Kindler, 1995). While exploration of art elements and media is an important goal for early childhood art, if children do not move beyond exploration they will not develop their full potential in the arts or be able to effectively use the arts as a tool for thinking, inquiry, and communication. Many artists contrast this to the approach used for verbal language, where adults model conversations, stimulate and challenge children, and present new language tasks. If adults were to take the same hands-off approach to learning language as some do to art, children would be extremely delayed in learning to talk.

Production-Oriented Approach

The teacher at ABC Academy is using the production-oriented approach to art. In this approach, the children complete prescribed teacher-directed art projects. There is little room for individuality. The focus of the activity is on producing a product that is predetermined by the teacher. When children are presented with models to copy, they will often use this identical form extensively, stunting their further development. For example, in drawing trees they will use the triangle method that they have been taught. They do not need to examine trees, think about the branches on the trees, or decide how to represent this three-dimensional object in a two-dimensional form. Teachers who use this method might plan art around holidays, planning one-time activities with no continuity or developmental progression (Bresler, 1995). Because the production-oriented art approach stifles creativity as well as cognitive and artistic growth, it is considered developmentally inappropriate (Copple & Bredekamp, 2009).

Teachers may provide production-oriented art because of their discomfort with art methods and processes. Additionally, some teachers use this approach so that they have products to send home to parents. Many parents were raised in schools where crafts or patterned activities were sent home as art and so they expect that their child will also come home with these. We can improve our own and families' understanding of creative art through sponsoring art workshops and guest speakers at the program. Rather than sending home production-oriented art, we can show the progress in children's art at home visits or parent-teacher conferences. We can also attach notes to children's artwork explaining what children have learned. Some teachers have developed notes and have them ready to attach at the appropriate time. For example, Bonnie teaches children who are ages 2 through 4. She has a note prepared when children first draw a tadpole person. "Today, Hope drew a tadpole person (a head with legs extending from it). People in all cultures and throughout history have drawn tadpole people as their first attempts to draw a person. This is an exciting step in Hope's development."

Art as Inquiry Approach

At the Nature Preschool, the teacher is using the inquiry approach to art. The art as inquiry approach involves active investigation, where children deepen their knowledge about art techniques as well as the art subject or topic as they engage in art. In this approach, art is viewed as a language to communicate thoughts, ideas, and feelings. The art is often related to an in-depth project with the children using art to express their knowledge. In the beginning stages, children still spend time exploring media and elements. However, teachers also scaffold children's learning by providing background experiences on the topic and through teaching art techniques. In this approach, children often revisit their artwork, allowing them to learn more about art, while deepening their knowledge of the world (Spodek, 2006). They will also revisit their ideas using multiple media. For example, in *To Make a Portrait of a Lion,* a video documenting a project at Reggio Emilia, children made field sketches of a lion statue, created paintings of the lion, and made the lion in clay.

Stages of Art in the Early Childhood Years

Several experts have studied the stages of children's art. Perhaps the most famous has been Victor Lowenfeld. We will examine the stages that Lowenfeld and Brittain (1987) found in children's art, focusing on the early childhood years.

Scribble Stage

The scribble stage typically occurs before the age of 4 and is often considered to be primarily kinesthetic. Children do not pre-plan their artwork or begin with a subject in mind. This stage is further divided into three substages: random, controlled, and naming. During the random scribble stage, children use their whole arm and may even draw off the paper. When children enter the controlled scribble stage, they begin to use their wrist. This allows them to make smaller marks and have more control in placing lines on their paper. During the naming scribble stage, children make a variety of different lines and shapes. They also begin to name their scribbles. Often children will begin to draw and then decide the scribble looks like something. They will then add further detail to enhance the appearance.

Preschematic Stage

In the preschematic stage, which typically occurs between ages 4 and 7, visual ideas are developing. At the beginning of this stage, children will often draw tadpole people, characterized by a head with lines coming directly from it, representing legs and sometimes arms. Tadpole figures are found in children's artwork throughout the world and have been documented in children's drawings for more than 100 years (Lasky & Muderji, 1987). In the preschematic stage, children often use a larger size for those things that are most important, powerful, or impressive to them. For example, a child who is fearful of a dog may draw a dog that is very huge with disproportionately large teeth.

Schematic Stage

Children at the schematic stage, which typically occurs between the ages of 7 and 9, have developed a schema for the way an object looks and may make the object the same each time they draw it. In this stage, children use baselines, skylines, and show beginning awareness of perspective. Many children will use "X-ray" drawings at this stage, drawing what they know rather than what they see. For example, they may draw clothes on a person but also draw the body underneath. Or, they may draw a person in profile but show both eyes. To see several examples of children's drawings of people look at *A Drawing of Dana and*

Dina, Baseball Player, A Drawing of Two Friends, Hand Stand Drawing, Happy Mom, Baby, and Sun, and *Tina's Self Portrait* on MyEducationLab. What stages of development are the children exhibiting?

Children who have rich art experiences continue to progress through additional art stages as they mature (dawning realism, pseudorealism).

How the Art Center Enhances Children's Development

Children increase their artistic knowledge, skills, and creativity while enhancing emotional, social, cognitive, and physical development as they participate in art. They also are more likely to develop a "love of the arts" when they are exposed to art at a young age.

Artistic Development

Although most children will not choose to be professional artists when they become adults, they will nevertheless be surrounded by images. To be literate in today's world, one must be able to understand, analyze, and critique these images. Through early childhood art, children can increase observation skills, learn art techniques, begin to understand the relationship of art to culture and history, and learn to appreciate and enjoy images and art. They will also have the experience of joy that comes from creating unique products (West, 2006).

Although the arts are often the first subjects to be eliminated when there are school funding cuts, Hetland and Winner (2001) make the following important point, "Cultures are judged on the basis of their arts; and most cultures and most historical eras have not doubted the importance of studying the arts" (p. 5).

Creative Development

Art enhances creativity, which is crucial for innovation and adaptation. Creative people have the ability to see multiple solutions to a problem, employ original thoughts, and use their imagination. As a field, art promotes these skills, encouraging unique and divergent responses and diverse ways of looking at things. To see two examples of creative artworks by young children view *One-Eyed Creature* and *Guitar Drawing* on MyEducationLab.

Many early childhood teachers previously thought the best way to enhance creativity in the arts was to use the noninterventionist approach. However, we have now come to realize the power and possibilities in the art as inquiry approach. As stated by HMIE (2006), a group in Scotland who researched creativity,

> As pupils acquire experience, develop skills, and broaden their knowledge and understanding, they are able to use their increased control of materials, movements, media, and ideas to demonstrate a more mature level of creativity. Ironically, in contrast with the view that a climate of 'anything goes' is conducive to creativity, the opposite is the case. Higher levels of creativity usually result from an interaction of considerable knowledge and skill with a willingness to innovate and experiment. (p. 3)

Land and Jarmin tested people's ability to think in divergent ways (creatively generate multiple solutions or ideas). Using the same instrument, they tested 1,600 children—first in preschool, then in elementary school, and finally in high school. When the group of children were tested as preschoolers, 98% were considered to be geniuses in divergent thinking. The test was repeated when the children were 8 to 10 years old and only 32% of the children still reached the genius stage. When the children were tested as 14- and 15-year-olds, only 10% still tested in the genius range for divergent thinking. Preschoolers who once had the ability to think in divergent ways had lost this ability through their school years (Robinson, 2005). While thinking divergently is only one characteristic

myeducationlab

Go to MyEducationLab and select the topic "Child Development." Under Activities and Applications, view the following artifacts: *A Drawing of Dana and Dina; Baseball Player; A Drawing of Two Friends; Hand Stand Drawing;* and *Happy Mom, Baby, and Sun.* Next, select the topic "Diversity." Under Activities and Applications, view the artifact *Tina's Self Portrait.*

myeducationlab

Go to MyEducationLab and select the topic "Child Development." Under Activities and Applications, view the artifact *Guitar Drawing.* Next, select the topic "Visual Arts." Under Activities and Applications, view the artifact *One-Eyed Creature.*

needed for creativity, it is critical, since the other characteristics of creative thinking are built upon this skill. It is crucial that we encourage divergent thinking in the arts, as well as in all curricular areas in the classroom.

According to Robinson and the National Advisory Committee on Cultural and Creative Education (1999), four characteristics are necessary for an activity to be defined as a creative process: thinking imaginatively; being purposeful; generating an original thought, idea, or product; and having this thought, idea, or product valuable in relationship to the task or objective. As we plan our art environments, we need to think about these characteristics. Children who have learned the artistic techniques needed to represent their ideas and have the opportunity to explore topics and media in-depth, to revisit and add to their work, and to examine the same idea in different media are more likely to embody these four characteristics.

Emotional Development

Art experiences can also assist children's emotional development. As children participate in art activities they gain self-confidence, feel pride in their work, and experience success (Koster, 2005). Art allows children to express strong emotions that they may have difficulty verbalizing. It may provide the child and others with insights into the child's thoughts and feelings, thus allowing for conversation and further discussion. For example, Gross and Clemens (2002) discuss how preschoolers in their class used drawings, paintings, and clay models to re-enact the destruction of the twin towers in New York. Re-enacting the scene was therapeutic for many children, allowing them to feel a sense of control, and opening up dialogue with the other children and adults in their lives.

Social Development

As children examine art from various artists, in different time periods and diverse cultures, they have the opportunity to learn about and to appreciate differences. They come to understand that people have unique values and see things in different ways.

In many classrooms, children also have the opportunity to collaborate with others on murals and other large art projects. Again, children learn about diverse views, practice negotiation, and have tangible proof of how their work, when combined with others, can create something beautiful.

Cognitive Development

Through art, children learn about the world, record thoughts and ideas, and enhance academic learning. "Artmaking is a form of inquiry and way of learning about oneself and the world" (Tarr, 1997, p. 2). For example, as a child observes a flower and then draws a sketch, he notices details he may not have considered before. Slight imperfections in the petals raise questions. What caused the holes in the petals? Why are some petals turning brown while others are not? He notes that the petal is a graduated color and must determine how he will portray this. When the child is done, he shares his work with others. "Through sharing and gaining others' perspectives, and then revisiting and revising their work, children move to new levels of awareness" (Edwards & Springate, 1995).

As with written language, the visual arts involve recording a thought or idea that then can be conveyed to someone else. For this reason, art is often considered the child's first written language (Koster, 2005). This window into the child's thinking makes her ideas visible to others. This allows others to engage in dialogue and ask questions that will assist the child to reflect even more deeply.

As children carefully study and discuss their art and the art of others, they are developing "visual perception or 'visual thinking' a cognitive process that takes images and gives them meaning" (Koster, 2005, p. 5). They are also seeing items from different vantage points and exploring spatial concepts (critical skills in geometry). In addition, while participating in art, children pose and solve problems, organize thoughts, and reflect on their learning. They learn about properties of materials and experiment with cause and effect. All of these skills are critical in other disciplines as well.

Physical Development

Art develops large and small muscles and eye-hand coordination. Unlike prescribed writing or art exercises, creative art provides a motivating climate for children to practice and perfect motor control. Some teachers use production-oriented art as a way of promoting fine motor control. However, children are typically more passionate about their own creative art. Therefore, they are often more committed to the repeated practice that is needed to master the skills.

As children participate in art they have opportunities to increase artistic skills, enhance creativity, and develop emotional, social, cognitive, and physical skills. However, for optimal development, the teacher must use the inquiry approach to art and must establish an environment that is conducive to learning. How does a teacher develop an art center that stresses the art as inquiry approach?

Designing an Effective Art Center

Art does not occur in only one area of the room. Children learn about art from picture books, pictures on the wall in other areas of the room, and the aesthetics of the room itself. However, it is also important to have a dedicated area where children can focus on producing and studying art. Art centers can be a separate room such as the *atelier* in the Reggio Emilia schools or they can be a center in the classroom. Whether a separate studio or a corner nook, art centers are most effective when they contain the following:

- Plenty of natural and artificial light (Pelo, 2007).
- Easy clean up with linoleum or tile floors, covered or easy-to-clean tables, and a close proximity to water.
- A quiet space that allows for focus and attention.
- Ample space so that children have room to create large projects and so that several children can work at a time.
- Space for drying creations and storing ongoing work.
- Space for displaying art creations (both two and three dimensional).
- An abundance of diverse materials. There may be a limited number of materials when children are first introduced to a medium. However, to allow for in-depth exploration and enhanced creativity, the range of materials should expand with the children's experiences.
- High-quality, authentic materials and tools in good working condition. Poor-quality tools inhibit children from expressing their talent. For example, trying to control the line of paint when the brush will not keep a point, can frustrate children's efforts to create the picture they are envisioning. Clogged glue bottles or scissors that don't cut can also be very frustrating.
- Safe and nontoxic materials. You can check for safe supplies at the Art and Creative Materials Institute (ACMI) website http://acminet.org/index.htm, or you can look for the ACMI-certified nontoxic label.
- Low, uncluttered shelves so that children have easy access to materials.

Notice how the mirrors on the second and fourth shelves reflect the light and highlight the materials in Brenna's home child care art area.

- Aesthetically displayed materials that invite children to investigate and use the media. As we are teaching children about aesthetics, we need to model it in the environment. Materials can be displayed in baskets, transparent bowls, and in beautiful containers. You can organize materials by color palette. For example, color crayons or color pencils can be displayed in clear jars. Each jar can contain a different color with many hues represented. Mirrors can be used to reflect the materials in a different way.

- An abundance of reference materials and materials for inspiration. Especially when children are creating representational drawings, it is important to provide them with real-life objects, pictures, photos, and reference books to use as resources. Even adult artists, who have years of observational training and increased ability to remember detail, use references when creating pictures. In addition, reference materials provide opportunities for children to examine and appreciate art.

- Storage for replenishing supplies.

When developing your art center, it is also important to consider art goals.

Art Goals: Creating and Appreciating Art

Colbert and Taunton (1992), who authored a National Art Education Association (NAEA) briefing paper on developmentally appropriate practices in art education for young children, identify the following art goals. Children need many opportunities to create art and they need many opportunities to appreciate art, to look at and talk about art, and to become aware of art in their everyday lives.

Provide Art Materials That Can Be Transformed

As mentioned in the opening story, production-oriented or patterned art is developmentally inappropriate in early childhood. Patterned art tends to produce nearly identical looking products. In some cases, the teacher has precut much of the product and the child's role is to assemble the pieces. For example, children create snowmen by gluing teacher-made construction paper circles together.

Whenever you choose an art project, you should consider whether you are expanding or limiting creativity and the cognitive thought process. For example, many teachers have children make caterpillars out of egg cartons. While children are allowed to decorate the caterpillars any way they wish, is this the best way to encourage children to closely observe caterpillars, to think about how caterpillars look, to decide what media would be best to create the caterpillar, or to contemplate how to capture the fluffiness of the caterpillar? Epstein and Trimis (2002) urge us to choose art projects carefully. According to them, a good rule of thumb is to avoid art materials that are "cute or novel." Instead, choose art materials that can be transformed and used by the child to express an idea or feeling (Epstein & Trimis, 2002).

Encourage In-Depth Artwork

Art experiences need to be thoughtfully planned to encourage in-depth artwork. The practice in some programs of an art activity each day does not allow children the in-depth development of the skills they need to portray their thoughts and ideas adequately. Repetition with media, revisiting the same piece of art, and creating an idea in different media contribute to deeper learning and enhanced artistic outcomes.

Revisit Media. To become proficient, children need many opportunities to use media over an extended period of time. This will allow children to move beyond exploration, which is the first phase when someone is introduced to a new media such as clay or watercolors.

Revisit Artwork. Just like professional artists, children need the opportunity to revisit their work. Artists often begin with a sketch, work on a number of pieces at once, revisit, and find ideas from a number of sources (Tarr, 1997). Most artists also name their work. Encouraging children to create names or titles for their creations helps them to reflect upon their art and is another way for children to revisit their work.

Revisit Ideas Using Different Media. Revisiting ideas through different media also helps children to reflect. When children use different media, they are challenged to think about the idea they are expressing in different ways. For example, a child might create a sketch of a caterpillar, then paint a picture of a caterpillar, and then create the caterpillar out of clay. Each media allows the child to represent his knowledge in a unique way and creates new questions and deeper thought. Todd was creating the caterpillar out of clay. He decided to use wire to represent the hairs on the caterpillar. This involved cutting the wire and placing each hair individually, causing him to focus on the hair. He had many questions. Does the hair grow straight up or does it curl slightly at the end? Are the hairs on all the caterpillars the same? Do they go in circles around the body or are they random? After closely observing the caterpillars for a length of time, he began to work. Forman (2006) suggests that to increase children's knowledge of their learning after they have created in different media, they should circle back and revisit their first drawing. "Children draw to learn as opposed to merely learn to draw. Children are revising their theories, not simply revising the accuracy of a copy" (Forman, 2006, p. 36).

The first goal of art for young children then is to allow them to create art in a developmentally appropriate way. This includes encouraging in-depth creative artwork through revisiting media, creations, and ideas. Second, children need to learn to appreciate art.

Appropriate Materials and Activities for Creating Art

When creating art, children first need the opportunity for in-depth experimentation with art media, tools, and elements. Teachers need to help children become competent in the use of art media so they can express ideas and thoughts in the way they intended (Spodek, 2006). As mentioned earlier, when children are first introduced to a media or tool, it is important to begin with a limited number of materials, allowing children to explore and master them before gradually introducing more materials (Spodek, 2006). "We must be careful in our zeal to provide children with a variety of art materials and experiences, we do not shortchange their time with each one" (Epstein & Trimis, 2002, p. 45). For example, Latoya, a teacher of 3-year-olds, introduces children to tempera paint by giving them just one color. After children have thoroughly explored this color, she adds white paint so that children can create a range of tints of this color. Eventually she adds additional colors. As children become proficient, she also provides additional types of paper and brushes.

A variety of different types of drawing implements are made more appealing and visible by displaying them by color palette in clear containers.

Art centers for young children will typically contain materials for drawing, painting, modeling, and creating sculptures and collages. Each of these media has different affordances, or differing physical properties and abilities to be transformed by a child's desire to represent an idea (Forman, 1994, p. 38).

Drawing

Children gain inspiration for drawing from a variety of sources: observation, experiences, memory, and their imagination (Bartel, 2006). However, their drawings are more in-depth when they are observing rather than relying on memory (Colbert & Taunton, 1988). To assist children in observational drawings, it may be helpful to provide observational tools, such as magnifying glasses to observe fine details. Another observation tool is a cardboard viewfinder that can help to narrow the child's focus. Mirrors can also be a helpful tool, allowing children to see objects from a different view. Additionally, like artists, children need the real object as well as representations of the object for inspiration while drawing.

TIP   You can make your own viewfinder by cutting the center from an 8" square rigid, piece of cardboard. Make the frame 2 inches wide. This creates a 4" interior square. Children can hold the viewfinder at eye level and look through it or place it on a picture to narrow the viewpoint.

Esmeralda, like many teachers, begins each year with a study of self. In the art area, she provides photos of each child and his or her family. She also provides photos that focus on one facial feature; for example, a close-up photo of eyes, ears, or teeth for each child. Mirrors of different sizes are available throughout the art area. Magnifying glasses for close examination are also available. On the walls of the art area are framed pictures from famous artists: Gainsborough's "The Blue Boy," Durveger's "Alone," and Cassatt's "Two Children Playing on a Beach." A viewfinder is hung next to each reproduction to assist children in narrowing focus. She also provides a three-dimensional bust and a hardwood 12" manikin for children to study.

The children make self-portraits beginning with sketches. Esmeralda adds skin tone paper and markers for the children to use if they wish. They then produce their portraits in paint and wire. Ultimately, the children make clay busts of themselves. They mix paints to match their skin tones and give each child's paint a creative, descriptive name (chocolate syrup, nutmeg, root beer float). They use these mixtures to paint their clay busts.

Esmeralda also adds a variety of costumes to the dramatic play area to help children extend the discovery of self. Children experiment with new identities through wearing the costumes—and often capture their transformations through their art.

Basic Drawing Materials

Art centers for preschool and early elementary age children should contain many types of drawing tools. Each tool has unique characteristics, allowing children to use them for different purposes. At a minimum, the center should contain different types of pencils, markers, chalk, and crayons.

Pencils. Pencils allow good control, produce precise lines, are clean to work with, and are readily available. Children can use drawing pencils, colored pencils, and pastel pencils.

Markers. Markers come in a wide variety of colors (skin tones, fluorescent, bold) and types (erasable, fabric, window). They allow smooth application, requiring little pressure. It is important to buy nonpermanent markers with a variety of different-sized tips. This allows children to use the markers for different purposes. For example, fine-tip markers are excellent for detailed work while thick markers can be used for coloring in the child's creation.

Chalk. Chalk is inexpensive, blends easily, and can be used either wet or dry. A fixative helps the chalk to adhere to the paper and reduces chalk dust. Two solutions that work well as fixatives are liquid starch (equal part water and liquid starch) or sugar water (three tablespoons sugar to one cup of water) solutions. The child can either brush the solution on the paper or dip the chalk into the solution. Inexpensive chalkboards can be created by painting a piece of wood or the back of a cabinet with chalkboard paint.

Pastels, while more expensive, provide a vibrant color, do not rub off like chalk, and can still be blended. They do, however, crumble and break easily.

Crayons. Crayons are inexpensive, have a wide range of vibrant colors, and come in a variety of kinds (metallic, multicultural, fabric, scented, glitter, anti-roll). Unlike markers, changes in pressure influence the outcome of the drawing. This allows children to use different amounts of pressure to create depth and shading.

In addition to placing pencils, chalk, markers, and crayons in the art area, these drawing materials are also typically available throughout the classroom to encourage writing, drawing, and sketching. For example, drawing materials and paper in the block area encourage the children to pre-plan their buildings and to document their buildings after they create them.

Painting

Tempera, watercolor, acrylic, and finger paints are appropriate for preschool and early elementary age children and should be available in the art center. An easel set up in the art center with a variety of paint hues provides an appropriate surface while enticing children to paint. The Helen Gordon Child Development Center uses an adult adjustable easel in their art area, finding that it can accommodate both larger and smaller pieces of paper.

This adjustable easel at the Helen Gordon Child Development Center accommodates children's artistic needs, becoming large enough for a giant mural or small enough for a mini picture.

Even very young children can use tempera paint and an easel. For example, the Birge Nest room in Early Head Start, serving children from birth to age 3, has an easel with several colors of paint that is continually available to children.

In many programs, children are encouraged to draw their pictures before painting them, allowing them to pre-plan their creations. The drawing may be made several days before or immediately before painting. Pencils and other drawing materials placed near the easel provide an invitation for children to draw before painting if they have not already done so.

It is critical to have quality brushes in a variety of sizes for children to paint with. The quality of the brush greatly influences the child's ability to manipulate the paints. If the child wishes to create a special effect, you might provide other items to paint with, including sticks, pastry brushes, feathers, sponges, small paint rollers, makeup brushes, toothbrushes, and vegetable brushes. For example, toothbrushes may be effective in creating a background for snow scenes.

Basic Painting Materials

Tempera Paints. Tempera paints are economical and come in a variety of colors, including metallic. You can buy tempera paints that are premixed, powdered, or in cakes. When buying the paint, choose a washable variety.

It is important to give children many opportunities to explore paint. You might begin by exploring these questions. How does paint work on different types of surfaces? What kind of lines can be produced with different size brushes? How can paint be made thicker (soap flakes), shiny (sugar), glittery (salt on wet paint), or gritty (sand)? What other substances can change the texture of the paint? What colors can be produced by mixing the paints? You can provide small clear glass or plastic containers for children to use for their experimentation. As children become more experienced, the teacher can also create mixing challenges such as trying to mix paint to match a paint chip. The mixed paints can be displayed in the art area and used for future paintings. The wide variety of hues in clear containers also adds an aesthetic element to the classroom.

Finger Paints. Finger paints are a creamy, thick consistency that also come in a variety of colors. You can purchase special paints or use thick tempera paint in finger painting. You can also finger paint with lotion, cold cream, or a mixture of liquid starch and tempera paint.

Acrylic Paints. Acrylic paints are water soluble and produce bright vibrant colors. They are very adhesive and flexible, allowing the child to successfully apply the paint to many surfaces, including plastic, metal, canvas, and boards. For example, at the Opal School in Portland, Oregon, children created beautiful, transparent murals by painting pictures on a clear plastic shower curtain using acrylic paints.

Watercolor. Watercolor is transparent, dries quickly, and is water-based for easy cleanup. Watercolors come in a variety of forms, including watercolor pencils, watercolor cakes (both student and professional), liquid watercolors, and watercolors in tubes. Special watercolor paper (textured and designed to absorb water) is typically used with this media. Because the paper is expensive, you might encourage children to take smaller pieces if they plan to create small images.

When learning about the properties of watercolor, children can experiment with different size brushes, create shades by adding an increasing amount of water, and experiment with wet versus dry paper. Wet paper allows the paint to spread out and often creates a misty or hazy look (Romberg, 2002).

Figure 13.1
Surfaces to Draw
and Paint On

Nearly any surface can be drawn or painted on with one's imagination being the only limit. In addition to providing different types of surfaces, it is also important to provide different sizes of surfaces, since different sizes suggest different types of strokes. As a rule of thumb, the younger the children the larger the surface will need to be for them to be successful. Some common surfaces are

manila paper	wallpaper
newsprint	foam board
construction paper	gift wrap
watercolor paper	cardboard
newspaper	sandpaper
computer print-out paper	bubble wrap
large rolls of craft paper	foil
shiny papers to finger paint on	fabric
such as butcher paper	felt
cellophane	tree bark
wax paper	wood
tissue paper	

For more transitory pictures, children can draw in sand or paint on tabletops. Transitory pictures can also be created using different items on a light table or overhead projector. The Children's Museum in Chicago provided children with a spray bottle of water, an abundance of cut and torn colored cellophane, and a Plexiglas easel. Children could create transitory pictures by spraying the Plexiglas with water and arranging the cellophane.

As children become more familiar with the media, they may wish to produce special effects such as blotting with a sponge to create texture or overlaying colors (paint with one color, let the painting dry, and then paint over the picture with another color).

In addition to having a variety of hues of watercolors and paintbrushes in the art center, you will also want to have paper towels available for children to remove water from their brushes. Small jars for water will also be needed.

Providing a variety of paints allows children to experiment with the different properties of each. It also allows children to choose the most conducive paint for their specific purpose and surface. Many surfaces can be used for drawing and painting. See Figure 13.1 for a list of some possible surfaces.

Collage

A collage is a composite of material or objects pasted onto a surface. It can be two or three dimensional. Collage materials are often recycled items such as newspaper clippings, beads, buttons, wallpaper, fabric, and items from nature.

Collages may be created around a theme. For example, Sarah has children create "All about me"

The array of collage materials becomes the focus of attention when displayed in clear containers.

A mirror reflects the natural collage materials, adding an aesthetic element to the display of materials.

collages that include magazine pictures, drawings, and items representing themselves. One child loved apple juice and added a small juice box to his collage. Another child included a clay model of a ladybug because she liked to collect bugs.

Infants can make collages by sticking items to clear contact paper. When the child is done, the teacher can place another piece of contact paper over the top of the picture, sealing the materials between the two layers.

Sculpture

A sculpture is a three-dimensional figure. Like collages they can be created from a variety of materials. Materials that are suitable for children include different sizes of wire, rolled up newspaper, boxes, wood, papier-mache, small appliance parts, and a variety of other recycled materials (see Figure 13.2 for ideas). You will also need the appropriate type of glue, tape, nails, and so forth to hold the sculpture together.

At the Mentor Graphics Child Development Center, children created bug sculptures following an in-depth study of insects. Children first drew their designs and then created the three-dimensional models using kitchen items such as forks, spoons, and colanders. After the bugs were completed, they were painted gold and were mounted to fence posts in the playground, becoming permanent art exhibits.

Modeling

Many early childhood programs provide play dough for children to use in modeling. While play dough allows children to experiment with modeling, clay provides several benefits not found with play dough. Clay is a natural material, coming from the earth. It

Figure 13.2
Recycled Materials
for Art Activities

Reusable resource centers are becoming popular throughout the United States and Europe. Businesses and individuals donate discarded materials, saving disposal fees while allowing the materials to be reinvented as resources for classrooms. For more information on reusable resource centers visit the Reusable Resources Association at www.reusableresources.org. Some programs are beginning their own resource centers, making the materials available to their staff and the community.

Some examples of recycled materials include

glass beads	wood	CDs
pipes	fabric—netting, velvet,	shredded paper
sockets	upholstery	Styrofoam
ceramic pieces	Mylar	craft sticks
paper	wire	cotton balls
cardboard	yarn	buttons
leather	foam	wire
rubber		

Natural items might also be used in collages and sculptures:

rocks	dried flowers	nuts
stones	shells	twigs
seedpods	leaves	wood shavings

allows for more detail than play dough and holds its shape, allowing the artist to create upright sculptures. Some teachers are concerned that young children may be unable to use clay successfully. However, in the book *Poking, Pinching, and Pretending,* Smith and Goldhaber (2004) demonstrate that even toddlers can successfully use this media.

In many classrooms, children are given cookie cutters to use with clay or play dough. However, Koster (2005), an early childhood art educator and author, equates this to giving children dittoes for drawing or coloring. Using cookie cutters often inhibits children from using the clay to develop three-dimensional models. It can also give children the impression they are not capable of producing the items on their own (Koster, 2005). Instead, provide clay cutting materials such as pizza cutters and plastic knives, rolling pins, ice cream scoops, and items to make impressions such as potato mashers. Make sure you wedge (knead) the clay to mix it well before giving it to the children.

In introducing clay, let the children first experiment without using tools. For example, the teacher might sit with the children during center time and provide exploratory exercises to help children discover ways to change the shape of the clay. This might include using hands to change the surface of the clay (handprints, fingerprints), poking holes in the clay, squeezing the clay into tall shapes, breaking clay into pieces, and constructing balls, coils, and slabs (Topal, 2006). Children can also add water to the clay, experimenting with the different effects.

In addition to providing an art medium, clay provides a rich sensory experience. Clay also encourages experimentation and revisiting. As long as it is still soft, clay sculptures can easily be changed, added to, or reinvented.

Art Tools and Paper

In addition to providing drawing, painting, collage, sculpture, and modeling materials you will also want to stock your art center with some basic materials and tools. Besides quality paintbrushes and clay tools, you will want

- Other basic tools (tape, stapler, hole punch, rulers, paper clips, glue and paste, and high-quality right- and left-handed scissors). Choose appropriate tools based upon the children's developmental level and their interests.
- Smocks to protect children's clothing, freeing them to focus on their artwork rather than worrying about keeping their clothes clean.
- A variety of types of paper (see Figure 13.1).

The art center or studio for preschool and early elementary age children needs to be well stocked with a variety of drawing, painting, collage, sculpture, and modeling materials that are aesthetically displayed. A variety of tools and types of paper will also be necessary. In addition, you might include materials for special projects such as printing, weaving, puppet-making, mask-making, beading, and jewelry-making.

Special Considerations and Materials for Infants and Toddlers

As soon as children begin to show interest, they are ready to begin drawing. Beginning at the age of one, most children can draw, make collages, paint, and model with clay or play dough (Koster, 2005). By age 2, most children are ready to explore printmaking, especially with body parts such as hands and feet (Koster, 2005).

One of the major art goals for children three and under is the exploration of media and tools. Toddlers need the opportunity to use paper and cardboard, clay, crayons and markers, and nontoxic paint. They can also begin to explore art elements, especially color (Gandini, 2006). If children have these opportunities as toddlers, they will be ready to use the media and tools to create representational and imaginative art when they are preschoolers. Since children this age may still be mouthing items, it is crucial that all materials are safe to ingest and do not pose a choking hazard.

> TIP   To prevent marker tops from being a choking hazard for infants and toddlers, place the tops upright into a plaster of paris mixture. After the mixture has dried, children can simply place markers onto the ummovable tops. Playcare teachers created the marker holder in a golden cookie tin and added glitter to the plaster to make it more attractive.

Even very young children can participate in long-term art explorations. For example, infants and toddlers in Reggio Emilia participated in an exploration of white. Young infants explored a multisensory landscape of white materials, each having different tactile and visual qualities. Children could crawl on the materials, try to tear them, mouth them, pick them up, and try to look through them. The toddler's explorations of white began by focusing on the properties of a white paper napkin. They continued exploring a variety of white materials (wool, cotton, paper, paper towels, plastic, slick paper, corn paper, tissue paper, sheer fabric, satin, and more). After repeated opportunities to explore, each child made her own individual creations that were included in a large, beautifully displayed composition (Vecchi & Giudici, 2004).

Apply Your Knowledge   Early childhood educators using the Reggio Emilia approach believe in introducing a variety of art materials to children at a young age. For example, in Reggio Emilia, toddlers use beautifully displayed drawing materials, earth clay, wire, natural collage materials, and glass containers filled with paints. However, some early childhood educators question the safety and appropriateness of these practices. How do these practices reflect the Reggio Emilia philosophy (see Chapter 1)? What would a teacher from Reggio Emilia say were the advantages of providing these materials to toddlers?

Appropriate Materials and Activities for Appreciating Art

Children need many opportunities to look at and talk about art, to appreciate art and to become aware of it in their everyday lives (Colbert & Taunton, 1992). This section will examine how the art center can assist in accomplishing these National Art Education Association (NAEA) goals.

Art appreciation has a long history in the United States, having been first introduced in American elementary schools in the 1880s (Kerlavage, 1995). Today we know that even toddlers exhibit the ability to make aesthetic choices, often showing preferences for specific colors and textures (Danko-McGhee & Shaffer, 2003). Generally, young children tend to prefer bright, saturated colors, pictures that have a familiar subject (either abstract or realistic) and simple compositions (Epstein & Trimis, 2002).

Without adult guidance, children tend to focus on the subject matter when discussing a work of art (Epstein & Trimis, 2002). However, when supported through open-ended questions, children can be guided to consider multiple aspects of a picture.

Most early childhood art centers focus on art production. However, you can add many materials to your art center that also introduce children to famous works of art and art appreciation. Often these will relate to the topics, media, or subjects that the children are exploring in their art production. You can accomplish this by doing the following:

- Display art from the community (weaving, pottery, quilts, jewelry).
- Over time provide a variety of art from different cultural groups and time periods featuring different art media and styles.

- Provide postcards featuring art to match and classify. At first children may match identical cards or sort cards by the subject matter. However, with the opportunity to explore different types of art and adult guidance they can learn to sort by the media or the type of art (oil, collage, drawing, fresco or wet plaster, pastel, print, sculpture, acrylic, mobile, drawing) or by the broad subject (abstract, cityscape, interior, landscape, portrait, seascape, still life) (Koster, 2005).

- Provide books with famous art reproductions.

- Use calendars of art prints to create puzzles.

- Provide a peek-a-boo window over an art print. The peek-a-boo window piques curiosity and helps children to closely examine one small part of the picture.

- Create bulletin boards of art featuring opposing concepts (realist/abstract) (Schiller, 1995).

- Place a picture frame in the art area that allows children or teachers to feature pictures (Schiller, 1995).

- Set up an inspirational display of nature as art (Epstein, 2005). For example, place rocks or shells in an interesting design or arrange a beautiful bouquet of flowers.

- Create a masterpiece corner to highlight a featured piece of artwork (Koster, 2005).

In the next section, we will examine the teacher's role in exposing children to art. As the teacher exposes children to art and then guides them to look at multiple aspects of a picture, their art appreciation as well as their art production is enhanced.

Teachers' Facilitation of Learning in the Art Center

The teacher is crucial in helping children gain optimal art skills, dispositions, and knowledge. She exposes children to different types of art, provides life experiences, discusses art with children, teaches children techniques, acknowledges the artist and his art, challenges children, and documents and assesses their learning. Through providing culturally relevant, developmentally appropriate materials and making modification as needed, she also meets the needs of all learners.

Expose Children to Art

In literacy, we rarely question that it is essential that children see adults and older children modeling reading and writing. We also believe that children need abundant exposure to high-quality literature. The same is true for art. Children need artist models and abundant exposure to art from the masters. Invite artists, sculptors, and potters to visit your program. They can model creating art and describe problems encountered as they work (Tarr, 1997). The artists can also work directly with the children modeling teaching techniques, art techniques, and art language for teachers and children (Bisgaier, Samaras, & Russo, 2005). In some instances, artists may work on a cooperative project with children (Tarr, 1997). You can also take children on field trips to art galleries and pottery studios.

Many children's books have wonderful illustrations providing another opportunity to expose children to art. For example, Caldecott-award-winning books are chosen based on their illustrations. When reading a book to children, discuss the pictures. What media or special techniques are used? How do the illustrations add to the story? Provide the background on the artist. Compare the illustrations in the book to illustrations in previous books you have read or to current work the children are engaged in. For example, Ezra Jack Keats uses a paper collage technique. When reading *The Snowy Day,* Lakisha discussed with the children how they also had been using the collage technique in creating pictures and discussed how their collages and Keats' were similar and different. She also used a Venn diagram as part of the discussion to help clarify and focus the conversation (see Chapter 3 for information on Venn diagrams). The diagram was also a way to create documentation of the dialogue.

Display Works of Art

It is important to expose children to a variety of art. The experiences children initially have with art will influence their tastes and preferences for art throughout their lives. These preferences are often resistant to change (Gardner, 1991). Introduce children to male and female artists from different cultures and time periods. Local art as well as art from the masters can be studied. Koster (2005) recommends that you carefully choose art that helps children to understand three things. First, art is made by people of all ages, in diverse geographic areas, and in different periods of time. Second, art can tell us about the lives of other people. Third, art is made from a variety of materials and is found throughout the environment (p. 229).

High-quality reproductions can be obtained from many sources. You can obtain inexpensive art from calendars, prints of great artists, art books, or magazines such as *The Smithsonian*.

Discuss Art with Children

Talk to the children about the art that is displayed, engaging children in both art history and art criticism. While art history is often reserved for older age levels, some art educators question this, stating that children in the early childhood years are ready for art history (Erickson, 1995). Erickson researched second-grade students' understanding of art history by asking three questions: "How was life different back then? How would life back then have made a difference in the way the painting looked? What question would you ask to help better understand the painting?" She found that children attempted to make sense of the subject matter, difficulty, and skill of the painter, and made hypotheses about why artists may have painted the way they did.

Teachers can also help children learn more about art history by learning as much as they can about the art, the artist, and the historical time period so that they have information to share with the children (Koster, 2005). "Teachers do not have to become art historians overnight, just experts on one piece of artwork at a time" (Koster, 2005, p. 229). Some programs prepare a little informational card to go with a posted print, so that teachers and volunteers have the needed background knowledge.

Teachers can also engage children in art criticism or "provocative art dialogues" (Cole & Schaefer, 1990; Spodek, 2006). According to Spodek (2006), art criticism includes the following four stages:

- Description of the artwork—subject matter, elements, medium
- Analysis—relationships between the elements
- Interpretation—ideas, feelings, mood conveyed by the artwork
- Judgment—based upon description, analysis, and interpretation

By using questioning, you can guide even young children through this process (Epstein, 2005). In discussing the art, you can discuss art elements and ask children questions about the subject, the artist's intentions, and how the art was made. You can compare this art piece to other works of art. You can also ask children how the artwork makes them feel. Another technique is to encourage children to pick a spot in the painting and imagine they were there (Newton, 1995).

It is also important to discuss reasons people make art. For example, artists might be expressing an idea, illustrating a book, recording what they see, depicting an emotion, or exploring visual relationships (Tarr, 1997, p. 3).

Provide Life Experiences

"To create art, children must first have a feeling, thought, or experience they want to express. Without meaningful and individual experiences, children tend to draw stereotypical objects" (Epstein, 2005, p. 53). Rather than creating art activities that are isolated from the rest of the curriculum, teachers can tie art to other areas of learning.

Children at All Stars Childcare Center were completing a project on flowers. Their study included a field trip to a greenhouse, visiting a field of wildflowers, interviewing gardeners, reading and looking at flower books, and ultimately creating their own flowerbed at the childcare centers. The children watered, fertilized, and cared for their flowers. They studied the flowers they grew, learning which ones lasted if they were picked and brought inside, which could be eaten, and which could be dried to form permanent bouquets. Using magnifying glasses, they carefully examined different types of petals, leaf patterns, and stamen. They also created their flowers in a variety of media, including representational drawings, paintings, and three-dimensional models in clay. As winter approached and with it freezing weather, children decided they wanted to preserve their garden by creating a mural. They drew sketches, transferred their sketches to canvas, and then painted their creation with acrylic paint, creating a beautiful, vibrant, permanent rendition of their flowerbed. Because children had participated in a long-term project studying flowers, the mural captured their in-depth knowledge of the subject as well as their feelings and experiences with their garden.

Teach Techniques

Early childhood practitioners must teach art techniques needed for children to be successful. For example, children need to know how to create a slip of water and clay to hold clay together or how to wet the paper when using watercolors. You can learn techniques yourself by taking a class or you can invite an art partner to assist. Local art groups may volunteer to help teachers and children learn art techniques (Lutton, Spade, & DeCheser, 2006).

Learning to use proper techniques assists children to advance their artistic skill, thereby allowing them the ability to express their creativity. For example, when children were given guided opportunities to experiment with clay, they created more advanced human figures than did children who had not had this exposure (Grossman, 1980).

Acknowledge Learners

There are many ways that we can acknowledge children's creations. These include attractive classroom displays or art shows featuring children's work, referring to children as artists, and discussing children's art with them (Thompson, 2005).

Attractively displaying children's work surrounds them with beauty, provides affirmation for the artists letting them know that they and their work is important, extends project work, provides a window into children's thoughts and soul, and provides information to other children, parents, and administrators (Seefeldt & Waites, 2002).

Make displays attractive and informational by doing the following:

- Frame the art with a mat, place it in a purchased frame, or create your own tagboard picture frame.
- Purchase several different sizes and colors of Plexiglas. Children's pictures can easily be taped to and removed from this surface.
- Use unusual backgrounds such as tinfoil or newspaper but only if it does not detract from the art.
- Include photos of children creating the art with their masterpiece.
- Include photos or still lives that children were using for inspiration or references as they were drawing or painting along with their finished product.
- Include a written description or dictation from the child about the artwork when you display it.

Allowing children to determine what to display causes them to reflect upon their work. You can help children learn about displays by discussing their purpose, visiting exhibits,

Providing a special shelf allows these preschool children to display their three-dimensional clay on tinfoil sculptures.

and making a list of criteria to consider when creating your own display (Clayton, 2002). Establishing a framing center in the classroom is another way to encourage children to be actively involved in creating the display. In addition to displaying children's art on bulletin boards, you might want to try one of the following:

- Create pedestals by stacking boxes or crates. Boxes can be arranged in numerous ways including pyramids or stair steps, or by stacking the same-size boxes on top of each other at different angles. Boxes and crates allow you to display art on all four sides and when stacked often provide room for three-dimensional displays. It might be necessary to weight the boxes to make them less likely to tip over.

- Use all available space. In small rooms, you may need to be creative. For example, consider using the backs of dividers for displays.
- Clip children's artwork to a clothesline hung across the wall or ceiling.
- Create a mobile out of coat hangers by taping them together to create a triangle or square. Children can clip their artwork to the hangers.
- Sew pockets on a clear shower curtain to display small works of art. These can be hung in a window or from the ceiling as a divider between centers.
- Create albums of children's work (include children's drawings, paintings, and photos of three-dimensional work).
- Use art as a permanent addition to the school. For example, children might make ceramic tables, sculptures, stepping-stones, or placemats.

Discuss Children's Art

Another important way of acknowledging children is to talk to them about their creations. The discussion can also help children verbalize their intent and cause them to think more deeply about their art. Through the discussion, you can assess the child's understanding and learning and provide additional relevant information. "For dialogue to promote learning, it needs to be thoughtfully structured around a sequence of questions that invite reflection" (Burton, 2000, p. 330).

It is important to refrain from asking the child what the picture is or trying to guess what it is. Many of us have been in the embarrassing position of guessing incorrectly and disappointing a child. Also, avoid judgmental statements (beautiful, good job, nice painting). These are not helpful to the child and are often statements used by adults when they have not taken the time to examine the artwork carefully. In addition, children may be dissatisfied with the results and wonder about your judgment when you state the art is beautiful. Instead, there are several ways you can discuss the work with the child.

- Ask the child to describe his work.
- Discuss the art elements; for example, line, color, shape, texture, form, pattern, and space (open area) (Tarr, 1997, p. 3). When you are describing the work use correct art terms when it is developmentally appropriate.
  - tint (white added)
  - primary color (red, yellow, blue)

- secondary color (purple, green, orange)

- hue (color)

- intensity (brightness or dullness of color)

- symmetry (same on both sides)

- Talk about the art subject (cityscape, landscape, portrait, abstract, still life). What is the subject and why was it chosen?

- Discuss the technique that was used. "How did you get the two pieces of clay to stick together?" "What colors did you combine to create the goldenrod color?"

- Discuss the effort the child put into the work. "You've worked on your clay bear for the last 3 days. Each day I've noticed that you've added new details like the lines for the fur."

- Discuss the artistic decisions (Koster, 2005). "You decided to use only yellow items in your collage."

- Describe your own feelings when looking at the work. "When I see your picture of the ocean, it reminds me of when I was young and would pick up seashells with my grandfather."

- Encourage children to notice and discuss other children's artwork.

Challenge Children

Teachers can challenge children to make sketches to capture memories, to draw ideas and theories, and to draw using different viewpoints. You can also encourage children to revisit their creations, exploring the media, the subject, or the current work of art in more depth. Additionally, teachers can challenge children to think about whether they have adequately portrayed their ideas and encourage them to continue to work on their art piece until they are personally satisfied with it.

Observe and Document Children's Art Processes and Products

There are many ways you can document children's artwork such as keeping the actual artifact, taking photos of three-dimensional work, and saving children's renditions of the same subject over time or the same idea in multiple media. Having older children write a description of why they chose the subject, the art process they used, and the challenges they encountered can add additional information. Younger children can be interviewed about their art piece and the information can be written by the adult. You might save children's artwork in portfolios, adding anecdotal records, photos of the child creating the work, and a description and analysis of the work. When observing and documenting children's work, consider the following questions:

- What ideas does the child express in her artwork? Is there a theme?

- What media does the child prefer using? Is the child able to use the media successfully?

- What art techniques does the child use (Koster, 2005)?

- What was the purpose of this specific piece of artwork (Koster, 2005)?

- Where did the idea for the art come from (Koster, 2005)?

- How long did the child work on the art? Did he revisit his creation? What changes were made as a result of the revisiting?

- Did he produce the theme or idea in different media? How did the idea change when different media were used?

- What is the child's stage of art development?
- Is the child able to describe the art? Does the child use any art terminology in the description?
- What physical skills does the child demonstrate while completing her art (cutting on a line, using a pincer grasp)?

Assessing and documenting the child's art development provides information to share with the child and family. Teachers can also use this information for planning appropriate materials and activities.

Meet the Needs of All Learners

Teachers need to make sure that the art center and materials reflect cultural diversity and meet the needs of learners with differing abilities. Art provides a wonderful opportunity to expose children to local culture, their own unique culture, and the culture of others. One preschool program, surrounded by sheep growers, brought in local culture by providing a variety of types of wool (wool that was unprocessed, carded, spun, and felted) for children to use in their art.

Tonisha, a teacher of first-grade children, invites families to share artwork they have created or collected. One family brought in tole painting they created and sold. Another family brought in a collection of quilts, telling children the stories of the different designs. Still another family shared a collection of American Indian art.

Displaying and discussing professional works of art from different cultures and by people with disabilities is still another way that children can learn about their own and other's cultures. Posting the picture of the artist with the work of art assists children to see this diversity.

Unfortunately, art activities can also perpetuate stereotypes. For example, some programs have children create totem poles when they study American Indians. This may cause children to think mistakenly that all American Indians created totem poles. Additionally in some cultures, the totem pole is sacred, and it is inappropriate for children to create one. Local artists or families from the culture being studied can often provide guidance on appropriate art activities.

We need to consider how to meet the needs of children with differing abilities, as well. See Figure 13.3 for an example of how one teacher met the needs of a young boy with cerebral palsy.

The teacher plays a crucial role in children's art development in a variety of ways. She provides an aesthetic, well-stocked art center and interacts with children while they use the center—discussing art history and criticism, teaching techniques, providing challenges, acknowledging children's work, and documenting their progress. The teacher provides background experiences and exposes children to art and artists.

Figure 13.3
Meeting a Child's
Special Needs

Thomas is a young child with cerebral palsy. He enjoys art but has difficulty grasping and controlling the materials. His parents, therapist, and teachers feel that Thomas will be successful with environmental support. They modify the art area by taping the paper to the table. They add foam curlers to the crayons, pencils, paintbrushes, and glue sticks to make them easier to grasp. They also provide a rotary cutting tool that is easier to use than scissors. Although these adaptations were added to the center specifically for Thomas, children in the classroom are allowed to experiment with the adaptive tools if they are interested (West, 2006).

Special Challenges in the Art Area
Storage for Continuing Projects

Sometimes it can be difficult to locate space for children to store works in progress. Following are some suggestions:

- Have children work on trays or cardboard so that it is easier to move the creation to another location.

- For smaller three-dimensional art use clear plastic boxes that can stack for storage.

- Store paintings and drawings on clotheslines. Several works by the same artist can be clipped together for later revisiting.

- Place crates containing artwork in progress on a large piece of plywood. Attach rope to each corner and use a pulley system to raise and lower the storage as needed.

- Reconsider existing art display areas to see if you can redesign them for works in progress. For example, one teacher replaced her bulletin board with shadow boxes. This created a display area that could also be used for three-dimensional work in progress, without sacrificing wall or floor space. Shadow boxes can also be placed in windows.

Using Food for Art Materials or Activities

Developmentally Appropriate Practices (Bredekamp & Copple, 1997) emphasizes that using food for art activities is inappropriate. The primary objection is wasting food when people are hungry. Since the value placed on a particular food varies among cultures, there is also the danger of offending people when a culturally valued food is used for play. Others assert that if teachers use food for art activities, it is difficult for children to make the distinction about when it is permissible to play with food and when it is not.

However, others state that food items provide a safe alternative to other art materials, are readily available, and may be less expensive than purchased art supplies. They also argue that many purchased art items such as glue and play dough contain food items (although these may be inedible residues) (Koster, 2005).

If you choose to use food items for art, it is important that you are sensitive to the children and families in your classroom. In many cases, nonfood items can be easily substituted.

Children Want You to Create for Them

If children ask you to draw for them, begin by trying to determine what underlying needs the children have. Do they need help with a specific technique? Do they want your attention? Are they having trouble determining how to begin their project? You will provide a different response depending upon each child's needs. For example, if the child does not know where to begin, you might offer suggestions or ask questions that will assist him. If he is drawing a person, you might suggest he begin with the head. You can then show him his face in a mirror, show him pictures, or discuss the facial features that can be added. In other cases, children might not understand the process. For example, they might be trying to paint at the easel and the paint runs because they are not wiping the brush after dipping it in the paint. In this case, it is important to teach children a more effective technique. Through careful analysis and problem solving the teacher can alleviate many challenges.

Outdoor Art Centers

The outdoor environment provides inspiration for artists, an abundance of natural materials that can be used to create art, and space for large and messy projects. The outdoors is also a wonderful place for permanent displays of children's art. Ideally, the outdoor art center is a permanent center, with ample storage for needed supplies. However, if this is not possible, a tote or bag can be used to transport needed materials outdoors. Following are some examples of outdoor art ideas.

- An easel placed under a tree can be used for quietly painting or drawing.
- A chalkboard with a bucket of colored chalk can be placed in the playhouse.
- A collage center can be created that is stocked with natural items (pinecones, twigs, dried berries, flower petals that have dropped off flowers, seedpods, nuts). Children can go on nature walks to replenish their supplies.
- A clay center can provide opportunities for making casts of trees, flowers, and pinecones as well as other clay creations.
- An outdoor loom stocked with natural materials (dried grasses, supple sticks) creates an invitation to weave.
- A sculpture center that includes a variety of similar items (bicycle parts, appliance parts, different sizes and shapes of wood) provides opportunities for large sculptures.
- An art sack or tote that contains clipboards, paper, pencils, and markers encourages children to make representational drawings.
- Sand, ice, and snow can provide the media for transitory sculptures.

Teachers can also display children's artwork to decorate the playground. For example, at Mentor Graphics Child Development Center, children working with an artist used strips of painted roofing paper to create three-dimensional art by weaving the strips through the fence. At the Helen Gordon Child Development Center, children created gigantic murals that were painted on a canvas and then covered with a polymer to protect them.

In the art area, children participate in self-expression, create unique visual images of their ideas and thoughts, and engage in problem solving and inquiry. As children create and study art they take part in a universal language that breaks cultural barriers and transcends the changes of time.

This child-created mural at Helen Gordon Child Development Center in Portland, Oregon, provides a vivid reminder of the children's work.

Sample Application Activities

1. View one of the following websites to learn about children's art.

   Visit the Learning Design website at www.learningdesign.com/Portfolio/DrawDev/ kiddrawing.html to learn about art stages.

Visit www.childart.indstate.edu/about.asp at Indiana State University to see a database of children's artwork.

To see a historical perspective on children's art throughout the twentieth century, visit the National Gallery of Australia at www.nga.gov.au/Derham/

2. Often we ask children to draw from memory. Choose an item, such as a flower, to draw from memory. Then draw the same item while examining a real object, a photo, or multiple illustrations. Compare your two pictures.

3. Assess an art center using the environmental assessment checklist found in Figure 13.4.

4. Classify children's artwork using the stages of art development.

5. Design a plan for an attractive display of children's artwork.

6. Begin a collection of artwork (calendars, postcards, magazine pictures).

7. Build your teaching skills in visual arts by completing an exercise on MyEducationLab. Select the topic "Visual Arts." Under Building Teaching Skills and Dispositions, complete the exercise "Learning to 'See': Integrating Visual Arts in the Classroom."

☐ Does the art center contain plenty of natural and artificial light?
☐ Are the floor and tables easy to clean?
☐ Is the center located in close proximity to water?
☐ Is the center placed in a quiet space that allows for focus and attention?
☐ Does the center provide ample work space so that children have room to work on large projects and so that several children can work at the same time?
☐ Is there storage for ongoing work?
☐ Is there storage for replenishment of supplies?
☐ Are there low, uncluttered shelves so that children have easy access to materials?
☐ Is there an abundance of diverse materials for drawing, painting, modeling, collage, and sculpture?
☐ Are there high-quality, authentic materials and tools that are in good working condition?
☐ Are materials safe and labeled nontoxic?
☐ Are materials displayed aesthetically?
☐ Is there an abundance of reference materials on art and on the current topic being explored?
☐ Are there pictures and displays to provide inspiration?
☐ Are there materials for art appreciation?
☐ Do materials encourage children to create their own artwork (no patterns, coloring pages, stencils, cookie cutters)?
☐ Is art displayed at the children's eye level, highlighting both their two- and three-dimensional work?
☐ Is the work of other artists (local artists, artists from other cultures, the masters) displayed?
☐ Is art displayed in an uncluttered and attractive way? For example, is the artwork framed or matted? Is a photo of the artist displayed with the work?

Figure 13.4
Environmental Assessment: Art Center

Source: Permission is granted by the publisher to reproduce this figure for evaluation and record-keeping. From Julie Bullard, *Creating Environments for Learning: Birth to Age Eight.* Copyright © 2010 by Pearson Education, Inc. All rights reserved.

chapter 14

Developing Music Centers

*I*n a small music center, a plastic basket of various instruments sits on a shelf. Beside the instruments sits a tape player and a few children's tapes. A keyboard with a missing key sits on the floor. The children rarely use the center, which has remained the same all year. At a staff meeting, Martha, the teacher, wonders if she should remove the music center, allowing more room for the nearby dramatic play area. She says, "Since the children seem uninterested in music, perhaps the space could be more wisely used."

Apply Your Knowledge Do you think the center should be removed? What are reasons other than disinterest that might inhibit the children from using this center? What are ways that the center could be enriched?

Music has a strong influence on us. Through music, we communicate powerful emotions, ideas, and thoughts. Throughout history, music has played an important role. For example, the early Greeks considered music to be the language of the gods (Carlton & Weikert, 1994). Music is significant in nearly all cultures, assisting in transmitting cultural beliefs, values, and heritage, and developing a culture's identity. Additionally, music is usually closely linked to our own personal histories. When we hear a particular song, it can bring us instantly back to the past, helping us remember other co-occurring events.

In early childhood settings, "music helps young children synthesize experiences, transition into new activities, calm down during naptime, share cultural traditions, and build self-esteem and a sense of community" (Shore & Strasser, 2006). Music also has academic benefits, such as boosting memory and improving spatial-perceptual development (Hetland & Winner, 2001; Sawyers & Hutson-Brandhagen, 2004). From the beginning of the early childhood education movement, Pestalozzi and Froebel advocated the study of music by young children (Fox, 2000).

Development of Music Skills

Children begin to experience elements of music even before birth. Did you know that the first inter-uterine sense to develop is hearing? By 26 weeks, fetuses will respond to sound stimulation with increased heartbeats (Federico, 2002). When infants are born, they will show preferences for not only their parents' voices but also songs that they heard in the final trimester of pregnancy (DeCasper & Spence, 1986; Shore & Strasser, 2006; Van de Carr & Lehrer, 1986). They will also respond differently to quiet and lively music (Jalongo, 1996). Beginning in infancy, caregivers around the world sing to children. These lullabies contain common characteristics, including simple melodies, a higher pitch, and a slower, more exaggerated rhythm than other songs (Trehub, 2001). The rationale for singing to infants is supported by research. Children are more attentive to mothers when they are singing versus speaking (Trehub, 2001). Studies indicate that premature infants who listen to vocal music have less stress reactions, maintained more of their birth weight, and have shorter hospital stays than those babies who do not listen to music (Caine, 1991).

Infants have innate musical behaviors, including using music as a form of communication (Fox, 2000). They spontaneously create music; cooing, singing, and banging items to create rhythm. By 7 months, infants can sing by matching or harmonizing to pitch 50% of the time (Ries, 1982). By 2½ years old, 75% of children sing spontaneous songs and 83% sing standard songs (Ries, 1982). By the age of 6, most children can sing in an accurate key and are able to use an increased singing range (Flohr, 2004). The majority of studies show that boys and girls sing equally well (Flohr, 2004).

Children also learn to keep rhythm. For example, 93% of 3-year-old children can keep a beat. However, this varies with the task. While 87% can clap hands to a beat and 67% can play an instrument to a beat, only 33% can march and clap to a beat. Fewer than half of 4-year-olds can march and clap to a beat (Frega, 1979). 4-year-olds, however, can determine when rhythm beats are the same or different, while 3-year-olds are not able to do this (Frega, 1979). By the time children are 5 years old, they can step and clap accurately to a beat and almost all of the children can also step and play an instrument to a beat (Frega, 1979).

As children develop musical skills, they also enhance many other areas of development. We will explore these next.

How the Music Center Enhances Children's Development

Children develop musical skills and appreciation as they interact in the music center. While participating in music activities, children are also enhancing physical, language, social-emotional, and cognitive development. In today's world of high-stakes tests, many are using music's enhancement of cognitive development as a rationale for including music in the curriculum. However, as stated by Hetland and Winner (2001), "The arts are a fundamentally important part of culture, and an education without them is an impoverished education leading to an impoverished society. Studying the arts should not have to be justified in terms of anything else. The arts are as important as the sciences: they are time-honored ways of learning, knowing, and expressing" (p. 5).

Music Skills and Appreciation

Even without adult intervention, children are natural, instinctive music makers. However, when we expose children to music through singing and playing instruments, they become more proficient and develop musical skills earlier (Kelley & Sutton-Smith, 1987).

When young children listen repeatedly to a style of music, they learn to prefer that music and these preferences become lifelong (Flohr, 2004; Peery & Peery, 1986). It is important, therefore, to expose children to music that broadens their repertoire. Learning to appreciate music from another culture or time period can also open the door to further interest and learning.

Cognitive Development

Many studies have found a correlation between music abilities and academic achievement (Shore & Strasser, 2006). Music can aid in all areas of the child's development. A study of 106 preschool children found that those exposed to a systematic and integrated music program significantly increased their motor, cognitive, language, and social-emotional scores as assessed by the Preschool Evaluation Scale (McCarney, 1992).

Singing relevant songs can help children to learn science, math, and language concepts (Miche, 2002). History and geography can also be enhanced by examining the music of the time period or geographic area. Music can also assist with memorization. When items to be memorized are set to music, children remember them more readily (Sawyers & Hutson-Brandhagen, 2004).

Music is organized mathematically; music and math support one another (Sawyers & Hutson-Brandhagen, 2004, p. 46). As children hear and move to a beat or read music, they use one-to-one correspondence skills. As they recall a series of sounds or actions (head, shoulders, knees and toes) they gain seriation skills.

There is also a strong relationship between music and spatial-temporal intelligence (the ability to visualize and mentally manipulate spatial patterns). A review of nineteen studies found this relationship was even stronger if children also learned music notation (Hetland & Winner, 2001). Other studies support these findings. When researchers assigned preschool children to computer lessons, piano lessons, singing lessons, or no lessons, those who received piano lessons showed a 34% increase in spatial-temporal intelligence while there was no change in children in the other groups (Shaw, 2003). Researchers found similar results in elementary age children (Schellenberg, 2004).

Although there were reports that children who listen to classical music at an early age show greater learning potential (sometimes referred to as the Mozart Effect), this claim has been refuted (Shonkoff & Phillips, 2000). Currently, there is no evidence to support a link between listening to music as an infant and brain size or school success (Fox, 2000; Hetland & Winner, 2001). However, one thing that we might learn from the study of music's effect on adults is that brain development appears to be related to active engagement with music (making music) rather than just passive listening to music (Fox, 2000).

Motor Development and Rhythm

As children create music, they improve fine motor skills, coordination, and rhythm. Music also entices one to move and dance. Participating in movement or dance activities while listening to music enhances children's ability to sequence sound, recognize and respond to rhythm patterns, and discriminate melodies (Ferguson, 2005). As children dance to music, they increase coordination, flexibility, and motor skills. They develop body awareness and self-confidence. Like music, dance is an art form and a means of communication. Through dance, children communicate feelings, thoughts, and cultural values and beliefs.

When Curious Minds provided dance props in the music area, the children became more interested in using the center. They would often dance in front of the three full-length mirrors while rhythmically moving streamers or scarves. At other times, they would dance while playing a musical instrument. Young children naturally respond differently to sound and silence, fast and slow music, and different musical styles (Metz, 1989). However, adults can enhance children's movement repertoire by describing what children are doing, making suggestions, and modeling movement. Adults are powerful models. In one study, children using a music center during free play copied two-thirds of the teacher's modeled movements (Metz, 1989).

Language Development

Like art, music is a form of communication conveying mood, ideas, and concepts (Ohman-Rodriquez, 2005). As children listen to music, they hear differences in sounds, assisting them not only with music making, but also with speech (Miche, 2002). Music can also help children develop fluency (smoothness of speech), pronunciation, enunciation (speaking clearly), and vocabulary (Aquino, 1991). For example, children who are involved in music activities such as reproducing sound sequences, melody discrimination, and singing combined with motor activities and visual stimuli display a significant increase in vocabulary (Moyeda, Gomez, & Flores, 2006).

Social Development

Music links children to their cultural heritage, assisting them to acquire cultural beliefs and values. Listening to music also exposes children to other times and cultures and provides the opportunity to gain appreciation for them. In addition, as children create music together, they engage in a metaphorical experience, where different instruments combine to make a unique sound that no individual instrument could produce. Through this process, they learn that to make beautiful music, you must have unity and work together.

Emotional Development

From the time of Plato and Aristotle, music has also been viewed as therapeutic. Today more than seventy universities offer degrees in music therapy (Greata, 2006). Music helps to create and manipulate moods. It "has the ability to relax, give pleasure, irritate and deafen us, stimulate, excite, make us feel happier or sadder" (Federico, 2002, p. 534). With these mood changes also comes physiological changes to our heartbeats, blood pressure, and breathing (Federico, 2002).

As we have learned, through music children not only gain music skills and appreciation but also enhance cognitive, motor and rhythm, language, social, and emotional development. While children and adults naturally engage in music, a well-planned center can enhance their development. What does a well-planned music center include?

Designing the Music Center

The National Council of Music Teachers (NCMT) standards stress that "every pre-kindergarten and kindergarten needs to have a music center where children can access music materials and listen to music" (Music Educators National Conference, 1994). The music center is most effective if the following guidelines are followed:

- The music center needs to be "an uncluttered area that can provide ample space for creative and structured movement activities" (Music Educators National Conference (MENC) 1994, p. 3).

- The center needs to be located away from quiet areas. Teachers should also attempt to reduce and absorb sound. This includes having earphones available for individually listening to music and providing sound-absorbing materials on the walls and ceilings of the music area.

- A variety of high-quality instruments should be available. It is important that instruments have a high-quality sound and do not break easily.

- Instruments need to be displayed so that children have easy access to them. They might be on labeled shelves, hung on hooks on the wall or on the back of a divider, or grouped in labeled baskets.

- Children need access to sound equipment that they can operate themselves (a tape recorder that has a green dot for start and a red dot for stop).

- A variety of exemplary music should be available for children to use in listening and playing instruments, and for dancing and moving. Music should be available from a variety of genres, cultures, and historical time periods.

- Choose high-quality, award-winning music. American Library Association's Notable Recordings, Parents' Choice Seal of Approval, National Parenting Publications Awards (NAPPA) program, Grammy Awards for best musical albums for children, Oppenheim Toy Portfolio Gold, and Earlychildhood NEWS Directors' Choice Awards all have lists of quality music. The Children's Music Web Awards (voted on by children) is another source for finding quality music.

- Written music should be in the center, including music books, children's storybooks with music notation, and written music that children can play. For preschool and elementary age children, written music should be available with any pitched instrument (keyboard, xylophone).

- There should be materials available so that children can write their own music (preschool and early elementary).

This display of children's CDs and music books allows children to clearly see their choices.

- Each item in the center should be fully developed. For example, if including cultural instruments, label the instrument so that adults and children in the classroom can learn the name of the instrument. A recording or short video of a musician playing the instrument is also helpful.

Music Standards

The National Standards for Arts Education (1994) lists four content standards or strands for early childhood music:

- Singing and playing instruments
- Creating music
- Responding to music
- Understanding music

A well-rounded early childhood music program includes each of these content standards. To help clarify how each of these can be promoted through music learning centers, the materials and activities for the center reflect these standards.

Appropriate Materials for the Music Center

Materials you choose to include in the music center must help children to develop competencies related to the content standards. Additionally, it is critical that the materials are appropriate for the children's developmental level and relate to their interests.

Antonio, a teacher of 4- and 5-year-old children, begins his circle each day by drumming a rhythm on the large gathering drum. As children join the circle, they also begin to play the rhythm.

Antonio noticed that several of the children were beginning to pound rhythms on other materials (tabletops, blocks, snack dishes). Expanding upon their interest, he introduced several different types of drums, and added the drums and drumming CDs to the music center. He also invited an American Indian drummer to spend the afternoon in the music center drumming with the children. Antonio initially sparked the children's interest in drumming by beginning circle time each day with a musical rhythm. However, when he observed the children's interest, he expanded upon it by adding new materials and resources.

Singing and Playing Instruments

Many of the achievement standards for singing and playing instruments can be met through the music center. See Figure 14.1 for a list of the standards for this area.

Figure 14.1   Achievement Standards for Singing and Playing Instruments

Children:
  a. use their voices expressively as they speak, chant, and sing
  b. sing a variety of simple songs in various keys, meters, and genres, alone and with a group, becoming increasingly accurate in rhythm and pitch
  c. experiment with a variety of instruments and other sound sources
  d. play simple melodies and accompaniments on instruments

Source: National Standards for Arts Education. Copyright © 1994 by Music Educators National Conference (MENC). Used by permission. The complete National Arts Standards and additional materials relating to the Standards are available from MENC: The National Association for Music Education, 1806 Robert Fulton Drive, Reston, VA 20191; www.menc.org.

Singing. Songs with or without words (boo, bow, bah) can be included in the music center. When you choose songs, keep children's interests and voice ranges in mind (D4–A4). Short repetitive verses, descending intervals, and skipping patterns are popular with young children (Flohr, 2004, p. 94). If you are singing with children keep your voice "high and light" to avoid damage to children's vocal cords (Shore & Strasser, 2006, p. 65). To promote singing in the music center the early childhood teacher can do the following:

- Provide earphones so that children can hear themselves singing. Teachers can create these by connecting two PVC joints to create a semi-circular shape. The child holds one end at his mouth and the other at his ear.
- Develop props that children can manipulate as they sing a song. For example, you might provide a plastic spider to use as children sing eensey, weensy spider.
- Provide echo toys that children can sing to and easily play back.
- Construct a stage with a microphone (the microphone does not need to work).
- Supply picture books containing songs and music.
- Provide purchased sing-along tapes.
- Create your own tape for the music center by recording the class singing familiar songs.

Playing Instruments. Music centers are ideal for letting children independently experiment with a variety of instruments. Through playing musical instruments, children learn about pitch (how high or low), timbre (quality of the sound such as the difference between a clarinet and saxophone), and texture (how instruments interact with each other) (Carlton, 2006). To assist children to move beyond experimentation, provide recordings they can use as accompaniment and simple written music to play. Listed here are materials and ideas that can be added to the music center to help children learn about instruments.

- Provide a variety of high-quality instruments. The National Association for Music Education (1994) recommends that "drums, rhythm sticks, finger cymbals,

A set of bells along with the music allow preschool children to play a song.

triangles, cymbals, gongs, jingle bells, resonator bells, step bells, xylophone-type instruments with removable bars, chorded zithers, fretted instruments, electronic keyboard instruments, and assorted instruments representing a variety of cultures" be available for young children (p. 3).

- Provide two sets of instruments with a screen between them. One child plays an instrument. The child on the other side of the screen tries to find the same instrument to play.

- Provide two sets of some instruments. One child can play a melody and another child can try to duplicate it.

- Provide music that children can play. Children can learn to play simple melodies on many different types of instruments if keys are color or number coded and the written musical notes are also color or number coded.

- Provide a tape recording of different beats for children to use when playing instruments.

- Make a tape with short, recorded rhythms. Include a pause after each rhythm so that children can create the same rhythm with their instrument.

- Encourage children to create their own instruments. It is important that the instruments are durable and easy to play if you want children to be able to successfully use them after they are created (see Figure 14.2 for several examples).

- Develop musical instruments out of household items. For example, you can add different levels of water to glasses or jars creating a homemade xylophone. Washboards, pots, pans, and wooden spoons can also be used as musical instruments.

- Provide instruments from different cultures. Authentic instruments can help children to learn about the cultures of others. Some cultural instruments that are appropriate for young children include marimbas, shaker eggs, tom-tom drums, African tongue slit drums, afusche casaba (Lang, 1999), gourd shakers,

---

- Shakers—provide film canisters and a variety of found items (sand, pebbles, small sticks, seedpods) that could be used to create shakers. Larger shakers can be created using lengths of PVC pipes and PVC pipe caps.
- Drums can be created by removing the top and bottom of a metal coffee can. The plastic lid can be used for a drumhead. Or for better sound, cut a circle one inch larger than the circumference of the can out of an inner tube, a heavy plastic bag, rawhide, or a heavy balloon (only for older children). Attach the circle to the drum by securing the top to the coffee can side with heavy tape. You can also make a top and a bottom, punch holes around each, and lace them onto the can.
- Rain sticks can be created by pounding nails into postage mailing tubes. The nails should be nailed in a spiraling pattern around the tube. When this is completed, experiment with adding different small items that will trickle through the nails. For example, different sizes of pebbles will create different sounds.
- Gourd rattles can be created by cutting off the end of a gourd, scooping out the inside, and letting the gourd dry in the sun. After it has dried, the children can return the seeds to the gourd or add other small items and glue the lid back on. The gourd can be decorated with string and small beads, which will add more sound.
- Children can string bells on elastic and tie them to make bracelets for their wrists and ankles.
- Children can also use found materials to create their own unique instruments.

Figure 14.2
Durable, Easy-to-Play Instruments That Children Can Create

tambourines, maracas, and rain sticks. Pictures of musicians playing the instruments along with short instrumentals can often be found on the Internet.

Maria, a teacher of first-grade children, labels each instrument with a picture of a musician playing the instrument on one side of a card and an outline of the country where the instrument is played on the other side. She adds a globe and a map so that children can locate the countries where the instruments come from. She also includes recordings of the different instruments being played and a computer game where children match the instrument to the recorded music.

- Hang a variety of bells from a frame (cowbells, jingle bells, hand bell) so that children can experiment with the different sounds.

Creating Music

Ohman-Rodriguez (2005) states that composing music allows children to be "music insiders." Like other written symbols, it is important for children to have opportunities to play with and use music symbols even if they are not connected to the sound the symbol represents (Ohman-Rodriguez, 2005). Children first learn to improvise music and then to write music. See Figure 14.3 for the standards related to this area. Following are materials teachers can add to the music center to assist children in creating music:

- Cards with a picture of a different body part on each card (hands, elbows, knees, feet). Children then draw a card and create body music using the body part shown on the card.
- Examples of printed music such as songbooks. Charts of printed music hung on the wall also can provide examples. It is especially effective if the teacher introduces and uses the chart during a group activity, following the song and the notes with her finger as the children sing it.
- Tape recorders and paper and pencils so that children can record their own songs. Campbell (1991) studied children ages 5 to 7 and found that their own songs were rhythmically more complex than children's songs in the Caucasian, Native American, Hispanic, or most world cultures.
- A variety of instruments that children can use for improvising and a tape recorder. This allows children to record themselves and listen to the music they have created. Children first begin to compose through improvising music.

Figure 14.3   Achievement Standard: Creating Music

Children:
a. improvise songs to accompany their play activities
b. improvise instrumental accompaniments to songs, recorded selections, stories, and poems
c. create short pieces of music, using voices, instruments, and other sound sources
d. invent and use original graphic or symbolic systems to represent vocal and instrumental sounds and musical ideas

- Staff paper and note stickers or stamps so children can create their own music. After improvising music, children begin to write musical notation. To maximize learning, children need to hear the music they have composed soon after it is created. The teacher can play the music for the child. Another alternative is for the children to use a computer program to create music. For example, Morton Subotnik's website features a free program that allows children to choose an instrument that will play the music that they have created at http://www.creatingmusic.com/.

Responding to Music

As we've discussed, children naturally respond to music from birth. However, for optimal development of listening and musical skills, children need the opportunity to actively engage with the music, attending to the sounds and the changes in the sounds (Fox, 2000). See Figure 14.4 for standards in this area. Below are several materials for encouraging this engagement in the music center:

- Tape recordings of different classroom and outdoor sounds such as a car starting, vacuum cleaner running, and bird singing. Add picture cards of each of the sounds so that children can display the correct card when they hear the sound.
- A bright light (overhead projector, a halogen flood light) so that children can shadow dance to the music (Stamp, 1992).
- A large doll to use as a dance partner.
- A podium, a conductor's baton, and a music stand so that children can be conductors.
- Cards with pictures of a ball bouncing, hands clapping, feet tapping, and so forth. Children draw a card and demonstrate the beat of the music using the method shown on the card.
- A dancing scarf doll. Create the doll by putting batting and a square of fabric on a wooden spoon to form the doll's head. Tie the head with ribbon. The children can move the doll to the beat of the music (Kenney, 2004).
- Flannel-board pieces and songs that tell a story such as "The Old Woman Who Swallowed a Fly." Older children may be able to use story props for less obvious music (*Peter and the Wolf*).
- Paper and markers for drawing the beat of the music. Although many early childhood teachers have children draw to music, Flohr (2004) stresses that this typically does not constitute a music listening experience since the music is often part of the background. To make it a musical listening experience, the music must be the primary activity.

Figure 14.4   Achievement Standard: Responding to Music

Children:
a. identify the sources of a wide variety of sounds
b. respond through movement to music of various tempos, meters, dynamics, modes, genres, and styles to express what they hear and feel in works of music
c. participate freely in music activities

Source: National Standards for Arts Education. Copyright © 1994 by Music Educators National Conference (MENC). Used by permission. The complete National Arts Standards and additional materials relating to the Standards are available from MENC: The National Association for Music Education, 1806 Robert Fulton Drive, Reston, VA 20191; www.menc.org.

Figure 14.5   Achievement Standard: Understanding Music

Children:
  a. use their own vocabulary and standard music vocabulary to describe voices, instruments, music notation, and music of various genres, styles, and periods from diverse cultures
  b. sing, play instruments, move, or verbalize to demonstrate awareness of the elements of music pitch (highness or lowness), rhythm (beat of the music), harmony (combination of notes played simultaneously), dynamics (loudness or softness), timbre (quality of a sound—why two different types of instruments playing the same note sound different), texture (number or parts or voices), form (predictability) and changes in their usage
  c. demonstrate an awareness of music as a part of daily life

Source: National Standards for Arts Education. Copyright © 1994 by Music Educators National Conference (MENC). Used by permission. The complete National Arts Standards and additional materials relating to the Standards are available from MENC: The National Association for Music Education, 1806 Robert Fulton Drive, Reston, VA 20191; www.menc.org.

Understanding Music

Many of the previously described activities also assist children in understanding music. See Figure 14.5 for the standards relating to this area. To further help children understand music the early childhood teacher can add the following materials to the center:

Infants point to the guitar when they want to play. This protects the instrument while still making it a visible choice.

- Instrumental music. Have pictures of each of the instruments being played. As children hear the instrument, they show the card (Flohr, 2004).
- Sound-matching games using film canister shakers containing different items.
- A tape with different pitches. Have a pause after each pitch so that children can try to imitate it.
- Games that children can play. For example, standing high for high notes or crouching low for low notes.
- Puzzles of different instruments.
- Variety of instruments with a few notes marked on each instrument so that children can listen to the same note on each of the different instruments.
- Tape of different recorded rhythms. Children can have a card that they turn over to indicate if the two rhythms are the same or different. After a pause, the tape can give the child the correct answer.

Special Considerations for Infants and Toddlers

Infants and toddlers are natural music makers. But, as with preschool age and early elementary age children, we can enhance this natural love. Teachers at Children's Place do this by providing a variety of instruments such as a lap harp, bongo drum, guitar, auto harp, basket of shaker eggs, and tambourine. They model how instruments are cared for and demonstrate ways the instruments might be played. The shaker eggs, lap harp, tambourines, and drums are left on a low shelf for children to explore. The guitar and autoharp are hung on the wall to be used with more adult supervision. Children point to them when they want to play.

Natasha, a teacher of infants, provides a basket of exploration items that make noise when banged. For example, she includes a basket of household items such as pots, pans, and metal and wooden spoons. She plays a variety of music for the children to listen to and dance to.

Tania has created a musical center for children who are just beginning to crawl. She found a play mat that makes sound when you crawl on the pad. She also has hung a bell at the top of the ramp to the climbing structure, so that when children crawl to the top they can ring the bell.

Each of these teachers has found ways to introduce active musical exploration in their settings. What are other ways that teachers help children to be successful in the music center?

This music center provides toddlers a variety of choices.

Teachers' Facilitation of Learning in the Music Center

Provide Musical Experiences

The early childhood years are perfect for introducing children to a wide range of musicians and musical experiences. If possible, have the musician sit in the music area with children coming and going as they wish. This allows children to interact with the musician individually and in small groups, according to their interests.

To provide children with opportunities to see musicians that are not available in your community you might provide short videotapes.

Thomas, a teacher of first graders, had visited Australia and returned with a didgeridoo. He brought the instrument into his classroom and introduced it by playing a short video of an Aborigine man playing the didgeridoo. Thomas left the didgeridoo in the music center for several days, allowing children to experiment with creating sound using the instrument. The children also looked up information about the didgeridoo on the Internet and learned the instrument's history.

There are many other options for exposing children to music. Amanda brings her preschool children to a music store where they get to examine instruments and hear different selections of music. Samantha, a teacher of kindergarten children, takes her children to visit the high school band room where students describe and play instruments for the children. Curious Minds, a program for preschool children, brings children to short musicals.

Include Music Throughout the Day

There are many opportunities throughout the day to incorporate music. Natalie, a teacher of preschool children, sings a special song for many classroom transitions. For example, she has a special song for cleaning up, beginning lunch, and going outside. She has special calming music that she plays at the beginning of rest time. Each day, Natalie also emphasizes music at the morning group time. During this time children might play instruments, sing songs, or dance to music. Through the music, Natalie also introduces other skills. For example, she often chooses songs that reinforce concepts she is working on with the children (learning each other's names, and learning colors, body parts, the alphabet, and numbers). She has written the children's beloved songs on a flip chart. When the children request a song, she can point to the words as they sing, exposing the children to written language.

Introduce New Instruments and Musical Activities

For children to take full advantage of materials available in the music area, you will need to introduce the materials and activities to them. For example, you will want to demonstrate how to use and care for instruments. You can introduce children to instruments and activities individually, in small groups, or at a group time. For example, during group time you can introduce a musical activity where children stand high for high notes and crouch low for low notes while singing the "Grand Old Duke of York." Then you can place the music in the music center with a picture of children standing high and crouching low to remind children of how to complete the activity.

Model Enjoyment of Music Yourself

Children pick up their cues from us. It is important to model enjoyment of a variety of types of music. It is also important to include singing in our curriculum. If you feel uncomfortable singing, rather than avoiding singing songs use a musical tape when singing with children.

Interact with Children to Deepen Their Knowledge

Your involvement can assist children in developing more advanced skills in music. For example, you might demonstrate how to play an instrument. You might also encourage children to take the next developmental step. For example, a child who has been improvising songs on a musical instrument may be ready to try to follow a pattern card or musical notes. Or, the child might be ready to write the notes down for others.

You might also present musical challenges. For example, you might ask, "What would happen if you played the drum with just your hands? Does it sound different than when played with a drumstick?" "What are all the different ways you can move to the music?"

Discuss Music and Model Musical Vocabulary

Children learn musical terms that are used by the adults in their environment. Following is a list of ways of increasing children's musical knowledge and vocabulary:

- Discuss the tempo, pitch, tonal quality, and rhythm of the music.
- Name musical terms (whole note, half note, quarter note, sharp, treble clef) (Ohman-Rodriquez, 2005).

- Miche (2002) recommends that we teach preschool children the following words for dynamic levels: piano (soft), mezzo (medium), and forte (loud). Elementary students can learn pianissimo, piano, mezzo piano, mezzo forte, forte, and fortissimo (p. 64).
- Discuss the size of the group that is playing (duet, orchestra, and band).
- Name the type of music being played (call and response, jazz, blues, western, classical).
- Identify the instruments.

Acknowledge Learners

Recognize children's musical abilities by describing what they are doing, asking for information, discussing the aesthetic elements of their music, or pointing out their progress and effort (Imiolo-Schriver, 1995). Another way to acknowledge learners is to video or audio tape them playing an instrument, singing, or moving to music. This allows children to revisit their work and share it with friends and family.

Observe and Document Children's Musical Skills

Children in the music area can be assessed on their ability to

- Move to music
- Use voices expressively
- Sing a variety of simple songs
- Sing in pitch
- Play a variety of instruments
- Keep rhythm when playing with a group or a recording
- Play simple melodies
- Improvise songs with their voice and instruments
- Represent music through original or standard systems
- Identify a variety of sounds
- Indicate preferences in music and instruments

For a very thorough examination of assessment methods, criteria, and rubrics see the MENC Performance Standards for Music: Grades PreK–12 at http://www.menc.org/resources/view/national-standards-for-music-education

Meet the Needs of All Learners

Supporting Children from All Cultures. It is important to include music and instruments in the classroom that represent children's cultural backgrounds.

The director at Birge Nest Early Head Start invited teachers to bring in their favorite child-friendly music to share with children. Since each of the three teachers had a different musical taste, this practice exposed children to a rich variety of music. However, one day Lisa, one of the teachers, heard Andre rapping and realized that none of their music represented his cultural music. She realized that we must be intentional in the music we choose or we risk not including all children.

Music provides the opportunity to learn about one's own culture and the culture of others. For example, children can study different instruments and songs, and the use of voice from different cultures gives a glimpse into the values and customs of the culture. Culture strongly influences how the voice is used (Flohr, 2004, p. 85). Some examples of this include Tuvan throat singing, Tibetan yodeling, and women singing in high pitches in Hindi music.

Children can also learn about the people in the community in which they live. Inviting families with musical skills and area musicians to visit the classroom can help children to learn about rich music opportunities within their geographic area. Even musical elementary, middle school, and high school visitors can provide opportunities for children to experience a range of songs and instruments.

Supporting Children with Special Needs. All children need the opportunity to interact successfully in the music center.

Tori, a child who is blind, enjoys music and playing musical instruments. Janelle, her teacher, has found many ways to assist Tori in independently using the center. Tori is beginning to learn Braille. Therefore, Janelle labeled the tapes, CDs, and location of each instrument in Braille. Janelle also created an outline of each instrument with sandpaper and placed it on the shelf. She labeled the tape recorder and CD player with tactile symbols. Through individually examining the needs of Tori, Janelle was able to make environmental modifications so that she could be successful.

Teachers play an important role in the music center, from setting up an appropriate music environment to introducing all children to music and successful musical experiences.

Special Challenges in the Music Center

There are two challenges that sometimes prevent teachers from developing a music center. These are a lack of instruments and the noise created by the center.

Lack of Instruments

You will need durable, quality-sounding instruments for your music center. If you cannot afford to buy instruments, there are many quality instruments that you or volunteers can make. Following are a few examples:

- Drums can be created with five-gallon buckets. To create a set of three drums with different pitches, you will need six buckets. Cut three buckets in half and throw away the bottom half. One drum will be a single whole bucket, the next drum will be a single whole bucket with a drum-half attached with wood screws, and the third drum will be a single whole bucket with two drum-halves attached (Kenney & Persellin, 2000). This website from the Texas School Music Project will provide additional directions for making drums: http://www.tsmp.org/elementary/ turner/turner_ building_centers_drums.html

- A xylophone can be created by cutting PVC pipe or ½" aluminum conduit pipe into different lengths and tying them onto a wooden frame or placing them on two strips of foam rubber. It is best if a little less than a third of the pipe extends off the frame. Xylophone pipes should be cut to the following lengths: 11", 10¼", 9¾", 9½", 8⅞", 8½", 7⅞", and 7⅝".

- Many instruments around the world are created from gourds, including water drums, temple gongs, stamping tubes, shakers, rattles, rain sticks, xylophones, drums, and lutes (Summit & Widess, 1999). For detailed directions on making all of the above instruments, see *Making Gourd Musical Instruments: Over 60*

String, Wind, and Percussion Instruments and How to Play Them (Summit & Widess, 1999).

- Tambourines may be made by tying flattened bottle caps with a hole in the center to the inside ring of an embroidery hoop and then fitting the rings together.

Excessive Noise

As we discussed in Chapter 6, excessive noise can increase stress in children and adults and can negatively affect learning. However, following are several ways to decrease noise in the music area.

- Encourage children to explore the texture of sounds with purpose, not just make noise.
- Choose appropriate indoor instruments. For example, you might avoid whistles, and select smaller drums.
- Provide earphones for listening to music.
- Keyboards often come with a jack for headphones. It is important to use them as a way of reducing any unnecessary noise.
- Be consciously aware of the level of noise when children are dancing or moving to music. You might want to place a symbol on the tape or CD player indicating where the volume dial should be set.
- Place sound-dampening materials on the floor, ceilings, and walls. For example, foam padding that is used under carpeting makes an excellent sound dampening material. You can staple the padding to the desired surface and paint it to add to the aesthetic quality.

Outdoor Music Centers

The outdoors provides a unique musical environment where there is less concern about noise, a larger space to move freely, and natural sounds. There are many ways to incorporate outdoor music. You can create a sound path, a music hut, a sound garden, or a soundscape with music interspersed throughout the playground. Rusty Keeler (2002), a playground designer, suggests hiding sound elements like wind chimes and different kinds of bells in trees, bushes, and flower and herb beds for the creation of ambient sounds. Children can also be encouraged to listen to natural sounds, like the sound of water in a fountain, birds in a tree, or wind rustling leaves. To assist with capturing sounds outside the fence, you can mount listening cones or traffic cones on the fence.

Children can experiment with sound through PVC talk tubes that they can use to throw their voices. These tubes are designed in a U shape and can be buried on the playground or installed overhead. You can also give the PVC pipes to the children and let them test different lengths and shapes of pipe.

Indoor instruments such as marimbas, rain sticks, and sound blocks can also be used outside. It is ideal if locked storage is available so that you can leave a collection of instruments in the play yard.

The play yard can also contain permanently installed instruments such as a giant "thunder drum" made from steel or plastic barrels (Keeler, 2002). You can create mallets by attaching softballs to each end of a dowel. To keep the mallets from being lost, attach them permanently to the drum (Keeler, 2002). Jumbo chimes from metal pipes, a giant wooden xylophone, triangles, and sound pipes hung in trees are also good playground choices. At Curious Minds, a college student created a hanging xylophone from different

Pots and pans provide an inexpensive outdoor music area.

sizes of wrenches. In Long Island, a program created a sound garden containing a music marimba, xylophone, mettalaphone, thunder wall, musical turtle, and arches with bamboo chimes and temple bells. When children climb a hill they can even find temple blocks (Schwartz, 2007). At Early Head Start, teachers created a music environment by hanging pots, pans, lids, and muffin tins along with strikers on the fence.

When establishing your outdoor environment, seriously consider a music center. As demonstrated by the examples, there are many creative outdoor music possibilities. Outdoor music provides the same rich advantages as indoor music in an environment with fewer constraints.

Throughout history, in all cultures, music has been a natural part of children's experiences. Music can enhance the quality of life, sometimes calming and other times exciting the participant. We can enjoy music alone or with others.

Music helps to form our identity, teaching us about our culture. Through music, children can also learn about other cultures. All areas of children's development are enhanced through music. The music center, based on our knowledge of music standards and the children's own unique talents and interests, can provide a world of musical opportunities for children.

Sample Application Activities

1. Make a homemade instrument to have for your classroom.
2. The school board in your community has just decided to cut the arts at the school. Write a short letter describing why the arts are important.
3. Make a list of songs that you could use during transition times.
4. Review songs that have won awards for children's music.
5. Assess a music center using the environmental assessment in Figure 14.6.
6. Make a list of instruments from different cultures that you would like to have in your classroom. Develop cards for each instrument with information about the instrument on one side and a picture of a musician playing the instrument on the other side.
7. To learn more about incorporating music into the curriculum visit the following websites:
   Best Children's Music at http://www.bestchildrensmusic.com
   The Children's Music Web at http://www.childrensmusic.org
   The National Association for Music Education (MENC) at http://www.menc.org

The music center

- ☐ Is an uncluttered area with space for movement
- ☐ Is located away from quiet areas
- ☐ Provides noise reduction through earphones and absorbent materials on floors, ceilings, and walls
- ☐ Includes a variety of instruments (drums, rhythm sticks, finger cymbals, triangles, cymbals, gongs, jingle bells, resonator bells, step bells, xylophone-type instruments with removable bars, chorded zithers, fretted instruments, electronic keyboard instruments, and assorted instruments representing a variety of cultures (MENC, 1994)
- ☐ Provides instrument storage that allows easy access for children
- ☐ Provides sound equipment that children can operate themselves
- ☐ Includes a variety of music to listen to and play instruments with, and for dancing and moving
- ☐ Includes music from a variety of genres, cultures, and historical time periods
- ☐ Provides high-quality, award-winning music
- ☐ Provides written music
- ☐ Contains materials so that children can write their own music (preschool and early elementary)
- ☐ Is fully developed with each musical activity having all needed materials such as an audiotape to play rhythm instruments with and written music for the keyboard
- ☐ Contains materials and activities in all four content standards (singing and playing instruments, creating music, responding to music, understanding music)

Figure 14.6
Environmental
Assessment: Music
Center

Source: Permission is granted by the publisher to reproduce this figure for evaluation and record-keeping. From Julie Bullard, *Creating Environments for Learning: Birth to Age Eight.* Copyright © 2010 by Pearson Education, Inc. All rights reserved.

chapter 15
Integrating Technology

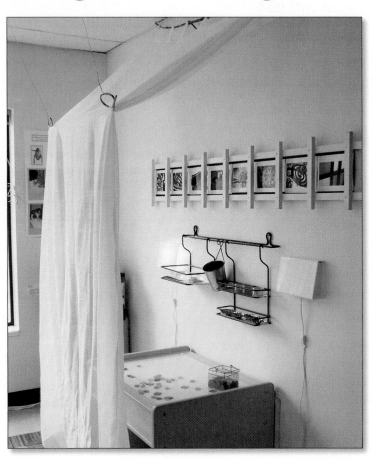

*T*erri, a teacher of preschoolers at Sunshine Academy, had a computer center
that contained three computers. The computers were popular with the children
and were always in use. However, Terri struggled with using the computers to
support the curriculum. For example, although the computers were loaded with software programs for children to use in creating books, the children usually played
games instead. Terri had loaded some streamed videos to support her farm animal
unit. However, few children had watched them.

Terri decided to experiment with moving the computers to different areas of the
classroom. She loaded programs onto the computer that would support the curriculum area where the computer was located and removed any unrelated programs. In
the music area she loaded short videos of people playing instruments, a game where

children matched sounds to the correct musical instrument, music that children could sing along with, and a program where children could write their own music and hear it played back. In the literacy center, she added KidPix (allowing children to write or dictate their story) and a drawing program (so they could add illustrations). They could also listen and follow along with computerized children's books. The computer in the science and math center included short videos on farm animals and webcams such as the Animal Planet horse cam. The Building Blocks math program was also available.

After making these changes, the children used the computers for a variety of purposes rather than just to play games. Terri felt the computers supported her curriculum and increased children's learning. She stated, "I now think of the computer as a tool that when used appropriately can enhance learning." She plans to change the computers to different areas as needed. For example, she is thinking about adding a variety of hats from different cultures to the dramatic play area. She thinks that the children's play and learning may be supported by streamed videos of the different cultures that are represented by the hats.

Today the majority of children in the early years use some type of technology. For example, 67% of preschool-age children and 80% of kindergarten-age children use the computer (DeBell & Chapman, 2006). However, the use of technology in the early childhood years continues to be debated, particularly in regard to computer use. For example, The Alliance for Childhood published a report entitled *Fool's Gold: A Critical Look at Computers in Childhood* declaring that computers were detrimental to children's physical health, creativity, and social well-being (Cordes & Miller, 2000). *Strip Mining for Gold: Research and Policy in Educational Technology—A Response to Fool's Gold* responded with the many educational and social benefits of computers for young children (Clements & Sarama, 2003). Organizations such as NAEYC have responded to this debate with position statements clarifying the appropriate use of computers. Many consider the computer to have no inherent value or ability to harm; instead, they view it as a tool that can be appropriately or inappropriately used. "Just as pencils do not replace crayons but rather provide additional means of expression, computers, or cameras or any other form of technology do not replace other tools but add to the array of tools available to children to explore, create, and communicate" (Scoter, Ellis, & Railsback, 2001, p. 25). In thinking about using any type of technology, it is important to consider the following:

- Is it the best tool for the job?
- Will it produce added value to the activity?
- Is the activity of benefit to the child?
- What is the cost benefit? In thinking about the cost benefit, it is important to balance the cost of technology with the need and cost of other classroom learning materials (NAEYC, 1996).

This chapter will examine classroom technologies including the digital camera, video recorder, overhead projector, light table, and computer.

How the Use of Technology Can Enhance Children's Development

Through the use of technology, children learn technology skills, while enhancing social and cognitive development.

Technology Skills

As children use the computer and other forms of technology, they have the opportunity to meet the following technology standards. Established by the International Society for Technology in Education (ISTE), these standards are for children ages prekindergarten through second grade (2000).

1. Use input devices (e.g., mouse, keyboard, remote control) and output devices (e.g., monitor, printer) to successfully operate computers, VCRs, audiotapes, and other technologies.

2. Use a variety of media and technology resources for directed and independent learning activities.

3. Communicate about technology using developmentally appropriate and accurate terminology.

4. Use developmentally appropriate multimedia resources (e.g., interactive books, educational software, elementary multimedia encyclopedias) to support learning.

5. Work cooperatively and collaboratively with peers, family members, and others when using technology in the classroom.

6. Demonstrate positive social and ethical behaviors when using technology.

7. Practice responsible use of technology systems and software.

8. Create developmentally appropriate multimedia products with support from teachers, family members, or student partners.

9. Use technology resources (e.g., puzzles, logical thinking programs, writing tools, digital cameras, drawing tools) for problem solving, communication, and illustration of thoughts, ideas, and stories.

10. Gather information and communicate with others using telecommunications, with support from teachers, family members, or student partners.

Social Skills

Though initially some educators expressed concern that computers might reduce socialization, researchers suggest that instead computers may increase the amount of communication and positive interaction between children (Clements, 1994; Haugland & Wright, 1997). For example, Muller and Perlmutter (1985) found that children participated in interactions with others during 63% of computer play versus 7% of puzzle play. Computers offer a unique environment that might encourage children who typically do not interact with others to do so. "For many children the computer is a catalyst for information sharing, language development, and decision making" (Tsantis, Bewick, & Thouvenelle, 2003, p. 7). Children engage in diverse social interactions when using the computer including asking for help; directing others' actions; providing information, assistance, and instruction; managing turn taking; acknowledging each other; commenting on each other's actions; and disagreeing (Heft & Swaminathan, 2002; Shahrimin & Butterworth, 2002). Although children seem to naturally assist each other when using the computer, one classroom developed rules to assure interaction. These included finding a friend (children were only allowed to play at the computer with a friend), helping a friend (pointing, discussing, providing information, and sharing the mouse), and taking turns (a timer helped to determine when it was the friend's turn) (Medvin, Reed, Behr, & Spargo, 2003).

Often computer "experts" arise in classrooms and become teachers of the other children. The experts are not assigned to this role by the teacher but instead the other children bestow this title on them. Surprisingly, the computer expert often does not have a computer at home. Experts are usually not the most proficient children at academics or social skills, but they do gain communication and social skills as they help other children (Hutinger, 1999). For example, in one kindergarten program the families were invited to send emails to their children. Since the children were not yet proficient readers, they had trouble reading the messages. That was when they discovered that Michael, a child with autistic behaviors, could read. Each day he went from classmate to classmate reading each of their messages. While in the past he'd been ignored by other children, he was now sought after.

Cognitive Skills

As a tool, the computer has several advantages that can aid in children's cognitive development.

- Computers are motivating for young children, increasing their time in on-task behavior. For example, one study found kindergarten children were on-task 90% of the time when they were on the computer (Bergin, Ford, & Hess, 1993).
- Computers provide consistent and frequent reinforcement (Parette, Hourcade, & Heiple, 2000).
- Computers allow children to work independently at their own pace (Parette et al., 2000).
- Software programs often provide extensive scaffolding of learning. Scaffolding is very important in developing cognitive skills.
- The computer provides unique opportunities that may enhance learning. For example, computers can allow children to access the "largest information bank—with the broadest range of quality and utility—the world has ever known" (Parette et al., 2000, p. 245). With the computer, children can participate in simulations and manipulate variables that might not be possible in the real world (Scoter et al., 2001).

The best academic results are found when the use of technology is clearly related to other classroom activities and curriculum. For example, when children are using a software program that manipulates items, the teacher places the concrete items on the table next to the computer or incorporates the items into classroom activities (Haugland, 1992). Research indicates that using a computer with supporting manipulatives increases children's skills more than using only the manipulatives or the computer alone (Clements, 1994; Haugland & Shade, 1994).

While there are many cognitive advantages to using computers, there is danger in using too much drill and skill software (Scoter et al., 2001). In one study, children's creativity was reduced by 50% after using this type of software (Haugland, 1992).

Using Technology in the Classroom

While technology can be a separate classroom center, ideally teachers integrate it into other existing centers. As illustrated in the opening scenario, when teachers place computers or other technology devices in existing learning centers, there is often a more direct relationship between the current curriculum and what is offered through the technology. The computer or other technology device is used as a tool that expands and extends the current curriculum, thereby increasing educational opportunities (Downes, Arthur, & Beecher, 2001). For example, Downes et al. (2001) suggest computers be moved to different centers as needed to facilitate learning. If computers are difficult to move, you might instead move the other centers around the computer. However, regardless of where the technology is placed, there are important criteria to consider in designing a setting to support technology use. We will examine these next.

Design the Setting for Children's Independent Use

Design the technology devices and center so that children can use them independently.

- Mark tape players, CD players, overhead projectors, and other electronic devices with easy to recognize symbols so that children can turn them off and on. In some toddler classrooms, teachers mark the stop with a red sticker and the play with a green sticker.

- When tapes and CDs are removed from covers they may be difficult to tell apart. Some teachers draw pictures on the CDs and tapes to help children to locate their favorites.

- Place materials that children need within easy reach.

- Label shelves so that children can return the materials to the proper place.

- Pre-load programs onto the computer. Label the programs with easy to understand icons. Haugland (1997) recommends a utility program such as KidDesk from Edmark.

- Provide a mouse for each computer. Keyboards should also be available for older children. Although they are more difficult to use than a mouse, they offer more options and are preferred by children (Robinson, 1999).

- Establish a separate computer folder for each child where she can save her digital pictures, drawings, and stories.

- Make sure that everything that is needed to effectively use the technology device is easily accessible. For example, blank tapes are located with the tape players. Extra paper is stored near the printer.

Choose Appropriate Media

Media such as computer programs and tape recordings need to be developmentally appropriate and high quality. They must also be free from bias. Ideally they should introduce children to other cultures.

It is also important to provide enough media. For example, at a minimum each computer should contain a drawing program and a word processing program. See Figure 15.1 for information on choosing appropriate computer software.

TIP Ways to Find Appropriate Software

- Buy award-winning programs—Some awards given for children's software include Oppenheim Toy Portfolio Software Awards, Parents' Choice Awards, EDDIE Award, BESSIE Award, All Star Software Awards, AEP (Association of Educational Publishers) Award, and the CODiE Award.

- Subscribe to a site that reviews software. (Children's Technology Review is an advertisement-free site that evaluates software programs for ease of use, educational value, design features, value for cost, and entertainment.)

- Review the program yourself using the checklist found in Figure 15.1.

Figure 15.1
Choosing Appropriate
Software

When screening software, consider the following criteria:

☐ Does the software have high educational or informational value? "Does this software program help create learning opportunities that did not exist without it" (Tsantis et al., 2003, p. 5)? Or, would this information be better presented in a different format?

☐ Is the program developmentally appropriate for the children using it? According to Haugland (2005), only 20% of software is developmentally appropriate. Appropriate software enhances learning and is more engaging for children. It is important that the program is not just an electronic worksheet page.

☐ Is the program designed so that the child can use the program independently (simple and precise directions, uses speech when appropriate, uses picture menus, organized for intuitive use) (Prairie, 2005)?

☐ Is the child able to exercise some control when using the software (sets the pace, can repeat a process, can stop and resume, can choose from multiple paths)?

☐ Does the program encourage active learning (requires active participation and encourages exploration and further investigation)?

☐ Is the program exciting and interesting?
  • utilizes many senses including sound, music, and voice
  • includes graphics and sounds that are motivating for young children (NAEYC, 1996)
  • relevant to the group of children using the program

☐ Does the program scaffold children's learning (provides increasing challenges and a variety of levels, provides nonthreatening feedback, does not penalize for mistakes)?

☐ Is the program anti-bias, containing respectful images of diverse cultures, multiple languages, people of different ages, abilities, colors, and diverse family structures (NAEYC, 1996)?

☐ Does the program promote pro-social values (no violence or implicit violence is present such as "blowing it up" to get rid of mistakes) (Tsantis et al., 2003)?

☐ Is the program preselected to match curricular goals and is the program tied closely to other curricular activities? Software should support or be supported by the curriculum (Haugland, 1997). Haugland (1997) describes "a flannel board of the weather reinforcing Sammy's Science House (from Edmark); dramatic play props including airplanes, a ticket counter, and brochures, reinforcing Let's Explore the Airport With Buzzy (from Humongous); and marbles, spinners, and dice, reinforcing Math Keys: Unlocking Probability (from The Learning Company)" (p. 15).

☐ Does the program contain an aesthetic screen with high-quality graphics and sounds? Graphics and sound need to add to the quality rather than being distracting.

☐ Is the program accessible for children with special needs?

Figure 15.1
Choosing Appropriate
Software

Provide for Health and Safety

It is critical that electronic devices are set up in a safe and healthy manner.

• Cords are placed to prevent tripping. For example, computer cords are bundled and placed at the back of the computer.

• To reduce overall classroom noise, earphones are used with electronic equipment. The earphones are closely monitored so that loudness does not cause hearing damage.

• Extension cords are never used.

• Electrical items are not placed near a water source.

- There is proper light for the computer center and the computer is placed to prevent glare.
- The computer station is designed to be ergonomic. This will help to prevent injuries. It can also help children to establish healthy computer habits that will aid them throughout life.
  - Workstations should be adjustable (18 to 26 inches). In a study of 18 children's settings, it was found that the monitor and keyboard or mouse were often too high. This can cause pain in the neck, shoulder, back, arm, and hand (Kemp, 1999).
  - If the workstation is not adjustable, it is important to provide adjustable chairs to raise or lower the child to the proper position. Footstools should also be provided so that children's feet are resting flat (Ergonomics for Children and Educational Environments, 2006).
  - The monitor needs to be directly in front of the child and the top of the screen should be below the child's eye level (Ergonomics for Children and Educational Environments, 2006).
  - The keyboard and mouse need to be 3 to 4 inches lower than the computer desk. The child's elbows should be bent at no more than 90 degrees when keyboarding.
  - Children should be encouraged to keep their wrists straight (Ergonomics for Children and Educational Environments, 2006).
  - Children should change positions every 15 to 20 minutes and take breaks every 30 to 60 minutes (Ergonomics for Children and Educational Environments, 2006).

Design the Setting to Encourage Social Interaction

Intentionally design the setting to encourage the children to interact while they are using the technology. For example, place two or three chairs at each computer station and place computers in areas where other children can watch (Clements, 1999). Research indicates that there are better outcomes when children use the computer together (Clements, 1999). Computers should be placed in an area that allows children to see the computers throughout the room. When computers are in an isolated corner, children tend to be separated into users and nonusers. When there is room around the computer, children can watch what other children are doing and provide support and encouragement. They can also learn by watching (Haugland, 1997).

To encourage social interaction and a shared story experience, add multiple earphones to the tape or CD player. However, there may be times when individual use is more appropriate, and you will want to set up an environment to support this. For example, if children are taping individual stories you might want to set up a private booth to assist in concentration and to improve sound quality.

Provide Equal Access to the Technology

Establish a management system to provide equal access to technology. Because computers and other technology devices are popular, it is often necessary to have a sign-up sheet so that everyone has an opportunity to use the equipment. Lists can prevent children from having to watch and wait their turn. Some early childhood classrooms use a timer to designate the amount of time that each child receives on the equipment. When the timer goes off the child using the computer or other popular equipment crosses his name off the list and goes to get the next child on the list. If the child is engaged in another activity and does not want to leave it, she can leave her name on the list but let the next person have a turn first. In most classrooms, there are times during the day when technology devices are not available. Becky, a teacher of preschool children, places a "computer sleeping" sign on the computer when it is not available.

Provide Ideas for Using the Equipment

Post ideas for use near the electronic device. You can use pictures to remind children of the different activities that they might accomplish with the device. For example, the tape player might be used to listen to music, listen to a story, record a story or song, or play a game of identifying sounds. Visual aids can help children to remember these varied choices.

Supply an Adequate Number of Computers and Other Technology Devices

There should be a computer for every four or five children. If this is not possible, you might consider combining your computers with those of other teachers and then rotating the computers on a predetermined schedule. Computer labs are not recommended for young children because when computers are not in the classroom there is often a disconnect between the computer and the rest of the curriculum.

You will want to analyze the use of other media to determine the number of items needed. For example, one toddler classroom found that the light table was so popular that they added another one.

Limit the Amount of Time Children Are Exposed to Media

Allow children to use the computers and other media devices for a brief period of time. It is recommended that media exposure from all sources be limited to 1 to 2 hours per day, since sedentary time displaces more physical activity. There is also concern that excessive computer use by young children might lead to repetitive stress injuries, eyestrain, and obesity (Cordes & Miller, 2000; Shields & Behrman, 2000).

Use the Internet Effectively

The Internet can be used to communicate with others, locate information, and share and publish projects. Research reveals that 23% of preschool children, 32% of kindergarten children, and 50% of third-grade children use the Internet at home or school (DeBell &

TIP Internet Sites to Consider for Young Children

- *The Children's Literature Web Guide* provides links to award-winning books, authors, and illustrators: http://www.acs.ucalgary.ca/~dkbrown
- *Webquest* provides computer activities for kindergarten through adulthood: http://webquest.org/search/index.php
- *Pitsco's Ask An Expert* provides an index of experts that are willing to answer questions: http://www.askanexpert.com/
- *Ask Jeeves for Kids* provides links that match children's questions http://www.ajkids.com/
- *Yahooligans* provides a variety of child-friendly links: http://www.yahooligans.com
- *KidsClick* provides a variety of websites divided into categories compiled by librarians: http://www.kidsclick.org/
- *SuperKids* provides a list of websites reviewed by teams of educators, parents, and children: http://www.superkids.com/aweb/pages/reviews/reviews.shtml

Chapman, 2006). It is important that parents and teachers review and preselect Internet sites for children in the early childhood years. In addition, you might want to add protective software such as Net Nanny or Cyber Patrol that will prevent children from inadvertently visiting inappropriate sites. Internet sites should meet the same criteria as listed for appropriate software. In addition, sites should be commercial free and should not request any personal information from the child.

Technology Activities to Support the Curriculum

Technology can be used to support all areas of the curriculum. Technology such as tape recorders, CD players, video recorders, light tables, overhead projectors, digital cameras, and computers are tools that can provide children unique learning experiences, allow them to document their learning, and aid them in reflection.

Using Tape Recorders and CD Players to Support the Curriculum

Tape recorders and CD players allow children to listen to stories, finger plays, or music. They also provide children with opportunities to engage in activities such as "guess the sound." With tape recorders, children are able to document their discussions, dramatic play episodes, story telling, and oral reading. These recordings can be used in a variety of ways. They can be

- Transcribed so children can see their ideas in print
- Used as documentation of children's learning
- Analyzed to determine children's current competencies
- Used for planning and facilitating deeper learning

Recordings of children playing musical instruments and singing songs are also valuable. Children enjoy listening to their creations. Additionally, when recordings are made over a period of time they can hear the improvement in their skills.

Using Video Recorders to Support the Curriculum

George Forman has labeled video recording "a tool of the mind" (1999), an aid for reflection for both teachers and children. For example, video recorders allow children to instantly revisit their experiences and to describe their thinking. It is easier for children to consider their thinking when they are not also engaged in the action. As children watch themselves participating in different interactions and then reflect upon them, they might also see the incident from another child's point of view. For example, they may see the look on the other child's face and hear the other child's statements better during reviewing.

Video recordings can also help children revisit group experiences. For example, Anya and her class of rural preschoolers were completing a project on tractors. As part of the project, they visited an implement dealer where they examined several different tractors and interviewed the manager. The children made a video of their visit. Upon returning to their program, they decided to make their own tractor. Over the next several weeks, they worked on it, frequently revisiting the tractors they had videotaped as dilemmas arose in their building.

As with tape recordings, video recordings can also be used to document children's learning. For example, Anya used video to document the children's questions and process as they created their tractor.

Using Light Tables to Support the Curriculum

Light tables (a box with fluorescent light tubes covered with an opaque Plexiglas cover) allow children to experiment with light and shadows, color, transparency, layering, and textures. "The light takes everyday items and recreates them into objects of beauty and wonder for children" (Whited, 2003, p. 39). A variety of materials can be placed in clear containers on a shelf by the light table for exploration, including

- Translucent items in different colors and shapes
- X-rays
- Sand
- Colored gems and flat marbles
- Colored cellophane and tissue paper
- Natural items such as agates, crystals, feathers, leaves, bugs, shedded snake skins, pressed flowers, dried rose petals, shells
- Found items such as bubble wrap and spiral pencil shavings (Cadwell, 2003)
- Interesting colored dishes
- Bottles of colored water

The light table highlights details in these natural items such as the different layers within the rocks and the veins of the leaves.

In addition to exploration, children can create interesting transitory designs with translucent objects, create masterpieces on the light table using art media (colored glue, shaving cream, and watercolors), mix colors in clear trays, trace items, or examine pictures, photos, and artwork that have been reproduced on transparencies.

Using Overhead Projectors to Support the Curriculum

Overhead projectors allow children the opportunity to explore color, transparency, and shadows. Because the overhead projector shines onto a wall, it can also be used as a light source for creating shadows with objects and bodies and for creating shadow puppet plays.

When I was teaching Head Start, a group of children became enthralled with the overhead projector, often bringing items from home to see them projected on the wall. For example, one day Amber brought her doll to the classroom. Initially she was surprised when she stood the doll on the projector that she did not see the shadow of the

Using the light table adds a new element to color mixing, with the light allowing the child to see the difference in even minor gradients of color.

entire doll. She spent the next half hour exploring shadows by positioning the doll in various poses to see the shadow that was created.

Adding a picture transparency to the overhead projector *can* provide inspiration for art or a new backdrop for drama. Transparencies can also be used so that children can see their artwork and photos enlarged, creating a sense of wonder and pride. Enlarging pictures can also allow children the opportunity to study a subject in more detail. For example, the parts of a flower become more obvious when they are enlarged.

Overheads can also be used as a tool to help children think more deeply. A long-term project resulted in establishing a playground for birds. As part of the study, preschool children were trying to figure out a way to make a fountain for the birds (Forman & Gandini, 1994). They visited the city water fountain and took pictures. When they returned the teachers put the photos on transparencies and shone them on the wall. They asked children to trace the fountain and show how they thought the water got into the fountain. This helped to make the children's thinking visible and also caused children to think more deeply about their theories.

Using Cameras to Support the Curriculum

Digital pictures can support the curriculum in a variety of ways. Photos can be used to do the following:

- Record and document children's learning. Digital pictures can be shared on documentation boards or in documentation notebooks, placed on bulletin boards, or entered into individual children's portfolios.
- Display results of science experiments over time (plants at different stages of growth, metamorphosis).
- Record visitors for future discussion and study (children's pets, insects that have been caught and released, birds that have visited the bird feeder).
- Provide nonverbal directions in a learning center.
- Provide the schedule for the day in picture form. See the photo at the beginning of Chapter 3 for an example.
- Show the steps needed to complete a process (washing hands, cooking snack).
- Show where items are to be placed on shelves and cupboards.
- Help establish management systems such as sign-up boards, attendance boards, and job charts. Some teachers place children's pictures on juice can lids and then use a magnetic board for their management systems.
- Revisit an experience such as a field trip.
- Create games and activities such as sorting, classifying, matching, graphing, expressing feelings, and puzzles.
- Help children to feel valued (pictures of children participating in various activities, pictures of children successfully accomplishing a task).
- Introduce the staff, children, and families to each other (Curious Minds creates a paper quilt of family pictures that hangs in the center).
- Soothe a child (individual family albums are available for children to look at and carry around).
- Make the transition from home to school easier. For example, Portland Oregon Public School Head Starts introduce the school to new children through sending photos to the child (Scoter et al., 2001, p. 28).
- Share information with parents and the community.

Some classrooms have a child assigned as the photographer for the day or the week. This child is available for taking requested pictures. If these children are able, they are also responsible for downloading the pictures onto the computer.

School-age children and preschoolers can successfully use digital cameras. For example, here are some ways that children have used cameras in different programs:

- Children at the Discovery Preschool went on a neighborhood walk and took pictures of different kinds of homes. These were placed in the block area to inspire their building.

- A series of different types of books were created by the preschool and kindergarten class in an urban private school. One of the books was a "Guess What I Am?" book. Each child took a picture using unusual angles or close-up shots to include in the book.

- Children at Burlington Little School took digital pictures of their pattern block designs. These were printed and placed in a three-ring binder for the children to revisit and use for future inspiration.

- In a kindergarten class where many children were homeless, the teacher gave each child a camera that he used to show his experiences. The photos were displayed in the school and in the community, highlighting the homeless experience through a child's eyes.

- Curious Minds has a stuffed bear named Tegar that travels to each child's house. A disposable camera and journal accompany the bear so that children can record the bear's adventures. The pictures are posted on a bulletin board in the program.

To see another example of how a teacher uses digital cameras to support the curriculum, watch the video *Technology* on MyEducationLab.

Go to MyEducationLab and select the topic "Math, Science, and Technology." Under Activities and Applications, watch the video *Technology*.

Using Computers to Support the Curriculum

Like tape recorders, video recorders, light tables, overhead projectors, and digital cameras, computers are tools that can support all areas of the curriculum.

To Support the Arts. Computers can support the arts by providing tools for creating art, informative games, and research for supporting the topic of study. Programs such as Kid Pix Studio or HyperStudio can be used for drawing and creating products. Children can also look up information about artists and see examples of the artists' work. For example, a preschool class was studying flowers and was able to examine more than 200 of Georgia O'Keefe's flower paintings at http://www.artst.org/okeefe/. They compared the flowers painted by Georgia O'Keefe, an American painter, with the flowers painted by Vladimir, a Russian artist.

Computer technology can also help children learn about music. With the computer, children can compose and record music and hear it played back using any instrument that they choose. They can play musical matching games, match instruments to their sounds, and hear and see musicians playing instruments including instruments from other cultures.

Dramatic play can also be enhanced with short, streamed videos of people using newly introduced props. For example, when Kirima introduced a fishing center she showed the children a short video of a fishing camp.

To Support Literacy. Computers can assist children with writing and reading by providing a motivating environment and tools that make the process easier. Research demonstrates that children write more when using computers than when using pencil and paper (Clements, Nastasi, & Swaminathan, 1993). This is most likely because writing is less laborious for children when they use the computer. The powerful editing tools can also help children to analyze and correct their work (Parette et al., 2000). Digital text can easily be arranged, rearranged, added to, and deleted (Ackermann, 2002).

Children as young as 3 can create and organize stories using story fragments and software such as Tell-Tale, Sprite, and PETS (Personal Electronic Teller of Stories) (Ackermann, 2002, p. 37). With the computer, the child can insert icons and pictures into her script, providing new avenues for creating books. The books can easily be printed and placed in the classroom literacy center. This provides additional classroom reading material, an acknowledgment of the writer, and an authentic reason to write.

Computers also offer the unique opportunity to switch text to speech and speech to text. Voice synthesizers can read children's storybooks or their written text while highlighting the text that is being read. This assists children to link the written and spoken word. Some software even changes the story to a different language.

Visiting an author or illustrator's website is another use of the computer to support literacy. This can add interest to an author's study. For example, Jan Brett, author of several children's books including *The Mitten,* provides information, games, and activities on her site. In addition, Hedgy, a character in her books, reads a story in a gravelly, hedgehog voice.

Computers also allow children to communicate with others from around the world, providing another authentic opportunity to read and write. Younger children might share digital pictures and drawings with pen pals.

Although there was initial concern that computers might decrease children's oral language, research shows that children use similar amounts of language at the computer center as they do at other learning centers (Kelly & Schorger, 2001). Children often engage in self-talk as they first figure out how to use the computer. They then progress to using communication to solve problems and to discuss cause and effect (Bhargava & Escobedo, 1997).

To Support Social Studies. Computer programs and the Internet can expose children to a world beyond their normal experience. For example, they can learn about and communicate with children from other places. Clark (1998) describes how four teachers (prekindergarten, kindergarten, and first grade) electronically linked their classrooms. The children helped to develop websites, choosing items to place on the site and favorite links to share. The children also shared information through e-mail, asking each other questions such as, "How many of you have pets?" In developing websites, children have the opportunity to think about what makes their community unique and how to capture that uniqueness to share with others.

To Support Science. Computers can support science learning in a variety of ways. For example, a second-grade class in Atlanta was studying marine life. They enriched their learning through a variety of technological activities.

- The children played a simulation game called *Odell Down Under,* where they became a fish and tried to survive in the ocean.
- They completed a web quest called Marine Life (Kadee McLaughlin, 2006). The web quest began by telling the child that one day she woke up to find that she had become a sea creature in her sleep. As she worked with her peers, she needed to figure out what marine animal she represented, how to survive, what she needed to eat, and who her enemies were.

- Before visiting the Georgia Aquarium, the children viewed webcams of the fish and learned about the fish through an online animal guide. Because of this exposure, they were prepared with a detailed list of questions to ask on their field trip.

- Working in pairs, the children wrote factual stories about a favorite sea animal using an online children's encyclopedia and pre-selected Internet sites (many featuring streaming videos) as references. They illustrated their storybooks and placed them in the class library for their classmates to read.

To Support Math. Computers can be successfully used with young children for a variety of math purposes, including self-guided instruction, exploration, problem solving, practice, and manipulation of math objects (Sarama & Clements, 2002). One advantage of using the computer for math is that children can manipulate math objects and easily save their work so they can continue it over a period of time. For example, when creating designs, they can continue to modify and add to them.

Several software programs have been developed to help young children learn math skills. One of these is *Building Blocks,* which combines manipulative and print activities, supported by computer learning. *Building Blocks* software provides activities and games including open-ended activities. Children's learning is scaffolded through a sequenced set of activities that provide needed encouragement and prompts as children progress through the program. This is a research-based, organized curriculum that helps to link children's formal and informal math knowledge. Research shows large gains for children who use the program versus those who do not (Sarama & Clements, 2004).

Special Considerations for Infants and Toddlers

Many experts do not recommend computer use for children under the age of 3 (Haugland, 2000; Scoter et al., 2001). However, infants and toddlers can take advantage of other forms of technology such as tape players, overhead projectors, and light tables.

Jennifer Whited from the Ohio University Child Development Center implemented a project on light with children age 6 months to 3 years. Over a period of time, they experimented with different types of technology, such as a light table. They examined different objects such as transparent blocks, colored dishes, and bottles filled with tinted water. Transparent tissue paper was used to create designs. They painted, mixed colors, and experimented with clay, discovering how they looked on the table.

Jennifer and her colleagues eventually established a separate room for the exploration of light that included different types of technology such as a light table, an overhead projector, flashlights, rope lights, and battery-operated lanterns. They added a variety of props for experimentation (transparent materials, fabric, fishing line, art media, hair gel, ribbons, and mirrors). Dark curtains shaded the windows and sheer dark fabric was suspended from the ceiling to darken the room and help children to focus on the light source. They continued to experiment with a variety of media such as drawing with markers, painting with watercolors, and making designs in shaving cream on the projector. Eventually the children understood that the design they were creating was the same as that transmitted onto the wall. Children also made designs with colored glue on Plexiglas and tissue paper on clear contact paper. The children placed their creations on the overhead projector enhancing the beauty of their designs. As stated by Whited, "Infants have a natural ability to reinvent the ordinary; boxes become houses, baskets become boats and plastic bottles become wonderful instruments. On the light table, plastic cups and plates become glowing blocks to build with" (2003, p. 39).

Apply Your Knowledge   List reasons why computer use is considered inappropriate for children under 3.

Teachers' Facilitation of Learning Through Technology

Teachers often take a hands-off approach to teaching technology. However, when teachers scaffold learning, children's knowledge increases. For example, children learn significantly more about computer technology and increase cognitive skills such as abstract thinking, vocabulary, planning, and visual motor coordination with teacher mediation (Shute & Miksad, 1997). Without teacher intervention, children often resort to trial and error "that is devoid of task conceptualization" (Samaras, 1996, p. 133).

Instruct, Model, Select Appropriate Technology, and Facilitate

According to Davis and Shade (1994), the teacher plays the following roles:

- Instructor who becomes familiar with technology, software, and websites. The instructor introduces new materials and software to children, providing initial instruction so that all children have an equal playing field. The instruction might be individual or small group. To be the most effective, children need to have the chance to actually use the technology while being instructed (Haugland, 1997).

- Role model. The teacher uses the computer and other technologies as classroom tools (creates portfolios, class books, classroom signs, and so on). Many schools are now creating electronic child portfolios that can easily be stored over a period of time. In many cases the portfolio is added to throughout the child's schooling years. The electronic portfolio can be easily shared with families, administrators, children, and future teachers. It also allows the insertion of video and sound recordings. As children and teachers work together on the creation of the portfolios, teachers have the opportunity to model the use of technology.

- Critic. The teacher carefully selects appropriate technologies, CDs, tapes, software, and websites. The critic thinks about whether this is the best tool to accomplish the goal. Is there value added by using technology?

- Mentor and facilitator. The teacher is a "sensitive observer, master questioner, and scaffolder of children's learning" (Samaras, 1996, p. 133). According to Nir-Gal and Klein (2004), the facilitator helps children to

  - focus on the task or the problem to be solved

  - expand their learning through discussion of what is happening, linking the learning to past experiences and knowledge, asking thought-provoking questions, providing challenges (What would happen if . . . ? Can you think of another way of . . . ?), discussing the thinking process, and helping children to predict outcomes

  - experience success

  - promote positive feelings through encouragement

  - regulate their behavior

Observe and Document Individual Children's Learning

It is important to observe and document children's technological learning to provide appropriate experiences, determine ways to facilitate their learning, and to document their current competency and growth in relation to technology. When observing children using technology, consider the following questions:

- Is the child able to effectively use the device (for example, turn the computer on and off, complete an activity independently and problem solve if an issue arises)?
- Does the child follow the rules for technology use (taking turns, treating materials respectfully)?
- Does the child use ergonomically correct posture?
- Does the child interact with others while using technology (discusses work with others, provides assistance, asks questions, shares ideas, works cooperatively)?
- What software can the child successfully use?
- Does the child use a systematic approach or a trial and error approach when using the device?
- Can the child use the tape or CD player to listen to her favorite tapes, to record a story?
- What activities does the child participate in at the light table or overhead projector?

Meet the Needs of All Learners

It is important that all children have the opportunity to become proficient in using the computer and other forms of technology. We will examine the digital divide where inequities exist due to race, parental educational levels, and income. We will also look at the ways that technology is being used to support learners with special needs.

The Digital Divide. Inequities in access to computers have created "the digital divide." While the digital divide is decreasing, computer and Internet use is still more common for Caucasians and Asians than for African Americans and Hispanics (U.S. Department of Commerce, 2004).

Children who have more highly educated parents are also more likely to have computer access. For example, children who have a parent who did not complete high school have a 35% rate of computer access in their homes compared with 88% if one parent attended graduate school. Higher family incomes are also associated with greater computer access. For example, 37% of children have home access if family incomes are below $20,000 and 88% of children in homes with incomes over $75,000 have computer access (DeBell & Chapman, 2006).

The children who do not have computers at home typically have at least some access to computers at school (DeBell & Chapman, 2006). There is still concern, however, that school computer use and software may vary based upon the socioeconomic status of the children attending the program. Programs serving low-income children use the computer for more drill activities while peers in higher income programs use the computers for problem solving. Using the computer for problem solving is found to have more positive academic impact. In addition, in some programs better-behaved children have more access to computers, since computers are used as rewards (NAEYC, 1996). As teachers, it is important that we assure that all children have equitable access to technology, especially those that might not have access in their home environments.

Technology as a Support for Children with Special Needs

Technology may be especially important for children with special needs, "Technology can be a powerful compensatory tool—it can augment sensory input or reduce distractions; it can provide support for cognitive processing or enhance memory and recall; it can serve as a personal "on demand" tutor and as an enabling device that supports independent functioning" (NAEYC, 1996, p. 13). For example, one study showed that a group of children with mild to moderate disabilities gained skills more rapidly in all developmental areas after the introduction of computers. Children's attention spans were also improved through using the computers (Hutinger, Rippey, & Johanson, 1999). Children who had behavior problems and those having autism exhibited less negative behaviors and communicated more while using the computer (Hutinger et al., 1999). Although there is potential for computers to assist children with disabilities, inadequate training and cost often prohibit the realization of this (Hasselbring & Glaser, 2000).

The teacher plays an important role in children's successful learning through technology. The teacher is an instructor, a role model, a critic who chooses appropriate technology, and a mentor and facilitator. She observes and documents children's individual learning and assures that she meets the needs of all learners.

With thoughtful planning, children can use technology as a tool of inquiry to answer questions, to enhance creativity, to see things in a new way, or to bring items to life (Mitchell, 2007). Integrating technology into the curriculum can provide children with highly motivating activities that promote their development, while preparing them for the future. By increasing our knowledge of appropriate technology resources and programs, we can be more effective in facilitating learning for all children, including those with special needs.

Sample Application Activities

1. Visit one of the Internet sites listed in this chapter. Make a list of ways that you could use the site.
2. Think of a topic of study. Look for technology and media that will support the topic.
3. Use the software evaluation in Figure 15.1 to critique three popular software programs for children.
4. Observe a classroom. What technology is being used? How is the adult supporting the children in using technology? Use the Environmental Assessment in Figure 15.2 to critique the environment.
5. To read several articles about computers and children, visit The Future of Children website at http://www.futureofchildren.org/pubs-info2825/pubs-info_show.htm?doc_id=69787

☐ Are there a variety of technology devices in the classroom that are available for children's use (computers, tape players, CD players, overhead projectors, light tables, digital cameras)?

☐ Can technology devices be used independently by the children?

☐ Do technology devices have the needed materials to make them effective such as tapes for tape players, paper, and extra ink cartridges for printers?

☐ Are the materials organized and easily accessible (stored within reach)?

☐ Are ideas for usage posted near the electronic device?

☐ Are there enough devices (computers, tape players) to prevent long waits?

☐ Is there a management system to provide equal access to technology?

☐ Are electronic devices used in a safe and healthy manner (earphones, proper light, cords placed to reduce tripping, no extension cords)?

☐ Is the computer center ergonomic (adjustable 18–26 inch workstation or footstools, monitors directly in front of children below child's eye level, keyboard and mouse 3 to 4 inches lower than a computer desk with children encouraged to keep wrists straight)?

☐ Are computer programs loaded on the computer with easy to read icons?

☐ Is there at a minimum a drawing program and word processing program on the computer?

☐ Is there a mouse available for the computer?

☐ Is a keyboard available for older children?

☐ Is there a separate computer folder so that children can store their work?

☐ Are computers placed so that children can see them throughout the room?

☐ Is computer usage monitored?

☐ Is the technology area designed to encourage social use (two or three chairs at the computer, multiple earphones for tape or CD player)?

☐ Is media developmentally appropriate?

☐ Is media free from bias?

☐ Does media introduce children to other cultures?

☐ Is media high quality?

☐ Are the media and technology devices accessible for children with special needs?

Figure 15.2
Environmental Assessment: Technology

Source: Permission is granted by the publisher to reproduce this figure for evaluation and record-keeping. From Julie Bullard, *Creating Environments for Learning: Birth to Age Eight.* Copyright © 2010 by Pearson Education, Inc. All rights reserved.

chapter 16
Special-Interest Centers

*M*iranda, a new preschool teacher, excitedly began the program year. However, in a few days she tearfully told the director that she was not sure that she could be a successful teacher. She said she had "several children who were out of control and nothing she did seemed to work." She described them as "very noisy, distractible, and destructive." The director agreed to observe the children and the environment. After the observation, the director and Miranda had a conference. The director suggested that Miranda add a classroom physical fitness area and a woodworking area that would provide for the high-energy needs of the children. Since the children were interested in taking things apart, the director also suggested that Miranda establish a special take-apart center. Miranda made these changes. She also began to observe each child more carefully, noting his or her interests and making sure all the classroom centers included materials of high interest to the children. After she implemented these changes, the children became more engaged and the behavioral issues were greatly diminished. Miranda, reflecting upon this, told her director, "I realize that when I initially set up the classroom, I put things out that I liked when I was young. I was a very quiet child who enjoyed passive activities. I had only prepared the environment to meet the needs of children who were just like me."

In this chapter, you will learn about several special-interest centers, including special theme and project-based centers, gyms and indoor physical centers, puppetry centers, cooking centers, and woodworking centers. These centers might occupy their own areas in the classroom or be included into other existing centers (puppetry with literacy, cooking in the science center). They may be permanent additions or used on a rotating basis.

Centers to Support Theme and Project-Based Learning

Project work and theme work usually integrated into existing centers are as illustrated in the following example.

Toddlers at Early Head Start had discovered bugs outside in the play yard and had become very interested in them. Emma, their teacher, brought some of the insects inside and placed them in a magnifying jar in the science center for temporary viewing. The children and Emma also created habitats for some of the different kinds of bugs they caught. These were also placed in the area along with magnifying glasses. The habitats allowed the insects to be on display for longer periods before the children released them outside. Emma also created a book containing pictures of insects found in the local area. Some of these were pictures she took herself, as children pointed out bugs on their walks or in the play yard. Collection items such as jars, nets, and a turbo vacuum bug catcher were also housed in this area.

Emma also added books on bugs and insect puppets to the reading area and an insect matching game and plastic bugs to the manipulative center. Because the children were very interested in pretending to be bugs, she also added bug costumes to the dramatic play center. She had purchased these inexpensively after Halloween. By changing the science center and adding materials to other existing centers, Emma was able to support the children's interest in insects.

However, sometimes, because of the nature of the project or the materials, a separate center is established.

Tessa, a teacher in a multi-age preschool classroom, lived in a community that had been plagued with forest fires. Recently, several houses had been evacuated and many families were being housed in a temporary shelter in the city hall. Many of the children had witnessed a helicopter filling a bucket with water from a nearby pond and flying with it. Children in Tessa's class were very worried and had many questions about the fire, the firefighters, and what happens if you have to leave your home. The group decided to make this the focus of their project and began to make a list of questions that they wanted to investigate. Since many of the questions focused on how the fire was fought, Tessa called the local ranger district to see what materials and tours might be available. She was told that the children could see a wild-land firefighting engine, tour a helicopter, and visit with a member of the helitack crew. In addition, a retired firefighter was willing to demonstrate the clothing, tools, and fire shelters that were being used. They could also let the children try some food from MREs (meals ready to eat). At the conclusion of the visit, the firefighter lent the program several props to display, including clothing, canteens, some tools, a fire tent, and MREs. Tessa wanted children to be able to look at the materials; however, they were not suitable for play. She decided to establish a special firefighting display and information center. The center included the authentic forest fighting equipment and tools, books on forest fires, pictures of the fire from the local newspaper, pictures of the city hall shelter, and a computer with information and streaming video on forest fires in their area. The children's questions and the answers they had discovered were also posted in this area.

In addition to this special display and information center, Tessa added materials to several existing centers. For example, she added firefighter and family finger puppets and a shoebox puppet stage to the literacy center. Model helicopters and firetrucks were added to the block center. The children and Tessa changed the dramatic play center into a firefighting camp that contained a dispatch center with a telephone and radios, clothing and backpacks, and firefighting tools created by the children.

Go to MyEducationLab and select the topic "Curriculum." Under Activities and Applications, watch the video *Birds: Parts 1 & 2.*

Emma and Tessa provide two examples of how project and theme work can be supported by the classroom learning environment. To see another example of the project approach, watch the video *Birds: Parts 1 & 2* on MyEducationLab. Pay special attention to the environmental changes that were made to support the project. Also note how art is used to enhance and demonstrate the children's knowledge in this project.

In these cases, the teachers used existing centers to support the topic. However, in Tessa's case it was also necessary to provide a special center. In some cases, teachers feel they must add materials to every center when they change to a new topic. However, this is not necessary. Instead, it is more important to determine what materials will assist children to learn about the topic and where these materials might logically be placed. The materials added, the centers used to support the project, and the need to add additional centers will vary based upon the topic.

Indoor Physical or Fitness Center

Physical activity is essential so that young children can develop motor skills and maintain a healthy lifestyle. Childhood inactivity is contributing to the rising rate of obesity in children (Sanders, 2002). Obesity places children both at immediate and future risk of Type II diabetes, high blood pressure, high cholesterol, orthopedic problems, gallbladder disease, sleep apnea, stroke, and premature death (Lynn-Garbe & Hoot, 2004, p. 74; USDHHS, 2001). For additional information about obesity and the critical need for physical activity see Chapter 17.

The National Association for Sport and Physical Education (NASPE) recommends an accumulation of 30 minutes per day of structured physical activity for toddlers and 60 minutes per day of structured physical activity for preschoolers and elementary age children (2002). In addition, they recommend that children participate in one to several hours a day of unstructured physical activity. Gyms or fitness centers can be one way to meet this need.

Establishing the Indoor Physical Activity Space

How you set up and use your indoor physical area will depend upon your answers to the following questions:

- What is the developmental level of the children?
- How much space is available for the center?
- Is the space a dedicated gross motor area or is the space dual purpose?
- Can you permanently set up the space or do you need to put away all the materials at the end of the session?
- What is the need for indoor gross motor? Are children able to play outside daily? Is the outside space established to promote physical activity?

Indoor physical centers might be placed in any large area such as a gym, lunchroom, or hallway. Generally, you will set up stations (similar to learning centers in the classroom) in this space. It is best to use the perimeter of the room for the stations, allowing several feet of space between each activity (Sanders, 2002). It is important that storage space is readily available. Hooks and shelves for storage at each station can make both set-up and clean-up more convenient (Sanders, 2002). However, if the space is a hallway or lunchroom you will need storage cabinets or closets for storing materials. For example, the Meadowlark Center has rolling carts and tubs that house materials for each of their six typical stations.

Indoor physical activities should be developed around the motor skill categories: locomotion skills such as running, hopping, skipping; stability skills such as bending, jumping, stretching, and balancing; and manipulative skills such as catching, throwing, rolling, and kicking. Ideally, if all the children are using the space concurrently, six to eight activity stations (or at a minimum one station for every three children) will be available (Sanders, 2002). Each station will typically focus on one or two skills such as throwing a ball at a target (Sanders, 2002). It is imperative that each station has enough equipment so that the children using the center will not have to wait for a turn (at least one ball per child at the target throwing center). When planning the stations, it is essential to consider the need for active adult supervision. Most centers will need to be planned so that children can complete the center independently, freeing the teacher to actively supervise the group.

Goodway and Robinson (2006) advocate that the teacher also establish a classroom physical fitness center. Ideally, this space is in a corner of the room. If a dedicated space in the classroom cannot be established, you might consider setting up a special gross motor activity each day in the circle area. Classroom fitness centers allow children to increase the overall time available to participate in physical activity and to practice motor skills. It also meets the needs of children with high levels of energy. Many of the activities listed in the next sections are appropriate for either a classroom fitness center or fitness stations in a gym.

Sample Fitness Materials and Activities: Locomotor

Following are suggestions for materials that you might include at fitness stations. Varying the materials helps to keep children interested while also creating new challenges.

Materials for jumping and hopping

- Bubble wrap to jump or hop on.
- Several hoops or circles to use for jumping or hopping from circle to circle. Lisa, a teacher of multi-age children, made laminated colored circles and then glued a bath mat with suction cups underneath each circle to prevent slipping on the linoleum floor.
- A box platform or aerobic step stairs to jump or hop onto and off of.
- Foam noodles that are taped to the floor or made into a low hurdle by placing the noodle on a cone that has been cut for children to jump over (McCall & Craft, 2004).
- Hanging objects that children can bump into as they jump.
- Secured mats for broad jumping.
- A timer so children can hop as far as they can before the timer goes off.
- Hopscotch squares. Karl, a teacher of kindergarten children, cut pieces of rug into small squares and wrote numbers on the back of each square. Children can place the rug squares into a hopscotch pattern or any other pattern that they choose. They use these on a carpeted surface. Having the rug square carpet face down prevents slipping.

Materials for walking and running

- A walking path with contact paper footsteps that show toes pointing in, toes pointing out, giant steps, short steps, etc.
- Pictures on cards of different types of walking such as uphill, downhill, lifting knees high, with floppy legs, with stiff legs, as if on ice, and on tiptoes. Children can draw a card and walk in the way shown from one side of the center to the other.
- A piece of tape or a 2 × 4 that children can use for walking heel to toe (as children become more proficient, they can walk backwards).
- An egg timer and mat so children can run in place until the timer goes off.
- A recorded drum beat, including fast and slow beats, beats that start and stop, for children to walk and run to.
- A course made from highway cones for children to run through.
- A course made of hanging empty plastic bottles with bells inside. The child tries to go through the course without ringing any bells or tries to ring every bell.

Materials for galloping and skipping

- A recorded drum beat or music with a skipping beat.
- Stick horses to ride.
- Music to gallop or skip to.

Materials for climbing

It is critical that climbing equipment have appropriate protective surfaces under them. See Table 17.2 for information on appropriate surfaces.

- Climbing structures.
- A climbing rope attached at both the top and bottom.
- A climbing wall mounted on the side of the gym.

Materials that combine movements

- Streamers or scarves, and music for dancing.
- Dance or exercise videotape.
- An obstacle course (such as a tunnel to crawl through, jumping platform to jump from, stick horse for galloping to a balance board, footsteps indicating running to the end of the gym).

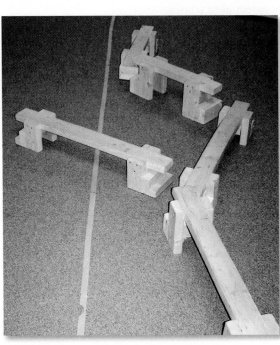

These teacher-made balance beams are used each day in the kindergarten hallway. When not in use they are stored under the hallway benches.

Sample Movement Materials and Activities: Stability Skills

Materials for bending and stretching

- Photos of children in yoga poses that children can copy.
- Activity records.
- Scooter boards for moving across the room.

Materials for balancing

- A timer that children can set to practice balancing on one foot. To help children remember the activity, Bellanca places a timer and a picture direction card in a basket. The picture direction card first shows a child setting the timer on one minute.

The next picture shows the child balancing on one foot. The next picture shows the child jumping in the air in a celebratory pose.

- Balance picture cards that children can follow. As children become familiar with following photos, you can make the pictures more abstract by replacing the photos with stick people, and eventually symbols such as an × for arms and feet spread apart.
- A balance beam—can be a 2×4 on the floor or a piece of tape. As children become more proficient, you can create additional challenges such as providing a narrower board. Children can also walk backwards or sideways on the board; step over an item like a bicycle tire or a traffic cone on the board; hold an item like a ball or beanbag while transversing the board; move to the center of the board, kneel down, and rise again; or hop on the beam. These various challenges can be provided in picture form.
- Animal cards in a basket that children can draw out and move like that animal.
- Tilt boards for learning to balance on an unstable surface.
- Stilts for walking on.
- Dumbbells for promoting stability skills and also strength and endurance. You can create dumbbells by filling two plastic bottles with sand and attaching one at each end of a dowel or old broomstick (Goodway & Robinson, 2006). Children can lift these from various positions—standing, sitting, lying on the floor, or squatting.

Sample Movement Materials and Activities: Manipulative Skills

Materials for Catching and Throwing. A large, soft ball is easiest to catch while a small light-weight ball is easiest to throw. Until children are proficient at catching and throwing, it can be frustrating for them to throw and catch with each other.

- Scarves for throwing and catching (this is especially helpful for children who are afraid of balls).
- Different sizes, types, and weights of balls.
- Different weights of beanbags. Beanbags can easily be made by cutting a child's pair of pant legs into a bean bag size, filling it with sand, and sewing the ends.
- Scoops such as one made from a plastic milk carton.
- Boxes or baskets for throwing into.
- Suspended hula hoops or a low basketball hoop for throwing beanbags and balls through.
- Targets taped to the wall for throwing at.
- A suspended, empty plastic bottle with a bell inside for hitting with a ball or beanbag (McCall & Craft, 2004).
- Rubber balls and plastic bottle bowling pins—sand can be placed inside the bottles to increase the challenge.
- Paper airplanes for throwing and catching.

Materials for Kicking. It is generally easier to kick a lighter-weight ball.

- A box of balls set near the corner of the room. The child kicks the ball into a corner so that the ball will come back to him.
- Targets to kick at.
- Obstacle course to dribble a ball through.
- Cards showing different parts of the foot—child practices dribbling the ball using that area of the foot.

exercise mats
step exerciser
plastic hoops
balls in a variety of kinds and sizes to meet children's needs
scoops
ribbon sticks
beanbags
balance beam
climbing structure
tunnels or tubes to crawl through
jump ropes
stilts in a variety of sizes for different levels of challenge. You can create stilts from cans
    by removing the tops, punching a hole on each side of the can, and tying on rope.
nylon batters
weights
climbing rope attached at both top and bottom
therapy balls
sweat and wrist bands
fitness books
CD player or tape player for listening to music
rolling boxes to store balls, hula hoops, etc.
wooden boxes or cardboard stuffed with newspapers for jumping platforms

Materials for Striking. The younger the child, the larger the striking object and instrument will need to be.

- Lightweight balls, a highway cone, and a plastic bat for hitting the ball off the cone.
- A foam noodle to bat a cloth-covered balloon or beach ball that is hung from the ceiling (McCall & Craft, 2004).
- A hockey stick and balls for hitting.
- Nerf balls or cloth-covered balloons and racquets. You can create racquets by bending a wire coat hanger into a circular form and covering the racquet with a discarded calf-length nylon stocking. Make sure to bend the handle of the hanger into a loop to prevent eye injuries.

As the preceding sections have illustrated, it is important to have a variety of equipment available to enhance children's physical skills. For a list of suggested physical equipment see Figure 16.1.

Special Considerations for Infants and Toddlers

Physical development rapidly occurs in the infant and toddler years. Children at this age need to practice skills such as climbing onto a couch and getting down repeatedly. Therefore, they need multiple areas in their classroom dedicated to physical development. Some areas infants and toddlers might use to practice their developing skills include classroom climbing structures; tunnels and low rectangular boxes to crawl in and out of; risers, mattresses, low couches, or futons to crawl or step onto; and when ready for the challenge, steps such as a turned over rocking boat to climb or a climbing rail mirror (Greenman & Stonehouse, 1996; Greenman, Stonehouse, & Schweikert, 2007). Climbing rail mirrors feature an unbreakable mirror that is attached to a wall along with a wide ladder, allowing children to see themselves as they climb. Young infants will use this piece of equipment to pull themselves up and look in the mirror. It is important to have mats below the climber. Securely anchored pull-up rails are another piece of equipment that is helpful for infants.

When children become more proficient at walking, push-and-pull toys can provide enjoyment as children practice. If there is room in the classroom, indoor riding toys can also be provided.

Meeting the Needs of Children with Disabilities

Sensory integration disorders are receiving attention in the early childhood field. One of these disorders involves the **vestibular system,** which includes the middle ears. This system allows us to detect movement and change the position of our head accordingly. Children with an over-active vestibular system disorder may be hypersensitive, exhibiting fear in normal situations such as swinging or walking on uneven surfaces. They often appear clumsy. Children may also have an underactive vestibular system, seeking continual vestibular stimulation such as spinning (Hatch-Rasmussen, 1995).

Another sensory disorder involves the **proprioceptive system**. This system provides a person with a subconscious awareness of body position, providing the ability to adjust one's body to new positions. A child with this disorder may have odd posture, look clumsy, fall frequently, lack aware-ness of her body in space, and demonstrate difficulty in planning and organizing motor tasks (Hatch-Rasmussen, 1995). While these disorders must be diagnosed by special-ists such as occupational or physical therapists, there are some activities that can help all children develop these systems. This includes providing ma-terials (available from school catalogs) such as the following that stimulate these areas:

Climbing is a favored activity of toddlers. This wall climber takes little space and provides the advantage of allowing the child to see his reflection.

- Tactile steppingstones
- Moon shoes—little trampolines attached to the feet
- Spinning disks or sit and spins
- Rocker or wobble boards
- Scooter boards
- Bouncing balls for children to sit on and bounce (typically they have a handle)
- Therapy balls or hot dog shaped balls for children to roll on
- Stilts to walk on
- Different types of sensory balls (nylon bath scrubbers, textured balls)

Teacher's Facilitation of Learning in the Fitness Center

For fitness learning stations to be successful, children will need to independently complete most of the activities. To assist children to reach this goal, you will need to introduce each activity over a period of time and assist children to understand how to complete the activ-ity and safely use any equipment. Once you are confident that children can do this, they will be ready for station activities. For successful stations, you will need to do the following:

- Have activities available as children enter the indoor physical fitness area. Some teachers handle this by having one teacher lead the children in a group activity as the other teacher sets up the stations. One or two children designated as helpers for the day assist in the station set up.

- Circulate among stations offering assistance.
- Assess children's progress.
- Provide encouragement.
- Help all children feel successful by:
  - setting up the environment to encourage the right level of challenge. For example, in setting up a center for throwing, you might have different sizes of targets for children to throw at and also encourage children to stand at any distance they wish from the target. Children will usually choose the right level of challenge for themselves, if allowed.
  - avoiding games or activities where children compete with each other.
  - avoiding having a leader choose other children for teammates. This can be an agonizing experience for children who are chosen last.
- Increase physical activity for all children through:
  - avoiding elimination games. The children who go out first are often the ones who need the exercise the most. In addition, these children may feel unsuccessful, increasing their desire to avoid physical activities.
  - analyzing games or activities to make sure they are encouraging activity. For example, in many circle games such as "Duck, Duck, Goose" only two children are running and the rest are sitting still.
  - eliminating waiting by having enough stations and materials.

Children need the opportunity to engage in daily physical activity. As they participate in the fitness center, they improve body composition, enhance physical skills, become more physically fit, and increase cardiovascular endurance, muscular strength, muscular endurance, and flexibility (Pica, 2006).

Puppetry Centers

With the help of a child, an inert puppet comes to life. Puppet centers can be as simple as a shoebox stage with a variety of finger puppets, or they can be as elaborate as a permanently established puppet center housing a variety of types of stages and puppets. Puppets can be placed in a center of their own, or they might be included in the dramatic play, music, literacy, or manipulative centers. The art center can provide materials so that children can create a variety of different kinds of puppets.

How the Puppetry Center Enhances Children's Development

Puppets encourage imaginative, improvisational play, and self-expression. They can enhance a story and encourage language development. Children can participate in informal dialogue, retell a favorite story, or make their puppet dance to the musical beat. Puppets allow children to act out a character causing them to think about how that character might act, what the character might say, and how that character might look. They encourage the child to experiment with a variety of different voices.

Puppets also encourage social and emotional development through allowing children an acceptable way to express feelings, by letting them act out situations that they are currently experiencing, and by helping them brainstorm solutions to current or future problems. Because puppets draw attention away from the speaker, they can encourage the shy or scared child to talk. Many children feel safer when talking to or through a puppet, viewing the puppet as a "nonthreatening, sympathetic friend that can be trusted with thoughts and feelings without fear of ridicule or reprimand" (Hunt & Renfro, 1982, p. 17).

Designing an Effective Puppetry Center

A puppetry center is one way to encourage children to use puppets. An effective puppetry center contains these elements:

- A quiet space away from traffic with enough room for an audience.
- A simple puppet stage. Puppet stages can help to define the puppet area and add a playful touch (Hunt & Renfro, 1982). They can be store-bought or you can make your own by cutting a window out of an appliance box, turning a table onto its side, or creating a fabric curtain that hangs between two chairs. Small stages for finger puppets can be constructed using shoeboxes. Enquiring Minds Child Care created a puppet stage by removing a door from a storage closet and replacing it with a curtain. The teacher cut a hole in the curtain for the puppet play. A flap of cloth over the hole allowed the puppeteers to keep the audience in suspense.
- A variety of puppets for children to use. Puppets can be closely aligned with books, such as a Clifford puppet to go with the Clifford books, or they can be

This outdoor stage encourages children to put on puppet shows.

generic. Animal, people, and insect puppets are especially appropriate for young children. Choose puppets that can easily be controlled by the child, are durable, and, if possible, washable (Hunt & Renfro, 1982).

- Storage that allows puppets to be visible, organized, and protected. You might put hand puppets into puppet tuckers such as milk cartons or soda bottles with the tops cut off, shoe bags, wine racks, or hanging baskets. Finger puppets might be stored in plastic divider boxes, muffin tins, or egg cartons (Hunt & Renfro, 1982).
- Materials for children to create their own puppets. Begin by making one type of puppet using simple materials (puppet made from a sock or paper bag). As children become more proficient, you can add materials to make new types of puppets as well as additional materials for decorating puppets. Children should create puppets that they can use in their productions. For example, it is easy to create a puppet from a box. However, these puppets can be difficult to use. Some puppets that are appropriate for both creating and then using are listed in Figure 16.2.
- A list with pictures of puppet activities that children can act out (look sad, move arm, give a hug, hop, clap).
- Books and tapes that children can use for puppet stories.

Role of the Teacher in Promoting Puppetry

If you have ever seen young children using puppets for the first time, you may have witnessed a scene similar to the following. Puppet number one, "Hi, how are you?" Puppet number two, "I'm fine." Then the puppets proceed to "wham-bam" each other. To prevent this, it is important to support the child's learning through introducing puppetry,

Figure 16.2
Child-Created
Puppets

There are many different types of puppets that young children can make. A few of these are as follows:

- Sock puppets—Children can glue eyes, ears, mouth, etc., onto the sock. For a more sophisticated puppet, children can cut the toe of the sock, and sew in a circle of fabrics to create a mouth.
- Mitten or glove puppets—Orphaned mittens and gloves can also become puppets. The thumb of the mitten can become the jaw allowing movement. Gloves might suggest unique types of puppets such as an octopus. Gloves can also be used for a family of finger puppets.
- Stick puppets—Puppets (often made from paper) attached to a Popsicle stick or rod can become a stick puppet. As children become more sophisticated puppet makers, they can use brads to create moving body parts. They can then attach each body part to a rod, allowing a range of movement.
- Finger puppets—Children can create finger puppets in a variety of ways. They can be made by creating a cone that fits on the finger, becoming the body of the puppet. They also can be created by attaching a small puppet to a felt ring that fits on the finger. The individual finger of a glove can also become the base for a finger puppet. For children who are beginning to create finger puppets, you can make it easier by providing the base (completed cone, felt ring, individual glove finger).
- Paper bag puppets—These puppets, made from small paper lunch bags, use the flap of the bag for the mouth. While these are simple to make, they are more difficult to use than sock puppets.

You will want to supply a variety of materials for decorating the puppets. These might include sequins, beads, discarded jewelry, feathers, movable eyes, buttons, cotton balls, rickrack, ribbon, yarn, pompoms, pieces of fabric, felt, colored foam, construction paper, tag board, markers, needle and thread, brad fasteners, and glue.

After children have created the puppets, encourage them to use the puppets to talk. Puppets can enhance language skills by encouraging children to communicate with others, practice dialogue, and tell stories.

providing information, and assisting children to learn techniques with puppets. To provide a successful puppetry experience you will want to proceed as follows:

- Introduce puppetry to children
  - Model puppet use.
  - Participate in puppet exercises with the children such as making the puppet talk. This can be a group activity with each child holding a generic mitten puppet to use for practice.
  - Have puppeteers visit the classroom.
  - Take children to puppet shows.
- Provide dramas for the puppet to act out. It is often easier for children to begin using puppets by only having to move the puppets without saying the words. As children become more proficient, they can do both.
  - Record the teacher telling a puppet story.
  - Provide recordings of other stories that lend themselves to puppet shows.
  - Provide a variety of books for children to act out with the puppets (*Caps for Sale; Five Little Monkeys Jumping on the Bed; Green Eggs and Ham; Mama, Do You Love Me; Noisy Nora; My Crayons Talk; Silly Sally; Where the Wild Things Are*) (Beaty, 2005, p. 106).
- Participate in puppet activities with individual and small groups of children.

- Renew interest in puppetry by providing new puppets, backdrops, and stories. You can also renew interest by introducing children to a new form of puppetry such as shadow puppetry.

- Use the puppets as a way of communicating with children. Many teachers have special puppets who have well-developed personalities. The puppet becomes a treasured classroom guest, interacting with individual children, small groups, and at times the entire class. The puppet frequently has dilemmas that children help to solve. Children's dilemmas might also be solved by talking to the puppet. Anthony, a teacher in Head Start, often used his wise owl puppet to visit with an individual child who was having a difficult time.

- As children become more skilled at puppetry, they will often begin to develop more elaborate scripts that they will be interested in performing. Make sure that children understand the variety of roles in puppetry. Some children may be interested in making backdrops, turning the backdrops, or writing scripts. In this way, many children can be included in a child-initiated puppet production.

> TIP   To create your own inexpensive puppets for children to use, remove the stuffing from a secondhand stuffed animal.

Puppetry can bring joy to the child puppeteer and the audience, allow avenues for self-expression and creativity, and encourage language. Puppetry can also become an integrated unit of study. In Claudia's third-grade classroom, children became very interested in the puppetry corner. They composed and wrote special stories to perform. Claudia also found that the children were often working cooperatively in designing puppets and backdrops, and in performing. As children displayed interest in the puppets, Claudia decided to make this a topic of study for social studies. She introduced different types of puppets and puppetry that were used throughout the world, showing children short videos and inviting puppeteers to the classroom. As children learned about the puppets, they also learned about stories and traditions from different cultures.

Cooking and Snack Centers

A cooking and snack center may be an established center in the classroom or it may be a center that is only set up for a specific time of the day. For example, Curious Minds Child Care sets up a snack center each afternoon so that children can individually prepare their afternoon snack during choice time. Weeping Willow Kindergarten sets up a snack center for those children who have not eaten breakfast before they come to school.

What Children Learn Through Interacting in the Cooking and Snack Center

When children engage in the cooking and snack area, they learn the following skills (Foote, 2001):

- Food preparation skills such as washing their hands before beginning to cook, measuring and mixing skills, using small appliances, and cooking safety.

- Math skills such as one-to-one correspondence, measuring, fractions, and counting.

- Science skills such as observing, measuring, predicting, physical properties of matter, and changes in matter.

- Literacy skills such as sequencing, left to right progression, word and letter identification, reading for information, and new vocabulary (directional words, sensory words).
- Fine motor skills. Cooking provides the opportunity to use hand strength and co-ordination (kneading, stirring), eye-hand coordination (pouring), and fine motor skills (cutting, peeling, using a melon baller) (Colker, 2005).
- Appropriate nutrition and healthy eating habits. Many children in the United States are not consuming a well-balanced diet. For example, they are eating too much fat and not enough vegetables (Colker, 2005). Food preferences begin when children are very young (Barbour, 2004). However, children are more likely to ex-periment with and taste food they have helped to prepare. Through discussing healthy food choices and providing children opportunities to prepare healthy foods, we can help children to develop lifetime healthy habits.
- Cultural knowledge. Through cooking, children can learn about their own and other's cultures.
- Socio-emotional development. As children cook, they develop initiative, respon-sibility, self-regulation, and a feeling of competence (Colker, 2005).

The cooking and snack center should include the following:

- An attractive place for a small group to sit and eat (you might add a tablecloth and a vase of flowers to the dining table).
- A counter or additional table for preparing the snack or setting out the tasting tray.
- A sink for ease of washing hands.
- A conveniently placed electrical outlet for the occasional use of a blender, toaster, or other small appliance.
- A system for designating the number of children that can use the center at one time. Some programs provide four aprons and require that all the children who are cooking wear an apron, others only set out four chairs at the table with the rule that you can only enter the area if there is an empty chair, others post a sign with the number of children allowed.
- Aprons that are hung on hooks or a child-size coat tree.
- Clean up supplies (covered garbage can, sponges, child-size sponge mop).
- Storage for small appliances, cooking equipment and utensils, and serving utensils.
- Recipe books, food magazines, and blank recipe cards for children to write their own recipes.
- Nutritional information (healthy-unhealthy snack poster, Food Guide Pyramid for Young Children poster).

Appropriate Cooking Center Activities

Many different types of activities can occur in the cooking center. The center might be used for preparing individual snacks (see Figure 16.3 for individual snack ideas), to pro-vide taste trays, or for small groups of children to prepare recipes.

One-Portion Recipes. Individual portion recipes allow many learning opportunities. Chil-dren are able to complete each step themselves, following sequenced directions, measur-ing and mixing ingredients, and finally eating the finished product. Because each child is completing the entire recipe, he is able to work independently as time is available,

Following are nutritious cooking activities that a child can complete independently during center time. None of the recipes involve cooking, so the child can assemble and then immediately eat her creation. These recipes can be tailored to the developmental level of the children. For example, 3-year-old children might assemble kebobs on toothpicks from pre-cut meat and cheese. Older children will be able to cut the meat and cheese into cubes for their kebobs before assembling them. Whenever you are planning cooking activities, it is very important to be aware of allergies in your classroom, so that you can avoid these foods.

These are the easiest recipes. They require few ingredients and involve spreading and mixing, but not cutting or blending.

- Ants on a log—stuff celery with soft cheese and add raisins.
- Ritz or other round cracker with faces created with cream cheese and decorations.
- Plain yogurt with a variety of stir ins (fruit, granola).
- Apple face—spread peanut butter on an apple half and use raisins to create a face.
- Tortilla spread with refried beans and grated cheese.
- Trail mix—mixture of raisins, nuts, dried fruits, cereal.

These recipes require children to follow more steps and to cut or blend ingredients.

- Fruit salad—older children can peel the fruit and make melon balls.
- Various types of kebobs—fruit, meat and cheese, cheese and cucumber.
- Peanut butter sandwiches—older children might make their own peanut butter by shelling one-quarter cup peanuts and putting them in the blender with ½ tablespoon of vegetable oil. Make sure you check for peanut allergies before you do this activity.
- Smoothies—usually contains milk, fruit, and yogurt.
- Peanut butter balls—mixture of peanut butter, honey, and dried milk, rolled in rice krispies.
- Ice cream for one—see the recipe in Figure 16.4.
- Pudding in a jar—shake 1 tablespoon plus 1 teaspoon of pudding mix in a baby food jar with ¼ cup milk.
- Boiled eggs to peel—after children have peeled the egg, they can follow the recipe to create egg salad sandwiches or deviled eggs.
- Peel carrots and make an individual portion of spinach dip.
- Raw vegetables with individually child-prepared bean or cottage cheese dip.
- Carrot raisin salad.

For additional recipe ideas, see *Cup Cooking, Individual Child-Portion Picture Recipes* by Barbara Foote or *The Cooking Book* by Laura Colker.

Figure 16.3
Examples of Individual Portion Recipes That Do Not Require Cooking

making it a perfect center activity. In addition, the child decides when he is hungry and prepares and eats the snack at that time rather than at a predetermined time established by someone else. This helps to establish a "healthy approach to eating" (Colker, 2005, p. 7). Occasionally, you may have a child who is compelled to overeat if food is continually available. In this case you will want to closely monitor the situation.

Recipes should be chosen that children can complete themselves during the allocated time, that they will enjoy eating, and that are nutritious, meeting childcare food program guidelines for a snack. Independent recipes are most successful if they can be completed in a few steps. Place each step of the recipe on a large index card that includes printed directions along with pictures or photos. You may want to laminate the cards to keep them for future cooking activities. Lay the cards out from left to right, beginning with a card that reminds children to wash their hands. Place the needed ingredients and measuring devices

Figure 16.4
Recipe for an
Individual Portion
of Ice Cream

1 small plastic freezer bag
1 large plastic freezer bag
½ cup milk or half and half
1 tablespoon sugar
¼ teaspoon vanilla
Ice cubes
6 tablespoons rock salt

Combine the milk, sugar, and vanilla in a small plastic freezer bag. Securely seal the bag. Combine the ice and salt in the large bag until the bag is half full. Put the small bag inside the large bag and then seal the large bag. Shake the bag until the mixture thickens. When the mixture is the consistency of ice cream, take the smaller bag from the large bag and enjoy. If children have a long-handled spoon they can eat the ice cream out of the plastic bag.

above each card. If the child is using measuring spoons or cups for more than one direction, it is helpful to have enough measuring devices that there can be one placed with each direction. See Figure 16.4 for a recipe that makes an individual portion of ice cream.

Taste Trays. Taste trays often provide three or more types of food for children to sample. At least some of these foods may be new to the children. The chosen foods often share some characteristic. For example, the taste tray might include a food item in different states (coconut in the shell, coconut milk, dried coconut). The highlighted foods might all come from one area of the food pyramid (different types of vegetables). Or the food might relate to a particular theme (foods from a certain area of the country, food that grows in trees, foods that are the same color, foods that grow underground) (Colker, 2005).

Taura sets up a taste tray each week in the cooking center. She first discusses the foods that will be present with the children at circle time and allows them to see the food in an uncut form. For example, when they were tasting pineapples, she passed the pineapple around the circle where the children smelled it and felt the bumpy skin and prickly leaves. She then cut the pineapple open so they could see the core and flesh. She then placed the fresh pineapple chunks, along with canned pineapple chunks and fried pineapple, on the taste tray.

Small-Group Cooking Activities. Many teachers plan a special small-group, supervised activity in their cooking area each week.

Dominique, a teacher of preschool children, valued the learning that occurred during cooking and had done this for several years. However, she was interested in helping children learn more about the diverse cultures in her community and wondered if cooking could be an avenue to explore culture. One day she and the children ate Irish soda bread for snack. Many of the children were unfamiliar with the bread and had questions about it. Dominique realized that perhaps beginning with breads would be a way to start to learn about different cultures. She invited families and community members to come in once a week and bake bread with the children in the cooking area. They then ate the bread for snack. Over the course of several months the children and their guests made scones (Scotland), tortillas (Mexico), chapattis (India), mandarin pancakes (China), okonomiyaki (Japan), pita bread (Middle East), crumpets (England), challah (Jewish braided bread), diphaphata (Botswana), and American Indian fry bread. Many of the guests also brought in cooking and eating utensils used by their culture, recipe books written in their native language, and other items such as photos of stoves and kitchens to show the children. As the children baked bread, they learned cooking techniques while also learning about other cultures.

Figure 16.5   One-Portion Recipe Setup

Role of the Teacher in the Cooking Center

Children need to be supported in the cooking center by adults who effectively organize the center, supervise it, offer assistance as needed, and promote learning through conversations with children. The adult in the cooking center should do these things:

- Organize the center so that children can use it independently when completing one-portion recipes (individual cards with words and pictures for each step of the recipe, all ingredients available and set out ahead of time beside each card). See Figure 16.5 for an example of how to set up a one-portion recipe activity. Even during small-group cooking experiences, it is important to have a recipe written so that children can follow it and to have all materials ready before beginning the activity.

- Teach the children the skills they need to be successful (demonstrate how to measure ingredients, use small appliances, and use unfamiliar techniques).

- Discuss the food and processes with the children. For example, you can discuss background information about the food, name the food and processes, discuss the attributes of the food such as the texture, ask open-ended questions, and listen to children describe the steps they have taken.

- Be available to offer assistance.

- Make sure the center is safe and healthy (food is kept at the correct temperature to reduce bacteria, children use healthy practices such as replacing a cooking spoon that has been dropped on the floor or has been licked, children use appliances and utensils in a safe manner).

A cooking center allows children the gratifying experience of creating their own snacks while learning about healthy food choices. Children also gain independence and apply literacy, science, and math skills as they cook.

Woodworking and Carpentry Centers

Although many teachers have concerns about the safety of woodworking, advocates stress that woodworking has many benefits and is a safe activity when children are taught the proper use of tools and there is adequate supervision. As children participate in woodworking, they enhance their creativity while practicing eye-hand coordination, large and fine motor skills, mathematical skills (measuring, one-to-one correspondence, angles), and science skills (properties of materials and the use of tools). Woodworking can also increase attention span and perseverance. For example, Thomas, a 4-year-old, normally flitted from activity to activity. However, the combination of a specific goal, obvious visual progress, and the physical activity inherent in woodworking allowed him to stay focused. At times, he spent half an hour working on a construction in the woodworking center. Like Thomas, many children find woodworking to be a preferred activity. Additionally, many programs find that woodworking has caused some of the previously uninvolved families to participate in the program. For example, at Beautiful Beginnings Child Care one father, who is a carpenter, now regularly brings in pieces of wood for the children to use. He carefully chooses wood that will be easy for the children to hammer and saw. He says, "I used to think that there was nothing I could contribute. But now that you've started the woodworking center, I can see a way I can help out." Two grandparents have been volunteering each week to assist in the woodworking center. One of the mothers, who makes wood signs, has invited the class to her workshop.

Young children's first woodworking attempts might be to pound golf tees or large flat-headed nails into Styrofoam. As children's skills increase, they are able to pound nails into wood. For example, in one early childhood program in Hawaii, teachers placed a coconut tree cut lengthwise into the outdoor play yard. Children have pounded nails into the tree for many years.

By the end of the preschool years, most children can develop and follow a plan to create a self-chosen product. They are able to use a variety of tools in their creations and develop these creations over a period of time (Wellhousen & Crowther, 2004). See Figure 16.6 for more information on the developmental stages of woodworking.

Designing the Woodworking Center

Since woodworking is noisy, the center needs to be placed outside or in a noisy area of the classroom. If the center is inside, it might be placed next to the creative art area, so that children can use the art materials to decorate their creations. An effective woodworking center includes the following:

- Enough space for two to four children to work without interfering with each other.
- A sturdy, stable woodworking bench (it should not move as children use it).
- Real tools (you might choose smaller-sized options). Appropriate tools for preschool and elementary children include hammers, pliers, vise grips, metal clamps,

Figure 16.6
Seven Developmental Stages of Children's Woodworking

Stage One—Becoming acquainted with tools and wood. Children in this stage are exploring wood and tools. They might pound nails into a piece of wood simply for the joy of pounding.

Stage Two—Making simple skill attempts. In this stage, children begin to hammer, saw, and glue. They will attempt to make projects. For example, they might try to connect two pieces of wood by nailing them together. However, they often are not successful.

Stage Three—Developing simple constructions. As children become more proficient in woodworking, they are able to design and build simple constructions.

Stage Four—Refining skills. After children have built many constructions, they may begin to refine their skills. For example, they may glue before they nail wood together.

Stage Five—Functional construction. At this stage, children make realistic objects.

Stage Six—Decorative combinations. Children in this stage will preplan their woodworking to intentionally create a project that they can use. For example, they might make a doll bench to use in dramatic play.

Stage Seven—Emergence of craft. In this stage, children try out new ideas, using carpentry for both functional and symbolic ideas (Huber, 1998, p. 75).

This preschool woodworking area has an abundance of tools. Note the storage for ongoing projects.

planes, levels, miter boxes, crowbars, files, handsaws (crosscut, keyhole, or compass), screwdrivers (standard and Phillips), drills (hand drill, brace, and bits), rulers, and tape measures (Huber, 1998, p. 74).

- An abundance of pieces of soft wood (pine or poplar) that are a manageable size for the age group (Sosna, 2000). Do not use hardwood (too difficult to nail into), plywood (can splinter), or treated wood (can contain harmful chemicals). You can often get free scrap lumber. However, Sosna (2000) recommends buying wood so that you get the type of wood you want.
- Wood glue, nails, screws, duct tape, wire.
- Items for decorating creations (spools, bark, discarded knobs, latches, paint).
- Items to use in building (wheels, latches, knobs).
- Sandpaper.
- Carpentry pencils for marking wood.
- Pencils and paper for drawing plans.
- Well-fitting safety goggles, work gloves (prevent blisters when sawing), and carpentry aprons (to hold nails) to provide for safety and convenience.
- A table covered with a plastic tablecloth for painting and gluing.
- Appropriate storage. All storage should be clearly labeled with an outline, photo, word, or in the case of small objects with the actual item (screws, nails).

  - Place for hanging the tools. An outline of the tool allows children to know where to return each one. Avoid toolboxes since it is difficult to find a tool in the box and children can become injured as they dig through the box.
  - Chest with clear drawers for nails and screws.
  - Storage area for wood.

- Shelf containing different baskets for goggles, hard hats (can be used to limit numbers), work gloves, and items that can't easily be hung, such as miter boxes.
- Place for children to display ongoing and completed work.
- A magazine stand to provide storage for books of woodworking ideas, tool catalogs, and binders containing photos of children's woodworking process and products. A wall-mounted magazine stand can be used to save room.

Role of the Teacher in the Woodworking Area

Teachers play a crucial role in the success of the woodworking center through establishing an effective center, keeping the center stocked with materials, providing instruction and encouragement, and teaching and monitoring for safety. In the woodworking area teachers do the following:

- Introduce the tools (provide the name, discuss when you would use the tool, and demonstrate the proper usage of the tool). You may want to introduce one tool at a time, allowing children the opportunity to become competent with that tool before introducing another. Often the first tool introduced is a hammer.
- Encourage safety rules (wearing goggles when using tools, using the tools in a responsible manner, keeping the work area clean, putting tools away when done, following the work area participant limit signs).
- Provide inspiration through visits to lumber yards and woodworking shops, allowing children to see tools being used in the real world (Huber, 1999). You can also invite carpenters and other woodworkers to visit the classroom.
- Keep the area interesting by adding new materials and tools and presenting challenges.
- Document children's woodworking process and products with photos. Many teachers create a book of the constructions.
- Provide encouragement for children to make creative constructions and, as they become more skilled, to follow a plan. Typically, children will design and build their own constructions. However, at times it is appropriate to have a model for children to follow so that they can learn to follow a plan that includes structured steps (Sosna, 2000). This can allow children to have a successful building experience. "Woodworking has not only a creative side but also a more structured side— following a design, pattern, set of instructions, or model" (Sosna, 2000, p. 38).
- Offer assistance so that the child can be successful (such as helping the child choose the appropriate tool for the job, assisting the child to use the tool in an effective manner such as pointing the saw down at an angle).
- Discuss constructions with children (ask children about the process used, the steps in the process, their next steps for continuing the project, and their challenges).
- Provide new vocabulary while talking with children (names of tools, types of wood, processes).
- Provide appropriate woodworking activities. Beginning woodworking activities need to be designed to acquaint children with tools and wood. It is important to provide activities that allow early success. These might include activities such as
  - nailing flat-headed nails into Styrofoam. You can provide colorful paper designs that children can nail around to increase motivation.
  - sawing pieces of Styrofoam. As children become more competent, they can begin to saw soft wood.

- using wood glue to create sculptures.
- sanding pieces of wood.
- nailing pre-set nails into wood and then pulling them out.

As children become more competent with woodworking, you will want to provide the additional tools and materials they need to be successful. For example, children might be interested in creating a particular product such as a bird house. You might provide some pieces of wood containing cut-out holes so that children can use them for their birdhouses. You might also provide simple plans or pictures of different types of simple birdhouses that the children can use for inspiration and guidance.

> TIP   To hold the nail steady, you might insert the nail through a large-tooth comb. The child can then hold the end of the comb. Alternatively, you might insert a piece of cardboard that will support the nail but will be torn away after the nail is securely imbedded in the wood. Teachers might also use an awl to punch a hole for setting the nail.

Woodworking is an engaging center for both children and families. This center, where children get the chance to practice real-world skills, "incorporates all the values that educators want to develop, including self-esteem, social skills, creativity, and physical abilities" (Foster & Hardison, 2000, p. 1).

Providing special interest centers can meet children's unique needs while providing many additional learning opportunities. Special interest centers can also help to prevent boredom. This is especially important for children who might be spending multiple years in the same classroom.

Sample Application Activities

1. Brainstorm a list of other special-interest centers. Choose one center and make a list of materials that would support the center.
2. Visit an early childhood classroom and observe the amount of physical activity that children receive during the day. Are they receiving the recommended amount? What options do you see for increasing indoor physical activity within the space?
3. Develop a cup-cooking recipe. Try the recipe with a group of children.
4. To learn more about puppetry throughout the world and how to create and use puppets, see the puppetry home page at http://www.sagecraft.com/puppetry/.
5. Develop a puppet show that you can use to introduce children to puppetry.
6. Observe a teacher who is using the project approach. What learning materials does she add to support the project?

chapter 17
Creating Outdoor Environments

*T*he playground at Sunshine Academy, a preschool program, was too small and was cluttered with materials that the children did not use. While there was a heavy focus on physical development, few other outdoor learning centers were available. However, even the physical area was not fully developed. The equipment consisted of small plastic climbing sets that did not create developmental challenges for the children. As a result, children often used the equipment in unintended, unsafe ways. Additionally, none of the equipment developed upper body strength. There were few natural materials in the playground and the ground cover, once grass, had become mainly dirt. When it rained or the snow melted, the playground became a muddy bog.

Three years later the playground is blooming with flower and vegetable gardens, new trees have been planted, and a variety of ground surfaces (sand, wood chips, pavers, grass) are evident. The playground, now much larger, is zoned into different areas and can be used in all types of weather.

To develop gross motor skills, tires are embedded on their side to create a tunnel, and different heights of stumps are upended to form a place to climb on and jump from. An extensive white cedar play set offers climbing, sliding, and swinging opportunities. A climbing wall, overhead ladder, fire pole, and knotted climbing rope all increase upper arm strength and development.

Creative arts are enhanced through a music area that is attached to the fence and an art studio that is tucked under a tree. A small house and a golf cart with wheels removed create dramatic play opportunities.

The gardens and a bird feeder attract birds to the playground. The bird feeder is hung in the tree with a rope and pulley, making it easier to fill the feeder while also teaching about simple tools. Under the tree sits a small table that contains binoculars and a bird book for watching and identifying birds. A small cabinet that can be locked at night contains other equipment for watching and investigating (magnifying glasses, bug jars, and butterfly nets). A hammock and a basket of books are also under the tree, providing a quiet retreat area.

The evolution continues. While the playground currently contains a construction area and a water table, further development of these areas is planned.

How did this transformation occur? First, the program developed a long-term plan. The plan began with what children needed and were interested in rather than what equipment to buy. A committee of parents, teachers, and administrators met over a period of several months to develop the plan. Children were asked for their ideas, playgrounds were thoroughly researched, visits were made to high-quality playgrounds, and goals and timelines were developed. Critical to the success of the plan was an increase in the size of the playground. There was an area adjacent to the playground that was not being used. Although there had been many previous unsuccessful attempts to obtain this space, the playground research and planning made it easier to convince the manager that this area should be used for the playground. Work was phased in over a period of time. Costs were reduced through donated labor (a youth group helped to bury the tires and stumps, a local college woodworking club built the playhouse) and materials. Finally, the administrator used the research the group had gathered to obtain a grant for the playground structure. Establishing long-term goals by involving all constituencies and seeking help from many sources allowed the program to transform their playground. Planning for children's needs and interests allowed the playground to become a fun, interesting, outdoor classroom filled with learning opportunities.

Value of Outdoor Play

There are many benefits to a well-planned outdoor space. Outside, children can play vigorously, use loud voices, release excess energy, and engage in large, messy projects. In the outdoors, children can experience climate, openness, messiness, wildlife, and different landscapes such as hills, holes, streams, and mud puddles (Greenman, 1991). They can test and strengthen their physical skills and engage in social, cognitive, and creative pursuits. Research indicates that children who play outdoors demonstrate better visual motor integration, imagination, and verbal and social skills than children who play inside (Yerkes, 1982). There are also health benefits to playing outdoors, including opportunities for exercise, exposure to sunlight necessary for the body to produce Vitamin D, and an environment with less-concentrated disease organisms than are found inside (American Academy of Pediatrics, American Public Health Association, & National Resource Center For Health and Safety in Child Care and Early Education, 2002).

The outdoors provides invaluable learning opportunities, promotes health, and encourages lifelong dispositions (Cuppens, Rosenow, & Wike, 2007). However, we need to protect this right to outdoor experiences.

Protecting Children's Right to Play Outdoors

As Rivken (1995), the author of *The Great Outdoors,* states, "Children's access to outdoor play has evaporated like water in sunshine. It has happened so fast, along with everything else in this speed-ridden century that we have not coped with it well. If someone had said to our grandmothers, 'Bet your great-grandchildren won't know where to find worms,' they would not have believed it" (p. 2). There is growing concern about the decrease in children's time outdoors. For example, between 1981 and 1997, the time children between the ages 6 to 8 decreased by 27% (Hoffert & Sandberg, 2000). In one study, 70% of mothers played outside everyday when they were young, while only 31% of their children do (Clements, 2004). Children today have limited opportunities for free play or exposure to nature due in part to a "culture of fear" (White, 2004). Eighty-two percent of preschool and elementary children's parents stated the main reason they do not allow children to play outside is concern about crime and safety (Clements, 2004). Parents are concerned about stranger danger, sun exposure, insect-carrying diseases, and pollution (Pyle, 2002; Wilson, 2000). The recent trend in some elementary schools to eliminate recess so that children can spend more time on academic skills has exacerbated the problem. This lack of free time to play outside has resulted in what some call a "childhood of imprisonment" (Stoecklin, 2000).

The trend to spend less time outside is also a concern in other countries. For example, the lack of time children spend outside, rising obesity, sedentary activities, and the amount of time children spend watching or using electronic media is a concern in Norway and several other Scandinavian countries (Fjortoft, 2001). To counteract this, some kindergartens in Scandinavian countries are provided entirely outdoors. Results show that children in these programs are more creative in play, engage in increased play activities, have less illness, and are more physically fit than their peers (Fjortoft, 2001, p. 112).

To gain full advantage from outdoor play, children need an appropriate space. "Space is the backdrop to play, supplying content, context, and meaning. It is bound to communicate a variety of possible messages to children (Titman, 1994): welcome, dismay, excitement, intimidation, warmth, coldness" (Cosco & Moore, 1999).

History of Playgrounds

Playgrounds in the United States began to appear in the 1800s (Moore, Bocarro, & Hickerson, 2007). Preschool playgrounds were influenced by Froebel, the father of kindergarten, and John Dewey, an American educator and philosopher who emphasized experiential learning. These playgrounds included gardens, sand play, woodworking, natural play materials, and equipment (Dempsey & Frost, 1993; Frost, Brown, Sutterby, & Thornton, 2004). The American parks movement, on the other hand, influenced elementary school playgrounds. These playgrounds emphasized equipment that contributed to physical development and were often placed on flat expanses of pavement or dirt (Dempsey & Frost, p. 316). What planners forgot in designing elementary school playgrounds is that this area is used not only for physical development but is like "the city square" where children meet, play, interact, and socialize (Sebba & Churchman, 1986).

Types of Playgrounds

Playgrounds have evolved from their early beginnings into several different types: traditional, contemporary, adventure, creative, and natural. Each type has advantages and disadvantages.

The traditional playground features fixed equipment such as jungle gyms, designed primarily for exercise. The contemporary playground often contains complex climbing equipment that is more aesthetically pleasing than the traditional. However, it may not be more advanced developmentally.

The adventure playground began in Europe after World War II when a designer noticed that children preferred playing with rubble and scraps rather than on traditional playground equipment. Using scraps of lumber, other building materials, nails, hammers, and saws, children build, design, and manipulate their own play environments. Adventure playgrounds are supervised by play workers or play leaders. While few exist in the United States, more than 1,000 adventure playgrounds exist in Europe (NPR, March 9, 2006).

The creative playground is a combination of contemporary and adventure playgrounds. It contains both equipment and open-ended materials (Dempsey & Frost, 1993).

Natural environments, sometimes called adventure gardens (Fjortoft, 2001), use the natural habitat instead of equipment for learning.

This natural playground provides climbing and balancing surfaces.

> Children want to play in unmanicured places. They want the adventure and mystery of hiding places and wild, spacious, uneven areas broken by clusters of trees and shrubs. In adventure gardens, children can experience other things that live in the outdoors, water/vegetation, including trees, flowers and long grasses; animals, including fish, frogs and other living things; sand; natural color; places and different features to sit in, on, under, and lean against, and that provide shelter and shade; different levels and nooks and crannies, places that offer privacy; structures, equipment and materials that can be changed, actually or in their imaginations. (White, 1997, p. 4)

The adventure gardens include elements such as water play in ponds and bogs, butterfly gardens, mud play, secret hiding places, tree houses, natural obstacles to climb on, animal farms, and musical experiences (White, 1997, p. 4). One example is the Environmental Yard in Berkeley, California.

There are limited research studies comparing child outcomes on different kinds of playgrounds. Furthermore, because these studies have typically compared and contrasted only two types of playgrounds, it is difficult to make comparisons across all types of playgrounds. However, to see the current research that does exist on playground types and child outcomes, see Table 17.1.

Table 17.1 Comparison of Playground Types

Type of Playground	Research Findings
Traditional	Children spend most of their time in physical activity, favors children with high levels of physical skills (Barbour, 1999; Frost & Campbell, 1985; Frost & Strickland, 1985).
Natural environment	More effective in developing motor fitness, balance, and coordination than traditional playground (Fjortoft, 2004).
Contemporary	Encourages children of all ability levels to interact. Children are more passive than in traditional playground. Children engage in more creative and pretend play than when playing on traditional playgrounds (Barbour, 1999; Hart & Sheeham, 1986; Susa & Benedict, 1994).
Adventure	Children engage in play for longer periods of time, engage in more cognitive play activities, participate in a wider range of activities, and participate in more adult interactions than in contemporary or traditional playgrounds (Hayward, Pathenberg, & Beasley, 1974; Moore, 1985).

How Playing in the Outdoors Enhances Children's Development

Children have the opportunity to gain a variety of skills while playing outdoors. These include greater physical fitness, increased exercise, reduced obesity, improved motor development, and enhanced social and intellectual development. They also develop an appreciation for nature. The emphasis on each of these areas will vary depending on the type of playground the child is using.

Physical Fitness

In the United States, 14% of children 2 to 5 years old are overweight (weight for height is equal to or greater than the 95th percentile) and 19% of children 6 to 11 are overweight (National Health and Nutrition Examination Survey [NHANES], 2003–2004). The percentage of overweight children is continuing to rise. For example, the prevalence of overweight children who were 2-to-5-years-old was only 5% in 1976–1980 compared with 14% in 2003–2004 (NHANES, 2003–2004). This increase is found in all ethnic and racial groups in the United States (Lynn-Garbe & Hoot, 2005). Other countries are also struggling with this epidemic. For example, in England nearly 30% of children ages 2 to 10 are overweight (Jotangia, Moody, Stamatakis, & Wardle, 2005).

Children who are overweight have a much greater risk of becoming overweight adults (Lynn-Garbe & Hoot, 2005). Approximately one-third of children who are obese as preschoolers will be obese as adults. Half of all children who are obese in their school years will be obese adults (Serdula et al., 1993). Children who are overweight face both immediate and lifelong health problems, including Type II diabetes, high blood pressure, high cholesterol, orthopedic problems, gallbladder disease, sleep apnea, stroke, and premature death (Lynn-Garbe & Hoot, 2005, p. 74; USDHHS, 2001). Children and adults who are overweight also face social discrimination including being stigmatized and labeled as lazy, stupid, and slow (Deitz, 1998). Peers consider children who are overweight to be less likable (Latner & Stundard, 2003). This discrimination often results in the child who is overweight having a lower self-concept (Davison & Birch, 2001; Smith, 1999). It is important to intervene early both to prevent and combat obesity in children. Intervening early provides immediate health and social benefits and enhances long-term health (Baranowski et al., 2000).

Excluding genetic factors, the strongest predictor for being overweight is lack of exercise (Nelson, Carpenter, & Chiasson, 2006). Early childhood programs can intervene by promoting higher activity levels and improving physical skills. In addition to the immediate advantages of exercise, physical skills and dispositions gained in early childhood can form a foundation for exercise throughout life.

Children engage in higher activity levels and burn more calories when they play outdoors rather than indoors (Sutterby & Frost, 2002). Children who spend more time outdoors are also more physically fit than their peers (Baranowski et al., 2000; Sallis et al., 1993). Ideally, the outdoor time is spent in child-chosen play, since this is the best way for children to accumulate physical activity (Pate, Baranowski, Dowda, & Trost, 1996). "For most children, outdoor play offers the only opportunity to engage in aerobic activities that enhance fitness, strength, flexibility, and endurance and helps compensate for faulty diets" (Sutterby & Frost, 2002, p. 38).

There is a special concern about early elementary children engaging in enough exercise. A study conducted in 2000 found that only 8% of elementary schools provided daily physical education (SHPPS, 2001). In addition, recess is only required in 4% of states (SHPPS, 2001). Most commonly, children have recess for less than 30 minutes per day. Even this amount is currently being decreased due to pressures from "No Child Left Behind" (Castle & Ethridge, 2003; Hardman & Marshall; 2006). Recess can significantly contribute to needed exercise requirements if children participate in moderate intensity play for 40% of the playtime (Ridgers, Stratton, & Fairclough, 2005). In addition, some children, especially those with attention deficit hyperactivity disorder (ADHD), have an increased need for physical activity. Increased opportunities for rough and tumble play may decrease these children's ADHD symptoms (Panksepp, Burgdorf, Turner, & Gordon, 2003).

Researchers have studied several interventions designed to increase playground activity. Successful interventions have included development of obstacle courses (Scruggs, Beveridge, & Watson, 2003); marking playgrounds with mazes, hop scotch, and snakes and ladders (Stratton, 2000); and game intervention (Connolly & McKenzie, 1995). When the ratio of equipment (balls, bats, and jump ropes) to children is improved, children also exercise more (Zask, van Beurden, & Barnett, 2001). Whatever intervention is planned, enjoyment is crucial if children are to continue the activity (Weis & Ferrer-Caja, 2002).

Motor Development

Children in the early childhood years are typically in the **fundamental movement** phase. Fundamental movements include running, walking, hopping, skipping, jumping, galloping, kicking, catching, striking, **dynamic balancing** (balancing while moving), **static balancing** (center of gravity remains stationary), and **axial movement** (such as bending, stretching, twisting, turning) (Frost et al., 2004, p. 25; Gallahue, 1993).

Mastery of the fundamental movements is critical to participate successfully in many recreational games, sports, and activities. If these skills are not mastered, it leads to failure and frustration. While it is possible to learn these skills later in life, "the individual is . . . beyond the sensitive period during which it is easiest to master these skills; as a result, the skills frequently do remain unlearned" (Gallahue, 1993, p. 24). As people get older, they often are more self-conscious about poor skills, fear injury and peer rejection, and must unlearn bad habits, making skill development more difficult (Gallahue, 1993).

While maturation plays a role in the development of movement, it is not enough to assure competence. Children need opportunities to practice skills, encouragement to do so, and instruction (Gallahue, 1993). Free play that includes a range of physically challenging activities and equipment is the best way to provide movement activities (Frost et al., 2004, p. 25). Teachers who interact with children during outdoor free play can provide encouragement and individualized instruction, further enhancing skill development.

Social Development

Children develop social skills as they interact freely with peers, organize games, develop rules for play, and resolve conflicts (Jarrett, 2002, p. 1). As children create their own rules, they learn that rules are "not fixed and immutable but are man-made and refutable" (Elkind, 2006, p. 8).

In many schools, the playground may provide one of the limited opportunities for children to play freely with peers. In addition, playgrounds often combine children from different classrooms allowing interaction with an expanded peer group.

Cognitive Development

Outdoors, children have unique intellectual learning opportunities. Through experience, they learn about the elements (earth, air, water, and fire) and cosmos (sun, moon, stars, and planets) (Elkind, 2006). They learn about **conservation** as they play. "Conservation, the understanding of continuity beneath apparent change, is a fundamental intellectual achievement aided and abetted by out-of-door experiences" (Elkind, 2006, p. 8). Additionally, as children interact in "rich" outdoor learning centers, they have opportunities to participate in math, science, music, art, and literacy, and to engage in communication and problem-solving skills.

Appreciation of Nature

A love of nature, and therefore the desire to preserve it, grows out of a child's frequent contact and play in the natural world (Schultz, Shriver, Tabanico, & Khazian, 2004; Sobel, 2004). If children do not have ample opportunities to play in the natural world in their early childhood years, they may never develop these attitudes (Sobel, 2002). Instead, children develop fears and phobias about nature and the natural world (Cohen, 1984), referred to as **biophobia** (Sobel, 1996). Children not regularly exposed to nature refer to nature as "diseased," "disgusting," and "dirty." They also show fear of plants and insects (Bixler, Carlisle, Hammitt, & Floyd, 1994). Because children often spend 40 or more hours a week in early childhood programs, these places may be "mankind's last opportunity to reconnect children with the natural world and create a future generation that values and preserves nature" (White, 2004, p. 3).

Nature provides differences within sameness. For example, slight changes are found in a babbling brook as water cascades over a little waterfall, becomes narrow through a canyon, or widens around a bend. "These moderate variations in sensory stimulation help maintain optimal levels of mental and physical alertness and foster feelings of comfort and playful attitudes toward events and materials" (Olds, 1987, p. 121).

Children learn to appreciate nature as they care for and observe the many different types of birds that visit bird feeders.

Nature is also often considered a healer. Olds (1989a) interviewed 300 adults and asked them to describe a healing place for a wounded person. Over 75% described outdoor environments. The remaining 25%, although describing indoor environments, still referred to elements related to outdoors. Studies show that nature helps to mediate stress (Wells & Evans, 2003), helps children develop a sense of season (natural cycles), gives children a sense of themselves as nurturers, and provides connection to something timeless and larger than themselves (Bohling-Phillippi, 2006, pp. 49–51).

Natural, ungroomed places are often favorites of children. When asked to recall favorite environments in childhood, adults tend to remember more natural places than other settings (Jenkins & Bullard, 2002). These are often places that they could manipulate (for example, build a fort) (Sobel, 1993).

Some programs have replaced blacktop, building natural environments that feature trees, ponds, and gardens. Studies in one school where this occurred showed that children had fewer playground injuries, and they experienced more joy, pride, and a sense of belonging after the transformation. In addition, there was a greater awareness of the environment (Moore, 1989).

You may be unable to transform the entire playground environment into a natural place. However, Frost et al. (2004) advocate designing a natural area in every playground, even if it is as simple as retaining an unmowed portion of grass to allow for wildflowers.

How do we develop a playground that will promote physical fitness, motor development, social development, and appreciation for nature? Are there other areas of development that can be enhanced through a well-designed playground? We will examine these questions next.

Designing an Effective Outdoor Environment

An effective outdoor environment protects children's safety and health. It also contains an effective playground design, providing enhanced learning opportunities and social interactions. We will have an in-depth discussion of these criteria next.

Provide a Safe Playground

Safety must be a major consideration in designing, installing, and maintaining playgrounds. The goal is to reduce hazards while maintaining challenges. "A hazard is something a child does not see; a challenge is a risk the child can see and chooses to undertake or not. Children need to take risks to challenge their skills and courage. A risk-free play area is neither possible nor desirable" (Kells, 2002, p. 22).

Each year in the United States, 200,000 children under the age of fourteen are treated in emergency rooms for playground-related accidents (Tinsworth & McDonald, 2001). Forty-five percent of these injuries are severe (Tinsworth & McDonald, 2001). Seventy-five percent of nonfatal injuries occur on public playgrounds (Tinsworth & McDonald, 2001). Most of these are in schools or in childcare centers (Phelan, Khoury, Kalkwarf, & Lanphear, 2001). In examining all playground injuries, girls are slightly more likely to be injured than boys (Tinsworth & McDonald, 2001) with children ages 5 to 9 being at greatest risk (Phelan et al., 2001).

There are more injuries on climbers than on other types of playground equipment (Tinsworth & McDonald, 2001) with 60% to 70% of all playground injuries due to falls and approximately 90% of serious injuries due to falls (Frost et al., 2004, p. 79). While many children experience fear that inhibits them from climbing higher than they can safely handle, two groups are at special risk—infants, because they are often not aware of the risk, and children with ADHD characterized by impulsiveness and lack of fear (Frost et al., 2004).

While the majority of injuries occur on public playgrounds, the majority of deaths occur on home playgrounds. Between 1990 and 2000, 147 children died of playground injuries and 103 of these deaths occurred on home playgrounds. Over half of the home playground deaths were caused by strangulation (Tinsworth & McDonald, 2001).

So how can you prevent injuries on the playground? The National Program for Playground Safety (NPPS) stresses S.A.F.E. (supervision, age appropriateness, fall surfacing, and equipment maintenance) as a way of protecting children. After S.A.F.E. was implemented in one school district, there was a 27% decrease in severity and frequency of injuries (Tipping, 2007).

Supervision. Close supervision to assure that rules are followed and that children are not participating in unsafe behaviors is very important. Teachers can also help children to feel emotionally and physically safe by helping to prevent and resolve conflict. Many conflicts can be prevented by having an effective environment and enough materials and equipment. When children do have conflicts that they are unable to successfully solve, it is important that the teacher assist the children in discussing and resolving the conflict.

Age Appropriateness. Nevertheless, while it is crucial to limit serious playground accidents, it is important to allow children to experience physical challenges that are appropriate for their age and developmental level. "Being able to make informed decisions based on previous experience and through learning to manage challenges that are obvious or foreseeable is an important learning experience for a child. It assists in contributing to a child's holistic development, formulating positive self-image as well as competent living skills" (Mitchell, Cavanagh, & Eager, 2006, p. 122).

Children seek physical challenges. If there are no legitimate ways to challenge their skill levels, children will invent their own, sometimes with unintended risk. To meet the needs of children's rapidly developing skills, playgrounds need to contain graduated challenges. For example, teachers can provide balance beams that are different widths.

Fall Surfacing. Since most public playground injuries relate to falls, it is critical that playgrounds have appropriate fall surfacing. In a survey of 1,000 playgrounds, only 25% met this criterion (Weintraub & Cassady, 2002). Appropriate surfaces (see Table 17.2) need to be installed under all equipment from which children could fall, including climbers, slides, swings, seesaws, and merry-go-rounds.

Table 17.2 Surface Materials

To use the table, find the surface material, read across the table to find the height of the equipment, and then read the heading at the top of the table to determine the depth needed. For example, if you have a surface of fine sand and your structure is 9 feet high, you would need 12 inches of uncompressed sand to provide a safe surfacing.

TABLE 1–CRITICAL HEIGHTS (in feet) OF TESTED MATERIALS

MATERIAL	UNCOMPRESSED DEPTH			COMPRESSED DEPTH
	6 Inch	9 Inch	12 Inch	9 Inch
Wood Chips*	7	10	11	10
Double Shredded Bark Mulch	6	10	11	7
Engineered Wood Fibers**	6	7	>12	6
Fine Sand	5	5	9	5
Coarse Sand	5	5	6	4
Fine Gravel	6	7	10	6
Medium Gravel	5	5	6	5
Shredded Tires***	10-12	N/A	N/A	N/A

* This product was referred to as Wood Mulch in previous versions of this handbook. The term Wood Chips more accurately describes the product.
** This product was referred to as Uniform Wood Chips in previous versions of this handbook. In the playground industry, the product is more commonly known as Engineered Wood Fibers.
*** This data is from tests conducted by independent testing laboratories on a 6 inch depth of uncompressed shredded tire samples produced by four manufacturers. The tests reported critical heights which varied from 10 feet to greater than 12 feet. It is recommended that persons seeking to install shredded tires as a protective surface request test data from the supplier showing the critical height of the material when it was tested in accordance with ASTM F1292.

Source: Handbook for Public Playground Safety (U.S. Consumer Product Safety Commission, 1997).

Equipment Maintenance. It is also important that the playground be well maintained. In a study of home child cares, 93% were found to be unsafe, containing debris, unsafe play equipment, and improper ground cover (Brink, Tortolero, O'Hara, Hammond, & Frankowski, 1991). Playgrounds need to be inspected daily for debris or obvious safety hazards. In addition, there should be a regularly scheduled safety inspection to examine all the equipment and measure the ground cover to determine if compaction has occurred.

It is also important to be aware of your state licensing regulations. For example, childcare licensing standards often require that playgrounds be fenced.

Protect Children's Health

As discussed previously, being outdoors provides many benefits to children's health including the opportunity to receive physical exercise. However, there are two potential concerns that we must be aware of so that we can provide protection against them. These are the use of arsenic on playground equipment and ultraviolet rays from the sun.

CCA. Arsenic from chromate copper arsenate (CCA), a pesticide used to treat wood in playground equipment, is a concern on children's playgrounds. The European Union banned CCA for residential use in 2003 (EC, 2003). Beginning in 2004, it became illegal for manufacturers to treat wood with CCA for most consumer uses in the United States (Hatlelid et al., 2004, p. 215). However, many playgrounds still contain CCA. Until the ban, CCA-treated wood was the most common wood used in playground construction (Hatlelid, Bittner, Midgett, Thomas, & Saltzman, 2004). Arsenic can cause skin, lung, and bladder cancer after ingestion (ATSDR, 2000). This is a special concern for young children who may have hand-to-mouth contact. Studies find that children ages 2 to 6 typically ingest half of whatever is collected on their hands (Kwon et al., 2004).

So what can you do if you have a wood playground structure that might contain arsenic? The most effective solution other than removing the equipment is to have everyone who plays on the equipment wash their hands. Washing hands removes most of the arsenic (Kwon et al., 2004).

Ultraviolet Rays. Another outdoor danger is ultraviolet rays. To protect children, it is important to provide shade on the playground. This can include both natural shade from trees and bushes, and human-made shade. Whenever possible, shades should be placed over areas where children will be spending extensive time, such as over platforms and sandboxes. In addition, it is important that all children wear sunscreen with UVB-ray and UVA-ray protection of SPF-15 or higher (American Academy of Pediatrics et al., 2002, p. 51). Sunscreen should be applied to all exposed skin, except eyelids, 30 minutes before going outdoors and every 2 hours while in the sun (American Academy of Pediatrics et al., 2002, p. 137). The American Academy of Pediatrics recommends that if children are playing outside between 10:00 AM and 2:00 PM that they also wear protective clothing, including hats, long-sleeve shirts, and long pants. These need to be light-colored and lightweight in warm weather (American Academy of Pediatrics et al., 2002).

Use an Effective Playground Design

The design of the space is as important outdoors as indoors. Optimal playground design allows the playground to be functional and safe while providing increased learning opportunities and improved social interactions.

Provide Adequate Space That Is Divided Into Zones. Most states require playgrounds to contain 75 square feet of space per child, but most experts recommend a minimum of 100 square feet (Pardee, Gillman, & Larson, 2005). When calculating the square feet needed, you must consider the maximum number of children that will be on the playground at any one time.

Most playground experts suggest that this space should be divided into zones that clearly delineate areas for different activities. Zones help to decrease conflicts, increase ability to focus, make areas more understandable, separate serene areas from more active areas, and keep areas from interfering with each other (Cuppens, et al., 2007). In one study, nearly half of the play occurred in 10% of the playground, that which provided an enclosed area (Kirkby, 1989). Through zoning, we provide many enclosed areas.

The type of zones you plan will be based upon the developmental level of the children that you serve. The NAEYC accreditation standards for early childhood programs require semiprivate areas that accommodate "motor experiences such as running, climbing, balancing, riding, jumping, crawling, scooting, or swinging. Activities such as dramatic play, block building, manipulative play, or art activities; exploration of the natural environment, including a variety of natural and manufactured surfaces and areas with natural materials such as nonpoisonous plants, shrubs, and trees" (NAEYC Program Standards and Accreditation Criteria, 2005). In planning where to place the zones, Pardee et al. (2005) suggest you consider the following:

- Environmental features—shape of the space, the topography, and the placement of natural items like trees. For example, slopes may be used for sliding, trees for climbing or for building a bench around for reading and watching.
- Sun patterns.
- Safety hazards such as overhead and underground lines.
- Points of access. Where will children enter the playground?
- How far will play materials need to be hauled before they can be used? (pp. 3–4)

Zones can be divided using low, fragrant, non-toxic plants (mint, anise); low earth berms; brick walls; or fences from natural materials (Cuppens et al., 2007, p. 7). Zones can also be separated by providing unique surfaces in different areas.

Provide Circulation Paths. Clear routes around the playground prevent children from interfering with other children's play. They also help children to avoid safety zones around equipment. Avoid long straight paths that encourage running. Instead, plan a looping path with no dead ends. By using a variety of materials (such as gravel, shredded wood bark, paving stones, sand, log cookies, or bricks) with different textures, you can create different moods and differentiate zones (Keeler, 2002). Paths can also be individualized by letting children create and decorate their own paving stone.

Design an Exciting Entry. It is ideal if classrooms can open directly onto playgrounds. As stated by Moore, "Progressive childcare programs are run outdoors as much as indoors . . . . Thus the need for wonderful visual and movement connections between in and out—low windows, wide doorways, etc." (2002a, p. 9).

However, if playgrounds do have separate entries, it is important to design the entryway. The entry provides "a visual clue that you are entering a special place" (Cuppens et al., 2007, p. 8). The entry welcomes children, helps to establish a mood, and controls the access into the area, encouraging children to create a thoughtful entry rather than a "mad dash" (Cuppens et al., 2007, p. 8). Entries might contain an arbor, interesting surface texture, or unique entry gate.

Provide Shade and Protection from the Elements. It is important to have protected areas on the playground, to maximize usage and to protect children from ultraviolet rays and inclement weather. Natural shade can be provided under trees or vine enclosures. Shade can also be provided under canopies, umbrellas, awnings, parachutes, or netting covered with leafy branches. Water misters might also be provided to help children cool down in hot climates.

Natural shade protects children from the sun in this appealing outdoor music center.

Include Sufficient Storage Areas. According to Nelson, an expert and author on outdoor environments, "lack of storage is the single most common playground design weakness discouraging teachers from being outside" (Nelson, 2006, p. 43). Needed materials must be readily available or they frequently are not used. Therefore, it is important to have storage throughout the playground. Appropriate storage is determined by what is being stored. For example, wood shelves with locking doors could store art or music supplies, storage benches might be used for loose parts, a low parking garage might house tricycles or bikes. A built-in cabinet under the woodworking bench could store carpentry tools.

Provide Access to Toileting, Hand Washing, and Drinking Water. Ideally, a bathroom or changing table (for children in diapers) is available on the playground. If possible, running water should also be available for washing hands and to provide drinking water. If running water is not available, it is important to bring pitchers of water and glasses outdoors.

Create an Aesthetically Pleasing Environment. While playgrounds need to be functional, they also should be aesthetic or beautiful. Aesthetic playgrounds welcome children and adults and show the value we place on both them and the setting. In an aesthetic environment, participants are more likely to care about the setting and vandalism is reduced (Kelling & Coles, 1996). To create an aesthetic playground, consider the following:

- Use the materials and colors from nature. To learn about the environment and experience what it can offer us, "children need daily chances to interact with materials found in nature . . . like wood, stone, water, grass and nonpoisonous trees and shrubs" (Wilke, 2006). Bright, bold colors, often found on plastic playground equipment, can be overstimulating and can detract from nature (Pardee et al., 2005). Instead, a variety of colors and textures can be introduced through different ground covers, plants, trees, and flowers.

- Personalize the playground with children's ideas and art (sculptures or murals created by children in the program). At the Helen Gordon Child Development Center in Portland, Oregon, children created gigantic murals on canvas. These hang in the playground enhancing the environment and providing documentation of children's learning.

- Design for rich sensory experiences—sound (wind chimes, water falling, leaves rustling), sight (flowers, trees that change color), smell (different fragrant herbs in different areas such as lavender, lemon balm, mint, creeping thyme, rosemary), tactile (different types of fencing, diverse elements like wood, rock, dirt, water) (Keeler, 2002).

- Provide a variety of ground covers.
- Pay attention to details (the water fountain can be beautiful as well as practical).
- Consider curved lines when creating walkways, flower beds, and divisions between zones.
- Create beauty (a basket of beautiful rocks, a miniature pond with floating plants, mosaic tables, gazing balls to reflect light).
- Make sure the playground is clean and uncluttered and that materials and equipment are in good repair.

Create a Sense of Place. Today, many American playgrounds are cookie cutter designs, untouched by the influence of the children that use them or the community in which the children live. Instead, playgrounds should provide a "sense of place" giving children a feeling of belonging, identity, and ownership (Cosco & Moore, 1999). Landscape architects stress that each outdoor environment should be individualized, reflecting the location, climate, culture, and values of the program. For example, at the East Stroudsburg University Childcare in Pennsylvania, a "sense of place" is created through playhouses representing those found on the Appalachian trail. A mosaic-backed stage created by a community artist, students, and children also helps to create a "sense of place" and provides a beautiful backdrop for impromptu plays.

In creating a "sense of place," incorporate program and community values, along with local materials, plants, and cultures. Involve all participants in the planning and ongoing development (children, parents, and teachers). Even children as young as three are able to provide valuable insights that help to produce playgrounds that meet their needs and interests (Whiren, 1995). When planning, immerse children in the idea. Take them on field trips to see other parks, gardens, and natural habitats. Look at pictures of playgrounds and natural play settings. Let children express their ideas by discussing their experiences, drawing playground designs, and building dioramas and models (Keeler, 2002). When children have a "sense of place" they honor that place, cherishing it, remembering it, and taking care of it.

Provide a Variety of Activity Areas

Playgrounds should contain a complete mix of activities: places to climb, crawl, swing, and slide; areas for riding wheeled toys; a large open area to run and play games; messy areas; places to play with water; places to grow things; places to observe nature; places to retreat; building areas; creative areas for music, movement, and art; and places for dramatic play (Greenman, 2005a). Areas need to be dynamic, allowing children and teachers to constantly reinvent the setting to meet the interests and the needs of the inhabitants.

Huge recycled tractor tires provide many climbing opportunities and are an inexpensive playground option.

Areas to Climb, Crawl, Develop Arm Strength, Jump, and Balance. As children climb, crawl, jump, and balance they master physical challenges, gain self-confidence, develop body awareness, and gain motor skills and fitness (agility, speed, balance, and coordination). They also develop spatial and directional awareness (Cuppens et al.,

2007; Frost et al., 2004). High places allow children to see what is occurring around them and gives them a sense of power.

Places to Climb. Most playgrounds feature a structure to climb on. You can purchase or build a stand-alone climbing structure. A variety of other climbing, jumping, and balancing options include

- Platforms built around or in a tree
- Tree stumps of different heights embedded into the ground
- Balance beams of different widths and heights
- Planks laid on cable spools turned sideways (Hogan, 1982)
- Suspension bridges made from tires placed side by side with a cable through the sides and attached to two poles at each end to hold the tires in place (Hogan, 1982)
- Suspension bridges from other materials
- Cargo nets on a frame to climb over (Hogan, 1982)
- Tire trees
- Tire walk made of tires set on the ground
- Climbing walls

Since children can climb up before they can climb down, make sure there is more than one way down, particularly on high structures (Pardee et al., 2005). For example, a child might climb up a climbing wall on a play structure and then climb down a set of steps. Also, "provide a means for children to display or announce the completion of a challenge. Possibilities include: platforms at the top of ropes and ladders; a bell to ring at the end of a complex route; banners to fly" (Olds, 2001, p. 421). When buying climbing equipment, you might have the option to include features such as dinosaur panels, alphabet cutouts, or spinning tic-tac-toe games. However, these "items which only have one use or purpose, may have limited lasting appeal" (Pardee et al., 2005, p. 8). Instead, you might buy buckets with pulleys so that items can be brought up and down from the structure, colored fiberglass panels that allow the children to experience the world in a different way, or telescopes.

Places to Crawl. Options for children to crawl through include

- Hollowed out logs (Cuppens et al., 2007)
- Translucent crawl-through tunnel under a hill (Cuppens et al., 2007)
- Tires laid on their side and embedded into the ground
- Concrete tunnel
- Living willow tunnel—At St. Peter Chanel Primary School in England, parents, children, and staff collaborated to build a 5-foot-tall, 50-foot-long tunnel on their playground. Living willow has several advantages. It provides a natural environment that is inexpensive. It can take a variety of forms. Children can experience the willows through changes of season. While children feel hidden, they can still be seen by adults (Danks, 2003).

Places to Develop Arm Strength. Overhead equipment such as ladders, track rides, and overhead rings develop upper body strength, coordination, lateral movement, and visual perception (Frost et al., 2004). Since children in the United States lack upper body strength (Frost et al., 2004), this type of equipment is especially important. Overhead equipment must be challenging, yet usable by all children. Challenges are greater for children when dynamic elements such as free moving rings are added or when spacing is uneven (Frost, 1992). Some overhead equipment is developed on an incline, becoming higher and more difficult as it ascends and allowing children with differing abilities to experience success. The equipment should be slightly above reaching height of 95% of the children using it (Frost, 1990, pp. 39–40). Balloon tires, standing upright, can be partially buried allowing a safe, accessible take off and landing platform (Frost & Kim, 2000). Preschool children need assistance and encouragement when they are first introduced to overhead equipment. However, in one study, once assistance was given, most of the 3- to 6-year-old children were able to use the overhead ladder successfully. Within one month, they were able to travel the full distance of the ladder on their own (Frost et al., 2004). To assist the child, hold her by the waist as she moves from rung to rung.

Places to Swing.

Swings are also important playground equipment. Swings encourage rhythmic motion that can be relaxing and improve balance and coordination. In addition, "The pendulum action, gravitational force and speed physically experienced while swinging quickly translate into feelings of falling and flying—sensations that inspire imaginations" (Sutterby & Thornton, 2006, p. 1). Swings also provide children the opportunity to share and to work together thereby assisting social development.

Providing a variety of swings can offer different advantages. For example, a horizontal tire swing allows several children to swing at once. Traditional swings allow children to swing back and forth under their own power. Adaptive swings allow children with disabilities to enjoy swinging. However, avoid heavy metal swings such as those shaped like animals that have been banned due to the high incidence of injuries.

Teachers can help children to be more successful in swinging by encouraging them to lean their torso in sync with pumping. In addition, extending legs to the apex on top of the forward swinging arc provides additional momentum (Frost et al., 2004).

Places to Slide.

Slides improve dynamic balance. In addition, unlike many other equipment options, slides present a low level of challenge to meet the needs of all children. Providing a variety of types of slides (spiral, tunnel, wide slides, and wave slides) in the playground adds interest and provides for children's differing ability levels. Slides can be provided as a stand-alone piece of equipment or attached to other equipment like a climber. For young children, embankment slides or slides placed upon a natural or human-made hill are often used, helping to prevent injury.

Area for Riding Tricycles, Scooters, Bikes, and Other Wheeling Toys.

As children ride wheeled toys, they improve physical skills, coordination, muscle strength, and spatial perception. In designing this area, a hard-surfaced path is critical. Paths that are meandering, containing small hills, ramps, and drive-through tunnels, can add interest and challenge, and increase exercise. Requiring helmets will protect children from head injury and teach lifetime safety skills.

A Large Open Area for Gathering and Large Motor Play.

The playground needs to include a large open area. Children can use this space as a gathering area. It also provides a place for playing games, running and dancing, flying kites, and throwing Frisbees and balls.

Messy Areas.

Today many children live in sterile environments, not having the opportunity to dig in the dirt, make mud pies, or dash through mud puddles. However, when adults were asked about fond childhood memories, playing in the mud was frequently mentioned (Jenson & Bullard, 2002). "Even as adults we continue to enjoy the sensory experience of mud through mud baths, mud facials, gardening, and barefoot walks with mud oozing through our toes" (Jensen & Bullard, 2002, p. 16). To provide children with this opportunity, one program created a mud center. The center included a real stove with an oven, an assortment of pots, pans, and cooking utensils, a variety of found items for decorating (sawdust, pine cones, dried berries, pebbles, crushed leaves), an area with water for cleaning up, and of course large buckets of dirt and water. As the mud play developed, the children collected an increasing variety of items for decorating and stirring into their inventions and experimented with a variety of mud creations (stuffed pies, layered pies, soups, birthday cakes). The mud center was open-ended and allowed for a range of challenges. It included many curriculum areas, and was a favorite center for both adults and children.

While many other substances can be used for digging and creating, sand is probably the most popular medium. Cuppens et al. (2007) suggest creating an L-shaped sandbox, which allows more children to be involved in digging than does a rectangular box. Sandboxes need to be covered when not in use. One technique is to cover the sand area with netting, allowing sand to air dry while keeping out cats.

Water Area. "Water comforts, fascinates, and instructs" (Rivken, 1995, p. 41). Although one must be cautious about water that is deep or stagnant, these restraints do not need to eliminate water play. Following are some suggestions on how to incorporate water play in the playground. Some of these suggestions may not be appropriate for areas that have limited water supplies. It is also important to check the licensing regulations in your state before developing a new water area.

- Allow children to run through a sprinkler.
- Provide water in tubs or water tables.
- Install an outdoor shower head.
- Provide a recirculating fountain. Depending on the size, children can observe and listen, or actually splash and wade into the fountain.
- Add a water source to your sand area; this can be as simple as a hose with a shut-off valve. By adding rain gutters or pipes, children can move water throughout the area. "The play value of sand is enhanced by the provision of a second fluid material, water" (Frost, 1992, p. 103). When children mold wet sand they can make the connection between the sand and the container's shape (McIntyre, 1982).
- Install outdoor sinks and faucets. At the Pacific Oaks Infant/Toddler Program, a series of sinks (each with its own unique type of faucet) stair step down a slight incline. Water overflows into a shallow stream bed allowing for more water adventures.
- Install a hand pump, this typically limits water consumption while providing exercise.
- Provide a very shallow creek. At a park in Salt Lake City, a very shallow creek meanders through the playground. Children learn hands-on physics as they experiment with large rocks they can move to divert the flow of water.
- Install a misting pipe from the side of a building or as a stand-alone structure.

Areas for Plants and Gardens. Caring for gardens allows children to gain a sense of responsibility, an enhanced appreciation and understanding of where food comes from, and increased knowledge of natural systems and seasons. Gardening can also help establish lifelong values. "If sustainable development values are to be created in society, we must recreate, as a matter of great urgency, viable educational habitat for children where they are able to learn on a daily basis the lessons of nature. Gardening is clearly an effective first step" (Moore, 1995, p. 68). Garden activities can also be a springboard for curriculum in math (charting, graphing), science (photosynthesis, plant needs, pests, composting,

This herb bed created by parent volunteers allows children to learn about gardening. Children care for the herb bed and pick the herbs to use in cooking projects. Also note in this photo how the bikes and helmets are stored in the bike corral.

observation), social studies (food in different cultures, mapmaking), art (garden design), literacy (sign making, reading books), and health and nutrition (Stoeklin, 2001). The San Francisco Environmental yard provides examples of the many activities that gardening can promote. Children experimented with plants growing under different conditions. They kept garden logs where they recorded observations and documentation such as heights of plants and weight of produce. They learned about insects that assist and harm plants and developed ways to preserve food (Moore, 1995).

Depending upon space, gardens can be planted directly into the ground, in raised beds, in child-size swimming pools, in tubs, or in flowerpots. Froebel believed that children should have both individual and group plots, promoting both responsibility and community (Brosterman, 1997).

In many communities, there are garden clubs and greenhouses that will provide advice and assistance. In San Antonio, master gardeners volunteered to help elementary schools establish gardens. Ten thousand children, most in inner-city schools, participated in gardening each week. Children learned about nature by caring for and nurturing living things. They also learned about the need for cooperation and delayed gratification. Children indicated that school was more pleasurable after the gardening project began. The gardening project also increased parent involvement (Alexander, North, & Hendren, 1995).

> TIP For a quick, easy, gardening bed, buy a bag of potting soil, cut holes on top to insert plants, and cut holes in the bottom for drainage (Rivken, 1995, p. 43).

Places to Observe and Interact with Insects, Animals, and Birds. Most playgrounds provide some exposure to living things. However, teachers can improve learning by attracting more birds, animals, and insects to the playground, and by providing tools to study what is found. Domesticated animals can also be part of the playground learning experiences.

To attract birds, animals, and insects, you must provide hospitable habitats. For example, teachers can provide bird feeders, birdhouses, and birdbaths; worm beds; squirrel feeders; and gardens and plants to attract butterflies and ladybugs. Long ungroomed grass and hedges for hiding might attract small native animals.

Binoculars, magnifying glasses, butterfly nets, and containers allow children a close-up view. Learning can be extended by providing resources for animal, bug, and bird identification. For very young children, it might be helpful to provide laminated pictures of birds, bugs, and animals typically found in your playground. As children become more skilled, they can graduate to children's guidebooks and then to adult guidebooks. Teachers can place these along with magnifying glasses and binoculars into plastic containers with tight-fitting lids to protect them from unexpected rain showers.

Some programs have domestic animals such as rabbits or chickens in their play yards. At one preschool, a large ground-level rabbit hutch, containing a small house to shelter the rabbit along with a fenced yard, is in the children's playground. Two children at a time are allowed to enter the yard to spend time with the rabbit. If the rabbit does not want contact, he can enter his house and children learn that if the rabbit goes in his house, he is not to be bothered. Several preschools and elementary schools have chicken coops on their playgrounds. Children participate in feeding the chickens and gathering eggs.

Plants, shrubs, and trees are also important for wildlife habitat. In addition, they provide beauty, shade, and exposure to nature. Choosing plants that are indigenous to the region ensures a proven survival rate and helps children to learn about plants and trees that are native to the area (Schappet, Malkusak, & Bruya, 2003).

A Place to Seek Refuge. Places to seek refuge, sometimes called stimulus shelters (Frost et al., 2004), are semi-private areas that allow a special place for dreaming and introspection, quiet exploration, solitary play, and a place to withdraw from the group when play becomes too intense. It also provides a place to watch others while deciding whether to participate with the group.

When planning a refuge, design it to be semi-enclosed so that adults can easily see inside the enclosure. Children also prefer semi-enclosed rather than fully enclosed structures. For example, when given a choice, 5- to 8-year-old children preferred semi-open rather than entirely closed structures by a five-to-one ratio (Dempsey & Frost, 1993).

Low platforms, areas screened by vegetation, a sunflower tepee, living willow hut, telephone booth, playhouse, tree house, or tent can all provide places of refuge. A ceiling or canopy also helps to create a sense of refuge. For example, a hammock under a tree with overhanging branches could be a quiet place to retreat. A small house with various peepholes can allow the child to seek a retreat while also viewing the world in interesting ways. A small Zen garden can help establish a contemplative mood.

Places to Sit. Many different seating options add versatility and interest to the playground, while providing appropriate space for a variety of activities. These can include picnic tables and benches, seats built around trees, or mosaic tables created by the children. Natural benches can be created from large, smooth boulders; logs placed on their side with a seat and back carved in; or log stools. Adult and child-sized tables and seating, when placed throughout the play yard, allow for a variety of activities—games, resting, reading, art, eating, and cooking.

Loose Parts for Enhancing Possibilities. Loose parts add flexibility, increase creativity, and enhance and extend play (Sawyer, 1994). A variety of loose parts should be readily available. If outdoor storage is not available, it may be necessary to have crates, tubs, or baskets filled with items that can be brought out when you play outdoors. Although the list is limited only by one's imagination, following are some examples of loose parts:

- Natural materials to collect, sort, and use for decorating—pinecones, seashells, stones, leaves, seed pods, moss, rocks, berries
- Materials for water and sand exploration—hoses, spray bottles, sprinklers, turkey basters, paintbrushes, rain gutter, plastic tubing, buckets, cups, bowls, shovels, sifters, containers in various sizes

The Mentor Graphics Child Development Center playground is adorned with art sculptures that were created by children and parents at the conclusion of a long-term project on bugs. Also note the child-painted strips of roofing material woven into the fence.

Outdoors provides opportunities for large musical instruments that might be too large or noisy for indoor play.

- Materials to explore nature—butterfly nets, magnifying glasses, magnifying boxes, binoculars, bird and insect identification books, jars
- Pulleys, ropes, and buckets for getting things in and out of tree houses and for getting bird feeders up and down
- Things to throw, kick, jump, and bat—variety of types of balls, Frisbees, bats, jump ropes, hoops
- Things to fly—kites, airplanes
- Things to ride and pull—trikes, bikes, wagons, pull toys
- Materials to build with—spools, boards, tires, crates, PVC pipe and elbows, plastic tubing, sheets or tarps
- Tools—hammers, saws, screwdrivers, nails, rope

Outdoor Learning Centers (Block and Building, Art, Music and Movement, Science and Math, Literacy, and Dramatic Play). Outdoor learning centers are important additions to playgrounds. Playgrounds typically contain a block and building center (see Chapter 11), areas for dramatic play (see Chapter 12), an art area (see Chapter 13), and music and movement center (see Chapter 14). Many programs also include science and math centers (see Chapters 9 and 10), and literacy centers (see Chapter 7). If outdoor centers are not yet permanent fixtures on your playground, you might develop play crates. These could include a dress-up crate, music crate, bubble crate, sand and water play crate, and gardening crate (McGinnis, 2002).

Generally, when planning outdoor centers, it is important to take advantage of the extra freedom, space, and items available in the natural environment rather than duplicating what is available indoors.

Through appropriate playground design, we can provide rich experiences in a safe, healthy outdoor environment. However, in developing an appropriate design we must also consider the specific age group that will be using the playground.

Designing Playgrounds for Specific Age Groups

Although there are basic areas found on playgrounds for all age groups, to provide for safety and appropriate activities and experiences we must specifically design the playground for the ages using it. Following are recommendations for infant and toddler, preschool, and early elementary playgrounds.

Infants and Toddlers

Infants and toddlers experience rapid development of motor skills, including locomotor (running, jumping, climbing), small motor (throwing, hitting, kicking), and stability (bending, balancing). Children at this age are often practicing skills and engage in much repetition. For example, a toddler may repeatedly climb up and down a set of steps. Pretend play is also beginning to emerge (Frost et al., 2004). Sensory learning is especially critical at this age. Since children this age often mouth items, it is important that everything in the playground be safe to eat and either large enough or small enough that it does not create a choking hazard (Greenman, 1991). Some unique features that are important to include in infant and toddler playgrounds are

- 14- to 16-inch barriers that children can lean against and use to pull themselves to a standing position.
- Grassy places to roll, crawl, and move.
- Meandering pathways to crawl on or walk on—dirt, stone, planks, wood rounds, half logs, brick (Greenman, 1991, p. 23).
- Different types of railing—poles, chains, iron, rope (Greenman, 1991, p. 23).
- A house or lean-to that babies can crawl or toddle into. Flexibility can be provided by using skeletal structures. For example, a wide A-frame stepladder allows children to climb over and under (Greenman, 1991). By adding fabric, the structure can also become a tent. Changing the type of fabric can provide additional variability.
- Items to challenge newly developed gross motor skills—steps, inclines, things to crawl over, jump over, and climb on.
- Climbers with "varying levels and means of entry and exit, bells or pulleys to make sounds, dynamic components such as steering wheels to manipulate, and slides or climbers to promote action" (Dempsey & Frost, 1993, p. 23).
- Colored panels in climbers or on fences that allow babies to see the world in a different way.
- Cradle or bucket seat swings (Greenman, 1991, p. 23).
- Short tunnels to crawl into and play peek-a-boo.
- Slides built into a hill.
- Elevated waterways with troughs to experiment with water.
- Things to hear—a variety of wind chimes, leaves rustling.
- Things to look at—mobiles, kites, banners, parachutes, wind socks, leaves, patterns of sun and shade.
- Different textures to feel—"smooth round boulders, coarse bark and smooth sensual wood, soft and not so soft pine needles, and other vegetation to feel and rub up against" (Greenman, 1991, p. 23).
- Places to keep cool—human-made and natural shade.
- Places to sit alone and to sit with adults such as small chairs, hammocks, porch swings.
- Loose parts—fabric; baskets or buckets for collecting items; natural items to collect, carry, and dump; mats; inner tubes; dramatic play props; art materials; sand and water toys; riding toys; toys to push and pull; balls.
- Diaper-changing tables.

To protect infants from older toddlers who may injure infants due to running and throwing items, nonmobile infants need separate spaces. In addition, children need to be protected from equipment or areas that they are not yet developmentally ready to use. One way to accomplish this is by providing challenges that children must successfully navigate to reach the area. For example, at the Pacific Oaks Infant/Toddler Program, children must crawl over a boardwalk to reach the sand pit. In addition, they must transverse an obstacle of tires to reach the climber (Striniste & Moore, 1989).

Preschool

Preschool children are in the fundamental movement phase of physical development, a phase of rapidly maturing physical skills. Sociodramatic play becomes more complex, with children participating in small-group cooperative play. Children at this age need additional challenges, more complex equipment, and a greater diversity of choices than do the infants and toddlers. All of the activity areas discussed earlier in the chapter should be included in the preschool playground.

Early Elementary

Children ages 6 to 8 are entering a more mature stage of fundamental movements (Gallahue, 1993) allowing them to learn new skills such as riding bikes or jumping rope. Games with rules become very important at this age. In addition to all the interest areas described earlier in the chapter, playgrounds need areas with firm surfaces for games such as basketball, hopscotch, and jump rope. Large surfaces are also needed for soccer, softball, and chase games.

Teachers' Facilitation of Learning in the Outdoor Environment

Teachers are critical, not only in the initial playground design, but also in making the playground a dynamic environment that meets the needs and interests of the current group of children. For this to occur, the teacher must recognize the importance of outdoor play. As with indoor play, the teacher is responsible for planning additional daily activities and interacting with children to scaffold learning, promote positive social interactions, and encourage safe play while outdoors.

Recognize the Importance and Possibilities of Outdoor Play

Many teachers hold misconceptions about outdoor play, believing that it is a time for children to release excess energy, a time for a break for children and adults, or a place to develop gross motor skills (Frost et al., 2004). While each of these is true, the misconception is that this is the sole purpose for outdoor time. When teachers hold these misconceptions, they are often not fully supporting children's development through a "rich" environment or through their interactions.

Create a Rich, Challenging Environment

The outdoor environment needs to be continually assessed and adapted to meet children's needs and interests. In many programs, the outdoor environment is an afterthought with little funding or planning. Play materials are static, rather than dynamic, and there are few playground enhancements (Nelson, 2006; Wilke, 2006). In planning the outdoor play yard, it might help to think of it as an outdoor classroom containing all of the design features and areas described earlier in the chapter (Nelson, 2006).

Provide a Schedule That Allows Time for Play Outdoors

When classrooms have adjacent playgrounds, children often are able to choose whether to play indoors or outdoors. When this is the case, outdoor play is available several hours a day. When it is not the case, it is important to have at least one period of extended outdoor play for a half-day program and two periods of extended outdoor play for a full-day program. With the emphasis on academic achievement, many elementary programs are reducing outside time, instead using this time for more structured learning activities. However, research demonstrates that children who take time for physical activity have increased physical fitness, better attitudes, and score at least as well, if not better, on academic tests as children who spend all their time inside working on academics (Sallis et al., 1999). A meta-analysis of nearly 200 studies examining the effect of physical activity on cognitive functioning supports this conclusion (Etnier et al., 1997). Taking time for physical activity also increases attention spans and reduces off-task behavior when children return to the classroom (Jarrett et al., 1998).

Children benefit from playing outdoors in most weather conditions. However, it is important that teachers and children are prepared with proper clothing. Many programs provide extra clothes for children who come unprepared.

If the weather does occasionally prohibit outdoor play, teachers should use a gym, hallway, or lunchroom to provide similar activities. If there is no access to these environments, active play can be planned for the classroom. For ideas on indoor physical play, see Chapter 16.

Plan Special Activities for Outdoor Time

Special daily activities should be planned for outdoors. These activities provide additional choices for children, while enhancing learning opportunities. The ideas are limitless. Following are a few ideas to use as a springboard for planning.

- Provide mazes and hopscotch on the playground
- Bury items in the sandbox, then give children brushes and screens to be archeologists or paleontologists
- Give children doll clothes to wash and hang out to dry
- Fill spray bottles with water and food coloring—spray on snow in winter or on an old sheet in summer
- Provide chalk for drawing around shadows
- Supply bubble mixtures and a variety of bubble wands
- Play games
- Hang a hoop from a tree for children to throw balls through
- Bring the musical instruments outside and have a band
- Create streamers with crepe paper, children can use them for dancing and experimenting with wind
- Provide kites to fly
- Provide sheets of paper of different weights and sizes to create paper airplanes or pinwheels
- Create challenges (a sand castle 2 feet high)

Obstacle courses are another way to provide variety. They can be created by teachers and children using the static features in the playground along with loose parts such as milk crates, tires, plastic hoops and bottles, planks, boxes, and cable spools. Tunnels can be created by cutting the bottom out of plastic trashcans. Plastic swimming pools can be filled with balls or Styrofoam to walk or crawl through (Griffen & Rinn, 1998). Obstacle courses can change and become more physically demanding when children master the current obstacle course or lose interest. Climbing, crawling, balancing, throwing, and kicking skills can all be incorporated into the obstacle course.

Provide Needed Props

Props can extend children's learning and can support children's developmental levels, interests, and program goals. For example, after a heavy rainstorm, water flooded into the basement in one child care. The children were very interested in building a dam outside to "save their school." The teacher provided a variety of different materials for the children to experiment with, including sand bags and hay bales. The children then became interested in other ways to divert water. Children built waterways in the sand area including lakes and streams using the plastic and piping the teacher provided.

Interact with Children

It is crucial that teachers interact with children in the outdoors if children are to gain the full value from the outdoor experience. There are many important roles that the early childhood professional performs in the outdoor environment, including the following:

- Playing with children (throwing balls, playing games, blowing bubbles).
- Demonstrating and teaching skills such as how to plant a garden or how to pump legs when swinging.
- Modeling enjoyment of nature and providing opportunities for children to experience nature. Rachel Carson, a well-known naturalist, stated, "If a child is to keep alive his inborn sense of wonder, he needs the companionship of at least one adult who can share it, rediscovering the joy, excitement, and mystery of the world we live in."
- Offering encouragement and providing recognition.
- Helping the excluded child to be included. For example, if you begin to play with the excluded child, often other children will join in the play. You can then continue to play, modeling appropriate interactions. Review Chapter 2 for a more in-depth discussion of this topic.

Meet the Needs of All Learners

It is important to provide special encouragement and opportunities to be active to those children at special risk. This includes children who have fewer opportunities for exercise outside of the early childhood setting, children who are overweight, and children who are naturally less active.

Supporting Children from All Cultures. Preliminary research indicates that physical activity levels may vary based upon ethnic background. For example, in one study European-Americans engaged in more physical activities than their Mexican-American peers (McKenzie et al., 1997). This may be due to fewer opportunities. Studies have found that "communities with low-SES populations and higher proportions of minority racial groups are also associated with the fewest community-level physical activity-related settings" (Powell, Slater, & Chaloupka, 2004, p. 143). For example, in Los Angeles, researchers conducted a study examining the acres of park per 1,000 people in different neighborhoods. Caucasian neighborhoods have 31 acres of parks, African-American neighborhoods have only 1.7 acres of parks, and Latino neighborhoods have only 0.6 acres of parks per 1,000 people (Clark, 2007, p. 54). These statistics are important since the number and size of parks is linked to the amount of physical activity that people receive (Clark, 2007). Playgrounds in low-income areas also have more maintenance hazards than playgrounds in high-income areas (Suecoff, Avner, Chou, & Crain, 1999). As a result, parents in the low-income areas might not use the parks.

It is important that all children have access to outdoor play. If this is not possible in the home environment, it is even more crucial that there is ample opportunity for outdoor play in the childcare or school environment.

Supporting Children Who Are Overweight. Lack of activity is one of the primary predictors of being overweight as a child (Nelson et al., 2006). Observing the level of physical activity of each individual child will assist you in knowing when it might be helpful to intercede. Teachers can assist children to be more active by

- Providing a range of challenges so all children can be successful (children who are overweight often have less developed physical skills than their peers)
- Setting up obstacle courses that everyone progresses through as they enter the playground
- Providing encouragement and support when children are physically active
- Engaging in physical activity with a child or small groups of children
- Assisting children to master physical skills
- Providing activities that appeal to a reluctant child's interests

Several studies have found that boys spend more time in vigorous physical activity than do girls (Finn, Johannsen, & Specker, 2002; Pellegrini, Kato, Blatchford, & Baines, 2002; Ridgers et al., 2005). Therefore, it might be necessary to provide encouragement for girls to be more physically active.

Supporting Children with Disabilities. In addition to encouraging and providing opportunities for children who might engage in less physical activity, we must make sure that our playgrounds are accessible for all children, including those with disabilities. Boundless Playgrounds, a national organization dedicated to creating barrier-free playgrounds, lists their dream as, "For every child, A place to play: Every child, Every ability, Every where." In early childhood playgrounds, we need to make sure that all children in our program are able to realize this dream. We can be more successful if we use the following process to help a child with disabilities access the playground. First, we need to gather information about the child's interests, strengths, and challenges. Second, determine what opportunities and barriers exist on the playground. And third, brainstorm modifications to enhance playground opportunities for the child (Flynn & Kieff, 2002). These modifications will vary from child to child. Following are a few examples of possible adaptations:

- Wind chimes, different textures to designate different platforms on a climbing structure, and different fragrant plants to mark different areas of the playground can help children with visual impairments to orient themselves (Moore, 1992).
- Circulation paths with firm surfaces that are 60 inches wide can accommodate a child in a wheelchair (Tipping, 2007).
- Multiple ways of getting on equipment, including ramps, allows access for children with reduced motor mobility.
- Structures with climbing and resting places at many levels help children who are physically challenged.
- Large swings with back supports allow children with physical disabilities to use swings.
- Various heights of water tables and sand tables allow children to stand or to sit in a wheelchair to access them.

- Side-mounted grips in tunnels allow children with limited use of their legs to still use the equipment.
- Wide slides allow children to slide down with someone else.
- Overhead ladders that are either low on one end or ramped allow use by children in wheelchairs.
- Adjustable-height basketball hoops allow all children to use them (Theemes, 1999).
- Low-demand activities encourage all children to participate and be successful. In one study, children with a range of disabilities were more likely to play cooperatively in low-demand activities (playing in the playhouse, swinging on a tire swing, climbing on equipment, or playing on slides) (Nabors et al., 1999).
- Peer buddies can help children with disabilities to be included in groups and can also provide needed physical assistance.
- Involvement in the play or activity by the teacher facilitates inclusion of children with special needs (Nabors et al., 1999).

For inspiration, you might consider the playground at Clemy Park in northern Virginia. The park features an accessible public playground that includes such unique features as a wheelchair drag race strip, a movable helicopter that allows a wheelchair to be attached, a flush-mounted carousel, spinning cups, and voice-activated components (Avrasin, 2007, p. 46).

Observe and Document Children's Learning

The outdoor environment provides an opportunity to observe many different skills. Two areas that are especially conducive to observing outdoors are gross motor skills and social/emotional development. While there are many ways to observe children outdoors, a checklist of physical skills may be helpful. As children demonstrate the skills in play, you can check them off the list. You might also set up an obstacle course and check the skills children use as they navigate the course. One way to document children's social skills is through anecdotal records. Following are a list of gross motor skills that can be observed on the playground.

- Walking
- Running
- Hopping
- Skipping
- Jumping
- Galloping
- Kicking
- Throwing
- Catching
- Striking (hitting with hand or object such as a bat)
- Dynamic balance (balancing while moving)
- Static balance (center of gravity remains stationary)
- Axial movement (bending, stretching, twisting, turning, etc.)
- Dominant hand and foot usage

Following are questions regarding social/emotional development that can be observed on the playground.

- Who does the child play with or does the child play alone?
- What are the child's favorite activities?
- How does the child gain play entry with his peers?
- What is the child's level of fear? Does the child seek new challenges?
- Is the child a leader or follower when participating in playground activities?
- Is the child able to take turns with others?
- Can the child negotiate and make compromises?
- Does the child express frustrations effectively?
- Does the child engage in appropriate interaction with new children and adults?

In well-designed outdoor play environments, children experience rich learning, developing intellectual, social, creative, and physical skills. In addition, they have opportunities to engage in vigorous physical activity and to experience nature in ways that are typically not available indoors.

In this day of increased obesity, physical exercise is critical. "To deny children the opportunity to reap the many benefits of regular, vigorous physical activity is to deny them the opportunity to experience the joy of efficient movement, the health effects of movement and a lifetime as confident, competent movers" (Gallahue, 1993).

As outdoor play times decrease and natural environments shrink, the playground becomes one of the few places that children might still experience nature. Nurturing the joy of nature creates lifelong dispositions that are necessary to preserve the natural environment for future generations.

Sample Application Activities

1. Take an online visit to playgrounds to gain inspiration (visit Planet Earth Playscapes for a look at several playgrounds http://www.planetearthplayscapes.com/)
2. Learn more about creating living willow structures by reading the article, *Green Mansions: Living Willow Structures Enhance Children's Play Environments* at colorado.edu/journals/cye/13_1/Volume13_1FieldReports/WillowArticleFinal.pdf
3. Brainstorm a list of outdoor activities.
4. Assess a playground using the environmental assessment in Figure 17.1.
5. Develop a model of your ideal playground.
6. Learn more about safe playgrounds by visiting http://www.playgroundsafety.org/standards/index.htm
7. Locate additional websites that picture interesting playgrounds and share them with your class. Determine what type of playground you are reviewing (traditional, natural, contemporary, creative, adventure, or a combination).
8. Locate grants (for example, check with state block grant funds) and other funding resources (Boy Scouts seeking to become Eagle Scouts will sometimes develop a playground as a project) for developing a playground.

Figure 17.1
Environmental Assessment: Playground

Playground design

☐ Is the playground S. A. F. E. (appropriate supervision, developmentally appropriate equipment, appropriate fall zones and surfaces, well-maintained equipment)?

☐ Is there enough space for the number of children using the playground? (To determine, tally the number of children that are in each playground area. Are there some areas that are crowded? Are there some areas with no children?)

☐ Are there safe, looping circular paths?

☐ Is the playground zoned?

☐ Are the zones visibly separated through different ground surfaces or dividers?

☐ Are nonmobile children protected from mobile children?

☐ Is there shade and protection from the elements?

☐ Is there sufficient storage space?

☐ Is the storage space located near the location where the materials will be used?

☐ Is there access to toileting, hand washing, and drinking water?

☐ Are a variety of activity areas present?
  • Areas to climb, crawl, jump, and balance
  • Areas to swing
  • Places to slide
  • Messy areas (mud, sand)
  • Water areas
  • Area for riding tricycles, scooters, bikes
  • Areas for plants and gardens
  • Places to observe and interact with insects, animals, and birds
  • Large area for gathering and for large motor play
  • Place to seek refuge
  • Many different places to sit
  • Outdoor learning centers
    ▪ Block and building
    ▪ Art
    ▪ Music
    ▪ Dramatic play
    ▪ Science and math
    ▪ Literacy

☐ Are there loose parts available to enhance possibilities?

☐ Does the playground have the right amount of challenge?

☐ Are there ways children can feel powerful (ringing a bell when they reach the top of a climbing structure)?

☐ Are there a range of activities to meet the needs of different skill levels (balance beams at different widths, different types of swings, different ways to climb a structure)?

☐ Are all children able to use the playground successfully (playground equipment accessible to all)?

☐ Is the playground aesthetically pleasing (materials and colors from nature, personalized with children's ideas and art, designed for rich sensory experiences, created with beauty in mind, clean, uncluttered, attention to detail, curved lines).

☐ Does the playground provide "a sense of place" (reflects location, climate, culture, values, local materials, and local plants)?

Adult/child interactions

☐ Are adults enforcing rules? If so, are the rules necessary for safety? Are children engaging in unsafe or harmful behavior that is being ignored?

☐ Are adults interacting with children? In what ways (for example playing, conversing, reading a book, disciplining)?

Figure 17.1
(Continued)

- ☐ Are adults scaffolding children's learning (for example helping a child transverse across an overhead ladder or providing additional information about a worm that was found in the playground)?
- ☐ Are adults nurturing dispositions (such as the love of nature, respect for living things)?
- ☐ How are children who are in conflict helped to solve the conflict (are children separated, punished, or forced to apologize, or are they helped to problem solve the issues) (Wohlwend, 2005)?
- ☐ Are adults helping excluded children to be included?

chapter 18
Creating Spaces for Families and Teachers

*E*nquiring Minds Early Childhood Center strived to meet the needs of children and adults in their program. In addition to children's classrooms, they had dedicated two rooms for adults, one for staff, and one for families. However, these rooms were very rarely used.

Katie, a new director, wanted to rejuvenate the rooms. She began by meeting with the staff and parents to ask what they needed to make their jobs (teaching or parenting) easier. The staff wanted a place where they could spend their breaks in a relaxing, rejuvenating environment. They also needed a workroom. However, they stated that when both of these occurred in the same space, it was often ineffective. For example, *staff found it difficult to relax when the copier machine was running. While the work-room needed to be functional with long tables, machines, and storage, the staff envi-sioned the relaxation room as a somewhat whimsical place with soft curtains and comfortable furnishings. The current room did not have space for both.*

Katie then interviewed the parents. She was surprised to find that parents also de-sired a quiet place to regroup after dropping children off or before picking them up. They, like the staff, had a need to access resources and materials. Both staff and fam-ilies concluded that designing the rooms to serve the needs of both groups would be the most effective way to use the space.

After brainstorming ideas for both rooms, Katie and a committee of staff and par-ents began the room design. In the relaxation room were plants, a coffee table hous-ing inspirational books, and comfortable chairs including one that vibrated. The windows were covered with sheer curtains that allowed the light to flow into the room. Crystals hung in the window creating rainbows on the floor and surrounding walls. There was a refreshment bar with many kinds of tea, an espresso machine, a coffee pot, a mini fridge for snacks, and a microwave. To increase relaxation, a fountain, headphones with relaxation tapes, and natural oils for aromatherapy were also avail-able. A bulletin board contained thank-you notes and an inspirational quote of the day. In addition, the bulletin board contained a brainstormed list of ten-minute relax-ation ideas generated by the staff and parents. Because physical exercise helped some staff and families relax, one corner was dedicated to more active pursuits such as jug-gling scarves, lifting weights, yoga, and stretching exercises. To make sure the room continued to meet staff and parents' needs, a suggestion box was added. Because of a suggestion from some fathers who felt the rooms needed more materials to meet their needs, a computer with Internet hookup and headphones was added to play games, listen to music, or check e-mail. In addition, books focused on fathers were added.

The workroom contained a resource library, family learning backpacks to check out, a variety of office supplies, and machines such as computers, a laminator, and a copier. To maintain confidentiality, individual children's files were kept in the class-rooms. The room had large worktables as well as individual carrels.

Although this room was designed for functionality, the staff and families also wanted the room to be aesthetically pleasing. Plants, framed pictures of children, fam-ilies, and staff and interesting baskets to hold supplies added to the aesthetics. One family donated a beautiful rug that also created a more pleasant ambiance.

Keeping the relaxation rooms and workrooms organized and clean had been a concern raised during the planning sessions. A group of parents and staff volunteered to take turns checking the rooms on a daily basis and cleaning them if necessary.

Because of these changes, the rooms were in constant use. Families tended to use the rooms more at the beginning and end of the day, while staff used the room in the middle of the day. An effective, organized workroom made it easier to accomplish tasks. The relaxation room provided an invitation and opportunity to relax and reju-venate. As families and staff began to use the rooms, a sense of community developed.

Apply Your Knowledge   This center had two rooms available for staff and parents. Many programs do not have this amount of space. What are ways that you could still meet the parents' and staff's needs for relaxation and work space in a setting that had very little space?

Your environment provides a message about the respect and the value you place on the adults in children's lives. Effective environments meet the needs of both children and adults. They are aesthetic, comfortable, and emotionally and physically safe. Materials and displays represent and recognize the inhabitants. Environments for adults, like children, should send the message, "This is a place where I belong, where I am valued, and where my basic needs are met. It is a place where I can receive and give information."

Meeting the Needs of Families

To be effective educators, we must form partnerships with families and the community. Under the best scenario, the teacher "functions as a member of the extended family for both the parent and child" (Riley, San Juan, Klinkher, & Ramminger, 2008, p. 7).

Value of Family Involvement

Regardless of socioeconomic status, parent's educational background, age, ethnic or racial background, or gender, numerous outcomes for children improve when families are involved (Carter, 2003; Diffily, 2004). Family involvement in the infant, toddler, and preschool years provides immediate benefits and sets the stage for future involvement. Children whose families are involved in the early school years experience greater school success and achievement in every academic area, higher motivation, improved behavior, and increased attendance and retention (Carter, 2003; Diffily, 2004). Family involvement is beneficial for several reasons. It can assist

- In establishing a more positive relationship between the home and school
- The educator to become more aware of home situations and the families' desires, values, and beliefs
- Families to become more aware of programs at the school
- In creating a bridge between what is taught at school and at home so that complementary learning can take place
- Families to become better teachers of their children
- In gaining support and resources for the early childhood program
- In linking families to needed community supports
- In offering families an opportunity for social interaction and a place to make adult friends

Types of Family Involvement

However, in planning for family partnerships, we must respect the many ways that families can be involved. Recognizing the different needs of families, Epstein (2001) identified six types of family involvement—parenting, communicating, volunteering, learning at home, decision making, and collaborating with the community. Each type serves a different purpose, meeting the needs of families and schools in different ways. A well-rounded program considers these six types of parental involvement and strives to provide opportunities for each in their environment. Each program needs to determine the emphasis and depth that is placed on each of the types of involvement based upon the parent population they serve.

Designing Effective Entries

Every program is unique in the amount of space available and the arrangement of this space. Some programs have long halls filled with child documentation, offices where par-

Curious Minds has developed a welcoming family space featuring documentation, a communication book, and parent information, even though they have very limited space.

ents are greeted, and well-stocked family resource rooms. In other programs, parents and children enter directly into the classroom. In still other programs, children arrive by bus. Each of these scenarios affects the placement of information for parents, the type of parental/child transition spaces, and the location of resources (such as literacy backpacks) for parents. For more information about designing entries, see Figure 18.1.

However, even with limited space, creative teachers find ways to meet family and program needs. Regardless of space, we must develop a respectful environment where families feel they are valued and belong, that meets the families' basic needs as both individuals and parents, and where families can share and receive information about

Figure 18.1
Entries

The entry into the building creates the first impression of your program. It reflects your philosophy and gives a message to families and children. It also acts as a transition place, particularly when parents transport children to the program. With thoughtful design, halls and entryways can be used to welcome and inform. Entries can provide different types of information, such as parent pamphlets, parent displays, project webs, or children's documentation.

While classrooms at Kid College were aesthetically pleasing, the entry had been ignored and was very unattractive. Realizing that this area was the place that parents spent the majority of their time, the staff decided that the entry needed an uplift. They covered the battered table that held the child and adult sign-in forms with a beautiful tablecloth, placed mirrors to reflect the light, and added plants and a tabletop fountain to provide a sense of nature and calmness. Families commented about the change, appreciating the effort and the result.

the child, parenting, and community services. Following are some suggestions for accomplishing this.

Establishing an Environment That Tells Families, "You Belong Here"

If we want families to feel that they belong in our programs we must be welcoming; make sure that our environments are inclusive of all cultures; assure that families recognize themselves in the images and information on our walls, in our materials, and in our different forms of communication; and reach out to under-represented groups. We will examine each of these criteria in the following sections.

Develop a Welcoming Environment. "I belong here" begins with signage that greets families as they enter the program. At one school the sign said, "Everyone must report to the office immediately upon entering the building." At another school the sign read, "Please come to the office so that we can have the opportunity to personally greet you." Both asked families to comply with the same request. However, one made them feel like intruders while the other conveyed the image of welcoming treasured guests. To be effective and welcoming, signs need to contain a positive tone and must be written in the families' native language.

Be Inclusive of All Cultures. Environments that denote belonging are inclusive of all cultures. In thinking of the culture, it is important to consider all dimensions of culture including ethnic, racial, linguistic, geographic area or region, religion, economic status, and family composition (Bradley & Kibera, 2006). These dimensions of culture can affect family values and beliefs, historical and social influences, communication, and attitudes toward seeking help (Bradley & Kibera, 2006, p. 36). Norms of privacy and beliefs about child development are also highly dependent on families' culture. It is important not to make assumptions about an individual family's culture based upon a particular characteristic. Instead, it is best to learn about the family by asking them to share information about their culture, values, beliefs, and desires for their children (Pipher, 2002, p. 353).

Assure That Images, Materials, and Communication Are Inclusive of All Families. To denote a sense of belonging we must make sure family resource materials, pamphlets, posters, flyers, newsletters, and children's books contain images that reflect cultural and family diversity, including fathers in caregiving roles and grandparents in the parenting role. We must also be conscious of the labels we apply to newsletters and bulletin boards. For example, family is more inclusive than mother, father, or parent. Paperwork can also give a sense of belonging or inclusion. Are the forms that families complete inclusive of all families (foster families, grandparents, gay or lesbian families)?

 Apply Your Knowledge Some schools have developed programs such as Muffins for Moms, where mothers are invited to school to have breakfast with their child and Donuts for Dads where fathers are invited to breakfast. What are the advantages and disadvantages of these programs? Are they inclusive of all families?

Using family photos is another way to include and highlight the diversity of families within your program. In one classroom, Becky, the teacher, made a family quilt. Each family created a quilt piece from construction paper that held a family picture and any other information or pictures the family wished to include. The teacher then laminated the papers and tied all the families' papers together with yarn to create the quilt. Becky displayed the quilt in the entry to the program.

In another program, each family is highlighted for one week. During this week, a showcase is provided for the family to share artifacts, pictures, and stories. Best Beginnings child care encourages families to set up special interactive displays for the children in the program. One family had just taken a vacation to the ocean. They brought back seashells and set up a display for the children.

Providing materials (newsletters, flyers, informational packets, parenting books) in the family's native language is also a way of letting families know that they belong, especially for parents who are just learning English. It is also an essential communication tool.

This display created by a parent highlights a special family activity.

Reach Out to Under-Represented Groups. In the past few years, there have been several national initiatives to reach out to fathers. National leaders have recognized that fathers play a unique role in children's development, parenting in a different but complementary way with mothers (Fagan & Palm, 2004). However, in two-parent homes, only 28% of fathers compared with 58% of mothers are highly involved in their children's education (attended parent teacher conferences and school events, volunteered) (Nord & West, 2001). In single-parent homes the involvement of the primary parent, whether mother or father, was similar (Nord & West, 2001). While parental involvement leads to higher academic outcomes for children, achievement is increased even further when both parents are involved (Nord & West, 2001). In designing environments for fathers, display images of fathers with their children, establish resource libraries that include information specifically designed for fathers, and spotlight examples of involved fathers. Some programs include a special column in their newsletter specifically devoted to dads.

It is also important to involve noncustodial parents. As children proceed through their school years, noncustodial parental involvement is linked to higher grades, and lower retention, suspension, and expulsion rates (Nord & West, 2001). Providing additional newsletters and print materials is one way to accomplish this. Some programs provide a mounted literature holder near their bulletin board with extra newsletters, flyers, and invitations. Other programs mail information to the noncustodial parent or prepare a separate folder for each of the child's households. Noncustodial parents also need to be considered in family–teacher conferences. For example, Happy Hands Kindergarten gives separated parents the option of coming to the conference together or having separate conferences.

Establishing an Environment That Tells Families, "You Are Valued"

When we value a person, we acknowledge that person, seek his or her ideas, involve the person in decision making, and appreciate and utilize his or her expertise.

Acknowledge Family Members. One way to acknowledge someone is to provide a greeting to the person. Every person entering a program needs to be greeted. A brief personal message as family members pick up and drop off children can help to build relationships and let them know that you value them as persons and as parents. For example, as family members drop off children, Tanya notices a mother's new coat, discusses a child's upcoming birthday with another mother, asks a grandmother who has been receiving treatment for cancer how she is feeling, and asks a father who was in a race over the weekend how it went.

Seek Input from Families. When we value someone, we seek his or her ideas and opinions. You can obtain families' ideas in a variety of ways. The Beaverhead Infant/Toddler Program added a box with a pad of paper and a pencil to their entry area so that families could express their joys and concerns. Parents posted the joys on a bulletin board. They placed concerns in a box. The staff addressed the concerns at the next staff meeting. The director then posted the concern and the solution on the bulletin board. At another center, idea lists are posted on the bulletin board. For example, the parents were asked about ideas for a playground renovation. As the project proceeded, the parent committee asked parents for fundraising ideas.

Involve Families in Decision Making. We also involve families in decision making when we value them. This includes decisions about their child and about the program. Many programs have parent committees that are actively involved in program operations and decision making. For example, the composition of Head Start Policy Councils is more than 50% parents. Families are involved in decisions about hiring new staff, budgets, and curriculum.

In one program, families were actively involved in facility design. At Birge Nest Early Head Start, in Brattleboro, Vermont, a parent committee developed the entry space. The program was housed in an old industrial building. Although the classrooms and offices had been remodeled, the entry had been left with cement floors and drab undecorated walls. The parents added several small café tables, a coffee bar, and a comfortable seating area where they could sit and read a book to their child or meet with other parents. Children's art work, a fountain, and a beautiful screen added to the ambiance.

To include more families in decision making, the Meadowlark School added poll boxes to the parent/child transition area. The current poll is whether to provide weekly potlucks at the center.

Recognize and Use Family Members' Expertise. We recognize and use others' expertise when we value them. In Ella's kindergarten room, family members are given a choice of activities when they volunteer in the classroom. She has established a volunteer station that includes a list of possible activities. All the materials and directions to complete needed tasks are at the station. She respects that families have different interests and skills and so provides materials for a variety of options. Parents help develop learning center materials, work with individual or small groups of children, and create homemade books and audiotapes. For example, two parents have been creating tapes in Spanish to use with some of the classroom books.

Brian, a teacher in a K–1 classroom, posts signs in each center with a list of what children are learning. Also posted are ways that adults can facilitate the learning. For example, he posts sheets with open-ended questions and background information in the science area. Brian states that since he has begun this, volunteers say that they feel more competent working with the children.

Amelia, a home childcare provider, posts a note on her door describing the theme she and the children are working on and invites parents to share materials, ideas, or expertise.

The first time she did this, the theme was firefighters. One parent brought in a toy fire truck, another shared an authentic fire hat, and another arranged a visit by an uncle who was a firefighter.

At Curious Minds, a project web is hanging in the area where parents enter. Like Amelia's note, the project web informs families about the progress of the current project. Family members are encouraged to suggest ideas and to provide materials or assistance.

Establishing an Environment That Meets Families' Basic Needs

New families have the immediate need to successfully navigate the early childhood building and locate parking. Families also have the need to have their physical needs met as they use the early childhood facility, to feel comfortable leaving their children in your care, to have a peaceful transition when leaving or picking up their children, to have their resources protected, and to be considered as individuals as well as parents.

Assist Families to Easily Navigate the Setting. Entering a large program or school and trying to find the office can sometimes be intimidating, especially when there are multiple entrances. Recently I visited four programs. Each had a sign posted stating the need to check in with the office. However, the office was not easily located in any of the programs. When families first begin a program, we are setting the stage for future interactions. This first impression helps to answer the question, "Will my needs be met in this program?" Families need to be able to easily navigate the setting—to locate the office, their child's classroom, the gym, the parent resource room, and so forth. Classrooms and offices should be labeled in the language or languages used by the families. Floor plans posted by the door or arrows can direct families and others to the office. Diagrams, verbal directions, or a personal guide can assist families and guests to locate other program spaces.

Provide Convenient Parking. Easy to locate, convenient parking spaces are also important. Imagine a mother with a 3-year-old and an infant. Even walking across a parking lot carrying the infant; a large bag of diapers; and a diaper bag with extra clothes, bottles, and formula, while trying to keep her 3-year-old safe from traffic, can be very difficult.

Provide for Adults' Physical Needs. Adult-size chairs in classrooms, offices, meeting rooms, gyms, and other play spaces are critical to meet adults' physical needs. Many adults have difficulty sitting in small chairs or in sitting or rising from the floor. Maria Montessori stressed the need for child-size furnishings as a way to demonstrate respect and provide comfort for the child. The same philosophy is true for adults. Adult bathrooms are also critical.

Assist Families to Feel Comfortable Leaving Children in Your Care. Families need to feel comfortable and safe leaving their children in your care. It is important for families to have information about the staff that works with their children. Many programs develop a showcase of staff, including cooks and janitors. The showcase often includes pictures and professional information such as degrees, how long they have worked in the field, and awards. It should also include personal information that helps the families learn about staff members as individuals. For example, Tina wrote about her fascination with children's development, let parents know she had a bachelor's degree in early childhood, and that she had been an early childhood teacher for 10 years. She also told about her interest in fly-fishing. This personal piece of information was a starting point for many conversations with families.

Assist with a Peaceful Transition. Families and children have a need for a peaceful transition from home to the program and from the program to home. To see an example of how one teacher assists families and children to transition from home to the center, watch the video *Saying Goodbye* on MyEducationLab.

Providing a quiet place where parents can engage in a transition activity such as reading a book can help to ease the transition for young children. Depending upon the climate and the child's age, you might need a place where parents can sit with children to help them remove boots and put on shoes or slippers. A waving window allows children and families to say their final goodbyes. For infants and toddlers, small, low windows can be placed slightly above the floor.

Help Protect Families' Resources. Families have the need to protect their resources. Having a lost and found box can help families find missing clothing, toys, and other items.

Meet the Needs of Parents as Individuals. Many programs also strive to meet the needs of parents as individuals. For example, each morning the Nurturing Center provides coffee and tea for families. They also provide a whiteboard for parents who wish to leave messages for other parents. Recently one parent wrote about a sale on children's clothing at a local store. Another parent let other families know about a free children's production at the local theatre.

Establishing an Environment That Allows the Family to Effectively Share and Receive Information About Their Child

There are many ways that we can encourage the sharing of information between families and staff. This includes providing multiple, frequent opportunities for two-way dialogue, taking advantage of daily communication opportunities, using your environment to provide information about what children are learning, and providing private places for conferences. We will examine each of these criteria in more depth in the following sections.

Provide Multiple, Frequent Opportunities for Two-Way Dialogue. The most effective family/teacher communication involves two-way dialogue and frequent contact using varied forms of interaction (Crosser, 2005). When there is regular, effective communication, families rate teachers higher, feel more comfortable with the school, and are more involved in the school (Caplan, Hall, Lubin, & Fleming, 1997). Family/teacher communication is encouraged through family/teacher conferences, home visits, open houses, phone calls, e-mail exchanges, newsletters, and family-program activities such as child art shows, culminating events to projects, and parent luncheons.

Take Advantage of Daily Communication Opportunities. Communication is also enhanced by having an environment that promotes daily interaction. It is important to design staff schedules so that someone is available to greet children and families as they arrive.

Family communication books or two-way journals are another way for families and teachers to exchange information. At the infant/toddler programs in Reggio Emilia, teachers and families create a "Notebook for Two Voices." These notebooks, which circulate between home and school, record children's developmental progression through notes, anecdotes, and personal reflections (Giovannini, 2001, p. 147). They also provide valuable documentation of the child's earliest years.

Individual family and teacher mailboxes can also be a place to share information. One program uses a hanging shoe holder for mailboxes. Another program uses plastic shoeboxes that are stacked on top of the children's cubbies. Both methods help to assure that families and teachers receive notes and other correspondence.

When children are transported to school on busses, regular communication is more difficult. Terri, a teacher of kindergartners, sews 9" × 12" fabric pockets (a different design for each child) to hold information that goes between the family and teacher. The pockets are durable and obvious, and so are not easily destroyed or lost in backpacks.

Use Your Environment to Provide Information About What Children Are Learning. Your environment can also inform families about what children are learning. Many programs post the classroom schedule and lesson or project plans for families and volunteers to see. Like Brian, you can also post signs on the walls of each learning center telling what children are learning in that area. Project notebooks, documentation panels, and albums also inform families of children's learning. At the Burlington Little School, Deb Curtis places documentation (photos, descriptions, and interpretations) of class activities as well as individual activities on 8½" × 11" paper that she places in plastic sleeves. She then posts these in the entry area for families to read. After all of the families have had a chance to read them, she places them in a three-ring binder that is also kept in the entry area. The Mentor Graphic Child Development Center has a file for each child that houses possible portfolio entries. The files and portfolios are placed next to the sign-in area, so that families can easily look at them. To see another example of ways that programs share portfolios with families, watch the video *Portfolio Exhibitions* on MyEducationLab.

Go to MyEducationLab and select the topic "Assessment/Documentation." Under Activities and Applications, watch the video *Portfolio Exhibitions.*

Many programs also provide parents with information about what their child does each day. For example, when families drop children off at Curious Minds, there is a statement posted, "Today we are going to . . . ." The families are encouraged to read the statement to their child or allow the child to read the statement to them. There is also a daily flash at the end of the day. On the "Daily Flash," the teacher lists at least one thing that the children did that day. A "Daily News Reporter," one of the children's rotating jobs, provides information from a child's point of view. In addition, teachers often place individual Happygrams, listing an accomplishment such as "Today I completed the ABC puzzle all by myself," in family mailboxes.

Teresa takes digital pictures on a daily basis. She then provides a slide show of images of the children engaged in activities, as families pick up their children.

Provide Private Places for Impromptu and Scheduled Conferences. Within the environment, it is also important to have a private place for impromptu and scheduled family conferences. Adult-size chairs and a round table can help to create a comfortable and egalitarian atmosphere. Sitting across from each other over a desk creates a barrier that some families might associate with the teacher having more power than they do.

Establishing an Environment Where the Family Can Gain Information and Materials That Will Assist Them in Providing for Their Child's Needs

Early childhood programs can be instrumental in providing information about parenting, home learning activities, and community resources. Each type of information can assist families in meeting children's needs.

Provide Parenting Information. You can share parenting information through parent lending libraries of books, tapes, and videos. You can also offer tip sheets, placed near the sign-in area, that provide easy to read information about common issues for the age group. For example, in an infant/toddler program you might have tip sheets about subjects like toilet

Figure 18.2
Family Bulletin Boards

Many programs have a family bulletin board. However, it is not worth a program's time to develop the board unless it meets the needs of families, and they find it useful. With family input, programs need to determine the purpose of the board and then to use design principles and placement so that the board is useful to families.

There are many purposes for bulletin boards (share information about events, share documentation of what children are doing, and provide parenting information). Bulletin boards might contain children's artwork, answers to a question, photos of children engaged in an activity, or a photograph of a learning center or activity and a description of what children learned. The bulletin board might also be a place to pick up an extra copy of a newsletter, announcement, book order, or permission slip.

Some programs have a "Give and Take Bulletin Board." Teachers divide the board into featured spaces. These include areas such as Give Us a Hand (accomplishments), Learning Opportunities (training events), Things You Always Wanted to Know (program information), How About a Hand (volunteer opportunities), Picture This (photos of children), and I've Got an Idea (suggestions). Paper, pushpins, tape, and markers are available so families can easily add information to the board (Child Care Plus, 1995).

The location of the bulletin board is critical. It must be placed in an area where families will notice it and have time to linger to read it. An infant/toddler program in Santa Rosa, California, has classrooms that face an interior open courtyard. The bulletin boards for each classroom are placed outside the door, facing the courtyard, and are covered with Plexiglas to protect them from the elements. Since the bulletin boards have been moved outside the classroom, families are able to linger and read them.

Bulletin boards need to be attractive, using design elements and colors effectively. They need to be noncluttered with short, easy-to-read phrases, and large type. It is important for the boards to be at the reader's eye level.

To catch the reader's attention, you might add interactive elements such as lifting a flap to find an answer to a question on the board. Display tables below the bulletin board allow the display of three-dimensional items and can draw the viewer to the board. Changing the background of the bulletin board can alert families that something new has been added. Bulletin boards can provide an effective means for communicating with families when designed appropriately.

learning, starting solid foods, encouraging language, and sleeping through the night. Information might also be placed on bulletin boards. See Figure 18.2 for information on designing family bulletin boards.

Provide Information on Home Learning Activities. Many programs also provide families with information and materials to assist with home learning activities. For example, Curious Minds creates math and literacy bags that include a children's book, a list of activities to use with the book, and all the materials to complete the activities. See the opening photo for an example of the bags. Backpacks or bags can also be used for art kits, game kits, and science kits. Other programs provide writing briefcases containing paper, journals, a variety of writing implements, and story starters that families can check out.

While many programs stress that families should read to children, this may not be possible for all families. For example, some families may have difficulty accessing books in their native language. Encouraging storytelling is a way of respecting families while also meeting children's literacy needs. One program encouraged families to engage in storytelling by providing a bag with a tape player and blank tapes. Blank books and art supplies were also included for writing and illustrating a book, if the family wanted. Some families then lent the books and tapes to the program so that other children could also listen to them.

Storytelling is also an important option for families with low reading skills. Through storytelling, children gain many of the same skills that they gain from being read to, including concept of story, the many strands of plot, internalization of character, prediction skills, the natural rhythms and patterns of language, listening and attending skills, vocabulary development, and learning figures of speech and metaphors. In addition, stories are often an important way of learning about and internalizing one's culture (Malo & Bullard, 2000).

Provide Information on Community Services. It is also helpful for programs to provide information about community services. Some programs sponsor one-stop services featuring a variety of social agencies in the family resource center (learn more about family resource centers by reading Figure 18.3). In other programs, teachers distribute booklets of available community services to each family. You might also display brochures from different community agencies in a prominent place.

This continually changing bulletin board is a favorite of parents.

Programs can assist families in many other ways as well. Some programs sponsor a clothing or toy exchange. For example, Santa Rosa Infant/Toddler Program has a clothing bin where families can drop off clean clothing. Any family can take clothing from the bin if they wish. Some programs provide families with the phone numbers of staff who are willing to provide after-hours or weekend child care (with staff permission) as another way to assist families.

Some programs provide family resource centers. In the centers, families can obtain information, take classes, meet other parents, access community services, and assist in projects to make the program higher quality (Little, 1998). Resource rooms might contain computers, libraries, clothing or toy exchanges, and private meeting spaces. In establishing a parent resource center, consider the following:

- Hold a meeting or survey families to see what they value in a resource center
- Make the center visible and easy to find
- Staff the center with volunteers
- Clearly label all materials in the center
- Make the center child friendly (even if families are using the center when their child is in the classroom, they might be bringing younger children with them)
- Provide multilingual information
- Provide a welcoming environment (noncluttered, adult-size soft furniture, coffee and tea pot)
- Provide informative posters, books, pamphlets
- Provide a suggestion box
- Provide name tags where families can write their name and the name of their child as a way to build community

Figure 18.3
Family Resource Centers

Meeting the Needs of Staff

Through your environment, you can help to motivate, empower, and appreciate staff. Your environment can assist in developing or discouraging a sense of community and can reduce or contribute to job stress. It also serves as a model. "If we want caregivers to offer well designed and pleasing learning environments for children, we need to design an environment like that for them" (Carter & Curtis, 1998, p. 124). Teachers often spend 8 or more hours in the early childhood setting. All aspects of the environment should allow staff to feel that this is a place where they belong, where their basic needs are met, where they are valued, where they can effectively share information with others, and where they can efficiently obtain the information and materials they need to be successful in meeting children's needs.

Reducing Burnout

Early childhood providers are particularly vulnerable to burnout (Evans, Bryant, & Owens, 2004). Leading researchers in the field describe burnout as including emotional exhaustion, depersonalization (distances self from others), and reduced accomplishment (Maslach, Jackson, & Leiter, 1996). Burnout leads to increased negativity about the job and children, a cynical attitude, feelings of inadequacy, and a reduced ability to cope. This has a negative impact on the care children receive in these environments (Evans et al., 2004).

There are many factors that contribute to early childhood practitioner burnout, including low wages, ambiguous job descriptions, poor communication among staff, and lack of involvement in decision making (Evans et al., 2004). The job itself is also very demanding. Children in the early childhood years require teachers who always have high energy, high interaction levels, and a high level of alertness.

One way that occupational burnout can be reduced is through adequate pay and benefits. One organization that is working on this issue is the Worthy Wage Network. For information about worthy wages and current wage initiatives see http://www.ccw.org/about_wage.html.

Occupational burnout can also be reduced through stress management, networking and communicating with others, informal coping networks, and resources and materials to meet the high demands of early childhood (Evans et al., 2004). An effective environment can assist in providing these.

Establishing an Environment That Tells Staff, "You Belong Here"

Staff, like children and families, experience a sense of belonging when they see reflections of themselves in the environment (Carter & Curtis, 1998). This includes images and favorite items.

A sense of belonging is also reinforced by having a place for storing personal belongings (coat, purse, etc.). This space needs to be secure so that children do not have access to medicines or other harmful items that might be found in purses or pockets. Teachers also need a space for storing personal teaching materials and private files and records.

Establishing an Environment That Tells Staff, "You Are Valued"

It is important to let staff know that they are valued. Some of the ways that we can do this is by providing a comfortable, aesthetic environment; showing consideration for their time; involving them in decision making, and showing appreciation for them. In the next sections we will examine each of these criteria more thoroughly.

Provide a Comfortable, Aesthetic Environment. Establishing comfortable, aesthetic, and clean adult environments (bathrooms, lounges, staff rooms) is one very basic way that we let staff know that they are valued. For example, Susan, a principal of a kindergarten school, realized that she had been stressing the need for aesthetic places for children, while ignoring the aesthetics and comfort of adult spaces in her school. She began by redecorating the institutional adult bathroom, adding mirrors, plants, and a hand-woven rug. She placed lavender liquid soap and lavender lotion by the sink. A parent, who worked in a floral shop, brought in discarded but still beautiful fresh flowers that Susan placed in the bathroom. Like children, adults spend many of their waking hours in the early childhood environment. They need to be surrounded by "softness, art, beauty, natural materials, and living things" (Carter & Curtis, 1998, p. 125). It is important to create an environment where adults and children want to spend their time, rather than just enduring the experience.

Show Consideration of Staff's Time. Being considerate of someone's time is another way that we value him or her. For example, in early childhood facilities, having organized and convenient storage for program materials and supplies saves time and makes working conditions easier.

Seek Staff Input When Making Decisions. Encouraging staff input into decision making is an important way to let staff know that we appreciate their expertise. This often results in better decisions as well. Some programs provide joys and concerns boxes for staff to express views. Others have a running dialogue on a staff bulletin board or discussion board. For example, one center was considering extending their hours. On the staff bulletin board was the question, "What are the pros and cons of extending our hours?" Sticky notes and pens encouraged staff to add their views. One of the teachers then typed the notes and they were used as a basis for discussion at a staff meeting.

Show Appreciation for Staff Members. Letting people know that we appreciate them is another way to say, "You are valued." The director at Tiny Tots uses a variety of ways to show appreciation. For example, she places fresh flowers in the staff room with an appreciation note. She began an appreciation bulletin board and encourages parents and staff to place notes on it. She collects free and inexpensive items and places them in a basket in the teachers' lounge for the teachers to take (sample lotions, pens, posters, magnets). She remembers birthdays with special treats. She also places individualized thank-you notes in teacher's mailboxes.

In a field with high turnover and high stress levels, it is important to remember to value staff. Establishing an environment of respect and appreciation, where all individuals are valued, can make the workplace more rewarding.

Establishing an Environment That Meets Staff's Basic Needs

Teachers, like children, have a basic need for a safe and healthy environment with a place to keep personal belongings and materials. They also need a comfortable place to take a break where they can relax and rejuvenate. Providing for these basic needs helps to relieve staff stress and create a more pleasant working environment. This can lead to higher quality care for children.

Provide a Safe Environment. The most common adult injuries in early childhood settings are back injuries (Wortman, 2001). Back injuries most frequently occur over a period of time rather than as an isolated incident (Wortman, 2001). To provide a comfortable environment and to protect teachers' backs, it is important to provide adult furniture (Wortman, 2001). If adults are sitting on the floor, backrests should be provided. Steps that children can climb for diaper changing can also protect adults' backs. Another option that some centers use to protect an adults' backs when changing toddlers is to have the toddler stand for diaper changes while the teacher sits on a low stool.

Provide a Healthy Environment.

It is also critical to protect adults' health. "Improving the health of adults who work in child care pays double dividends. It not only helps the individual, but also everyone who depends on them" (Aronson, 2001, p. 1). Adequate airflow and noise, temperature, and humidity control, are also important in protecting health for adults and children (see Chapter 4 for more information).

To protect from blood-borne diseases, it is imperative to have gloves easily available. Many centers have a supply of gloves in every room (classroom, bathrooms, gym, and lunchroom) and a fanny pack with gloves for taking outside. Teachers are more likely to use gloves when they are readily accessible.

To prevent illness, adults need to wash hands many times a day (for example, when they enter the program, before food preparation, whenever assisting children with toileting or blowing noses). Since all the hand washing can lead to dry and cracked hands, it is important to have lotion available at every sink.

Assist Teachers to Reduce Stress.

To be effective with children and to prevent burnout, staff need breaks from children. As discussed in the scenario at the beginning of the chapter, a comfortable lounge can decrease stress and assist staff to return to the children refreshed.

Some directors have found innovative ways to reduce stress for teachers. For example, the director at the First Steps Infant/Toddler Program brainstormed ways that she could support teachers and reduce their stress. Many of the teachers were single parents with multiple demands on their time. She realized that each day the program threw away quantities of food, since any food placed in serving bowls could not be reserved. She encouraged staff to take home the remaining food at the end of the day. This saved the staff time and money while providing a nutritious meal for their family. The director also provided free yoga classes once a week that staff could attend with their children.

Establishing an Environment That Allows the Staff to Share Information with Others

Establishing a lounge and furniture groupings that encourage interaction can facilitate staff networking, sharing ideas, and problem-solving issues (Bentham, 2008). As people have the opportunity to know each other, they often form informal mentoring and support networks. While this is usually positive, at times it can become negative. When the Fifth Avenue School staff discussed creating a staff lounge, one of the teachers mentioned that in a previous school the lounge was dominated by negative talk about children and parents. She said that she ended up staying in her classroom during breaks rather than be influenced by the lounge atmosphere. The Fifth Avenue staff decided that they would prevent the possibility of this occurring by creating and posting a list of ground rules in the lounge. Two of their rules were, "Freely share positive information about children, parents, and coworkers," and "Any problems or issues that are discussed are for the purpose of brainstorming solutions, no names will be used." The staff also made a commitment to remind each other of the rules. These guidelines have helped the Fifth Avenue School to have a positive staff lounge.

Individual staff mailboxes are also helpful in organizing and systematically getting mail and messages to staff members. Some programs also provide a list of staff phone numbers (with their permission) so that people can easily contact each other outside of work hours.

Curious Minds, a college lab school, has many students who work in the center each day. At the staff sign-in area, there is a communication book where the director, teachers, and lab and work-study students write pertinent information. This might include reminders about upcoming events, information a parent has provided that needs to be passed on to other staff members, a thank-you, and so forth.

Establishing an Environment Where the Staff Can Gain Information and Materials They Need to Provide for Children's Needs

To meet children's needs, teachers must have access to children's records, materials and supplies, references, and a work area for creating their own materials and supplies.

Provide Ready Access to Children's Files. Parents often fill out enrollment information that includes information about their child's interests, their goals for the child, and special talents they may have. If directors keep this information in a central office, teachers may never have the time to look at the material. Instead, locked files in each classroom can allow teachers to keep information readily available.

Provide Organized, Abundant Materials and Supplies. Teachers need enough materials and supplies to meet children's needs. While teachers will keep some of these in the classroom, there should also be storage for materials bought in bulk (paints, paper) and for recyclables. Supplies and materials should be visible, organized, and distributed fairly. Keeping a running list of additional materials, with the person's name requesting it, can help the person purchasing supplies get what teachers need. A workroom with a large table, copying machine, computer, and laminating machine can assist teachers in preparing additional materials.

Provide Teaching Resources. As demonstrated in the opening scenario, a resource area with a reference library, current educational journals, and access to a computer can help teachers in planning classroom activities and researching a topic for their own background knowledge. These resources are also helpful in learning about new techniques or accessing information to meet the needs of a child or family with special needs. Some programs highlight new materials or books by placing them on an attractive display table (Bentham, 2008).

At the Kids World Learning Center, staff took turns writing a "Did you know . . .?" on the resource room whiteboard. These tidbits of information provided teachers with educational ideas. For example, "Did you know that we should use one ounce of sunscreen per child at least 20 minutes before going outside?"

The resource area can also contain announcements. For example, announcements about upcoming staff training, community workshops, and college courses can keep staff informed about educational opportunities.

To reduce adult stress and burnout and to provide high-quality care for children, parents and staff must have their needs met. An early childhood setting needs to provide an environment within its program that meets adults' needs, encourages communication, provides access to resources, and lets adults know they belong and are valued.

Figure 18.4
Environmental Assessment: Meeting the Needs of Families and Teachers

While there are many ways that we involve and appreciate adults, this checklist will focus on those that would be noticeable if you were observing the environment.

Does the program meet the needs of families through

☐ Representing families in the program through photos, displays, and artifacts?

☐ Assuring that all materials used in the program represent cultural and family diversity (forms, posters, brochures, children's books, family resource books)?

☐ Providing materials in the families' native language?

☐ Seeking family input (for example, a suggestion box)?

☐ Involving families in decision making?

☐ Valuing families' expertise (such as a volunteer center, signs letting families know what the children are learning and how they can support the learning posted in learning centers, project webs with an invitation to add to it)?

☐ Easy-to-locate offices and classrooms?

☐ Signage that welcomes families in their native language?

☐ Convenient parking spaces?

☐ Adult-size furniture and bathrooms?

☐ Staff displays that provide information to families about the people who are working with their children?

☐ Providing a space for peaceful transitions?

☐ Meeting the needs of parents as individuals (warm personal greetings, coffee and tea, parent lounge for relaxing)?

☐ A welcoming, informative entryway?

☐ Providing mechanisms for two-way communication (such as family mailboxes, communication books, individual greetings)?

☐ Providing information about what children are learning (for example, documentation panels, portfolios, daily flashes, happygrams)?

☐ Private places for conferences?

☐ Providing information that will assist families in providing for their child's needs (lending libraries, literacy backpacks, family resource centers, community pamphlet displays)?

Does the program meet the needs of staff through

☐ Providing reflections of staff (such as images and favorite items)?

☐ Supplying a place to store personal belongings and personal teaching materials?

☐ Providing a lounge for teachers to relax and rejuvenate?

☐ Providing adult-size bathrooms?

☐ Valuing staff time by providing organized and convenient storage?

☐ Allowing staff input into decision making (such as joys and concerns boxes)?

☐ Appreciating staff's work (for example, posted thank-you notes, highlighting accomplishments on bulletin boards)?

☐ Protecting adults from back injuries by providing adult furniture, backrests for floor sitting, and diaper-changing steps?

☐ Improving the health of staff and children with adequate airflow, temperature, humidity, and noise control?

☐ Protecting staff from blood-borne diseases by having readily available gloves in every room?

☐ Encouraging hand washing through easily available sinks and providing lotion for protection from cracked hands?

☐ Providing a pleasant, aesthetic classroom environment?

☐ Supporting staff interactions (for example, a staff lounge, staff mailboxes, staff communication book)?

☐ Easily accessible children's files so that teachers have needed information?

☐ Providing enough materials and supplies so adults can meet children's needs?

☐ Providing teacher resources (such as a reference library, educational journals, computer with Internet access)?

Sample Application Activities

1. Brainstorm a list of relaxing activities that can be completed in 10 minutes.

2. Discuss ways that you would develop a welcoming environment for a family who does not speak English.

3. Brainstorm ways that stress could be reduced for staff in the program where you are working or completing labs.

4. Visit a program. Make a list of all environmental cues that tell families they belong in the program and that they are valued.

5. Use the environmental assessment in Figure 18.4 to critique an early childhood environment.

6. To learn more about strategies and resources for meeting the needs of families, visit one of these websites:

   Harvard Family Research Project
   http://www.hfrp.org/family-involvement

   National Coalition for Parent Involvement in Education
   http://www.ncpie.org/

   State Parent Resource Centers to serve children and families with disabilities
   http:// www.taalliance.org/ptidirectory/index.asp

chapter 19
Meeting Environmental Challenges

*A*n Early Head Start program invited a consultant to their classroom to help design their small space. The teachers were concerned because the mobile infants, who were beginning to crawl and walk, had limited space to move and play. In addition, there were no centers in the classroom, so it was difficult for children to find quiet places to look at a book or complete a simple puzzle. The room contained four highchairs, a large ramped loft, a small table and chairs, two adult-size rocking chairs, and several teacher cabinets. A partial wall enclosed a sleeping area containing five cribs.

Although initially the teachers thought there was a need for each piece of equipment since at times they had five babies who were in cribs, after further analysis it was determined that equipment that was not in current use could be disassembled and stored elsewhere. This eliminated two cribs and two highchairs. Placing plastic storage bins under two of the remaining cribs eliminated the need for one of the teacher cabinets. High storage built on the wall eliminated the need for another *storage cabinet. The removal of the equipment and storage cabinets created significantly more space for children to play.*

The large loft could not be removed from the classroom, having been assembled within the space. However, the teachers felt that currently the loft wasn't being used to its full space potential. They decided to divide the loft platform with a gauzy curtain. They furnished the back half of the loft with soft cushions and books, creating a cuddly reading area. The bottom of the loft had been fully enclosed. A carpenter cut two child-size holes into this area, making it usable for children to crawl in and out of.

The teachers also provided an illusion of more space by adding more mirrors to the walls and the ceiling. The napping area had a heavy wooden half door. This was replaced with a Plexiglas door, allowing children to see in and out of the napping area and also providing more light for this space.

By removing equipment that was not currently being used, rethinking storage options, reexamining their current space, and creating an illusion of space, the teachers were able to transform the room. Children and staff felt less confined in the newly designed room and children had more room for movement and play.

This chapter will examine a variety of challenges that programs face, including challenges with space, limited budgets, having an early childhood business in your home, and the need to share space.

Creating Centers in Small Spaces

Although most programs must meet minimum state standards for space of 35 square feet per child, most experts recommend a per child minimum of 50 square feet (White and Stoecklin, 2003). If you have only the minimum amount of space that is required by law, arranging your room can be challenging. However, there are several strategies to use if you are in this situation. They include removing any equipment or materials that you are not currently using, using all available space throughout the day, increasing space in a variety of innovative ways, using vertical surfaces, and creating an illusion of more space.

Effectively Use All Available Space

As in the opening scenario, as teachers we sometimes become so familiar with the equipment, materials, and space arrangement in our classrooms that we need to take a fresh look to determine if our space is being used to its full advantage. Some hints to take advantage of space include the following:

- Collect data on the space use. For example, every 10 minutes during center play, tally where each child is playing. Are the children using every area within the classroom? If not, what changes could be made to better utilize the space?
- Remove all equipment and materials that are not in current use.
- Reduce clutter (clutter takes space and makes small spaces seem smaller).
- Provide portable centers (a tote containing math manipulatives can be brought out and placed on the snack table during free play, a beanbag throw can be placed in the circle area during this time). The Oak Street Afterschool Learning Program provided additional space by having a play table that mounted to the ceiling with a pulley. The table was used for a train set. Children were taught to carefully lower the table for play and then raise it to provide space for circle time activities.

- Use tops of shelving for centers. For example, a science center might be placed on the top of the manipulative shelf.
- Think creatively, examine every space for possible use (bathrooms, closets, nap rooms, coatroom). Can you replace a closet door with a curtain and use it for a puppet area? If there is a teacher's desk in the room, could an alone area be placed under the desk? Could the hall be used for cubbies, storage, or a separate center? For example, Karl Wolf, a teacher of kindergarten children, has a woodworking center and a gross motor area in the hallway outside his classroom.

Increase Usable Space

Programs might increase usable space in a variety of ways. This can include creating lofts, developing centers outdoors, carefully considering furniture options, and designing storage spaces that do not take floor space.

Create Lofts. Lofts allow centers to be placed in the upper platform and underneath. One Head Start program created an inexpensive option by converting bunk beds into lofts. When creating lofts, make sure that you contact your licensing agent or health department for requirements. You will also want to make sure that you have appropriate fall zones and surfaces.

Create Outdoor Centers. You might also be able to effectively use the outdoors for some of your centers. Many programs allow children to freely move back and forth between indoor and outdoor centers. If the weather allows you to spend significant time outside and space is an issue, you would not need to have the same centers inside and outside.

Floating shelves and an easel attached directly to the wall allow a home childcare provider to develop a functional, aesthetic art center in a very small space.

Use Dual-Purpose Furniture. Programs can also economize space by using movable or dual-purpose equipment. Blissful Beginnings Child Care has a lunch table that folds and latches against the wall when it is not needed for eating. The back of the table is a whiteboard that is used for drawing and writing when it is folded up. They also have a parent sign-in table that folds down for use and then folds and latches along the wall for the remaining part of the day. Another program uses folding chairs that they fold up when not in use, to create more play space. Central Preschool has a specially designed sensory table with a lid that extends beyond the table. When the lid is placed on the sensory table, it can be used as a lunch table.

Use Smaller Furniture. Smaller furniture can also economize space. For example, a rectangular table takes less space than a kidney shaped table. Typical shelves are wider than needed. Purchasing or building narrower shelving can save space.

Reconsider Storage Options. Effectively organizing and using storage can often eliminate floor storage. For example, like Andrea, consider using spaces under tables, cribs, or furniture for storage or placing storage high on the walls. Storage can also be increased by using the inside of cabinet doors, adding shelves between shelves that are spaced far apart, adding rotating trays, and using square rather than round storage containers. For inspiration on storage options, you might want to visit an RV dealership. RVs are typically built to take advantage of all possible storage spaces.

Use Vertical Space Whenever Possible

Vertical space is an often-forgotten area for centers. Wall-pockets, magnetic surfaces, and whiteboards can all be used for activity centers. These can be mounted to the wall, on the front of cabinets, or on the ends and backs of bookshelves. Pegboards mounted on the wall can provide access to materials (dramatic play props, carpentry tools, art supplies) for many centers. Wall-mounted short lengths of rain gutter can be used to hold books or displays. Books can be hung in pockets on a divider, thus eliminating a bookshelf. You can mount easels on walls, as another way to preserve floor space (Wellhousen, 1999).

Create the Illusion of More Space

Mirrors can make a room feel larger. Placing the mirrors so that they reflect an outdoor scene can be especially effective. Keeping windows unobscured allows the outside in, which also creates a feeling of more space. Painting everything in the room the same light color (including walls and furniture) can also provide an illusion of greater space.

To create centers in small spaces, effectively use your available space and think creatively. One program had separate classrooms for 3- and 4-year-olds and for 4- and 5-year-olds. The classrooms were small and placed side by side. The teachers decided to share the classrooms, placing quiet areas (reading, art, manipulative, literacy, science) in one classroom and active areas (blocks, dramatic play, music, art) in the other. This allowed the teachers to provide every center and to make each center larger.

Free and Inexpensive Materials to Assist a Limited Budget

Teachers in early childhood classrooms are frequently looking for ways to expand their supply budget. You can obtain free and inexpensive materials by borrowing or creating materials, seeking donations of materials, buying materials secondhand, or through special fund-raisers, contributions, or grants. Repairing what you have also reduces the need for a replacement.

Borrow Materials

- Literacy—check out books and tapes from the local library. Some children's librarians will have the books ready if you call ahead with a list or a topic.
- Resource trunks—check with your local resource and referral agency and museums. Many have materials that can be checked out by teachers.
- Exchange with other childcare providers—in one community, family childcare providers meet monthly to exchange toys, manipulatives, and books. They also pooled their money to buy an indoor climber that they each take turns using.

Create Materials

Many materials can be handmade. One center had a committee of family and community volunteers who created and renovated materials. There were retired carpenters as well as people who enjoyed sewing and creating crafts. Throughout this book are ideas for materials to create, including musical instruments, blocks, manipulatives, gross motor equipment, and puppets. Following are some ideas for creating furniture:

- Create child-size tables using old doors and screw-on legs. Another option is to shorten the legs on an adult table.
- Resurrect old furniture by painting or covering it with a cloth.
- Create shelving by using bricks and boards, stackable crates, or heavy boxes duct taped together and spray-painted.
- Make your own pillows or beanbag chairs using packing filling for the stuffing (Wellhousen, 1999).
- Create furniture from cardboard (heavy-weight cardboard, when placed in layers at 90-degree angles, is very strong). To learn more about creating cardboard furniture for children and to get free patterns visit the About.com: Furniture website http://furniture.about.com/ and conduct a search for cardboard furniture. Or visit The Fold School Website at http://www.foldschool.com/_about/about_start/about_start.html

Seek Donations

Stores are often willing to donate unsold merchandise, samples, or promotional material. For example, after Halloween you might be able to obtain quality costumes and face paint either free or very inexpensively. Lumberyards, home improvement stores, and furniture outlets often have product samples (paint chip, counter, wallpaper, wallboard, rug, fabric). As these become outdated, the store is often willing to donate them to you. Many businesses are also willing to donate promotional items to programs. For example, a bank had their name printed on Frisbees. They donated 25 to the local child care. Another time, they donated sticky notes that the teachers and children used in a variety of ways.

Merchants might also be willing to donate ends of rolls (fabric, paper, plastic, carpet, contact paper). As you shop, look for items that are sold in rolls. If there are materials that you could use, ask the store if they would be willing to donate the roll ends to you. Also, ask for donations of other items that are typically thrown away, such as film canisters or reject keys.

In their book, *Beautiful Stuff: Learning with Found Materials,* Cathy Topal and Lella Gandini (1999) describe their invitation to children and parents to collect materials. Children helped to brainstorm a list of found and recyclable materials that they would like and the teachers sent home bags to hold the items. The returned bags were clipped shut until the grand opening, creating a sense of eager anticipation. When the bags were opened, the children determined ways to sort and classify the materials. Ultimately, the materials were displayed in clear or white containers. This allowed the children to see the contents, placed the emphasis on the materials rather than the container, and created a beautiful, enticing display. The materials became part of the classroom art studio.

Some communities have Reuse Centers. These centers are stocked with reusable materials that are typically given free to teachers (see Chapter 13 for more information).

Buy Secondhand Materials and Equipment

Make a list of needed items that could be purchased secondhand. The Mother Goose Center had the following materials on their list: lamp, small loveseat, beanbag chairs, parent sign-in table, beautiful trays, crystal dishes, interesting containers, children's books, toys, and manipulatives. They had several parents who volunteered to look for these items when they went to garage sales and secondhand stores. By the end of the summer, they had found everything on their list. Craigslist.org or other similar online exchanges are another source for secondhand materials.

You might also be able to make special arrangements with a secondhand store for reduced rates or donations. Nearly New, a consignment store, allowed donations of used items to be credited to a local child care. This allowed the staff to receive items from the store for free.

Engage in Special Fund-Raisers and Seek Contributions and Grants

Some programs have parents who engage in fund-raisers and seek contributions. It is often easier to receive contributions or to engage in fund-raising if you have a specific project in mind. For example, you might be able to seek contributions for a specific piece of equipment, to paint the center, or to create a new learning center. This allows those donating to know how you will use their money. It also gives those participating in the fundraising a sense of accomplishment when the goal is met. When fund-raising, you will want to make sure that the fund-raiser fits with your organization's philosophy and mission. For example, many early childhood programs do not sell candy, since they have a goal of promoting healthy eating.

You might also receive needed program materials as gifts. For example, during the winter holiday season, many families give gifts to teachers. At one program, the teachers asked that instead, families donate a puzzle, toy, or book to the center.

Grants can also assist in meeting program goals. As the need for quality early childhood programs becomes more visible, many states, corporations, and foundations are placing emphasis on this area. You might begin to look for grants by contacting your local resource and referral agency and inquiring about childcare block grants, state initiatives, and local businesses and foundations that award grants. To learn more about corporate and federal grants and to receive grant writing tips visit the Grants Alert website at http://www.grantsalert.com/.

Repair What You Have

Repairing what we have helps with limited budgets and demonstrates to children that we can be good stewards of resources. A program in Oregon contacted a local woodworking group, who agreed to repair any broken wooden items.

Another program had an "I Need Fixing Table" that families walked by as they dropped off and picked up their children. Families would often take an item home, repair it, and return it to the "I'm Fixed Box" that sat under the table.

Using found items, sharing materials, seeking donations of materials that would otherwise be thrown away, and repairing and fixing items we already own are earth-friendly ways to help our budget, while supplying children with innovative, open-ended materials. Special fundraisers, contributions, and grants can help us to purchase materials that we cannot create or scrounge.

Teachers in this Head Start program find an innovative use for their surplus cubbies.

Establishing an Early Childhood Program in Your Home

More than 1.5 million children are cared for in family childcare homes (Census Bureau, 2005), making it the most common type of childcare arrangement (Burchinal, Howes & Kontos, 2002). Family childcare home providers have the advantage of owning their own business, creating a naturally intimate environment for children, and establishing long-term relationships with children and families. However, creating a business within your home is sometimes challenging, with family childcare providers reporting more stress than either mothers working outside the home or non-employed mothers (Atkinson, 1992). To some extent, all members of the family are affected by the business. While many family childcare providers begin care when their children are young, having your own children in the program can sometimes be stressful. Children who are used to having their own space must now share space as well as their parent's time. In family child care, providers play a multitude of roles (cook, janitor, administrator, teacher) and may work extended hours. This also increases stress levels.

The family childcare home typically includes a smaller group size and a wider range of ages (babies to after school) than a typical classroom. This allows families to keep all their children together, increasing sibling interaction and providing extended continuity of care with one provider. Because of the different age ranges, there may be less competition for the same toy or materials (Ferrar, Harms, & Cryer, 1995). However, mixed-age grouping also creates a need for a wider developmental range of materials. If the range includes infants and toddlers with older children, you must provide materials for the older children, while protecting the younger children from choking hazards.

Provide Appropriate Materials, Activities, and Environments.

Whether children are in family childcare homes or centers, they have the same need for appropriate activities, experiences, and environments. According to the National Association of Family Child Care (2005), children in family child care need materials for large- and small-muscle development, literacy, art, math, science, and dramatic play. They also need child-size furnishings and quiet alone areas. For example, as with center care, children in family care have a need for retreats or alone spaces where they can seek solitude, escape noise and social interaction, release emotions, and calm themselves (Weinberger, 2000, 2006). Retreats in homes can be created by placing a lacy curtain over a table, adding space behind a couch or chair, replacing a closet door with a gauze curtain, or adding a play tent or loft (Weinberger, 2000).

Previous chapters devoted to individual learning centers apply to family child care as well as centers and schools. Therefore, this section will address a unique issue for home child cares—how to meet the needs of the provider's family and also a mixed-age group of children.

Meeting the Needs of Children in Care and the Provider's Family

In addition to providing developmentally appropriate materials, activities, and environments for the children in care, the family childcare provider must also meet the needs of her family. Research indicates that this is best accomplished through clearly designating family and childcare space, protecting the private space and possessions of the provider's children, and assuring that the provider spends daily one-on-one time with the children she is taking care of (Goelman, Shapiro, & Pence, 1990).

Clearly Designate Childcare and Family Space. The environmental design of family child cares varies greatly. Some providers have a separate designated space for the childcare. Many have some separate designated space and some shared space. In other programs, all space used by the child care is shared with the family. To provide for everyone's needs, it is important to clearly define what space will be used for the child care and what space will be used by the family (Goelman et al., 1990). More than half the providers in one study felt that lack of clearly designated spaces was an issue for them (Atkinson, 1988). Keisha has solved this problem in her childcare home by placing a smiley face on rooms that are designated as childcare space and a stop sign on doors that are not used for child care. This made it clear to all, including Keisha's teenage children, that their private spaces will be protected. With shared space, it is also important to decide who is responsible for cleaning up the area.

Protect the Private Space and Possessions. of the Home Provider's Child Many providers have young children who must learn to share their space and their parent. It is important to make sure the child's possessions are respected, that they have their own private space, and that they have special time with their parent each day (Goelman et al., 1990). Some providers have a special closet or room for their child's toys. The same rule applies to these toys as to toys that children bring from home. For example, Amy had the rule that if any toys were brought from home then that meant the child was willing to share that toy with others. This same rule applied to Christina, her daughter.

A beautiful individual sand tray provides children with an enticing retreat activity.

Provide Parent/Child One-on-One Time. All children need the opportunity to have one-on-one time with their parent. Amy found that if she set aside 15 minutes to spend with Christina before the other children arrived each morning, then Christina was willing to share her mother the rest of the day.

The Story of Maria's Family Childcare Home

Each family child care faces unique environmental challenges. We will examine the challenges faced by one family childcare provider, Maria. She faces particularly difficult issues due to having a very small home, where most spaces need to be shared by the childcare business and by the family. This is made more challenging by the family's desire to have a home that does not look like a child care during the evenings and weekends. Let's examine how Maria handles these challenges.

Maria had worked in a childcare center for several years. However, now that she had her own young child she had decided to begin a family childcare business. Maria knew that she needed child-size furnishings and learning centers to meet the needs of the children in the family child care. However, she lived in a small house and she and her husband, Rafael, entertained their friends frequently. They wanted their house to look like a home rather than a family childcare business during the evenings and weekends. Although they had turned the guest bedroom into a dedicated space for child care, they also needed to use the living room, kitchen, and bathroom as shared space. They decided that their bedroom and Juliana's bedroom would be dedicated family spaces.

Because the kitchen had a linoleum floor, Maria used this area for art, sensory play, and snacks and meals. A rolling cart (stored in the pantry when not in use) contained art supplies. The kitchen contained two child-size tables. When children were not using them for eating, one was used for art materials and the other held tubs for sensory play. Maria and Rafael could fold the tables and place them on the porch if they needed extra room for entertaining friends.

The living room was used for reading, writing, a quiet space, and a computer area. Beanbag chairs provided comfortable seating for both children and adults. Maria sewed several plastic pockets onto pieces of canvas to hold books and writing materials. Grommets at the top of the canvas slipped over nails on the wall. Maria could easily remove the pockets from the wall, fold them, and place them in the living room closet. She placed extra books in a basket by the beanbag chairs. Children used the living room coffee table for their writing activities.

The children's playroom contained dramatic play, block, and music areas. Knowing the importance of displaying children's images and work, Maria also added several bulletin boards to this room. One of Maria's concerns with this space was how to allow the older children to use the small manipulatives while protecting the infants and toddlers from choking hazards. She considered placing a partial door or gate on this room and only allowing the older children to use it. However, the toddlers loved to play with blocks and to dress up and Maria felt that developmentally they needed these opportunities. Maria solved the dilemma by building a loft in the room. The upper deck of the loft housed the manipulatives. A gate prevented the toddlers from using this area. Under the loft was an area enclosed on three sides, creating an intimate space for dramatic play. Framed children's artwork decorated the dramatic play area.

Children and families entered the child care through the front door. At this door, a small porch contained a hook for children's coats and a plastic tub for each child's extra belongings. The porch entered into the living room. Maria purchased a secondhand roll top desk and used this for the parent sign-in area. The desk had cubicles that served as parent mailboxes. She placed a bulletin board above the desk where she posted menus, her weekly plans, and other parent information. At the end of the day, Maria closed the desk and flipped the bulletin board over. On the other side of the bulletin board was a collage of family pictures.

Maria found that sometimes neighbors and relatives would drop in to visit during the day, not understanding that she was working. She created a sign to help solve this problem. On one side, the sign said "Welcome to our home." On the other side of the sign she wrote, "Maria's Child Care." Maria let friends and relatives know that they were welcome to visit when the welcome sign was displayed, but she was working when "Maria's Child Care" was displayed.

Through creative development and planning, Maria was able to develop a space that met the needs of her family and the childcare business. This allowed her to be an entrepreneur in a business that she found rewarding and that served a critical need.

Sharing Learning Spaces: Afterschool Programs

Many programs are challenged by needing to offer services in a shared space. For example, a morning and afternoon teacher may share a classroom, or a program may meet in a church space requiring teachers to put everything away each weekend. However, one of the most challenging space-sharing situations is one faced by many afterschool programs who meet in gyms or cafeterias. They have to set up and put away all materials on a daily basis. The Central Avenue Afterschool Program faced these challenges. They served approximately 30 children ages 5 to 8 each day in the school cafeteria, setting up several tables with different activities on them (art, reading, games). There was no clear division of space. The cafeteria also lacked soft spaces or places for children who wanted privacy. Because no active activities were available, some children invented their own. Children played tag, raced around the room, and slid under tables, bumping into other children and jarring tables. This led to arguments.

Tanya, a new teacher in the program, faced the challenge of how to change this pattern of behavior, while offering the children a quality program. She began by holding a circle time and asking children what they would like to do when they came to the afterschool program. She also had a meeting that included the afterschool and the cafeteria staff. A final meeting was held with parents. After she received input from the different constituencies, she made a list of criteria. The space needed to

- Be easy to set up and take down.
- Contain many varied activities (both quiet and active). There had been a request for a gross motor area and a woodworking area.
- Be divided into centers to allow for uninterrupted work.
- Provide a place for solitude.
- Contain storage for materials and also works in progress.

Designing the Afterschool Space

In planning for the space, the teachers and children first determined what specific centers to include. They decided on the following areas:

- Woodworking—The woodworking area was stationary. It included a woodworking bench, a variety of tools, and scraps of wood. A broom and dustpan allowed each woodworker to clean up when he or she was finished.
- Large motor—A rolling cart held a variety of activities including balls, plastic hoops, beanbags, a lawn dart game, and a bowling game.
- Theatre—A trunk held a variety of costumes and pieces of fabric that children could use to create their own costumes. The theatre was located on the stage and the trunk was stored there.
- Art and writing—The art materials were stored on a multi-shelf rolling cart. A tablecloth to protect the lunch tables was also stored on the cart.
- Hobby and game—These were placed on open shelves. The shelves had casters that could be closed and latched when not in use.
- Reading area—A wagon carried baskets of books and two beanbag chairs to the reading area. This area also served as a space where children could be alone.
- Fantasy play—A rolling cart held a wooden barn with realistic-looking animals, people, and accessories such as fencing, wagons, and milk cans; matchbox cars with a variety of play sets; and a Victorian dollhouse with furniture and dolls. Several lightweight, nonslip rugs were placed on the floor to define the area and to make floor play more comfortable.

The teachers used two open shelves that they currently owned and several lunchroom tables as part of the room design. They ordered a woodworking table and had a local carpenter create several rolling dividers. These dividers not only divided the

Figure 19.1
Classroom Dividers

> Robert Sheehan and David Day (1975) suggest several ways of creating dividers. Portable walls on casters (4 feet wide by 6 feet high), hanging curtains from guide wires, or creating a canopy over an area are all ways to separate and differentiate space. You can also make your own dividers from a trellis, a large cardboard box, pegboard, or old doors. A board painted with chalkboard or magnetic paint can serve a dual purpose as an activity center or divider. Placing locking wheels on dividers or shelving makes it easy to move them, creating extra flexibility.

space, but they were designed to serve at least one other function. For example, one divider had a white board on the side that faced the art area and book pockets on the side that faced the reading area. Another divider contained a parent bulletin board on one side and children's work on the other. To learn more about creating classroom dividers see Figure 19.1. The program also purchased several rolling carts. At the end of the day, the children and teachers placed all the rolling carts around the woodworking table. They rolled the dividers over to the area, forming a barrier around the carts. This kept the materials from being disturbed when the space was used for other purposes.

The teachers were stymied by how to store children's on going work (models, clay sculpture, beading). One of the cafeteria staff mentioned that they had an extra 6-foot-high rolling cart that held lunch trays. The teachers and children found this to be the perfect solution. Children placed their work on lunch trays and stored them on the cart.

After the redesign of the space, children were more engaged in activities, there were less discipline problems, and children and teachers enjoyed their time together more. There are many techniques that the Central Avenue Afterschool Program used that can be helpful to other programs seeking transformation. These include

- Involving all constituents in the planning
- Providing a variety of engaging activities, both quiet and active
- Separating the space according to use
- Using portable screens for dividers that, whenever possible, were used for a dual purpose (whiteboard, bulletin board, holding book pockets)
- Having adequate, convenient storage for putting materials away at the end of the day
- Providing rolling carts, wagons, and shelving with wheels to make it easier and faster to move materials
- Involving the children in setting up and taking down the space so that more of the teachers' time could be devoted to planning and preparing activities

When facing a challenge, it is wise to involve all constituencies. Receiving input can result in better designs and more support for the project. With the creative thinking generated by the group, even challenging spaces can be transformed to meet the needs of children and adults.

Many programs face environmental challenges. Through critically examining your space, creatively using materials, and involving others in problem solving, solutions can typically be found.

Sample Application Activities

1. Visit a thrift store to see what might be available to furnish a classroom. Make a list of materials that would be beneficial for an early childhood program.

2. Make a list of 10 materials that you could create for an early childhood setting. Make one of the materials and bring it to class to share with your classmates. Bring directions on how to create the item. These can be collected and made into a class booklet.

3. Visit a classroom or, if you are currently working with children, analyze the classroom that you are in. Make a list of innovative ways that the classroom could provide more play space for children.

4. Interview a teacher or visit an afterschool program that is located in a gym or cafeteria. How have they managed this space challenge?

5. Visit a home child care. How have they designed the space to meet the needs of their family and the children in child care?

References

Abrams, R. M. (1995). Some aspects of the fetal sound environment. In I. Deliage & J. A. Sloboda (Eds.), *Perception and cognition of music* (pp. 83–101). Philadelphia, PA: Psychology Press.

Ackermann, E. (2002). Language games, digital writing, emerging literacies: Enhancing kids' natural gifts as narrators and notators. In A. Dimitracopoulou (Ed.). *Information and communication technologies in education.* Proceedings of 3rd Hellenic Conference, with international participation, 26–29/9/2002, University of Aegean, Rhodes, Greece, Kastaniotis.

Adams, M. J. (1990). *Beginning to read: Thinking and learning about print.* Cambridge, MA: MIT Press.

ALA (American Lung Association). (2007). *Asthma in children fact sheet.* New York: American Lung Association. Retrieved from http://www.lungusa.org/asthma/ascpedfac99.html

Alkon, A., Genevro, J. L., Tschann, J. M., Kaiser, P., Ragland, D. R., & Boyce, W. T. (1999). The epidemiology of injuries in four child care centers. *Archives of Pediatric and Adolescent Medicine, 153,* 1248–1254.

Al-Mohaisen, A., & Khattab, O. (2006). Green classroom: Daylighting conscious design for Kuwait autism center. *Global Built Environment Review, 5*(3), 11–19.

Alexander, J., North, M., & Hendren, D. K. (1995). Master gardener classroom garden project: An evaluation of the benefits to children. *Children's Environments, 12*(2), 123–133.

American Academy of Pediatrics, American Public Health Association, & National Resource Center for Health and Safety in Child Care and Early Education. (2002). *Caring for our children: National health and safety performance standards: Guidelines for out-of-home child care programs* (2nd ed.). Elk Grove Village, IL: American Academy of Pediatrics and Washington, DC: American Public Health Association. Retrieved from http://nrc.uchsc.edu

American Association for the Advancement of Science (AAAS). (1993). *Benchmarks for science literacy: Project 2061.* New York: Oxford University Press.

Andrews, A. O. (1999). Solving geometric problems by using unit blocks. *Teaching Children Mathematics, 5*(6), 318–325.

Anti-Defamation League. (2003). Assessing children's literature. *New York State Association for the Education of Young Children (NYSAEYC) Reporter.* Retrieved from http://www.adl.org/education/ assessing.asp

Aquino, F. (1991). *Songs for playing.* Mexico, D.F.: Trillas.

Aronson, S. S. (1999). The ideal diaper changing station. *Child Care Information Exchange, 130,* 92.

Aronson, S. S. (2001). Taking care of caregivers: Wellness for every body. *Child Care Information Exchange.* Retrieved from https://secure.ccie.com/catalog/search.php?search=taking+care+of +caregivers&category=50

Atkinson, A. M. (1988). Providers' evaluations of the effect of family day care on own family relationships. *Family Relations, 37,* 399–404.

Atkinson, A. M. (1992). Stress levels of family day care providers, mothers employed outside the home, and mothers at home. *Journal of Marriage and the Family, 54*(2), 379–386.

ATSDR. (2000). *Toxicological profile for arsenic.* Atlanta, GA: U.S. Department of Health and Human Services—Prepared by Syracuse Research Corporation for Agency for Toxic Substances and Disease Registry.

Avrasin, M. (2007). Creating a powerhouse of play. *Parks and Recreation, 42*(4), 42–47.

Bafile, C. (2004). The prop box: Setting the stage for meaningful play. *Education World.* Retrieved from http://www.educationworld.com/a_curr/profdev101.shtml

Bakawa-Evenson, L., Oesterreich, L., & Ouverson, C. (1995). *Making blocks.* Ames: Cooperative Extension Service, Iowa State University.

Bandura, A., & Locke, E. A. (2003). Negative self-efficacy and goal effects revisited. *Journal of Applied Psychology, 88*(1), 87–99.

Bandura, Albert (1993). Perceived self-efficacy in cognitive development and functioning. *Educational Psychologist, 28*(2), 117–148. Retrieved from http://www.informaworld.com/10.1207/ s15326985ep2802_3

Baranowski, T., Mendlein, J., Resnicow, K., Frank, E., Cullen, K. W., & Baranowski, J. (2000). Physical activity and nutrition in children and youth: An overview of obesity prevention. *Preventive Medicine, 31,* S1–S10.

Baratta-Lorton, B. (1972). *Workjobs: USA:* Addison-Wesley.

Barbour, A. (1999). The impact of playground design on the play behaviors of children with differing levels of physical competence. *Early Childhood Research Quarterly, 14*(1), 75–98.

Barbour, A., Desjean-Perrotta, B., & Rojas, M. (2002). *Prop box play: 50 themes to inspire dramatic play.* Ranier, MD: Gryphon House.

Barbour, J. (2004). *Children's eating habits in the U.S.: Trends and implication for food marketers.* Rockville, MD: Packaged Facts. Retrieved from www.packagedfacts.com

Bartel, M. (2006). *Teaching creativity.* Retrieved from http://www.goshen.edu/~marvinpb/arted/tc.html#skills

Bartlett, S. (1993). Amiable space in the schools of Reggio Emilia: An interview with Lella Gandini. *Children's Environments, 10*(2), 23–38.

Beaty, J. J. (2005). *50 early childhood literacy strategies.* Upper Saddle River, NJ: Merrill/Pearson.

Beilinson, J. S., & Olswang, L. B. (2003). Facilitating peer-group entry in kindergartners with impairments in social communication. *Language, Speech, and Hearing Services in Schools, 34,* 154–166.

Benbow, M. (1990). *Loops and other groups, a kinesthetic writing system.* Tucson, AZ: Therapy Skill Builders.

Beneke, S. J., Ostrosky, M. M., & Katz, L. G. (2008). Calendar time for young children: Good intentions gone awry. *Young Children, 63*(3), 12–16.

Bentham, R. (2008). Rich environments for adult learners. *Young Children, 63*(3), 72–74.

Berger, A., Tzur, G., & Posner, M. I. (2006). Infant brains detect arithmetic errors. *Proceedings of the National Academy of Sciences of the United States of America (PNAS), 103*(33), 12649–12653.

Berger, K. S. (2006). *The developing person through childhood* (4th ed.). USA: Worth Publishers.

Bergin, D. A., Ford, M. E., & Hess, R. D. (1993). Patterns of motivation and social behavior associated with microcomputer use of young children. *Journal of Educational Psychology, 85*(3), 437–445.

Berk, L. E. (1976). How well do classroom practices reflect teacher goals? *Young Children, 32,* 64–81.

Bhargava, A., & Escobedo, T. H. (1997, March). *What the children said: An analysis of the children's language during computer lessons.* Paper presented at the Annual Meeting of the American Educational Research Association, Chicago, IL (ERIC Reproduction Service No. ED409561).

Biddle, B. J., & Berliner, D. C. (2002). Small class size and its effects. *Educational Leadership, 59,* 12–23.

Bisgaier, C. S., Samaras, T., & Russo, M. J. (2005). Young children try, try again: Using wood, glue, and words to enhance learning. In D. Koralek (Ed.), *Spotlight on young children and the creative arts* (pp. 12–18). Washington, DC: National Association for the Education of Young Children.

Bishop, R. S. (1992). Multicultural literature for children: Making informed choices. In V. J. Harris (Ed.), *Teaching multicultural literature in grades K–8* (pp. 37–53). Norwood, MA: Christopher-Gordon.

Bixler, R. D., Carlisle, C. L., Hammitt, W. E., & Floyd, M. F. (1994). Observed fears and discomforts among urban students on field trips to wildland areas. *Journal of Environmental Education, 26*(1), 24–33.

Bodrova, E., & Leong, D. J. (1998). Development of dramatic play in young children and its effects on self-regulation: The Vygotskian approach. *Journal of Early Childhood Teacher Education, 19*(2), 115–124.

Bodrova, E., & Leong, D. J. (2007). *Tools of the mind: The Vygotskian approach to early childhood education* (2nd ed.). Upper Saddle River, NJ: Merrill/Pearson.

Bodrova, E., Leong, D. J., Hensen, R., & Henninger, M. (1999). *Scaffolding early literacy through play: How to strengthen play, increase oral language, encourage symbolic thinking, and support the development of print and writing concepts.* New Orleans, NAEYC Conference.

Bogart, V. S. (2002). *The effects of looping on the academic achievement of elementary school children* (Doctoral dissertation, East Tennessee University). Retrieved from http://etd-submit.etsu.edu/etd/theses/available/etd-0820102-105005/unrestricted/BogartV082302a.pdf

Bohling-Philippi, V. (2006). The power of nature to help children heal. *Child Care Exchange, 171,* 49–53.

Bohn, C. M., Roehrig, A. D., & Pressley, M. (2004). The first days of school in the classrooms of two more effective and four less effective primary-grade teachers. *The elementary school journal, 104*(4), 269–287.

Bondavalli, M., Mori, M., & Vecchi, V. (Eds.). (1993). Children in Reggio Emilia look at their school. *Children, Youth, and Environments, 10*(2), 39–45.

Boutte, G., Scoy, I. V., & Hendley, S. (1996). Multicultural and nonsexist prop boxes. *Young Children, 52*(1), 34–39.

Bowman, B. (2006). Resilience: Preparing children for school. In B. Bowman & E. K. Moore (Eds.), *School readiness and social-emotional development: Perspectives on cultural diversity* (pp. 49–57). Washington, DC: National Black Child Development Institute.

Bowman, B., Donovan, M., & Burns, M. (2001). *Eager to learn: Educating our preschoolers.* Washington, DC: National Academy Press.

Bowman, O. J., & Wallace, B. (1990). The effects of socioeconomic status on hand size and strength, vestibular function, visuomotor integration, and praxis in preschool children. *American Journal of Occupational Therapy, 44,* 610–621.

Bradley, J., & Kibera, P. (2006). Closing the gap: Culture and the promotion of inclusion in child care. *Young Children, 61*(1), 34–40.

Braswell, J. S., Lutkus, A. D., Grigg, W. S., Santapau, S. L., Tay-Lim, B., & Johnson, M. (2001). *The nation's report card: Mathematics 2000* (NCES 2001–517). Washington, DC: National Center for Education Statistics.

Brendtro, L., & Larson. S. (2006). *The resilience revolution.* Bloomington, IN: National Educational Service.

Brendtro, L. K., Brokenleg, M., & Van Bockern, S. (2002). *Reclaiming youth at risk: Our hope for the future* (Rev. ed.). Bloomington, IN: Solution Tree.

Bresler, L. (1995). The case of the Easter bunny: Art instruction by primary grade teachers. In C. Thompson (Ed.), *The visual arts and early childhood learning* (pp. 63–66). Reston, VA: The National Art Education Association.

Brink, S. G., Tortolero, S. R., O'Hara, N., Hammond, M. V., & Frankowski, R. F. (1991). Injury hazards in outdoor play areas of family day care homes. *Children's Environments Quarterly, 8*(3), 62–68.

Brokering, L. (1989). *Resources for dramatic play.* Belmont, CA: Fearon Teacher Aids.

Bronfenbrenner, U. (1979). *The ecology of human development: Experiments by nature and design.* Cambridge, MA: Harvard University Press.

Brosterman, N. (1997). *Inventing kindergarten.* New York: Harry N. Adams.

Brown, P., Sutterby, J., & Thornton, C. D. (2001). Dramatic play in outdoor play environments. *Today's Playground, 1*(0), 10–11.

Brown, S. E. (1982). *One, two, buckle my shoe: Math activities for young children.* Ranier, MD: Gryphon House.

Bruce, T. (1992). Children, adults, and blockplay. In P. Gura (Ed.), *Exploring learning: Young children and block play* (pp. 14–26). Paul Chapman Publishing.

Bruni, M. (1998). *Fine-motor skills in children with Down syndrome: A guide for parents and professionals.* Bethesda, MD: Woodbine House.

Buck, G. (1999). Smoothing the rough edges of classroom transitions. *Intervention in School and Clinic, 34*(4), 224–227.

Buckley, J., Schneider, M., & Shang, Y. (2004). *The effects of school facility quality on teacher retention in urban school districts.* Washington, DC: National Clearinghouse for Education Facilities.

Bullard, J., & Hitz, R. (1997), Early childhood education and adult education: Bridging the cultures. *Journal of Early Childhood Teacher Education, 18*(1), 15–22.

Burchinal, M., Howes, C., & Kontos, S. (2002). Structural predictors of child care quality in child care homes. *Early Childhood Research Quarterly, 17,* 87–105.

Burke, D. L. (1996). Multi-year teacher/student relationships are a long-overdue arrangement. *Phi Delta Kappan, 77*(5), 360–361. EJ 516 053.

Burke, K., & Burke-Samide, B. (2004). Required changes in the classroom environment: It's a matter of design. *Clearing House, 77*(6), 236.

Burton, J. (2000). The configuration of meaning: Learner-centered art education revisited. *Studies in Art Education, 41*(4), 330–342.

Butin, D. (2000). *Early childhood centers.* Washington, DC: National Clearinghouse for Education Facilities.

Butterfield, P. M. (2002). Child care is rich in routines. *Zero to Three, 22*(4), 29–32.

Cadwell, L. B. (2003). *Bringing learning to life: The Reggio approach to early childhood education.* New York: Teachers College Press.

Caine, J. (1991). The effects of music on the selected stress behaviors, weight, caloric and formula intake, and length of hospital stay of premature and low birth weight neonates in a newborn intensive care unit. *Journal of Music Therapy, 28*(4), 180–182.

Calabrese, N. M. (2003). Developing quality sociodramatic play for young children. *Education, 123*(3), 606–608.

Campbell, P. S. (1991). The child-song genre: A comparison of songs by and for children. *International Journal of Music Education, 17,* 14–23.

Caplan, J., Hall, G., Lubin, S., & Fleming, R. (1997). *Literature review of school-family partnerships.* Retrieved from http://www.ncrel.org

Carlton, E. B. (2006). Learning through music: The support of brain research. In B. Neugebauer (Ed.), *Curriculum: Art, music, movement, drama: A beginnings workshop book* (pp. 45–48). USA: Exchange Press.

Carlton, E. B., & Weikart, P. S. (1994). *Foundations in elementary education music.* Ypsilanti, MI: High/Scope Press.

Carnegie Task Force on Learning in the Primary Grades. (1996). *Years of promise: A comprehensive learning strategy for America's children: The report of the Carnegie Task Force on Learning in the Primary Grades.* New York: Carnegie Corp. of New York.

Carter, M., & Curtis, D. (1998). *The visionary director.* St. Paul, MN: Redleaf Press.

Carter, S. (2003). *The impact of parent/family involvement on student outcomes: An annotated bibliography of research from the past decade.* Consortium for "Appropriate Dispute Resolution in Special Education." http://www.directionservice.org

Cartwright, S. (1988). Play can be the building blocks of learning. *Young Children, 43*(5), 44–47.

Cartwright, S. (1990). Learning with large blocks. *Young Children, 45*(3), 38–41.

Casey, B., & Bobb, B. (2003). The power of block building. *Teaching children mathematics.* Reston, VA: National Council of Teachers of Mathematics.

Castle, K., & Ethridge, E. A. (2003). Urgently needed: Autonomous and effective early childhood teacher educators. *Journal of Early Childhood Teacher Education, 24*(2), 111–118.

Caulfield, R. (2000). Number matters: Born to count. *Early Childhood Education Journal, (28)*1, 63–65.

CDC Developmental Milestones. (2007). *Learn the signs.* Retrieved from www.cdc.gov/actearly

Center for Accessible Housing. (1992). Accessibility Standards for Children's Environments. Architectural and Transportation Barriers Compliance Board. US: Department of Education.

Ceppi, G., & Zini, M. (Eds.). (1998). *Children, spaces, relations: Mataprojects for an environment for young children.* Washington, DC: Reggio Children.

Chalufour, I., Hoisington, C., Moriarty, R., Winokur, J., & Worth, K. (2004). The science and mathematics of building structures. *Science and Children, 41*(4), 30–34.

Chalufour, I., & Worth, K. (2004). *Building structures with young children.* St. Paul, MN.: Redleaf Press.

Chalufour, I., & Worth, K. (2005). *Exploring water with young children.* St. Paul, MN: Redleaf Press.

Chard, D. J., & Dickson, S. V. (1999). Phonological awareness: Instructional and assessment guidelines. *Intervention in School and Clinic, 34*(5), 261–270.

Charlesworth, R. (2005). Prekindergarten mathematics: Connecting with national standards. *Early Childhood Education Journal, 32*(4), 229–236.

Charlesworth, R., & Lind, K. (2007). *Math & science for young children* (5th ed.). USA: Thompson Delmar.

Child Care Plus. (1995). Keys to building partnerships with families. *Child Care Plus Newsletter, 5*(2), 1–4. Retrieved from http://www.ccplus.org/newsletters/5-2.pdf

Chirichello, M., & Chirichello, C. (2001). A standing ovation for looping: The critic responds. *Childhood Education, 78,* 2–9.

Christie, J. F., & Wardle, F. (1992). How much time is needed for play? *Young Children, 47*(3), 28–32.

Church, E. B., & Miller, K. (1990). *Blocks: A practical guide for teaching young children: Learning through play.* New York: Early Childhood Division, Scholastic.

Clark, L. (1998). *When young children use the Internet: A report of benefits for families, children and teachers.* Retrieved from http://www.wiu.edu/users/mimacp/wiu/articles/

Clayton, M. K. (2002). Displaying student work: An opportunity for student-teacher collaboration. *Responsive Classroom Newsletter, 14*(4), 1–4.

Clements, D. (2004). Major themes and recommendations. In D. H. Clements & A. DiBiase (Eds.), *Engaging young children in mathematics: Standards for early childhood mathematics education* (pp. 7–72). Mahwah, NJ: Lawrence Erlbaum Associates.

Clements, D., & Sarama, J. (2003). Strip mining for gold: Research and policy in educational technology: A response to "Fool's Gold." *AACE Journal, 11*(1), 7–69.

Clements, D. H. (1994). The uniqueness of the computer as a learning tool: Insights from research and practice. In J. L. Wright & D. D. Shade (Eds.), *Young children: Active learners in a technological age* (pp. 31–49). Washington, DC: National Association for the Education of Young Children.

Clements, D. H. (1999). Young children and technology. *Dialogue on early childhood science, mathematics, and technology education.* Washington, DC: American Association for the Advancement of Science, Project 2061. Retrieved from http://www.project2061.org/newsinfo/earlychild/experience/clements.htm

Clements, D. H. (2004). Part one: Major themes and recommendations. In D. H. Clements, J. Sarama (Eds.), & A. M. DiBiase (Assoc. Ed.), *Engaging young children in mathematics: Standards for early childhood mathematics* (pp. 1–72). Mahwah, NJ: Lawrence Erlbaum Associates.

Clements, D. H., Nastasi, B. K., & Swaminathan, S. (1993). Young children and computers: Crossroads and directions from research. *Young Children, 48*(2), 56–64.

Clements, D. H., & Sarama, J. (2000a). The earliest geometry. *Teaching Children Mathematics, 7*(2), 82–86.

Clements, D. H., & Sarama, J. (2000b). Standards for preschoolers. *Teaching Children Mathematics, 7*(1), 38–41.

Clements, D. H., & Sarama, J. (2000c). Young children's ideas about geometric shapes. *Teaching Children Mathematics, 6*(8), 482–488.

Clements, D. H., & Stephan, M. (2004). Measurement in pre-K–2 mathematics. In D. H. Clements, J. Sarama (Eds.), & A. M. DiBiase (Assoc. Ed.), *Engaging young children in mathematics: Standards for early childhood mathematics* (pp. 299–317). Mahwah, NJ: Lawrence Erlbaum Associates.

Clements, R. (2004). An investigation of the status of outdoor play. *Contemporary Issues in Early Childhood, 5*(1), 68–80.

Cody, D. (1989). The building blocks of childhood. *Sky Magazine, 18*(11).

Cohen, J. (1988). *Statistical power for the behavioral sciences* (2nd ed.). Hillsdale, NJ: Lawrence Erlbaum Associates Inc.

Cohen, M. J. (1984). *Prejudice against nature.* Freeport, ME: Cobblesmith.

Colbert, C. B., & Taunton, M. (1988). Problems of representation: Preschool and third grade children's observational drawings of a three dimensional model. *Studies in Art Education, 29*(2), 103–114.

Colbert, C. B., & Taunton, M. (1992). *Developmentally appropriate practices for the visual arts education of young children.* Reston, VA: National Art Education Association.

Cole, E., & Schaefer, C. (1990). Can young children be art critics? *Young Children, 45*(2), 33–38.

Colker, L. J. (2005). *The cooking book: Fostering young children's learning and delight.* Washington, DC: National Association for the Education of Young Children.

Colvin, G., Sugai, G., Good, R. H., & Lee, Y. (1997). Effect of active supervisions and precorrection on transition behaviors of elementary students. *School Psychology Quarterly, 12,* 344–363.

Conezio, K., & French, L. (2003). Science in the preschool classroom: Capitalizing on children's fascination with the everyday world to foster language and literacy development. In D. Koralek & L. J. Colker (Eds.), *Spotlight on young children and science* (pp. 4–16). Washington, DC: National Association for the Education of Young Children.

Connolly, P., & McKenzie, T. L. (1995). Effects of a games intervention on the physical activity levels of children at recess. *Research Quarterly for Exercise and Sport, 66* (Suppl.):A60.

Cooper, P. M., Capo, K., Mathes, B., & Gray, L. (2007). One authentic early literacy practice and three standardized tests: Can a storytelling curriculum measure up? *Journal of Early Childhood Teacher Education, 28*(3), 251–275. Retrieved from http://www.informaworld.com/10.1080/10901020701555564

Cooper, R. G., Jr. (1984). Early number development: Discovering number space with addition and subtraction. In C. Sophian (Ed.), *Origins of cognitive skills* (pp. 157–192). Mahwah, NJ: Lawrence Erlbaum Associates.

Coopersmith, S. (1981). *The antecedents of self-esteem.* Palo Alto, CA: Consulting Psychologists Press. (Original work published 1967.)

Copley, J. V. (2000). *The young child and mathematics.* Washington, DC: National Association for the Education of Young Children.

Cordes, C., & Miller, E. (2000). *Fools gold: A critical look at computers in childhood.* College Park, MD: Alliance for Childhood.

Cosco, N., & Moore, R. (1999). *Playing in place: Why the physical environment is important in playwork.* 14th Playeducation Annual Play and Human Development Meeting: Theoretical Playwork. Ely, Cambridgeshire, UK. Retrieved from www.naturalearning.org/PlayingPaper.html

Council for Professional Recognition. (1995). *CDA assessment observation instrument: Preschool, infant/toddler, family child care.* Washington, DC: Author.

Crandell, C., Smaldino, J., & Flexer, C. (1995). *Sound field FM amplification: Theory and practical applications.* San Diego, CA: Singular Press.

Crosser, S. (1994). Making the most of water play. *Young Children, 49*(5), 28–32.

Crosser, S. (2005). *What do we know about early childhood education?: Research based practice.* Clifton Park, NY: Thomson Delmar Learning.

Cryer, D., Hurwitz, S., & Wolery, M. (2001). Continuity of caregiver for infants and toddlers in center-based care: Report on a survey of center practices. *Early Childhood Research Quarterly, 14*(4), 497–514.

Cryer, D., & Phillipsen, L. (1997). Quality details: A close-up look at child care program strengths and weaknesses. *Young Children, 52*(5), 51–61.

Cullen, C. (1998). *An investigation of the long-term effects of middle school looping programs.* Master of Arts Degree in Education Thesis, University of Connecticut.

Cuppens, V., Rosenow, N., & Wike, J. (2007). *Learning with nature idea book: Creating nurturing outdoor spaces for children.* Lincoln, NE: National Arbor Day Foundation.

Curtis, D., & Carter, M. (2005). Rethinking early childhood environments to enhance learning. *Young Children, 6*(3), 34–38.

Danko-McGhee, K., & Shaffer, S. (2003). *Looking at art with toddlers.* Smithsonian Early Enrichment Center. Retrieved from http://www.seec.si.edu/resources.htm

Danks, S. G. (2003). Green mansions: Living willow structures enhance children's play environments. *Children, Youth and Environments, 13*(1). Retrieved from http://cye.colorado.edu

Danoff-Burg, J. (2003). Be a bee and other approaches to introducing young children to entomology. In D. Koralek & L. J. Colker (Eds.), *Spotlight on young children and science* (pp. 33–37). Washington, DC: National Association for the Education of Young Children.

Davidson, J. (1982). Wasted time: The ignored dilemma. In J. F. Brown (Ed.), *Curriculum planning for young children* (pp. 196–204). Washington, DC: National Association for the Education of Young Children.

Davis, B. C., & Shade, D. D. (1994). *Integrate don't isolate: Computers in the early childhood curriculum.* ERIC Digest. EDO-PS-94-17. Urbana, IL: ERIC Clearinghouse on Elementary and Early Childhood Education, University of Illinois.

Davison, K. K., & Birch, L. L. (2001). Weight status, parent reaction, and self-concept in five-year-old girls. *Pediatrics, 107*(1), 46–53.

Day, C. B. (2006). Leveraging diversity to benefit children's social-emotional development and school readiness. In B. Bowman & E. K. Moore (Eds.), *School readiness and social-emotional development: Perspectives on cultural diversity* (pp. 23–32). Washington, DC: National Black Child Development Institute.

DeBell, M., & Chapman, C. (2006). *Computer and Internet use by students in 2003: Statistical analysis report.* Institute of Education Sciences. National Center for Education Statistics. Retrieved from http://purl.access.GPO/LPS74345

DeCasper, A., & Spence, M. (1986). Prenatal maternal speech influences newborns' perception of speech sounds. *Infant Behavior and Development, 9,* 133–150.

Deitz, W. H. (1998). Health consequences of obesity in youth: Childhood predictors of adult disease. (The causes and health consequenses of obesity in children and adolescents.) *Pediatrics, 101*(3), 518–525.

Dempsey, J. D., & Frost, J. L. (1993). Play environments in early childhood education. In B. Spodek (Ed.), *Handbook of research on the education of young children* (pp. 306–321). New York: Macmillan Publishing.

Denton, K., & West, J. (2002). Children's reading and mathematics achievement in kindergarten and first grade. *Education Statistics Quarterly, 4,* 19–26.

Derman-Sparks, L. (1989). *Anti-bias curriculum: Tools for empowering young children.* Washington, DC: National Association for the Education of Young Children.

DeVries, P., & Kohlberg, L. (1987). *Constructivist early education: Overview and comparison with other programs.* Washington, DC: National Association for the Education of Young Children.

DeVries, R. (2004). What is constructivist about constructivist education? *The Constructivist, 15*(1), 1–26.

Diffily, D. (2004). *Teachers and families working together.* Upper Saddle River, NJ: Merrill/Pearson.

Diller, D. (2003). *Literacy work stations: Making centers work.* Portland, ME: Stenhouse.

Dinwiddie, S. A. (1993). Playing in the gutters: Enhancing children's cognitive and social play. Retrieved from http://communityplaythings.com/resources/articles/sandandwater/PlayGutters.html

Doctoroff, S. (2001). Adapting the physical environment to meet the needs of all young children for play. *Early Childhood Education Journal, 29*(2), 105–109.

Douglas-Hall, A., & Chau, M. (2007). Basic facts about low-income children: Birth to age 18. *National Center for Children in Poverty.* Retrieved from http://www.nccp.org/publications/pub_762.html

Downes, T., Arthur, L., & Beecher, B. (2001). Effective learning environments for young children using digital resources: An Australian perspective. *Information Technology in Education Annual.*

Retrieved from http://64.233.179.104/scholar?hl=en&lr=&q=cache:VjxPqeQJaN4J:www.aace.org/dl/files/ITCE/ITCE2001-139.pdf+

Dreier, E. (1996). Blocks in the elementary school. In E. S. Hirsch (Ed.), *The block book* (Rev. ed., pp. 103–116). Washington, DC: National Association for the Education of Young Children.

Dunlap, G., DePerczel, M., Clarke, S., Wilson, D., Wright, S., White, R., & Gomez, A. (1994). Choice making to promote adaptive behavior for students with emotional and behavioral challenges. *Journal of Applied Behavior Analysis, 27*(3), 505–518.

Dunn, J. (2004). *Children's friendships: The beginning of intimacy.* Malden, MA: Blackwell Publishing.

Earthman, G. I. (2004). Prioritization of 31 criteria for school building adequacy. Retrieved from www.schoolfunding.info/policy/facilities/ACLUfacilities_report1-04.pdf

EC (European Commission). (2003). Commission Directive 2003/2/EC of 6 January 2003 relating to restrictions on the marketing and use of arsenic (tenth adaptation to technical progress to Council). Retrieved from http://eurlex.europa.eu/LexUriServ/LexUriServ.do?uri=OJ:L:2003:004:0009:0011:EN:PDF

Edwards, C. P. (1995). *Encouraging creativity in early childhood classrooms.* ERIC Digest. ERIC Clearinghouse on Elementary and Early Childhood Education, Urbana, IL.

Elias, C. L., & Berk, L. E. (2002). Self-regulation in young children: Is there a role for sociodramatic play? *Early Childhood Research Quarterly, 17,* 216–238.

Elkind, D. (2006). The values of outdoor play. *Exchange Press, 171,* 6–11.

Environmental Protection Agency (EPA). (2000). *Indoor air quality and student performance.* EPA report number EPA 402-F-00–009. Washington, DC: Author. Retrieved from http://www.epa.gov/iaq/schools/performance.html

Environmental working group (EWG). (2006). *Shopper's guide.* Retrieved from http://www.foodnews.org/

Epstein, A., & Trimis, E. (2002). *Supporting young artists: The development of the visual arts in young children.* Ypsilanti, MI: High/Scope Press.

Epstein, A. S. (2005). Thinking about art: Encouraging art appreciation in early childhood settings. In D. G. Koralek (Ed.), *Spotlight on young children and the creative arts* (pp. 52–57). Washington, DC: National Association for the Education of Young Children.

Epstein, A. S. (2007). *The intentional teacher: Choosing the best strategies for young children's learning.* Washington, DC: National Association for the Education of Young Children.

Epstein, J. L. (2001). *School, family, and community partnerships: Preparing educators and improving schools.* Boulder, CO: Westview Press.

Ergonomics for children and educational environments. (2006). *General recommendations for computer use.* Retrieved from http://www.iea.cc/ergonomics4children/guidelines.html

Erickson, M. (1995). Art historical understanding in early childhood. In C. Thompson (Ed.), *The visual arts and early childhood learning* (pp. 63–66). Reston, VA: The National Art Education Association.

Espinosa, L. M. (2006). Social, cultural, and linguistic features of school readiness in young Latino children. In B. Bowman & E. K. Moore (Eds.), *School readiness and social-emotional development: Perspectives on cultural diversity* (pp. 33–47). Washington, DC: National Black Child Development Institute.

Ethridge, E. A., & King, J. R. (2005). Calendar math in preschool and primary classrooms: Questioning the curriculum. *Early Childhood Education Journal, (32)*5, 291–296.

Etnier, J. L., Salazar, W., Landers, D. M., Petruzzello, S. J., Han, M., & Nowell, P. (1997). The influence of physical fitness and exercise upon cognitive functioning: A meta-analysis. *Journal of Sport and Exercise Psychology, 19*(3), 249–277.

Evans, G. D., Bryant, N., & Owens, J. S. (2004). Ethnic differences in burnout, coping, and intervention acceptability among childcare professionals. *Child Youth Care Forum, 33*(5), 349–371.

Evans, G. W. (2001). Environmental stress and health. In A. Baum, T. Revenson, & J. E. Singer (Eds.), *Handbook of Health Psychology* (pp. 365–386). Mahwah, NJ: Erlbaum.

Evans, G. W., Hygge, S., & Bullinger, M. (1995). Chronic noise and psychological stress. *Psychological Science, 6*(6), 333–338.

Evans, G. W., & Maxwell, L. (1997). Chronic noise exposure and reading deficits: The mediating effects of language acquisition. *Environment and Behavior, 29*(5), 638–656.

Exner, C. E. (1992). In-hand manipulation skills. In J. Case-Smith & C. Pehoski (Eds.), *Development of hand skills in children* (pp. 35–45). Bethesda, MD: American Occupational Therapy Association, Inc.

Fachner, J., & Aldridge, D. (Eds.). 2002. *Dialogue and Debate—Conference Proceedings of the 10th World Congress on Music.* Witten, Germany: Music Therapy World.

Fagan, J., & Palm, G. (2004). *Fathers and early childhood programs.* Canada: Thomson Delmar.

Farran, D. C., Aydogan, C., Kang, S. J., & Lipsey, M. W. (2006). Preschool classroom environments and the quantity and quality of children's literacy and language behaviors. In D. K. Dickinson & S. B. Neuman (Eds.), *Handbook of early literacy research* (pp. 257–268). New York: The Guilford Press.

Federal Interagency Forum on Child and Family Statistics. (2005). *America's children: Key national indicators of well being 2005.* Washington, DC: U.S. Government Printing Office.

Federico, G. F. (2002). Fetal responses to a musical stimulation. *Music Therapy and Pregnancy.* In J. Fachner & D. Aldridge (Eds.), *Dialogue and Debate Conference Proceedings of the 10th World Congress on Music* (pp. 530–546). Witten, Germany: Music Therapy World.

Feldman, R. S. (2007). *Child development* (4th ed.). Upper Saddle River, NJ: Prentice Hall.

Ferguson, C. J., & McNulty, C. P. (2006). Learning through sociodramatic play. *Kappa Delta Pi Record, 58*(3), 60–64.

Ferguson, L. (2005). The role of movement in elementary music education: A literature review. *Applications of Research in Music Education, 23*(2), 23–33.

Ferrar, H., Harms, T., & Cryer, D. (1996). *Places for growing: how to improve your family child care home.* Princeton, NJ: Mathematica Policy Research.

Fielding, R. (2006). *Learning, lighting and color: Lighting design for schools and universities in the 21st century.* Retrieved from http://www.designshare.com/articles/1/133/fielding_light-learn-color.pdf

Finn, J. D., & Achilles, C. M. (1999). Tennessee's class size study: Findings, implications, misconceptions. *Educational Evaluation and Policy Analysis, 21*(2), 97–110.

Finn, K., Johannsen, N., & Specker, B. (2002). Factors associated with physical activity in preschool children. *The Journal of Pediatrics, 140*(1), 81–85.

Fisher, J. (2006). *Creating place identity: It's part of human nature.* Retrieved from http://environmentpsychology.com/place_identity.htm

Fjørtoft, I. (2001). The natural environment as a playground for children: The impact of outdoor play activities in pre-primary school children. *Early Childhood Education Journal, 29*(2), 111–117.

Fjørtoft, I. (2004). Landscape as playscape: The effects of natural environments on children's play and motor development. *Children, Youth and Environments, 14*(2), 21–44. Retrieved from http://www.colorado.edu/journals/cye/

Flohr, J. W. (2004). *The musical lives of young children.* Upper Saddle River, NJ: Pearson.

Flynn, L. L., & Kieff, J. (2002). Including everyone in outdoor play. *Young Children, 57*(3), 20–26.

Foote, B. J. (2001). *Cup cooking: Individual child-portion picture recipes.* Mt. Ranier, MD: Gryphon House.

Forman, G. (1994). Different media, different languages. In L. G. Katz & G. Cesarone (Eds.), *Reflections on the Reggio Emilia approach* (pp. 37–46). Urbana, IL: ERIC Clearing House on Elementary and Early Childhood Education.

Forman, G. (1999). Instant video revisiting: The video camera as a "Tool of the Mind" for young children. *Early Childhood Research and Practice, 1*(2), 1–6. Retrieved from http://ecrp.uiuc.edu/v1n2/forman.html

Forman, G. (2006). Negotiating with art media to deepen learning. In B. Neugebauer (Ed.), *Curriculum: Art, music, movement, drama* (pp. 34–36). Redmond, WA: Exchange Press.

Forman, G., & Gandini, L. (1994). *The amusement park for birds* (video). Amherst, MA: Performanetics.

Forthum, L. F., & McCombie, J. W. (2007). A preliminary outcome study of Response Ability Pathways training. *Reclaiming Children and Youth, 16*(2), 27–35.

Foster, R. R., & Hardison, R. (2000). Can a woodworking center be safe? *Healthy Child Care: Health and Safety Ideas for the Young Child, 3*(4). Retrieved from http://www.healthychild.net/articles/sf16wood.html

Fox, S. B. (2000). Music and the baby's brain: Early experiences. *Music Educators Journal, 87*(2), 23–27.

Fraser, S., & Gestwicki, C. (2002). *Authentic childhood: Exploring Reggio Emilia in the classroom.* Canada: Delmar.

Frega, A. L. (1979). Rhythmic tasks with 3-, 4-, and 5-year-old children: A study made in Argentine Republic. *Bulletin of the Council for Research in Music Education, 59,* 32–34.

French, L. (2004). Science as the center of a coherent, integrated early childhood curriculum. *Early Childhood Research Quarterly, 19*(1), 138–149.

Froebel, F. (1912). Froebel's chief writings on education. Retrieved from http://core.roehampton.ac.uk/digital/froarc/frochi/

Fromberg, D. P. (2002). *Play and meaning in early childhood education.* Allyn and Bacon: Boston.

References

Frost, J. G., Wortham, S., & Reifel, S. (2001). *Play and child development.* Upper Saddle River, NJ: Merrill/Prentice Hall.

Frost, J. L. (1990). Young children and playground safety. In J. Frost & S. Worthman (Eds.), *Playgrounds for young children: National survey and perspectives* (pp. 29–48). Reston, VA: American Alliance for Health, Physical Education, Recreation and Dance.

Frost, J. L. (1992). *Play and Playscapes.* Albany, NY: Delmar.

Frost, J. L., & Campbell, S. D. (1985). Equipment choices of primary-age children on conventional and creative playgrounds. In J. L. Frost & S. Sunderlin (Eds.), *When children play* (pp. 89–92). Wheaton, MD: Association for Childhood Education International.

Frost, J. L., Brown, P., Sutterby, J. A., & Thornton, C. D. (2004). *The developmental benefits of playgrounds.* Olney, MD: Association for Childhood Education International.

Frost, J., & Kim, S. (2000). *Developmental progress in preschool-age children's using an overhead bar.* Unpublished manuscript.

Frost, J. L., & Strickland, E. (1985). Equipment choices of young children during free play. In J. L. Frost & S. Sunderlin (Eds.), *When children play. Proceedings of the International Conference on Play and Play Environments.* Wheaton, MD: Association for Childhood Education International.

Gallahue, D. L. (1993). Motor development and movement skill acquisition in early childhood education. In B. Spodek (Ed.), *Handbook of research on the education of young children* (pp. 24–41). New York: Macmillan.

Gallenstein, N. (2005). Never too young for a concept map. *Science and Children, 43*(1). 44–47.

Gallenstein, N. L. (2004). Creative discovery through classification. *Teaching Children Mathematics, 11*(2), 103–108.

Gandini, L. (1984). Not just anywhere: Making child care centers into "particular" places. *Beginnings: the Magazine for Teachers of Young Children, 1,* 17–20.

Gandini, L. (1998). Educational and caring spaces. In C. Edwards, L. Gandini, & G. Forman (Eds.), *The hundred languages of children* (pp. 161–178). Greenwich, CT: Ablex Publishing Corporation.

Gandini, L. (2004). Foundations of the Reggio Emilia approach. In J. Hendrick (Ed.), *Next steps toward teaching the Reggio way* (pp. 13–26). Upper Saddle River, NJ: Merrill/Pearson.

Gandini, L. (2006). Teachers and children together: Constructing new learning. In B. Neugebauer (Ed.), *Curriculum: Art, music, movement, drama* (pp. 26–29). Redmond, WA: Exchange Press.

Gandini, L., & Edwards, C. P. (2001). *Bambini: The Italian approach to infant/toddler care.* New York: Teachers College Press.

Garcia, E. (2003). Respecting children's home languages and cultures. In C. Copple (Ed.), *A world of difference: Readings on teaching young children in a diverse society* (p. 16). Washington, DC: National Association for the Education of Young Children.

Garcia, E. E. (1993). The education of linguistically and culturally diverse children. In B. Spodek (Ed.), *Handbook of research on the education of young children* (pp. 372–384). New York: Macmillan.

Gardner, H. (1991). *The unschooled mind.* New York: Basic Books.

Gareau, M., & Kennedy, C. (1991). Structure time and space to promote pursuit of learning in the primary grades. *Young Children, 46*(4), 46–51.

Gartrell, D. (2007). *A guidance approach for the encouraging classroom* (4th ed.). Albany, NY: Thomson Delmar Learning.

Gasper, K. (1995). Liberating art experiences for preschoolers and their teachers. In C. Thompson (Ed.), *The visual arts and early childhood learning* (pp. 44–48). Reston: VA. The National Art Education Association.

Gelman, R. (2005). Learning from children—Research in preschool settings. In A. Beatty (Rapporteur), *Mathematical and scientific development in early childhood* (pp. 5–7). Washington, DC: The National Academies Press.

Gelman, R., & Brenneman, K. (2004). Science learning pathways for young children. *Early Childhood Research Quarterly, 19*(1), 150–158.

Gelman, S. A. (1999). Concept development in preschool children. In *Dialogue on early childhood science, mathematics, and technology education* (pp. 50–61). American Association for the Advancement of Science. Washington, DC: AAAS.

General Accounting Office. (1995). *School facilities: America's schools not designed or equipped for 21st century.* GAO report number HEHS-95-95. Washington, DC: General Accounting Office. (ED383056)

General Services Administration (GSA). (2003). *Child care center design guide.* Retrieved from http://www.gsa.gov/gsa/cm_attachments/GSA DOCUMENT/designguidesmall_R2FD38_0Z5RDZ-i34K-pR.pdf

Genesee, F., Paradis, J., & Crago, M. (2004). *Dual language development & disorders: A handbook on bilingualism and second language learning.* Baltimore: Paul H. Brookes Publishing.

Geoff, C., Sugai, G., Good, R. H., & Lee, Y. (1997). Using active supervision and precorrection to improve transition behaviors in an elementary school. *School Psychology Quarterly, 12*(4), 344–363.

George, J. (1995). A loft-y idea for learning. *Educational Leadership, 53*(3), 56–57.

George, P., Spreul, M., & Moorefield, J. (1987). *Long term student teacher relationships: A middle school case study.* Columbus, OH: National Middle School Association.

Giagazoglou, P., Fotiadou, E., Angelopoulou, N., Tsikoulas, J., & Tsimaras, V. (2001). Gross and fine motor skills of left-handed preschool children. *Perceptual and Motor Skills, 92,* 1122–1128.

Gifford, R. (1994). Scientific evidence for claims about full-spectrum lamps: Past and future. In J. A. Veitch (Ed.), *Full-spectrum lighting effects on performance, mood, and health* (pp. 37–46). Ottawa, Ontario, Canada: Institute for Research in Construction.

Gilbert, M. B. (2004). *Communicating effectively: Tools for educational leaders.* Lanham, MD: Scarecrow Education.

Ginsburg, H. P. (2006). Mathematical play and playful mathematics: A guide for early education. In D. G. Singer, R. B. Golinkoff, & K Hirsh-Pasek (Eds.), *Play = learning: How play motivates and enhances children's cognitive and social-emotional growth* (pp. 145–167). New York: Oxford University Press.

Giovannini, D. (2001). Traces of childhood: A child's diary. In L. Gandidi & C. P. Edwards (Eds.), *Bambini.* New York: Teacher College Press, 146–151.

Girolametto, L., Hoaken, L., Weitzman, E., & van Leishout, R. (2000). Patterns of adult-child linguistic interaction in integrated day care groups. *Language, Speech, and Hearing Services in Schools, 31,* 155–168.

Glenn Commission. (2000). *Before it's too late: A report to the nations from the National Commission on Mathematics and Science Teaching for the 21st century.* Washington, DC: U.S. Department of Education.

Goelman, H., Shapiro, E., & Pence, A. R. (1990). Family environment and family day care. *Family Relations, 39*(1), 14–19.

Golbeck, S. L. (2005). Building foundations for spatial literacy in early childhood. *Young Children, (60)*6, 72–83.

Goodway, J. D., & Robinson, L. E. (2006). SKIPing toward an active start: Promoting physical activity in preschoolers. *Beyond the Journal.* Retrieved from http://www.journal.naeyc.org/btj/200605/GoodwayBTJ.asp

Gramza, A. F. (1970). Preferences of preschool children for enterable play boxes. *Perceptual and Motor Skills, 31,* 177–178.

Grant, J., & Johnson, B. (1995). Looping, the two grade cycle: A good starting place. In J. Grant & B. Johnson (Eds.), *A common sense guide to multiage practices, primary level* (pp. 33–36). Columbus, OH: Teacher's Publishing Group.

Graves, G. (1985). Shedding light on learning. *American School and University, 57*(7), 88–90.

Greata, J. D. (2006). *An introduction to music in early childhood education.* Clifton Park, NY: Thomson Delmar Learning.

Grebennikov, L., & Wiggins, M. (2006). Psychological effects of classroom noise on early childhood teachers. *The Australian Educational Researcher, 33*(3), 35–54.

Greenman, J. (1991). Babies get out: Outdoor settings for infant toddler play. *Child Care Information Exchange, 79,* 21–24.

Greenman, J. (2005a). *Caring spaces, learning places: Children's environments that work.* Redmond, WA: Exchange Press, Inc.

Greenman, J. (2005b). Places for childhood in the 21st century: A conceptual framework. *Beyond the Journal, Young Children, 60*(3), 1–7.

Greenman, J. (2006). The importance of order. *Exchange, 170,* 53–55.

Greenman, J., & Stonehouse, A. (1996). *Primetimes: A handbook for excellence in infant and toddler programs.* St. Paul, MN: Redleaf Press.

Greenman, J., Stonehouse, A., & Schweikert, G. (2007). *Prime times, 2nd ed: A handbook for excellence in infant and toddler programs.* St. Paul, MN: Redleaf Press.

Griffen, C., & Rinn, B. (1998). Enhancing outdoor play with an obstacle course. *Young Children, 53*(3), 18–23.

Gronlund, G. (1992). Coping with Ninja Turtle play in my classroom. *Young Children, 48*(1), 21–25.

Gross, T., & Clemens, S. G. (2002). Painting a tragedy: Young children process the events of September 11. *Young Children, 57*(3), 44–51.

Grossman, E. (1980). Effects of instructional experience in clay modeling skills on modeled human figure representation in preschool children. *Studies in Art Education, 22*(1), 51–59.

Gura, P. (1993). Becoming connoisseurs and critics: Making sense of blockplay. *Early Child Development and Care, 92,* 69–81.

Guralnik, M. J., & Hammond, M. A. (1999). Sequential analysis of the social play of young children with mild developmental delays. *Journal of Early Intervention, 22*(3), 243–256.

Gurunathan, S., Robson, M., Freeman, N., Buckley, B., Roy, A., Meyer, R., Bukowski, J., & Lioy, P. J. (1998). Accumulation of chlorpyrifos on residential surfaces and toys accessible to children. *Environmental Health Perspectives, 106*(1), 9–16.

Guthrie, J. T. (2000). Contests for engagement and motivation in reading. *Reading Online, 4*(8). Retrieved from http://www.readingonline.org/articles/handbook/gunthrie/

Haight, W., Black, J., Ostler, T., & Sheridan, K. (2006). Pretend play and emotion: Learning in traumatized mothers and children. In D. G. Singer, R. B. Golinkoff, & K. Hirsh-Pasek (Eds.), *Play = learning: How play motivates and enhances children's cognitive and social-emotional growth* (pp. 209–230). New York: Oxford University Press.

Halle, T., Calkins, J., Berry, D., & Johnson, R. (2003, September). Promoting language and literacy in early childhood settings. *Child Care and Early Education Research Connections,* 1–17.

Hampton, F., Mumford, D., & Bond, L. (1997, March). *Enhancing urban student achievement through family oriented school practices.* Paper presented at the Annual Meeting of the American Educational Research Association, Chicago, IL.

Hanline, M. F., Milton, S., & Phelps, P. (2001). Young children's block construction activities: Findings from 3 years of observation. *Journal of Early Intervention, 24,* 224–237.

Hannibal, M. A. (1999). Young children's developing understanding or geometric shapes. *Teaching children mathematics, 5*(6), 353–358.

Hanson, B. J. (1995). Getting to know you multiyear teaching. *Educational Leadership, 53*(3), 42–44.

Hardman, K., & Marshall, J. (2006). The state and status of physical education in school in international context. *European Physical Educational Review, 6*(3), 203–219.

Hart, B., & Risley, T. R. (1995). *Meaningful differences in the everyday experience of young American children.* Baltimore, MD: Brookes Publishing Company.

Hart, C. R., & Sheehan, R. (1986). Preschoolers' play behavior in outdoor environments: Effect of traditional and contemporary playgrounds. *American Educational Research Journal, 23*(4), 668–678.

Hasselbring, T. S., & Glaser, C. H. (2000). Use of computer technology to help students with special needs. *The Future of Children, 10*(2), 1–21.

Hatch-Rasmussen, C. (1995). *Sensory integration.* Autism Research Institute. Retrieved from http://www.autism.org/si.html

Hathaway, W., Hargreaves, J.,Thompson, G., & Novitsky, D. (1992*). A study into the effects of light on children of elementary school age—a case of daylight robbery.* Edmonton, Canada: Alberta Department of Education.

Hatlelid, K. M., Bittner, P. M., Midgett, J. D., Thomas, T. A., & Saltzman, L. E. (2004). Exposure and risk assessment for arsenic from chromated copper arsenate (CCA)-treated wood playground equipment. *Journal of Children's Health, 2*(3), 215–241. Retrieved from http://www.informaworld.com/10.1080/15417060490930056

Haugland, S. (2005). Selecting or upgrading software and web sites in the classroom. *Early Childhood Education Journal, 32*(5), 329–340.

Haugland, S. W. (1992). Effects of computer software on preschool children's developmental gains. *Journal of Computing in Childhood Education, 3*(1), 15–30.

Haugland, S. W. (1997). Computers in the early childhood classroom. *Early Childhood News, 9*(4), 6–17.

Haugland, S. W., & Shade, D. D. (1994). Software evaluation for young children. In J. L. Wright & D. D. Shade (Eds.), *Young children: Active learners in a technological age* (pp. 63–76). Washington, DC: National Association for the Education of Young Children.

Haugland, S. W., & Wright, J. L. (1997). *Young children and technology: A world of discovery.* Boston, MA: Allyn and Bacon.

Hayward, D. G., Rothenberg, M., & Beasley, R. R. (1974). Children's play and urban playground environments: A comparison of traditional, contemporary, and adventure playground types. *Environment and Behavior, 6*(2), 131–168.

Hazen, N. L., & Black, B. (1989). Preschool peer communication skills: The role of social status and interaction context. *Child Development, 60,* 867–876.

Heath, P., & Heath, P. (1982). The effect of teacher intervention on object manipulation in young children. *Journal of Research in Science Teaching, 19*(7), 577–585.

Hedge, A. V., & Cassidy, D. J. (2004). Teacher and parent perspectives on looping. *Early Childhood Education Journal, 32*(2), 133–138.

Heft, T. M., & Swaminathan, S. (2002). The effects of computers on the social behavior of preschoolers. *Journal of Research in Childhood Education, 16*(2), 162–174.

Heisner, J. (2005). Telling stories with blocks: Encouraging language in the block center. *Early Childhood Research & Practice, 7*(2). Retrieved from http://ecrp.uiuc.edu/v7n2/heisner.html

Herbert, J. (1984). Why do some children have trouble learning measurement concepts? *Arithmetic teacher, 331,* 19–24.

Heschong Mahone Group. (2003). *Windows and classrooms: A study of student performance and the indoor environment.* California Energy Commission.

Hestenes, L. L., & Carroll, D. E. (2000). The play interactions of young children with and without disabilities: Individual and environmental influences. *Early Childhood Research Quarterly, 15*(2), 229–246.

Hetland, L., & Winner, E. (2001). The arts and academic achievement: What the evidence shows. *Arts Education Policy Review, 102*(5), 3–6.

Higgens, S., Hall, E., Wall, K., Woolner, P., & McCaughey, C. (2005). *The impact of school environments: A literature review.* CfBT: Research and Development. Retrieved from http://www.ncl.ac.uk/cflat/news/DCReport.pdf

Hill, D. M., & Berlfein, J. (1977). *Mud, sand, and water.* Washington, DC: National Association for the Education of Young Children.

Hill, D. M., & Berlfein, J. (2000). *Mud, sand, and water, 3rd edition.* Washington, DC: National Association for the Education of Young Children.

HMIE (Her Majesty's Inspectorate of Education) (2006). *Emerging good practice in promoting creativity: A report by HMIE.* Retrieved from http://www.hmie.gov.uk/documents/publication/hmieegpipc.html

Hoffert, S., & Sandberg, J. (2000). *Changes in American children's time 1981–1997.* Center for the Ethnography of Everyday Life. Retrieved from ceel.psc.isr.unich.edu/pubs

Hogan, P. (1982). *The nuts and bolts of playground construction.* West Point, NY: Leisure Press.

Hohmann, M., & Weikart, D. P. (2002). *Educating young children: Active learning practices for preschool and childcare programs.* Ypsilanti, MI: High/Scope Educational Research Association.

Honig, A. S. (2002). *Secure relationships: Nurturing infant/toddler attachment in early care settings.* Washington, DC: National Association for the Education of Young Children.

Honig, A. S., & Thompson, A. (1994). Helping toddlers with peer group entry skills. *Zero to Three, 14*(5), 15–19.

Houle, G. B. (1984). *Learning centers for young children.* West Greenwich, RI: Consortium Publishing.

Howe, A. (1993). Science in early childhood education. In B. Spodek (Ed.), *Handbook of research on the education of young children* (pp. 227–235). New York: Macmillan.

Howes, C. (1989). Friendships in very young children: Definition and functions. In B. H. Schneider, G. Attili, J. Nadel, & R. P. Weissberg (Eds.), *Social competence in developmental perspective* (pp. 107–121). Dordrecht, Netherlands: Kluwer Academic Publishers.

Howes, C., & Hamilton, C. E. (1993). The changing experience of child care: Changes in teachers and in teacher-child relationships and children's social competence with peers. *Early Childhood Research Quarterly, 8*(1), 15–32.

Howes, C., Unger, O., & Seidner, L. B. (1989). Social pretend play in toddlers: Parallels with social play and with solitary pretend. *Child Development, 60*(1), 77–85.

Huber, L. (1999). Woodworking with young children: You can do it! *Young Children, 54*(6), 32–34.

Huber, L. K. (1998). Woodworking in my classroom? You bet! *Early Childhood News, 10*(2), 72–75.

Huber, L. K. (2000). Promoting multicultural awareness through dramatic play centers. *Early Childhood Education Journal, 27*(4), 235–238.

Huffman, C. (2006, July). Supportive care for infants and toddlers with special health needs. *Beyond the Journal: Young Children on the Web,* 1–8.

Hunt, T., & Renfro, N. (1982). *Puppetry in early childhood education.* Puppetry in education series. Austin, TX: N. Renfro Studios.

Hutinger, P. (1999). *Preschool classroom computer experts.* Retrieved from http://www.wiu.edu/users/mimacp/wiu/articles/

Hutinger, P., Rippey, R., & Johanson, J. (1999). Findings of research study on effectiveness of a comprehensive technology system demonstrate benefits for children and teachers. Retrieved from http://www.wiu.edu/users/mimacp/wiu/articles/

Iatridis, M. (1984). Teaching science to preschoolers. In M. McIntyre (Ed.), *Early childhood and science*. Washington, DC: National Science Teachers Association.

Imiolo-Schriver, D. A. (1995). *Developmentally appropriate practice: The creation, implementation, and assessment of learning centers in the kindergarten music curriculum*. St. Paul, MN: University of St. Thomas.

International Ergonomics Association. (2006). *Ergonomics for children and educational environments: General recommendations for computer use*. Retrieved from http://www.iea.cc/ergonomics4children/guidelines.html

International Society for Technology in Education. (2000). *ISTE national educational technology standards (NETS)*. [Eugene, OR]: The Society. Retrieved from http://cnets.iste.org/index.html

IRA/NAEYC. (1998). Learning to read and write: Developmentally appropriate practices for young children joint position statement. In S. B. Neuman, C. Copple, & S. Bredekamp (Eds.), *Learning to read and write: Developmentally appropriate practices for young children* (pp. 3–28). Washington, DC: National Association for the Education of Young Children.

Isbell, R., & Raines, S. (2003). *Creativity and the arts with young children*. Clifton Park, NY: Thomson Delmar Learning.

Isbell, R., & Isbell, C. (2003). *The complete learning spaces book for infants and toddlers*. Beltsville, MD: Gryphon House, Inc.

Isbell, R. T., & Raines, S. C. (1991). Young children's oral language production in three types of play centers. *Journal of Research in Childhood Education, 5*(2), 140–146.

Isenberg, J., & Jalongo, M. (2001). *Creative expression and play in early childhood* (3rd ed.). Upper Saddle River, NJ: Merrill/Pearson.

Jalongo, M. R. (1996). Using recorded music with young children: A guide for nonmusicians. *Young Children. (51)*5, 6–14.

Jalongo, M. R. (2003). *Early childhood language arts* (3rd ed.). Boston: Allyn and Bacon.

Jalongo, M. R. (2008). *Learning to listen, listening to learn: Building essential skills in young children*. Washington, DC: National Association for the Education of Young Children.

Jarrett, O., Maxwell, D., Dickerson, C., Hoge, P., Daview, G., & Yetley, A. (1998). Impact of recess on classroom behavior: Group effects and individual differences. *The Journal of Educational Research, 92*(2), 121–126.

Jarrett, O. S. (2002). *Recess in elementary school: What does the research say?* Champaign, IL: ERIC Clearinghouse on Elementary and Early Childhood Education. Retrieved from http://purl.access.gpo.gov/GPO/LPS43139

Jenson, B. J., & Bullard, J. A. (2002). The mud center: Recapturing childhood. *Young Children, 57*(3), 16–19.

Jimerson, S. R., Pletcher, M. W., Graydon, K., Schnurr, B. L., Nickerson, A. B., & Kundert, D. K. (2006). Beyond grade retention and social promotion: Promoting the social and academic competence of students. *Psychology in the Schools, 43*(1), 85–97.

Johansson, R. S., Westling, G., Bäckström, A., & Flanagan, J. R. (2001). *The Journal of Neuroscience, 21*(17), 6917–6932.

Johnson, H. M. (1996). The art of block building. In E. S. Hirsch (Ed.), *The block book* (Rev. ed., pp. 9–26). Washington, DC: National Association for the Education of Young Children.

Johnson, J. E., Christie, J. F., & Wardle, F. (2005). *Play, development, and early education*. Upper Saddle River, NJ: Merrill/Pearson.

Johnson-Pynn, J., & Nisbet, V. (2002). Preschoolers effectively tutor novice classmates in a block construction task. *Child Study Journal, 32*(4), 241–255.

Jordan, N. C., Levine, S. C., & Huttenlocher, J. (1994). Development of calculation abilities in middle- and low-income children after formal instruction in school. *Journal of Applied Developmental Psychology, 15,* 223–240.

Jordan-DeCarbo, J., & Nelson, J. A. (2002). Music and early childhood education. In R. Colwell & C. Richardson (Eds.), *The new handbook on music teaching and learning: A project of the music educators national conference* (pp. 210–242). New York: Oxford University Press.

Jotangia, D., Moody, A., Stamatakis, E., & Wardle, H. (2005). *Obesity among children under 11.* London: Department of Health.

Juel, C. (1988). Learning to read and write: A longitudinal study of 54 children from first through fourth grades. *Journal of Educational Psychology, 80*(4), 437–447.

Justice, L. M. (2004). Creating language—rich preschool classroom environments. *Teaching Exceptional Children, 37*(2), 36–44.

Kantrowitz, E. J., & Evans, G. W. (2004). The relations between the ratio of children per activity area and off-task behavior and type of play in day care centers. *Environment and Behavior, 36*(4), 541–557.

Karre, A. (2003). *Lighting design and installation.* Cranhassen, MN: Creative Publishing International, Inc.

Katz, L., & Chard, S. (1996). *The contribution of documentation to the quality of early childhood education.* ERIC Digest. (ED393608)

Keeler, R. (2002). *20 ways to create play environments for the soul.* Retrieved from http://www.planetearthplayscapes.com/20souls.html

Kelley, L., & Sutton-Smith, B. (1987). A study of infant musical productivity. In J. C. Peery, I. W. Peery, & T. W. Draper (Eds.), *Music in child development* (pp. 35–53). New York: Springer-Verlag.

Kelling, G. L., & Coles, C. M. (1996). *Fixing broken windows: Restoring order and reducing crime in our communities.* New York: The Free Press.

Kells, P. (2002). Safety vs. challenge—The playground dilemma. *Interaction, 16*(2), 21–22.

Kelly, K. L., & Schorger, J. R. (2001). "Let's play 'puters": Expressive language use at the computer center. *Information Technology in Childhood Education Annual, 13,* 125–138.

Kemp, C. (1999). Computer stations get failing grade. *American Academy of Pediatrics News, 15*(5), 2.

Kennedy, M. (2001). Into thin air. *American School & University, 73*(6), 32.

Kenney, S. (1989). Music centers: Freedom to explore. *Music Educators Journal, 76*(2), 32–36.

Kenney, S. (2004). The importance of music centers in the early childhood class. *General Music Today, 18,* 28–37.

Kenney, S. H., & Persellin, D. (2000). *Designing music environments for early childhood.* Reston, VA: The National Association for Music Education.

Kerlavage, M. (1995). A bunch of naked ladies and a tiger: Children's responses to adult works of art. In C. Thompson (Ed.), *The visual arts and early childhood learning* (pp. 56–62). Reston, VA: The National Art Education Association.

Kieff, J. (2004). Winning ways with word walls. *ACEI Exchange.* 84 I–K.

Kilgore, C. (2005). Toys' noise exceeds OSHA thresholds (Occupational Safety and Health Administration). *Pediatric News, 39*(7), 44.

Kim, S. (1999). The effects of storytelling and pretend play on cognitive processes, short-term and long-term narrative recall. *Child Study Journal, 29*(3), 175–191.

Kindler, A. L. (2002). *Survey of the states' limited English proficient students and available educational programs and services: 2000–2001 summary report.* Washington, DC: National Clearinghouse for English Language Acquisition.

Kindler, A. M. (1995). Significance of adult input in early childhood artistic development. In C. Thompson (Ed.), *The visual arts and early childhood learning* (pp. 10–14). Reston, VA: National Art Education Association.

Kirkby, M. (1989). Nature as refuge in children's environments. *Children's Environments Quarterly, 6*(1), 7–12.

Kissel, B. T. (2008). Apples on train tracks: Observing young children reenvision their writing. *Young Children, 63*(2), 26–32.

Kissinger, K. (1994). *All the colors we are.* St. Paul, MN: Redleaf Press.

Klein, E. R., Hammrich, P. L., Bloom, S., & Ragins, A. (2000). Language development and science inquiry: The head start of science and communication program. *Early Childhood Research and Practice.* Retrieved from http://ecrp.unic.edu/v2n2/klein.html

Klibanoff, R., Levine, S., Huttenlocher, J., Vasilyeva, M., & Hedges, L. (2006). Preschool children's mathematical knowledge: The effect of teacher "math talk." *Developmental Psychology, 42*(1), 59–69.

Koch, C. J. (n.d.). *Not just for sand & water anymore: Your ultimate guide to sensory tables.* Retrieved January 15, 2008, from http://www.preschooleducation.com/ebook.shtml

Kolbe, L. J., Kann, L., & Brener, N. D. (2000). SHPPS: School Health Policies and Programs Study. *Journal of School Health, 71*(7), 253–259.

Kostelnik, M. J., Whiren, A. P., Soderman, A. K., & Gregory, K. M. (2009). *Guiding children's social development & learning* (6th ed.). Clifton Park, NY: Delmar.

Koster, J. B. (2005). *Growing artists: Teaching art to young children.* Clifton Park, NY: Thomson Delmar Learning.

Kotch, J., Isbell, P., Weber, D., Nguyen, V., Savage, E., Gunn, E., Skinner, M., Fowlkes, S., Virk, J., & Allen, J. (2007). Hand-washing and diapering equipment reduces disease among children in out-of-home child care centers. *Pediatrics, 120*(1), 29–36.

Krafft, K. C., & Berk, L. E. (1998). Private speech in two preschools: Significance of open-ended activities and make-believe play for verbal self-regulation. *Early Childhood Research Quarterly, 13*(4), 637–658.

Kriete, R. (2002). *The morning meeting book.* Turners Falls, MA: Northeast Foundation for Children.

Krogmann, J., & Van Sant, R. (2000). Enhancing relationships and improving academics in the elementary school setting by implementing looping. PS-028-718. Master's Action Research Project, Saint Xavier University and SkyLight Field-Based Masters Program. ERIC ED 443 557.

Kryter, K. D. (1985). *The effects of noise on man* (2nd ed.). New York: Academies Press.

Kuschner, D. (1989). Put your name on your painting, but the blocks go back on the shelves. *Young Children, 45*(1), 49–56.

Kwon, E., Zhang, H., Wang, Z., Jhangri, G. S., Lu, X., Fok, N., Gabos, S., Li, X., & Le, X. C. (2004). Arsenic on the hands of children after playing in playgrounds. *Environmental Health Perspectives, 112*(14), 1375–1380.

Lang, S. (1999). *Cornell University child-care center rings with music to develop young brains.* Retrieved from http://www.planetearthplayscapes.com/soundart.html

Lantz, D. (1979). A cross-cultural comparison of communication abilities: Some effects of age, schooling, and culture. *International Journal of Psychology, 14*(3), 171–183.

Lasky, L., & Muderji, R. (1980). *Art: Basic for young children.* Washington, DC: National Association for the Education of Young Children.

Latner, J. D., & Stundard, A. J. (2003). Getting worse: The stigmatization of obese children. *Obesity Research, 11,* 452–456.

Leach, K. (1997). In sync with nature: Designing a building with improved indoor air quality could pay off with improved student health and performance. *School Planning and Management, 36*(4), 32–37.

Legendre, A. (1999). Interindividual relationships in groups of young children and susceptibility to an environmental constraint. *Environment and Behavior, 31*(4), 463–468.

Legendre, A. (2003). Environmental features influencing toddlers' bioemotional reactions in day care centers. *Environment and Behavior, 35*(4), 523–549.

Levin, D. (2003). Beyond banning war and superhero play: Meeting children's needs in violent times. *Young Children, 58*(3), 60–64.

Levy, A. D., Wolfgang, C. H., & Koorland, M. A. (1992). Sociodramatic play as a method for enhancing the language performance of kindergarten age students. *Early Childhood Research Quarterly, 7,* 245–262.

Lincoln, R. (2000). Looping at the middle school level: Implementation and effects. *ERS Spectrum, 18*(3), 19–24.

Lind, K. (1999). Science in early childhood: Developing and acquiring fundamental concepts and skills. In *Dialogue on Early Childhood Science, Mathematics, and Technology Education* (pp. 73–83). Washington DC: American Association for the Advancement of Science.

Lind, K. K. (2005). *Exploring science in early childhood education: A developmental approach.* Albany, New York: USA: Thomson Delmar Learning.

Little, P. (1998). *Family resource centers: Where school readiness happens.* Cambridge, MA: Harvard Family Research Project.

Loo, C. M., & Kennely, D. (1979). Social density: Its effects on behaviors and perceptions of preschoolers. *Environmental Psychology and Nonverbal Behavior, 3*(3), 131–146.

Losse, A., Henderson, S. E., Elliman, D., Hall, D., & Knight, E. (1991). Clumsiness in children—do they grow out of it? A 10-year follow-up study. *Developmental Medicine and Child Neurology, 33*(1), 55–68.

Lou, Y., Abrami, P. C., & Spence, J. C. (2000). Effects of within-class grouping on student achievement: An exploratory model. *The Journal of Educational Research, 94*(2), 101–112.

Lowenfeld, V., & Brittain, W. L. (1987). *Creative and mental growth* (8th ed.). New York: Macmillan.

Lowry, P. (1993). Privacy in the preschool environment: Gender differences in reaction to crowding. *Children's Environments, 10*(2), 46–61.

Lu, C., Fenske, R., Touchstone, J., Moate, T., Kedan, G., Knutson, D., & Box, D. K. (1999). National school IPM toolbox. *Preprints of Extended Abstracts, 39*(2), 131–132.

Lucas, T., & Katz, A. (1994). Reframing the debate: The roles of native languages in English-only programs for language minority students. *TESOL Quarterly, 28*(3), 537–561.

Lutton, A., Spade, G., & DeCheser, A. (2006). Look, there is blue: A community of artists, teachers, and children. In B. Neugebauer (Ed.), *Curriculum: Art, music, movement, drama* (pp. 7–10). Redmond, WA: Exchange Press.

Lynn-Garbe, C., & Hoot, J. L. (2004). Weighing in on the issue of childhood obesity: An overweight child often becomes the target of discrimination and ridicule on the playground: Clearly, the problems that overweight children encounter go beyond the physical. *Childhood Education, 81*(2), 70–77.

MacDonald, S. (2006). *The portfolio and its use: A road map for assessment* (2nd ed.). Little Rock, AR: Southern Early Child Association.

MacDonald, S., & Davis, K. (2001). *Block play: The complete guide to learning and playing with blocks.* Beltsville, MD: Gryphon House.

Malcom, S. (1999). Making sense of the world. In *Dialogue on early childhood science, mathematics, and technology education* (pp. 8–13). American Association for the Advancement of Science. Washington, DC: AAAS.

Malo, E., & Bullard, J. (2000). Storytelling and the Emergent Reader. (ED448464) Paper presented at the International Reading Association World Congress on Reading, Aukland, New Zealand.

Manav, B. (2007). Color-emotion associations and color preferences: A case study for residences. *Color Research and Application, 32*(2), 144–150.

Marion, M. (2007). *Guidance of young children* (7th ed.). Upper Saddle River, NJ: Merrill/ Pearson.

Marotz, L. R. (2009). *Health, safety, and nutrition for the young child* (7th ed.). Clifton Park, NY: Thomson Delmar Learning.

Marr, D., Cermak, S., Cohm, E. S., & Henderson, A. (2003). Fine motor activities in Head Start and kindergarten classrooms. *The American Journal of Occupational Therapy, 57*(5), 550–557.

Marshall, H. H. (2003). Cultural influences on the development of self-concept: Updating our thinking. In C. Copple (Ed.), *A world of difference: Readings on teaching young children in a diverse society* (pp. 167–170). Washington, DC: National Association for the Education of Young Children.

Martens, F. L. (1982). Daily physical education—a boon to Canadian elementary schools. *Journal of Physical Education, Recreation, and Dance, 53*(3), 55–58.

Maslach, C., Jackson, S. E., & Leiter, M. P. (1996). *Maslach burnout inventory manual* (3rd ed.). Palo Alto, CA: Consulting Psychologists Press.

Maxwell, L., & Evans, G. W. (1999). Design of child care centers and effects of noise on young children. DesignShare.com Retrieved from http://www.designshare.com/index.php/articles/chronic-noise-and-children/

Maxwell, L. E. (1996). Multiple effects of home and day care crowding. *Environment and Behavior, 28*(4), 494–511.

Maxwell, L. E. (2003). Home and school density effects on elementary school children. *Environmental Behavior, 35*(4), 566–578.

Maxwell, L. E. (2007). Competency in child care settings: The role of the physical environment. *Environment and Behavior, 39*(2), 229–245.

Maxwell, L. E., & Evans, G. W. (2000). The effects of noise on pre-school children's pre-reading. *Journal of Environmental Psychology, 20,* 91–97.

Mazzuchi, D., & Brooks, N. (1992). The gift of time. *Teaching Pre K–8, 22*(5), 60–62.

McCall, R. M., & Craft, D. H. (2004). *Purposeful play: Early childhood movement activities on a budget.* Champaign, IL: Human Kinetics.

McCarney, S. B. (1992). *The preschool evaluation scale.* Columbia, MO: Hawthorne Educational Services.

McCune-Nicolich, L. (1981). Toward symbolic functioning: Structure of early pretend games and potential parallels with language. *Child Development, 52*(3), 785–797.

McDevitt, T. M., & Ormrod, J. E. (2007). *Child development and education* (3rd ed.). Upper Saddle River, NJ: Merrill/Pearson.

McDougall, S. (2006). Furniture for the future. *21st Century Schools, 2*(1), 48–51.

McGinnis, J. L. (2002). Enriching outdoor environments. *Young Children, 57*(3), 28.

McHale, K., & Cermak, S. (1992). Fine motor activities in elementary school: Preliminary findings and provisional implications for children with fine motor problems. *American Journal of Occupational Therapy, 46,* 898–903.

McIntosh, K., Herman, K., Sanford, A., McGraw, K., & Florence, K. (2004). Teaching transitions: Techniques for promoting success between lessons. *Teaching Exceptional Children, 37*(1), 32–38.

McIntyre, M. (1982). Early childhood: Discovery through sand play. *Science and Children, 19*(6), 36–37.

McLaughlin, K. (2006). *Marine life Webquest.* Retrieved from http://webquest.org/questgarden/lessons/14095-060117134552/

McKenzie, T. L., Sallis, J. F., Elder, J. P., Berry, C. C., Hoy, P. L., Nader, P. R., Zive, M. M., & Broyles, S. L. (1997). Physical activity levels and prompts in young children at recess: A two-year study of a bi-ethnic sample. *Research Quarterly for Exercise and Sport, 68*(3), 195–202.

References

McKenzie, T. L., Sallis, J. F., Kolody, B., & Faucette, N. (1997). Long-term effects of a physical education curriculum and staff development program: SPARK. *Research Quarterly for Exercise and Sport, 68*(4), 280–291.

McWilliam, R. A., Scarborough, A. A., & Kim, H. (2003). Adult interactions and child engagement. *Early Education and Development, 14*(1), 7–28.

Medvin, M. B., Reed, D., Behr, D., & Spargo, E. (2003). Using technology to encourage social problem solving in preschoolers. In G. Marshall & Y. J. Katz (Eds.). *Learning in school, home and community: ICT for early and elementary education,* International Working Conference on Learning with Technologies in School, Home and Community, Manchester, United Kingdom.

MENC. (1994). *National standards for arts education.* (1994). Reston, VA: Music Educators National Conference. Retrieved from http://www.menc.org

Mendell, M. J., & Heath, G. A. (2005). Do indoor pollutants and thermal conditions in schools influence student performance? A critical review of the literature. *Indoor Air, 15*(1), 27–52.

Metz, E. (1989). Movement as a musical response among preschool children. *Journal of Research in Music Education, 37*(1), 48–60.

Miche, M. (2002). *Weaving music into young minds.* Australia: Delmar Thomson Learning.

Milburn, D. (1981). A study of multi-age or family-grouped classrooms. *Phi Delta Kappan, 62*(7), 513–514. EJ 242 413.

Miller, D. F. (2004). Science for babies. *Montessori Life, 16*(2), 25–27.

Miller, K. (2005). *Simple steps: Developmental activities for infants, toddlers, and two-year-olds.* Beltsville, MD: Pearson Education, Inc.

Mitchell, R., Cavanagh, M., & Eager, D. (2006). Not all risk is bad, playgrounds as a learning environment for children. *Injury Control and Safety Promotion, 13,* 122–124.

Mix, K. S., Huttenlocher, J., & Levine, S. C. (2002). *Quantitative development in infancy and early childhood.* New York: Oxford University Press.

Moffitt, M. (1996). Children learn about science through block building. In E. S. Hirsch (Ed.), *The block book* (Rev. ed., pp. 27–34), Washington, DC: National Association for the Education of Young Children.

Montessori, M. (1995). *The absorbent mind.* New York: Henry Holt Company. (First published 1967.)

Moolenaar, R., Crutcher, J., San Joaquin, V., Sewell, L., Hutwagner, L., Carson, L., Robison, D., Smithee, L., & Jarvis, W. (2000). A prolonged outbreak of pseduomonas aeruginosa in a neonatal intensive care unit: Did staff fingernails play a role in disease transmission? *Journal of Infection Control and Hospital Epidemiology, 21*(2), 80–85.

Moon, R. Y., Sprague, B. M., & Patel, K. M. (2005). Stable prevalence but changing risk factors for sudden infant death syndrome in child care settings in 2001. *Pediatrics, 116*(4), 972–977.

Moon, R. Y., Weese-Mayer, D. E., & Silvestri, J. M. (2003). Nighttime child care: Inadequate sudden infant death syndrome risk factor knowledge, practice, and policies. *Pediatrics, 111,* 795–799.

Mooney, C. G. (2000). *Theories of childhood: An introduction to Dewey, Montessori, Erickson, Piaget & Vygotsky.* St. Paul, MN: Redleaf Press.

Moore, G., Lane, C. G., Hill, A. B., Cohen, U., & McGinty, T. (1994). *Recommendations for child care centers.* Milwaukee: University of Wisconsin-Milwaukee, Center for Architecture and Urban Planning Research.

Moore, G. T. (1986). Effects of the spatial definition of behavior settings on children's behavior: A quasi-experimental field study. *Journal of Environmental Psychology, 6*(3), 205–231.

Moore, G. T. (2002). Designed environments for young children: Empirical findings and implications for planning and design. Retrieved from http://www.arch.usyd.edu.au/documents/staff/garymoore/111.pdf

Moore, R. (1985). Neighborhoods as childhood habitats. Special issue. *Children's Environments Quarterly, 1*(4).

Moore, R. (1992). Helping children to understand and love planet earth: *International Federation of Landscape Architects Handbook.* ASLA, Washington, DC.

Moore, R. C. (1995). Children gardening: First steps towards a sustainable future. *Children's Environments, 12*(2), 66–83.

Moore, R. C., Bocarro, J., & Hickerson, B. (2007). Natural surroundings. *Parks and Recreation, 42*(4), 36–41.

Morrow, L., & Gambrell, L. (2001). Literature-based instruction in the early years. In S. Neuman & D. Dickinson (Eds.), *Handbook of early literacy research* (pp. 348–60). New York: Guilford.

Morrow, L. M. (1990). Preparing the classroom environment to promote literacy during play. *Early Childhood Research Quarterly, 5,* 537–554.

Morrow, L. M. (2001). *Literacy development in the early years: Helping children read and write.* Boston, MA: Allyn and Bacon.

Morrow, L. M., & Rand, M. K. (1991). Promoting literacy during play by designing early childhood classroom environments. *The Reading Teacher, 44*(6), 396–402.

Morrow, S. B. (2006). The knowledge gap: Implications for early education. In S. Neuman & D. Dickinson (Eds.), *Handbook of early literacy research* (pp. 348–360). New York: Guilford.

Mott, L. (1997). *Our children at risk: The 5 worst environmental threats to their health.* National Research Defense Council. Retrieved from http://www.nrdc.org/health/kids/ocar/ocarack.asp

Moyeda, I., Gomez, I., & Flores, M. (2006). Implementing a musical program to promote preschool children's vocabulary development. *Early Childhood Research and Practice, 8*(1), Retrieved from http://ecrp.uiuc.edu/v8n1/galicia.html

Muller, A. A., & Perlmutter, M. (1985). Preschool children's problem-solving interactions at computers and jigsaw puzzles. *Journal of Applied Developmental Psychology, 6,* 173–186.

Music Educators National Conference (U.S.). (1994). *Opportunity-to-learn standards for music instruction: Grades pre-K-12: curriculum and scheduling, staffing, materials and equipment, facilities.* Reston, VA: Music Educators National Conference.

Myers, C. A. (1992). Therapeutic fine-motor activities for preschoolers. In J. Case-Smith & C. Pehoski (Eds.), *Development of hand skills in children* (pp. 47–61). Bethesda, MD: American Occupational Therapy Association, Inc.

Nabors, L., Willoughby, J., & Badawi, M. A. (1999). Relations between activities and cooperative playground interactions for preschool-age children with special needs. *Journal of Developmental and Physical Disabilities, 11*(4), 339–352.

NAEYC (National Association for the Education of Young Children). (1996). *Technology and young children—ages 3–8* [Position statement]. Washington, DC: Author. Retrieved from http://www.naeyc.org/resources/position_statements/pstech98.htm

NAEYC (National Association for the Education of Young Children). (2005). *Early childhood program standards and accreditation criteria: The mark of quality in early childhood education.* Available from http://www.naeyc.org/academy/NAEYCAccreditationCriteria.asp

NAEYC (National Association for the Education of Young Children). (2006). *Imitating superheroes: Early years are learning years.* Washington, DC: Author.

NAEYC (National Association for the Education of Young Children) & NCTM (National Council of Teachers of Mathematics). (2002). *Early childhood mathematics: Promoting good beginnings: A joint position statement of the National Association for the Education of Young Children (NAEYC) and the National Council of Teachers of Mathematics (NCTM).* Retrieved from http://www.naeyc.org/about/positions/psmath.asp

National Academy of Science. (1996). *National science education standards.* Washington, DC: National Academy Press.

National Advisory Committee on Creative and Cultural Education. (1999). All our futures: Creativity, culture and education. *Report to:* the Secretary of State for Education and Employment and the Secretary of State for Culture, Media and Sport. Retrieved from http://www.cypni.org.uk/downloads/alloutfutures.pdf

National Association for Family Child Care (NAFCC). (2005). *Quality standards for NAFCC accreditation* (4th ed.). Author.

National Association for Sport and Physical Education. (2002). *Active start: A statement of physical activity guidelines for children birth to five years.* Reston, VA: Author.

National Center for Education Statistics. (1996). *Pursuing excellence: A study of U.S. eighth-grade mathematics international context.* Washington, DC: NCES.

National Center for Health Statistics (NCHS). (2001). *Vital statistics system: 10 leading causes of death, United States 2001, all races, both sexes.* Retrieved from http://webappa.cdc.gov/cgi-bin/broker.exe

National Council of Teachers of Mathematics. (2000). *Principles and standards for school mathematics.* Reston, VA: Author. Retrieved from www.nctm.org

National Institute for Occupational Safety and Health (NIOSH). (2007). *Reducing pesticide exposure at school.* Washington, DC: Author.

National Research Council. (1993). *Pesticides in the diets of infants and children.* Washington, DC: National Academy Press. Retrieved from http://www.nap.edu/catalog.php?record_id=2126#toc

National Research Council (U.S.), Bowman, B. T., Donovan, S., & Burns, M. S. (Eds.). (2001). *Eager to learn: Educating our preschoolers.* Washington, DC: National Academy Press.

References

National Research Council. (2005). *Mathematical and scientific development in early childhood: A workshop summary.* Alix Beatty (Rapporteur). Mathematical Sciences Education Board, Board on Science Education, Center for Education, Division of Behavioral and Social Sciences and Education. Washington, DC: The National Academies Press.

National Safety Council. (2001). *Injury facts: 2001 edition.* Chicago: Author.

National Scientific Council on the Developing Child. (2004a). *Young children develop in an environment of relationships working paper No. 1.* Retrieved from http://www.developingchild.net/pubs/wp/Young_Children_Environment_Relationships.pdf

National Scientific Council on the Developing Child. (2004b). *Children's emotional development is built into the architecture of their brains working paper No. 2.* Retrieved from http://www.developingchild.net/pubs/wp/Childrens_Emotional_Development_Architecture_Brains.pdf

National Scientific Council on the Developing Child. (2006). *Early exposure to toxic substances damages brain architecture working paper No. 4.* Retrieved from http://www.developingchild.net/pubs/wp/Toxins.pdf

Neeley, P. M., Neeley, R. A., Justen, J. E., & Tipton-Sumner, C. (2001). Scripted play as a language intervention strategy for preschoolers with developmental disabilities. *Early Childhood Education Journal, 28*(4), 243–246.

Nelson, E. (2006). The outdoor classroom: No child left behind. *Child Care Exchange, 171,* 40–43.

Nelson, J. A., Carpenter, K., & Chiasson, M. A. (2006). Diet, activity, and overweight among preschool-age children enrolled in the Special Supplemental Nutrition Program for Women, Infants, and Children (WIC). *Preventing Chronic Disease.* Retrieved from http://www.cdc.gov/pcd/issues/2006/apr/05_0135.htm

Nelson, P. B., Soli, S. D., & Seltz, A. (2003). *Classroom acoustics II: Acoustical barriers to learning.* Melville, NY: Acoustical Society of America.

Neuman, L. B., Celano, D., Greco, A., & Shue, P. (2001). *Access for all: Closing the book gap for children in early education.* Newark, DE: International Reading Association.

Neuman, S., & Roskos, K. (1990). Play, print and purpose: Enriching play environments for literacy development. *The Reading Teacher, 44*(3), 214–221.

Neuman, S. B. (2006). Building vocabulary to build literacy: Creating a world of words in the classroom. *Early Childhood Today, 21*(2), 9.

Neuman, S. B., Copple, C., & Bredekamp, S. (2000). *Learning to read and write: Developmentally appropriate practices for young children.* Washington, DC: National Association for the Education of Young Children.

New, R. S. (1998). Theory and praxis in Reggio Emilia: They know what they are doing, and why. In C. Edwards, L. Gandini, & G. Forman (Eds.), *The hundred languages of children* (pp. 261–284). Greenwich, CT: Ablex Publishing Corporation.

Newburger, A., & Vaughan, E. (2006). *Teaching numeracy, language, and literacy with blocks.* St. Paul, MN: Redleaf Press.

Newton, C. (1995). Language and learning about art. In C. M. Thompson (Ed.), *The visual arts and early childhood learning* (pp. 80–83). Reston, VA: National Art Education Association.

NHANES (2003–2004). *NHANES data on the Prevalence of Overweight Among Children and Adolescents: United States, 2003–2004.* CDC National Center for Health Statistics. Retrieved from http://www.cdc.gov/nchs/products/pubs/pubd/hestats/overweight/overwght_child_03.htm

Nir-Gal, O., & Klein, P. S. (2004). Computers for cognitive development in early childhood: The teacher's role in the computer learning environment. *Information Technology in Childhood Education Annual, 16,* 97–119.

Nord, C. W., & West, J. (2001). *Fathers' and mothers' involvement in their children's schools by family type and resident status,* NCES 2001–032, Washington, DC: U.S. Department of Education National Center for Education Statistics.

NPR (Producer). (2006, March 9). Fun & Games: Adventure playgrounds a dying breed in the U.S. Retrieved from http://www.npr.org/templates/story/story.php?storyId=5254026

O'Hara, P., Demarest, D., & Shaklee, H. (2005). Early math skills: Building blocks for Idaho's future. *Parents as Teachers Demonstration Project.* University of Idaho.

Oderdorf, C. D., & Taylor-Cox, J. (1999). Shape up! Geometry and geometric thinking: Children's misconceptions about geometry. *Teaching Children Mathematics, 5*(6), 340–346.

Odom, S. L., Zercher, C., Li, S., Marquart, J. M., Sandall, S., & Brown, W. H. (2006). Social acceptance and rejection of preschool children with disabilities: A mixed-method analysis. *Journal of Educational Psychology, 98*(4), 807–823.

Ohman-Rodriguez, J. (2005). Music from the inside out: Promoting emergent composition with young children. In D. G. Koralek (Ed.), *Spotlight on young children and the creative arts* (pp. 44–49). Washington, DC: National Association for the Education of Young Children.

Olds, A. (1987). Designing settings for infants and toddlers. In C. Weistein & T. David (Eds.), *Spaces for children: The build environment and child development* (pp. 117–138). New York: Plenum Press.

Olds, A. R. (1989a). Nature as healer. *Children's Environments Quarterly, 6*(1), 27–32.

Olds, A. R. (1989b). Psychological and physiological harmony in child care center design. *Children's Environments Quarterly, 6*(4), 8–16.

Olds, A. R. (2001). *Child care design guide.* New York: McGraw-Hill.

Operation Physics. (1998). Children's misconceptions about science. Retrieved from http://www.amasci.com/miscon/opphys.html

Oregon Environmental Council. Eco-healthy childcare. Retrieved from http://www.oeconline.org/our-work/kidshealth/ehcc

Owocki, G. (2005). *Time for literacy centers: How to organize and differentiate instruction.* Portsmouth, NH: Heinemann.

Panksepp, J., Burgdorf, J., Turner, C., & Gordon, N. (2003). Modeling ADHD-type arousal with unilateral frontal cortex damage in rats and beneficial effects of play therapy. *Brain and Cognition, 52*(1), 97–105.

Pardee, M. (2005). *Equipping and furnishing early childhood facilities: Community investment collaborative for kids resource guide.* Local Initiatives Support Corporation. Retrieved from http://www.lisc.org/content/publications/detail/813

Pardee, M., Gillman, A., & Larson, C. (2005). *CICK resource guide—volume 4: Creating playgrounds for early childhood facilities.* Local Initiatives Support Corporation. Retrieved from http://www.lisc.org/content/publications/detail/814/

Parette, H. P., Hourcade, J. J., & Heiple, G. S. (2000). The importance of structured computer experiences for young children with and without disabilities. *Early Childhood Education Journal, 27*(4), 243–250.

Parten, M. B. (1932). Social participation among preschool children. *Journal of Abnormal and Social Psychology, 27,* 243–269.

Pasnak, R., Madden, S. E., Martin, J. M., Malabonga, V. A., & Holt, R. (1996). Persistence of gains for instruction in classification, seriation, and conservation. *Journal of Educational Research, 90,* 87–92.

Pasnak, R., McCutchen, L., Holt, R., & Campbell, J. W. (1991). Cognitive and achievement gains for kindergartners instructed in Piagetian operations. *Journal of Educational Research, 85,* 5–13.

Pate, R. R., Baranowski, R., Dowda, M., & Trost, S. G. (1996). Tracking of physical activity in young children. *Medicine and Science in Sports and Exercise, 28*(1), 92–96.

Patton, J. E., Snell, J., Knight, W. J., & Gerken, K. (2001). A survey study of elementary classroom seating designs. Paper Presented at the Annual Meeting of the National Association of School Psychologists. Apr 17, 2001. Retrieved from http://eric.ed.gov/ERICDocs/data/ericdocs2/content_storage_01/0000000b/80/26/1e/37.pdf

Peery, J. C., & Peery, I. W. (1986). Effects of exposure to classical music on the musical preferences of preschool children. *Journal of Research in Music Education, 34*(1), 24–33.

Pellegrini, A. D. (1985). Social-cognitive aspects of children's play: The effects of age, gender, and activity centers. *Journal of Applied Developmental Psychology, 6*(2–3), 129–140.

Pellegrini, A. D., Kato, K., Blatchford, P., & Baines, E. (2002). A short-term longitudinal study of children's playground games across the first year of school: Implications for social competence and adjustment to school. *American Educational Research Journal, 39*(4), 991–1015.

Pelo, A. (2007). *The language of art: Inquiry-based studio practices in early childhood settings.* St. Paul, MN: Redleaf Press.

Petrakos, H., & Howe, N. (1996). The influence of the physical design of the dramatic play on children's play. *Early childhood research quarterly, 11,* 63–77.

Phelan, K. J., Khoury, J,. Kalkwarf, H. J., & Lanphear, B. P. (2001). Trends and patterns of playground injuries in United States children and adolescents. *Ambulatory Pediatrics, 1*(4), 227–233.

Piaget, J. (1947/62). *Play, dreams, and imitation in early childhood.* London: Routledge.

Piaget, J. (1954). *The construction of reality in the child.* New York: Basic.

Piaget, J. (1964). Three lectures in Piaget rediscovered. R. E. Ripple & U. N. Rockcastle (Eds.). Ithaca, NY: Cornell University Press.

Piaget, J. (1967). *Play, dreams, and imitation in childhood.* New York: Norton.

Pianta, R., Howes, C., Burchinal, M., Bryant, D., Clifford, R., Early, D., & Barbarin, O. (2005). Features of pre-kindergarten programs, classrooms, and teachers: Do they predict observed classroom quality and child–teacher interactions? *Applied Developmental Science, 9*(3), 144–159. Retrieved from http://www.informaworld.com/10.1207/s1532480xads0903_2

Pica, R. (2004). *Experiences in movement: Birth to age 8.* Clifton Park, NY: Thomson/Delmar Learning.

Pica, R. (2006). Physical fitness and the early childhood curriculum. *Young Children, 61*(3), 12–19.

Pickett, L. (1998). Literacy learning during block play. *Journal of Research in Childhood Education, 12*(2), 225–230.

Pipher, M. (2002). *The middle of everywhere: Helping refugees enter the American community.* Orlando, FL: Harcourt.

Post, J., & Hohmann, M. (2000). *Tender care and early learning: Supporting infants and toddlers in child care settings.* Ypsilanti, MI: High/Scope Educational Research Foundation.

Potter, J., Johanson, J., & Hutinger, P. (2001). Creative software can extend children's expressiveness. The center for best practices in early childhood. Retrieved from http://www.wiu.edu/users/mimacp/wiu/articles/software4.html

Powell, L. M., Slater, S., & Chaloupka, F. J. (2004). The relationship between community physical activity settings and race, ethnicity and socioeconomic status. *Evidence-Based Preventive Medicine, 1*(2), 135–144.

Prairie, A. P. (2005). *Inquiry into math, science, and technology for teaching young children.* Clifton Park, NY: Thomson/Delmar Learning.

Pressley, M., Rankin, J., & Yokoi, L. (1996). A survey of instructional practices of primary teachers nominated as effective in promoting literacy. *The Elementary School Journal, 96*(4), 363–384.

Provenzo, E. F., & Brett, A. (1983). *The complete block book.* Syracuse, NY: Syracuse University Press.

Pyle, R. (2002). Eden in a vacant lot: Special places, species and kids in community of life. In P. H. Kahn & S. R. Kellert (Eds.), *Children and nature: Psychological, sociological and evolutionary investigation* (pp. 305–328). Cambridge: The Massachusetts Institute of Technology Press.

Ramsey, P. G. (2003). The stress of poverty. In C. Copple (Ed.). *A world of difference: Readings on teaching young children in a diverse society* (pp. 86–87). Washington, DC: National Association for the Education of Young Children.

Rankin, B. (2004). Dewey, Piaget, Vygotsky: Connections with Malaguzzi and the Reggio approach. In J. Hendrick (Ed.), *Next steps toward teaching the Reggio way* (pp. 27–36). Upper Saddle River, NJ: Merrill/Pearson.

Ray, A., Bowman, B., & Brownell, J. O. N. (2006). Teacher-child relationships, social-emotional development, and school achievement. In B. Bowman & E. K. Moore (Eds.), *School readiness and social-emotional development: Perspectives on cultural diversity* (pp. 7–22). Washington, DC: National Black Child Development Institute.

Read, M. A. (2003). Use of color in child care environments: Application of color for wayfinding and space definition in Alabama child care environments. *Early Childhood Education Journal, 30*(4), 233–239.

Read, M. A., Sugawara, A. I., & Brandt, J. A. (1999). Impact of space and color in the physical environment on preschool children's cooperative behavior. *Environment and Behavior, 31*(3), 413–428.

Readdick, C. A. (1993). Solitary pursuits: Supporting children's privacy needs in early childhood settings. *Young Children, 49*(1), 60–64.

Readdick, C. A., & Bartlett, P. M. (1995). Vertical learning environments. *Childhood Education, 71,* 86–90.

Reed, B., & Railsback, J. (2003). *Strategies and resources for mainstream teachers of English language learners.* Portland, OR: Northwest Regional Educational Laboratory.

Reifel, S. (1984). Block construction: Children's developmental landmarks in representation of space. *Young Children, 40*(1), 61–67.

Reifel, S., & Yeatman, J. (1991). Action, talk and thought in block play. In B. Scales, M. Almy, A. Nicolopoulu, and S. Ervin-Tripp (Eds.), *Play and the social context of development in early care and education* (pp. 156–172). New York: Teachers College Press.

Reutzel, D. R., & Morrow, L. M. (2007). Promoting and assessing effective literacy learning classroom environments. In J. R. Raratore & R. L. McCormack (Eds.), *Classroom literacy assessment* (pp. 33–49). New York: The Guilford Press.

Reynolds, J. C., Barnhart, B., & Martin, B. N. (1999). Looping: A solution to the retention vs. social promotion dilemma? *ERS Spectrum, 17*(2), 16–20.

Richgels, D. J. (2001). Invented spelling, phonemic awareness, and reading and writing instruction. In S. B. Neuman & D. Dickinson (Eds.), *Handbook of early literacy research* (pp. 142–55). New York: Guilford.

Ridgers, N. D., Stratton, G., & Fairclough, S. J. (2005). Assessing physical activity levels during recess using accelerometry. *Preventative Medicine, 41*(1), 102–107.

Ries, N. L. L. (1982). *An analysis of the characteristics of infant-child singing expressions.* Thesis (Ed.D.), Arizona State University, Abstract from ProQuest File: Dissertation Abstracts Item: 8223568.

Riley, D., San Juan, R. R., Klinkner, J., & Ramminger, A. (2008). *Social & emotional development: Connecting science and practice in early childhood settings.* Washington, DC: National Association for the Education of Young Children.

Rimm-Kaufman, S. E., La Paro, K. M., Downer, J. T., & Pianta, R. C. (2005). The contribution of classroom setting and quality of instruction to children's behavior in kindergarten classrooms. *Elementary School Journal, 105*(4), 377–394.

Rinaldi, C. (2001). Reggio Emilia: The image of the child and the child's environment as a fundamental principle. In L. Gandini & C. P. Edwards (Eds.), *Bambini: The Italian approach to infant/toddler care* (pp. 49–54). New York: College Press.

Rivken, M. S. (1995). *The great outdoors: Restoring children's right to play outside.* Washington, DC: National Association for the Education of Young Children.

Robinson, K. (2005). *Education Commission of the States 2005 National Forum of Education Policy Chairman's Breakfast.* Denver, CO.

Robinson, L. (1999). *Engaging young children in computer activities.* Retrieved from http://www.wiu.edu/users/mimacp/wiu/articles/

Rogers, L. (1988, October). Classroom management: Transitions and preschoolers. *Dimensions,* 7–8.

Romberg, J. (2002). *Hooked on art!: 265 ready-to-use activities in seven exciting media.* Paramus, NJ: Prentice Hall.

Rosen, K. G., & Richardson, G. (1999). Would removing indoor air particulates in children's environments reduce rate of absenteeism—a hypothesis. *The Science of the Total Environment, 234*(3), 87–93.

Rosenblatt, E., & Winner, E. (1988). The art of children's drawing. *Journal of Aesthetic Education, 22*(1), 3–15.

Rosenblum, S., Weiss, P. L., & Parush, S. (2003). Product and process evaluation of handwriting difficulties. *Educational Psychology Review, 15*(1), 41–81.

Roskos, K. A., Christie, J. F., & Richgels, D. J. (2003). The essentials of early literacy instruction. *Young Children Beyond the Journal.* Retrieved from http://www.journal.naeyc.org/btj/200303/Essentials.pdf

Rule, A. C., & Stewart, R. (2002). Effects of practical life materials on kindergartners' fine motor skills. *Early Childhood Education Journal, 30*(1), 9–13.

Ruopp, R., Travers, J., Glantz, F., & Coelen, C. (1979). *Children at the center: Summary findings and their implications.* Final Report of the National Day Care Study. Cambridge, MA: Abt. Associates.

Rushton, S. P. (2001). Applying brain research to create developmentally appropriate learning environments. *Young Children, 56*(5), 76–81.

Russ, S. W., Robins, A. L., & Christiano, B. A. (1999). Pretend play: Longitudinal prediction of creativity and affect in fantasy in children. *Creativity Research Journal, 12*(2), 129–140.

Russell, S. J. (1991). Counting noses and scary things: Children construct their ideas about data. In D. Vere-Jones (Ed.), *Proceedings of the Third International Conference on Teaching Statistics* (pp. 158–164). Voorburg, Netherlands: International Statistical Institute.

Rybczynski, M., & Troy, A. (1995). Literacy-enriched play centers: Trying them out in "the real world." *Childhood Education, 72*(1), 7–12.

Sacks, J., Goldman, J., & Chaille, C. (1984). Planning in pretend play: Using language to coordinate narrative development. In A. D. Pellegrini & T. D. Yawkey (Eds.), *The development of oral and written language* (pp. 119–128). Norwood, NJ: Ablex.

Saegert, S. (1978). High density environments: The personal and social consequences. In A. Baum & Y. M. Epstein (Eds.), *Human response to crowding* (pp. 257–281). Hillsdale, NJ: Lawrence Erlbaum.

Sainato, D. (1990). Classroom transitions: Organizing environments to promote independent performance in preschool. *Education and Treatment of Children, 13*(4), 288–297.

Sainato, D., & Lyon, S. (1983). A descriptive analysis of the requirements for independent performance in handicapped and nonhandicapped preschool classrooms. In P. S. Strain (Chair),

Assisting behaviorally handicapped preschoolers in mainstream settings: A report of research from the Early Childhood Research Institute. Symposium presents at the HCEEP/DEC Conference, Washington, DC.

Sala, E., Laine, A., Simberg, S., Pentti, J., & Suonpää, J. (2001). The prevalence of voice disorders among day care center teachers compared with nurses: A questionnaire and clinical study. *Journal of Voice, 15*(3), 413–423.

Sallis, J., McKenzie, T., Kolody, M., Lewis, M., Marshall, S., & Rosengard, P. (1999). Effects of health-related physical education on academic achievement: Project Spark. *Research Quarterly for Exercise and Sport, 70*(2), 127–134.

Sallis, J., Nader, P., Broyles, S., Berry, C., Elder, J., McKenzie, T., & Nelson, J. (1993). Correlates of physical activity at home in Mexican-American and Anglo-American preschool children. *Health Psychology, 12*(5), 390–398.

Samaras, A. P. (1996). Children's computers. *Childhood Education, 72,* 133–136.

Sandall, S. R., & Schwartz, I. S. (2002). *Building blocks for teaching preschoolers with special needs.* East Peoria, IL: Paul H. Brookes Publishing Company.

Sanders, S.W. (2002). *Active for life: Developmentally appropriate movement programs for young children.* Washington, DC: National Association for the Education of Young Children.

Saracho, O. (2002). Young children'creativity and pretend play. *Early Child Development and Care, 172*(5), 431–438.

Sarama, J., & Clements, D. (2002). The role of technology in early childhood learning. *Teaching Children Mathematics, 8*(6), 340–343.

Sarama, J., & Clements, D. H. (2004). Building blocks for early childhood mathematics. *Early Childhood Research Quarterly, 19*(1), 181–189.

Sawyer, W. E. (2004). *Growing up with literature.* Albany, NY: Delmar Learning.

Sawyers, K., & Hutson-Brandhagen, J. (2004). Music and math: How do we make the connection for preschoolers? *Exchange, 158,* 46–49.

Saxe, G. B., Guberman, S. R., & Gearhart, M. (1987). Social processes in early number development. *Monographs of the Society for Research in Child Development, 52*(2), 153–159.

Schappet, J., Malkusak, A., & Bruya, L. D. (2003). *High expectations: Playgrounds for children of all abilities.* Bloomfield, CT: National Center for Boundless Playgrounds.

Schellenberg, E. G. (2004). Music lessons enhance IQ. *Psychological Science, 15*(8), 511–514.

Schiller, M. (1995). Reggio Emilia: A focus on emergent curriculum and art. *Art Education, 48*(3), 45–50.

Schneider, M. (2002). *Do school facilities affect academic outcomes?* Washington, DC: National Clearinghouse for Educational Facilities.

Schultz, P. W., Shriver, C., Tabanico, J. J., & Khazian, A. M. (2004). Implicit connections with nature. *Journal of Environmental Psychology, 24*(1), 31–42.

Schunk, D. H. (1989). Self-efficacy and cognitive achievement: Implications for students with learning problems. *Journal of Learning Disabilities, 22,* 14–22.

Schwartz, B. (2007). Planting the seeds for a sound garden. In P. Kern (Ed.), *Early Childhood Newsletter, 13,* 12. Silver Springs, MD: American Music Therapy Association.

Schwartz, S. L. (1994). Calendar reading: A tradition that begs remodeling. *Teaching Children Mathematics, 1*(2), 104–109.

Schwarz, N. (2007). *Sensory play: Not just sand and water anymore.* Wabasso, MN: JonTi-Craft.

Schwebel, D. C., Brezausek, M. S., & Belsky, J. (2006). Does time spent in child care influence risk for unintentional injury? *Journal of Pediatric Psychology, 31*(2), 184–193.

Scoter, J. V., Ellis, D., & Railsback, J. (2001). *Technology in early childhood education: Finding the balance.* Portland, OR: Northwest Regional Educational Laboratory.

Scruggs, P. W., Beveridge, S. D., & Watson, D. L. (2003). Increasing children's school time physical activity using structured fitness breaks. *Pediatric Exercise Science, 15*(2), 156–169.

Searfoss, L. W., Readence, J. E., & Mallette, M. H. (2001). *Helping children learn to read: Creating a classroom literacy environment* (4th ed.). Needham Heights, MA: Allyn and Bacon.

Sebba, R., & Churchman, A. (1986). Schoolyard design as an expression of educational principles. *Children's Environments Quarterly, 3*(3), 70–76.

Seefeldt, C., & Galper, A. (2004). *Active experiences for active children: Mathematics.* Upper Saddle River, NJ: Merrill/Pearson.

Seefeldt, C., & Waites, J. (2002). *Creating rooms of wonder: Valuing and displaying children's work to enhance the learning process.* Beltsville, MD: Gryphon House.

Seldin, T., & Wolff, J. (2007). *The exercises of practical life.* The Montesorri Foundation. Retrieved from http://www.montessori.org/story.php?id=58

Seo, K. H., & Ginsburg, H. P. (2004). What is developmentally appropriate in early childhood mathematics education? Lessons from new research. In D. H. Clements & J. Sarama (Eds.), *Engaging young children in mathematics: Standards for early childhood mathematics education* (pp. 91–104). Mahwah, NJ: Lawrence Erlbaum Associates.

Serdula, M. K., Ivery, D., Coates, R. J., Freedman, D. S., Williamson, D. F., & Byers, T. (1993). Do obese children become obese adults? A review of the literature. *Preventive Medicine, 22*(2), 167–177.

Sgarlotti, R. (Ed.). (2004). *Creating a sacred place for students in mathematics K–12.* Polson, MT: National Indian School Board Association.

Shahrimin, M. I., & Butterworth, D. M. (2002). Young children's collaborative interactions in a multimedia computer environment. *Internet and Higher Education, 4,* 203–215.

Shaw, G. (2003). *Keeping Mozart in mind* (2nd ed). San Diego: Academic.

Sheehan, R., & Day, D. (1975). Is open space just empty space? *Early Childhood Education Journal, 3*(2), 10–13.

Sherwood, I. (2005). The early years. *Science and children, 43*(3), 20–23.

Shield, B. M., & Dockrell, J. E. (2003). The effects of noise on children at school: A review. *Journal of Building Acoustics, 102,* 97–116.

Shields, M. K., & Behrman, R. E. (2000). Children and computer technology: Analysis and recommendations. *Children and Computer Technology, 10*(2), 4–30.

Shore, R., & Strasser, J. (2006). Music for their minds. *Young Children, 61*(2), 62–67.

Shute, R., & Miksad, J. (1997). Computer assisted instruction and cognitive development in preschoolers. *Child Study Journal, 27*(3), 237–253.

Simel, D. (1998). Education for Bildung: Teacher attitudes toward looping. *International Journal of Educational Reform, 7*(4), 330–337.

Slack-Smith, L., Read, A., & Stanley, F. J. (2002). A prospective study of absence for illness and injury in childcare children. *Child Care Health & Development, 28*(6), 487–494.

Sluss, D. J. (2005). *Supporting play: Birth to age eight.* Canada: Thomson Delmar Learning.

Smilansky, S., & Shefatya, L. (1990). *Facilitating play: A medium for promoting cognitive, socioemotional, and academic development in young children.* Gaithersburg, MD: Psychosocial and Educational Publications.

Smith, C. B. (2003). *Skills students use when speaking and listening.* Bloomingdale, IN: ERIC Clearinghouse on Reading, English, and Language.

Smith, D., & Goldhaber, J. (2004). *Poking, pinching & pretending: Documenting toddlers' exploration with clay.* St. Paul, MN: Redleaf Press.

Smith, E., Lemke, J., Taylor, M., Kirchner, H. L., & Hoffman, H. (1998). Frequency of voice problems among teachers and other occupations. *Journal of Voice, 12*(4), 480–488.

Smith, J . C. (1999). *Understanding childhood obesity.* Jackson, MS: University Press of Mississippi.

Smith, P. K. (2000). Bullying and harassment in schools and the rights of children. *Children & Society, 14*(4), 294–303.

Smith, P. K., & Connolly, K. J. (1986). Experimental studies on the preschool environment: The Sheffield Project. *Advances in Early Education and Day Care, 4,* 27–66.

Snow, C. E., Burns, M. S., & Griffin, P. (Eds.). (1998). *Preventing reading difficulties in young children.* Washington, DC: National Academy Press.

Sobel, D. (1993). *Children's special places: Exploring the roles of forts, dens, and bush houses in middle childhood.* Tucson, AZ: Zephyr Press.

Sobel, D. (1996). *Beyond ecophobia: Reclaiming the heart in nature education.* Great Barrington, MA: The Orion Society.

Sobel, D. (2002). *Children's special places: Exploring the role of forts, dens, and bush houses in middle childhood.* Detroit, MI: Wayne State University Press.

Sobel, D. (2004). *Place-based education, connecting classrooms & communities.* Great Barrington, MA: The Orion Society.

Sosna, D. (2000). More about woodworking with young children. *Young Children, 55*(2), 38–39.

Spodek, B. (2006). Educationally appropriate art activities for young children. In B. Neugebauer (Ed.), *Curriculum: Art, music, movement, drama* (pp. 23–25). Redmond, WA: Exchange Press.

Sprung, B. (2006). Yes you can: Meeting the challenge of math and science. *Scholastic Early Childhood Today, 20*(4), 44–51.

Sprung, B., & Froschl, M. (2006). Building diversity through science and science through diversity. *Connect, (19)*4, 7–10.

Stamp, L. N. (1992). Music time? All the time! *Early Childhood Education Journal, 19*(4), 4–6.

Standing, E. M. (1957). *Maria Montessori: Her life and work.* New York: Plume.

Stevens, C. (2004). Playing in the sand. *The British Gestalt Journal, 13*(1), 18–23.

Stoecklin, V. (2001). *Developmentally appropriate gardening with children.* White Hutchinson Leisure and Learning Group. Retrieved from http://www.whitehutchinson.com/children/articles/gardening.shtml

Stoecklin, V. L. (2000). Creating playgrounds kids love. White Hutchinson Leisure & Learning Group. Retrieved from http://www.whitehutchinson.com/children/articles/playgrndkidslove.shtml

Stratton, G. (2000). Promoting children's physical activity in primary school: An intervention study using playground markings. *Ergonomics, 43*(10), 1538–1546.

Strickland, D. S., & Riley-Ayers, S. (2006). Early literacy: Policy and practice in the preschool years: Preschool Policy Brief. *National Institute for Early Education Research, 10,* 1–11.

Striniste, N. A., & Moore, R. C. (1989). Early childhood outdoors: A literature review on the design of childcare environments. *Children's Environments Quarterly, 6*(4), 25–31.

Strong-Wilson, T., & Ellis, J. (2007). Children and place: Reggio Emilia's environment as third teacher. *Theory into Practice, 46*(1), 40–47.

Stroud, J. E. (1995). Block play: Building a foundation for literacy. *Early Childhood Education Journal, 23*(1), 9–14.

Suecoff, S. A., Avner, J. R., Chou, K. J., & Crain, E. F. (1999). A comparison of New York City playground hazards in high and low-income areas. *Archives of Pediatrics and Adolescent Medicine, 153,* 363–366.

Summit, G., & Widess, J. (1999). *Making gourd musical instruments: Over 60 string, wind & percussion instruments and how to play them.* New York: Sterling Publishing Co., Inc.

Susa, A. M., & Benedict, J. O. (1994). The effects of playground design on pretend play and divergent thinking. *Environment and Behavior, 26*(4), 560.

Sutterby, J. A., & Frost, J. L. (2002). Making playgrounds fit for children and children fit for playgrounds. *Young Children, 57*(3), 36–40.

Sutterby, J., & Thornton, C. D. (2003, September). Swinging stimulates both bodies and brains. *Today's Playground, 3*(5), 10–11.

Sveinsson, A., & Morris, R. (2006). School bullying and victimization of children with disabilities. In R. J. Morris (Ed.), *Disability research and policies: Current perspectives* (pp. 187–204). Mahwah, NJ: Lawrence Erlbaum Associates.

Sweedler-Brown, C. O. (1992). The effect of training on the appearance bias of holistic essay graders. *Journal of Research and Development in Education, 26*(1), 24–29.

Tarr, P. (1995). Creating connections: Adding "art" to your art program. *Interaction Canadian Child Care Federation. Summer,* 37–40.

Tarr, P. (1995). Preschool children's socialization through art experiences. In C. Thompson (Ed.), *The visual arts and early childhood learning* (pp. 23–27). Reston: VA. The National Art Education Association.

Tarr, P. (1997). Creating connections: Adding "art" to your art program. *Canadian Child Care Federation.* Retrieved from http://www.cccf-fcsge.ca/docs/cccf/00000980.htm

Tarr, P. (2001). Aesthetic codes in early childhood classrooms: What art educators can learn from Reggio Emilia. *Art Education, 54,* 33–39.

Tarr, P. (2004). Consider the walls. *Beyond the Journal,* 1–6. Retrieved from http://www.journal.naeyc.org/btj/200405/ConsidertheWalls.pdf

Task Force on Sudden Infant Death Syndrome. (2005). American Academy of Pediatrics policy statement: Organizational principles to guide and define the child health care system and/or improve the health of all children. *Pediatrics, 116*(5), 1245–1255.

Taylor-Cox, J. (2003). Algebra in the early years? Yes. *Young Children, 58*(1), 14–21.

Teets, S. (1985). Modification of play behaviors of preschool children through manipulation of environmental variables. In J. L. Frost & S. Sunderlin (Eds.), *When children play* (pp. 265–272). Wheaton, MD: Association for Childhood Education International.

Tegano, D. W., & Burdette, M. P. (1991). Length of activity periods and play behaviors of preschool children. *Journal of Research in Childhood Education, 5*(2), 93–99.

Texas Child Care. (2005). Manipulatives: Big learning from little objects. *Texas Child Care,* Fall, 30–37.

Theemes, T. (1999). *Let's go outside! Designing the early childhood playground.* Ypsilanti, MI: High/Scope Press.

Thompson, S. C. (2005). *Children as illustrators: Making meaning through art and language.* Washington, DC: National Association for the Education of Young Children.

References

Thorne, G. (2006). Graphomotor skills: Why some kids hate to write. Center for development and learning. Retrieved from http://www.cdl.org/resource-library/articles/graphomotor.php?type= recent&id=Yes

Timm, S., & Schroeder, B. L. (2000). Listening/nonverbal communication training. *International Journal of Listening, 12,* 109–128.

Tinsworth, D., & McDonald, J. (2001). *Special study: Injuries and deaths associated with children's playground equipment.* Washington, DC: U.S. Consumer Product Safety Commission.

Tipping, E. (January, 2007). Safe ground: Building, maintaining and inspecting playgrounds to ensure all kids can play safely. *Recreation Management.* Retrieved from http://www.recmanagement.com/features.php?fid=200701fe01&ch=5

Titman, W. (1994). *Special places, special people. The hidden curriculum of school grounds.* WWF UK (World Wide Fund for Nature)/Learning Through Landscapes.DOI: 10.1080/03004430214553

Tomes, R. E. (1995). Teacher presence and child gender influences on children's activity preferences in preschool settings. *Child Study Journal, 25*(2), 123–140.

Tompkins, G. E. (2005). *Literacy for the 21st century: A balanced approach.* Upper Saddle River, NJ: Merrill/Pearson.

Topal, C. W. (1983). *Children, clay and sculpture.* Worcester, MA: Davis Publications.

Topal, C. W. (2006). Fostering experiences between young children and clay. In B. Neugebauer (Ed.), *Curriculum: Art, music, movement, drama* (pp. 30–33). Redmond, WA: Exchange Press.

Topal, C. W., & Gandini, L. (1999). *Beautiful stuff: Learning with found materials.* Italy: Davis Publications.

Torelli, L. (2002). Enhancing development through classroom design in Early Head Start. *Children and Families.* Retrieved from http://www.spacesforchildren.com/enhanc.html

Torelli, L., & Durrett, C. (1996). Landscape for learning: The impact of classroom design on infants and toddlers. *Early Childhood News, 8*(2), 12–17.

Torelli, L., & Durrett, C. (2000). *Landscapes for learning: Designing group care environments for infants, toddlers and two-year-olds.* Retrieved from http://www.spacesforchildren.com/impact.html

Trancik, A. M., & Evans, G. W. (1995). Spaces fit for children: Competency in the design of daycare center environments. *Children's Environments, 12*(3), 43–58. Retrieved from http://www.colorado.edu/journals/cye/

Travers, J., & Ruopp, R. R. (1978). *National day care study: Preliminary findings and their implications.* Cambridge, MA: Abt Associates.

Trawick-Smith, J. (2006). *Early childhood development: A multicultural perspective* (4th ed.). Upper Saddle River, NJ: Merrill/Pearson.

Trehub, S. (2001). Musical predispositions in infancy. *Annals of the New York Academy, 930,* 1–16.

Trick, W., Vernon, M., Hayes, R., Nathan, C., Rice, T., Peterson, B., Segreti, J., Welbel, S., Solomon, S., & Weinstein, R. (2003). Impact of ring wearing on hand contamination and comparison of hand hygiene agents in a hospital. *Clinical Infectious Diseases, 36*(6), 1383–1390.

Tsantis, L. A., Bewick, C. J., & Thouvenelle, S. (2003). Examining some common myths about computer use in the early years. *Beyond the Journal, Young Children.* Retrieved from www.journal.naeyc.org/btj/200311

Tu, T. (2006). Preschool science environment: What is available in a preschool classroom? *Early Childhood Education Journal, 33*(4), 245–251.

Tulve, N. S., Jones, P. A., Nishioka, M. G., Fortmann, R. C., Croghan, C. W., Zhou, J. Y., Fraser, A., Cave, C., Friedman, W., & Tulve, N. S. (2006). Pesticide measurements from the First National Environmental Health Survey of Child Care Centers using multi-residue GC/MS analysis method. *Environmental Science and Technology, 40*(20), 6269–6274.

United Nations Convention on the Rights of the Child. (1989). UN General Assembly Document A/RES/44/25 *USA IPA* http://www.ipausa.org/ipadeclaration.html

U.S. Census Bureau. (2005). *Who's minding the kids? Child care arrangements.* Washington, DC: U.S. Government Printing Office. Retrieved from http://www.census.gov/population/www/socdemo/childcare.html

U.S. Consumer Product Safety Commission. (1999). *Safety hazards in child care settings.* Washington, DC: Author.

U.S. Department of Commerce. (2004). *A nation online: Entering the broadband age.* Retrieved from http://www.ntia.doc.gov/reports/anol/index.html

U.S. Department of Health and Human Services, Public Health Service, Office of the Surgeon General [USDHHS] (2001). *The Surgeon General's call to action to prevent and decrease overweight and obesity 2001.* Rockville, MD: Author.

Van de Carr, R., & Lehrer, M. (1986). Enhancing early speech, parental bonding, and infant physical development using prenatal intervention in standard obstetric practice. *Pre- and Perinatal Psychology Journal, 1*(1), 20–30.

Vecchi, V., & Giudici, C. (2004). *Children, art, artists: The expressive languages of children, the artistic language of Alberto Burri.* Reggio Children Modena: Italy.

Vincent, S. (Ed.). (1999). *The multigrade classroom: A resource handbook for small, rural schools. Book 2: Classroom organization.* Portland, OR: Northwest Regional Educational Lab.

Vygotsky, L. (1986). *Thought and language.* Cambridge, MA: MIT Press.

Vygotsky, L. S. (1976). Play and its role in the mental development of the child. In J. S. Bruner, A. Jolly, & K. Sylvia (Eds.), *Play: Its role in development and evolution* (pp. 536–552). New York: Basic Books.

Vygotsky, L. S. (1978). *Mind and society: The development of higher mental processes.* Cambridge, MA: Harvard University Press. (Original work published in 1930–1933, 1935.)

Vygotsky, L. S. (1978). *Mind in society: The development of higher psychological processes.* Cambridge, MA: Harvard University Press.

Wadsworth, B. J. (1989). *Piaget's theory of cognitive and affective development* (4th ed.). White Plains, NY: Longman.

Waldecker, M. (2005). High class: Furniture and equipment selection. *American School and University, 78*(2), 30–34.

Walker, L. (1995). *Block building for children.* Woodstock, NY: Overlook Press.

Walsh, M. (2007). Making the cut: Better understanding fine motor skill development in kindergarten students. Retrieved from http://origen.ed.psu.edu/pds_download/2007InquiryProjects/WalshMinquiry0607.pdf

Wardle, F., & Cruz-Janzen, M. (2004). *Multiethnic and multiracial children in schools.* Boston: Allyn and Bacon.

Wehrmann, S., Chiu, T., Reid, D., & Sinclair, G. (2006). Evaluation of occupational therapy school-based consultation service for students with fine motor difficulties. *The Canadian Journal of Occupational Therapy, 11,* 225–236.

Weinberger, N. (2000). Overcoming obstacles to create retreats in family child care. *Young Children, 55*(5), 78–81.

Weinberger, N. (2006). Children's use of retreats in family child care homes. *Early Education & Development, 17*(4), 571–591.

Weinstein, C. S. (1987). Designing preschool classrooms to support development. In C. S. Weinstein & T. G. David (Eds.), *Spaces for children: The built environment and child development* (pp. 159–185). New York: Plenum.

Weintraub, R., & Cassady, A. (2002). *Playing it safe: The sixth nationwide safety survey of public playgrounds.* Retrieved from http://www.consumerfed.org/backpage/PlayingItSafeJune2002.pdf

Weiss, M. R., & Ferrer-Caja, E. (2002). Motivational orientations and sport behavior. In T. S. Horn (Ed.), *Advances in sport psychology* (pp. 101–183). Champaign, IL: Human Kinetics Publishing.

Wellhousen, K. (1999). Big ideas for small spaces. *Young Children, 54*(6), 58–61.

Wellhousen, K., & Crowther, I. (2004). *Creating effective learning environments.* New York: Delmar Learning.

Wellhousen, K., & Giles, R. M. (2005). Building literacy opportunities into children's block play: What every teacher should know. *Childhood Education, 82*(2), 74–79.

Wellhousen, K., & Kieff, J. E. (2001). *A constructivist approach to block play in early childhood.* Albany, NY: Delmar.

Wells, N. M., & Evans, G. W. (2003). Nearby nature: A buffer of life stress among rural children. *Environment and Behavior, 35*(3), 311–330.

West, J., Denton, K., & Germino-Hausken, E. (2000). *America's kindergartners.* Washington, DC: National Center for Education Statistics, U.S. Department of Education.

West, N. T. (2006). Art for all children: A conversation about inclusion. In B. Neugebauer (Ed.), *Curriculum: Art, music, movement, drama* (pp. 15–19). Redmond, WA: Exchange Press.

West, S., & Cox, A. (2001). *Sand and water play: Simple, creative activities for young children.* Beltsville, MD: Gryphon House.

Whiren, A. P. (1995). Planning a garden from a child's perspective. *Children's Environments, 12*(2), 250–255.

White, R. (1997). Sometimes, you just gotta make mud pies: Children's adventure play gardens. *Tourist Attractions and Parks Magazine.* Retrieved from http://www.whitehutchinson.com/leisure/articles/84.shtml

References

White, R. (2004). Adults are from earth; Children are from the moon; Designing for children: A complex challenge. Retrieved from http://www.whitehutchinson.com/children/articles/earthmoon.shtml

White, R., & Stoecklin, V. (2003). *The great 35 square foot myth.* Kansas City, MO: White Hutchinson Leisure & Learning Group.

Whited, J. (2003). Experiences with light. Retrieved from http://www.ohiou.edu/childdevcenter/DOCUMENTS/lightbook.pdf

Wien, C. A. (1996). Time, work, and developmentally appropriate practice. *Early Childhood Research Quarterly, 11*(3), 377–403.

Wien, C. A. (2004). From policing to participation: Overturning the rules and creating amiable classrooms. *Young Children Online,* 1–7. Retrieved from http://www.journal.naeyc.org/btj/200401/wien.asp

Wien, C. A., Coates, A., Keating, B., & Bigelow, B. C. (2005). Designing the environment to build connection to place. *Young Children, 60*(3), 16–24.

Wiggins, G., & McTighe, J. (1998). *Understanding by design.* Alexandria, VA: ASCD.

Wilke, J. (2006). Why outdoor spaces for children matter so much. *Child Care Exchange, 171,* 44–48.

Williams, R. A., Rockwell, R. E., & Sherwood, E. A. (1987). *Mudpies to magnets.* Mt. Rainier, MD: Gryphon House.

Wilson, N. K., Chuang, J. C., Lyu, C., Menton, R., & Morgan, M. K. (2003). Aggregate exposures of nine preschool children to persistent organic pollutants at day care and at home. *Journal of Exposure Analysis and Environmental Epidemiology, 13,* 187–202.

Wilson, R. A. (2000). *Outdoor experiences for young children* (ERIC Digest). Charleston, WV: ERIC Clearinghouse on Rural Education and Small Schools (ERIC Identifier ED 448013).

Wittmer, D. S., & Honig, A. S. (1991). Convergent or divergent? Teacher questions to three-year-old children in day care. *Early Child Development and Care, 68*(1),141–147.

Wohlwend, K. E. (2005). Chasing friendship: Acceptance, rejection, and recess play. *Childhood Education, 81*(2), 77–82.

Wohlwill, J. F., & van Vliet, W. (1985). *Habitats for children: The impact of density.* Hillsdale, NJ: Lawrence Erlbaum.

Wolfgang, C. H., Stannard, L. L., & Jones, I. (2001). Block play performance among preschoolers as a predictor of later school achievement in mathematics. *Journal of Research in Childhood Education, 15,* 173–180.

Wolpert, E. (2005). *Start seeing diversity: The basic guide to an anti-bias classroom.* St. Paul, MN: Redleaf Press.

Worth, K., & Grollman, S. (2003). *Worms, shadows, and whirlpools: Science in the early childhood classroom.* Portsmouth, NH: Heinemann.

Wortman, A. M. (2001, July). Preventing work-related musculoskeletal injuries. *Child Care Exchange,* 50–53.

Wynn, K. (2000). Addition and subtraction by human infants. In D. Muir & A. Slater (Eds.), *Infant development: The essential readings in developmental psychology* (pp. 185–192). Oxford, UK: Blackwell.

Yang, X. (1997). *Educational benefits in elementary school through looping and Friday in-services.* San Diego, CA: National Association for Year Round Education.

Yerkes, R. (1982). *A playground that extends the classroom.* ERIC Document 239802.

Yochman, A., Ornoy, A., & Parush, S. (2006). Perceptuomotor functioning in preschool children with symptoms of attention deficit hyperactivity disorder. *Perceptual and Motor Skills, 102,* 175–186.

Young-Loveridge, J. M. (2004). Effects on early numeracy of a program using number books and games. *Early Childhood Research Quarterly, 19*(1), 82–98.

Zask, A., van Beurden, E., Barnett, L., Brooks, L. O., & Dietrich, U. C. (2001). Active school playgrounds: Myth or reality? Results of the 'Move It Groove It' project. *Preventive Medicine, 33*(5), 402–408.

Zur, O., & Gelman, R. (2004). Young children can add and subtract by predicting and checking. *Early Childhood Research Quarterly, 19*(1), 121–137.

Index